Bahamas
Turks & Caicos

Christopher P Baker

LONELY PLANET PUBLICATIONS
Melbourne • Oakland • London • Paris

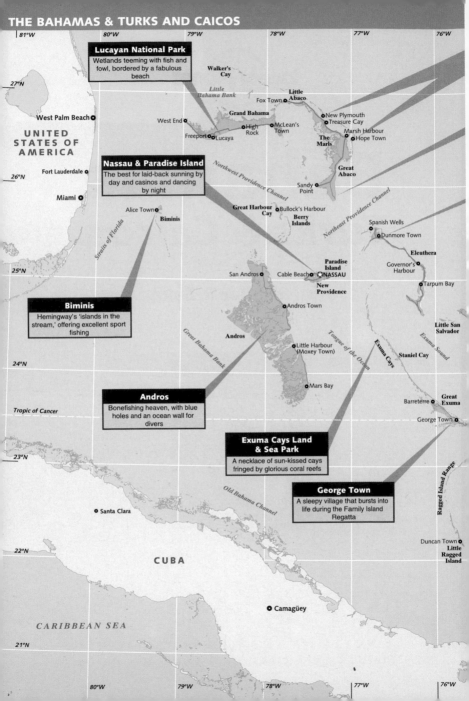

THE BAHAMAS & TURKS AND CAICOS

81°W · 80°W · 79°W · 78°W · 77°W · 76°W

27°N

26°N

25°N

24°N

23°N

22°N

21°N

Lucayan National Park
Wetlands teeming with fish and fowl, bordered by a fabulous beach

Nassau & Paradise Island
The best for laid-back sunning by day and casinos and dancing by night

Biminis
Hemingway's 'islands in the stream,' offering excellent sport fishing

Andros
Bonefishing heaven, with blue holes and an ocean wall for divers

Exuma Cays Land & Sea Park
A necklace of sun-kissed cays fringed by glorious coral reefs

George Town
A sleepy village that bursts into life during the Family Island Regatta

UNITED STATES OF AMERICA

West Palm Beach

Fort Lauderdale

Miami

Walker's Cay

Little Bahama Bank

Fox Town

Little Abaco

West End

Grand Bahama

High Rock

McLean's Town

New Plymouth

Treasure Cay

Freeport · Lucaya

The Marls

Marsh Harbour

Hope Town

Great Abaco

Northwest Providence Channel

Sandy Point

Alice Town

Biminis

Straits of Florida

Great Harbour Cay

Bullock's Harbour

Berry Islands

Spanish Wells

Dunmore Town

Eleuthera

Governor's Harbour

Northeast Providence Channel

San Andros

Cable Beach

Paradise Island

NASSAU

New Providence

Tarpum Bay

Andros Town

Great Bahama Bank

Andros

Little Harbour (Moxey Town)

Mars Bay

Tongue of the Ocean

Little San Salvador

Exuma Sound

Exuma Cays

Staniel Cay

Barreterre

Great Exuma

George Town

Tropic of Cancer

Old Bahama Channel

Santa Clara

Ragged Island Range

Duncan Town

Little Ragged Island

CUBA

CARIBBEAN SEA

Camagüey

80°W · 79°W · 78°W · 77°W · 76°W

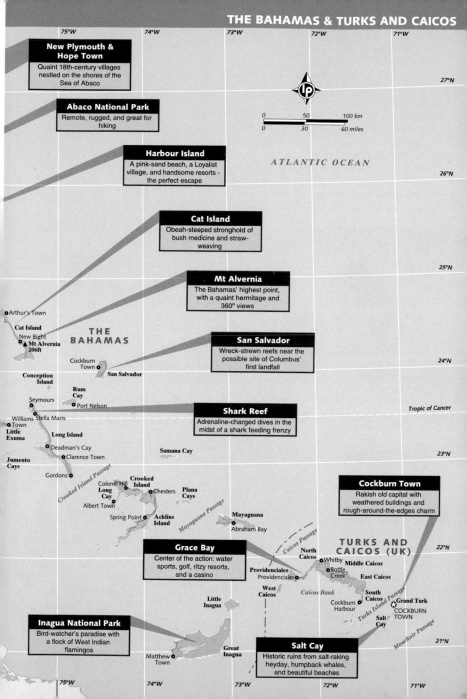

THE BAHAMAS & TURKS AND CAICOS

New Plymouth & Hope Town
Quaint 18th-century villages nestled on the shores of the Sea of Abaco

Abaco National Park
Remote, rugged, and great for hiking

Harbour Island
A pink-sand beach, a Loyalist village, and handsome resorts - the perfect escape

Cat Island
Obeah-steeped stronghold of bush medicine and straw-weaving

Mt Alvernia
The Bahamas' highest point, with a quaint hermitage and 360° views

San Salvador
Wreck-strewn reefs near the possible site of Columbus' first landfall

Shark Reef
Adrenaline-charged dives in the midst of a shark feeding frenzy

Cockburn Town
Rakish old capital with weathered buildings and rough-around-the-edges charm

Grace Bay
Center of the action: water sports, golf, ritzy resorts, and a casino

Inagua National Park
Bird-watcher's paradise with a flock of West Indian flamingos

Salt Cay
Historic ruins from salt-raking heyday, humpback whales, and beautiful beaches

ATLANTIC OCEAN

0   50   100 km
0   30   60 miles

THE BAHAMAS

Arthur's Town
Cat Island
New Bight
Mt Alvernia 206ft
Cockburn Town
San Salvador
Conception Island
Rum Cay
Seymours
Port Nelson
Williams Town
Stella Maris
Little Exuma
Long Island
Deadman's Cay
Clarence Town
Samana Cay
Jumento Cays
Gordons
Crooked Island Passage
Colonel Hill
Crooked Island
Long Cay
Chesters
Plana Cays
Albert Town
Spring Point
Acklins Island
Mayaguana Passage
Mayaguana
Abraham Bay
Caicos Passage
North Caicos
Whitby
Middle Caicos
East Caicos
Providenciales
Bottle Creek
West Caicos
Caicos Bank
Little Inagua
South Caicos
Cockburn Harbour
Grand Turk
COCKBURN TOWN
Turks Island Passage
Salt Cay
Matthew Town
Great Inagua
Mouchoir Passage

TURKS AND CAICOS (UK)

Tropic of Cancer

27°N
26°N
25°N
24°N
23°N
22°N
21°N

75°W   74°W   73°W   72°W   71°W

Bahamas, Turks & Caicos
2nd edition – June 2001
First published – May 1998

Published by
Lonely Planet Publications Pty Ltd ABN 36 005 607 983
90 Maribyrnong St, Footscray, Victoria 3011, Australia

Lonely Planet Offices
Australia Locked Bag 1, Footscray, Victoria 3011
USA 150 Linden St, Oakland, CA 94607
UK 10a Spring Place, London NW5 3BH
France 1 rue du Dahomey, 75011 Paris

Photographs
Many of the images in this guide are available for licensing from
Lonely Planet Images.
W www.lonelyplanetimages.com

Front cover photograph
Columbus Memorial, San Salvador (Christopher P Baker)

ISBN 1 86450 199 5

text & maps © Lonely Planet Publications Pty Ltd 2001
photos © photographers as indicated 2001

Printed by The Bookmaker International Ltd
Printed in China

Contents

ELEUTHERA 312

EXUMAS 338

CAT ISLAND 359

SAN SALVADOR, RUM CAY & CONCEPTION ISLAND 373

LONG ISLAND 384

CROOKED ISLAND DISTRICT 395

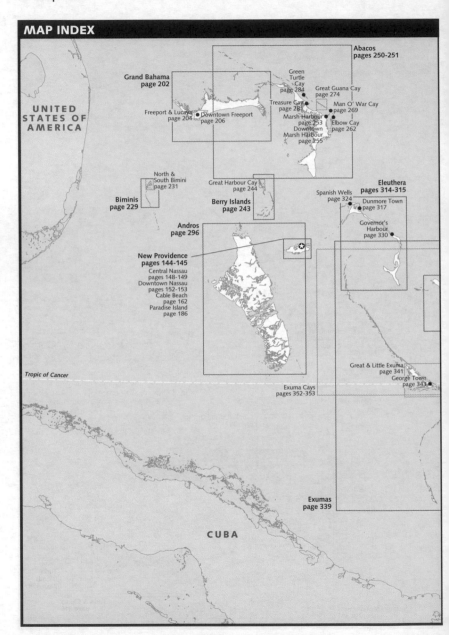

MAP INDEX

UNITED STATES OF AMERICA

Abacos
pages 250-251

Grand Bahama
page 202

Green Turtle Cay
page 284

Great Guana Cay
page 274

Freeport & Lucaya
page 204

Downtown Freeport
page 206

Treasure Cay
page 281

Man O' War Cay
page 269

Marsh Harbour
page 253

Elbow Cay
page 262

Downtown Marsh Harbour
page 255

North & South Bimini
page 231

Great Harbour Cay
page 244

Eleuthera
pages 314-315

Spanish Wells
page 324

Dunmore Town
page 317

Biminis
page 229

Berry Islands
page 243

Governor's Harbour
page 330

Andros
page 296

New Providence
pages 144-145

Central Nassau
pages 148-149
Downtown Nassau
pages 152-153
Cable Beach
page 162
Paradise Island
page 186

Tropic of Cancer

Great & Little Exuma
page 341

George Town
page 343

Exuma Cays
pages 352-353

Exumas
page 339

CUBA

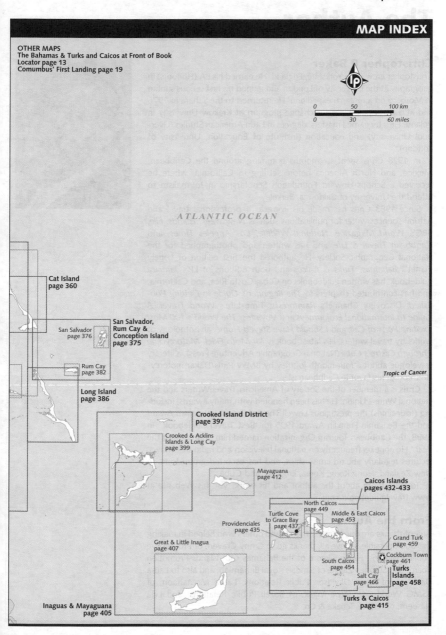

MAP INDEX

OTHER MAPS
The Bahamas & Turks and Caicos at Front of Book
Locator page 13
Comumbus' First Landing page 19

ATLANTIC OCEAN

0   50   100 km
0   30   60 miles

Cat Island
page 360

San Salvador
page 376

San Salvador,
Rum Cay &
Conception Island
page 375

Rum Cay
page 382

Tropic of Cancer

Long Island
page 386

Crooked Island District
page 397

Crooked & Acklins
Islands & Long Cay
page 399

Mayaguana
page 412

Caicos Islands
pages 432-433

North Caicos
page 449

Middle & East Caicos
page 453

Turtle Cove
to Grace Bay
page 437

Providenciales
page 435

Grand Turk
page 459

Cockburn Town
page 461

Great & Little Inagua
page 407

South Caicos
page 454

Turks
Islands
page 458

Salt Cay
page 466

Inaguas & Mayaguana
page 405

Turks & Caicos
page 415

The Author

Christopher P Baker

Christopher grew up in Yorkshire, England. He earned his BA (Honours) in geography at the University of London and gained his first serious suntan in Morocco on a research expedition. He returned to the Sahara in 1976 and also participated in an exchange program at Krakow University in Poland. He later earned masters' degrees in Latin American Studies (Liverpool University) and education (Institute of Education, University of London).

In 1978 Chris spent six months bumming around the Caribbean, Mexico, and North America before settling in California, where he received a Scripps-Howard Foundation Scholarship in Journalism to attend the University of California, Berkeley.

Since 1983 Chris has made his living as a professional travel and natural sciences writer for publications such as *Newsweek*, *Islands*, *Elle*, BBC's *World Magazine*, *National Wildlife*, *Los Angeles Times*, and *Caribbean Travel & Life*, and has written and photographed for the National Geographic Society. He authored the first edition of Lonely Planet's *Bahamas, Turks & Caicos* and both editions of LP's *Jamaica* guidebook, has written guidebooks on Cuba, Costa Rica, and California, and has contributed chapters to *The Beginner's Guide to Getting Published*; Discovery Channel's *Rainforests*; Time-Life's *World Travel: A Guide to International Ecojourneys* and *Voyages: The World's 100 Most Exciting Ports of Call*; and *I Should Have Stayed Home*, an anthology of works by travel writers. His latest book is *Mi Moto Fidel: Motorcycling Through Castro's Cuba* (National Geographic Adventure Press), a literary travelogue about a four-month journey by BMW Paris/Dakar motorcycle through his favorite Caribbean isle.

Chris is a member of the Society of American Travel Writers and the National Writers Union. He has been honored with many awards, including (four times) the prestigious Lowell Thomas Travel Journalism Award and the Benjamin Franklin Award 1995 for 'Best Travel Guidebook.' In 1998, the Caribbean Tourism Organization named him 'Journalist of the Year.' He appears frequently on national television and radio talk shows, lectures regularly aboard cruise ships, and has escorted group tours to New Zealand, Hong Kong, Korea, England, and Cuba.

To learn more about the author and his work, visit his Web site at www.travelguidebooks.com.

From the Author

Ardent thanks are due to many friends and others who helped in making this book possible. Above all, thanks go to Ginny Craven, of Progressive Public Relations, Helen Filmore of the Bahamas Out Islands Promotion Board, and Stephen Zaidie, of Sandals Royal Bahamian; and also to Laura Davidson of Laura Davidson Public Relations; Laura McMahaon, of BSMG Worldwide; Rene Mack, of Bozell Public Relations; and Lyla Naseem, of Patrice Tenaka & Co.

I'd also like to thank the following: Karen Adderley; Marion Adira, of the Nassau Marriott; the Armbrister family, of Fernandez Bay Village; Charity Armbrister, of the Ministry of Tourism; Jeff Birch, of Small Hope Bay Lodge; Carla Caccavale, of the British Colonial Hilton; Mona Lisa Cassar; Sean Cooper, of Point Grace; Gregory Curry, of Cafe Matisse; Claudette Davis, of the Nassau Promotion Board; Jean and Dan Davies, of Laughing Bird Apartments; Peter Douglas, of the Andros Tourist Board; Wynsome Ferguson, of the Abaco Tourist Office; Louise Fletcher; Gail Forrester, of Beaches; Enrico Garzarolli, of Graycliff; Ralph Higgs, of Turks & Caicos Islands Tourism Board; Elaine Hokin, of Island Outpost; Laurie Kaiden, of Jensen/Boga Inc; Michele Lee Landa, of BSMG Worldwide; Stacy Lewis, of Murphy O'Brien Public Relations; Danny & Judy Lower, of Orange Hill Beach Inn; Marilyn Marx, of Marilyn Marx Public Relations; Mikala Moss, Miss Bahamas 1999; Ann Mullin, of The Cove, Eleuthera; Eoin O'Sullivan, of Beaches, Providenciales; Claudia Outten; Shantini Ramakrishnan, of Spring O'Brien Public Relations; Alyssa Rogers, of Jensen/Boga, Inc; Ryvis Sierra, of Sandals; Rachela Tirelli, of Atlantis; Priscilla Williams, of the Bahamas Ministry of Tourism; and many others whom I may have forgotten to credit by virtue of oversight or senility…to one and all, a hearty thank you.

Thanks, too, to all those other Bahamians who displayed great warmth and generosity in various ways, and to the many fellow travelers who shared insights and experiences along the way. And lastly, I wish to acknowledge Ginny and Jim Craven, who opened their hearts and their home to me; and to all my other personal friends who have lavished their support and forbearance, whether knowingly or not. Above all, my dear friend and attorney Sheri Powers, who selflessly took care of my affairs during my lengthy research trips; and most fervently to Maureen Collins – friend, inspiration, teacher – whose memorably passionate contributions proved the adage that it really is 'Better in the Bahamas.'

Dedication
To Maureen Collins

This Book

This 2nd edition of *Bahamas, Turks and Caicos* was edited and produced in Lonely Planet's Oakland office by a team large enough to populate a small Family Island. Erin Corrigan was the editor; Rachel Bernstein proofed most of the book; Vivek Wagle, Gabi Knight and Erin also did some proofing. The senior editor was at various times Tom Downs, Robert Reid, Kate Hoffman and Michele Posner. Miss Maria Donohoe also provided helpful insight, as always. The colorful cover was created by design manager Susan Rimerman. The book itself and the colorwraps were designed and laid out by Josh Schefers; Wendy Yanagihara cast her careful eye over all his work. The illustrations were drawn by Justin Marler and Beca Lafore. The detailed mapping was done by cartographer Kat Smith; senior cartographer Monica S Lepe gave Kat guidance when needed. The many other cartographers who helped with this book were Tessa Rottiers, Ed Turley, Justin Colgan, Dion Good, Nao Ogawa and Andrew Rebold. And finally, the index was created by Ken 'The Pro' Della Penta.

Foreword

ABOUT LONELY PLANET GUIDEBOOKS

The story begins with a classic travel adventure: Tony and Maureen Wheeler's 1972 journey across Europe and Asia to Australia. Useful information about the overland trail did not exist at that time, so Tony and Maureen published the first Lonely Planet guidebook to meet a growing need.

From a kitchen table, then from a tiny office in Melbourne (Australia), Lonely Planet has become the largest independent travel publisher in the world, an international company with offices in Melbourne, Oakland (USA), London (UK) and Paris (France).

Today Lonely Planet guidebooks cover the globe. There is an ever-growing list of books, and there's information in a variety of forms and media. Some things haven't changed. The main aim is still to help make it possible for adventurous travelers to get out there – to explore and better understand the world.

At Lonely Planet we believe travelers can make a positive contribution to the countries they visit – if they respect their host communities and spend their money wisely. Since 1986 a percentage of the income from each book has been donated to aid projects and human-rights campaigns.

Updates Lonely Planet thoroughly updates each guidebook as often as possible. This usually means there are around two years between editions, although for more unusual or more stable destinations the gap can be longer. Check the imprint page (following the color map at the beginning of the book) for publication dates.

Between editions, up-to-date information is available in two free newsletters – the paper *Planet Talk* and email *Comet* (to subscribe, contact any Lonely Planet office) – and on our website at www.lonelyplanet.com. The *Upgrades* section of the website covers a number of important and volatile destinations and is regularly updated by Lonely Planet authors. *Scoop* covers news and current affairs relevant to travelers. And, lastly, the *Thorn Tree* bulletin board and *Postcards* section of the site carry unverified, but fascinating, reports from travelers.

Correspondence The process of creating new editions begins with the letters, postcards and emails received from travelers. This correspondence often includes suggestions, criticisms and comments about the current editions. Interesting excerpts are immediately passed on via newsletters and the website, and everything goes to our authors to be verified when they're researching on the road. We're keen to get more feedback from organizations or individuals who represent communities visited by travelers.

> Lonely Planet gathers information for everyone who's curious about the planet – and especially for those who explore it firsthand. Through guidebooks, phrasebooks, activity guides, maps, literature, newsletters, image library, TV series and website, we act as an information exchange for a worldwide community of travelers.

Research Authors aim to gather sufficient practical information to enable travelers to make informed choices and to make the mechanics of a journey run smoothly. They also research historical and cultural background to help enrich the travel experience and allow travelers to understand and respond appropriately to cultural and environmental issues.

Authors don't stay in every hotel because that would mean spending a couple of months in each medium-size city and, no, they don't eat at every restaurant because that would mean stretching belts beyond capacity. They do visit hotels and restaurants to check standards and prices, but feedback based on readers' direct experiences can be very helpful.

Many of our authors work undercover; others aren't so secretive. None of them accept freebies in exchange for positive write-ups. And none of our guidebooks contain any advertising.

Production Authors submit their raw manuscripts and maps to offices in Australia, the USA, the UK or France. Editors and cartographers – all experienced travelers themselves – then begin the process of assembling the pieces. When the book finally hits the shops, some things are already out of date, we start getting feedback from readers and the process begins again....

WARNING & REQUEST

Things change – prices go up, schedules change, good places go bad and bad places go bankrupt – nothing stays the same. So, if you find things better or worse, recently opened or long since closed, please tell us and help make the next edition even more accurate and useful. We genuinely value all the feedback we receive. A well-traveled team reads and acknowledges every letter, postcard and email and ensures that every morsel of information finds its way to the appropriate authors, editors and cartographers for verification.

Everyone who writes to us will find their name listed in the next edition of the appropriate guidebook. They will also receive the latest issue of *Planet Talk*, our quarterly printed newsletter, or *Comet*, our monthly email newsletter. Subscriptions to both newsletters are free. The very best contributions will be rewarded with a free guidebook.

We may edit, reproduce and incorporate your comments in all Lonely Planet products, such as guidebooks, Web sites and digital products, so let us know if you don't want your comments reproduced or your name acknowledged.

Send all correspondence to the Lonely Planet office closest to you:

Australia: Locked Bag 1, Footscray, Victoria 3011
USA: 150 Linden St, Oakland, CA 94607
UK: 10a Spring Place, London NW5 3BH
France: 1 rue du Dahomey, 75011 Paris

Or email us at: talk2us@lonelyplanet.com.au

For news, views and updates, see our Web site: www.lonelyplanet.com

HOW TO USE A LONELY PLANET GUIDEBOOK

The best way to use a Lonely Planet guidebook is any way you choose. At Lonely Planet, we believe the most memorable travel experiences are often those that are unexpected, and the finest discoveries are those you make yourself. Guidebooks are not intended to be used as if they provided a detailed set of infallible instructions!

Contents All Lonely Planet guidebooks follow the same format. The Facts about the Country chapters or sections give background information ranging from history to weather. Facts for the Visitor gives practical information on issues like visas and health. Getting There & Away gives a brief starting point for researching travel to and from the destination. Getting Around gives an overview of the transport options available when you arrive.

The peculiar demands of each destination determine how subsequent chapters are broken up, but some things remain constant. We always start with background, then proceed to sights, places to stay, places to eat, entertainment, getting there and away, and getting around information – in that order.

Heading Hierarchy Lonely Planet headings are used in a strict hierarchical structure that can be visualized as a set of Russian dolls. Each heading (and its following text) is encompassed by any preceding heading that is higher on the hierarchical ladder.

Entry Points We do not assume guidebooks will be read from beginning to end, but that people will dip into them. The traditional entry points are the list of contents and the index. In addition, however, some books have a complete list of maps and an index map illustrating map coverage.

There may also be a color map that shows highlights. These highlights are dealt with in greater detail later in the book, along with planning questions and suggested itineraries. Each chapter covering a geographical region usually begins with a locator map and another list of highlights. Once you find something of interest in a list of highlights, turn to the index.

Maps Maps play a crucial role in Lonely Planet guidebooks and include a huge amount of information. A legend is printed on the back page. We seek to have complete consistency between maps and text, and to have every important place in the text captured on a map. Map key numbers usually start in the top left corner.

Although inclusion in a guidebook usually implies a recommendation, we cannot list every good place. Exclusion does not necessarily imply criticism. In fact, there are a number of reasons why we might exclude a place – sometimes it is simply inappropriate to encourage an influx of travelers.

Introduction

Strewn like pearls in a 750-mile arc from the south tip of Florida to the north shore of Haiti is a low-lying archipelago made up of two distinct nations: the independent Commonwealth of The Bahamas (more than 700 islands spread over 100,000 sq miles of ocean – about the same size as the UK) and, immediately to the southeast, the half-dozen or so relatively small islands that make up the Turks and Caicos, a crown colony of the UK. Contrary to popular opinion, both countries lie outside the Caribbean Sea; they are washed on the north and east by the Atlantic and on the south and west by the Gulf Stream.

Many visitors think of The Bahamas as a single (and small) island destination and know little of the diversity of its individual islands. Some are quite large: Eleuthera, the

longest, is 100 miles long. Andros, the largest, covers 2300 sq miles. Though the islands have some things in common, each has its own character and often a distinct culture, usually with a timeless charm and several layers of life to discover.

The Bahamas has long been the major tourist destination in the Caribbean region. In a recent survey of US citizens, the islands ranked as the 'most desirable Caribbean island vacation destination' for winter months. The Turks and Caicos are far less well known, sparking the nation's tourism board to come up with a marketing slogan: 'Where on earth are the Turks and Caicos?'

The popularity of The Bahamas was tarnished in the 1980s, when it became known as the prime staging point for the South America-to-US drug trade. Political

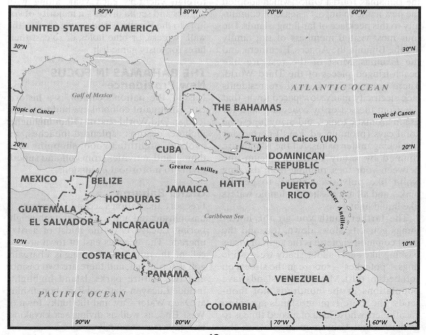

corruption and deteriorating social conditions also fostered surliness among the people of Nassau (capital of The Bahamas), one felt by tourists. Visitors began to stay away. Fortunately, The Bahamas has bounced back – the mood is now benign and welcoming. And several upscale new properties have energized the marketplace, setting off a scramble among hoteliers to refurbish and renovate.

There are two sides to these islands, but only one is celebrated – the cruise-ship-run-aground world of rum-swizzle excursions, water sports, and bargain Bulgari shopping…and the James Bond world of casinos, luxury yachts, golf courses, and grandiose mansions. That's New Providence, especially Nassau; Grand Bahama, seen by 3 million visitors a year; and Providenciales (Turks and Caicos).

The other side of the coin – one you don't hear much about – is the Out Islands, or Family Islands, the name preferred by the Bahamas Tourist Office, which adopted the new name to impart a sense of community to this necklace of far-flung islands. The four most-visited members of the family are the Biminis, the Abacos, Eleuthera, and the Exumas. Most of the rest are like beach-fringed pieces of the Third World. There are many pockets where residents lack electricity, many slow-paced towns that live from the sea or by collecting bark for use in aromatic tonics, and many lonesome coral cays (pronounced 'keys') perfect for picnicking under palms. All the islands are rimmed by sandy beaches, talcum-fine between your toes, running from dazzling white like pulverized sugar, to peachy pink…and all are washed by limpid waters like liquid light.

The farther south you go, the hotter things get. Life slows down, too, and the most common vignette is the sight of locals basking like seals under shady trees while dogs – 'potcakes' – snooze in the streets on soft beds of dust. Most Family Islands have populations in the hundreds, not thousands. The more remote islands appeal to vacationers whose idea of a good time is to go with local fishermen far out on the green-blue, where they gather conchs or lobsters on the sandy sea bottom. Attractions are limited to a few Victorian-era lighthouses, roofless plantation houses, and old cannons. And don't expect rousing nightlife. Celebrating the sunset is a prelude to simple evenings spent sampling rum cocktails and listening to native rake 'n' scrape combos.

Though the focus is on sun, sand, and 'sin,' opportunities for ecological adventures abound. Great Inagua, for example, has a wildlife reserve with one of the largest flamingo flocks in the world. And sea kayaking and even biking and hiking programs are taking off, as are whale-watching trips and dolphin swims. The government is wooing ecosensitive hoteliers and tour operators. The Turks and Caicos – abounding with wildlife – have made even greater strides in preserving their natural heritage in parks.

Both countries draw thousands of foreign yachters each year, along with anglers and scuba divers – a majority of visitors to the Family Islands come to dive 'the wall,' wrecks, or blue holes, or to cast their lures for feisty game fish.

THE BAHAMAS IN FOCUS
New Providence

Nassau, the nation's capital, is a historic city with quaint colonial-era buildings that lend an Old World charm. Other highlights include casinos, splendid beaches, an evolved nightlife, good shopping and dining, and activities from golf and superb diving to motorboat excursions.

Grand Bahama

Freeport, the nation's second-largest city, is unsophisticated and soulless, though neighboring Lucaya is in the midst of a ritzy upgrade. The beaches east of town are excellent, the duty-free shopping is a bargain, golf is top-notch, and there are two casinos and two nature parks. Island highlights include Lucayan National Park, bonefishing at Deep Water Cay, and the funky town of West End, as well as diving, sea kayaking, and day-cruise excursions.

Biminis

The prime attraction is sport fishing – the island group is the site of many annual fishing tournaments. The bars spill over during spring break, when college kids flock from Florida. The bonefishing is acclaimed and the diving splendid, and Hemingway's haunts are still frequented by tourists and locals alike.

Berry Islands

These small islands appeal for sport fishing and a few lonesome beaches. Facilities are minimal.

Abacos

This island group is the third-most-visited area in the country. Its Loyalist villages (on a series of cays – Green Turtle, Great Guana, Man O' War, and Elbow) are the prettiest in The Bahamas, with Cape Cod–style clapboard architecture, museums, art galleries, glorious beaches, and a caught-in-time lifestyle. Waters in the lee of the cays are an acclaimed yachting playground. The east shore is stunning. West of Great Abaco – the main island – are The Marls, with superb bonefishing.

To the south lies Abaco National Park, a pristine site for bird watchers and hikers. Whales pass by offshore. A string of small isles north of Great Abaco ends at Walker's Cay, a prime sport-fishing and dive site.

Andros

Relatively undeveloped for tourism, Andros – comprising three islands – offers superb bonefishing and diving in blue holes and on the wall along the world's third-longest barrier reef. Andros is smothered in pine forests, thick undergrowth, and marshy wetlands.

Eleuthera

Once popular with wealthy vacationers, mainland Eleuthera has declined in recent years. The happening scene is now the offshore cay of Harbour Island, the choicest place in The Bahamas, boasting Pink Sands, the nation's finest resort; Dunmore Town, a Loyalist village with 200-year-old architecture; and Pink Sands Beach, one of many blush-hued beaches running Eleuthera's length. Eleuthera also offers scenic headlands and sea-scapes, plus interesting towns such as Spanish Wells, Governor's Harbour, and quaint Tarpum Bay.

Exumas

A prime cruising ground, the Exumas are a 100-mile-long string of pristine cays. The Exuma Cays Land & Sea Park protects many of these cays and offshore waters. The diving is first class and the bonefishing on the flats west of Great Exuma is acclaimed. Site of the annual Family Island Regatta, George Town briefly becomes the liveliest place in The Bahamas.

Cat Island

The heart of traditional Bahamian culture still beats on Cat Island, one of the isles least touched by tourism. Obeah (a form of African-based ritual magic) and bush medicine are still practiced, and many locals make a living from their basketry. Cat has several interesting historic sites, including plantation ruins and the hermitage of Father Jerome. Diving, bonefishing, hiking, kayaking, and bird watching are excellent.

San Salvador

This small island claims (but cannot prove) that it's the site of Columbus' 1492 New World landfall. The island is also known for sport fishing and superb diving. The birding is good and there's a working lighthouse.

Long Island

This aptly named island is virtually un-touched by tourism. The main base is Stella Maris, the setting for acclaimed diving, sport fishing, and bonefishing. Its beaches are sublime. Long Island offers intriguing churches, hidden beaches, fine coastal vistas, caves, and blue holes. In May the island awakens for the Long Island Regatta.

Crooked Island District

Remote and unspoiled, the island group has few facilities. Attractions are limited to a few splendid beaches, bat caves, and an abandoned lighthouse on an offshore cay. Its birds – especially flamingos – are a good reason to visit. Turtles nest here in season.

Inaguas & Mayaguana

Semiarid, scrub-covered Great Inagua receives few tourists. Beaches, too, are few, but the island boasts the largest flock of flamingos in the Western Hemisphere. Inagua National Park has dozens of other bird species. The island, which has meager tourist facilities, is dominated by the salt industry. Neighboring Mayaguana is even less prepared for tourism but is slated to become a nature reserve.

TURKS AND CAICOS IN FOCUS
Providenciales

'Provo,' the main island, boasts a score of resorts along one of the world's most incredible beaches. There are good birdwatching sites, lonesome beaches, and spectacular Chalk Sound. The island offers splendid bonefishing at Sapodilla Bay, plus a rugged drive to Northwest Point Marine National Park.

West Caicos

This rugged island south of Provo is known for fantastic diving. It's a popular spot for picnics. Iguanas and flamingos abound and there are isolated beaches.

North Caicos

This island has minimal tourist facilities but an abundance of plantation ruins and lakes with flamingos and other waders. Seabirds nest in the wetlands of the south shore.

Middle & East Caicos

Middle Caicos, the largest island, features a dramatic coastline, limestone caves, remains of an Indian ballcourt, dense vegetation, secluded beaches, and the country's only developed hiking, the Middle Caicos Reserve & Trail System. The south shore, lined with wetlands, is fabulous for bird watching. East Caicos is a virtually uninhabited, down-at-the-heels island with caves, beaches, and large wetlands.

South Caicos

South Caicos, the center of the fishing industry, is a mecca for bonefishermen and home to the Commonwealth Regatta. There are flamingos and a protected reef close to funky Cockburn Harbour, which has fine historic buildings and an earthy appeal.

Grand Turk

Turks and Caicos' surprisingly small capital, Cockburn Town, is quaint and somnolent, with antique, weather-beaten buildings and the Turks & Caicos National Museum. If you like sand-blown streets, you may love its rugged, against-all-odds charm. The wall diving is superb. There are also good beaches, bird watching, and windsurfing.

Salt Cay

This tiny cay was once the world's largest salt producer. Steeped in the history of the Turks and Caicos, it boasts fascinating industrial ruins, historic buildings, and great beaches and swimming.

Facts about The Bahamas

HISTORY
The Lucayans

The original inhabitants of the Bahamas were the Lucayans, a tribe of the Arawak Indian group. The Lucayans (a word derived from *lukku-caire*, or 'island people,' the Indians' name for themselves) arrived near the turn of the 9th century, at the end of the great migration of Arawaks from South America. Fleeing the advance of the more militaristic, cannibalistic Caribs, they leapfrogged from one Caribbean island to another. The Caribs never reached the Bahamas. (Some archaeologists argue that the Lucayans were a separate group altogether and had migrated from the North American continent.)

The peaceful Lucayans lived primarily off the sea. They made bread from manioc and grew corn, yams, and other vegetables. They also evolved skills as potters, carvers, weavers, and boatbuilders, and they spun and wove cotton into clothing (which they traded with neighboring islands) and hammocks. The Indians also wove ropes, carpets, and watertight roofs from the bark of the calabash tree. They got fired up by drinking corn alcohol, smoking dried leaves, and using a powdered drug, blown up the nostrils through a meter-long tube called a *tabaco*. The Lucayans, however, had no conception of the wheel and no written language, and they did not use beasts of burden or metals.

Christopher Columbus, arriving in 1492, considered them 'well-proportioned and good looking.' The Indians, whom he described as the same color as the people of the Canaries ('neither black nor white'), went about painted. Flattened heads were considered beautiful, and babies' heads were thus encased between boards to restrict their development.

They lived in egalitarian communities in caves and thatched shelters. Their villages were comprised of several family clans, each headed by a *cacique*, whose largely nominal title was passed down by primogeniture.

Arawak society was communal, and materialism an alien concept.

Religion played a central role in Arawak life. They worshiped various gods who were thought to control the rain, sun, wind, and hurricanes. They believed in a glorious afterlife and would sometimes strangle dying chieftains to speed them to heaven (called *coyaba*).

Dozens of Lucayan sites have been unearthed, although only a few have been seriously excavated. The little that remains of their culture is limited to pottery shards, petroglyphs, and English words such as 'canoe,' 'cannibal,' 'hammock,' 'hurricane,' and 'tobacco.'

The Coming of Columbus

Native Americans had occupied the Bahamas for at least 500 years by the time Christopher Columbus first sighted the New World on October 12, 1492, during the first of his four voyages to find a westward route to the East Indies.

Though taunted with skepticism and ridicule, Columbus pressed his plan to sail west from Europe to the Orient. King Ferdinand and Queen Isabella of Spain granted him two caravels and he gained the patronage of the powerful Pinzón family. Finally, on August 3, 1492, Columbus and his crew set out from Spain aboard *Santa María*, the flagship, accompanied by two caravels, the *Niña* and *Pinta*, about 20 'friends of the Crown,' and a crew of 90, including a translator versed in Chinese and Arabic.

The expedition sailed west, following the latitude of Japan and China. On October 12, after 33 days and more than 3000 miles, the shout of *'Tierra!'* went up and an island gleamed in the moonlight. Columbus planted the Spanish flag and named the island San Salvador. (The people who already inhabited it called their island 'Guanahaní.') From here, the fleet sailed south to an island Columbus named Santa María de la Concepción, then west to a large island he named Fernandina.

The First Landfall

No one disputes that Columbus' first landfall was in The Bahamas (except residents of the Turks and Caicos). But the question of *which* island it was has aroused considerable controversy. Several islands claim the prize.

Columbus and the priest-historian Bartolomé de las Casas kept assiduous records, but, much to historians' regret, no evidence exists to prove where Columbus *first* stepped ashore. (The original record vanished after being dispatched to Queen Isabella.) Investigators have spent centuries sleuthing for clues to put the argument to rest.

Nine first landfalls have been proposed and defended. Today's Samana Cay was strongly favored at an early stage, but in 1942 Admiral Samuel Eliot Morison, a noted biographer of Columbus, declared that Watling Island (which in 1926 was renamed San Salvador – the name that Columbus bestowed on his first landfall) was the hallowed island. Watling Island was accepted for years as the first landfall, although, incredibly, no one had taken into account 'dead reckoning' – the cumulative effect of current and leeway (wind-caused slippage) on a vessel's course – in tracing the route of the round-bottomed fleet. Columbus' course took him along the southern half of the North Atlantic gyre, a then-undiscovered slow clockwise swirl of winds and currents that sweeps in a southwestern direction from the Madeira Islands to The Bahamas.

In November 1986, following five years of extensive study by Joseph Judge and a team of scholarly interests under the aegis of the National Geographic Society, *National Geographic* magazine announced that it had solved the 'grandest of all geographic mysteries.' Judge ordered a new translation of the Columbus diaries, drew the first-ever track of the log, then input all the variables into a computer to adjust for leeway, current, and magnetic variation, and traveled to the islands to find actual evidence. See the Columbus' First Landing map for a comparison of Judge's and Morison's proposed tracks.

Judge's team also was the first to track Columbus' course using the Spanish league (2.82 nautical miles), *not* the English league (2.5 nautical miles) previously used. *Presto!* The *exact* landing spot turns out to be latitude 23°09′00″N and longitude 73°29′13″W...the island of Samana Cay.

Turning southeast, they touched at a fourth island, christened Isabela, then sailed southwest to today's Ragged Island Range.

The Columbus' First Landing map shows two courses, each of which has been proposed as the one that Columbus traveled during his exploration. The first, the 'Morison track,' was proposed by Admiral Samuel Eliot Morison, one of the explorer's biographers, and shows Columbus' first landfall as the present-day island of San Salvador. The second, supported by a National Geographic Society study, is the 'Judge track.' It proposes Samana Cay as the first landfall. In parentheses below the modern-day names of the landfall islands are the names that Columbus assigned to them.

Everywhere he landed, Columbus found indigenous people who came out to greet the vessels, bearing gifts. He recorded that 'they should be good servants....With fifty men they would all be kept in subjection and forced to do whatever may be wished.'

Columbus and his fellow expeditionaries were underwritten by monarchs and merchants whose interest was economic. Gold, or at least the thought of it, filled the sails. The Spaniards did not linger in these barren coral islands. The Indians told Columbus that gold might be found in Cubanacan (middle Cuba), which he translated as 'Kublai Khan.' Columbus spent 15 days sailing from island to island before cutting south to 'discover' Cuba and Hispaniola,

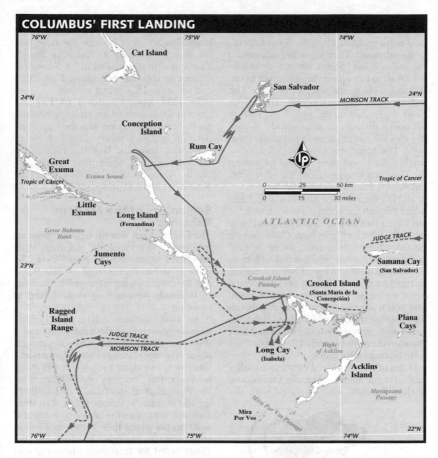

COLUMBUS' FIRST LANDING

where he wrecked the *Santa María* on a reef. Columbus then took command of the *Niña*, left his crew marooned, and headed back to Europe to report his exciting find. (When he returned to Hispaniola in 1493, the 43 stranded crew members were dead.)

Until his death, Columbus was convinced that these islands were the easternmost outposts of Asia. Since he had traveled west to reach them, he named them the West Indies. Thus their inhabitants became known as 'Indians.'

Despite three more voyages, he discovered no gold, ivory, or other wealth in any quantity, and his underwriters withdrew their support. On May 20, 1506, he died, powerless and relatively poor.

Early Colonial Years

In 1495 Spanish colonialists established the first settlement in the archipelago. The small stockade, at the southeast corner of today's Cat Island, was named Columba in honor of the explorer. It served as a shipping point for Lucayan Indians, enslaved by the Spaniards and bound for Hispaniola.

There were then perhaps 50,000 Lucayans in the Bahamian islands and only a limited quantity of gold, obtained in trade with other islands. Hispaniola, to the south, held more promise. Here the Spaniards established mines. They so swiftly decimated the native Taino Indians, whom they shackled for slave labor, that they returned to the Bahamian chain and seized Lucayans. The Indians were worked to death. Those who resisted perished by the sword, the rest by European diseases or mass suicide. Within 25 years the entire Lucayan population was gone. The Spaniards casually sailed away, leaving the island chain devoid of human life. Columba struggled along for a few years but was eventually abandoned.

In 1513 the Spaniard Juan Ponce de León sailed through the archipelago searching for the fabled Fountain of Youth. Instead Ponce de León, who had been with Columbus on his second expedition, came across the fast-moving Gulf Stream, which whisked him to Florida and his 'discovery' of North America. In rapid succession, Spanish explorers came upon the treasure-filled empires of Central and South America. Soon Spanish galleons were passing by the reef-encrusted Bahamas laden with treasure bound for Spain. Many foundered, and the waters of the archipelago were littered with wrecks.

Tales of treasure lured pirates and other adventurers, such as Francis Drake and Walter Raleigh, who operated with the

Juan Ponce de León

sanction of Queen Elizabeth I and used the Bahamian islands as hideaways and bases. San Salvador became the base, too, for Raleigh's colony at Roanoke Island, England's first settlement in America. Otherwise the islands remained unsettled and unclaimed for over a century.

In 1629 King Charles I of England granted the islands to his attorney general, Sir Robert Heath, along with the Carolinas, part of Britain's newly founded North American colonies. But the islands remained neglected, while their neighbors – North America, Hispaniola, Cuba, and Jamaica – grew and prospered.

Beginnings of the Modern Bahamas

The English Civil War brought religious intolerance and persecution, and many Puritans fled England for the New World. The wave of intolerance arrived in their wake, and the colonies were infected. The Puritans of Bermuda were among those forced to move on.

In 1648 William Sayle, the Puritan founder-governor of Bermuda, outfitted a ship named the *William* and set out with about 70 other islanders, mostly farmers and fishermen, intent on founding a colony of tolerance. The Company of Adventurers for the Plantation of the Islands of Eleuthera arrived at today's Abacos. Political rivalries forced a split, and the majority continued south to the island then known as Cigatoo (the founders renamed it Eleuthera, the Greek word for freedom), where the ship ran aground and sank, taking with it all their provisions. Sayle and a few survivors set out by rowboat to enlist support. They made it to Jamestown, Virginia, whose residents sent provisions to the marooned, who then founded the first independent republic in the New World.

Unfortunately, the thin Bahamian soil allows root crops little chance to flourish, and the islanders soon began to starve. Some gave up and sailed back to Bermuda (in 1657 Sayle himself left). Others hung on and were supplied by the Puritans of Massachusetts, who received in exchange a large quantity of native hardwoods, which funded creation of Harvard College. Other nonconformists arrived, including freed slaves seeking a home.

In 1649, the year the Adventurers founded their republic, Oliver Cromwell's Puritans proved victorious and Charles I lost his head – literally. In 1654 Cromwell devised his ill-fated 'Grand Western Design' to destroy the Spanish trade monopoly and secure English holdings in the Caribbean by enticing settlers with land grants and promises of supplies. Puritan settlers were sponsored in the islands. Many of the settlers were free blacks and troublesome slaves evicted from Bermuda and North America.

In 1681 Cromwell's reign ended, and Charles II, ignoring the Puritan government of Eleuthera, doled out the islands among six nobles led by Lord Ashley, Lord Proprietor of South Carolina, and sponsored 300 settlers loyal to the crown. New settlements consolidated their hold, notably Charles Town, which was founded in 1666 and favored by its well-sheltered harbor. (In 1695 the town was renamed Nassau in honor of the new king of England, William III, formerly Prince of Orange-Nassau.) Soon seafaring rogues were attracted to the new port.

Alas, the six Proprietors were absentee landlords. Charles appointed a governor, who died en route. Meanwhile the populace elected their own governor, Captain Hugh Wentworth, foretelling the troubles that ensuing Royal appointee-governors would have in establishing their authority. The city had descended into a 'lewd, licentious' lifestyle. When Wentworth decided to take his duties seriously by collecting taxes, he was forcibly removed from office. A replacement was sent from England, but he, too, was sent packing.

Charles Town – an assemblage of sordid elements who gained their livelihood from the salvage trade – grew and prospered. Lacking accurate maps and subject to the vagaries of hurricanes, hundreds of ships foundered in these reef-strewn waters. When times were slow, 'wreckers' would lure hapless ships to their fate by placing shore lights amid the reefs and then brutishly pick over the bones. Ever-increasing numbers of ruffians came to Charles Town, where the governor served his time at the behest of pirates and outlaws.

Rise of Piracy

During the 17th century, England was constantly at war with France or Spain. Since the Royal Navy couldn't effectively patrol the Caribbean, the crown sponsored privateers to do the job. Its Letters of Marque authorized privateers – many of them pirates, or 'buccaneers' – to capture enemy vessels and plunder cities. Gradually they replaced their motley vessels with captured Spanish ships and the pirates grew into a powerful force. The Bahamas, with hundreds of islets, cays, and complex shoals and channels, lay in the path of treasure fleets bound for Europe and thus was an ideal base. Charles Town took to piracy on an almost industrial scale.

Spain, of course, was outraged, especially since it still claimed title over the Bahamas, and on at least four occasions attacked and razed Charles Town, beginning in 1684, when the town was destroyed. Charles Town was rebuilt and returned to its wicked ways.

In 1701 the War of the Spanish Succession broke out, with England pitted against France and Spain. In 1703 a joint French and Spanish fleet destroyed Nassau. Again the pirates and privateers returned. This time, without a governor to control things, they proclaimed a 'Privateer's Republic' without laws or government. This state of affairs lasted until 1714 (Nassau survived Spanish naval assaults in 1704 and 1706), when the three nations signed the Treaty of Utrecht.

No longer under royal patronage, pirates became outlaws. For the next century, even while attempts were made to suppress them, they plundered ships of all nations and raided towns and plantations in the Caribbean and the Carolinas.

The most important pirate in Bahamian history was Henry Jennings, a privateer who arrived in Nassau in 1715 and rapidly rose to become its de facto leader. Under his tutelage, the town prospered as a pirate capital, and its wealth attracted merchants, rum traders, vintners, prostitutes, and countless others. Townsfolk even invested in the expeditions in exchange for a share of the booty. No number of taverns and whorehouses seemed enough to slake their thirsts.

Several other pirates rose to infamy, including 'Blackbeard' (Edward Teach), who terrorized his victims by wearing flaming fuses in his matted beard and hair. Teach proclaimed himself magistrate of Nassau and used his unique brand of discipline to maintain harmony among the irreverent rabble.

Pirates Expelled

In 1718 King George II decided to make the Bahamas a royal colony with direct rule from England. Governor Woodes Rogers (himself a former privateer) was appointed by the king to suppress piracy and install a viable administration. Rogers arrived with three warships and issued the king's ultimatum to pirates: 'death or pardon.' A brief battle ensued, and the royal forces were victorious. Most pirates wisely opted to abandon their lifestyle. Several who refused were promptly

Blackbeard

hanged. The city settled into a period of relative calm. Rogers described his own tenure in words that became the nation's motto: *Expulsis Piratis – Restituta Commercia* (Pirates Expelled – Commerce Restored), words that still adorn the official seal of The Bahamas.

England was soon again at war with Spain. Governor Rogers fortified the city. When the Spaniards made another raid on New Providence in 1720, cannon volleys and well-trained former pirates repulsed them.

In 1729 Rogers convened an assembly of prominent Bahamians – the progenitor of one of the oldest parliaments in the New World. It remained virtually unchanged in form until independence in 1973. Rogers' Bahamian assembly was notably oligarchic. The elite often acted in their own interests and were frequently and obstinately at loggerheads with the governor and the English crown, setting a tone that lasted two centuries.

Privateering was legalized whenever wars broke out with France or Spain (as in 1738, 1748, and 1756), and Nassau benefited from brief bursts of prosperity. But in times of peace, Nassau and the colonies were depauperate, and the islanders scraped by through turtle trapping, salt farming (collecting salt from evaporation pans), and, most importantly, wrecking. Rogers' attempts to foster agriculture foundered.

The authorities set up strict rules to govern wrecking, or 'salvage,' as they preferred to think of it. Historian John Oldmixon, in his *History of Providence* (1780), wrote:

As for Wrecks, all that came ashore was Prize, and if a Sailor had, by better Luck than the rest, got ashore as well as his Wreck, he was not sure of getting off again as well.... The Inhabitants looked upon every thing they could get out of a Cast-away Ship as their own, and were not at any Trouble to inquire about the owners.

By 1850 as much as half of the islands' population made a livelihood from wrecking – as did the government, which took 15% customs duty on the proceeds of sales from salvaged goods. The governor took an additional 10%. The industry became so well organized that many people had a vested interest in causing a ship's demise, including unscrupulous skippers eager to share in the booty.

Those Damned Yanks

The Bahamas lay close to the North American colonies, and the outbreak of the American Revolution in 1775 put the Bahamas in the firing line. The islands' ties to the 13 colonies were intimate, for Charles I's original grant to Sir Robert Heath had lumped the Carolinas and the Bahamas together. Trade and family ties bound the islands to the colonies. Inevitably, although most islanders remained loyal to the crown, sympathies for the rebels ran deep.

When the 13 colonies declared independence, England blockaded North America's eastern seaboard, cutting off trade with the Bahamas, which at the time relied on food imports from North America. The American Navy fell upon Nassau, intent on capturing arms and explosives (the first-ever foreign invasion by US forces). The Yankees occupied Nassau, carousing their way through Bay St's brothels and bars before sailing away two weeks later.

Nassau again fell victim to the rebels in 1778, and in 1782 a joint Spanish-French-US force took advantage of England's weakened position to capture the city. Spain declared possession of the Bahamas and proceeded to make life intolerable for Nassau's inhabitants. US colonel Andrew Deveaux, a Loyalist, took it upon himself to recapture the Bahamas for England. He arrived in 1783 with 200 pro-British mercenaries. The Spaniards watched from afar as longboats ferried soldiers ashore. As the landing point was hidden from view, the soldiers stood up for the journey to shore and then the same men lay out of sight for the journey back to the ship, repeatedly. Thus the Spaniards gained the impression that thousands of troops were landing. The Spaniards packed their belongings and set sail for Cuba.

The Treaty of Versailles formally ceded the Bahamas to England from Spain.

Loyalist 'Invasion'

With the American colonies now independent, English Loyalists began washing up in the Bahamas: more than 8000 Loyalists and their slaves resettled in the Bahamian islands between 1783 and 1785, tripling the existing population.

A Loyalist became the new governor. Lord Dunmore, an autocratic and corrupt Scottish earl, had been governor of New York and then Virginia until he was chased out by George Washington's men. In a rage, Dunmore had his ships destroy Norfolk before fleeing to Nassau, where he erected Fort Fincastle and Fort Charlotte to defend against retribution. Dunmore spent lavishly on himself, eventually erecting property on Harbour Island and overseeing construction of a Loyalist settlement that he named Dunmore Town. Dunmore's dissolute ways led to his replacement in 1796.

King George III had guaranteed each of the Loyalist settlers a plot of land. The newcomers – now important landholders – demanded political representation and were supported by Lord Dunmore, who had doled out crown land liberally to gain their support. Soon they were at loggerheads with the existing families, whom the *arrivistes* considered a less noble breed (the Loyalists called them 'conchs,' after the lowly mollusks).

The Loyalists introduced two things that would profoundly shape the islands' future: cotton and slaves. They set up plantations modeled on those in the Carolinas. However, most of the settlers were merchants and craftsmen with little knowledge of farming, and the land was ill suited to cotton. Most of the farms failed within a few years. Many settlers gradually drifted back to the US or to England. Others stayed, rising to prominence in Nassau and the Abaco Cays.

Plantation Era

Slavery was introduced relatively late to the Bahamas and here differed from that on neighboring islands or in the US South. The infertile soils of the Bahamas precluded large-scale agriculture. Vast plantations with huge slave populations and their attendant need for barbarous suppression never evolved. Nor did a large slave trade evolve. It was, relatively speaking, a more humane affair.

Overnight the islands' population became predominantly black, and African heritage was woven into the weft of English culture. By 1788 the population of the islands was estimated at about 11,200, 75% of whom were black (of these, 25% were freemen, many of whom were themselves slaveowners). That year, almost 1 million pounds of cotton were exported to Britain. The plantation system, however, was comparatively short lived. In 1789, the plantations were struck by an infestation of chenille worms and most failed within a few decades.

Ambitious public-works programs were initiated to keep slaves employed, resulting in the erection of the fine stone edifices that still grace downtown Nassau.

Demise of Slavery

This period coincided with a time of growing antislavery sentiment. The British Parliament banned the slave trade throughout the empire in 1807, and Royal Navy vessels intercepted slavers on the high seas. Their captive cargoes were liberated and deposited in the Bahamas.

Parliament abolished slavery on August 1, 1834. After emancipation, many Loyalists bequeathed their lands to their former slaves, who turned, like the free blacks around them, to fishing and subsistence farming. The transition went smoothly. Freemen founded new settlements throughout the islands. And from the very first election, black members were voted into the House of Assembly.

Full equality and political rights, however, proved more elusive, for the postslavery era was marked by continued colonialism and class and racial discrimination. Voting districts and requirements were gerrymandered to ensure that blacks would be outnumbered in the Assembly. A minority white elite of merchants and administrators ruled over an ill-represented black majority, a state of affairs that would last for more than a century.

For most of the 19th century, the economy muddled along based on subsistence agriculture, fishing, wrecking, smuggling, and sponging. Thousands of Bahamians – black and white – made a living diving for sponges, which briefly became the islands' most prominent industry under the tutelage of Greeks, who arrived in large numbers. In 1938 a blight killed the sponges and the industry withered. See the boxed text 'Sponging' in the Andros chapter for more information.

As the century progressed, fruit farming evolved as demand for pineapples and citrus blossomed in England and America…until the latter enacted ruinous tariffs. Meanwhile the British erected lighthouses and drew up accurate maps that provided for safer sea passage, bringing on the virtual demise of wrecking.

The US Civil War (1861–65) gave the Bahamas a boost when President Abraham Lincoln imposed a naval blockade on the Southern states. The British textile industry relied upon cotton from the South; thus Britain favored the Confederacy, and the Bahamas became the major trading center for the South. Ships such as the *Ballymena* became infamous blockade-runners, running supplies to the South and returning with holds full of cotton. Author Margaret Mitchell, in *Gone with the Wind*, presents Rhett Butler as a well-known figure in Nassau, where he loaded his schooner with luxuries for the Confederacy.

Nassau boomed. Fine edifices were erected and the population swelled as out-islanders flocked to reap their share of smuggling fortunes. But the end of hostilities burst Nassau's bubble again, and the ensuing decades witnessed an exodus of migrant labor to the US.

A reverse flow also evolved. The US' rapidly growing wealth created a burgeoning class of people with discretionary money. Many sought vacations in balmy climes. By the turn of the century, Florida was a tourist hot spot and the Bahamas were catching the spin-off.

A Rum Deal

By now Bahamians of all shades had evolved a fiercely patriotic identity as a British colony. When WWI erupted in 1914, thousands of Bahamians volunteered and gave their lives while serving in the British West Indies regiment.

The war killed the embryonic tourism trade, but in 1920 the islands were again granted divine deliverance – the 18th Amendment to the US Constitution, otherwise known as Prohibition. The Bahamas were ideally situated for running illicit liquor into the US aboard speedboats and the Nassau waterfront soon resembled a vast rum warehouse. Millions of gallons of alcohol were whisked across the water to Florida or New Jersey's Rum Row.

On Nassau and, to a lesser degree, other islands, construction boomed. New public buildings arose. Hotels blossomed like mushrooms on a damp log. And the islands' first casino opened, attracting gamblers and gangsters alongside a potpourri of the rich and famous.

The British Parliament and Bahamian Assembly were hesitant to act against the trade. Heck, importing and exporting spirits was no crime. And there were English and Scottish distilleries to support.

In December 1933 the repeal of Prohibition again burst Nassau's bubble. The Depression followed, and the Bahamas hit skid row.

The Bahamas as Duchy

In 1940 the Duke and Duchess of Windsor arrived as governor and governess. Formerly King Edward VIII of England, the duke and Mrs Wallis Simpson (the American divorcée he had married) gave the islands new luster, ensuring that the rich and famous would pour into Nassau in postwar years.

Edward, who had suffered great humiliation in Britain, proved as controversial in the Bahamas as he had at home. Some claim that he made strides to right the colony's backward and racist politics. Others believe he endorsed the corrupt ways of the 'Bay Street Boys,' an oligarchy of white lawyers and merchants that dominated the islands' assembly for many years.

It is argued that the duke, who abdicated the throne in 1936 to marry 'the woman I love,' was given the governor's position – considered lowly – as a punishment. There was, however, evidence that on the eve of WWII, the Nazis were planning to kidnap the duke – who had settled in the south of France – and restore him to the throne as a puppet after Hitler's forces had conquered Great Britain. Edward had shown sympathies toward Nazism. Winston Churchill, the prime minister, urged King George VI to send his brother to the Bahamas to place him out of harm's way.

Nonetheless, the duke was beloved by many, black and white alike, and became the topic of several endearing songs and poems. One of his favorites was a ditty by Blake Higgs:

It was Love, Love alone
Cause King Edward to leave the throne.
It was Love, Love alone
Cause King Edward to leave the throne.
We know that Edward was good and great
But it was Love that cause him to abdicate.

Strategic Importance & Civil Unrest

During WWII the islands served as a base for Allied air and sea power. The war also revived the tourism industry. Exhausted Yankee GIs came to the islands to recuperate, joined by wealthy Americans and Canadians seeking a sunny winter retreat.

Joint US-UK naval bases were established on five islands, including a major air base (today's Nassau International Airport) on New Providence. Local laborers, predominantly black, were hired for military construction at appallingly low (albeit legal) wages, causing a riot that erupted into full-scale racial strife. Eventually the riot was quelled and the workers were appeased when wages were raised from four shillings a day to five shillings and free lunch. Nonetheless, as in the US, black Bahamians (many of whom valiantly risked their lives in WWII) were still restricted from entering hotels, restaurants, and theaters…a color bar that persisted until 1956.

Tourism Blossoms

It was clear in the slump that followed the end of WWII that the Bahamas' future lay in the still-embryonic tourism industry. Canadian entrepreneur and philanthropist Sir Harry Oakes, who owned one-third of New Providence and built the Cable Beach Golf Course, the Bahamas Country Club, and much of the tourist infrastructure, had lain the foundation. Oakes' brutal murder in his bed on July 7, 1943, and the subsequent trial of his son-in-law, Duke Alfred de Marigny, reverberated around the world as 'The Crime of the Century,' putting the Bahamas back on the map. The son-in-law was acquitted and the case remains unsolved.

The decision to promote tourism coincided with the arrival of the jet age and the Cuban Revolution in 1959. During the 1950s, Havana was the mecca for US tourists. In 1961, when Fidel Castro spun Cuba into Soviet orbit, the subsequent US embargo forced revelers to seek their pleasures elsewhere.

Enter Sir Stafford Sands, a wealthy Bahamian who established the Bahamas Development Board. Sands seized the opportunity. The US air base was expanded and reopened as Nassau International Airport. The harbor was dredged and Prince George Wharf rebuilt to lure cruise ships. A massive advertising campaign was launched.

Sands' board also decided to establish the Bahamas as a corporate tax haven, aided by statutes modeled on Switzerland's secrecy laws. The government promoted the nascent banking industry. Tourism and finance bloomed together, with a steadily increasing source of loan capital to support the development boom, further fostered by an influx of capital from British investors escaping onerous taxes imposed by Britain's Labour government. The Bahamas began to prosper, aided by the patronage of many European blue-blood vacationers. Several ultraexclusive resorts were spawned to cater to royals and the social elite.

A major leap forward in tourism was the transformation of Hog Island, facing Nassau Harbour, into chic Paradise Island. A new city – Freeport – sprang up on Grand Bahama under the patronage of the prominent businessman Wallace Groves. Sands' goal of attracting 1 million tourists was reached in 1968.

Independence Soon Come

The upturn in fortunes coincided with (and perhaps helped spark) the evolution of party politics and festering ethnic tensions, as the white elite and a growing black middle class reaped profits from the boom.

Only a small number of black representatives (mostly wealthy black businessmen) sat in the assembly, which remained dominated by the Bay Street Boys and by British appointees sent over from London. Middle-class blacks' aspirations for representation coalesced with the pent-up frustrations of their brethren who remained impoverished.

In 1953 a local firebrand named Lynden Pindling formed the Progressive Liberal Party (PLP) to seek justice for the nation's majority at the ballot box. In response, the Bay Street Boys and other establishment groups formed the United Bahamian Party (UBP), igniting a long and tenacious feud.

In 1963 the tensions bubbled up into a violent national strike supported by the PLP. A new constitution, proposed by Britain, was drawn up with the aim of creating a more representative legislature and providing for internal self-government. The UBP, led by white Bahamian Roland Symonette, gained power in national elections by a slender majority, and Symonette became premier. The close race allowed for white dominance to be somewhat diluted, but black aspirations had barely been appeased, particularly since voting was restricted to male property owners, a provision overwhelmingly favoring whites.

Pindling and his party followers refused to recognize the parliamentary speaker's authority. In 1967 the PLP finally boycotted Parliament altogether, but not before winning an elimination of the property-ownership qualification. A new election was held, and Pindling's PLP came to power, a position it would maintain for the next 25 years.

Britain agreed that the islands were ready for independence, and a new constitution was drawn up, granting islanders autonomy in many internal matters. The independence issue fiercely divided the nation. The PLP was in favor; the UBP, meanwhile, had allied with other minor opposition parties to form the Free National Movement (FNM), which opposed independence. In Eleuthera and the Abacos, ardent descendants of Loyalists plotted to secede and declare their loyalty to Britain if independence were granted. In the September 1972 election, Pindling's party won resoundingly, and the people of the Bahamas prepared themselves for nationhood.

On July 10, 1973, the islands of the Bahamas officially became a new nation, The Commonwealth of The Bahamas, ending 325 years of British rule. That night, thousands of Bahamians gathered at Fort Charlotte to watch the Union Jack lowered a final time and the new flag of The Bahamas raised in its place.

Pindling Era

Pindling initially continued the progressive economic policies first adopted by Sands and Symonette, based on tourism and finance. However, foreign-owned development interests enjoyed preferential treatments that had fostered land speculation (much of the islands' best land had been bought for development or simply to 'land bank' for speculative investment) and abusive labor practices. Pindling's moves to redress these problems led to a real-estate slump. The economy stalled.

In 1983 the premier became *Sir* Lynden Pindling, knighted by the Queen for his services. The Pindling regime, however, had lost its direction and integrity. The administration had become mired in corruption. Kickbacks to government members had become a staple of political life. The international drug business was also booming, and The Bahamas, with hundreds of islands, marinas, and airstrips, had become the frontline staging post for narcotics en route to the US. Bahamians from all walks of life made hay on the trade, and

the government seemed disinclined to crack down on it (it was a boon to the nation during a time of shaky financial conditions worldwide).

In 1984 it was revealed that Colombian drug barons had corrupted the government at its highest levels, and the country's drug-heavy reputation tarnished its image abroad. Tourism and financial investment declined, so the government belatedly launched a crackdown led by the US Drug Enforcement Agency (US DEA).

Pindling's tenure ended on August 19, 1992, when voters gave the conservative FNM and its leader, Hubert A Ingraham, a resounding victory. The new, intensely probusiness government is generally credited with having put the bounce back in the Bahamian economy and restoring a sense of pride. It was returned to power in a landslide victory in March 1997. (See the Government & Politics section later in this chapter.)

In 1997, a government inquiry found Pindling (who had returned from cancer treatment in the US) guilty of corruption, but no charges were filed. Several cabinet ministers resigned, similarly charged.

Governmental change was followed by environmental disaster. In August 1999, Hurricane Dennis raked the Abacos and Grand Bahama. Then, in September 1999, Hurricane Floyd – a 600-mile-wide whopper – pounded the islands with winds up to 155 mph. The storm center passed over Cat and San Salvador islands, then swept over (and passed between) Abaco and Eleuthera, all of which sustained considerable damage. Many houses and public buildings were destroyed. Roads were washed away. Many communities were left without water due to extensive salt pollution to cisterns. And Nassau erupted in widespread looting and mayhem by gangs of local teens. Amazingly only one person lost his life, despite a storm surge that reached up to 20 feet in places.

GEOGRAPHY

The Bahamas archipelago rises from the Bahama Banks, a vast and uniformly flat underwater platform, and consists of some

700 islands and nearly 2500 small islets or cays sprawled across roughly 100,000 sq miles of ocean.

The archipelago stretches 750 miles south from Walker's Cay, about 75 miles east of Florida's Palm Beach (United States), to the Ragged Island Range, which lies 50 miles northeast of Cuba and 55 miles north of Haiti. In all this vastness, the islands together add up to no more than 5363 sq miles of land, about the size of the US state of Connecticut. The largest island, Andros, takes up 2300 sq miles.

The mostly linear islands are strewn in a general northwest-southeast array. Several – Great Abaco, Eleuthera, Long Island, Andros – are as much as 100 miles long. Few, however, are more than a few miles wide. All are low lying, the terrain either pancake-flat or gently undulating. Cat

In or Out?

The Bahamas is geographically *not* part of the Caribbean, as many people think it is. It's part of the North American plate and is bordered on the east by the Atlantic Ocean and on the west by the 'great ocean river,' the Gulf Stream. The *Concise Oxford Dictionary* says that The Bahamas 'is in the West Indies,' the name given to all the islands between North and South America. In general parlance, however, the West Indies is considered to be those islands that encircle and lie within the Caribbean Sea: the Greater Antilles (Cuba, Hispaniola, Jamaica, and Puerto Rico) and Lesser Antilles (the islands between Puerto Rico and Venezuela).

Politically, The Bahamas *is* considered part of the Caribbean (not least by its own government), although the usual reference is to 'The Caribbean and The Bahamas.' The British High Commission in Nassau emphatically denies that The Bahamas is in the Caribbean, for the reasons stated above. The US Information Service considers it 'outside the designated Caribbean zone.' It's all a question of perception versus reality!

Island's Mt Alvernia, the highest point in The Bahamas, is only 206 feet above sea level.

Virtually all the islands are surrounded by coral reefs and sand banks. Most islands have barrier reefs along the length of their windward (east) shores, anywhere from 200 yards to 2 miles out, that offer protection from Atlantic wave action. These shores are lined virtually their entire lengths by white- or pinkish-sand beaches – about 2200 miles in all – shelving into turquoise shallows. In a few places, notably parts of Eleuthera and Cat Island, the Atlantic rollers break through the reefs and crash ashore at the base of limestone cliffs.

The protected sandbanks and shallows extend for miles leeward (west) of most islands. They are usually swampy close to shore, with vast wetlands dissected by serpentine channels. (The Spaniards called the waters *baja mar*, or 'shallow sea'; hence the Bahamas islands are the islands of the shallow sea.) Some islands are separated by great trenches, such as the Tongue of the Ocean, a Grand Canyon–scale crevasse more than 5 miles deep.

GEOLOGY

The Bahamas archipelago sits atop and is formed by one of the greatest masses of limestone in the world: a reef-shelf of solid sea fossils 20,000 feet thick, rising sheer-sided from the seabed. Beneath the sea, division and redivision of the mountainlike landmass formed 20 or so flat-topped summits separated by deep-water gorges. The largest mass is the Great Bahama Bank, encompassing the islands from the Biminis and the Berry Islands south to the Ragged Island Range and Long Island. In the north, Grand Bahama and the Abacos rise from the Little Bahama Bank. Crooked Island and those islands to the south and east sit atop their own separate platforms.

The Bahamian islands are composed primarily of oolitic limestone, a sedimentary rock laid down in almost perfect layers and formed by chemical processes in the shallow seas (rather than through the building action of coral normally associated with

limestone formation). Over eons, countless tiny marine organisms grew atop the stone and added their skeletal remains to those of their forebears. About 6 miles of limestone rock lie beneath the present-day Bahamas, the result of nearly 150 million years' deposits. The islands as we know them today began to take their present form only about 500,000 years ago.

During the course of millions of years, the region underwent alternating periods of uplift and submergence as the earth's temperature changed.

Oolitic limestone is relatively soft and crumbly and is easily dissolved by rain and seawater, as is evidenced by the honeycombed nature – treacherous to unwary hikers – of the weathered surface rock and, most dramatically, by the numerous caves and 'blue holes' found throughout the islands. Since limestone is unusually porous, rainfall tends to soak into the rock rather than form rivers (the lack of rivers and the silt they deposit into seas helps explain the remarkable clarity of The Bahamas' ocean waters). The limestone filters rainfall, purifying the islands' water supply. The islands' surfaces bear only a thin cover of soil.

Blue Holes

The islands are pocked by giant sinkholes – water-filled, often fathomless circular pits that open to underground and submarine caves and descend as much as 600 feet.

Sinkholes are formed by rainwater combining with carbon dioxide to form a mild carbonic acid. The acidic freshwater solution dissolves surface rock. Some depressions and pore spaces are enlarged quickly and attract more water, which then further erodes the rock. These holes join into a large depression that grows ever deeper with time. Eventually the fresh water meets saltwater that has seeped into the substrate limestone from the ocean.

Fresh water forms a lens above the separate body of saltwater (the juncture is called a 'halocline'), and the two mingle at their boundary to form a corrosive mixture capable of dissolving limestone more quickly than either the fresh or saline layers. Since saltwater is denser than fresh water, organic detritus that sinks through the upper layers hits the halocline and stops; here bacteria break it down, generating heat, coloring the water orange, and producing a mild but even more corrosive sulfuric acid. This creates an unnerving environment for divers descending into blue holes to find the narrow sinkholes that lead to chambers below.

Unique creatures have evolved to exist solely within the gloom of the underwater caverns, including blind, pigmentless fish. There are corals and other familiar marine creatures skulking in the enclosed depths, too. And local lore attributes deadly mermaids, mermen, and sea monsters to many of the holes.

For further information, read *Deep into Blue Holes*, by cave explorer Rob Palmer, or contact The Bahamas Caves Research Foundation (☎ 242-257-0532, fax 242-355-5557, bahamacave@aol.com).

CLIMATE

Upon visiting the Bahamian archipelago in the 1760s, George Washington referred to it as the 'Isles of Perpetual June.' Indeed, the sun shines an average of 320 days a year, with seven hours of sunshine daily in Nassau. Officially, the climate is a tropical maritime wet-and-dry climate. In general, the islands are balmy year-round, with cooling, near-constant trade winds blowing by day from the east. However, the islands are bisected by the tropic of Cancer and span 6 degrees of latitude, a distance north to south of almost 500

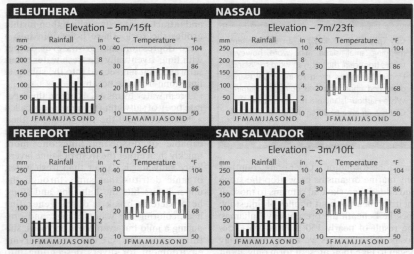

miles. Hence significant regional and seasonal variations occur.

Temperature

Rarely do temperatures drop below 60°F in winter or rise above 90°F in summer (the coldest recorded temperature is 41.4°F on January 20, 1981). Nationwide, daytime temperatures in the peak-season winter months (December to April) average 70°F, with cooler evenings. However, midwinter temperatures in the northern and western islands can be surprisingly cold, especially when northeasters that bring freezing weather to Florida blow in. Then temperatures can plummet into the 50s. In summer the days, averaging 80°F, are breezy and balmy...the best time of all.

Temperatures increase from northwest to southeast, ordinarily reaching 90°F in New Providence and regularly exceeding 100°F in the Inaguas and Turks and Caicos in midsummer.

The breezes generally blow from the east, but tend to become southeasterly May to September and northeasterly October to April, when they can whip in at 25 knots.

The surrounding waters are equally balmy, ranging from about 74°F in midwinter to about 80°F.

Rainfall

Yearly rainfall averages 52 inches. Northern islands receive considerably more rain than do those to the south.

A rainy season begins in May or June and ends in November. About 80% of annual rain falls in these months, normally in short, heavy showers (often accompanied by thunderstorms that typically develop in midafternoon) and occasionally in protracted rainfall over several days.

Summertime sometimes also brings squalls and hurricanes. Still, rain can fall at any time of year. In Nassau rainfall averages 2 inches a month November to April and 6 inches monthly May to October. The islands north of New Providence tend to get more; the southernmost islands receive half that amount and are virtually rain-barren in summer, often experiencing drought.

Humidity in the northern islands is relatively high year-round, ranging from about 65% to 75% in Nassau – slightly less humid than Florida. Humidity declines from northwest to southeast.

Hurricanes

The Bahamas lies outside the Caribbean belt and statistically has received fewer hurricanes than the Caribbean islands (on average, once every nine years). The past few years have been an exception, and several hurricanes have swept through the country.

The official hurricane season lasts from June 1 to November 30. August and September are peak months. Usually only one or two islands, or portions of them, are affected by an individual hurricane.

The Meteorological Service in Nassau (☎ 915) has weather forecasts available 24 hours a day, as does the Nassau Marine Operator (channel 27). Radio Bahamas ZNS1 (1540 kHz) offers regular weather broadcasts 24 hours a day. Hurricanes are tracked by the US National Hurricane Center in Miami. Satellite weather forecasts provide advance warning, but it is

Big Blows

The hurricane season in The Bahamas, like that of the eastern USA, is from June to November, with most activity occurring in August and September. Hurricanes can also appear outside the official season but are much less frequent. While the annual average is only about five hurricanes per year, the frequency can vary greatly from year to year.

Hurricanes are defined as storms that originate in the tropics and have winds in excess of 120km/hr (74mph). Those that hit The Bahamas form off the coast of Africa and whip in a westerly direction across the Atlantic. The winds of these hurricanes revolve in a counterclockwise direction around a center of lower barometric pressure, picking up energy from warm waters and moisture as they approach the Caribbean.

The first stage of a hurricane's approach is called a tropical disturbance. The next stage is a tropical depression. When winds exceed 64km/hr, the system is upgraded to a tropical storm and is usually accompanied by heavy rains. The system is called a hurricane if wind speed exceeds 120km/hr and intensifies around a low-pressure center called the eye of the storm.

The strength of a hurricane is rated from one to five. The mildest, a Category 1 hurricane, has winds of at least 120km/hr. The strongest and rarest hurricanes, the Category 5 monsters, pack winds that exceed 250km/hr; Hurricane Mitch, which killed more than 10,000 people in Central America in late 1998, was a rare Category 5 hurricane. Hurricanes travel at varying speeds, from as little as 10km/hr to more than 50km/hr.

If you are caught by an approaching hurricane, stay calm and follow local warnings. Hotels are typically of concrete and steel construction capable of withstanding strong winds with minimal damage. However, in low-lying areas ocean swells can also pose a hazard – if you have an oceanfront room it's a wise precaution to relocate to a unit farther inland. Most hurricane injuries are the result of flying debris, so don't be tempted to venture outside in the midst of a storm. If a hurricane warning is announced, stay sober. A hurricane is no time to be partying. You'll need your wits about you both during and after the storm.

difficult to predict a storm's path. For current weather information, you can visit *The Miami Herald*'s Web site (www .herald.com) and scan the menu for hurricane and storm information. Another excellent place to find current English- and Spanish-language tropical-storm information is the National Hurricane Center's Tropical Prediction Center Web site (www.nhc.noaa.gov/), maintained by US National Oceanic and Atmospheric Administration.

ECOLOGY & ENVIRONMENT

Coastal mangrove and wetland preserves, pine forests, and other wild places are strewn throughout the archipelago, yet – with the notable exception of the underwater world – few travelers visit the islands to get close to nature. Ecological treasures such as Inagua National Park – protecting the hemisphere's largest colony of West Indian flamingos – go untapped. Ecoconsciousness among the local population is at best embryonic, and existing legislation, while well-intentioned, has often been ineffectual (see the next section).

The past few years, however, have seen a stirring of ecoawareness. The island governments have adopted a more sensitive approach to development. And entrepreneurs are beginning to open up nature spots to a more sophisticated audience that wants to escape the resort routine.

The archipelago does not display the lushness and physical diversity of neighboring Caribbean islands. But if you're keen to get close to nature, you'll find plenty to keep you enthralled. You'll also be doing the islands a good turn. Nature tourism is one of the most practical ways to save wild places and their wildlife from erosive exploitation: It provides a way of reconciling economic development with species protection while giving local communities a stake in conservation.

Ecological Treasures

The Bahamian archipelago has beaches, but it also has bush. You can forsake sandals for hiking boots to follow coastal trails, explore caverns, and shoot birds through the lens of a camera. Bird watchers are particularly favored. Virtually every island is a birder's haven, for the vegetation is relatively open.

The island ecology displays a gradual yet marked change from the northwest to the southeast, becoming more arid and less vegetated as you move south, where hardy drought-resistant scrub and cacti predominate and brackish lakes and ponds are favored by flocks of flamingos. This simple transition masks a more complex matrix of ecosystems, which range from the dense pine forests of Great Abaco and Grand Bahama in the north, to the mangrove swamps and wetlands of Andros and North and Middle Caicos, to the intricate and absorbing coral reefs.

The Bahamas and Turks and Caicos governments take their role as guardians of their ecology seriously and work in cooperation with several worldwide conservation bodies. Both nations have designated large areas of land and sea as national parks.

The Bahamas in particular has a long history of conservation activities. As early as 1905, for example, concern was expressed for the West Indian flamingo population in the Caribbean. That year, at the first annual meeting of the National Audubon Society, a plea was made to The Bahamas' government for the birds' legal protection, and the Wild Birds (Protection) Act was passed. Nonetheless, the late 1940s and '50s saw a sudden decline in the flamingo population. The Audubon Society sent a team to Great Inagua in an attempt to prevent the birds' seemingly fast-approaching extinction. After three years' research, the Society for the Protection of Flamingos was formed in 1951 and wardens were hired (paid for by the Audubon Society).

Meanwhile increasing development elsewhere in the island chain was having a damaging effect on other animal and plant life. A proposal was made to establish buffer zones, and in 1955 the Crown Lands Office set aside 22 miles of the Exumas for

Cleaning fish in Potter's Cay

New Plymouth, Green Turtle Cay

The Nassau straw market

West Indian flamingo

Snowy egret

Brown pelicans

Allan's Cay iguana

Ten Tips for Environmentally Conscious Travelers

1. *Don't litter.* Remember: Take only photographs, leave only footprints. If you see litter, pick it up. Support recycling programs.

2. *Respect others' property.* Never take 'souvenirs' such as shells, plants, or artifacts from historical sites or natural areas. Treat shells, sea urchins, coral, and other marine life as sacred.

3. *Don't buy products made from endangered species.* Many species of plants and animals are killed to make trinkets for tourists. By buying products made of tortoiseshell, coral, bird feathers, or similar materials, you are contributing to the decimation of wildlife. Shop with a conscience.

4. *Keep to the footpaths.* When you're hiking, always follow designated trails. Natural habitats are often quickly eroded and animals and plants disturbed by walkers who stray off the beaten path.

5. *Don't touch or stand on coral.* Coral is extremely sensitive and is easily killed by snorkelers and divers who fail to honor this law of nature: Human contact is deadly. Boaters should never anchor on coral – use mooring buoys. That's the law!

6. *Sponsor environmental consciousness in others.* Try to patronize hotels, tour companies, and merchants that act in an environmentally sound manner. Consider their impact on waste generation, noise levels and other pollution, energy consumption, and the local culture.

7. *Help local communities gain a share of tourism revenues.* Many local communities are hard pressed to survive and derive little benefit from tourism profits. Educate yourself on community tourism and ways you can participate. Use local guides whenever possible.

8. *Respect others' privacy.* Don't intrude into people's lives or privacy. Ask permission before taking photographs of individuals and before entering private property.

9. *Respect the community.* Learn about the customs of the region and support local efforts to preserve its environment and traditional culture.

10. *Tell others.* Politely intervene when other travelers act in an environmentally or socially detrimental manner. Educate them about the potential negative effects of their behavior.

a study (under the auspices of the New York Zoological Society) that spawned the creation in 1958 of the Exuma Cays Land & Sea Park, the first of its kind in the world. One year later, Parliament created a body charged with the park's management and conservation.

Outside the national park system, inappropriate development, pollution, and overexploitation increasingly threaten wildlife and marine resources. Although The Bahamas was the first Caribbean nation to outlaw long-line fishing, a threat to the marine ecology, the islands' stocks of grouper, spiny lobster, and conch all face the consequences of overfishing. Commercial poaching, mostly by Cuban-Americans from Florida in the west and by Dominicans in the east, has been a significant problem. In the late 1970s the problem stirred several

island communities to establish their own reserves, independent of the government.

In 1996 a new government office, Ambassador of the Environment, was created, while the Ministry of Tourism announced a new department to develop ecotourism.

Bahamas National Trust

Today over 238,000 acres of national parks and protected areas are under the jurisdiction of the Bahamas National Trust (BNT), a nonprofit, nongovernmental organization established in 1959. Its headquarters (☎ 242-393-1317) is The Retreat, on Village Rd in Nassau (mailing address PO Box N-4105, Nassau, The Bahamas). It has a second office (☎ 242-352-5438) at the Rand Memorial Nature Centre (mailing address PO Box F-43441, Freeport). It is the major force for conservation in The Bahamas and has been at the forefront of saving hundreds of thousands of acres of valuable wetlands, forests, and islands as protected areas.

In addition to an ongoing education campaign, the BNT has achieved such celebrated successes as the preservation of the white-crowned pigeon and repopulation of the endangered hutia, as well as performing important turtle conservation work. The BNT's park management has brought the West Indian flamingo from near extinction to a thriving colony of 50,000 birds in Inagua National Park. Now it hopes to achieve similar success with the endangered Bahama parrot on Great Abaco.

The BNT has developed a National Strategy for Environment & Development. It is also involved in historic preservation.

FLORA

Compared to neighboring islands, The Bahamas is not species-rich; the thin, rocky soil, underlain by limestone, is not conducive to lush vegetation. Nonetheless, the islands together boast more than 1370 species of trees and plants, including 121 endemics, such as Bahamian mahogany and Bahamian pine.

The dominant ecosystem in the northern and western Bahamas is pine forest, characterized by a shrubby understory of palmetto, cabbage palm, and fern, and low-growing thatch palm whose large leaves are used for thatching and weaving. The Caribbean (Cuban) pine and thatch palm have adapted to withstand the wildfires that decimate competing hardwoods, a natural occurrence that maintains the ecosystem. The red blooms of *Exogonium*, brilliant magenta milk peas, and strange devil's potato flowers entwine the pines.

The forests today bear little resemblance to the original primary cover of subtropical hardwood forests of mahogany, strangler fig, lignum vitae, and gumbo limbo. Most of those forests were felled for boatbuilding and to clear ground for short-lived cotton plantations. Secondary pine forests grew in their place, many of which (especially those on Grand Bahama, Great Abaco, and Andros) were heavily logged in the decades following WWII.

Mahogany, once common, is now rare, as are ebony (recognizable by its burst of vermilion-bright flowers after rains) and lignum vitae, the beautiful purplish hardwood – and national tree – that you may recognize by its clusters of dark-blue blooms. Its timber is the heaviest of all known woods and much in demand among carvers (its bark, gum, fruit, leaves, and blossoms also serve useful purposes, including medicines for gout and syphilis).

Poisonwood, in the same family as poison ivy, is a very common tree. The waxy branches of the candlewood tree, another endemic species, were once lit as torches by Lucayan Indians. Other natives include the massive silk cotton, the huge buttress flanks of which are unmistakable, and the strangler fig (or ficus), which begins life as an epiphyte on the branches of other trees. It sends down woody roots that attach themselves to the ground and expand – as if in some horror movie – to totally engulf the host tree. Eventually they smother the host, which may die and rot away, leaving a thriving, freestanding fig, the hollow trunk of which may become a habitat for bats, rodents, and other species.

Australian pines (or casuarinas) grow everywhere along the windward (eastern) shores, providing welcome shade and laying down soft carpets of pine needles. These graceful evergreens are introduced to the islands to anchor the dunes. They outcompeted native vegetation and spread along the coasts, where they exclude understory vegetation.

Mangroves fringe many of the leeward shores. All four New World species are found here. The hardy plant puts down a circumference of slender stilt roots, forming a great tangle that helps build up the shoreline and prevents erosion. It also provides rich compost for algae and other microorganisms that draw crustaceans and spawning fish in vast numbers. The trees are replaced in the semiarid southern islands by thorny scrub and cactus.

Coconut palms are not as ubiquitous as you may imagine – there are many islands where you are hard pressed to find a single one.

Blooming Lovely

Flowers abound every month of the year. Many are associated with trees, such as the Pride of India, a large tree that when in flower becomes a cloud of lavender. In spring all the islands are ablaze with the orange blossoms of the croton and the dramatic vermilion of the *Spathodea*, or flame-of-the-forest, also known as the African tulip tree and, locally, the Jesus Christ tree because it blooms blood-red at Easter. It is commonly found outside churches.

Another blooming beauty is the blue mahoe, an endemic form of hibiscus with a ruler-straight trunk reaching 70 feet. Mahoe blossoms blaze from yellow to red.

Ground-loving plants include whisk-broom fern, while ernodea and shy little straw-lilies peep up from the pine forest floors.

The long, thin, twirled leaves of the sisal (which rattles in the wind and is therefore also known as mother-in-law's-tongue) are common along roadsides. Sisal is used for making the baskets you see in the straw markets. Agave leaves have been used for generations by islanders as natural needles and threads. And berry- and pod-bearing plants are abundant. Many have uses, such as sea grape, ubiquitous along the shores; its fruits often end up in jams and jellies.

Many plants have long been used for bush medicines, a practice that continues today. Five-finger (also known as chicken-toe) is used to make a tea that relieves body ache. The aromatic leaves of white sage are used as a salve for chicken pox and measles. Wild guava is used to treat diabetes. And several plants are considered to be aphrodisiacs: 'A lot of men lose love life, and they want to make love again. So you boil Gamalamie and strongback and drink a couple of gallons of that, and that straightens you right out – you make love like mad,' says Maggie Nixon of Little Farmer's Cay.

Several species are exotics introduced from abroad, including bougainvillea, whose tissue-paper blossoms blaze purple, pink, and orange, and the frangipani. Pineapple, a bromeliad, is native. Honeysuckle, jasmine, morning glory, night-blooming cereus, passionflowers, and the rose veil of corallita also mingle their perfumes with the fragrant air. The national flower is the yellow elder, a tubular yellow flower with delicate red stripes on each petal.

Flowering cacti flourishing in the parched south, notably in the Turks and Caicos, where the national symbol is the Turk's head cactus, named for the similarity of its flower to a fez. Opuntia, or prickly pear cactus, is also common and is popular with poorer island residents, who roast and eat it.

FAUNA
Land Mammals

The archipelago has only 13 native land mammal species, all but one being bats. All are endangered. The most common is the leaf-nosed bat. Bats consume large amounts of insects, especially mosquitoes, and act as important seed dispersers and pollinators for flora.

The only native terrestrial mammal is the endangered hutia, a cat-size brown rodent akin to a guinea pig, and a sub-species of a large rodent also found in Cuba and Jamaica. Once a favorite food of Arawak Indians, the hutia was hunted to near extinction by humans and feral dogs and cats and was thought to be extinct until rediscovered in the mid-1960s on East Plana Cay near San Salvador. A population has been re-established on a small cay in the Exumas in an attempt to diversify their range.

Wild boar roam the backcountry on larger islands. And feral cattle, donkeys, and horses, released after the demise of the salt industry, outnumber humans on the southern islands, including the Turks and Caicos.

You might be surprised to find North American raccoons on Grand Bahama. They were introduced during Prohibition (they were popular as pets among Yankee bootleggers). Many raccoons escaped or were released, and the population is now well established.

Marine Mammals

The Caribbean monk seal, once common in the southern waters, was hunted to local extinction during the last century. The endangered West Indian manatee has suffered a similar fate. Humpback whales, however, pass through the waters windward of The Bahamas and Turks and

Whales Ahoy!

The Bahamas Marine Mammal Survey Team (☎ 242-393-1317), PO Box N-4105, Nassau, The Bahamas, part of the Bahamas National Trust, asks mariners to report *any* sightings of whales, dolphins, manatees, and even seals in Bahamian and adjacent waters. You're asked to report the location, date, time, species, size, color, number of animals, and other pertinent information. Take photographs if possible.

Caicos en route to their mating grounds in the warm waters of the Mouchoir Banks, south of Grand Turk. Blue whales are also frequently sighted.

Atlantic bottle-nosed dolphins frequent these waters, as do the less often seen Atlantic spotted dolphins. Several individual dolphins, such as 'JoJo' in the Turks and Caicos, have taken a fancy to hanging out with humans in the wild – you may be lucky enough to have one approach you while you're snorkeling. (For information on interacting with dolphins, see Dolphin Encounters in the Outdoor Activities chapter.)

Amphibians & Reptiles

The islands have plenty of slithery and slimy things, including 44 species of reptiles. Lizards (29 species) are seen everywhere in their dusky brown, sky-blue, and rainbow-colored suits. The Bahamas' symbol could well be the curly-tailed lizard, a critter found throughout most of the islands and easily spotted sunning on rocks; its tail is coiled like a spring over its back. Each island has its own subspecies. Some grow to 12 inches in length.

The quick-moving blue-tailed lizard and the well-camouflaged anole are also common. My favorites are the geckos, charming but noisy little creatures that often can be seen hanging by their suction-cup feet.

None of the islands' 10 species of snakes are poisonous. Brown racers and corn snakes are often seen, as are native Bahamian pigmy boas and blind worm snakes. Snake populations are dwindling, mostly due to the ravages of feral cats.

Many islands have endemic species of reptiles, such as Cat Island, home to the Cat Island terrapin. Great Inagua also has its own terrapin.

There are frogs, too, including the Cuban tree frog, whose mucus is poisonous. The Bahamian crocodile is extinct.

Iguanas Dragonlike iguanas, the archipelago's largest native land animals, can reach 4 feet in length. Iguanas are shy and harmless vegetarians, feeding mainly on leaves, fruits, and berries. The islands host several

Cute little geckos can climb anywhere.

separate iguana subspecies, though humans and feral dogs and cats (the iguanas' only natural predators are larger birds of prey) have completely eradicated iguana populations on virtually every inhabited island. They are now relegated to the outlying isles and cays.

The Central Exuma iguana is known on five small adjacent cays of the Exuma chain; the White Cay iguana is found only on that particular isle, and the Allan's Cay iguana lives on Allan's and one adjacent cay. San Salvador has an endemic subspecies, as do two cays in the Bight of Acklins. Andros has a severely threatened endemic species, and the Bartsch's rock iguana is found only on one cay off Mayaguana.

Crustaceans

Several species of crabs are found in the Family Islands, including giant ochre-hued land crabs. You may see locals chasing them down for the pot. There are also tiny hermit crabs, which make their homes in shells on the beaches. Several species of crayfish (lobsters) inhabit the coral reefs.

Insects

Insects are an obvious presence, notably mosquitoes, which can be ferocious on certain islands in the rainy season. Their presence is limited near the breezy shores, as well as near Nassau and Freeport, where spraying is done to kill larvae. No-see-'ums (almost microscopic sand flies with a bite that belies their diminutive size) are ubiquitous on beaches around dusk.

The air thrums, too, with the buzzing of bees and paper wasps and the steady cadence of cicadas. Grasshoppers are plentiful, as are dragonflies. The Bahamas also has several species of ants and spiders.

About 60 species of butterflies waltz through the islands. Pure yellow sulfurs are common, capering across the roadways in tens of thousands in springtime. You can't miss the zebra longwing, either, with its narrow wings and black and white stripes. The rarely seen giant swallowtail, a mammoth among insects, has a slow-gaited flight and long, sensual tips on its black-and-yellow hind wings.

Moths abound, notably the giant, dark-brown nocturnal fruit moth, called a 'bat' locally and easily mistaken for one because of its size.

Birds

The Bahamas is a bird watcher's paradise, with about 230 species of birds. Only a few are endemic, including the Bahama swallow, Bahama parrot, and the Bahama woodstar hummingbird. The majority of birds in the northern Bahamas are of North American origin. From September through May, the forests swarm with migrants. Vireos, flycatchers, thrushes, and plovers visit, migrating between summer and winter habitats. Birders also can spot Bahama whistling ducks, guinea fowl, quails, snipes, coots, herons, and gallinules in the wetlands.

The pinelands of the northern Bahamas support a wide variety of resident summer nesters, plus migratory songbirds in winter. With luck, you might see a tiny yet noisy blue-gray gnatcatcher picking insects off trees, or the red-legged thrush going about the same business on the ground (another small undergrowth bird is the Bahama yellowthroat; the male has a banditlike black mask). The brown-and-white crested stolid flycatcher prefers its food on the wing, as does the Greater Antillean peewee, a small, yellowish-brown flycatcher with white eye rings. Stripe-headed tanagers perch in the pines. The white-crowned pigeon is ubiquitous, though the great lizard cuckoo is a secretive bird that you are not likely to see.

The red-tailed hawk is one of several birds of prey commonly seen soaring high overhead, as is the jet-black turkey vulture, unmistakable with its undertaker's plumage and bald red head. The beautiful and diminutive osprey and kestrel prefer to spy from atop telegraph poles.

The islands are also home to the burrowing owl and the barn owl. Both are protected species. Alas, a third species – the flightless barn owl – is extinct. It died out about 300 years ago, and the memory of it probably gave rise to the legend of the 'chickcharnie,' the nasty, leprechaunlike figure of Andros in whose existence many Androsians firmly believe.

Everywhere you'll see snowy-white cattle egrets. Roseate spoonbills can be seen in the southern brine lakes, especially on Great Inagua, ornithologically the richest island and boasting a large portion of the world's population of reddish egrets.

At sea, large, graceful pelicans can sometimes be seen diving for fish, while frigate birds – sometimes called 'man o' war' birds – soar high above. Offshore cays vibrate with the caterwauling of terns, tropicbirds, and boobies, common in the southern islands.

Flamingos The West Indian (Caribbean) flamingo – the national bird – inhabits Crooked Island, Long Cay, Great Inagua, and, in the Turks and Caicos, Providenciales and North and Middle Caicos. You can also see the birds in botanical gardens and preserves on New Providence and Grand Bahama. Great Inagua has a sanctuary with over 50,000 West Indian flamingos, the largest flock in the hemisphere.

Their orange-pink coloration results from absorption of carotene, a substance found naturally in their diet of shrimp, crustaceans, and tiny algae and insect larvae. Males are generally larger and more brightly colored than females.

Bahama Parrots The only species of parrot in The Bahamas is a close relative of the Amazon parrots of Cuba and the Cayman Islands. The green-and-red parrots were so numerous five centuries ago that Columbus recorded in his log of 1492 that their flocks 'darkened the sun.' Today two distinct populations of this endangered subspecies live on the islands of Great Inagua and Great Abaco. Oddly, there's a genetic split between the two: The Abaco parrots are ground nesters, while the Inagua parrots nest in trees.

Abaco National Park was created in Great Abaco to preserve its small parrot population, which faces a new threat: Raccoons were introduced into Little Abaco in recent years, and it is only a matter of time before they spread to Great Abaco and begin disturbing parrots' nests and eating eggs, further endangering the birds' survival.

Hummingbirds Restricted to the New World, most hummingbirds are tropical and subtropical, though they thrive in a wide range of climates. There are 163 tropical species, three of which live in The Bahamas.

The only species endemic to The Bahamas is the Bahamian woodstar, known locally as the God bird and found on most Bahamian islands. It weighs less than a US nickel yet is pugnacious. The male has a snow-white underbody, red-purple throat, and metallic bronze-green plumage. The female is less ornately adorned, as is typical among hummers.

The ruby-throated hummingbird is found only in Cuba, Hispaniola, and The Bahamas. The bright metallic-green Cuban emerald also inhabits Grand Bahama, Green Cay, Great Abaco, and Andros. It darts about like a dragonfly, hovering close to intruders with complete fearlessness and – more peacefully – sipping nectar at flowers. See the beautifully illustrated *Hummingbirds of the Caribbean* by Esther and Robert Tyrrell for more information on hummers.

Marine Life

The region's marine life is as varied as the islands and coral reefs themselves. Depending on whom you believe, The Bahamas has between 900 and 2700 sq miles of coral reef.

The undersea world is enthralling. Frondlike orange gorgonians (named for the trio of snake-haired sisters of Greek mythology) spread their fingers up toward the light. There are contorted sheets of purple staghorn and lacy outcrops of tubipora, resembling delicately woven Spanish mantillas; sinuous, boulderlike brain corals; and soft-flowering corals that sway to the rhythms of the ocean currents. Then there are the sponges, living pumps that take in water through their outer pores, extract the nutrients, and expel the residue.

Countless species of fish zip in and out of the exquisite reefs and swarm through the coral canyons: snapper, bonito, kingfish, jewelfish, deep-blue Creole wrasse, inflatable porcupine fish, moray eel, parrotfish with sharp teeth and a body of iridescent plumpurple and blue-green, and scores of others whose names you may never learn but whose beauty you will forever remember. Their

The Conch

The queen conch *(Strombus gigas),* a large marine snail with a spectacular pink shell, grazes on seagrasses and looks like a mossy rock crawling slowly along the seabed. The animal doesn't glide like most snails. It uses its large muscular foot to hop along the sea floor. It has a stalked eye to either side of its ungainly proboscis, which it extends like an elephant's trunk to smother a convenient morsel.

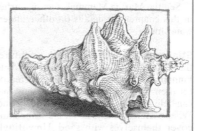

The conch, which can live for 20 years and attain a length of 12 inches and weigh half a pound, begins life as a larvalike creature called a 'veliger,' smaller than a pinhead. It swims at the surface, eating phytoplankton and drifting with the currents. At one month, when it is about 1.2 mm long, it settles to the bottom and undergoes a metamorphosis that includes development of a shell. By night it crawls along the seabed eating algae; by day it burrows. When it is about a year old, it migrates deeper into the ocean to live amid the seagrass meadows, where it continues to feed on algae.

A conch grows its shell in a clockwise direction. The shell expands in order to make way for its growing body. The process lasts for four years, until it is a full-lipped adult with upward-pointing spires. An irregular pink pearl is sometimes found in the shell. The characteristic shell lip forms at about 3½ years, when the animal approaches sexual maturity.

The male and female, now between 8 and 12 inches long apiece, mate sexually and spawn in summer. (Intercourse is a dangerous time for males: The penis, alas, is considered a delicacy by eels, which can often be seen nibbling at copulating couples!) The female lays egg masses up to 10 times a year on the clean coral sands. Each crescent-shaped egg mass may contain up to 300,000 eggs, bonded in a single strand. Only a fraction survive to adulthood – the conch has many predators, including spotted eagle rays, loggerhead turtles, octopi, porcupine fish, spiny lobsters, crabs, and, chiefly, humans.

The conch is the primary source of protein for islanders. It is widely sought after for its sweet white meat, which tastes somewhat like a rubbery scallop. Growing demand for conch has raised the price, leading to overexploitation and the gathering of immature snails. In 1992 the Convention on International Trade in Endangered Species listed the conch one category below threatened status.

For more information, contact the Caribbean Marine Research Center (☎ 561-741-0192, fax 561-741-0193, cmrc@cmrc.org), 250 Tequesta Dr, suite 304, Tequesta, FL 33469, USA.

stained-glass brilliance contrasts with the understated colors of the reefs. The smaller fry are preyed upon by giant groupers, sharks, tarpons, and barracudas, exquisitely patient and facing the current as if they had been frozen by time.

The marine world also moves by night, when bioluminescent creatures flit through the dark depths and small transparent fish and shrimp can be seen swimming through the scuba diver's light beam. Lobsters prowl the seabed. Cardinal fish and squirrelfish are also active, scanning the reef with their big, night-perfect eyes.

See the Marine Mammals section earlier in this chapter for details on other underwater life.

Stingrays Some of the islands' creatures thrive in part because they pose hazards to humans. Stingrays, for example, are feared for their whiplike tails, bearing a spine that can deliver an excruciatingly painful wound. When resting, the rays lie on the seabed and cover themselves with sand. Unwittingly step on one and its tail will whip around and plant a razor-sharp spine in your leg. For your troubles, the 6-inch-long spike is tipped with poison.

Up to 5 feet across, stingrays are in fact quite gentle. As they gather around you, they become gentle birds of the sea. You can even stroke them. These natural bottom-feeders will take food from your hand, though the ray never actually sees its food. Since its eyes are on top of its body and its mouth and nostrils below, it relies on highly developed electroreceptors and a keen sense of smell to find its food.

Sharks Several species of shark – predominantly nurse, tiger, and Caribbean reef sharks – abound in these waters. *Agh!*...those teeth! Sharks' razor-sharp, serrated teeth might have kept us rooting for harpoonists and fishermen, but the fact is that more people are killed in The Bahamas by falling coconuts than by sharks.

Though decades of shark-hunting have led to the near decimation of many species, a new appreciation has emerged of late as scientists have come to realize the shark's crucial role at the top of the marine food chain. Now the quest is on to learn how sharks live, reproduce, feed, and survive. Scientists based at Walker's Cay (Abacos) have been surprised, for example, to discover that male sharks migrate seasonally in winter, leaving female sharks in feeding zones.

Coral Ecology A coral is a tiny animal with a great gaping mouth, surrounded by tentacles for gathering food, at one end. The polyps, which resemble flowers or cushions upholstered with plush fabric, live protected by external skeletons, the production of which is dependent upon algae that live inside the polyps' tissue. The creatures live in vast colonies that reproduce both asexually by budding, and sexually through a synchronous release of spermatozoa that turns the surrounding sea milky. Together they build up huge frameworks – the reefs.

A reef is usually composed of scores of species of coral, each occupying its own niche. However, all corals can flourish only close to the ocean surface, where they are nourished by sunlight in clear, unpolluted waters above 70°F. Each species has a characteristic shape – bulbous cups bunched like biscuits in a baking tray for the star coral; deep, winding valleys for the well-named brain coral. Deeper down, where light is scarcer, massive corals flatten out, becoming more muted in color. Deeper still, soft corals – those without an external skeleton – predominate. These lacy fans and waving cattails look like plants, but a close perusal shows them to be menacing animal predators that seize smaller creatures, such as plankton.

Coral reefs are the most complex and sensitive of all ecosystems. Taking thousands of years to form, they are divided into life zones gauged by depth, temperature, and light. When a coral polyp dies, its skeleton turns to limestone that another polyp may use to cement its own skeleton. The entire reef system is gnawed away by parrotfish and other predators. A few areas have witnessed destruction by anchors dropped from boats. And in recent years Bahamian fishermen have begun destroying some of the reefs by squirting chlorine bleach into the reefs' nooks and crannies to drive out lobsters. The biggest culprit, however, is Mother Nature: Hurricanes cause as much devastation as a minor war.

For more information on the fragile reef ecology, pick up Dr William S Alevizon's superb *Caribbean Reef Ecology* (Pisces Books).

The Bahamas Reef Environment Educational Foundation (☎ 242-326-7938, fax 242-326-7443, breef@bahamas.net.bs; PO Box N-7776, Nassau, The Bahamas) is a nongovernmental body dedicated to protecting the reefs.

Marine Turtles Three species of marine turtles – green, loggerhead, and, more rarely, hawksbill – use the islands' beaches as nest sites. Turtles migrate thousands of miles to nest and lay the eggs for tomorrow's turtles, as they have for at least 150 million years.

Lucayan Indians considered them a delicacy. The Lucayans' subsistence needs had as little effect on the vast aquatic herds as the Plains Indians' had on the buffalo. The 'discovery' of the West Indies, however, opened up the waters to rapacious hunting of turtles, which are now endangered.

The Dept of Fisheries (☎ 242-393-1777), on E Bay St in Nassau, has established regulations to protect the species, although local fishermen still catch turtles legally for meat. Turtling is prohibited April 1 to July 31. At other times no turtles may be taken on a beach, no eggs may be taken, and no green turtles below 24 inches and no loggerheads below 30 inches may be taken. Hawksbills are protected year-round. Remember: It is strictly illegal to purchase turtle-shell products, which US or other customs agents are likely to confiscate. You can write the Dept of Fisheries at PO Box N-3028, Nassau, The Bahamas.

NATIONAL PARKS

The Bahamas has 12 national parks and protected areas. The newest among them is Abaco National Park, created in 1994 to protect the Bahama parrot. An additional 51 areas in the country are proposed for protection, and large sections of barrier reef off the east shore of Andros are slated to receive national park status.

The 175-sq-mile **Exuma Cays Land & Sea Park**, beginning 30 miles southeast of Nassau, was created in 1958 as the first marine fishery reserve in the world. The park teems with prehistoric life forms, coral reefs, turtles, fish, the endangered rock iguana, and the hutia.

Grand Bahama has **Lucayan National Park**, about 40 miles east of Freeport. This 40-acre ecojewel is leased to the BNT by the Grand Bahama Development Company and boasts 6 miles of underground caverns – one of the most extensive systems in the world – plus large mangrove swamps and native coppice.

Peterson Cay National Park preserves a 1½-acre cay and surrounding coral gardens off the leeward shore of Grand Bahama.

Also on Grand Bahama is the **Rand Memorial Nature Centre**, a 100-acre reserve of rare palms and native woodland in Freeport, with a captive flamingo flock and populations of native boa constrictors and curly-tailed lizards. Similarly, **The Retreat** is an 11-acre garden of rare palms, native coppice, and exotic plants in residential Nassau. The headquarters of the BNT is here.

The Abacos boast two national parks, including the 2100-acre **Pelican Cays Land & Sea Park**. It contains extensive coral reefs and undersea caves and abundant terrestrial plant and animal life. The 32-sq-mile **Abaco National Park** encompasses the breeding and foraging grounds – some 5000 acres of forest – of the Bahama parrot. The Abacos also have **Black Sound Cay**, off Green Turtle Cay, comprising a thick stand of mangrove vegetation and an important wintering habitat for waterfowl and avifauna, and **Tilloo Cay**, a 20-acre area of pristine wilderness that is a vital nesting site for tropic birds.

The 287-sq-mile **Inagua National Park**, on Great Inagua, protects the world's largest breeding colony of West Indian flamingos, while the 7-sq-mile **Union Creek Reserve** (at the park's northwest corner, yet separately administered) is an important tidal-creek research site for studying marine turtles.

Green turtles also get star billing at **Conception Island Land & Sea Park**, which is also a sanctuary for seabirds. It lies between Long Island and San Salvador.

See the island chapters for more information on the parks.

GOVERNMENT & POLITICS

Political stability has been a hallmark of the parliamentary democracy that has existed in The Bahamas for almost three centuries. The Commonwealth of The Bahamas has been independent since July 10, 1973, when the current constitution was adopted. The country inherited its political institutions from the UK, attested to by the parliamentary speaker's white wig and the gold scepter at his side.

The Bahamas is part of the Commonwealth of Nations (formerly the British Commonwealth). The British monarch is head of state and is represented by a Bahamian-born governor-general. Duties of this largely ceremonial post include appointing the prime minister, who is always the leader of the party that has won a majority in the last national election. Sir Orville Turnquest (deputy prime minister, minister of foreign affairs, and attorney general 1992–95) has been governor-general since 1995.

Executive power resides with a ministerial cabinet appointed and led by the prime minister and responsible to Parliament. Parliament consists of a bicameral legislature – the 49-member elected House of Representatives and the nominated 16-member Senate, nine members of which are appointed by the prime minister, four by the leader of the opposition, and three by mutual consent. All cabinet ministers must be members of Parliament.

The House may override a Senate veto, but any amendment to the constitution must be approved by a two-thirds majority vote in both houses of Parliament and by a national referendum.

A full parliamentary term is five years. The governor-general, however, may call a national election at his discretion at any time at the request of the prime minister (that usually means when timing seems propitious for the ruling party) and, in extreme cases, may even dismiss the government.

The political apparatus has traditionally been beset with cronyism and patronage (the ruling party usually dispenses government posts and public-service contracts to favored companies, family members, and friends).

The national flag is a black equilateral triangle on a background of three horizontal bands of equal size: a gold stripe sandwiched between stripes of aquamarine. Black supposedly represents the 'vigor and strength of a united people.' The triangle represents the 'enterprise and determination of the Bahamian people,' and the gold and aquamarine represent the land and sea. The nation's motto is 'Forward, Upward, Onward, Together.'

Party Politics & Elections

Island politics was for three decades intimately associated with Sir Lynden Pindling, who led the fight for independence and who served as prime minister from 1967 to 1992. Pindling headed the PLP, which historically has carried the banner of the underprivileged class.

Bahamians have traditionally been fiercely partisan about their politics. However, many traditional PLP voters finally came to realize that the Pindling government had become steeped in corruption. In 1992 the PLP's rival, the FNM, took power for the first time, with a 56% majority, under the leadership of the present prime minister, Hubert A Ingraham.

The FNM's prudent policies have made it a beacon of economic stability. Ingraham's first FNM administration spent much of its energy cleaning up the mess created by the 25 years of PLP rule. A majority of Bahamians feel that things improved markedly under Ingraham's tenure (the Family Islands in particular witnessed a wholesale laying of paved roads and an improvement in services). As a result, the FNM was reelected in March 1997 by a landslide, winning an 85%

majority with 34 of 40 seats – an unprecedented victory. In the Family Islands the *only* PLP member to win a seat was Sir Pindling, who announced his retirement soon after the election (the FNM captured his seat in the ensuing by-election).

The islands become charged with election fever. Politics are hotly debated between ordinary citizens, who are generally extremely knowledgeable about local issues. All adults older than 18 may vote. The din of disputes on the street astounds many visitors to the islands, who are sure that the arguments must end in fisticuffs. On election day voters clog the streets, stand in groups to argue, and display their purple-stained thumbs with pride. Turnout for the 1997 election was more than 90%.

Judiciary

The Bahamian judicial system is based on UK common law and practice. A large body of Bahamian statute law also exists.

Magistrates' courts and Family Island commissioners administer summary justice at the local level. There are 10 such courts on New Providence (plus two traffic courts and three drug courts). A superior magistrate reviews appeals, which can then be appealed to the Supreme Court. Further appeal can be made to the Bahamas Court of Appeal and, finally, to Her Majesty's Privy Council in the UK.

The prison system is one of The Bahamas' more feudalistic institutions and has been decried for its deplorable conditions.

Royal Bahamas Defence Force

Ostensibly The Bahamas has no army, navy, or air force. But in fact, the Royal Bahamas Defence Force, created in 1980 and comprising approximately 1200 members, is a well-armed military unit with its own coast guard and air wing. Its primary duty is maritime law enforcement, with a strong focus on drug-traffic interdiction. Its headquarters is in Coral Harbour (New Providence).

ECONOMY

The Bahamas is far more developed than most of its Caribbean neighbors (it is defined by the US Dept of Commerce as a 'stable upper-middle-income, developing nation,' with a gross domestic product (GDP) estimated at US$5.58 billion). Per-capita income is more than US$11,000, one of the highest in the region. Its economy has flourished, thanks to its stable political climate, liberal laws designed to attract investment, and, undoubtedly, its proximity to North America. The US is the nation's largest trading partner, accounting for 80% of exports and 65% of imports (excluding oil).

The country's wealth rests on the triumvirate of tourism, banking, and shipping, in addition to – unofficially yet indisputably – drug trafficking. Tourism is the driving engine, generating about 60% of the GDP and employing about 50,000 people (half of the national workforce).

One of the country's assets is its large, skilled, well-educated workforce, 10% of which is employed in banking and insurance industries. Another one-third is employed by the government.

The wealth is concentrated in Nassau, so there are plenty of pockets of poverty, especially in the Family Islands, where unemployment is high and much of the local economy operates on a barter basis. Thousands of Bahamians earn their income as itinerant vendors.

Government Policy

The FNM's policies have brought public spending and foreign debt under control. The nation's trade imbalance and huge budget deficit (the FNM government inherited a US$1.1 billion national debt) have been reduced. Inflation is low. And unemployment, previously escalating, was reduced to 10% by mid-1997 and has since remained relatively stable. Appropriately, in 1994 the Ministry of Tourism changed its slogan to: 'The Islands of The Bahamas…It Just Keeps Getting Better.'

A Tax Shelter in the Sun

The Bahamas is one of the world's premier tax-free havens. The integral policy creates a win-win situation for gamblers who get lucky at the gaming tables or for cannier bettors who bone up on tax laws by the hotel pool before hitting the slots. Incentives offered to investors attract millions of dollars every year.

The Bahamas levies no taxes on personal or corporate income, capital gains, dividends, interest, royalties, sales, estates, inheritances, or payrolls. The repatriation of foreign investment funds, foreign assets and dividends, and profits arising from investments is permitted tax-free. Bahamian law strongly protects clients' right to confidentiality and privacy.

The Bahamas Investment Authority (☎ 242-327-5970, fax 242-327-5907), PO Box CB-10980, Nassau, The Bahamas, is a 'one-stop shop' for international investors who need information and assistance.

Major Industries

Tourism Tourism is by far The Bahamas' largest industry, accounting for US$1.6 billion in 1999 and producing much of the government's tax revenue. Annual visitor numbers have grown from 1 million in 1970 to 3.5 million (including cruise-ship day-trippers) in 1999, and there is no sense of coming close to saturation, because many Family Islands remain virtually undeveloped. About 80% of its visitors come from North America.

Cruise-ship passengers make up a major portion of these visits: Passenger arrivals in 1998 totaled 1,729,894, up from 1.6 million in 1996. In fact, The Bahamas (predominantly Nassau) is the number-one Caribbean cruise destination. Most such visitors spend only a day or two ashore.

Tourist facilities (hotels, restaurants, etc) are as good as any in the region, reflecting an investment of more than US$2 billion in tourist infrastructure since 1994.

Although only about 250,000 visitors a year visit the Family Islands (that is, all the islands other than New Providence and Grand Bahama), the government sees these outlying islands as the future. To support development, the government is investing in new infrastructure and promoting eco-tourism and 'meet-the-people' programs that foster cultural interchange between visitors

and residents (see the 'People to People' boxed text in the Facts for the Visitor chapter). And a provision in the Hotels Encouragement Act (which exempts hoteliers from property taxes) was designed to spur growth of small properties, to generate tourism at local levels, to stem migration from the Family Islands, and to absorb some of the pressure on the two main islands.

Banking & Finance The Bahamas – specifically Nassau – is one of the world's principal international financial and insurance centers. Over 400 banks from 36 countries are licensed to do business within or from The Bahamas. Almost 200 banks have a physical presence in the islands. Together they manage more than US$200 billion in assets. Financial services annually contribute about US$200 million to the economy. Financial markets are regulated by the independent Central Bank of The Bahamas.

The system primarily serves as a tax-planning haven and place of asset security; financial records cannot be subpoenaed or released. Although the FNM government made sweeping changes in banking laws to help the US DEA and the US Internal Revenue Service combat money laundering (Bahamian-held assets are no longer secure from US federal agencies), in 2000 the 26-country International Financial Action Task Force named The Bahamas among a 'black list' of 15 nations failing to cooperate in the fight against money laundering.

Agriculture & Fishing Less than 5% of the workforce is employed in agriculture, which contributes only 3% of the GDP, mostly from fruit crops. Only about 12,000 acres – 1% of the land area – is farmed.

Pineapples were once a staple of the economies of Eleuthera, Long Island, and Cat Island, which were briefly the world's leading suppliers of the fruit (the islands supplied the US before the plant was introduced to the Hawaiian Islands in the 1890s). They are still grown, though in vastly reduced quantities. Citrus fruits are important on Great Abaco (where 98% by value of agricultural exports are grown). Other fruits, tomatoes, cucumbers, onions, potatoes, and pigeon peas are grown commercially on Great Abaco and North Andros.

The Bahamas has large tracts of unused fertile land and plentiful supplies of fresh water on Grand Bahama and in the Family Islands, where a large percentage of the population raises crops on a level barely above subsistence, usually in rock-strewn patches, often coaxing their products to ripen in the bottom of limestone pits where soil and water collect.

Logging, once a major industry, has declined markedly in recent years. A cattle industry that evolved on Eleuthera in the years following WWII is now defunct. However, chickens are commercially reared on Great Abaco.

Countless Family Islanders derive their income from the sea. Conch and scale fish are taken year-round, mostly for local needs. Commercial fishing is of only marginal importance. Fisheries' major export is lobster. The seasonal trade involves thousands of small-scale fishermen as well as locally owned, capital-intensive, large-scale operations based in Spanish Wells (Eleuthera).

The FNM government continues to invest in schemes to hold farmers and fishermen in the Family Islands and has made promoting agricultural investment a major goal.

Manufacturing The major industries are brewing and rum manufacture (valued at US$37 million in annual exports) on New Providence, and petrochemicals on Grand Bahama. Annual crude salt exports, predominantly from Great Inagua, are valued at more than US$20 million.

Drug Trade

No discussion of the economy would be complete without an account of the vast impact of narcotics and drug money. Domestic drug sales are slight. But many islanders are involved in illicit narcotics trading, using boats or planes to whisk drugs flown in from Colombia and other drug-producing nations to the US. An estimated 50% of the cocaine entering the US passes over or through The Bahamas.

Eluding drug-enforcement authorities is made easy by dozens of remote airstrips on the countless tiny cays and by the thousands of miles of indented shoreline that are impossible to police.

The traffic evolved during the late 1970s and peaked in the early '80s, when drug-laden planes and cigarette boats zipped in and out 24 hours a day. Thousands of Bahamians were involved in the trade, even otherwise respectable, church-going citizens and high-ranking government officials. Everyone else turned a blind eye...the legacy of a long history of wrecking and smuggling.

Following a scandal in 1984, when it was revealed that drug money had tainted the highest levels of government, the US DEA and Royal Bahamas Defence Force initiated a massive enforcement program. The DEA put three AEROSTAT surveillance balloons over Grand Bahama, Great Exuma, and Great Inagua to track air traffic (the balloons have since been replaced by radar). In 1987 the Biminis were quarantined, as US Coast Guard vessels were given permission to search every vessel entering and leaving the islands.

Despite the government's efforts to eradicate the trade, drug trafficking is still very much alive, pumping millions of dollars into the economy each year.

Wrecking still occurs, too. When a ship wrecks – albeit less often than in days of yore – skiffs from local hamlets (called 'settlements') can soon be seen piled high with brass fittings and other treasure plundered from the wreck. 'It's the law of the land,' say the locals.

POPULATION & PEOPLE

The Bahamas has approximately 294,982 people (2000 estimate), up from 210,000 in 1980. The last census took place in summer 2000.

Life expectancy is 74 years for women and 68 for men. The birth rate is a low 20 per 1000, and population growth is only 1.01% (until the advent of television, The Bahamas had the second-highest birth rate in the world). More than 64% of the population is younger than 30.

About 80% of the population is urban. Nearly two-thirds of residents live in Nassau, and approximately 40,000 live in Freeport, the only other major city.

The remainder of the population is scattered among about a dozen Family Islands (islands other than Grand Bahama and New Providence; predominantly the Abacos, Andros, and Eleuthera, each with about 10,000 people) and a few dozen offshore cays. The islands tend to be less populated as you move south, and the southern islands are suffering significant declines in population.

About 85% of the population is black (including 'browns,' who have a multiracial ancestry). Whites constitute 12% of the population; most are of British and to a lesser degree US, Irish, and Greek descent. The minuscule remainder are of Asian, Hispanic, or other descent.

The Bahamas prides itself on its harmonious race relations. Indeed, the islands are refreshingly free of racial tensions and class divisions are markedly *less* related to color than on many neighboring islands. Everyone can socialize together.

Nonetheless, color is still perhaps the ultimate status symbol in a society that exhibits great admiration for status symbols. Many darker Bahamians (who make up a good portion of the poorer classes) attempt to 'lift' their color by marrying a lighter-skinned person. On some of the Abaco Cays, few white descendants of Loyalists would even dream of dating or – heaven forbid! – marrying a black person, though the two groups get along fine. The most virulent prejudice – among both black and white Bahamians – is against Haitians, a recent immigrant underclass.

The nation's politics and businesses were, until independence, dominated by whites and light-skinned 'brights,' otherwise known as Long Island or Eleuthera 'reds' (Bahamians whose predominantly white ancestry, with a dash of black, is reflected in their mahogany complexions).

There are no descendants of the indigenous Lucayans. But around Red Bay

(Andros), you may note the distinct features of Seminole Indians, whose forefathers fled Florida and settled here two centuries ago.

Bahamian Blacks

The vast majority of blacks trace their ancestry to slaves brought from the Carolinas. They in turn were drawn predominantly from West African tribes such as the House, Ibo, Mandingo, and Yoruba.

The Bahamas' black population has grown out of several events. When Loyalists arrived in the islands, they brought with them their most trusted and able slaves. In other cases, slavetraders called into Nassau en route to other destinations and sold Africans to local slaveholders. Scores of free blacks fled the US for the islands, where many became large landholders (often slaveowners themselves) and prominent citizens. Additional thousands of runaway slaves – people of immense courage and imagination – and blacks liberated from slave ships by the British also landed in the islands as free people.

Bahamian Whites

Outside Nassau, most whites concentrate in a few settlements where they are a conspicuous majority: Marsh Harbour, Cherokee Sound, and Treasure, Green Turtle, Great Guana, Elbow, and Man O' War Cay (Abacos); and Spanish Wells and Harbour Island (Eleuthera). Each settlement has only a few family names – virtually everyone is an Albright on Man O' War. Other Loyalist names are Malone, Pinder, Sawyer, and Saunders.

Most whites in these settlements can claim descent from the earliest English settlers, Loyalists who fled the American Revolution. Others claim descent from Southerners escaping the US Civil War. A few like to claim ancestry from the English ruling elite. A far greater number are descended from pirates and vagabonds.

Nassau's white community remains somewhat clannish and dominates the upper echelons of economic life. The British tend to excel in the financial industry. Greeks, Jews, and Lebanese (who form less than 1% of the population) have been successful in their own businesses and are insular and protective of their cultural heritage.

Then there are the thousands of part-time and full-time residents – predominantly North Americans – who have chosen The Bahamas as an escape from the prying eyes of the world. Expats' houses are sprinkled throughout the archipelago.

Conchy Joes

Every Loyalist descendant and other Caucasian born in the islands is known as a 'Conchy Joe.' Family Island Conchy Joes are readily identifiable by their distinctive features: usually blue or green eyes, freckled skin, and blondish hair. They follow their own patterns of dress, speech, and behavior, distinct from those of black Bahamians and rather similar to stereotypical middle-American ways. For a hilarious look at what it means to be a Conchy Joe, see Patricia Glinton-Meicholas' *How to Be a True-True Bahamian* (Guanima Press).

Haitians

The islands have been 'invaded' in recent years by thousands of job seekers from other islands, predominantly Haiti and, to a lesser degree, the Dominican Republic and Jamaica. Most are illegal immigrants seeking a better life. The Bahamian government tried repatriating the early refugees, but Haiti refused them.

Haitians (sometimes called 'Hyshuns' locally) perform menial tasks – farm labor, domestic work – that few Bahamians are willing to do. Thus they are hired illegally and exploited at below-minimum wages. Nonetheless, there is lingering resentment among Bahamians, who look down on Haitians and even despise them, based on the old bugbear that the immigrants have 'stolen jobs.' The prejudice, however, perhaps derives from a sense of racial superiority: Haitians are in general darker-skinned and shorter than are Bahamians.

Many Haitians and 'Bahatians' (Haitians born in The Bahamas) live in squalid conditions, often without sanitation or utilities. A Human Rights Watch report revealed that 90% of prisoners in The Bahamas are Haitians. The government seems to have given little thought to the problem.

EDUCATION

During the late 19th century, the British established the foundations of The Bahamas' admirable education system, based on their own model of schooling. More than 98% of the population is literate. However, Bahamians are not big readers, and book and magazine sales among the population are minimal.

School attendance is compulsory through age 16. Some 80% of schools are government run. Most independent schools – called colleges – are affiliated with a church body. Students work toward earning the Bahamas General Certificate of Secondary Education in each subject (it is equivalent to the English GCE 'O' level but encompasses a broader range of abilities). All students wear uniforms. Each school district has its own colors.

There are four bodies of higher learning. The University of the West Indies (UWI) has a campus in Nassau, attracting students from English-speaking Caribbean nations. It has a Center for the Hotel & Tourism Industry. The government-run College of the Bahamas, with two campuses in Nassau and one in Freeport, offers advanced-level ('A') certificates, diplomas, and degrees in the arts, sciences, humanities, and banking and finance. The Bahamas Hotel Training College provides training in hospitality fields. The Industrial Training Programme offers training in trade skills.

ARTS

Relative to its neighbors, The Bahamas' intellectual tradition is comparatively weak and for a capital city, Nassau is surprisingly unsophisticated in the visual and performance arts. A wider search, however, reveals an evolving artistic tapestry. Quintessential Bahamian styles *have* evolved in music, dance, drama, and fine arts.

Music

From hotel beach parties to the raw sound system dance clubs of Over-the-Hill,

Nassau's poorer quarter, The Bahamas reverberates to the soul-riveting sounds of calypso, soca, reggae, and its own distinctive music, which echoes African rhythms and synthesizes Caribbean calypso and soca and English folk songs into its own *goombay* beat.

Goombay This type of music – the name comes from an African word for 'rhythm' – derives its melody from a guitar, piano, or horn instrument accompanied by any combination of goatskin goombay drums, maracas, rhythm (or click) sticks, rattles, conch-shell horns, fifes and flutes, and cowbells to add a uniquely Bahamian *kalik-kalik-kalik* sound. It's typified by a fast-paced, sustained, infectious melody. Goombay is to The Bahamas what reggae is to Jamaica.

Goombay draws on a heritage of folk music introduced by African slaves from North America, Jamaica, and other neighboring islands. Particularly important are the 'talking drums,' once used to pass along information, and folk songs developed in the cane fields to ease the backbreaking labor. Over generations, European elements, such as the French quadrille introduced by planters, were absorbed as well, creating a unique style.

Goombay is most on display during Junkanoo celebrations (see the boxed text 'Junkanoo' in the Facts for the Visitor chapter). The terms 'goombay' and 'Junkanoo' have become virtually interchangeable: 'Junkanoo' is often used to refer to this type of music, but it means, more strictly, the quintessential African-Bahamian celebration held at Christmastime.

Almost every major resort hotel has a goombay band or show, with male musicians and dancers of both sexes dressed in bright flounced costumes.

The Obeah Man, alias Tony Mackay, a flamboyant performer and musical superhero from Cat Island (he now lives in Miami), has become a bit of a cult figure in the US. His wild costume includes waist-length braided hair – 'Junkanoo locks' – an elaborate hat, and bells and other musical contraptions strapped to his body. His

Masked Junkanoo reveler

music is pure goombay. His recordings are available on the Mercury Records label and Mackay's own Nassau label. In 1987 he was awarded the British Empire Medal, thus becoming Sir Tony. 'No, no, no,' he laughs, 'Grassroots, man. Gotta stay with de people.'

Rake 'n' Scrape The Bahamas' down-home, working-class music is rake 'n' scrape, usually featuring a guitar, an accordion, shakers made from the pods of poinciana trees, and other makeshift instruments, such as a saw played with a screwdriver.

Rake 'n' scrape music can be heard at local bars throughout the islands.

Other Sounds Spirituals were brought to the islands by Southern Loyalists' slaves, then adapted to incorporate purely Bahamian 'call and answer' techniques, rhyming exchanges of voices. Many secular versions took on a quasicalypso or bluesy beat and addressed local events, be it a sex scandal or local superstition, and have lyrics that often pay respect to the sea. Bahamian folk music is rooted in spiritual and gospel hymns often performed in 'rhymin' style. Androsian folk-singer Joseph Spence was the islands' master of folk and blues.

Though calypso and reggae are more closely associated with Trinidad and Jamaica, many hotels feature a steel-drum band or reggae musicians in their weekly repertoire of entertainment.

The 1990s witnessed an upwelling of Bahamian popular music, and this diversity was carried to Nassau's radio stations. The music blends reggae and rap with goombay, and lyricists turn to praise of God, fast sex, and the female form. The calypso-soca songs of popular local artist KB, for example, have titles like 'She Fat,' 'Juicy Suzy,' and 'Only Meat,' which bring on a good chuckle among hip Bahamians, reflecting as they do a preference among Bahamian men for full-bodied women.

Sexual relations are a steadfast source of musical inspiration. One of the nation's most popular songs is 'Shame and Scandal in the Family,' an amusing and lively ditty about 'outside' children, those birthed or sired by someone other than the mother's or father's spouse.

Dance hall, a kind of Caribbean rap and the in-vogue working-class music of formerly British Caribbean islands, has evolved its own style in The Bahamas, where it is known as 'chatting.' It is performed entirely in local dialect. The music has its origins in US urban ghettos of the 1990s, and usually has a monotonous yet fast-paced, compulsive beat, often with vocals added to the rhythms. It is most often performed by local DJs with their own mobile discos. The lyrics are generally sexually explicit and often glorify violence. Check out Tony Mackay's 'Natty Bon Dey' on his *Canaan Lane* album (1994).

Chatting has an ancestor known as 'rigging' – see the Traditional Culture section, later in this chapter.

Literature

While The Bahamas has produced no writer of world renown, the nation does have its literati. Few, however, are known even within the Caribbean region.

An exception is Brian Antoni's *Paradise Overdose*, about the 1980s drug- and sex-addled Bahamian high-life and the redemptive power of love.

The most popular body of homegrown work draws on The Bahamas' unique Loyalist history. The authors themselves tend to be descendants of Loyalists. A good example is Captain Leonard M Thompson, a WWII Royal Canadian Air Force veteran and former prisoner of war who is considered the father of modern tourism in The Bahamas. His autobiographical *I Wanted Wings* is a splendid introduction to Bahamian history and ways.

Bahamian Anthology (College of The Bahamas) is a selection of poetry, stories, and plays by Bahamian writers. In a similar poetic vein, try *Bahamas: In a White Coming On* by Dennis Ryan (Dorrance).

Other works view Bahamian society through the eyes of foreigners who have traveled through the islands or settled there in recent decades. Perhaps the most famous example is *Out Island Doctor* by Evans Cottman, a Yankee teacher who fell for Crooked and Acklins Islands in the 1940s.

Architecture

The islands have their own architectural styles reflecting the influences of early Bermudian settlers and US Loyalists.

Most plantation and government buildings were built of local sandstone and limestone, as were the homes of the wealthy. The stones were fixed and finished by mortar and plaster containing lime produced by burning conch shells. Being thick – sometimes as much as 3 feet – these massive walls became temperature sinks, keeping the building relatively cool even during the heat of midday. To assist in cooling, breezes were permitted to flow through trellised windows, louvers, grills, and partition walls that didn't quite reach the ceiling.

On many islands, wooden houses are more prevalent. On Eleuthera and the Loyalist Cays of the Abacos, a distinctive style evolved that has been likened to that of Cape Cod in Massachusetts. The most splendid examples are in Dunmore Town and Spanish Wells (Eleuthera) and in Hope Town, New Plymouth, and Man O' War Cay (Abacos). The Bahamian clapboard house has been widely copied throughout the Caribbean. In the Turks and Caicos a uniquely Bermudian influence has been at work. Often the houses are made of ship-timber driftwood and planking, the framework filled with cemented rubble rock and finished in plaster. A close look at many of the pitched roofs reveals them to be stone that is stepped in the Bermudian fashion.

Smaller wooden homes in The Bahamas were elevated atop a masonry ground floor, with balconies supported by stilts or masonry pillars. Not only did this allow airflow beneath the living quarters, it also kept them above water level in the event of a hurricane surge.

The Family Islands are also peppered with tiny square stone buildings – 'slave homes' – that have survived decay and natural disasters. Many are still inhabited. Each is the size of a pillbox, with a steep-angled, four-sided roof and an open kitchen in back, but no toilet. Communal outhouses (they, too, still stand) were built along the shore, where one would make a deposit straight into the sea.

Paint finishes were produced from linseed oil, wood spirits, or turpentine derived from pine and mixed with ochre, sienna, and other mineral or organic pigments: iron oxides for barn red, copper oxides for green, cobalt for blue, and zinc for white. The latter two were expensive, and a white house with blue shutters became a true status symbol.

Two common features on historic buildings are steep-pitched roofs and an absence of roof overhangs. Designed to reduce wind resistance during hurricanes, the steep pitch aids in rigidity and also prevents airfoil uplift (the process that 'lifts' an aircraft off the ground) when strong winds blow across it. The lack of overhang prevents the wind from peeling back the roof. Those shady verandahs you see everywhere are invariably separate 'sacrificial' extensions to the roofs, designed so that the wind may tear them away without taking the roofs as well.

The passage in 1998 of the Antiquities, Monuments & Museums Act led to creation of several historic districts, and restoration work has been initiated.

Modern homes pay little homage to time-tested design; instead they are universally air-tight, with minimal windows and reliant upon air-conditioning.

Visual Arts

The islands' plastic arts (ceramics, sculpture, painting, woodcarving, and textiles) have been late in flowering.

Bahamian art has its origins in the 18th and 19th centuries, when itinerant English and American artists visited the islands and recorded their impressions in pen-and-ink sketches and paintings that reflected a Eurocentric point of view that totally ignored or mocked the African heritage.

Until recently there were very few artists painting full time: Brent Malone, Max Taylor, Rolph Harris, and Alton Roland Lowe – The Bahamas' artist laureate for more than three decades – come to mind. But today local talent is blooming. A collective visual style is evident, tending to portray a simple, idyllic notion of The Bahamas: shining-white clapboard houses, lush gardens, evanescent skies and seas, royal poincianas ablaze with orange. Junkanoo dancers and revelers are a common subject, as are sponge collectors, children fishing, and church congregations.

The oils of Alton Lowe, a seventh-generation Loyalist Abaconian, are much sought after by blue bloods and corporations. Another of the leading artists is Eddie Minnis, a cartoonist, songwriter, and recording artist who is inspired by his devotion to the church of Jehovah's Witnesses. His limited-edition prints are popular, and his original oils, works of intricate detail and vibrant color (he paints less than a dozen per year), command thousands of dollars.

Minnis' two daughters, Nicole and Roshanne, have followed in his footsteps. Nicole is acclaimed for her depictions in oils of people and traditional island life. Roshanne's works tend to depict ocean scenes in soft pastels.

The so-called father of Bahamian art is Amos Ferguson, the foremost folk artist. Like Minnis, Ferguson is intensely spiritual. His naive, palette-bright canvases focus upon religion, history, nature, and folklore, or 'ol' story.' Though crude – oil-based paint on cardboard, bearing his trademark child-like signature: 'Paint by Mr Amos Ferguson' – his works wear price tags of US$1500 or more. Recently Ferguson has begun making bird figurines, tumblers, and jars for the tourist trade. You can see a permanent collection of his works in the Pompey Museum in Nassau.

Ferguson's abstract expressionism ripples through the world of Bahamian art, influencing important young artists such as Eric Ellis, two generations his junior.

The most noteworthy experimental artist is Janine Antoni, from Grand Bahama. Antoni made headlines at the Whitney Biennial in 1993 when she lowered her naked body into a bathtub filled with animal fat. Antoni's unique art includes painting the floor with her hair and gnawing on huge blocks of chocolate and lard. 'A confectioner's day ruined by a beaver,' reported one witty reviewer.

Another artist is Sonia Isaacs, who is famous for her paintings' bright tropical colors and for her unglazed pottery. Isaacs depicts local culture and personalities in a kind of paint-by-numbers style, with a uniquely intuitive, often hallucinogenic manner.

The Doongalik Studios (☎ 242-394-1886), in Nassau, has brought together many leading contemporary artists under one roof.

Ceramics has blossomed in recent years, thanks in large part to the influence of Denis Knight, a septuagenarian British expat acclaimed for his ceramic murals, which adorn several public buildings. Several other expats have brought their own influences.

A splendid coffee-table book on the subject is *Bahamian Art* by Patricia Glinton-Meicholas, Charles Huggins, and Basil Smith (The Counsellors Press, Nassau).

Crafts

Bahamian artisans produce basketry and other straw-work from native thatch palm. But as tourism has increased, cheap straw goods have been imported from Asia to augment local supplies. These imports have virtually killed off native weaving. Pockets of weavers remain, particularly on Cat Island and in Red Bay, where beautiful watertight straw baskets are woven. See the Shopping section in the Facts for the Visitor chapter for more information.

With the exception of straw-work, the crafts industry is relatively undeveloped. It has been influenced in recent years by the influx of Haitians, who have inspired intuitive hardwood carvings, often brightly painted and highlighted by pointillist dots.

Film & Theater

The Bahamas is relatively theater-starved. There is no homegrown movie industry, although the islands are a popular locale for shoots (see the Films section of the Facts for the Visitor chapter). Hence the Bahamas Tourist Board doubles as the Bahamas Film & Television Commission.

SOCIETY & CONDUCT
Traditional Culture

Few traces remain of the indigenous Lucayan Indian culture, though many words have been passed down into common parlance. Much of what remains of traditional culture is a legacy of the slave era: African slaves brought their beliefs, folktales, music, and religious customs.

Folktales Bahamian folktales have an oral tradition dating back to African slave days. Folk stories bear a similarity to those of black residents of the US South. Particular favorites are tales of animal trickster-heroes such as Bredda (Brother) Rabbie and

Bredda Bookie, who survive against the odds by virtue of quick wit, intelligence, cunning, and ingenuity.

Other purely local figures have evolved and found their way into folktales, many of which are firmly believed as fact, such as the mischief-making chickcharnie of Andros and the sirens and Loch Ness Monster–like creatures of the blue holes of Andros and Cat Island. The 'bunce' is a bogeyman, an evil spirit that inhabits forests.

Ad-libbing or 'rigging' lyrics as part of the chanting and telling of myths has traditionally been used to pass down morals to children. Spiritual and folkloric figures abounded in rigged tales. Bahamian adults, as salacious in past years as now, were subtle in disguising much that was implied in the songs. Thus guileless children could hardly guess the truth of things when they heard that 'Mama look up in daddy's face all night long.'

Several books trace the evolution and meaning of Bahamian folktales, including *Bahamian Lore: Folk Tales and Songs* by Robert Curry and *An Evenin' in Guanima: A Treasury of Folktales from The Bahamas* by Patricia Glinton-Meicholas.

Spirit Beliefs Many Bahamians still keep spirit beliefs held over from slave days, when African religions melded with Christianity. Rooted in the animist beliefs of West Africa (animism has nothing to do with animal spirits; the name is derived from the Latin word *anima*, meaning 'soul'), they are based on the tenet that the spiritual and temporal worlds are a unified whole.

A core belief is that spirits live independently of the human or animal body and can inhabit inanimate objects. They can communicate themselves directly to humans and are usually morally neutral; it is the service to which humans call them that determines whether they will be a force of good or evil. Cantankerous, onerous people beget evil 'sperrids'; kind and thoughtful people beget good spirits. Spirits particularly like to live in silk cotton trees, of which many Bahamians are extremely wary.

Spirits reveal themselves on a whim; not being able to see them doesn't mean they aren't there. Many Bahamians believe that if you take the 'bibby' (mucus) from a dog's or horse's eye and put it in your own, you can actually see a spirit.

All kinds of practices have evolved to guard against evil spirits. Even physicians are known to tie a black cord around a newborn baby's wrists to guard against evil spirits. A Bible is often placed at the head of a sleeping child for the same reason. And if this fails, a Bahamian may attempt to dispel a malicious spirit by marking Xs all around and repeating the all-powerful phrase, 'Ten, ten, the Bible ten.'

To learn more, see the boxed text 'Obeah' – the practice of African witchcraft – in the Cat Island chapter, and pick up *Ten, Ten, the Bible Ten – Obeah in The Bahamas* by Timothy McCartney.

Bush Medicine Traditional folk healing is still alive, especially in the Family Islands, where locals have a suspicion of doctors and cling to folk remedies. Bush-medicine healers, often respected obeah practitioners, rely on native herbs, which they mix into concoctions, or potents, using recipes that have been handed down through many generations.

The sovereign ingredient is cerasee *(Mormodica charantia)*, an orange-fruited vine credited with resolving every imaginable human ailment. Aloe is also used for curing many ills, from sunburn to insect bites. Breadfruit leaves are said to cure high blood pressure. Not all the cures use berries and leaves. For example, 'goat nanny' (goat droppings) is said to cure whooping cough, while congested air passages are cured by pouring 'chamber lye' on the head. This golden liquid is named for the pot into which a person relieves himself at night when not blessed with an indoor toilet.

A good reference is *Bush Medicine in The Bahamas* by Leslie Higgs.

Modern Culture

Contemporary Bahamian culture revolves around the family, the church, and the sea.

Many cultural influences seep in from the US. The proximity of North America has had a profound influence on contemporary life and society. North American material values and consumer tastes have especially influenced youth and the monied classes. Fast-food franchises abound. A mobile telephone is considered de rigueur (The Bahamas has more satellite systems per capita than any other nation). And the destination of choice is Florida, where Bahamians flock to malls and car dealerships.

National Character The population is perhaps the *least* Caribbean in style and attitude of any in the region. The culture might strike the experienced traveler as rather soft-edged, devoid of nuance and piquancy. The islanders have not developed a uniquely identifiable character as have the Rastafarians of Jamaica, nor an intellectualism as in Cuba.

In some ways Bahamians of Nassau are terribly British. During the colonial era, white society was divided between Bahamian whites, or 'colonials' (those born in the islands), and English émigrés, who considered themselves an elite. Many wealthy Bahamian whites were accepted into the latter class, which established strict barriers to maintain the purity of the social hierarchy. To progress in society required one to become as British as possible in all spheres of life. Although the nation has been independent since 1973, many British traditions and attitudes remain (perhaps this is why Bahamians are notably quiescent and non-committal), although they have melded their Britishness with certain classically Caribbean behaviors.

For cultural inspiration, today's Bahamians look west, however, not across the Atlantic. Baseball caps…cars from Detroit…US fast-food chains. Nonetheless, they move with an air of un-American casualness, carrying on their affairs with a benign, nonchalant calm. Bahamians are relatively undisciplined and very relaxed toward rules and regulations, and they seem to regard set times for appointments as general guidelines. 'Fashionably late' is the white Bahamians' term for this attitude;

black Bahamians call it 'BT' (Bahamian Time).

Wit & Humor Though Bahamians have no great love for drama, they *do* appreciate a somewhat understated yet sardonic wit and keen sense of humor, preferably laced with sexual undertones. They like to make fun of people, usually in the subtlest way, but they accept being the butt of others' humor in good grace. Individual foibles and physical abnormalities are good sources of fun.

Being a reticent people, however, Bahamians will rarely direct their humor at you, the foreign visitor. If they do, take it in good humor. Their deprecating and self-deprecating wit is never meant to sting. You'll be an instant hit if you give as good as you get, but the key is subtlety, not malice.

Work & Social Ethic In general, the Bahamians are relatively contented, with few of the anguishes suffered by other island peoples in the region. The work ethic is pronounced. One rarely sees the malingerers of other countries, such as work crews snoozing beside the road. And most service staff display eagerness to please. The Bahamas offers service with a smile – it just might take a while.

Most Bahamians understand that their lifeblood is tourism. This recognition bolsters their natural sense of courtesy and a desire to please. But they are a proud, self-secure people who request the same respect that they willingly offer to tourists. Most Bahamians do not tolerate even a hint of condescension. Anyone who treats hotel staff like hired help is likely to be told, 'Don't disrespect me. Make me feel like you know me.'

Urban Culture There are really two Bahamian cultures: that of Nassau and Freeport and that of the more lackadaisical Family Islands.

In Nassau and Freeport most working people are employed in banking, tourism, or government work and live a nine-to-five lifestyle. The maturation of the banking and finance industries has fostered the growth of a large professional class, many of whom have become extremely wealthy: The streets thrum with expensive new cars and city workers dressed in fine togs bought on shopping sprees in Miami. Bright colors and tight clothes are de rigueur for younger women, as are Nike and Fila athletic shoes, oversize shirts, baggy jeans, and ostentatious displays of gold among young males. The elderly among the poorer classes, when 'dressed to the nines,' tend to adopt a 1960s hip look – a polyester suit, white tie over black shirt, alligator shoes, and fedora are typical for older Bahamian men.

It is generally acknowledged that Nassau and Freeport went through a crisis of character in the 1980s, when a surly mood was evident. Past visitors and local businesspeople alike will tell you that until a few years ago, many people in Nassau and Freeport were cursed with an aggressive, devil-may-care attitude that contributed to a bad reputation abroad.

Today people are markedly friendlier and the level of service is very high, although far too many Bahamians, both male and female, come across as sullen and unfriendly. To cement the turnaround, the FNM government has initiated programs to get locals involved in tourism and educate them about its fragility. 'Tourism 2000' gives hospitality employees and students a chance to be hotel guests themselves. And the 'People-to-People' program (see the boxed text on the program in the Facts for the Visitor chapter) matches tourists with locals for meals, religious services, and other aspects of daily life.

Alas, pretentious bravado is seeping into the behavior of younger adults. A growing number of younger Bahamian men, influenced by the symbolism of US and Jamaican gangsta rappers, have an 'I' mentality, act arrogantly, and, alas, adopt a threatening swagger. Elderly Bahamians increasingly complain that civilities are breaking down, pointing to increased lawlessness, laziness, and lack of discipline among young adults who have grown up in a generation that has known only the good life. Fortunately, there are still plenty of genuinely charming people with a friendliness that never pales.

Family Islanders The folks of the Out Islands – the Family Islanders – live languid lives in the sun and are altogether more at ease and neighborly than people in Nassau and Freeport. Unspoiled by city life, Family Islanders are friendliness personified, displaying a gentle wisdom and ever-present caring for other people. They take time to chat and to invite strangers to their homes. Traditional courtesies and a sense of integrity and dignity remain firm, untainted by tourism, which has barely touched many islands.

Family Islanders are an honest, hardworking lot. Many have little in the way of material goods, but 'their character and dignity are gold,' says author Harvey Lloyd. They have manners and pride. They are also far more traditional in outlook than their urban counterparts. Thus the practice of obeah, bush medicine, and folkloric songs and tales still infuse their daily lives, reflecting their bonds with nature.

After emancipation, most former slaves turned to fishing and subsistence farming. Many families still get by through fishing, catching conch and lobster, and raising corn, bananas, and other crops for the kitchen. Some earn a little from straw weaving; many still hunt tusked wild boar with dogs in the scrub and pinelands.

There is plenty of poverty in the Family Islands where local economies are underdeveloped. Most people live a hand-to-mouth existence alleviated by the government's social security system. In recent decades a desire for paid jobs has shrunk the settlements. Nassau has absorbed half of all Bahamians. Those who remain still live in the close-knit, tiny villages where they were born. They're curiously uncurious about life in distant places.

The islanders are raised from torpor by the unpredictable arrival of the mail boat, upon which most of them rely to ship their fruit, vegetables, and straw-work to market and to deliver basic necessities. The circus often begins even before the boat docks, as everyone gathers, carrying burlap sacks of potatoes or balancing their bundles and boxes.

Children Bahamian children are one of the joys of the islands. Raised with love and firm discipline, schoolchildren with cheery smiles and uniforms stream up and down the streets on the way to or from school. They are orderly and courteous; you'll rarely see bad behavior among children of school age. In groups, they are not wild or out of control.

Tittle-Tattle Isolation and the small scale of things have fostered another integral component of Bahamian culture: gossip, called 'sip-sip,' incorporating everything from political events to who's sleeping with whom. Everybody knows everyone else's business. And they're sure to share it. The more salacious, the better.

Patricia Glinton-Meicholas, author of The Island Life Series of books about The Bahamas, says that men tend to talk about 'women, sex, sports, politics, cars, and money,' and, more specifically, 'fast women, clandestine sex, fast sports, clandestine politics, fast cars, and fast and clandestine money.' Women like to talk about 'their weight, their clothing, their men, their marriage, their children, their hair, their religions, their careers, their education,' and, more specifically, 'other women's men, marriages, children, hair, religion, careers, and education.'

Names Black Bahamians hold great store by Christian names, and the biblical patriarchs and matriarchs offer steadfast favorites. A 'true-true' Bahamian may also be named for a celebrated personality or event or may have a purely homegrown name that combines established favored syllables.

For girls, favored prefixes are 'La,' 'De,' 'Sham,' or 'Sha,' followed by a favored suffix such as 'kera,' 'meka,' 'nika,' 'tika,' 'tishka,' 'neisha,' 'tisha,' or 'essa.' Thus you may meet Shanae, Latishka, Shameka, Denae, or Shakera. Any combination is permitted. The same prefixes are favored for boys, often with such suffixes as 'ario,' 'ardo,' 'ron,' and 'vaughn,' forming popular names like Danardo, Devon, Demark, and Shevaughn.

White children are usually given plain, old-fashioned English names (Andrew, Charles, William, Edward, Susan, Elizabeth), or other names drawn from the land of their cultural heritage.

You'll see the same surnames over and over again, regardless of color. Many Bahamian blacks inherited their last names from slaveowners. On Great Exuma, where Lord Rolle had his estates, half the population still bears his name.

Pastimes On weekends Bahamians follow social pursuits similar to those of Europeans or Floridians, taking to the basketball court, soccer field, or the beach, where they may gather the family, set up a barbecue grill, and turn up the goombay music. Bahamians tend to avoid touristed beaches in favor of more secluded spots. They spend a lot of time just hanging about in the water (the ocean shallows are also favored for making love). Bahamians, however, are *not* swimmers, although they are great sailors and fisherfolk. Every second household seems to have a boat or Jet Ski.

Bahamian kids play basketball with a passion. The islands' patron saint is Mychal Thompson, a Los Angeles Lakers player from Harbour Island and the first Bahamian to make it to the NBA. Most towns have a small court with makeshift stands. Bahamians follow the US basketball and baseball leagues with intensely loyal fervor.

Hardly a weekend goes by without a beauty pageant or 'sexiest swimsuit' (interpret that as 'sexiest body') contest. 'Sexiest male' competitions are equally popular, when otherwise discreet Bahamian women jostle for seats and whoop and scream at every flex of a muscle.

And no excuse is needed for a family cookout. Weddings, birthdays, christenings, and other family events bring in the most distant of blood relatives. Bahamians are also great joiners of choirs, youth groups, and above all, church groups and charity organizations. Fraternal lodges such as the Rotary Club are particularly popular among both males and females; you'll often see lodge members marching down the street in groups. Bahamians regularly perform acts of great kindness, and not only toward those they know – the calendar is filled with events in aid of charity.

Sex & Family Life Despite their Christian beliefs and demure exterior, Bahamians are relatively sexually promiscuous, beginning at an early age. (Couples may marry as young as 15 with parental consent, and as young as 13 by special permission of the courts.) The joy of sex seems to be acknowledged as one of God's blessings. Extramarital affairs are common, as are unwed mothers. About 57% of all births in The Bahamas are to single females, 24% of whom are teenagers.

Though Bahamian men tend to act publicly with due respect toward women, the women live unhappily with the knowledge that a large percentage of island males are philanderers. Many, it seems, hope for a better man to come their way; hence they, too, are prone to discreet trysts. It is part of the accepted way. Traditionally, 'outside children,' the offspring of an illicit union between a married man and a woman other than his wife, have been accepted into the man's home (his wife often ends up raising the child). A woman who becomes pregnant by another man, however, is usually cast out of the house. Thus the standard joke: 'You can ask who yo mama is, but don't ask who yo daddy is!'

Again, there are differences between blacks and whites and between the urbane of Nassau and the Family Islanders. Conchy Joes, it is claimed, retain more courtly habits between the sexes.

Women Bahamian women are strong and fiercely independent, again a legacy of surviving the hardships of a slave society. Although the first female member of Parliament, Janet Bostwick, was elected only in 1982, women have progressed markedly in recent years in politics and business.

Despite progress, The Bahamas remains a chauvinistic place. The menfolk, for example, expect their working spouses to cook their meals and clean house. Younger women in particular frequently complain

that local males treat them as chattel, talking down to them and ordering them about.

Female visitors to the islands, however, should have little problem. (See Women Travelers in the Facts for the Visitor chapter.)

Dos & Don'ts

Do relax. Time (and service) seems to move at a slower pace in the islands. 'Soon come,' a favorite expression, means 'it'll happen when it happens.' Don't expect that you can improve the situation by being rude or throwing tantrums. Most Bahamians will simply shrug their shoulders.

Don't call Bahamians 'natives.' Bahamians may be natives of the islands, but the term is laden with racial connotations that can be taken as slurs. 'Islanders' (or simply 'Bahamians') is more appropriate.

Do ask before snapping a photo. Most Bahamians enjoy being photographed, but occasionally you may find someone who prefers not to pose for tourists.

Don't teach children to beg. Begging is virtually unheard of in The Bahamas. However, in the Family Islands children often ask tourists for money. Giving it sets a bad precedent. If your conscience is tweaked, it is far better to give a useful item, preferably something educational.

Treatment of Animals

Bahamians are not particularly sentimental about animals, although many keep dogs as pets. Often, dogs are used solely to guard property. There are few wild dogs and most animals are respected, including the wild donkeys found on many islands.

RELIGION

The Bahamian people are almost pathological in their religious fervor. The overwhelming majority of islanders are devout believers who profess to live by the word of God. Every coincidence, good piece of luck, stroke of ill fortune, or other noteworthy occurrence is credited to His will or that of Satan.

Virtually every taxi driver has a Bible at hand, as do many office workers. State functions and the school day begin with prayers. Church affairs make headline news, while major international events are relegated to the inside pages. Every political speech is peppered with biblical quotations. And the nation claims the greatest number of churches per capita in the world.

The vast majority of Bahamians are mainstreamers – Baptists (32%), Anglican (20%), Catholic (19%), or Methodist (6%). The official state religion is the Anglican Church. Many Christian priests hedge their bets and mix a little good-willed obeah into their practice.

Every island is a veritable jumble of chapels and churches – usually Baptist revival centers, referred to as 'jumper churches' by locals – with every conceivable body in the world represented (one of my favorites is the Feed My Sheep Church of God). Often you'll see as many as a dozen churches in settlements with barely 200 people. Fundamentalists have made serious inroads in recent years. Some Family Islands have been won over by a single church (Seventh-Day Adventists, for example, predominate on Crooked Island).

The smallest congregations are often served by itinerant priests who make the rounds between islands. Sometimes you might come across a lay preacher giving a sermon beneath a shade tree, complete with amplifier and speakers, the better to attract the masses with his hip 'chattin' rap in praise of 'de Lord.'

On Sunday every church in the country seems to overflow with the righteous. The women arrive in high heels, glittering silk dresses, and fancy hats, accompanied by girls in white dresses trimmed with ruffled lace. The boys and men don their best suits and ties to attend church, holding their Bibles and braving the infernal heat.

The old fire-and-brimstone school of sermonizing is still the preferred mode. Crowded church pews rock with rapturous clapping and lusty hymn after hymn until it seems they'll raise the dead. Bible-waving congregations sway to and fro, roll their heads, and wail, 'Hallelujah!' and 'Amen, sweet Jesus!' while guitars, drums, and tambourines help work the crowds into a

frenzy. Often a church will have its own five-piece electric band.

The Bible is taken as divine instruction, not just a good-living guidebook written by the ancients, but some patterns of daily behavior don't square well with professed Christian tenets. Witness, for example, the astonishing degree to which God-fearing islanders are involved in the drug trade. A far more righteous attitude is displayed toward alcohol than toward narcotics. These hypocrisies are especially apparent on Saturday; many believers hold that though Sunday is dedicated to the soul and the Lord, the first day of the weekend may be given to the pursuit of pleasure.

Funerals

Some of the most important events on a Bahamian family calendar are funerals. The national newspapers dedicate a huge percentage of space to announcing deaths and funerals (weddings get little play). Radio programs are frequently interrupted by death and funeral announcements that mournfully recite tedious lists of all the bereaved family members and friends.

Bahamian funerals are grand social events. People buy new clothes to wear. Musicians are hired, politicians fly in to offer eulogies, and the affairs are often dragged out for a full day (that's why they're almost always held on weekends). Some funerals are straight out of a melodramatic Hollywood epic, with alternating frenzies of exaltation and fits of tribulation that seem designed to send weak-hearted members among the mourners into the grave, too. When things die down, someone may sing a traditional dirge, says Patricia Glinton-Meicholas, in 'a voyeuristic urge to see the floodgates open in a proper display of grief.' The mourners descend into a miasma of wailing so as not to be accused of lacking respect for the dead.

Bahamians keen like the Irish. Usually the wake has light-hearted moments, when tongues loosed by an excess of cheap rum tell tales of the deceased's past deeds and misdeeds. Six-handkerchief tributes – billed under the title 'As I Knew Him' in funeral programs – are offered, in which the deceased's good character is often embellished to such a degree that a spouse or close friend may be tempted to check the coffin to make sure it is occupied by the correct person. Tributes sound like idyllic nursery rhymes laced with lurid metaphor. The only thing missing is the gypsy violin. As soon as the funeral is over, the competing family groups begin gossiping about how such-and-such looked or behaved (see the Tittle-Tattle section earlier in this chapter).

LANGUAGE

English, the official language and that of business and daily life, is spoken by everyone but a handful of Haitian immigrants, who speak their own creole.

'True-true' Bahamians, mostly black, usually speak both Bahamian Standard English (BSE) and their own distinct island patois, a musical Caribbean dialect with its own rhythm and cadence. Though there are variances among the islands and between blacks and whites, all sectors of Bahamian society understand patois, the language of the street. Even polite, educated Bahamians, who tend to speak in a lilting Queen's or Oxford English, lapse into patois at unguarded moments.

See Books in the Facts for the Visitor chapter for titles on Bahamian English and patois.

Understanding Patois

When Bahamians speak patois, foreigners may find the discussion difficult to follow. However, rarely is it entirely incomprehensible, as it is, say, in Jamaica.

Bahamians have difficulty pronouncing 'th' and often drop the 'h,' as they may also do in words such as ''ouse' (for 'house'). Hence, 't'ree' for 'three,' 't'anks' for 'thanks,' and 'rat' for 'wrath.' 'The' is often pronounced as 'de' and 'them' as 'dem.' They also sometimes use 'v' in lieu of 'w' or drop the 'w,' as in ''ooman.' And the 's' sometimes disappears from the beginnings of words, as when cars ''mash up.' It also frequently disappears from the ends of plurals, which are thus pronounced as singulars.

Bahamians often use transliteration, such as 'flim' for 'film.' They rearrange syllables and give them their own inflection, such as 'fillymingo' for 'flamingo.' 'Only' becomes 'onliest.' And 'fishing' is 'fishenin'.' The 'ed' is often dropped from the end of verbs – thus a 'slipped disc' becomes a 'slippy dick.' And someone with an 'onion' is really suffering from a hernia.

A word is often repeated for emphasis, as in 'true-true.' Verbs are often deleted entirely: 'How de children?'

Patois is not gender specific. People and things are simply ''im' or 'dem;' possessive pronouns such as 'my' and 'mine' are often replaced by these words.

Hand-Me-Down Words

Many words in the Bahamian lexicon are carryovers from the early English colonial days – true Shakespearean English. The language is imbued with terms otherwise considered archaic. You may, for example, be served a drink in a 'goblet.'

Other words have been passed down from Africa, such as 'bo-bo' (fool) and 'nyam' (to eat).

A Manner of Speech

Female friends and acquaintances tend to address each other as 'chile' (for 'child'). Males prefer to use the term 'man.' Both words liberally spice general conversations. Both men and women commonly refer to members of the other gender (even strangers) as 'baby,' 'darling,' 'honey,' 'my love,' and similar endearing terms without any hint of sexist connotation or flirtation.

When Bahamians 'conversate,' they tend to inquire about the background of people they talk to, usually as a matter of establishing possible kinship. This is especially true of fellow Bahamians, who may be asked, 'Man, where you people from?' Likewise, 'Who yo daddy is?' and 'I bet you know my gran'daddy' are typical attempts to find some blood linkage.

Bahamians have a highly colloquial style of phrase. For example, typical greetings are: 'All is well?' (male) or 'Hey man, what happ'nin'?' and 'Chile, how you do? Me don't know de las' time I see you' (female). Expect to hear rejoinders such as: 'Tryin' to keep up wid' you rich people' or 'Right 'ere 'mong de strong.'

A woman with an ample posterior has a 'peas 'n' rice boungy.' A 'Gussy Mae' is a term of affection meaning a portly woman and reflecting the Bahamian male's penchant for flesh. And a Bahamian who intends to party is about to go 'spillygatin'.' No matter how wild they get, on Sunday Bahamians 'dress down to a fowl feather' for church service.

Bahamians have their own medical lexicon, too, such as 'cascating' for 'vomiting' and 'bound' for 'constipated.'

Another phrase you'll hear often is 'reach,' meaning 'arrive.' Thus 'de plane dun reach' means 'the airplane hasn't arrived.'

Talking Conchy Joe

Conchy Joes have evolved their own unique dialects that, in general, sound vaguely Australian and have been described by several writers as Elizabethan in form and cadence. Personally, I detect a Cornish or Somerset accent (the closest English dialect to Elizabethan English) on Harbour Island and in Spanish Wells. For example, listen for 'horbor' for 'harbor,' 'cor' for 'car,' and 'Cholly' for 'Charlie.' Typically the 'h' is dropped from words and added to others where it doesn't belong. Thus, ''am and heggs.'

Conchy Joes also have their own colloquialisms, such as 'A'am got to go.' They don't sound at all like black Bahamians.

Facts for the Visitor

THE BEST

Dolphin Encounters Nothing can prepare you for the thrill of an exalted encounter with dolphins on their own terms and on their own turf. Several operators offer swim-with-wild-dolphins trips (see the Outdoor Activities chapter).

Abaco National Park Few spots are as dramatic and serene as the lonesome headland at Hole-in-the-Wall, highlight of this forested park – a last refuge for the Bahama parrot. The hiking is splendid. It's a true escapists' dream for those who don't mind rustic accommodations.

Abacos' Loyalist Villages The fistful of bicentenary Loyalist villages on Elbow, Man O' War, and Green Turtle cays exude irresistible charm. Splendidly preserved, gaily decorated clapboard houses have been pickled in aspic, and the Loyalists' descendants add a living-museum quality.

Inagua National Park If the rewards of standing in the midst of the Western Hemisphere's largest flock of flamingos weren't enough for bird watchers, Great Inagua's saline ponds also attract countless other water birds.

Journeying by Mail Boat Far from cushy, this is down-to-earth travel guaranteed to show you a side of life far from the tourist mainstream, and it's sure to bond you to the Bahamian people.

Family Island Regatta Put yourself in a party mood and fly down to Great Exuma for the best time in the islands. This traditional sailing regatta pits local skippers against each other, while onshore the crowds whoop it up in a four-day party.

Harbour Island Besides the charming historic village of Dunmore Town, 'Briland' boasts a stunning pink-sand beach, great nightspots, and a choice range of accommodations, including Pink Sands, my favorite spot in the entire Bahamian chain to lay my head.

Sport Fishing Fisherfolk swear that wrestling a big one from the 'great blue river' is a tip-top thrill. If you can stomach it, your options are legion. Or for smaller yet no less challenging fry, try your hand at bonefishing; adherents swear that even great sex can't compare. You decide!

Swimming with Sharks Phewee! You can swim with sharks while they feed. At Stella Maris and Walker's Cay, you can witness a feeding frenzy just a few feet away. At Freeport and Nassau the sharks are hand-fed by a diver clad in chain mail. It's not for the timid!

Compass Point Pay one visit to this brazenly colorful, unpretentious gem west of Nassau – a sibling to Pink Sands (see Harbour Island, above) – and you'll understand why I try to end every Bahamas vacation here.

Cuba Excursions If you like The Bahamas, you'll *love* Cuba, a one-hour flight away and deservedly popular as a weekend excursion among Bahamians. Several tour companies offer single- to multiday excursions to this fascinating and friendly island of sensual charms. See the *¡Cuba Sí!* sidebar in the New Providence chapter.

THE WORST

This is where I lose friends and make enemies. Many hotels and attractions are dismal let-downs, despite being lauded. Here are a few of my least favorite things:

Bahamasair Sure, it's improved in recent years and continues to do so, but locals still call it 'banana air.' Bahamians don't ask if their flight is on time; they ask, 'How late is the flight today?' Often flights are canceled. Just when you figure you have it worked out and can afford to dally on the way to the airport, the plane will take off 20 minutes early! Guaranteed, the next flight is in two days' time. Do you laugh or cry?

Conch What *is* the big deal?

Downtown Freeport Some people love it, but I find it hard to say much that's encouraging about the town itself. 'Creeping, soulless, and dead as a doornail' about sums it up, though the golf courses are acclaimed and the duty-free shopping is passable. Overall it's a poor man's Las Vegas. Lucaya, with its spiffy new look and fine beaches, makes amends.

Island Transportation Getting around on most of the islands is a harpy. In general, there's no such thing as public transportation: The taxi drivers' union won't permit it. And name-brand car-rental companies give most of the islands a wide birth. Thus entrepreneurs have you by the short hairs and charge accordingly for beat-up vehicles that can't be guaranteed to last out the day.

SUGGESTED ITINERARIES

The following itineraries are for travelers *not* pursuing a particular interest (such as sailing, sport fishing, or scuba diving) and who are arriving and traveling by air. Scheduled air service between islands is limited (see the Getting Around chapter) and has not been factored into the itineraries below.

Weekend in Nassau

Assuming that you don't simply want to laze by the hotel pool sipping cocktails and getting a tan, I recommend the following plan:

Day One Take a walking tour of downtown Nassau, checking out Bay St for shopping, the Straw Market, and the Pompey Museum; the Pirates of Nassau museum; the Junkanoo Expo; and Rawson Square and Fort Fincastle for historical highlights. Climb the water tower for a bird's-eye view. Better yet, hire a surrey (horse-drawn cab) and get a guided tour.

Day Two Assuming you don't scuba dive, take a water taxi from Prince George Wharf and visit the marine park at Atlantis on Paradise Island. At night, visit the casino and/or take your pick of the King & Knights Club (for native dance show), The Zoo (for disco), or the 601 Club (for upscale disco).

Week in Nassau

Assume two or three days at the beach, and use the weekend itinerary above as a base:

Day Three Visit Ardastra Gardens and the nearby Botanical Garden to check out displays of The Bahamas' wildlife. Have a lunch of cracked conch at Arawak Cay, then visit Fort Charlotte.

Day Four Rent a car and drive around the island, with a stop for lunch and drinks at Compass Point. In the afternoon, take a boat ride from Paradise Island to Blue Lagoon Island, where you can swim with dolphins.

Day Five Play a round of golf or tennis, followed by a colorful, comfortable underwater adventure aboard the *Seaworld Explorer* submarine.

Day Six Enjoy a full-day powerboat ride to the Exumas, where you'll snorkel and meet the iguanas. Treat yourself to dinner at Graycliff, followed by a Cuban cigar.

Day Seven Regretfully, you're out of here!

Weekend in Freeport

This one is easy:

Day One Laze a little on the beach (preferably Taino); then maybe go shopping for duty-free goods at the International Bazaar or Port Lucaya Marketplace. Enjoy lunch at Kaptain Kenny's at Taino Beach. If gambling is your thing, take in The Lucayan Casino.

Day Two Perhaps a round of golf. Later, sign up with UNEXSO for a dolphin encounter.

Week in Freeport

Away from Freeport and Lucaya (two towns in one), Grand Bahama offers limited attractions but enough to fill a week if you're active. Building on the weekend itinerary, try the following plan:

Day Three Head to Rand Memorial Nature Centre, the Garden of the Groves, and Lucayan National Park to get close to nature. Pack a picnic and spend the afternoon at Gold Rock Beach, fronting the park.

Day Four Take a glass-bottomed boat ride from Port Lucaya Marina. Then, how about horseback riding at Pinetree Stables? Or sign up for a ride aboard the *Bahama Mama*.

Day Five Head to McLean's Town, and then take a water taxi to the Deep Water Cay Club for lunch. Spend the afternoon bonefishing or lazing in a hammock. Or sign up at Port Lucaya Marina to go sport fishing.

Day Six Go sea kayaking in the mangroves, picnic lunch included.

Would-be scuba divers should pencil in three full days for certification training. Make sure to head to Taino Beach on Wednesday night for the traditional fish fry.

Week in the Abacos

Two or three islands should do it. Here's my recommendation:

Day One Fly to Marsh Harbour and take a water taxi to Elbow Cay. Explore the Loyalist village of Hope Town. Eat dinner at Hope Town Harbour Lodge.

Day Two Laze on the beach. Explore the island by bicycle.

Day Three Return to Marsh Harbour. Take a guided snorkel or dive trip, or go fishing. Alternately, rent a boat and go to Man O' War Cay to visit Joe Albury's boatbuilding studio or to Great Guana Cay for lunch at Nipper's.

Day Four Rent a car and drive south to Little Harbour. Visit the studio and museum of Randolph Johnston, and enjoy a cocktail and lunch at funky Pete's Pub. Continue south to Different of Abaco (an alternate spot for lunch). Spend the afternoon bonefishing here or at Cherokee

Sound, or continue south and endure the bone-rattling drive through Abaco National Park to the lonesome lighthouse. Take a coastal hike.

Day Five Drive or take a taxi to north of Treasure Cay and a ferry ride to New Plymouth on Green Turtle Cay.

Day Six Explore the Loyalist village of New Plymouth. Tonight, have a Goombay Smash or two at Miss Emily's Blue Bee Bar and swing your hips at The Rooster's Restaurant.

Day Seven Return to Marsh Harbour and – *sigh!* – home.

12 Days in the Family Islands

Let's assume you want a rounded and diverse experience taking in three or four islands. I recommend the following plan:

Day One Fly to Marsh Harbour and take a water taxi to Elbow Cay. Explore the Loyalist village of Hope Town. Have dinner at Hope Town Harbour Lodge.

Day Two Laze on the beach. Explore the island by bicycle. Check out the local night scene.

Day Three Return to Marsh Harbour. Fly to Cat Island, using Fernandez Bay Village as your base.

Day Four Rent a car and explore the island, stopping to chat with locals. Don't fail to climb Mt Alvernia to marvel at the hermitage of Father Jerome.

Day Five Go snorkeling, diving, or fishing. Relax. Down a beer or two and play pool with locals.

Day Six Fly to Stella Maris (Long Island). Go snorkeling at Cape Santa Maria and eat a picnic lunch; if you're hearty and hearty, ride a bicycle to the Columbus Memorial.

Day Seven Go diving. If you're certified, pay a visit to Shark Reef.

Day Eight Rent a car and explore south to enjoy the seascapes, stopping at the Wild Tamarind Pottery & Gallery, the bat caves, Turtle Cove, and Clarence Town. Alternately, you may wish to overnight on Days Six through Eight at Lochabar Beach Lodge, spending your time relaxing, diving, snorkeling, and exploring.

Day Nine Take the high-speed ferry to Harbour Island, off North Eleuthera. If your budget allows, stay at Pink Sands. At the very least, dine here tonight.

Day 10 Laze on Pink Sands Beach and explore Dunmore Town. Tonight, check out the action at the Vic Hum Club.

Day 11 Take a day excursion to Spanish Wells.

Day 12 Time to head home.

For the Offbeat Traveler

To be a 'true-true' offbeat traveler, you'll move around by mail boat, and you'll need considerable time to do so (at least a day *each way* per island). Hence, here's a medley of recommended things to do:

Abacos Join Abaco Outback and go kayaking, snorkeling, bird watching, hiking, and even swimming with dolphins. At Walker's Cay, dive with the sharks at the famous Shark Rodeo, and then hitch a ride to Grand Cay and spend a few days fishing and hanging out with the locals.

Cat Island Go hiking at Turtle Cove and canoeing at Armbrister Creek. Have a local guide take you bonefishing. Take time to get scuba certified. Immerse yourself in obeah culture.

Eleuthera Hang with surfers at Surfer's Beach. Go sponging and lobstering with locals in Gregory Town.

Exumas Go blue-hole diving and visit the cays for birding and local wildlife. Deposit yourself for a few days at Bowe Cay, where you can live a simple lifestyle by your lonesome, like Robinson Crusoe.

Great Inagua Donate some time at the turtle reserve at Union Creek. Go bird watching in Inagua National Park, where a hike takes you into the heart of the flamingo preserve. Overnight at the rustic camp.

PLANNING
When to Go

The Bahamas is a year-round destination. Its trade breezes ensure cool temperatures, so weather isn't a strong factor in determining when to go unless you're visiting the southern islands, especially Turks and Caicos, which get infernally hot in summer. Winter months are preferable, with balmy weather and fewer mosquitoes.

The so-called rainy season extends from May to November. This time of year is more humid than winter and receives 80% of the total annual precipitation, though usually rain falls only for short stints in late afternoon. Occasionally prolonged rain may fall for several days. Hurricanes are a slim possibility, and when they strike the entire island chain can come to a virtual standstill. Flights and sea traffic cease operation. You may wish to ensure that you have a few days' leeway during these months. Also see Climate in the Facts about The Bahamas chapter.

The peak season typically runs from mid-December to mid-April, when hotel prices are highest. Some hotels are booked solid around Christmas and Easter. In the low or off season (the remainder of the year), many hotels reduce their rates by as much as 60%.

Some Family Island hotels close for the low season.

What Kind of Trip

Travelers have few options for bumming around on the cheap – the island group is too expensive to do so with ease. At the other extreme, it's easy to find trendy beach resorts where you might find yourself sunning alongside your favorite Hollywood star.

Above all, The Bahamas are about sun, sand, and sea, and most people visit simply to laze on a beach, sip rum cocktails, and get a tan. The experience can be a canned, idealized version of paradise: goombay bands, rum swizzles, and never a care in the world. Your contact with the *real* Bahamians may be limited unless you make a point to get out and explore.

A more enriching experience comes from immersing yourself in the islands. Playing dominoes at a local bar or satellite lounge, going fishing or crabbing with locals, or – whether religious or not – getting into the

spirit at a revivalist meeting. Your best choice for this is to escape to the Family Islands, where the pace slows and life still wears a traditional cast.

Many people come for the sailing, sportfishing, and diving. All are world-class. Scores of marinas and dive shops cater to watersports–seeking visitors. Otherwise the islands aren't particularly well set up for special-interest vacations, with the exception of golfing. Horseback riding is available on most islands. But birders and hikers aren't well catered to, and others with special interests will find relatively few tour companies to satisfy their needs.

Maps

The Bahamas Tourist Office (see Tourist Offices, later in this chapter) distributes a pocket-size map to the islands that is widely available at hotel tour desks and tourist-information booths. It is a handy general reference, though many roads are inaccurately drawn.

Several companies sell a series of Bahamas maps, including a 1:1,000,000 physical map, separate 1:500,000 road maps of the northern and southern Bahamas, a Nassau city atlas, and detailed 1:25,000 topographic maps.

You'll need a good road map for getting around New Providence. The most accurate and detailed map of New Providence is the 1:32,000 scale road map, with a 1:7000 scale inset of downtown Nassau, published by Island Maps, PO Box WK485, Warwick WKBX, Bermuda. It's available at a few stores in Nassau or from Holdfast Productions (☎ 242-323-7421), PO Box N-9562, Nassau. Dupuch Publications (☎ 242-323-5665, fax 242-323-5728) publishes *Bahamas Trailblazer Maps*, detailed street maps for Nassau and Freeport. These are readily available at tour desks in major hotels and resorts.

On the main islands, you'll find tourist newspapers with maps of varying accuracy (see the island chapters for information on tourist publications).

Few trustworthy maps of the Family Islands are available. The Bahamas Out Islands Promotion Board (see the Tourist

Offices section) can supply *The Bahama Out Islands Travel & Map Guide*, a handy newspaper-size foldout with maps and descriptions of hotels, airlines, and other services. You can order it from Star Publishers (☎ 242-322-3724, fax 242-322-4527, boipb@ix.netcom.com), PO Box N-4855, Nassau.

Detailed maps of individual islands (except for the cities of Nassau and Freeport) are mostly limited to navigation maps and charts for pilots and mariners. See the Private Yacht section in the Getting There & Away chapter for information about maritime maps and charts; see the Private Plane section in that chapter for information about aeronautical charts.

The islands are neither mountainous nor challenging enough to require detailed Ordnance Survey maps. Still, if you plan to explore the more remote wilds, there are no better maps to be had. You can order individual Ordnance Survey sheets from the following companies:

Australia
Travel Bookshop (☎ 02-241-3554) 20 Bridge St, Sydney, NSW 2000

Canada
ITMB Publishing (☎ 604-687-5925) 530 W Broadway, Vancouver, BC Canada V5Z 1E9; www.itmb.com

France
Espace IGN (☎ 01-43-98-85-00, fax 01-43-98-85-11) 107 rue la Boétie, 75008 Paris; www.ign.fr/fr/

New Zealand
Specialty Maps (☎ 9-307-2217) 58 Albert St, Auckland

UK
Ordnance Survey International (☎ 084-5605-0505, fax 023-8079-2615) Romsey Rd, Southampton, UK, SO16 4GU; www.ordsvy.gov.uk/
Sanfords (☎ 020-7836-1321, fax 020-7836-0189) 12-14 Long Acre, London WC2E 9LP

USA
Map Link (☎ 805-692-6777, fax 805-692-6787) 30 S La Patera Lane, Unit No 5, Santa Barbara, CA 93117; www.maplink.com
Omni Resources (in the US ☎ 800-742-2677, fax 910-227-3748) PO Box 2096, Burlington, NC 7216; www.omnimap.com
South Trek (☎ 512-440-7125, fax 512-443-0973) 1301 Oxford Ave, Austin, TX 78704

What to Bring

Travel light! The Bahamas generally basks in subtropical warmth, and you shouldn't need much clothing. If you can't take your main bag as a carry-on onto an aircraft, you've packed too much for a one-week visit. I manage to survive adequately with a single small piece of luggage for a month or longer. The fancier the resort, the more you will want to pack a selection of fancy clothes.

Clothing Loose-fitting, lightweight cotton clothing is best because it allows air to flow in the hot and sometimes humid climate. Tight clothing tends to make you sweat more and can get uncomfortable, as do synthetics like nylon. T-shirts, tank tops, and short-sleeved Hawaiian shirts are the perfect wear for outdoors and are best worn without being tucked in.

White is the best color for reflecting the sun's rays but has the disadvantage of getting dirty quickly. You're going to sweat a lot, so unless you plan on doing laundry, consider darker colors that hide the stains! A long-sleeved shirt and long pants are useful in case you get sunburned.

Don't forget one or two pairs of shorts, which can be your normal daywear, plus swimwear. Dress modestly in towns.

A light sweater might prove handy at night and in winter months, when it can get surprisingly cool.

Some hotels require casual eveningwear (including long pants) at dinner, as do more upscale dance clubs and nightclubs. Several of the posher hotel restaurants even require jackets (and ties in winter) for men and elegant dresses for women. Elsewhere fancy togs may be taken as a statement of the wearer's insecurities or snootiness. The casinos permit casualwear, but tank tops and skimpy clothes are frowned upon. You should also pack several fancy items if you're traveling on a cruise ship. Each company will provide specific information on dress formalities, and I've tried to note which clubs and restaurants require more dressy attire.

You'll get by with a pair of sneakers, and sandals or flip-flops (thongs), plus lightweight casual shoes for eveningwear.

Friendly fruit seller in Potter's Cay market

The cutest girls anywhere!

Gone fishin'

Cat Island junkanoo practice

Barbie of the Bahamas: resplendent in straw

Albert Lowe Museum, Green Turtle Cay

If you plan on hiking, bear in mind variable weather conditions. Rain can fall at any time of year. Check the forecast and dress accordingly. Usually lightweight cotton clothing will suffice. Trousers rather than shorts are best for hiking through bush, as they protect against thorns. Often sneakers or tennis shoes are fine for hiking, but lightweight canvas hiking boots are better: you'll want something sturdier than sneakers to handle the sharp limestone found on many islands. And sturdy sandals are perfect for walks around the mud flats and coral shorelines.

Toiletries Toiletries are widely available in Nassau and Freeport; however, bring them along if you plan on spending most of your time in the Family Islands.

Generally only the top hotels in The Bahamas provide complimentary toiletries. Don't forget a washcloth: Many hotels don't have them. Unless you're staying at an upscale hotel, bring a beach towel or buy one in The Bahamas.

Supplies Bring a flashlight to use in the event of a blackout and to find your way along lightless streets or paths at night. I also consider a Swiss Army knife essential. Other essentials include zip-lock bags (for toiletries), a small laundry bag (for dirty and/or wet clothes), a small fold-up umbrella (which will also prove a handy parasol), plus a wide-brimmed sun hat or baseball cap for shade (alternately, you can buy a straw hat in The Bahamas). Make sure your hat fits snugly; it's often breezy.

Camping & Sports Gear The Bahamas actively discourages campers. See the Accommodations section later in this chapter for information.

Some resorts with golf or tennis facilities rent equipment, as do scuba diving and snorkeling outlets. However, you may wish to bring your own.

RESPONSIBLE TOURISM

While tourism brings desperately needed foreign income, it has many potentially negative side-effects. How you behave abroad is critical. For example, visitors are often tempted to buy souvenirs made from black coral and other endangered oceanic wildlife without realizing the devastating impact this has on local ecology. See the Ecology & Environment section and the related boxed text in the Facts about The Bahamas chapter.

Drug use also raises certain moral dilemmas. Buying ganja or cocaine is not only illegal but also helps foster drug-trafficking and its concomitant hand-maiden...crime. Prostitution is not tolerated, although it exists around the casinos in tourist resorts. Sexual activity with a minor carries heavy penalties, as well as being morally reprehensible.

The Center for Responsible Tourism (1765-D LeRoy Ave, Berkeley, CA 94709, CRTourism@aol.com) publishes guidelines for tourists and works to mitigate the negative impacts of tourism. Its equivalent in the UK is the Centre for the Advancement of Responsive Travel (☎ 01732-352757).

The following guidelines will help ensure that your visit has a minimal impact:

• Travel with a spirit of humility and a genuine desire to meet and talk with local people.
• Be aware of the feelings of others. Act respectfully and avoid offensive behavior, particularly when taking photographs and with regard to dress codes.
• Cultivate the habit of actively listening and observing rather than merely hearing and seeing. Avoid the temptation to 'know all the answers.'
• Realize that others may have attitudes and concepts of time that are different – not inferior – to those you inherited from your own culture.
• Instead of looking only for the exotic, discover the richness of another culture and way of life.
• Learn local customs and respect them.
• Remember that you are only one of many visitors. Do not expect special privileges.
• When bargaining with merchants, remember that the poorest one may give up a profit rather than his or her personal dignity. Don't take advantage of the desperately poor. Pay a fair price.
• Keep your promises to people you meet. If you cannot, do not make the promise.
• Spend time each day reflecting on your experiences in order to deepen your understanding. Question whether your enrichment is beneficial for all involved.

• If you truly want a 'home away from home,' why travel? Be aware of why you are traveling in the first place.

TOURIST OFFICES

The Bahamas Tourist Office (BTO; ☎ 242-322-7501, fax 242-328-0945; in the US ☎ 800-422-4262; in Canada ☎ 800-667-3777), PO Box N-3701, Nassau, publishes maps, directories, guides, and brochures on the islands. It has offices in most major tourist destinations, and its staff is usually very helpful. The office itself does *not* act as a reservation service, but it has a reservation service, Bahamas Reservations (in North America ☎ 800-700-4752). For general tourist information, you can visit the official Bahamas Web page at www.bahamas.com; it has an overview of the islands, tourist and business information, and hotel listings, among other things.

The Nassau/Paradise Island Promotion Board (in the US ☎ 305-931-1555, fax 305-931-3005), 19495 Biscayne Blvd, suite 809, Aventura, FL 33180, USA, serves a function similar to the BTO.

In addition, the Family Islands are represented by the Bahamas Out Islands Promotion Board (in the US ☎ 305-931-6612, 800-688-4752, fax 305-931-6867, info@bahama-out-islands.com; in Germany ☎ 06131-99330, fax 06131-99331), at 19495 Biscayne Blvd, No 809, Aventura, FL 33180, USA. It represents the interests of member hotels and other tourism suppliers. It also serves as a one-stop reservation center and should be the first place to call when planning a vacation to the Family Islands. The staff are incredibly helpful and will send you hotel brochures, lists of marinas and other special-interest facilities, the *Bahama Out Islands Travel & Map Guide*, and the Family Islands *Getaway* magazine.

See also Information & Reservations under Accommodations, later in this chapter.

Local Tourist Offices

BTO
(☎ 242-377-6806) Airport Arrivals Terminal, Nassau

(☎ 242-326-9781) Rawson Square, Bay St, Nassau
(☎ 242-352-8044) International Bazaar, Freeport
(☎ 242-367-3067) Queen Elizabeth Drive, Marsh Harbour, Abacos
(☎ 242-332-2142) Queen's Hwy, Governor's Harbour, Eleuthera
(☎ 242-333-2621) Bay St, Harbour Island, Eleuthera
(☎ 242-336-2430) Queen's Hwy, George Town, Exumas

Grand Bahama Island Tourism Board
(☎ 242-352-8044, fax 242-352-2714) International Bazaar, PO Box F-40252, Freeport, Grand Bahama

Nassau/Paradise Island Promotion Board
(☎ 242-322-8383/8381, fax 242-326-5346) Hotel's House, Dean's Lane, Nassau

Tourist Offices Abroad

The BTO has a central information office in the US that sends out literature (☎ 800-422-4262). There are regional offices in the US and offices in other countries as well:

Canada
(☎ 416-968-2999, fax 416-968-6711) 121 Bloor St E, No 1101, Toronto, ON M4W 3M5

France
(☎ 01.45.26.62.62, fax 01.48.74.06.05) 60 rue Saint Lazare, 75009 Paris

Germany
(☎ 69-970-8340, fax 69-970-8343) Leipzigerstrasse 67D, 60487 Frankfurt Main

Italy
(☎ 2-72-02-30-03, fax 2-72-02-31-23) via Cusani N7, 20121 Milano

UK
(☎ 01483-448900, fax 01483-448990) 3 The Billings, Walnut Tree Close, Guildford, Surrey GU1 4UL

USA
California: (☎ 213-385-0033, fax 213-383-3966) 3450 Wilshire Blvd, suite 1204, Los Angeles, CA 90010
Florida: (☎ 305-932-0051, fax 305-682-8758) 1 Turnberry Place, 19495 Biscayne Blvd, Aventura, FL 33180
Illinois: (☎ 773-693-1500, fax 773-693-1114) 8600 W Bryn Mawr Ave, No 820, Chicago, IL 60631
New York: (☎ 212-758-2777, fax 212-753-6531) 150 E 52nd St, 28th floor, New York, NY 10022

Other tourist information bureaus in the US include the Grand Bahama Island Tourism Board (☎ 800-448-3386) and the Nassau/Paradise Island Promotion Board (☎ 305-931-1555, fax 305-931-3005), sharing the BTO's regional office in Aventura, FL (see above).

VISAS & DOCUMENTS
Passports & Visas
Canadians and citizens of the UK and Commonwealth countries may enter The Bahamas without a passport or visa for up to three weeks. For longer stays, a passport is required. However, UK citizens need to show a passport to re-enter their home country. US citizens do not need a passport for stays of less than eight months but must show proof of citizenship (a passport, voter registration card, etc). Regardless, it is wise to travel with your passport.

Visitors from most European countries, Turkey, and Israel require passports but no visas for stays up to three months. Citizens of most Central and South American countries, including Mexico, require passports but no visas for stays up to 14 days. Visas are required for longer stays.

Citizens of the following countries require passports and visas for stays of any duration: Dominican Republic, Haiti, South Africa, and all communist countries. Citizens of all other countries should check current entry requirements with the nearest Bahamian embassy or with the Immigration Dept (☎ 242-322-7530, fax 242-326-0977), PO Box N-831, Hawkins Hill, Nassau.

If you lose your passport while in The Bahamas, you'll need to visit your embassy, consulate, or high commission. There's a list of them later in this chapter; if your country has no such facility in The Bahamas, contact the Ministry of Foreign Affairs (☎ 242-322-7624/7590) on E Hill St in Nassau. Its postal address is PO Box N-3746, Nassau.

Travel Permits
No travel permits are required for standard visitors. However, you'll need to fill out an immigration card upon arrival (usually this is handed out onboard the aircraft, but if not, you'll find it in the arrivals lounge). You must show it when you depart. Cruise-ship passengers are cleared en masse by the cruise company.

Private skippers need a cruising permit, issued upon arrival (see the Getting There & Away chapter).

Onward Tickets
Immigration formalities require that air passengers have in their possession a return or onward airline ticket when arriving in The Bahamas. You will also be asked to declare where you'll be staying.

Travel Insurance
However you're traveling, it's worth taking out travel insurance. You may not want to insure that grotty old army surplus backpack, but everyone should be covered for the worst possible event: an accident, for example, that requires hospital treatment and a flight home. If you are planning to travel for a long time, travel insurance may seem rather expensive, but think of it this way: If you can't afford insurance, you certainly won't be able to afford a medical emergency overseas.

A travel insurance policy that covers theft, loss of luggage, and medical treatment is a good idea. You might also consider trip-cancellation insurance if you have booked a prepaid package with cancellation penalty clauses. Any travel agent can recommend an appropriate package. The international student travel policies handled by STA Travel and other student travel organizations are usually a good value.

Check the fine print to see if there are exclusions for any 'hazardous activities' you may be contemplating, such as riding motorcycles, scuba diving, or hiking.

In the US, the following companies are leading travel insurance suppliers:

American Express
  (☎ 800-234-0375) PO Box 919010, San Diego, CA 92190
Travelers
  (☎ 203-277-0111, 800-243-3174) 1 Tower Square, Hartford, CT 06183

TravelGuard International
   (☎ 715-345-0505) 1145 Clark St, Stevens Point,
   WI 54481

In the UK, contact Campus Travel (☎ 020-7730-8111), Endsleigh Insurance (☎ 020-7436-4451), or STA Travel (☎ 020-7361-6262). The Association of British Insurers (☎ 020-7600-3333), 51 Gresham St, London EC2V 7HQ, can recommend other travel insurance brokers.

   In Australia call AFTA (☎ 02-9956-4800), Cover More (☎ 02-9968-1333, 800-251881), or UTAG (☎ 02-9819-6855).

Driver's License & Permits

To drive in The Bahamas, you must have a current license for your home country or state. A visitor can drive on his or her home license for three months. An International Driver's License, required for longer stays, can be obtained in The Bahamas for US$50 from the Road Traffic Dept, Clarence A Bain Bldg, Thompson Blvd and Moss Rd, Nassau (see the Central Nassau map). You can also obtain an International Driver's License by applying with your current license at any American Automobile Association (AAA) office or an Automobile Association office in the UK. In the US it costs US$10 and can be issued on the spot at AAA offices (two passport photographs are required).

Other Documents

The Bahamas has no youth hostel system, though there *is* a hostel in Nassau – International Traveller's Lodge – that at press time was planning to become a member of the International Youth Hostel Association (IYHA).

   The same is true for student, youth, and seniors' cards. Virtually nobody in The Bahamas honors them.

Copies

You should make two photocopies of your most valuable documents before leaving home. Make sure you include your passport data page and visa page, credit cards, travel insurance policy, air/bus/train tickets, hotel vouchers, health insurance, etc. Keep one copy at home. Carry the second copy

with you, but keep it separate from the originals.

   It's also a good idea to store details of your vital travel documents in Lonely Planet's free online Travel Vault in case you lose the photocopies or can't be bothered with them. Your password-protected Travel Vault is accessible online anywhere in the world – create it at www.ekno.lonelyplanet.com.

EMBASSIES & CONSULATES
Bahamian Embassies & Consulates

Canada
   Bahamas High Commission: (☎ 613-232-1724, fax 613-232-0097) 50 O'Connor St, suite 1313, Ottawa, ON K1P 6L2, Canada

UK
   Bahamas High Commission: (☎ 020-7408-4488, fax 020-7499-9937) 10 Chesterfield St, London W1X 8AH, England

USA
   Washington, DC: (☎ 202-319-2660, fax 202-319-2668) Embassy of The Commonwealth of The Bahamas, 2220 Massachusetts Ave NW, Washington, DC 20008, USA
   Florida: (☎ 305-373-6295, fax 305-373-6312) Bahamas Consulate General, 25 SE 2nd Ave, suite 818, Miami, FL 33131, USA
   New York: (☎ 212-421-6925, fax 212-759-2135) Bahamas Consulate General, 231 E 46th St, New York, NY 10017, USA

Embassies & Consulates in The Bahamas

Most countries are represented by honorary consuls, individuals appointed to represent the respective country. They change frequently. Check the New Providence section of the phone book under Diplomatic & Consular Representation. Exceptions are the following:

British High Commission (☎ 242-325-7471) Bitco Bldg, East St, Nassau

Canadian Consulate (☎ 242-393-2123/4, fax 252-393-1305) Shirley St Plaza, Nassau

US Embassy & Consulate (☎ 242-322-1181/2/3, fax 242-328-7838) Mosmar Bldg, Queen St, Nassau

The US Embassy & Consulate in Nassau is also responsible for consular services in the Turks and Caicos.

Your Own Embassy

It's important to realize what your own embassy – the embassy of the country of which you are a citizen – can and can't do to help you if you get into trouble. Generally speaking, it won't be much help in emergencies if the trouble you're in is remotely your own fault. Remember that you are bound by the laws of the country you are in. Your embassy will not be sympathetic if you end up in jail after committing a crime locally, even if such actions are legal in your own country.

In genuine emergencies, you might get some assistance, but only if other channels have been exhausted. If you need to get home urgently, a free ticket home is exceedingly unlikely – the embassy would expect you to have insurance. If all your money and documents are stolen, it might assist you with getting a new passport, but a loan for onward travel is out of the question.

Some embassies used to keep letters for travelers or have a small reading room with home newspapers, but these days most of the mail-holding services have been stopped and even newspapers tend to be out of date.

CUSTOMS
Entering The Bahamas

All baggage is subject to customs inspection, and Bahamian Customs officials are serious about their business. Although foreign visitors are usually waved through after a cursory inspection, you should not be surprised if your luggage is searched. All visitors are required to complete a Baggage Declaration Form.

Individuals are allowed to import US$10,000 cash, plus 50 cigars, 200 cigarettes, or 1 lb of tobacco, plus 1 quart of spirits free of charge. Purchases of US$100 are also allowed for all arriving passengers. You are allowed to bring in a reasonable amount of personal belongings free of charge. However, you may need to show proof that laptop computers and other expensive items are for personal use. You should declare these upon arrival.

Excess items deemed to be imported goods are subject to 35% duty (25% for clothing). The tariff varies up to 300% for certain items.

The following items are restricted: firearms, drugs (except prescription medicines), flowers and plants, honey, fruits, coffee, and meats and vegetables (unless canned).

Also see the Getting There & Away chapter for information for private skippers and pilots.

Bahamian citizens are limited to importing US$300 worth of items duty free. All excess items are subject to duty, beginning at 35%. Since most Bahamians do their big-ticket shopping in Florida, their luggage is usually searched upon returning to The Bahamas. You may be approached by a Bahamian asking you to carry his or her possessions through customs as your own. Consider the risks!

Leaving The Bahamas

US citizens can return with up to US$600 of goods duty free per person, provided they have not used the allowance within the last 30 days. In addition, they may each import 200 cigarettes, 100 (non-Cuban) cigars, plus 1 liter of liquor or wine. Artworks, handicrafts, antiques, and certain other items are exempt from duties under the Generalized System of Preferences. For more specific information, contact the US Customs Service (☎ 202-566-5268), 1301 Constitution Ave NW, Washington, DC 20229, or see its Web site at www.customs.ustreas.gov/travel/travel.htm for further regulations.

Canadian citizens are once a year allowed a C$300 allowance, plus 200 cigarettes, 50 cigars, 2 lbs of loose tobacco, and 40 ounces of liquor. In addition, they can mail unsolicited gifts valued up to C$40 per day. The booklet *I Declare* provides more information; contact the Revenue Canada Customs Dept (☎ 613-993-0534), Communications Branch, Mackenzie Ave, Ottawa, ON K1A 0L5.

British citizens may import goods worth up to £200 in addition to 100 cigarettes, 50 cigars or 250 grams of loose tobacco, and 2 liters of wine plus 1 liter of spirits (depending on alcohol proof). For further information, contact Her Majesty's Customs & Excise

Office (☎ 020-7202-4227), New King's Reach House, 22 Upper Ground, London SE1 9PJ.

Australian citizens are permitted to bring back A$400 of gifts and souvenirs, plus 250 cigarettes or 250 grams of tobacco, and 1125 ml of alcohol. For specifics, contact the Australian Customs Service, Box 8, Sydney, NSW 2001 (☎ 02-9213-2000, fax 02-9213-4000).

New Zealand citizens may bring back NZ$700 worth of souvenirs, plus 200 cigarettes or 50 cigars, and 4.5 liters of beer or wine and 1125 ml of spirits. For specifics, contact the New Zealand Customs, Custom House, 50 Anzac Ave, Box 29, Auckland (☎ 09-359-6655).

Visitors departing Nassau and Freeport International Airports for most US destinations clear US Customs and Immigration prior to departure. No further customs formalities are required upon arrival in the US. All other passengers clear customs and immigration upon arrival at their destinations.

MONEY
Currency & Exchanging Money

The legal currency of The Bahamas is the Bahamian dollar. Bahamian coins are issued in denominations of 1¢, 5¢, 10¢, 15¢, 25¢, and 50¢. Notes are issues in denominations of 50¢, $1, $3, $5, $10, $20, $50, $100, and $500.

The currency is linked one-to-one with US dollars, so you can operate with US currency everywhere and will need only to change other foreign currencies into either Bahamian or US dollars. You can do this at any bank. Note that you may exchange only up to $70 in Bahamian currency for US dollars or foreign currency equivalent. The only bank permitted to exchange greater amounts is the Central Bank of The Bahamas on Market St in Nassau. Hence it's a good idea to spend all your Bahamian dollars prior to departure. Also, you might have difficulty getting locals to accept US$50 and US$100 bills. There are too many counterfeits in circulation.

Major commercial banks maintain branches throughout the islands, although in the Family Islands they are thin on the ground. Those in major towns maintain a foreign exchange booth, and foreign currency may be exchanged for US or Bahamian dollars during regular business hours. See Business Hours, this chapter, for bank hours.

You'll usually get the best exchange rate at banks. You also can change money at most hotels or at licensed exchange bureaus in the airports. Many hotels offer the same rates as banks. Others offer rates 2% to 5% lower.

Traveler's Checks Traveler's checks are widely accepted throughout The Bahamas except on more remote Family Islands, although some hotels, restaurants, and exchange bureaus charge a hefty fee for cashing traveler's checks. Banks do not generally charge commission but levy a tax (usually no more than US$1 for each check). You will need to show your passport.

You can purchase checks at virtually any bank, lending institution, or currency-exchange service worldwide prior to departing for The Bahamas, as well as at banks in the islands.

To report lost American Express traveler's checks in The Bahamas, contact Playtours (☎ 242-322-2931) at 303 Shirley St in Nassau; in the US call ☎ 800-221-7282. For lost Thomas Cook checks, call ☎ 800-223-7373.

ATMs Automated teller machine (ATM) cards are a good way to obtain incidental cash. There are ATMs in the leading tourist centers. Most accept Visa, MasterCard, and American Express via international networks such as Cirrus and Visa/PLUS. Check with your local bank before departing for The Bahamas to find out how you can use your ATM card.

Credit & Debit Cards Major credit cards are widely accepted throughout the islands. Visa and MasterCard are the mostly commonly accepted, followed by American Express, Diners Club, and Discover. Credit cards are *not* widely accepted for general transactions in the more remote Family Islands. You can use your credit card to get cash advances at most commercial banks. You'll usually be charged a small transaction fee.

Companies that accept credit cards may add an additional charge of up to 5%. You can challenge these charges, which the credit-card companies generally do not permit. If this doesn't work, you can challenge the charge with the credit-card company, but you will need to show original documentation of all relevant transactions.

To report lost or stolen credit cards, call the following numbers:

American Express	☎ 800-528-4800
American Express Gold	☎ 800-528-2121
MasterCard	☎ 800-826-2181
Visa	☎ 800-336-8472
Visa Gold	☎ 800-847-2911

International Transfers If you need an emergency injection of cash, you can arrange a telegraphic or mail transfer from your account in your home country or from a friend or family member. You can also arrange a transfer in advance through your local bank. A fee of 5% to 12% applies.

Western Union has offices on Frederick St in Nassau (☎ 242-325-3273) and on E Mall Drive in Freeport (☎ 242-352-6676). It also has agents throughout the Family Islands. In North America call Western Union Financial Services (☎ 800-325-6000/4176).

Security

Carry as little cash as needed when away from your hotel. Keep the rest in a hotel safe. You can rely on credit cards and traveler's checks for most of your purchases. However, you'll need cash for most transactions in rural areas and at gas stations.

Don't carry your cash where it can be seen. Avoid carrying wallets in your back pockets. Put them in your *front* pocket. Even better, you should carry cash in a money belt or pouch, worn *inside* your clothing. Set a small sum (say US$100 or so) aside for emergencies in case you get ripped off.

Costs

The Bahamas and Turks and Caicos are not for the budget-conscious! The islands are very expensive. How much you spend, however, depends on your sense of style.

Even hardcore budget travelers will need at least US$70 a day. Most foodstuffs and other items are imported from the US (other than seafood, virtually all foods are imported), with shipping costs and a whopping 35% import duty added. You can expect to pay at least 50% more for any item than you would in the US.

Roadside stalls and budget restaurants sell conch and other local meals for as little as US$3. More restaurants, even those serving a mostly local clientele, are expensive: Expect to pay at least US$8, for example, for lunch or dinner in modest restaurants and at least twice that in more upscale joints. You should budget US$15 to US$30 for the average meal.

Transportation costs vary. A mail-boat journey (for hardy travelers only) will cost at least US$25 one-way, per island. Air service between islands costs between US$25 and US$150 one-way, according to distance. However, if you plan on island-hopping, you're usually at the mercy of the hub-and-spoke system: you'll have to keep returning to Nassau for your next leg, adding to the expense (see the Getting Around chapter). Likewise, except for Nassau and Freeport, there is no public bus system; you're reliant on taxis (which are super-expensive) or rental cars, which cost upwards of US$60 per day, plus gas.

Accommodations will be your biggest expense (the *average* room rate is considerably more than US$100). A few budget accommodations go for as little as US$30 a night, though standards are dour. Most budget properties charge US$50 or more, even for mediocre conditions. Medium-range hotels cost US$60 to US$85, though even here, standards are often motley. Deluxe properties begin at about US$150 nightly. Ultradeluxe accommodations can run as high as US$500 nightly, but some are worth every penny! (Also see the Accommodations section later in this chapter.)

Discounts Consider visiting in 'summer,' or low season (mid-April to mid-December), when hotel prices drop significantly and airfares are often reduced. Then, the Bahamas

Ministry of Tourism issues a 'Bahamas Getaway' booklet with coupons offering discounts at up to 30 participating hotels, retailers, dive shops, etc, in cooperation with American Express. They're available at Ministry of Tourism information booths.

Another good way to spread your dollars is to rent a villa or cottage with several other people. Happy hours and free Ladies' Nights in bars offer further savings for the impecunious. Most of the hip nightspots offer nightly specials and you'll find discount coupons being handed out in Nassau and Freeport, tempting you to eat or shop at specific places. Similarly, tourist publications offer discounts.

Many larger resorts offer 'Dine-Around' packages for guests to sample local restaurants. These are usually good bargains.

Tipping & Bargaining

Tipping is expected, and certain US standards are followed. However, tipping hasn't reached the crazed levels of the US.

The generally accepted rule in restaurants is a 10% to 15% tip. However, many hotels and restaurants automatically add a service charge (usually 15%) to cover gratuities. This will be displayed on your bill. There is no need to offer additional tips unless you believe you have received exceptional service. But it is questionable whether a tip charged to your credit card will ever reach the service staff. Pay restaurant and hotel tips directly to the staff, and ask to have the service charge removed from your bill.

Most prices are fixed, and bargaining is less of a common practice than it is on Caribbean islands. Feel free to bargain, however, at straw markets and crafts stalls.

Taxes & Refunds

A hotel and room tax of at least 8% applies (the tax is only 4% for hotels that are not members of a major hotel association or promotion board). An additional 2% to 5% charge for housekeeping service is often added. This may be in the form of a daily flat rate of US$4 to US$12 per person, per day.

As there is no sales tax, no tax refunds are offered to visitors. However, if you were charged a customs fee for bringing an expensive item such as a cell phone into The Bahamas, this will be refunded when you leave the country with it.

POST & COMMUNICATIONS

Every settlement has a post office. The smaller ones issue stamps and receive and send letters but otherwise have few facilities. Larger post offices, found only in major settlements, are full service, with telegram facilities and often fax facilities.

Most post offices are open 8:30 am to 5:30 pm Monday to Friday and until 12:30 pm Saturday. Some have restricted hours.

Postal Rates

US stamps are *not* accepted by Bahamian post offices. Postcards to the UK, US, or Canada cost 40¢. Airmail letters cost 55¢ per half-ounce to the US and Canada; 60¢ to the UK and Europe; and 70¢ to Africa, Asia, or Australasia. Domestic mail costs 25¢ per ounce.

High-speed delivery costs $1.20 more than ordinary delivery. A 'Speed Mail' service is offered ($5 plus regular postage).

Airmail parcels below 1 lb in weight cost $4.15 to Canada, $5.25 to the US, and $9.25 to the UK. Each extra pound costs $2.45 to Canada and US, and $4.15 to the UK.

Sending Mail

You will need to go to a post office to mail your postcards and letters. Alternately, you can leave them with the front desk clerk at most hotels.

Alas, the Bahamian postal service is not noted for efficiency. Always use airmail unless you have a valid reason not to, and be sure to mark your mail 'Airmail.' Airmail to North America usually takes about 10 days to six weeks, despite the proximity. Allow longer to Europe. Surface mail can take forever (at least two months). Even a letter sent from one Bahamian island to another can take a week or longer.

Ensure that parcels are adequately secured. Postal theft is rare, but don't tempt fate by mailing loosely taped packages. *Never* enclose cash or valuables. If you want to mail valuable documents, use an express-mail service such as DHL, UPS, or Federal Express.

The weight limit is 22 lbs. Parcels cannot exceed a combined dimension of 6 feet 7 inches.

When sending mail to The Bahamas, always include the addressee's name, address or post office box, town, and island, plus 'The Bahamas.'

Express-Mail Services These are listed in the yellow pages. DHL, Federal Express, and UPS have headquarters in Nassau, plus agents on many Family Islands. UPS offers a money-back guarantee of 24-hour delivery to North America and parts of Europe, plus free customs clearance, for packages sent from Nassau.

Note that 24-hour service is not usually guaranteed from the Family Islands, as the express-mail services tend to rely on Bahamasair or an air-charter service.

Receiving Mail

You can have mail addressed to you 'Poste Restante' care of 'The General Post Office,' E Hill St, Nassau, The Bahamas. Mail should be marked 'To be collected from the General Delivery desk.' All correspondence is retained for three weeks.

Receiving parcels is a pain in the arse. You'll have to go down to customs to clear your package. Incoming packages are charged US80¢, plus any customs assessment. Packages are delivered at Parcel Post after customs is cleared and payment is made.

Postal codes refer to the post office boxes. Thus on New Providence 'N' refers to downtown Nassau, 'SS' to Shirley St, 'CB' to Cable Beach, 'FH' to Fox Hill, and 'GT' to Grant's Town.

You can also receive mail and telegrams via American Express Travel Services in Nassau and Freeport by prior arrangement with AmEx (☎ 800-221-7282) in North America. There's no charge for holders of American Express cards or traveler's checks.

Telephone

Telephone service throughout The Bahamas is controlled by the government-owned Bahamas Telecommunications Corporation (BaTelCo; ☎ 242-302-7000), which has its headquarters on John F Kennedy Drive on New Providence. BaTelCo has a local office on most islands.

Telecommunications services are up to date, with instantaneous international links provided via a 100% digitized switching system. However, in the Family Islands many communities still lack telephone hookups. Several remote settlements have only radio links, so be prepared for delays in getting your call through. Some hotels have a single phone, often antiquated.

Phone booths are ubiquitous throughout the islands, and even the smallest settlement usually has at least one roadside phone. Most accept only prepaid phonecards (see below). Some booths still accept US25¢ coins but often don't permit long-distance calls except through an operator or calling-card company.

The Bahamas country code is 242.

The following are handy numbers:

Current Time & Temperature	☎ 917
Directory Assistance	☎ 916
Emergency Assistance	☎ 911
in the Family Islands	☎ 919
International Operator Assistance	☎ 0
Weather by Phone	☎ 915

Calling Cards The majority of public telephones accept only prepaid phonecards issued by BaTelCo (☎ 242-302-7827), available at stores and other accredited outlets near phonecard booths. You simply insert the card into a slot in the phone and the cost of your call is automatically deducted from the value of the card until its value is used up. Some cards can be recharged. Others are nonrechargeable debit cards. The cards are sold in denominations of US$5, US$10, and US$20.

Domestic Calls Local calls are free of charge. Direct-dialed long-distance calls cost

US40¢ per minute. Operator-assisted calls cost US$1.80 per three-minute minimum, then US60¢ per minute.

You will need to dial ☎ 1-242, then the seven-digit local number for all interisland calls. Local calls to another number on the same island do not require you to dial the 1-242 prefix.

International Calls Many phone booths and all BaTelCo offices permit direct dial to overseas numbers. It is far cheaper to call direct from a phone booth than to call from your hotel. Typical costs from The Bahamas to the US (the cost is the same whether to California or Florida) are US99¢ for the first minute and US80¢ per minute thereafter. Rates to Canada are US$1.25 and US$1.15 respectively, and to Europe, US$2.75 and US$2 to US$2.75 respectively. Lower rates are charged after 11 pm on weekdays. Operator-assisted calls to the US cost US$4.50 to US$8.25 for three minutes, depending on zone. A similar call to Europe or Australia will cost you a whopping US$15.

Almost all the larger or more upscale hotels have direct-dial calling; elsewhere you may need to go through the hotel operator or even call from the front desk. Hotels generally add a government tax for overseas calls. They also impose their own service charge – as much as 500% (that's why the rates pages are torn out of the telephone book in your hotel room)! Some hotels even block access to direct services so that they can jack up your bill. Many hotels also charge for an unanswered call after the receiving phone has rung five times.

There's a wide range of local and international phonecards. Lonely Planet's eKno Communication Card is aimed specifically at independent travelers and provides budget international calls, a range of messaging services, free email and travel information – for local calls, you're usually better off with a local card. You can join online at www.ekno.lonelyplanet.com. To use eKno from The Bahamas once you have joined, dial ☎ 1-800-389-0209.

Check the eKno Web site for joining and access numbers from other countries and updates on super budget local access numbers and new features.

You can save money by using eKno, which is a prepaid phone card, or any of the home-direct services listed below, which bill the call to another number. You dial an access number from any telephone to reach a US operator, who links your call. You can bill to your home phone, phonecard, or collect to whomever you're calling. AT&T phone booths are located at several key places in The Bahamas, and most upscale hotels have signed up with AT&T to offer direct service from room phones. However, many hotels impose a US$5 surcharge for calls made using your calling card or charge card. *Never* give your calling-card number to anyone other than the operator, as scams are frequent. To place collect or calling-card calls, simply dial the appropriate code below:

AT&T USA Direct	☎ 800-225-5288
MCI	☎ 800-950-5555
Sprint	☎ 800-877-4646
Canada Direct	☎ 800-389-0004
UK Direct	☎ 800-839-4444

Most North American toll-free numbers cannot be accessed from The Bahamas. Usually you must dial ☎ 1-880, plus the last seven digits of the number. You'll be charged US$1 per minute (sometimes more).

Cellular Phones You can bring your own cellular phone into The Bahamas, but you may be charged a customs fee upon entry (refunded upon exit). Your phone will not operate on BaTelCo's cellular system unless you rent temporary use of a 'roaming' cellular line through BaTelCo (US$3 per day and US99¢ per minute, plus normal cellular rates). Callers must then dial ☎ 242-359-7626 to access your line, followed by your 10-digit number. Call your cellular company to determine if it has an agreement with BaTelCo.

Cable & Wireless Caribbean Cellular provides no-fee preregistration for your cellular, giving you a Caribbean number before you depart home. There's a US$5 daily activation fee. To get a local Caribbean number, call ☎ 800-262-8366 in the US, ☎ 800-567-

8366 in Canada, or ☎ 1-758-453-9922 elsewhere. If you're already in the islands, call ☎ 0 and SND.

Boatphone, a subsidiary of London-based Cable & Wireless, also provides a cellular network throughout the Caribbean for yachts and cruise ships. By dialing ☎ 0-SND in The Bahamas, you can register your cellular phone for instant service. For information, call the Cable & Wireless Caribbean Cellular telephone numbers, above.

Fax
In Nassau, BaTelCo has a fax bureau on East St and at its offices on Blue Hill Rd and Shirley St and in Golden Gates and Fox Hill.

Many other towns have private offices offering fax services; these are listed in the island chapters. You can also send faxes from hotels, major post offices, and regional BaTelCo centers.

Telegraph
You can send telexes from BaTelCo centers. The cost per minute for a telex is US$2.34 to the US, US$3.50 to Canada, and US$4 to the UK, Europe, and Australia.

The post office handles all telegram services, which cost US24¢ a word from Nassau and Freeport.

Email & Internet Access
In The Bahamas many of the modern and larger resorts have facilities for plugging in your laptop to gain access to the Internet. Some have business centers that offer Internet access through the hotel's own computer system. Most major islands have one or more 'electronic cafes' or Internet service providers catering to itinerant needs.

VHF Radio
Virtually every business (and many homes in the Family Islands) communicates by VHF radio, which is usually faster and more flexible and often easier to use than the telephone. Most folks have a call name for their house, boat, or business. The 'coconut telegraph' accounts for the rapid dissemination of news, information, and gossip (you have

to assume that many people are listening in to conversations).

Each island has a particular channel for making contact; other channels are then selected for communication.

If you use VHF, remember this steadfast rule: *Be brief.* The channels can get crowded.

INTERNET RESOURCES
The explosion in recent years of communications in cyberspace has fostered dozens of travel sites on the Internet. They are no substitute for a good guidebook, but many provide excellent information for planning your trip. On the Web, you can research your trip, hunt down bargain airfares, book hotels, check on weather conditions and chat with locals and other travelers about the best places to visit (or avoid!).

There's no better place to start your Web explorations than the Lonely Planet Web site (www.lonelyplanet.com). Here you'll find succinct summaries on traveling to most places on earth, postcards from other travelers and the Thorn Tree bulletin board, where you can ask questions before you go or dispense advice when you get back. You can also find travel news and updates for many of our most popular guidebooks, and the subWWWay section links you to the most useful travel resources elsewhere on the Web.

Sites specific to The Bahamas include BahamasNet at www.bahamasnet.com, which offers the usual tourism overview plus links to restaurants' menus, hotel Web pages, ferry schedules, and information about national parks and other 'Eco-Bahamas' topics. The Bahamas Out Islands Promotion Board at www.bahama-out-islands.com offers information about the Family Islands, including air travel providers and a listing of events. The official Bahamas Web site is at www.bahamas.com; it has an overview of the islands, tourist and business information, and entry requirements, among other things.

BOOKS
Information on bookstores throughout The Bahamas can be found in the island chapters. When searching for books recommended here, you should remember that

most books are published in different editions by different publishers in different countries. As a result, a book might be a hardcover rarity in one country but readily available in paperback in another. Fortunately, bookstores and libraries can search by title or author, so your local bookstore or library is best placed to advise you on the availability of the following.

Macmillan Caribbean, a division of Macmillan Press, publishes a wide range of general guides and special-interest books about the Caribbean, including *The Bahamas: A Family of Islands* and *The Turks & Caicos Islands: Lands of Discovery*. You can order a catalog by writing Macmillan Caribbean, Houndmills, Basingstoke, Hampshire RG21 2XS, England.

The books listed below provide worthwhile background reading.

Lonely Planet

Eastern Caribbean by Glenda Bendure and Ned Friary, *Cuba* by David Stanley, and *Jamaica* by yours truly are invaluable if you're planning to island-hop through the Caribbean. Other LP publications that might come in handy if you're traveling around the islands are *Dominican Republic & Haiti* by Scott Doggett and Leah Gordon and *Puerto Rico* by Randall Peffer. Likewise, pick up Nick and Corinna Selby's *Florida* for visits to the nearby Sunshine State or their *Miami* guide if you'll be spending much time there.

If you are going to The Bahamas to dive, you'll want to get the Pisces guides specific to the region. *Diving & Snorkeling Bahamas* by Michael Lawrence and *Diving & Snorkeling Turks & Caicos Islands* give detailed specifics on individual dives, dive site maps, and gorgeous full-color underwater photographs.

Guidebooks

Private Yacht No sailor should set out without the excellent *Yachtsman's Guide to The Bahamas and Turks & Caicos*, edited by Meredith Helleberg Fields. It provides detailed descriptions of just about every possible anchorage in the archipelago, and lists full information on marinas throughout the islands as well as approaches and other invaluable information. It's available at book-

stores and marinas in The Bahamas or by mail from Tropic Isle Publishers (in the US ☎ 305-893-4277), PO Box 610938, N Miami, FL 33261, USA.

Likewise, the splendid *Bahamas Cruising Guide* by Mathew Wilson also includes the Turks and Caicos Islands. It's published by Dolphin-Nomad, Magraw-Hill, PO Box 547, Blacklick, OH 43004, USA.

In a similar vein, refer to Julius Wilensky's *Cruising Guide to the Abacos and the Northern Bahamas*. It and other regional guides can be ordered from White Sound Press (in the US ☎ 217-423-0511, fax 217-423-0522), 1615 W Harrison Ave, Decatur, IL 62526, USA. Likewise, Stephen J Pavlidis' *On and Off the Beaten Path: The Central and Southern Bahamas Guide* and *The Exuma Guide: A Cruising Guide to the Exuma Cays* are both excellent yachters' guides.

Private Plane If you plan to pilot your own plane, purchase Betty and Tom Jones' superb *The Pilot's Guide to The Bahamas and Caribbean* (Pilot Publishing), 500 pages of listings on 60-plus airstrips, with details on which have jet fuel and Avgas. It also tells you everything you need to know about permits, entry and departure procedures, customs and immigration regulations, and essentials on ground transportation, etc. Contact Pilot Publishing (in the US ☎ 800-521-2120), PO Box 88, Pauma Valley, CA 92061, USA, which also sells a recently updated sectional covering the entire chain, *The Bahamas Air Navigation Chart*, as well as the *Bahamas & Caribbean Pilots Aviation Guide*.

Also try *Flying The Bahamas: The Weekend Pilot's Guide* by Frank K Smith (TAB Books). The Aircraft Owners & Pilots Association (AOPA) publishes the *AOPA Flight Planning Guide: Bahamas* and the *AOPA Bahamas Flying Kit*, available for US$8 from the AOPA flight-operations center (in the US ☎ 800-872-2672), 421 Aviation Way, Frederick, MD 21701, USA.

Travel

The Bahamas Re-Discovered by Dragan and Nicolas Popov is a coffeetable book with text on the history and contemporary scene. Harvey Lloyd's *Isles of Eden* is a splendid coffeetable book about life in the southern Family Islands.

Out Island Doctor by Evans Cottman is an excellent read, profiling the life of a US teacher who takes on the role of doctor when he settles in the Crooked Island District in the 1940s.

In the same genre try *Artist on His Island: A Study of Self-Reliance* by Randolph W Johnston (Little Harbour Press, Marsh Harbour), which tells of his and his family's lives in the Abacos.

History & Politics

For a general overview of Bahamian history, I recommend *The Story of The Bahamas* by Paul Albury and *A History of the Bahamas* by Michael Craton (San Salvador Press).

The Lucayans by Sandra Riley relates the sad tale of the extermination of the indigenous population by ruthless Spanish conquistadores. *Buccaneers of America* is an entertaining eyewitness account told by John Esquemeling, who took part in the misdeeds. It was first published in 1684.

Two recommended books tracing the traumas of the slave era are Gail Saunders' *Bahamian Loyalists and Their Slaves* and *Slavery in the Bahamas*. Colin Hughes' *Race and Politics in The Bahamas* takes a more contemporary viewpoint.

For a look at the Duke of Windsor's highly controversial time in The Bahamas, see *The King Over the Water* by Michael Pye and *The Duke of Windsor's War* by Michael Bloch. Likewise, I recommend James Leasor's *Who Killed Sir Harry Oakes?*, a serious look at the infamous, unsolved murder of one of The Bahamas' leading figures and the basis for the TV series *Murder in Paradise*.

Want to know more about drug trafficking in The Bahamas? Check out *The Cocaine Wars* by Paul Eddy, Hugo Sabogal, and Sara Walden.

Grand Bahama by PJH Barratt is an account of the history, geography, wildlife, development, and potential of Grand Bahama. Two similar, excellent books on the Biminis are Ashley B Saunders' *History of*

Bimini and *Sources of Bahamian History* by Philip Cash, Shirley Gordon, and Gail Saunders. Likewise, look for *Man O' War: My Island Home* by Haziel Albury. The founding era is traced in Everild Young's *Eleuthera: The Island Called Freedom* (Regency Press).

Junkanoo: Festival of the Bahamas by Clement Bethel examines the history of this Bahamian festival.

Flora & Fauna

A good starting point is David G Campbell's *The Ephemeral Islands: A Natural History of The Bahamas*. Likewise, check out *Native Trees of The Bahamas* by Jack Patterson and George Stevenson, *Tropical Flowers of the Bahamas* by Hans Hannau, and *Flora of the Bahama Archipelago* by Donovan and Helen Correll, which has a section on the Turks and Caicos.

For a general overview, *Caribbean Flora* by C Dennis Adams has detailed descriptions of individual species, accompanied by illustrations. In a similar vein are *Flowers of the Caribbean* and *Trees of the Caribbean: The Bahamas and Bermuda*, both by GW Lennox and SA Seddon.

Birders should pick up *Birds of New Providence and the Bahama Islands* by PGC Brudenell-Bruce. Also try *Natives of the Bahamas: A Guide to Vegetation and Birds of Grand Bahama*, a nifty pocket-size booklet by Erika Moultrie.

If you're into snorkeling or diving, a standard reference should be Eugene Kaplan's *Peterson's Field Guide to Coral Reefs*. In the same series is *Fishes of the Caribbean* by Ian Took. Academics might peek inside the massive *Fishes of the Bahamas & Adjacent Tropical Waters* by James E Bohlke and Charles C Chaplin.

Dee Carstarphen's *The Conch Book: All You Ever Wanted to Know About the Queen Conch from Gestation to Gastronomy* is a veritable feast of information on the ubiquitous marine snail.

Cookbooks

There are several books on Bahamian cooking that will help you recreate your favorite island dishes in your own kitchen.

Two of the best are *Bahamian Cuisine* by Jeanette Thompson and *Gourmet Bahamian Cooking* by Marie Mendelson and Marguerite Sawyer (Best-Way Publishing, Iowa).

Also look for *Cooking with Caribbean Rum* by Laurel-Ann Morley.

Art & Architecture

Bahamian native artist Amos Ferguson defines his love of the islands in *Under the Sunday Tree: Paintings by Mr Amos Ferguson*, with poems by Eloise Greenfield.

Several books have been written on Caribbean and Bahamian architecture, notably *Caribbean Style* by Suzanne Slesin and Stafford Cliff and its pocket-size companion, *Essence of Caribbean Style*. The lively text is supported by stunning photography.

Nassau's Historic Buildings by Seighbert Russell (Bahamas National Trust) provides a detailed review of individual buildings in the capital city.

The Hermit of Cat Island, by Peter F Anson, tells the biography of Father Jerome, the hermit architect who blessed Cat and Long Islands with splendid churches.

Folklore & Folktales

Telcine Turner's *Once Below a Time: Bahamian Stories* is an illustrated collection of short stories for children. Likewise, youngsters might enjoy *Climbing Clouds: Stories & Poems from The Bahamas*, also edited by Turner, and *An Evenin' in Guanima: A Treasury of Folktales from The Bahamas* by Patricia Glinton-Meicholas.

Bush Medicine in The Bahamas by Leslie Higgs (Nassau Guardian) provides recipes for curing everything from warts to a broken heart. Obeah and other Bahamian folk religions are the subject of *Ten, Ten, the Bible Ten – Obeah in The Bahamas* by Timothy McCartney.

General

Want to find a place or statistic? You'll find it in the *Atlas of the Commonwealth of The Bahamas* (Ministry of Education, Nassau).

Actor Sidney Poitier tells of his upbringing on Cat Island in his autobiographies, *This Life* and *The Measure of a Man*.

Ernest Hemingway's *Islands in the Stream* provides a fictitious but accurate look at Biminis life and his own bohemian ways during WWII. In a similar fictional vein, James Frew's *In the Wake of the Leopard* tells of heroes and Nazi villains playing cat-and-mouse in The Bahamas.

Bahamas Crisis by Desmon Bagley is a murder thriller that provides a behind-the-scenes look at the tourism industry. Remar Sutton's *Boiling Rock* is set on Grand Bahamas. And Brian Antoni's *Paradise Overdose* weaves a passionate love story set in an erstwhile Grand Bahamas steeped in sex and drugs.

Robert Wilder's *Wind from the Carolinas* is a historical novel that tells of the settlement of The Bahamas in the form of a generational saga. And Barbara Whitnell's *The Salt Rakers* follows suit. A hilarious, more contemporary romp is Herman Wouk's *Don't Stop the Carnival*, the tale of a publicist who gives it all up to open a hotel on a fictitious Caribbean isle.

To understand what makes Bahamians tick, check out *How to Be a True-True Bahamian* by Patricia Glinton-Meicholas (Guanima Press). To understand something of the local dialect, refer to *Talkin' Bahamian*, also by Patricia Glinton-Meicholas, and *The Dictionary of Bahamian English* by John Holm and Alison Shilling.

FILMS

The Bahamas has had star billing in dozens of movies and is a favorite of Hollywood, particularly for underwater scenes.

The islands have had strong links to James Bond movies ever since novelist Ian Fleming concocted the suave, macho spy 007. Fleming was so taken by the islands that he made them the setting for several Bond novels in which 007 seduced glamorous women and, of course, hauled in big cash in the casinos of Nassau. Fleming made Great Inagua the setting for *Dr No*, one of his early 007 novels.

Perhaps the movie most associated with the islands, however, is *Thunderball*, filmed in The Bahamas in 1965. The screenplay took full advantage of the islands' beauty. Who can ever forget the love scene between James Bond (Sean Connery) and Domino (Claudine Auger), when they meet in an undersea coral garden and swim to a perfect beach to make love on the sugary sand beneath the shade of tall palms? *Phew!* The film starred many local notables in tuxedos and ball gowns, stepping from their yachts to dine on caviar and champagne at the Café Martinique on Paradise Island. Talk about boosting tourism!

Scenes from *For Your Eyes Only* and *The Spy Who Loved Me* were also filmed in The Bahamas. In 1983, 007 returned to the islands in *Never Say Never Again*.

Scenes from *Jaws; Splash!; Wet Gold; Cocoon; My Father, the Hero; Flipper; Zeus & Roxanne*; and even *20,000 Leagues Under the Sea* were filmed in The Bahamas. In fact, The Bahamas was the setting for the first undersea motion picture in history, filmed by John Ernest Williamson in 1914.

CD-ROMS

Virtually There: Caribbean is a CD-ROM designed to take you on a 'virtual vacation.' The CD-ROM, issued by Sabre Interactive, is intended primarily for travel agents to show their clients. You can also buy it through retail computer stores.

The *Bahamas Reference Library* is available on CD-ROM from Benchmark Publishing (☎ 242-323-3398, fax 242-326-2020), PO Box N-7937, Nassau. It includes encyclopedic information.

NEWSPAPERS & MAGAZINES
Foreign Publications

Leading international newspapers and magazines and other general-interest publications are stocked by many hotel gift shops, pharmacies, and stationery stores in Nassau, Freeport, and Marsh Harbour. However, you'll be hard pressed to find even a local newspaper on some of the more remote islands.

Caribbean Travel & Life is a beautiful full-color bimonthly magazine covering travel throughout the Caribbean. *Caribbean World* comes out quarterly and has a snooty focus. *Islands Magazine* is published eight times a year and includes news and listings of rental accommodations.

Caribbean Week is a high-quality bi-weekly news magazine that covers travel, politics, fashion, economics, and other trends throughout the region. *Caribbean Today*, published in Trinidad, is similar.

Bahamian Publications

The two leading dailies are the morning *Nassau Guardian* and the afternoon *Tribune*. Both are published Monday to Saturday and cost US50¢. They are readily available in Nassau, Freeport, and Marsh Harbour, but have delayed and limited circulation in the Family Islands.

The daily *Freeport News* and twice-monthly *Freeport Times* serve Grand Bahama.

The Bahama Journal is a national weekly, as is the British-style tabloid *The Punch*, replete with scantily dressed 'Page 3' equivalents: the 'Beauty of the Week' and 'Hunk of the Week.'

Profile, published by the *Nassau Guardian* in small newspaper format, focuses on tourism, with feature articles and plenty of practical information. You can pick it up free at hotels and other locales.

Der Inseln der Bahamas is a German-language tourist newspaper available free at some hotels.

Island Scene is the official magazine of The Bahamas. The slick, full-color magazine is written for travel professionals. The same company publishes another glossy publication, *Islander Magazine*, aimed at the traveler. *Getaway Magazine* is the official magazine of the Bahama Out Islands Promotion Board.

RADIO & TV

The government-owned Bahamas Broadcasting Corporation (BBC) has a virtual monopoly on radio and television broadcasting.

Radio is the most important news medium for islanders. Expect to hear far less music and far more local news items and call-in banter than you may be used to. There is considerable political debate and airing of parochial grievances.

Radio Bahamas operates four stations using broadcast designation ZNS, for Zephyr (a balmy breeze) Nassau Sunshine. ZNS-1 (AM 1540 kHz and FM 107.1 MHz), in New Providence, broadcasts throughout the islands 24 hours a day. It is described as 'adult contemporary,' with an eclectic base of music, political analysis, call-in discussions, and tedious lists of funerals and personal announcements. ZNS-2 serves New Providence and has a heavy religious and educational bent. ZNS-FM (104.5) offers mostly contemporary music and has a focus on sports news. ZNS-3, Radio Bahamas Northern Service, offers a similar service to ZNS-1, transmitting from Freeport to the northern islands.

There are also three private radio stations inclined more toward entertainment and contemporary music: LOVE 97 FM and MORE 94.9 FM, and JAMZ at 100 FM, which plays jazz.

BBC operates the only local TV station, on Channel 13, which airs six hours daily on weekdays and 10 hours on weekends. Most homes have satellite or cable access to US programs. The Bahamas Travel Channel broadcasts on Channel 36.

Most hotels offer satellite or cable TV, and CNN, HBO, and ESPN are staples.

VIDEO SYSTEMS

Video cameras and tapes are widely available in photo supply stores in Nassau, Freeport, and main settlements. Prices are significantly higher than you may be used to in North America or Europe. VHS is standard.

PHOTOGRAPHY & VIDEO

The Bahamas is supremely photogenic. You'll want plenty of film. The seascapes are fabulous, as are the sunsets.

Film & Equipment

You'll find camera stores in Nassau, Freeport, and Marsh Harbour, where duty-free shops sell cameras and lenses at prices that offer marginal savings. You may be able to get better deals at discount mail-order photography suppliers in your home country. Check prices before leaving home.

There are few outlets away from major tourist centers.

Film is expensive – about half again what you'd pay in North America – so ensure that you bring enough to last. Most photo supply stores and drugstores sell a limited range of film. Print film is widely available, but slide (transparency) film is rare.

Many out-of-the-way places leave film sitting in the sun; avoid this like the plague, as heat and humidity rapidly deteriorate film. Don't forget to check the expiration date, too. You want film that's as fresh as possible. Once you've finished a roll of film, try to keep it cool; don't leave it sitting in the sun. And have it developed as soon as possible. Waiting one or two weeks is OK, but if you'll be traveling around for several weeks, consider having your film developed on the islands or mailing it home for development (you can purchase prepaid mailers for this purpose).

Likewise, don't leave your camera sitting around in the sun. Most shops sell a range of basic filters, including UV and polarizing filters – essentials for getting the most out of the subtropical conditions.

Technical Tips

Your greatest potential disappointment when you receive your processed photographs is a washed-out look. This is due to overexposure. The bright tropical light can fool all but the most sophisticated light-metering systems. Your meter may not be set up to register the dazzling ambient light surrounding the subject from which it's reading. Sand and water are particularly reflective.

It's often a good idea to 'stop down' one f-stop to reduce the light and thereby get richer color saturation, or 'push' your film by adjusting the ASA to read for a higher-speed film. Most effective of all is taking photographs in early morning and late afternoon to avoid harsh shadows and the glare of the sun, and to take advantage of warmer tones.

Your choice of film will also make a huge difference to the color rendition. Fujichrome Velvia gives the best color saturation of any film. It's not cheap, but it pays big dividends.

Kodachrome 25 and 64 also give excellent color rendition; the former is good for bright conditions but is too fast to handle dark conditions or great contrast of light and shade.

You'll need to take into consideration the intensely bright sun and the shadows and contrasts it creates. Many modern cameras have a fill-in flash for this purpose. Alternately, invest in a small hand-held reflector.

Photographing People

The majority of Bahamians delight in having their photographs taken and will be happy to pose for your camera. However, many Bahamians do not like having their pictures taken, especially if they're not dressed in their Sunday best. Others have religious proscriptions. If they don't want to be photographed, they may let you know this and can get quite volatile if you persist. Honor their wishes with good grace.

It is a common courtesy to ask permission. On rare occasions you may be asked to pay a small 'donation' to take photographs. Whether you agree to this is a matter of your own conscience: If you don't want to pay, don't take the shot!

In markets, it is considered good manners to purchase a small item from whomever you wish to photograph. Don't forget to send a photograph to anyone to whom you've promised one.

Airport Security

Your baggage will be inspected when departing Nassau and Freeport airports on international flights. It's a good idea to have your film inspected by hand, since x-ray machines can fog films. Most modern x-ray machines will not produce any noticeable fogging if your film passes through only once or twice, but why take the risk? If your baggage will be passed through several x-ray machines during the course of your travels, you should definitely have it checked by hand or invest in a lead-lined film pouch, which you can buy at most camera stores.

Don't forget to have your camera hand-inspected if it has film inside.

X-ray machines are not used nor are security checks made on domestic flights.

TIME

The Bahamas and Turks and Caicos operate on Eastern Standard Time (EST), five hours behind Greenwich Mean Time (GMT). Hence, they are in the same time zone as New York City and Miami, and three hours ahead of California.

Both nations operate daylight saving time, or EDT (four hours behind GMT), from the first Sunday in April to the last Sunday in October, the same as in the US.

ELECTRICITY

Most hotels operate on 110 volts (60 cycles), the same as in the US and Canada.

Sockets throughout the country are usually two- or three-pin US standard. If you're bringing electrical equipment from North America, you will not need to bring adapters. However, you will need a transformer and adapter for electrical appliances from the UK and certain other countries. Most upscale hotels can supply these to guests, but don't expect more moderate properties to do so.

WEIGHTS & MEASURES

The Bahamas uses the British Imperial System, although tentative moves to shift to the metric system have been made. Distances are still shown in miles and inches on most maps, although some official documents now speak of kilometers and centimeters. Road speed limits are given in miles per hour. Most measurements in this book are given in imperial.

Liquids are generally measured in pints, quarts, and gallons, and weight in grams, ounces, and pounds.

LAUNDRY

Most large hotels offer laundry and dry-cleaning services at extra charge. A few hotels, and many self-catering units, have coin-operated laundromats on-site. You'll also find local laundries in most settlements; where there is none, there'll be someone willing to wash your clothes for a few dollars.

Dry-cleaning services are available in most major settlements.

HEALTH

The Bahamas poses few health risks. The water is potable almost everywhere and food hygiene standards are generally high. However, most local water supplies come from ground wells that draw water directly from the limestone substrata. It will probably taste slightly brackish. This usually poses no health risk, but beware water that smells or tastes foul. Obviously, if the ground near the water source is contaminated by leaking sewers, then you're asking for trouble if you drink that water. I suggest you check with your hotel reception desk before drinking tap water (but bottled water is available at most resorts).

Your greatest threats, however, are dehydration and an excess of sun and booze.

Predeparture Preparations

Health Insurance A travel insurance policy to cover medical problems is a wise idea. There are a wide variety of policies, and your travel agent will have recommendations. For more details about health insurance, see Travel Insurance in the earlier Visas & Documents section, and Medical Assistance Organizations at the end of this section.

Medical Kit A small, straightforward medical kit is a good thing to carry. A possible kit list includes the following:

- Aspirin or Panadol (Tylenol) for pain or fever.
- Antihistamine (such as Benadryl), useful as a decongestant for colds and allergies, to ease the itch from insect bites or stings, and to help prevent motion sickness. Antihistamines may cause sedation; alcohol will increase this effect.
- Antibiotics are useful if you're traveling well off the beaten track, but they must be prescribed and you should carry the prescription with you. Some individuals are allergic to commonly prescribed antibiotics such as penicillin or sulfa drugs; it's sensible to always carry this information when traveling.
- Kaolin preparation (Pepto-Bismol), Imodium, or Lomotil, for stomach upsets.
- Rehydration mixture for treatment of severe diarrhea. This is particularly important if traveling with children but is recommended for everyone.

- Antiseptic, such as Betadine, for cuts and grazes.
- Calamine lotion to ease irritation from bites or stings.
- Bandages for minor injuries.
- Scissors, tweezers, and a thermometer (note that mercury thermometers are prohibited by airlines).
- Insect repellent, sunscreen, suntan lotion, and lip balm.
- Water-purification tablets.

If a medicine is available in The Bahamas, it will generally be available over the counter. However, be careful to ensure that the expiration date has not passed and that correct storage conditions have been met. It may be better to leave extra medicines, syringes, etc, with a local clinic, rather than carrying them home.

Immunizations No vaccinations are required to enter The Bahamas. However, a yellow-fever vaccination certificate is required for travelers arriving within seven days of traveling in the following countries: Bolivia, Brazil, Burkina Faso, Colombia, Gambia, Ghana, Nigeria, Peru, Sudan, Zaire, and any other infected areas. Vaccination protection lasts 10 years.

Other Preparations Make sure you're healthy before you travel. If you are embarking on a long trip, make sure your teeth are OK. You don't want to seek dental care in The Bahamas, as the cost is equivalent to that in the US.

If you wear glasses, bring a spare pair and your prescription. Losing your glasses can be a problem, although you can get new ones made up cheaply and competently in Nassau or Freeport.

If you require a particular medication, take an adequate supply, as it may not be available locally. Take the prescription or, better still, part of the packaging showing the generic rather than the brand name (which may not be locally available), as it will make getting replacements easier. It's a wise idea to have a legible prescription with you to prove that you legally use the medication.

Basic Rules

Food & Water Care in what you eat and drink is the most important health rule; stomach upsets are the most likely travel health problem, but the majority of these upsets will be relatively minor. Don't become paranoid – trying the local food is part of the experience of travel, after all.

The Bahamas has its own natural purification system in its limestone base, through which rainwater percolates. Water is usually safe to drink from faucets throughout the islands, but this is not guaranteed. If you don't know for certain that the water is safe, always assume the worst.

Reputable brands of bottled water or soft drinks are generally fine. Only use water from containers with a serrated seal – not tops or corks. Take care with fruit juice, particularly if water may have been added. Boiled milk is fine if it is kept hygienically, and yogurt is always good.

Salads and fruit should be washed with purified water or peeled when possible. Ice cream is usually OK, but beware of street vendors and of ice cream that has melted and been refrozen. Thoroughly cooked food is safest, but not if it has been left to cool or if it has been reheated. Conch and other shellfish are usually OK. However, be cautious about eating larger fish species such as barracuda, amberjack, and certain groupers, which have been known to cause potentially deadly ciguatera poisoning.

Bahamian restaurants pose relatively few hygiene problems. If a place looks clean and well run and if the vendor also looks clean and healthy, then the food is probably safe. In general, places that are packed with travelers or locals will be fine, while empty restaurants are questionable. Busy restaurants mean the food is being cooked and eaten quickly with little standing around and is probably not being reheated.

Nutrition If your food is poor or limited in availability, if you're traveling hard and fast and therefore missing meals, or if you simply lose your appetite, you can soon start to lose weight and place your health at risk.

Make sure your diet is well balanced. Eggs, tofu, beans, lentils, and nuts are all safe ways to get protein. Fruit you can peel (bananas, for example) is always safe and a good source of vitamins. Try to eat plenty of grains (like rice) and bread. Remember that although food is generally safer if it is cooked well, overcooked food loses much of its nutritional value. If your diet isn't well balanced or if your food intake is insufficient, it's a good idea to take vitamins and iron pills.

The Bahamas has a hot climate so make sure you drink enough – don't rely on feeling thirsty to indicate when you should drink. Not needing to urinate or very dark-yellow urine is a danger sign. Always carry a water bottle with you on long walks.

Everyday Health Avoid overexposure to extremes: Keep out of the sun at its peak. Avoid potential diseases by dressing sensibly. You can get infections through dangerous coral cuts by walking over coral without shoes, though you should not be walking on coral anyway! You can avoid insect bites by covering bare skin when insects are around, by screening windows or beds, or by using insect repellents. Seek local advice. In situations where there is no information, discretion is the better part of valor.

Medical Problems & Treatment

An embassy or consulate can usually recommend a good place to go for medical advice. In the Family Islands, medical service is generally offered through clinics, and you should bring sufficient supplies of any prescription medicines.

Also see the Medical Facilities listing later in this section.

Climatic & Geographical Considerations

Sunburn In the tropics you can get sunburned surprisingly quickly, even through clouds. Many people ruin their holidays by getting badly burned soon after they arrive. *Don't underestimate the power of the sun*, no matter how dark your skin color. Use a sunscreen with a protective factor (SPF) of 15 or more. Take extra care to cover areas that don't normally see sun – like your feet. Build up your exposure gradually. A hat provides added protection, and you should also use zinc cream or some other barrier cream for your nose and lips.

Aloe vera is good for mild sunburn.

Prickly Heat Prickly heat is an itchy rash caused by excessive perspiration trapped under the skin. It usually strikes people who have just arrived in a hot climate and whose pores have not yet opened sufficiently to cope with greater sweating. For relief until you acclimatize, keep cool, bathe often, use a mild talcum powder, and resort to air conditioning.

Dehydration & Heat Exhaustion You'll sweat profusely in The Bahamas. Take time to acclimatize to high temperatures and make sure you drink sufficient liquids. You'll lose quite a bit of salt through sweating. Salt deficiency is characterized by fatigue, lethargy, headaches, giddiness, and muscle cramps, and in this case, salt tablets may help. Vomiting or diarrhea can also deplete your liquid and salt levels. Anhydrotic heat exhaustion, caused by an inability to sweat, is quite rare. Unlike the other forms of heat exhaustion, it is likely to strike people who have been in The Bahamas' hot climate for some time rather than newcomers.

Maintain an adequate level of liquids. Avoid booze by day, as your body uses water to process alcohol. Drink water, soft drinks, or – best of all – coconut water straight from the husk.

Heat Stroke This serious, sometimes fatal, condition can occur if the body's heat-regulating mechanism breaks down and body temperature rises to dangerous levels. Long, continuous periods of exposure to high temperatures can leave you vulnerable to heat stroke.

The symptoms are feeling unwell, not sweating very much or at all, and a high body temperature. Where sweating has ceased, the skin becomes flushed and red. Severe, throbbing headaches and lack of co-ordination will also occur, and the sufferer may be confused or aggressive. Eventually the victim will become delirious or convulse. Hospitalization is essential, but meanwhile, get victims out of the sun, remove their clothing, cover them with a wet sheet or towel, and fan them continuously.

Fungal Infections Hot-weather fungal infections are most likely to occur on the scalp, between the toes or fingers (athlete's foot), in the groin area (jock itch or crotch rot), and on the body (ringworm). You get ringworm (which is a fungal infection, not a worm) from infected animals or by walking on damp surfaces, like shower floors.

To prevent fungal infections, wear loose, comfortable clothes, avoid artificial fibers, wash frequently, and dry carefully. If you do get an infection, wash the infected area daily with a disinfectant or medicated soap and water, and rinse and dry well. Apply an antifungal powder like the widely available Tinaderm. Try to expose the infected area to air or sunlight as much as possible, and wash all towels and underwear in hot water; change them often.

Motion Sickness Eating lightly before and during a trip will reduce the chances of motion sickness. While in transit, find a place that minimizes disturbance – near the wing on aircraft, close to midship on boats, near the center on buses. Fresh air usually helps; reading and cigarettes don't. Commercial anti–motion-sickness preparations, which can cause drowsiness, have to be taken before the trip commences; when you're feeling sick, it's too late. Ginger is a natural preventative and is available in capsule form.

Diseases of Poor Sanitation

Diarrhea Despite all your precautions, you may still have a bout of mild traveler's diarrhea, but a few rushed toilet trips with no other symptoms are not indicative of a serious problem. Dehydration is the main danger with any diarrhea, particularly for children, for whom dehydration can occur quite quickly. Fluid replacement remains the mainstay of treatment. Weak black tea with a little sugar, soda water, or soft drinks allowed to go flat and diluted 50% with water are all good. With severe diarrhea, a rehydrating solution is necessary to replace minerals and salts. Stick to a bland diet as you recover.

Lomotil or Imodium can be used to bring relief from the symptoms, although they do not actually cure the problem. Only use these drugs if absolutely necessary – for example, if you *must* travel. For children Imodium is preferable, but under all circumstances fluid replacement is the main message. Do not use these drugs if the person has a high fever or is severely dehydrated.

Giardiasis The parasite causing this intestinal disorder is present in contaminated water. The symptoms are stomach cramps, nausea, a bloated stomach, foul-smelling diarrhea, and frequent gas. Giardiasis can appear several weeks after you have been exposed to the parasite. The symptoms may disappear for a few days and then return; this can go on for several weeks. Tinidazole, known as Fasigyn, or metronidazole (Flagyl) are the recommended drugs for treatment. Either can be used in a single-treatment dose. Antibiotics are of no use.

Diseases Spread by People & Animals

Tetanus This potentially fatal disease is present in The Bahamas. It is difficult to treat but preventable by immunization. Tetanus occurs when a wound becomes infected by a germ that lives in the feces of animals or people, so clean all cuts, punctures, or animal bites. Tetanus is also known as lockjaw, and the first symptom may be discomfort in swallowing or stiffening of the jaw and neck; this is followed by painful convulsions of the jaw and whole body.

Sexually Transmitted Diseases There are numerous sexually transmitted diseases, and for most of these effective treatment is available. However, there is currently no cure for herpes or AIDS.

Condoms are widely available in pharmacies and general stores throughout the islands. Nonetheless, they may not be available when you need them. It's a good idea for both men and women to take condoms on their trip.

HIV/AIDS The human immunodeficiency virus (HIV) may develop into acquired immune deficiency syndrome (AIDS). HIV is a not insignificant problem in The Bahamas. The World Health Organization's UNAIDS Report from 2000 estimated that 4.1% of Bahamian adults and children, or 6900 people, were infected with HIV. The disease is rarer in the Turks and Caicos: The first case was diagnosed in 1985, and since then there have been approximately 130 cases. Any exposure to infected blood, blood products, or bodily fluids may put you at risk. In The Bahamas transmission is predominantly through heterosexual sexual activity. Apart from abstinence, the most effective preventative is to always practice safe sex using condoms. It is impossible to detect the HIV status of an otherwise healthy-looking person without a blood test.

Insect-Borne Diseases

Malaria Fortunately, malaria isn't present in The Bahamas. Among Caribbean islands, it's relegated to Hispaniola (Haiti and Dominican Republic) and, to a lesser degree, Cuba.

Dengue Fever Although extremely rare, dengue fever is present on all Caribbean islands, and 1997 saw a marked outbreak in eastern Cuba and Haiti. There is no prophylactic available for this mosquito-spread disease. A sudden onset of fever, headache, and severe joint and muscle pains (hence its colloquial name, 'broken-bone disease') are the first signs before a rash starts on the trunk of the body and spreads to the limbs and face. After a few more days, the fever will subside and recovery will begin. Serious complications are not common.

The mosquitoes that transmit dengue fever most commonly bite from dusk to dawn, and during this period travelers are advised to wear light-colored long pants and long-sleeved shirts, use mosquito repellents containing the compound DEET on exposed areas, avoid highly scented perfumes or aftershaves, and use a mosquito net – it may be worth taking your own.

Cuts, Bites & Stings

Cuts & Scratches Skin punctures can easily become infected in hot climates and may be difficult to heal. Treat any cut with an antiseptic such as Betadine. When possible, avoid bandages, as they can keep wounds wet, and clean any cut thoroughly with sodium peroxide if available.

Bites & Stings Bee and wasp stings are usually painful rather than dangerous. Calamine lotion will give relief and ice packs will reduce the pain and swelling.

There are various fish and other sea creatures that can sting or bite or are dangerous to eat. Again, local advice is the best preventative. Fortunately, The Bahamas has no venomous snakes.

No-see-'ums These well-named irritants are almost microscopically small fleas that hang out on beaches and appear around dusk (especially after rain) with a voracious appetite. Their bite is out of all proportion to their size. You'll rarely, if ever, see the darn things, despite the fact that they seem to attack en masse, usually when you're not looking. Cover your ankles if possible. Most insect repellents don't faze them. A better bet is a liberal application of Avon's Skin So Soft (SSS), a cosmetic that even the US Marine Corps swears by.

Jellyfish Local advice is the best way of avoiding contact with these sea creatures and their stinging tentacles. Dousing in vinegar will deactivate any stingers that have not fired. Calamine lotion, antihistamines, and analgesics may reduce the reaction and relieve the pain.

Bedbugs & Lice Bedbugs live in dirty mattresses and bedding. Spots of blood on bedclothes or on the wall around the bed can be read as a suggestion to find another hotel. Bedbugs leave itchy bites in neat rows. Calamine lotion may help.

All lice cause itching and discomfort. They make themselves at home in your hair (head lice), your clothing (body lice), or your pubic hair (crabs). You catch lice through direct contact with infected people or by sharing combs, clothing, and the like. Powder or shampoo treatment will kill the lice; infected clothing should then be washed in very hot water.

Scabies Scabies is an infestation of microscopic mites and is acquired through sexual contact, but it may also be transmitted through linen, towels, clothing, or upholstery. Scabies is common among people living in rustic conditions and is endemic throughout The Bahamas and the Caribbean.

The first sign – severe itching caused by eggs and feces left under the skin – usually appears three to four weeks after infestation (as soon as 24 hours for second infestations) and is worse at night. Scabies infestation appears as tiny welts and pimples, often in a dotted line, most commonly around the groin and lower abdomen, between the fingers, on the elbows, and under the armpits.

Treatment is by pesticide-containing lotions (prescription-only in the US) sold over the counter at local pharmacies in The Bahamas. The entire body must be covered. Personal hygiene is critical to exterminating the mites. At the same time that you use the treatment, you must also wash *all* your clothing and bedding in hot water. Any sexual partners must do the same.

Medical Facilities

The Ministry of Health and Environment administers a nationwide health service. You'll find government health clinics in settlements throughout the islands, plus private clinics in major towns. Many large hotels also have resident nurses, and doctors on call. For anything other than minor problems, you'll need to fly to Nassau or Freeport. For major treatments, the best advice is to get on a plane and fly home.

A visit to the outpatient clinic at Princess Margaret Hospital in Nassau costs US$10, although the wait is usually several hours. A room in Princess Margaret Hospital costs US$75 to US$100. Private doctor's office visits average US$30 to US$60.

The following are the leading hospitals:

Freeport
    Rand Memorial Hospital (☎ 242-352-6735)

Nassau
    Doctor's Hospital (☎ 242-322-8411)
    Lyford Cay Hospital (☎ 242-362-4025)
    Princess Margaret Hospital (☎ 242-322-2861)

Doctor's and Lyford Cay are both private hospitals.

Medical Assistance Organizations

Many companies offer medical assistance for travelers. Most maintain 24-hour emergency hot-line centers that connect travelers to professional medical staff worldwide. Many also provide emergency evacuation, medical attention, and payment of on-site medical treatment. Some provide services for a set annual membership fee; others offer varying coverage levels.

The Council on International Education Exchange (CIEE) offers low-cost, short-term insurance policies called 'Trip Safe' to holders of the International Student Identification Card (ISIC), International Youth Card (IYC), and International Teachers Identification Card (ITIC).

North American medical assistance organizations include:

Air Ambulance Professionals (in the US ☎ 954-491-0555, 800-752-4195), Ft Lauderdale Executive Airport, 1575 W Commercial Blvd, annex 2, Ft Lauderdale, FL 33309, USA. You can receive 24-hour worldwide medical transportation, with all flights staffed by 'aeromedically certified medical attendants.'

International Association for Medical Assistance for Travelers (IAMAT; in the US ☎ 716-754-4883), 417 Center St, Lewiston, NY 14092, USA. IMAT is an information service to assist travelers needing medical attention.

International SOS Assistance (in the US ☎ 215-244-1500, 800-523-8930, fax 215-244-0165,

corpcomm@internationalsos.com), 8 Neshaminy Interplex, suite 207, Trevose, PA 19053-6956, USA. This service provides 24-hour emergency services for insured members, with various plans at reasonable rates.

WOMEN TRAVELERS

Many Bahamian men accept a commonly held stereotype that foreign women are promiscuous. This is believed to be especially true of foreign women seen alone in bars or dance clubs. Fortunately, most Bahamian men are not pushy. They understand the meaning of 'no' and will usually take a rejection in good humor.

Bahamian men and women of all ages indulge in salacious dancing, even with complete strangers. Be aware that if a Bahamian man invites you to dance, he will probably 'wine' you – make sexual contact – from front or behind.

Safety Precautions

Sexual assault is comparatively rare in The Bahamas and is almost unheard of in the Family Islands. It is safe to walk virtually anywhere by daylight, although you should be cautious along E Bay St and Delancy St (to be avoided) and in the Over-the-Hill district of Nassau. The Family Islands pose few problems, although even here it is wise to avoid walking alone or hitchhiking at night in remote areas. If you're driving alone, be discreet about those you choose to pick up.

It is wise not to walk around in beachwear away from the beach. You'll *never* see a Bahamian woman in a bikini top around town.

Organizations & Resources

The Women's Crisis Centre (☎ 242-328-0922), on Shirley St in Nassau, can assist in an emergency or if you need emotional support.

The Women's Health & Diagnostic Centre (☎ 242-322-6440), at 1st Terr, Collins Ave, and Women's Health (☎ 242-328-6636), on Collins Ave, are useful resources.

Good resources include the International Federation of Women's Travel Organizations (in the US ☎ 602-956-7175), 4545N 36th St, No 126, Phoenix, AZ 85018, USA. The *Handbook for Women Travelers* by

Maggie and Gemma Ross and *The Traveling Woman* by Dena Kaye are also replete with handy tips and practicalities.

GAY & LESBIAN TRAVELERS

Although Bahamians are generally an extremely tolerant people, the pervasiveness of fundamentalist religious beliefs has fostered bigotry and intolerance of progressive lifestyles, particularly toward gays and lesbians. Most Bahamian gays are still in the closet, and the nation has draconian laws against homosexual activity, which is punishable by prison terms. Laws are strictly enforced; public expressions of affection between gays may well bring trouble. In 1998 a group of religious bigots called Save the Bahamas made waves when it angrily protested the arrival of a gay charter-cruise, and compounded the negative press by also protesting the arrival of Holland America's *Veendam*, which they mistakenly believed was chartered by a gay group, causing Bahamian Prime Minister Hubert Ingraham to issue a public apology.

According to the group Bahamian Gays & Lesbians Against Discrimination (see below), ClubMed, Super Club Breezes, and Atlantis resorts are gay-friendly, but Sandals Royal Bahamian forbids same-sex couples. In Nassau, the nightclubs Endangered Species (☎ 242-327-0127), on W Bay St, and The Drop Off (☎ 242-322-3444) are considered to be gay- and lesbian-friendly.

Organizations & Resources

The following organizations can provide information and assistance in planning a trip:

Bahamian Gays & Lesbians Against Discrimination (☎ 242-327-1249, bahamianglad@yahoo.com). BGLAD is a support/advocacy group that also staffs a hotline 9am to midnight daily. It can give you a detailed, if short, list of gay/lesbian-friendly establishments in The Bahamas. Web site: www.bglad.org

Damron Company (in the US ☎ 415-255-0404, 800-462-6654), PO Box 422458, San Francisco, CA 94142-2458, USA. Damron's Web site has a useful, searchable database that is truly international and can provide you with contact information for gay and lesbian advocacy groups, night clubs, hotels, etc, in cities and countries around the world. Web site: www.damron.com

International Gay & Lesbian Travel Association (in the US ☎ 954-776-2626, 800-448-8550, fax 954-776-3303, iglta@iglta.org), 4431 N Federal Hwy No 304, Ft Lauderdale, FL 33308, USA. IGLTA has a list of hundreds of travel agents, tour operators, and tourism industry professionals all over the world, as well as an international calendar of events, a country-by-country world survey of the legal position of GLBT people, a directory of local organizations, and ways of finding out about the local scene. Web site www.iglta.org

Women's Traveller with listings for lesbians and *Damron's Address Book* for men, are both published by Damron Company (see above). Ferrari Publications produces several travel guides for gays and lesbians, including the *Spartacus International Gay Guide* (in the US ☎ 602-863-2408, 800-962-2912, fax 602-439-3952, ferrari@q-net.com) PO Box 37887, Phoenix, AZ 85069, USA. Another valuable resource is *Odysseus: The International Gay Travel Planner* (in the US ☎ 516-944-5330, 800-257-5344, fax 516-944-7540, odyusa@odyusa.com) PO Box 1548, Port Washington, New York, NY 11050, USA.

Scuba divers should contact Undersea Expeditions (in the US ☎ 858-270-2900, 800-669-0310, fax 858-490-1002), which plans trips to The Bahamas for gays and lesbians. Web Site: www.underseax.com

DISABLED TRAVELERS

Disabled travelers will need to plan their vacation carefully, as few allowances have been made for them in The Bahamas and Turks and Caicos.

Only a small percentage of hotels have facilities for travelers who use wheelchairs. Check with the individual hotel before making your reservation. Fortunately, many hotels are one-story buildings or have ramp access or elevators, and the casinos have ramp access.

The tourist board can provide a list of hotels with wheelchair ramps, as can the

Bahamas Council for the Handicapped (☎ 242-322-4260) and the Bahamas Association for the Physically Disabled (☎ 242-322-2393, fax 242-322-7984), on Dolphin Drive in Nassau. Its mailing address is PO Box N-4252, Nassau.

The Bahamas Association for the Physically Disabled provides a minibus for disabled tourists and will arrange airport transfers and a guided island tour.

New construction codes mandate ramps and parking spots for disabled people at shopping plazas and other select sites. Larger hotels are beginning to introduce features such as Braille instructions and chimes for elevators, bathrooms with grab bars, and ramps. However, only the most recent structures in Nassau and, to a lesser degree, Freeport have adopted these features.

Organizations

Contact the following for more information:

Society for the Advancement of Travel for the Handicapped (in the US ☎ 212-447-7284, fax 212-725-8253), 347 Fifth Ave, No 610, New York, NY 10016, USA. Annual membership costs US$45. It publishes a quarterly magazine, *Open World*.

American Foundation for the Blind (in the US ☎ 212-502-7600, 800-232-5463, afbinfo@afb.org) 11 Penn Plaza No 300, New York, NY 10001, USA.
Web site: www.afb.org

Flying Wheels Travel (in the US ☎ 507-451-5005, 800-535-6790, fax 507-451-1685), PO Box 382, Owatanna, MN 55060, USA. This is a full-service travel agency for the physically challenged.

SENIOR TRAVELERS

One-third of travelers worldwide are older than 50, and travel companies court seniors with discounts, usually passed on to members of seniors' organizations. Most US airlines offer senior discount programs for travelers 62 or older. Some car-rental companies also extend discounts.

Unfortunately, The Bahamas seems virtually exempt from seniors' discounts. Only a handful of hotels offer them. There's no harm in asking, but don't be surprised to hear 'no' for an answer.

Organizations & Resources

The American Association of Retired Persons (AARP) offers discounts on hotels, car rentals, etc, through its Purchase Privilege Program (in the US ☎ 800-424-3410), 601 E St NW, Washington, DC 20049, USA. It also arranges travel for members through AARP Travel Experience. Annual membership costs US$8. The Golden Age Travelers Club (in the US ☎ 415-296-0151, 800-258-8880, fax 415-776-0753, tourmanager@gatclub.com), Pier 27, The Embarcadero, San Francisco, CA 94111, USA, offers similar services and has special programs aboard cruise ships. The Web site is www.gatclub.org.

Another handy source of tips on seniors' discounts is the monthly newsletter of the National Council of Senior Citizens (in the US ☎ 301-578-8800, 800-373-6407, fax 301-578-8999) 8403 Colesville Rd, No 1200, Silver Springs, MD 20910-3314, USA.

TRAVEL WITH CHILDREN

The Bahamas pursues the family traveler aggressively, and the larger hotels compete by providing facilities for children. Most hotels provide a babysitter or nanny by advance request. Most large resorts – such as Atlantis, with its Discovery Channel Camp – cater to families and have a full range of activities and amenities for children. And most hotels also offer free accommodations or greatly reduced rates for children staying in their parents' rooms (a child is usually defined as being 12 years or younger, but some classify those 16 or younger as children).

It's a good idea to prearrange necessities such as cribs, babysitters, and baby food.

Rental villas and apartments are good options for families. Most come fully staffed, allowing you to leave the children with the housekeeper.

Rascals in Paradise (in the US ☎ 415-978-9800, 800-872-7225) specializes in family vacation planning and offers all-inclusive group trips to several Family Island destinations; trips include a tour guide-cum-nanny. Premier Cruises (in the US ☎ 407-783-5061, 800-327-7113), specializes in family cruises, as does Walt

Disney Cruises (in the US ☎ 407-566-3500, 800-511-8444).

The Bahamas Ministry of Tourism's Children-to-Children program links visiting children with local kids, who can participate in activities together and learn from one another.

Travel with Children, by Lonely Planet co-founder Maureen Wheeler, gives you the low-down on preparing for family travel, as well as basic health advice. Other handy resources are *The Family Travel Guide Catalog* and *Family Travel Times Newsletter* (☎ 212-477-5524, 888-822-4388), 40 5th Ave, New York, NY 10011, on the Web at www.familytraveltimes.com.

For encouragement, you might also check out Nancy Jeffrey's *Bahamas – Out Island Odyssey*, her tale of traveling through the islands with two teenage sons and an infant.

USEFUL ORGANIZATIONS
Bahamas Historical Society
This nonprofit cultural and educational organization is dedicated to stimulating interest in Bahamian history. It publishes a regular journal and maintains a museum at its headquarters (☎ 242-322-4231) at Shirley St and Elizabeth Ave in Nassau; its mailing address is PO Box SS-6833, Nassau.

Dept of Archives
This department (☎ 242-393-2175, fax 242-393-2855), on Mackey St in Nassau, serves as a repository for government records and archives. It has a microfilm collection of historical documents dating back to 1700, plus a photographic archive and a large collection of maps and charts. It publishes books and booklets relating to historical and cultural aspects of the islands. The department is open 10 am to 4:45 pm daily except holidays. Its mailing address is PO Box SS-6341, Nassau.

DANGERS & ANNOYANCES
The US State Dept publishes travel advisories that alert US citizens to trouble spots. Advisories are available by recorded telephone message (in the US ☎ 202-647-5225, fax 202-647-3000), at US embassies and consulates abroad, and on the Web at http://travel.state.gov/bahamas.html. Contact the Citizens Emergency Center, room 4811, State Dept, Washington, DC 20520-4818. The US Centers for Disease Control posts information concerning travel to the Caribbean region on its Web site at www.cdc.gov/travel/caribbean.htm.

Natural Hazards
Undertows & Currents Those gorgeous coral reefs beg to be explored, and the turquoise waters are seductive sirens. However, many places have dangerous undertows and currents. Seek local advice about conditions before swimming.

Hurricanes Public warnings will be issued if a hurricane is due to come ashore. In the event of a hurricane, seek shelter in the sturdiest structure you can find. (For more on hurricane seasons, see Climate in the Facts about The Bahamas chapter, as well as the boxed text 'Big Blows.')

Manchineel Trees The manchineel tree, which grows along the Bahamian shoreline, produces small, applelike green fruits. Don't eat them – they're highly poisonous! The sap is also irritating. Take care not to sit beneath the tree, as even raindrops running off the leaves onto your skin can cause blisters.

Social Hazards
Soon Come! This is the Caribbean…well, almost. Service may sometimes be slower than you're used to at home. That's fine! You're *not* at home. You're on vacation. So slow down, relax, and go with the Bahamian flow.

Harassment Most Bahamians are cheery, helpful, law-abiding folks concerned with making the foreign visitor's experience as positive as possible. The Bahamas is relatively free of hustlers, the scourge of neighboring islands such as Jamaica. Nonetheless, The Bahamas is not immune, although hustlers are almost entirely restricted to Nassau and, to a lesser degree, Freeport. Here hustlers walk the streets looking for potential customers to whom to sell crafts, jewelry, or drugs; they also offer to wash cars, give aloe massages, act as guides, or perform a thousand varieties of service.

Aggressive persistence is key to their success. Play to the islanders' innate sense of humor. A wisecrack can often break the icy confrontation and earn you respect.

Drugs Marijuana *(ganja)* and cocaine are prevalent in The Bahamas, which is used as a transshipment point for drug traffic into North America. At some stage, you may be approached by hustlers selling drugs.

Possession and use of drugs and the 'facilitation of drug trafficking' in The Bahamas are strictly illegal and penalties are severe. The islands are swarming with US Drug Enforcement agents, and purchasing drugs is a risky business. Foreigners *do not* receive special consideration if caught. Bahamian prisons are notoriously nasty places. Likewise, US customs agents are on the alert – and well trained – to spot drug smugglers. *Caveat emptor!*

Crime Most Bahamians are extremely law-abiding citizens. Their sense of honor and pride runs deep, and their tolerance of thieves and criminals is extremely low. The Bahamas as a whole is relatively crime-free, and the vast majority of travelers return home without having suffered any mishaps whatsoever.

Nassau is a distinct exception, where shootings and violent robberies are frequent …and rising rapidly! Many of the murders are related to the drug trade. They occur overwhelmingly in the low-income and shantytown area south of downtown and to a lesser degree in parts of Freetown. Even the mellow Family Islands have seen noticeable increases in crime levels in recent years, notably in Marsh Harbour, Abacos.

Most crime against travelers is petty opportunistic crime, and is overwhelmingly relegated to Nassau and Freeport, where pickpockets – the foreigner by your side could be one – are busy in the casinos.

Take sensible precautions with your valuables. Hold handbags close to your body.

Carry your wallet in your front pocket. Leave jewelry in your hotel safe. Never leave valuables in view in your car, and always keep car doors locked. Steer clear of poorer quarters of Nassau and Freeport, including downtown, at night. And don't wander on unlit streets at night; stick close to main thoroughfares.

Keep hotel doors and windows securely locked at night. Don't open your door at night to anyone who cannot prove his or her identity.

EMERGENCIES

You can summon an ambulance or the police anywhere in The Bahamas by dialing ☎ 911, except in the Family Islands, where you dial ☎ 919. In Nassau the number for public ambulances is ☎ 242-322-2221; for the police, dial ☎ 322-4444.

For an ambulance in Freeport, call ☎ 242-352-2689. In the event of an emergency at sea, contact the following organizations:

Bahamas Air-Sea Rescue Association (BASRA; ☎ 242-322-3877, VHF channel 16, co@basra.org), PO Box SS-6247, Nassau

Nassau Marine Operator (VHF channel 27 or 2198 SSB)

US Coast Guard, 7th Coast Guard District, (in the US ☎ 305-415-6800, 2182 SSB), 100 MacArthur Causeway, Miami Beach FL 33139, USA

Each can arrange air transportation to the nearest medical facility. You can also reach the Royal Bahamas Defence Force at VHF channel 22A.

A private ambulance service, National Air Ambulance (☎ 954-359-9900, 800-525-0166), operates from Fort Lauderdale International Airport.

LEGAL MATTERS

Bahamian drug and drunk-driving laws are strictly enforced. Don't expect leniency because you're a foreigner. A jail term can ruin your vacation…and your life! Still, if you run afoul of the law and are arrested, insist on your right to call your embassy or consul to request their assistance. They should be able to help with finding a lawyer, advising relatives, and providing counsel. But that's about as far as they'll go.

BUSINESS HOURS

Government and private business offices tend to be open 9 am to 5 pm weekdays.

In Nassau and on Grand Bahama, banks are open 9:30 am to 3 pm Monday to Thursday and Friday 9 am to 3 pm. Some banks close at 2 pm and reopen from 3 to 5 pm on Friday, when they can be very busy. In the Family Islands, bank hours vary widely. Usually local banks are open only one or two days a week for two or three hours. A few local banks open 9 am to noon on Saturday. See island chapters for details.

In Nassau and Freeport most stores are open 9 am to 5:30 pm weekdays and 10 am to 5:30 pm Saturday. Often they close for lunch. Few stores are open on Sunday, except boutiques and gift shops in Nassau and Freeport, and then only when cruise ships are in town. In the Family Islands, hours are similar, although more fluid.

Post offices are usually open 8:30 am to 5:30 pm weekdays and until 12:30 pm Saturday. Most restaurants are open seven days a week. Hours vary.

PUBLIC HOLIDAYS & SPECIAL EVENTS

Bahamian national holidays include the following:

New Year's Day January 1
Good Friday Friday before Easter
Easter Monday Monday after Easter
Whit Monday Seven weeks after Easter
Labour Day First Friday in June
Independence Day July 10
Emancipation Day First Monday in August
Discovery Day October 12
Christmas Day December 25
Boxing Day December 26

Holidays that fall on Saturday or Sunday are usually observed on the following Monday.

Special Events

The BTO (☎ 242-322-7501, fax 242-328-0945, also see Tourist Offices, earlier in this chapter) publishes a monthly list of events, plus a pin-up calendar of events, available from its offices worldwide. It also provides phone numbers and dates for specific events. The Ministry of Tourism (☎ 242-322-7500) is often the place to call for general and specific information about Bahamian events.

Most events run on a predictable schedule. Many annual events occur at the cusp of months, so the specific month may vary from year to year.

No traditional African festivals were retained in The Bahamas. Nonetheless, several folk festivals evolved from the brief slave era, notably Junkanoo (see below) and Emancipation Day. On these days workers on New Providence put down their tools and walk with their families to Fox Hill, going from church to church and ending the day in merrymaking and traditional dancing.

Junkanoo

The nation's most famous festival has been called 'the centerpiece of Bahamian culture.' The event is hosted at various venues around Christmas and New Year's Day, when streets and settlements resound to the calliope of cowbells, whistles, and goatskin goombay drums, drawing in thousands of foreign visitors. Mostly it is a big blow-out for the local masses, a tropical Mardi Gras with quintessential Bahamian flavor. The festival is a street event, so there is no entrance charge.

Be prepared to throw inhibitions to the wind. Bahamians are not shy about wearing as little as possible, nor about wining (making sexual contact while dancing) with complete strangers.

The main festival is held in Nassau, beginning before sunrise on Boxing Day. As many as 20,000 locals and tourists party the night away or are up before dawn for the parade. Similarly, on Grand Bahama the parade is held on W Sunrise Hwy in Freeport on New Year's Day at 5 am.

In the Exumas a few local characters (such as Josh, 'King of the Junkanoo') add to the color of the festival. It begins at 3 am on Boxing Day (the day after Christmas). Eleuthera's Junkanoo celebration begins at 5 am on Boxing Day. In the Abacos the parades take place on both Boxing Day, when individual settlements celebrate, and

Junkanoo

You feel the music before you see it…a frenzied barrage of whistles and horns overriding the *ka-LICK-ka-LICK* of cowbells, the rumble of drums, and the joyful blasts of conch shells. Then the costumed revelers stream into view, whirling and gyrating like a kaleidoscope in rhythm with the cacophony. This is Junkanoo, the national festival of The Bahamas, its equivalent of Carnival or Mardi Gras.

Junkanoo is a traditional Christmas celebration in which revelers parade through the streets dressed in masquerade. It was once the major celebration on the slave calendar and dates from the 18th century, when slaves were granted three days off for Christmas.

The name, pronounced *junk-uh-NOO*, is thought to come from a West African term for 'deadly sorcerer.' Others say the festival is named for John Canoe, a tribal leader who demanded that his enslaved people be allowed to celebrate a holiday. Junkanoo, which had its origins in West African secret societies, evolved on the plantations of the British Caribbean among slaves who were forbidden to observe their sacred rites. The all-male cast of masqueraders hid their identity, following West African mask-wearing tradition. (The costumes resembled those of the Yoruba tribe, notably the Egunguns, a secret group that worshipped ancestral spirits. An Egungun mask often covers the entire body and usually represents the spirit of a particular person.) Some dressed as demons, others wore horse heads, and many were on stilts. The elaborate carnival was accompanied by musicians with drums, fifes, flutes, and rattles.

At first Junkanoos were suppressed by the Bahamian colonial government, which feared they might get out of hand and lead to slave uprisings. Later planters encouraged them. Creole elements found their way into the ceremony, and Morris dancing, polka, and reels were introduced. On Jamaica and other islands, Junkanoo was suppressed to the point of virtual extinction, but in The Bahamas it became an integral part of the culture.

Every major hotel now has a Junkanoo band, and no major event on the tourist calendar is complete without Junkanoo music and dancing. But the greatest spectacle is reserved for year's end, when Junkanoo parades flood down Bay and Shirley Sts in Nassau and erupt on other islands with all the energy of an atomic explosion.

In Nassau the first 'rush,' as the parade is known, takes place on Boxing Day (December 26); the second occurs on New Year's Day. Both parades begin at about 3 am and last beyond dawn. By noon on New Year's Day, the parades are over. The costumes are abandoned. Scraps of crepe paper float down Bay St.

Junkanoo is fiercely competitive and participants practice year-round. Many marchers belong to 'shacks,' organized groups with members from many social classes. The shacks vie to produce the best performance, costume, and music. The most elaborately costumed performers are one-person parade floats and are often sponsored by individual companies or stores. Each costume can weigh over 200lb, although they're crafted from crepe paper pasted on cardboard or Styrofoam. Most costumes depict exotic scenes or social themes, with plentiful beads, foils, and rhinestones added for glittery accent. Many people spend the entire year planning their costumes, keeping their designs a carefully guarded secret.

New Year's Day, when they come together in New Plymouth. There are *three* Junkanoo celebrations in Alice Town in the Biminis: on Boxing Day, New Year's Day, and July 10, in recognition of independence.

Caribbean Muzik Fest

This weeklong festival, held in late May or early June in Nassau, is an annual jam with reggae, soca, Junkanoo music, and dance hall under the same billing, showcasing the best talent from the Caribbean's cornucopia of musical genius. Little-known but top-notch locals also perform. The event is held at the Queen Elizabeth Sports Centre and traditionally lasts from 8 pm until dawn.

Homecomings & Regattas

Most Family Island towns have 'homecomings,' the very heart of the Bahamian social scene, when family members return from Nassau, other islands, or the US. Usually these homecomings are associated with national holidays, so that participants can stretch the festivities for three to five days. They're social parties, full of Bahamian bonhomie, and a good excuse for local men to get drunk. Other homecomings are 'dry' (the character of a celebration depends on the town: Harbour Island's homecoming is a bit of a revel, with sexy-swimsuit contests and no small amount of salacious fun; that of nearby Current is more of a church-supper affair).

Many of the homecomings are associated with sailing regattas, when locally made sailing craft compete for prizes and partying is taken to its limit. These numerous, fun events are mentioned in the island chapters. The more famous regattas – the Family Island Regatta in the Exumas (April) and the Long Island Regatta (May) – are tourist staples and have been summed up in three words: 'boats, bikinis, and booze.'

Other Happenings

See the island chapters for contact information and details on these events, or contact the Ministry of Tourism (☎ 242-322-7500) or the BTO (☎ 242-322-7501, fax 242-328-0945, also see Tourist Offices, earlier in this chapter) directly. For a listing of fishing tournaments, turn to the Outdoor Activities chapter.

January

Bahamia Pro-Am Golf Tournament – This tourney is held mid-month at the Emerald & Ruby Golf Courses, Grand Bahama. For information call ☎ 242-352-9661.

Classic Cars Race – Lovers of flashy vintage cars should head to Nassau for this four-day, mid-month festival. Rare Ferraris, Jaguars, and other classics dating back to the 1920s gear up for a race along Cable Beach.

Ebony Fashion Fair – The fair (hosted by *Ebony* magazine) draws Nassau's socialites and would-be models to 'ooh' and 'aah' at the latest creations of world-famous designers. In 2001, the Ebony Fashion Fair will be at Super Club Breezes on January 31.

February

International Food Fair – Local Bahamian fare comes to the streets of Nassau, with cookouts and competitions highlighting the bounty of the sea and land.

People of the Bahamas Annual Archives Exhibition – Held in Nassau, the exhibition features exhibits showcasing the contributions of various ethnic groups to the historical and cultural development of the nation.

March

Freeport Rugby Club Annual Easter Rugby Festival – Grand Bahama hosts 15 of the world's top rugby teams, as players from as far afield as Argentina and Wales gather to tussle for the grand prize.

Grand Bahama 5K Road Race – World-class athletes compete alongside locals, with a grand opening featuring spoofy costumes and bed races.

April

Family Island Regatta – This four-day extravaganza of sailboat races and general merrymaking is a highlight of the Bahamian social calendar. It takes place in George Town (Great Exuma), and thousands fly in for the lively social scene, which includes beauty pageants, cooking demonstrations, and plenty of drinking and dancing.

Snipe Winter Sailing Championships – These races pit homemade sailing craft against one other in Montagu Bay, off Nassau Harbour.

May

Bimini Festival – A popular sport-fishing tournament is the highlight of this festival in mid-May, featuring barbecues, cookouts, and general merriment.

Long Island Regatta – A smaller-scale version of the Family Island Regatta, this festivity, which coincides with Whit Monday, sees up to 50 traditional sailing vessels competing for honors. Rake 'n' scrape bands, native food stalls, and party games round out the carnival-like ambience.

June

Bahamas Boating Flings – Each June through mid-August, a lead boat guides a flotilla of yachts and other craft from Fort Lauderdale into the Biminis; see the Getting There & Away chapter for details.

Goombay Summer Festival – Nassau hosts a midyear Junkanoo, with round-the-clock festivities for summertime visitors.

Annual Eleuthera Pineapple Festival – This annual festival, held in early June in Gregory Town (Eleuthera), combines music, games, and festivities with cooking contests, 'best pineapple' contests, beauty pageants, and the highlight – the crowning of the young Pineapple Queen.

July

All Eleuthera Regatta – This sailing affair melds three days of racing with a festive atmosphere replete with fashion shows, music, and contests. Islanders flock to Rock Sound for the family fun.

August

Emancipation Day – Held the first Monday in August to commemorate the emancipation of slaves in 1834. A highlight is an early-morning 'Junkanoo Rush' at 4 am in Fox Hill.

Fox Hill Day Celebration – Held a week after Emancipation Day, this celebration recalls the day on which residents of Fox Hill learned of emancipation.

Great Abaco Triathlon – Athletes descend on Marsh Harbour to test their mettle. The event includes a kids' triathlon and Sprintman race.

Miss Bahamas Contest – Over a dozen finalists vie for the coveted title of Miss Bahamas in a much-anticipated gala evening mid-month in Nassau featuring star-spangled entertainment. The winner represents The Bahamas in the Miss Universe contest. For more information call ☎ 242-393-4041.

September

Bahamas Atlantis Superboat Challenge – Life is never so fast in Nassau as in late September, during this annual professional powerboat race. Forty or more teams compete in boats that are to smaller speedboats what dragsters are to the family sedan.

Ladies' Futures ProAm Golf Tournament – This is a challenging 54-hole tourney for top-ranked international golfers, traditionally hosted at the Paradise Island Golf Club (New Providence).

October

Annual Grand Bahama Triathlon – Athletes compete in the challenging 1½-mile swim, 15-mile bike race, and 3-mile run.

Annual McLean's Town Conch Cracking Contest – Participants in this contest on Grand Bahama compete to extract the highest number of conchs from shells in the shortest possible time. Politically incorrect as well as profligate? Ah, well…there's 'greasy pole' climbing and other inane amusements to keep everyone happy.

European Golf Weeks – Grand Bahama hosts a monthlong series of golf tournaments for amateurs at the Lucaya Golf & Country Club.

Great Bahamas Seafood Festival – The Arawak Cay Seafood Market in Nassau is the setting for this annual four-day culinary and cultural extravaganza, featuring concerts, Junkanoo, and plenty of food.

International Cultural Weekend – Bahamians celebrate unity among the many nationals residing in the islands with a mid-month weekend of float parades, food fests, arts and crafts displays, and concerts, held in Nassau.

International Mixed Championship Golf Tournament – This is a weeklong 54-hole event for amateurs traditionally held at the Paradise Island Golf Club.

North Eleuthera Sailing Regatta – This three-day racing pageant features scores of locally built sloops vying for the championship. Onshore festivities include entertainment by local bands, regional cuisine, and fashion shows. For more information call ☎ 242-394-0445.

World Invitational Bonefishing Championship – Top international anglers compete with the winner of the Bahamas National Bonefish Championship. It takes place in Exuma.

November

Annual Grand Bahama Conchman Triathlon – Over 200 athletes gather in Freeport to compete in swimming, bicycling, and running. There's a party, too, at Taino Beach.

Guy Fawkes Night – On November 5, Bahamians celebrate retribution for the Gunpowder Plot of 1605 – when Catholic plotters attempted to blow up the Houses of Parliament in London – by lighting bonfires and burning the lead villain, Guy Fawkes, in effigy, accompanied by requisite fireworks. Nassau has a nighttime parade.

December

Christmas Concert Under the Stars – The Garden Theatre, on Green Turtle Cay (Abacos), plays host to an open-air concert of traditional Christmas music and other performances.

Annual Christmas Day Parade – Bimini hosts a 5 am parade with music and festivities.

Plymouth Historical Weekend – Residents of Green Turtle Cay celebrate their Loyalist heritage with musical concerts, theater, art exhibits, and barbecues.

Police Band Annual Christmas & Classical Concert – The Royal Bahamas Police Force Band performs holiday classics at the Atlantis resort on Paradise Island, with accomplished local musicians assisting.

WORK

There are strict legal limitations against foreigners seeking work in The Bahamas. Competition for itinerant work is extremely high, so no expatriate may be offered employment in a post for which a suitably qualified Bahamian is available. However, a work permit application may be considered if you have already entered the country as a visitor. A permit relates to a specific job for which an employer must show proof of having made adequate attempts to recruit a Bahamian. Permit requests must be made through the Immigration Dept (☎ 242-322-7530), PO Box N-831, Nassau.

A good start would be to contact the Bahamas Employment Agency (☎ 242-328-4325), PO Box N-7250, Nassau; or the Bahamas Hotel Employer's Association (☎ 242-322-2262, fax 242-322-8381), PO Box N-7799, Nassau.

ACCOMMODATIONS

The Bahamas has a range of accommodations, from quaint family-run guesthouses and cozy inns to superdeluxe resorts. Where you stay can make or break your vacation, so it pays to research thoroughly. Price is only one guide – many hotels of similar price vary dramatically in ambience and value. Basically, you have two choices as far as location goes: windward or leeward. The former usually means miles-long beaches washed by Atlantic rollers; the latter means smaller coves, usually secluded, lapped by mint-green waters.

Rates & Seasons

Prices throughout this book are normally for double rooms year-round unless otherwise stated. Many hotels have a price system tiered into peak, shoulder, and low season

rates. Low or off season (summer) is usually mid-April to mid-December; high or peak season (winter) is the remainder of the year, when hotel prices increase by 40% or more.

Prices begin at about US$30 a night for budget, no-frills properties, usually swarming with mosquitoes. You're hard-pressed to find even a room in a modest middle-of-the-road hotel or guesthouse for less than US$60, which seems to be an island price-standard for even the most mediocre properties. Fortunately, you can also find a few gems in this range. Ocean-view rooms are usually more expensive than other rooms. Upscale resort hotels are priced from about US$80, deluxe ones from US$150. Ultra-deluxe hotels begin at about US$200 and run upward of US$500 nightly. If you have to ask…!

If you stay at an all-inclusive resort, you'll pay one price for as much food, booze, and activities as you wish to indulge in, and these resorts can therefore be great bargains. Check the fine print; some all-inclusives charge for diving and other services.

You might also consider buying a package, which most resorts and upscale hotels offer. It's possible to buy a three-day/two-night package from New York or Miami for US$199 to US$399, and a seven-day/six-night package for as little as US$399. Special packages are also offered to honeymooners, golfers, and divers. Some properties also discount room rates based on the number of nights you stay. *Ask what discounts may be available and feel free to suggest your own.*

Unless otherwise stated, prices refer to room only, or European Plan (EP). Some hotels will quote rates as Continental Plan (CP; room and breakfast), Modified American Plan (MAP; room plus breakfast and dinner), or American Plan (AP; room plus three meals daily). Don't forget to check if the quoted rate includes government tax, which can be as high as 12%, and service charge. Consider, too, whether breakfast is included. In addition, some hotels add miscellaneous charges such as an energy surcharge, 'resort levy,' or a per-diem fee for housekeeping service (US$3.50 is typical). You may challenge these questionable charges. The housekeeping service charge is legal, but the energy tab is left over from the oil crisis days of the mid-'70s and is definitely illegitimate.

The more popular hotels are often booked solid in peak season, when it is advisable to book several months in advance, especially if you're relying on the mail, which can take several weeks. It's best to phone, fax, or use email, or use a travel agent or hotel representative (see Information & Reservations) in your home country.

Hotel Discounts

Several organizations offer discounted room rates at savings of up to 50%. Most offer discounts to fee-paying members only, but joining is easy. Contact the following US organizations:

Entertainment Publications (☎ 248-637-8400, fax 248-637-3992), 2125 Butterfield Rd, Troy, MI 48084

Quest International (☎ 509-248-7512, 800-560-4100, fax 509-248-4050), 402 E Yakima Ave, suite 1200, Yakima, WA 98901

The Room Exchange (☎ 800-846-7000, fax 212-760-1013)

Information & Reservations

The BTO (☎ 242-322-7501, fax 242-328-0945) publishes a guide and rate sheet to leading hotels and guesthouses across the islands. You can obtain it from BTO offices worldwide (see Tourist Offices, earlier in this chapter) or from the BTO information booths at Nassau and Freeport airports. All the establishments listed have been inspected and are 'BTO approved.' (Many accommodations that have not been BTO approved are perfectly OK.)

You can make reservations directly with hotels, but you'll find it just as easy to use travel agencies or hotel representatives, notably the Bahamas Out Islands Promotion Board (see Tourist Offices).

The BTO's Bahamas Reservations is linked to the Charms reservation system (in North America ☎ 800-700-4752).

The Bahamas Hotel Association (☎ 242-322-8381, fax 242-326-5346), Hotel's House, Dean's Lane, Nassau, represents hoteliers and other accommodations owners and tourism service providers.

Camping

The Bahamas is not developed for campers, who are disdained by tourism officials. A handful of budget properties will let you pitch a tent on their lawns for a small fee. However, camping on the beaches is illegal and there are no official campsites, even in wilderness areas.

If you insist on camping, bring everything you need. Make sure your tent is bug-proof and capable of withstanding a good downpour. Don't count on there being a restaurant nearby. You'll need to bring cooking gear if you plan on camping in the boondocks.

Hostels

The Bahamas has no youth hostel association. However, there's a youth hostel in Nassau (see the New Providence chapter).

Guesthouses

These are the accommodations of choice for Bahamians when traveling. Usually they're small, no-frills, family-run properties.

Standards and prices vary enormously. Some are exquisite, with a live-in owner who provides breakfast and sometimes dinner on-site. Many are no more than a couple of dingy rooms with shared bathrooms and plenty of mosquitoes and a small stove and refrigerator. Others are self-contained apartments. Still others are indistinguishable from hotels or motels. They're good places to mix with locals, but choose carefully.

The *Nassau Guardian* and the *Tribune* newspapers list guesthouses under 'Boarding Accommodation' and 'Guesthouse' headings in their classified-ad sections.

Hotels

Bahamian hotels run the gamut, but it is unwise to rely solely on a hotel's brochure or promotional literature. Knowing whether a hotel has air-con, TVs, and a swimming pool tells you nothing about its true atmosphere, so I've tried to provide in-depth descriptions of hotels to help you make a more informed decision based on ambience as much as amenities.

All-Inclusive Resorts

These resorts are cash-free, self-contained hotels or village resorts; you pay a set price and (theoretically) pay nothing more once you set foot inside the resort.

Caution is needed when choosing a resort, for various reasons. Many properties have jumped onto the 'all-inclusive' bandwagon for marketing purposes. Club Med (☎ 800-258-2633), for example, has two properties in The Bahamas and one in the Turks and Caicos and is considered an all-inclusive chain, but in reality you will have to pay for booze and some extras, such as scuba. Check carefully for hidden charges for water sports, laundry, and other activities or services *not* included in the price. Rates begin at about US$100 per day at the less expensive resorts. The Web site is www.clubmed.com.

A Jamaican company, Sandals (www.sandals.com), dominates the Caribbean scene and has fostered the highest standards. Sandals' resorts, marketed as 'ultra-inclusives,' boast the highest occupancy rates of any hotels in the Caribbean. The Sandals Royal Bahamian, its flagship resort on New Providence, is for hetero couples only; its Beaches property, on Providenciales, is for singles, couples, and families. According to BGLAD, ClubMed, Super Club Breezes, and Atlantis resorts are lesbian/gay-friendly, but Sandals Royal Bahamian forbids same-sex couples, and will not allow two people of the same gender to share a room.

Homestays & Home Exchanges

The Ministry of Tourism's 'People-to-People Programme,' while not specifically designed to provide accommodations with families, is a good starting point. Participants have been screened by the ministry, which can assist in arranging overnight stays. It also offers a Children-to-Children program. See the boxed text 'People to People' for more information.

A similar international organization that arranges for homestays is Interculture GB (in the UK ☎ 020-8534-4201, ext 271), c/o CRS Ltd, 78–102 The Broadway, Stratford, London E15 1NL.

Another option is to exchange homes with a family in The Bahamas. One company that specializes in handling this is Intervac (in the US ☎ 800-756-4663). The Web site is www.intervac.com.

People to People

The Bahamas Ministry of Tourism would like you to meet the locals and discover their warmth and congeniality. It has developed the 'People-to-People Program' to enable visitors to interact with Bahamians and gain an appreciation for island life. Normally, participants attend an afternoon tea, dinner, or cocktail party; join a family at a church service or social or civic club; go sightseeing; or even spend a few hours sharing their hosts' work environments.

Visitors are matched with host families that share the visitors' interests or professions. Volunteer hosts are all approved by the ministry and their homes inspected to ensure that they meet the program's standards. Most are middle-class citizens.

The program is offered on New Providence, Grand Bahama, the Abacos, the Biminis, the Exumas, and San Salvador. There's no charge, but bringing a small gift (or at least picking up the tab) is considered a common courtesy.

Contact the Manager, People-to-People (☎ 242-326-5371, fax 242-328-0945), PO Box N-3701, Nassau, The Bahamas; or the Coordinator, People-to-People (☎ 242-352-8044), PO Box F-40251, Freeport, Grand Bahama, The Bahamas. You can also register at the tourism information booths at Nassau International Airport and in Nassau's Rawson Square.

The governor-general's wife hosts a People-to-People tea party on the last Friday of each month (January to August) at Government House in Nassau.

Rental Accommodations

The Bahamas boasts hundreds of private houses for rent, from modest cottages to lavish beachfront villas, often attached to resort hotels to which you have access. These units are a great way to establish your independence and are very cost-effective if you're traveling with your family or a group of friends.

Many are self-catering apartments in plain condo-style units. Most have a fully equipped kitchen; some have only a kitchenette, often tiny, with a small one- or two-ring gas burner. A few have their own swimming pool, tennis court, and/or boat jetty. Check carefully as to the number of bedrooms and beds, and ask whether a third and fourth person will sleep on a sofa bed or Murphy bed. Check for incidentals.

Upscale villas are almost always fully staffed with a housekeeper and cook and sometimes with a gardener and night watchman. Your rental agency should supply you with details on staff, including tipping guidelines.

Rental rates begin at US$100 per week for budget units with minimal facilities. More upscale villas begin at about US$750 weekly for a two-bedroom cottage and can run US$5000 or more for a four-bedroom estate sleeping eight or more people. Rates fall as much as 30% in summer. You'll pay a premium for being down by the beach. Expect to pay more, too, if your villa is provisioned with food. It's usual to buy your own food (costs generally run about US$100 per person per week). Your cook may stock the food for your first dinner and breakfast and should be reimbursed. He or she normally accompanies you on your shopping spree – a great way to learn about local food items and Bahamian dishes. If you let the cook do your shopping, give explicit written instructions and ask for a strict accounting.

Good sources are the classified-ad sections of *Caribbean Travel & Life* and *Islands* magazines. You can browse some of the classifieds online at www.caribbeantravelmag .com and www.islands.com, respectively.

In the UK a good starting point is TC Resorts (☎ 020-7486-3560, fax 020-7486-4108), 21 Blandford St, London W1H 3AD. In the US rental companies include the following:

At Home Abroad (☎ 212-421-9165, athomeabrod@ aol.com), 405 E 56th St, No 6H, New York, NY 10022

Villas International (☎ 415-499-9490, 800-221-2260, fax 415-499-9491, villas@villasintl.com), 950 Northgate Drive, suite 206, San Rafael, CA 94903.
Web site: www.villasintl.com

Once in The Bahamas, you can make arrangements through the following organizations:

Caribbean Management (☎ 242-393-8618, fax 242-393-0326), PO Box N-1132, Nassau

Grosham Property (☎ 242-327-0806, fax 242-327-0808), PO Box N-8189, Nassau

FOOD

The Bahamas' cuisine is a fusion of several ethnic traditions. The indigenous population was fond of seafood and callaloo, cassava, corn, sweet potatoes, and tropical fruits. English and US settlers adopted native spices, enhanced by spices brought from Africa. And basic roasts and stews followed the flag during British rule, as did meat pies and hot cross buns.

The Bahamians melded all these influences into their dishes, although in recent decades many ingredients have been ousted by North American fare. Most Bahamian food has little edge or nuance and is comparatively dull. Visitors who ask for spicy food may be handed a bottle of Tabasco.

Traditional cuisine is undergoing a renaissance, however. A new generation of Bahamian chefs is reinterpreting traditional dishes and creating new ones. A distinct Bahamian cuisine is emerging, sponsored by the Ministry of Tourism's annual Great Bahamas Seafood Festival culinary competition (see the Special Events section earlier in this chapter). Imagine crab-stuffed sweet potato with pineapple and papaya salsa, blackened conch with pigeon-pea relish and pepper coulis, and whelks seasoned in Kalik beer.

Out to Eat

There's a full gamut of restaurant types, from funky seafood shacks and burger joints to ritzy restaurants with candelabras. Restaurants range from wildly expensive (the norm) to humble roadside stands where you can eat simple Bahamian fare for as little as US$3. Small hole-in-the-wall restaurants often serve fabulous local fare; don't be put off by their often basic appearance (unless they're overtly unhygienic).

Most restaurants serve at least one vegetarian meal. Larger resorts have a choice of restaurants, with one always serving buffets. The ultradeluxe hotels have restaurants that are among the best on the islands, but they can't replicate the taste and atmosphere of small, locally run eateries.

Some all-inclusive resorts that are otherwise only for guests sell evening passes that allow you to eat and drink in their restaurants, bars, and nightclubs for a single fee. Hotel may also offer bargain-priced 'Dine-Around' programs, sometimes included in the hotel rate.

Many of the restaurants geared to the tourist trade are overpriced. See Costs, earlier in this chapter, for some examples.

Groceries are also expensive. Many canned and packaged goods are imported and cost up to three times what you might pay at home. With the exception of Nassau, you'll be hard pressed to find fresh fruits, vegetables, and spices at markets and roadside stalls. Consider taking favorite food items with you.

If your luck runs thin with rod and reel, you'll find fresh fish sold everywhere in the islands. Most settlements have either a makeshift market – where fishermen filet and sell their fresh catches of dolphin (the fish), grouper, conch, and lobster (in season) – or a cache in someone's home.

Snacks

Bahamians have taken to processed snack foods in a big way, and even the most faraway spot is sure to have a local shack selling snacks, from candy bars to cookies and other packaged snack foods. Nassau and Freeport also count dozens of name-brand fast-food outlets.

Very few food outlets open on Sunday. I've lost count of the number of times I was reduced to a lunch of peanuts, a Snickers bar, orange juice, and water while researching this book.

Main Dishes

Rice (imported) is the dietary staple, usually eaten with peas, such as red beans, pigeon peas, or lima beans. Another favorite is grits (ground corn), also usually mixed with peas. Peas find their way into hearty soups along with okra, meats, and vegetables. Potato salad often takes the place of rice.

Breakfasts tend toward US style, often with grits. Local breakfast favorites are tuna and grits, corned beef hash and grits (one of my favorites), and eggs and grits.

Seafood   Conch, crab, grouper, jack, lobster, shrimp, snapper, turbot, and tuna are all daily staples of Bahamian cooking, often cooked with carrot, cassava, cucumber, grits, guinea corn, okra, plantain, and wild spinach.

The sovereign dish is conch (pronounced 'conk' in The Bahamas). This tough mollusk is served pounded, minced, and frittered; marinated and grilled; or even raw as a ceviche or conch salad (diced with onions, celery, pepper, and cucumber, and soaked in lime juice). 'Scorched' conch is not sizzled by flames; it's a conch salad in which the conch is scored, not diced. Almost every eatery in the nation serves 'cracked conch' (battered and deep-fried), conch chowder, and conch fritters ('rhythm pills,' named for their aphrodisiac properties) fried on a grill. Often it is steamed or stewed in brown gravy.

It is somewhat rubbery and relatively tasteless. So why the fuss? Probably because it is considered an aphrodisiac capable of 'givin' men a strong back.' (Recall the scene in *Thunderball* where James Bond offers his delectable dining companion a bowl of conch chowder? She declines, hinting that 007's libidinous allure needs no artifice.)

Lobsters (crawfish) are other favorites, though being pricey they are not as important a staple as you may imagine.

Land crabs are also highly prized (and highly priced). Don't be surprised to see a car come to a screeching halt and its occupant hop out to chase down a land crab on the road. Baked crab is most popular, often with crab roe and meat mixed together, seasoned with bread crumbs.

The favorite fish is grouper, a mild-flavored white fish, often served poached, grilled, or steamed in a mildly spiced sauce. It's often eaten as 'grouper fingers' – thin, battered strips that are deep-fried.

A favorite breakfast dish is 'boil' fish,' a bouillabaisse of grouper boiled with salt pork, onion, potato, and seasonings. It is usually served with grits or johnnycakes (the Bahamian equivalent of Irish soda bread or American biscuits).

The Exumas are renowned for their turtle dishes. Turtles are a local delicacy, and each community swears by its own version of preparing the meat, which has a high scent that must be eliminated. The turtle is usually marinated and preseasoned, then chilled in aluminum foil to prevent freezer burn. It is served steamed or broiled.

Meat Chicken and pork are staples and tend to be fried, grilled, barbecued, or steamed, meaning braised in a broth of meat drippings, tomato, onion, and herbs. By far the most ubiquitous dish is fried chicken and fries (often packaged).

'Mutton' – frequently seen on menus – can be goat or lamb and is frequently served curried.

Weekends (especially Saturday, when many Bahamians shun the home kitchen) are the time for souse, a clear 'mess of pottage' (meats boiled in saltwater) seasoned with lime juice and pepper. The meat is usually that of a sheep, including tongue, trotters, and all. Local men consider it a good cure for a hangover.

Desserts

The trademark Bahamian dessert is duff or guava duff, a fruit-filled jelly pudding served with sauce made of sugar, egg, butter, and rum. It can be steamed, baked, or even boiled. Another favorite is coconut tart, a thin baked pie filled with sweetened shredded coconut filling.

Fruit & Vegetables

The islands are not the tropical Eden of exotic fruits one might expect. At one time rare and exotic fruits were synonymous with The Bahamas, most notably pineapple, which during the 19th century enjoyed a worldwide reputation. Only minuscule quantities are produced today, but look for the Eleutheran sugar loaf or Spanish scarlet varieties, considered especially delicious.

In New Providence, tiny roadside shacks proffer papayas, mangoes, pineapples, limes, and bananas. But have you ever tried jujubes, star apples, pigeon plums, Surinam cherries, sapodillas, or soursops? The following fruits are tropical favorites, and should you come across any of them, I recommend them:

ackee – A tree-grown fruit (native to Africa), the ackee has a daffodil-yellow flesh that bears an uncanny resemblance to scrambled eggs when cooked. Served with johnnycakes and callaloo and flaked saltfish with onion, it makes a fantastic breakfast. It is poisonous when unripe. It is rarely served in The Bahamas.

guava – A small ovoid or rounded fruit with an intense, musky, sweet aroma, it has a yellow-green skin and pinkish, granular flesh studded with regular rows of tiny seeds. It is most commonly used in nectars and punches, syrups, jams, chutney, and even ice cream.

guinep – This small green fruit grows in clusters, like grapes. Each 'grape' bears pink flesh that you plop into your mouth whole. It's kind of rubbery and juicy, and tastes like a cross between a fig and a strawberry. Watch for the big pit in the middle. It peaks in July and August, when every Bahamian seems to have some in his or her hands.

jujube – Similar to the guinep, this grape-size fruit is green when ripe, with yellow meat and a small pit inside.

mango – The mango is a lush fruit that comes in an assortment of colors. You should massage the glove-leather skin to soften the pulp, which can be sucked or spooned like custard. Select your mango by its perfume. Ripe mangoes smell unmistakably exquisite.

papaya – The papaya's cloak of many colors (from yellow to rose) hides a melon-smooth flesh that runs from citron to vermilion. The central cavity is a trove of edible black seeds. Tenderness and sweet scent are key to buying papayas. They are commonly served with breakfast plates, in fruit salads, in jams and ice cream, and baked in desserts.

soursop – This is an ungainly, irregularly shaped fruit with cottony pulp that is invitingly fragrant yet bland to acidic in taste, hinting at guava and pineapple. It's most commonly used for puddings, ice cream, canned drinks, and syrups.

star apple – This is a leathery, dark-purple, tennis-ball-size, gelatinous fruit of banded colors (white, pink, lavender, purple). Its glistening seeds form a star in the center. The fruit is mildly sweet and understated. Immature fruits are gummy and unappetizing. You should feel for some give when buying.

sugar apple – 'Sugar apple' is a strange name for a fruit that resembles a giant pine cone, with sections that separate when the fruit is ripe. The gray, juicy flesh is sweet and custardy and shot with watermelon-like seeds.

tamarind – There's no mistaking the pendulous 6-inch-long pod that hangs from tamarind trees. When brown, it is ready for picking. The shell will crack open to reveal a sweet green meat that is often used in sauces.

ugli fruit – This fruit is well named. It is ugly on the vine – like a deformed grapefruit with warty, mottled green or orange skin. But the yellow-golden pulp is delicious: acid-sweet and gushingly juicy.

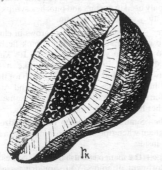

Luscious papaya stars at breakfast.

You may also come across breadfruit in various guises. This starchy fruit is popular throughout the islands and grows wild. The round fruits weigh up to 4 lbs. Young or immature fruit is either added to soups or served as an accompaniment to main dishes. The mature (but not yet ripe) fruit is roasted or deep-fried.

Among vegetables, the Irish potato has traditionally had pride of place, although more creative chefs are now using pumpkin, plantain, and sweet potato.

DRINKS
Nonalcoholic Drinks

Coffee drinkers be forewarned: Coffee in The Bahamas is *awful!* The problem is caused by the brackish local water. Few resorts have cottoned on to making coffee with bottled, purified water. Outside upscale hotels and restaurants, most coffee is instant, such as Sanka or Nescafé, served from a jar and whitened with sweetened condensed milk. Only a handful of places serve espresso or cappuccino.

Tea is served to US standards: a cup of hot water with a teabag on the side. It's enough to make a Brit's heart sink. Bush teas are still commonly brewed by locals, but you'll rarely see these offered commercially.

Soft drinks are readily available. In addition to North American favorites such as Coca-Cola and 7-Up, an assortment of local equivalents are offered, such as Goombay Punch. Ginger ale is very popular, as is nonalcoholic malt stout. Fruit juices are widely available, as is bottled water.

Alcoholic Drinks

The Bahamas rightfully claims one of the world's premier brews: Kalik. This light, sweet, lager-style beer is perfect for hot days (3.5% alcohol). It sells for US$1 to US$3 a bottle, depending on the standard of bar. The more robust and superb Kalik Gold is twice the strength and guaranteed to give you a buzz. Lucayan Lager was introduced in 1999; it's brewed by the Grand Bahama Brewing Co, which also brews Hammerhead Beer. Bahamians also drink locally brewed Heineken, plus Amstel and

US and Canadian beers. Bottled Guinness is popular.

The second drink of choice is rum. The poorer classes tend to shoot shots of cheap, overproof white rum, but there is an excellent range of quality rums, including Bacardi, which has a factory on New Providence.

Various locally produced rum liqueurs also find their way into cocktails. Nassau Royale is a rumlike liqueur with a hint of vanilla, good on the rocks or mixed with light rum to make a Rum Royal. Other flavored rums include coconut rum, banana rum, and pineapple rum sold under the Ricardo label.

Many bars serve a house libation, often concocted through weeks-long taste tests. Some drinks, though widely copied, have become synonymous with their place of origin, such as the Goombay Smash, invented by Miss Emily's Blue Bee Bar on Green Turtle Cay and consisting of coconut rum, Bacardi Gold, and fruit punch. Most seek to produce an effect – from a mild glow to complete disorientation – by using copious amounts of rum, often married to tequila, whiskey, or vodka. The concoctions – usually combining three flavors of rum – are disguised with fruit juice to cut the alcohol flavor and lend sweetness.

Each drink's name is a good guide to its potency. Thus, despite banana rum, coconut rum, gin, scotch, vodka, *and* 151-proof rum, the Tranquil Turtle (the house drink at the Bluff House on Green Turtle Cay) is 'very nice because it's not lethal. You can actually get up and walk around after four or five and not make a fool of yourself,' claims manager Martin Havill. Yeah, right! The neighboring Green Turtle Club makes no such claim for its Tipsy Turtle.

Cocktails range from US$3 in local bars to twice that in ritzier hotels.

Wines are widely available but costly. Often they have not been well protected from the heat. Wine connoisseurs should head to Graycliff in Nassau; its owner, Enrico Garzaroli, claims the largest wine collection in the Caribbean, with some rare vintages offered at US$5000.

ENTERTAINMENT
Pubs & Bars
In downtown Nassau there are several English-style pubs and others with an international flavor. These get a mixed crowd, as do hotel bars, which range in decor from rustic to elegant, often in a nautical theme.

Throughout the islands, locals tend to sup in 'satellite lounges' (the name refers to a satellite TV on the premises; watching basketball and other US sports is the main activity of the Bahamian men who hang out in bars, though pool and dominoes are also popular). Most bars are of this type. A rake 'n' scrape band is often featured. Visitors are always welcome. Very few bars are to be feared.

You'll rarely see Bahamian women drinking alone in bars, although frequently they'll visit with their boyfriend or spouse (or someone else's).

Discos & Clubs
Nassau and Paradise Island have numerous dance clubs popular with foreign visitors and urbane locals. The more upscale clubs boast modern decor and are ridiculously expensive. Here dress codes are enforced. These places are for serious dancing. Few such clubs get going before 11 pm and most usually stay open until 4 am.

More downscale clubs in Nassau and Freeport tend to attract a lot of fun-loving college types, especially during spring break. Wet T-shirt contests and beer-drinking contests are standard fare. One even has bungee-jumping…after half a dozen beers, *I don't think so!*

All dance clubs offer Ladies' Nights with free admission for women.

The Family Islands are altogether more down-to-earth affairs. Clubs tend, in general, to cater to the local crowd and often feature a live band.

Larger upscale resorts usually have their own clubs for patrons, but they're invariably open to the public for a small cover charge.

Casinos & Floorshows
Gambling is legal, and thousands of people visit The Bahamas to try their hand with

Lady Luck. The games include baccarat, blackjack, craps, roulette, and video poker. Some casinos have a Big Wheel and a sports book section.

You must be at least 18 years old to gamble. Only foreigners may gamble; Bahamians may enter casinos but cannot gamble. Admission is free. Free drinks are provided while you play. Bare feet and swimwear are not permitted and skimpy clothing is frowned upon, although tastefully elegant minimalism seems to be welcomed. Casinos are open 10 am to 4 am daily; the slot machines are open 24 hours a day.

At press time there were three casinos in The Bahamas:

The Casino at Atlantis, (☎ 242-363-3000) Paradise Island, New Providence

The Casino at Bahamia, (☎ 242-352-6721) Freeport, Grand Bahama

Crystal Palace Casino, (☎ 242-327-6200) Cable Beach, New Providence

Additional casinos were under construction at The Lucayan, on Grand Bahama, and at the Four Seasons Great Exuma, on Great Exuma.

The casinos each have Las Vegas–style revues featuring comedians, a magician, crooners, and song-and-dance routines.

Rock

This is not the music of the islands. Acclaimed rock performers rarely visit, and DJs are disinclined to play rock music. The more popular dance clubs in Nassau and Freeport occasionally intersperse favorite rock tunes from the 1960s and '70s.

Many bars have jukeboxes, usually with some rock sounds.

Jazz

The genre is growing in popularity. Several venues in Nassau and Freeport cater to jazz lovers, and leading jazz artists occasionally perform. An international jazz festival is held each summer in Nassau.

Folk & Traditional Music

Traditional rake 'n' scrape music is a highlight of many local bars and festivities such as Family Island regattas. The musical form has been incorporated into a handful of 'native shows.'

Opera & Classical Music

Nassau and Freeport each have venues offering classical music. See the regional chapters for details.

The benefit season gets into swing in winter, when concerts are as thick as baubles on a fir tree. At Christmas you can hear the Royal Bahamas Police Force Band and local musicians perform holiday classics at the Police Band Annual Christmas & Classical Concert.

Occasional soirées may be hosted locally. Keep your eyes on local notice boards and newspapers.

Gambling

Daunted by the sight of suave sophisticates calmly moving their tokens into place on the mysteriously patterned green felt of a gaming table? Then take a class. The Casino at Atlantis on Paradise Island (see the New Providence chapter) offers a crash 'Gambling 101' course each afternoon at 3 pm. You can take a visual tour of the casino at www.atlantis.com.

The hour-long sessions are guaranteed to help you take a step up from the slots. The course includes important aspects of casino etiquette. For example, never *ask* the dealer for a card; instead, tap the table lightly. Don't say 'no' or shake your head if you don't want a card; instead, give a slight sideways hand signal 1 inch above the table.

Here are three rules to remember:
• You are playing a game. It's for enjoyment.

• Make a budget for each day of play. Establish one budget for winning and one for losing.
• Don't touch tomorrow's money.

Cinemas

There are cinemas in Nassau, Freeport, and Abaco. First-run Hollywood hits are strongly favored. There are very few cinemas in the Family Islands.

Theater, Ballet & Contemporary Dance

The theatrical arts are quite lively in Nassau and, to a lesser degree, in Freeport; must less so on Family Islands. See the regional chapters for details.

Watch for performances by the Nassau Players, Bahamas School of Theater, Dundas Repertory Company, and, on Grand Bahama, the Freeport Players Guild and Grand Bahama Players.

Traditional Bahamian dialect is increasingly being honored on stage, headlined by the James Catalyn and Friends company in Nassau.

The National School of Dance, Nassau Civic Ballet, and New Breed Dancers are among the leading dance companies.

Check local newspapers for current and forthcoming performances.

SPECTATOR SPORTS

The Bahamas is not a major venue for spectator sports. The BTO (☎ 242-322-7501, fax 242-328-0945) can provide a calendar of major events, as can Bahamas Sports Marketing (☎ 242-322-4267).

Baseball is the primary team sport, and you may chance upon games on any of the islands. Bahamians are also fond of cricket, though not as much as you'd imagine for a former British colony. And rugby is popular: The Bahamas hosts the Freeport Rugby Club Annual Easter Rugby Festival on Grand Bahama in March.

Regattas are held on most of the major islands and feature locally made sailing craft vying against each other. A powerboat race is held off Nassau each September.

Track and field events are hosted at the Queen Elizabeth Sports Centre (☎ 242-323-5163) on Thompson Blvd in Nassau. Several road races are also held (see the Special Events section earlier in this chapter).

SHOPPING
Duty-Free Goods

The two main resort towns, Nassau and Freeport, and major settlements have a wide choice of duty-free stores stocked with perfumes, Cuban cigars, Italian leathers, Colombian emeralds, plus china, crystal, gold, silverware, linens, watches, and silks.

Since uncut gemstones can be exported duty free, jewelry constitutes a major trade item. Need a new watch? This could be the place for a first-class Swiss model. Many items can be bought at up to 30% below US or European retail prices. Prices vary between stores, however, so it pays to comparison-shop. No domestic sales tax is charged on duty-free purchases.

Destination Bahamas, a coffeetable book found in many hotel rooms, provides comprehensive information on where to shop for duty-free goods.

Paying by credit card is best, as this protects you if the item is defective (some card companies provide buyers' insurance). Most items are not bonded: You simply take your purchase away. In certain cases you may find that you cannot walk out with your purchase; instead, the goods will be delivered to your hotel or cruise ship.

For further information, contact the Nassau Tourist Development Board (☎ 242-394-3575), PO Box SS-5256, Nassau, which accredits merchants meeting required levels of quality and authenticity. Look for the pink-flamingo logo.

Warning: Not all duty-free items are bargains. Check the price of items prior to leaving your home country so that you can determine your actual savings.

Arts & Crafts

The Bahamas is well known for its busy straw markets, as Bahamian weavers were among the first in the Caribbean region to take their skills to commercial heights. You'll find crafts stores virtually everywhere, selling baskets, bags, mats, dolls, and hats woven from the top fronds of coconut palms. Other straw crafts are woven from silver-top or pond-top palm, harvested during a new moon according to tradition.

The local weaving industry has withered in recent decades, and much of the strawwork for sale in Nassau is actually imported from Taiwan and the Orient (yes, even if it has 'Made in Bahamas' stitched across the front in blazing colors)! Fortunately, traditional art has begun to make a comeback, especially on Long Island, which is renowned for its more than two dozen plaiting styles. Andros also claims its own unique style of basketry, often decorated with locally made Androsia batik, a colorful, handmade, authentically Bahamian product from which Androsians fashion clothing and fabrics representing the simplicity and beauty of the Family Islands.

There are dozens of art galleries throughout the chain. The Abacos are particularly blessed, for here reside some of the islands' most famous artists; originals by collector-name artists can be had for a relative steal.

Cigars

Fine handmade cigars from Cuba are all the rage in The Bahamas. Many locals smoke 'em, and many US visitors like to blow smoke at the four-decade-stale US embargo by drawing on a communist stogie.

Virtually every giftshop worth its salt sells top-class Havana cigars at bargain prices (you can purchase a box of 25 cigars for as little as US$45). Nassau and Freeport boast well-stocked tobacco shops dedicated to cigar lovers.

US citizens should know that it is illegal to purchase any Cuban-made product without a license to do so, whether you're buying inside or outside Cuba. Your Cuban cigars will be confiscated by US customs agents if discovered (only rarely is anyone ever arrested or prosecuted, and then only for attempting to smuggle large volumes). Even foreign citizens are barred from bringing goods of Cuban origin into the US…including passengers in transit! No worries: The Graycliff Cigar Co in Nassau makes cigars hand-rolled by Cuban workers under the tutelage of Fidel Castro's ex-roller. These Bahamian cigars, sold under the Graycliff and Bahiba labels, are perfectly legal.

Outdoor Activities

The Bahamas and the Turks and Caicos have a panoply of sports and special-interest activities for those to whom beach bumming spells boredom. The island chapters have more specific information, including details on sites of particular interest for each activity and contact information for local activity tour operators.

FISHING
Bonefishing
The gin-clear waters of the sandbanks that shelve the perimeters of most islands are made for battles with the bonefish: pound for pound, one of the world's fighting champions. The archipelago's sandy flats and channels are rated as perhaps the world's greatest location for stalking the wary *Albula vulpes*, a saltwater specter. The large-eyed, fork-tailed critter, a relative of the herring, is named for its complex skeletal structure. It makes for bony eating.

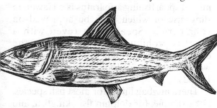

The fish, which average 5 to 10 lbs apiece, are bottom-feeders and pockmark the sandy ocean floor with their snoutlike mouths as they forage for crabs and shrimp, which they root out like vacuums. The fish is also called the 'white fox' or 'gray ghost,' for its flanks are silver mirrors – uncannily efficient camouflage – and when it forages over the green turtle grass, it is nearly invisible. Hushed anglers cast in waters so clear that they can see the fish's shadow before the fish itself appears. It spooks easily, however, and is hard to hook, which adds to the thrill of the chase. The slightest noise will scatter an entire school. All you'll see is a puff of silt where the fish had been.

Finding the fish is half the fun...or frustration. The bone is nomadic and fickle about tides, feeding at the flow of one site and the neap of another. It is also highly sensitive to water temperature and will desert waters below 70°F. You can't zip in with an outboard. You need to punt along with a long pole in about 3 feet of water, your osprey-eyed guide standing in the prow. Once the fish is found, you'll have one chance to strike...something sure to humble even the most experienced caster and a sure bet for piscatorial anecdotes over a consolation cocktail.

Since the fish look down to feed, your bait or fly must be presented below them. You should consult local guides for advice about tackle. Once a fish is hooked, you cannot risk the slightest fault. Despite its small size, it is considered the most sporting of quarries. Once you hook one, it'll tear away with 150 yards of your line and you'll think it will never stop. Sometimes it won't. Touch the reel when it flies and the fish may break your line. But once you've won the battle – and to ensure their survival (most bonefish are released) – you must reel them in quickly.

Light, drab-colored clothing is essential. You'll also need polarized sunglasses and a long-peaked hat, ideally with a dark underside to improve vision. You don't need a permit.

Bonefish can be caught year-round, but April and May – spawning time – are the most productive months: Large numbers shoal, and the flats may become cloudy. Such hot spots are called 'muds,' and here you can expect brisk sport. Look for a tell-tale uniform ripple, or 'nervous water,' on the shallows.

Many lodges are dedicated to bonefishing. The Peace & Plenty Bonefish Lodge on Great Exuma even sponsors an intensive fishing course in April and November (see the Exumas chapter).

There are local bonefishing guides on all islands. Rates begin at about US$150/250 half/full day for two anglers. If you prefer to go out on your own, bait and tackle are sold and rods rented at many fishing lodges.

The prime bonefishing tournaments are the Annual Staniel Cay Bonefish Tournament in the Exumas in August; the Annual Bahamas Bonefish Bonanza at George Town (Great Exuma) in October; and the annual invitation-only Bahamas National Bonefishing Championships, with a changing venue.

The Bahamas gets the fanfare for bonefishing, but the Turks and Caicos give it a run for its money. There are 2000 sq miles of flats between Grand Turk and Provo! No wonder a *Sports Illustrated* writer called the area 'the ultimate bonefishing flat.' You'll find guides on all the islands.

Sport Fishing

As fans of Ernest Hemingway know, the archipelago's ocean waters are a pelagic playpen for schools of blue and white marlin, dolphin fish, wahoo, and tuna. And reef or bottom fishing for snapper, yellowtail, or grouper the size of VW Beetles is sure to bring a succulent taste to your dinner table.

Where & When Any island is good at any time of year. However, individual species have prime seasons and locations:

amberjack – Favors reef areas and wrecks; November to May

barracuda – Favors reefs but found all over, including shallow water; year-round

blackfin tuna – Found all over but especially plentiful near Nassau; May to September

blue marlin – Gulf Stream waters from the Biminis to Walker's Cay, Chub Cay, the Tongue of the Ocean off Andros, both sides of Exuma Sound, and the Atlantic from Green Turtle Cay (Abacos) to south Eleuthera; year-round, especially June to August

bluefin tuna – Gulf Stream waters from the Biminis to Walker's Cay; especially May and June

dolphin fish – All deep-water regions; winter and spring

grouper – All reef areas; year-round

kingfish – Throughout the region, especially the Berry Islands and western Abacos; May to July

sailfish – Berry Islands, Gulf Stream waters from the Biminis to Walker's Cay, and Exuma Sound; summer and fall

tarpon – Andros and Biminis; year-round

wahoo – San Salvador, waters south of Cat Island, Exuma Sound, south Eleuthera, and Providence Channel; November to April, especially January and February

white marlin – Northwest Providence Channel and the Atlantic from Walker's Cay to Exuma Sound; winter and spring

Regulations Fishing is strictly regulated. Visiting boaters must have a permit to engage in sport fishing (US$20 per trip or US$150 yearly for up to six reels). Vessels with more than six reels are charged US$10,000 annually! No foreign vessels may fish commercially.

You can obtain a permit at your port of entry or in advance from the Director of Fisheries, Dept of Fisheries (☎ 242-393-1777), PO Box N-3028, Nassau, The Bahamas, who can also supply current fishing rules and regulations.

Scuba equipment and air compressors may not be used to catch fish. The only permitted spearfishing apparatus is a Hawaiian sling, use of which must be approved on your permit. Spearfishing (even with a sling) is prohibited within 1 mile of the coasts of New Providence and Freeport and within 200 yards of the coasts of all Family Islands.

There are bag limits for most fish species. For example, for dolphin fish, kingfish, and wahoo, only six fish (any combination) per person on a vessel are permitted. All other migratory fish *must* be released to the sea without undue injury. Only 20 bonefish per person are permitted. You may catch only 10 conchs, all of which must have a well-formed lip; lobster catch (in season only) is limited to six per person at any one time, and no egg-bearing 'crawfish' may be taken.

The capture, possession, or molestation of coral, marine turtles, and marine mammals is forbidden, as is long-line and net fishing. Other restrictions exist.

Charters Dozens of commercial operators offer sport-fishing charters. Rates begin at

US$200 for a half-day and US$350 for a full day, with bait and tackle provided. You normally provide your own food and drinks. Most charter boats require a 50% deposit (if you cancel, you should do so at least 24 hours before departure to avoid losing your deposit). Some operators keep half the catch. Discuss terms with the skipper prior to setting out. Never book your trip or negotiate arrangements with bystanders on the dock or beach.

Tours Several companies offer fishing tours to The Bahamas. Try the following:

Angler Adventure
(in the US ☎ 860-434-9624, 800-628-1447, fax 860-434-8605, inq@angleradventures.com) PO Box 872, Old Lyme, CT 06371, USA
Web site: www.angleradventures.com.

Fishing International
(in the US ☎ 707-539-3366, 800-950-4242, fax 707-526-3474, fishint@fishinginternational.com) PO Box 2132, Santa Rosa, CA 95405, USA
Web site: www.fishinginternational.com

Frontiers International
(in the US ☎ 724-935-1577, 800-245-1950, fax 724-935-5388, info@frontierstravl.com) PO Box 959, Wexford, PA 15090, USA
Web site: www.frontierstravl.com

Gillie Fly-Fishing Vacations
(in the US ☎ 800-441-3032, fax 914-632-2712, gillieny@aol.com) The Gillie, 781 Pelham Road, Suite 1G, New Rochelle, NY 10805
Web site: www.gillie.com.

Pan-Angling Travel Service
(in the US ☎ 312-263-0328, 800-533-4253, fax 312-263-5246, experts@panangling.com) 180 N Michigan Ave, suite 303, Chicago, IL 60601
Web site: www.panangling.com

Tournaments The Bahamas hosts dozens of major fishing tournaments every year (most are April to June), from big-game contests for serious contenders to laid-back, family-oriented tournaments.

Key contests include the following:

February
Bahamas Wahoo Tournament, Biminis

March
Bacardi Rum Billfish Tournament, Biminis
Hemingway Billfish Tournament, Biminis

April
Bimini Break (Blue Marlin) Rendezvous, Biminis
Boat Harbour All Fish Tournament, Marsh Harbour (Abacos)
Chub Cay Championship (Bahamas Billfish Championships), Berry Islands
North Abaco Championship (Bahamas Billfish Championships), Marsh Harbour (Abacos)

May
Green Turtle Club Fishing Tournament, Green Turtle Cay (Abacos)
Treasure Cay Fishing Tournament (Bahamas Billfish Championships), Treasure Cay (Abacos)
Walker's Cay Billfish Tournament, Walker's Cay (Abacos)

June
Boat Harbour Championship (Bahamas Billfish Championships), Marsh Harbour (Abacos)
Cat Cay Billfish Tournament, South Cat Cay

July
Chub Cay Blue Marlin Tournament, Berry Islands
Harbour Island Championship, Eleuthera

August
Big Game Club Family Tournament, Biminis
Bimini Native Fishing Tournament, Biminis

September
Big Game/Small BOAT Tournament, Biminis

November
All Wahoo Fishing Tournament, Biminis

December
Adam Clayton Powell, Jr, Memorial Fishing Tournament, Biminis

Turks and Caicos The Turks and Caicos lie on a major route for migrating Atlantic blue marlin, passing by in fantastic numbers from June to August. All the other game fish of The Bahamas can be caught here, too.

Provo boasts several marinas where fishing boats can be chartered (see the Caicos Islands chapter). Prices are similar to those in The Bahamas.

A permit is required. No spearfishing (including Hawaiian slings) or scuba gear is allowed, nor may visiting vessels take conch or lobster. Information on regulations can be obtained from the Dept of Environment and Coastal Resources, c/o Ministry of Natural Resources (☎ 649-946-2801, fax 649-946-2751).

The island nation hosts several annual competitions, including the Turks and Caicos International Billfish Tournament, held the second week of July on Provo, followed by an Invitational Billfish Tournament. Together they comprise the Turks and Caicos Billfish Challenge. The annual Grand Turk Game Fishing Tournament is held at the end of July or in early August.

Marlin fishing is excellent here.

BOATING & SAILING

With more than 3000 islands and cays scattered over 100,000 sq miles of ocean, the region is a boater's dream.

Favored areas are the protected waters of the Sea of Abaco (between Great Abaco and the Abaco Cays) and Exuma Sound. Both are good for beginning sailors, as the waters are shallow and sheltered and sailors are always within sight of land. The Sea of Abaco has the advantage of Marsh Harbour, capital of boating in The Bahamas, which is a departure point for sailing to the Loyalist Cays. The Exumas have fewer resorts and marinas

but compensate with the Exuma Cays Land & Sea Park.

You *must* have up-to-date charts. The meager shallows, sculpted by chaotic currents and treacherous shoals, are reshaped after each storm. Absolutely indispensable guidebooks are the *Yachtsman's Guide to The Bahamas and Turks & Caicos* and *The Bahamas Cruising Guide*. See the Books section in the Facts for the Visitor chapter for more recommendations, and also check the Private Yacht section of the Getting There & Away chapter for details on cruising permits and customs regulations, as well as a list of designated ports of entry.

The Turks and Caicos also offer excellent boating and sailing opportunities. See the Getting There & Away section in the Turks and Caicos introductory chapter for some details on boating rules and regulations in the islands.

Boat Charters

Both experienced sailors and novices can charter sailboats, yachts, and cruisers by the day or week. Most marinas offer boats with a skipper and crew, as well as 'bareboat' vessels on which you're your own skipper. You'll need to be a certified sailor to charter bareboat; usually you'll have to demonstrate proficiency before being allowed to sail away. All boats are fully stocked with linens and other supplies. You provide your own food, however. You can hire a cook if you want for about US$100 a day. A security deposit will be required.

Bareboat charters are usually by the week; prices begin at US$1200, depending on size. Crewed charters normally cost about double that. Skippers can be hired for about US$200 a day.

Two leading companies have home bases in the US plus bases in the islands:

Florida Yacht Charters
 Florida: (☎ 305-532-8600, 800-537-0050, fax 305-535-3179, charter@floridayacht.com) 1290 5th St, Miami Beach, FL 33139, USA
 The Bahamas: (☎ 242-367-4853, fax 242-367-4854) PO Box AB-20511, Marsh Harbour, Abaco, The Bahamas. The Web site is www.floridayacht.com.

The Moorings
Florida: (☎ 727-535-1446, 888-952-8420, fax 727-530-9747) 19345 US Hwy 19 N, Clearwater, FL 33764, USA
The Bahamas: (☎ 242-367-4000, fax 242-367-4004) Conch Inn Marina, PO Box AB-20469, Marsh Harbour, Abaco, The Bahamas
Web site: www.moorings.com

Also see Activities sections in the island chapters for details on local charter companies.

Alternately, you can use a broker, much like a travel agent, who works with a variety of boat companies for a commission. A broker will prearrange a crewed or bareboat charter based on your budgetary and other requirements, usually without charging a fee. Try the following:

Ed Hamilton & Co
(in the US ☎ 207-549-7855, 800-621-7855, fax 207-549-7822, hamilton@gwi.net) 28 Nilsen Lane, Whitefield, ME 04353, USA
Web site: www.ed-hamilton.com

Lynn Jachney Charters
(in the US ☎ 781-639-0787, 800-223-2050, fax 781-639-0216, ljc@boston.sisna.com) PO Box 302, Marblehead, MA 01945, USA
Web site: www.lynnjachneycharters.com

Nicholson Yacht Charters
(in the US ☎ 617-661-0555, 800-662-6066, fax 617-661-0554, nikyacht@tiac.com) 29 Sherman St, Cambridge, MA 02138, USA
Web site: www.yachtvacations.com

Small Sailboats & Motorboats

Most resorts provide small sailboats called Sunfish, either as part of the hotel package rate or for an hourly rental fee.

You also can rent motorboats, from small fry such as Boston Whalers to giant luxury cruisers with price tags to match, from local marinas. See island chapters for details.

DIVING

The islands are rimmed by coral reefs and offer some of the most spectacular and diverse scuba diving in the world, with 2500 miles of ocean wall drop-offs, underwater caverns, and blue holes (see below). Many blue holes are accessible from underwater caverns.

To the west, the warm waters of the nutrient-rich Gulf Stream protect The Bahamas from Florida's rain and river runoff, ensuring that the sea remains crystal clear and the coral reefs pristine.

The waters offer exceptional visibility – up to 100 feet or more, although winter fronts can stir up lingering silt. Water temperatures range from 74°F to 85°F year-round. Wet suits are not required, though they can prevent scrapes from coral.

The Bahamas boasts a dazzling display of colorful sealife, ranging from the exotic to the eerie. All the favorite stars are on show: moray eels, grunts, barracudas, stingrays, turtles, queen triggerfish, sand tigers, parrotfish and angelfish flashing their neons, and an impressive array of hard and soft coral formations. The north, central, and south islands (including the Turks and Caicos) each have their own special attractions. Most islands offer shallow and deep reefs, plus seemingly bottomless drop-offs.

There are plentiful wrecks, including ships, planes, and – *wow!* – even a wreck of an 1865 train off Eleuthera. The Bahamas even claims part of the 'lost city' of Atlantis, just off the Biminis.

Above all, The Bahamas is renowned for wall dives – descents of the sheer-faced walls at the edges of the Bahama Banks. A wall dive is said to be like 'flying a small plane into the Grand Canyon – and the descent is like falling down a huge mountain face.' Most commercial wall dives go to about 185 feet. The effects of pressure and the dangerous euphoria known as nitrogen narcosis begin to appear at these depths, and your stay is limited to only a few minutes.

Diving is especially spellbinding March to June, when the marine life is spawning and producing megaschools.

Everything that is true of diving in The Bahamas (including prices) holds for the Turks and Caicos, which boast some of the most spectacular wall diving in the world. The deep waters of the Turks and Caicos provide endless stretches of walls, breathtaking drop-offs, and a myriad of marine life and wrecks (such as the British warship

HMS *Endymion*, which went down in 1790 and still proudly displays her cannon). By some estimates, as many as 1000 wrecks may still await discovery amid the 230 miles of unplundered reefs.

The best diving is from June to August. Winter is a time of exquisitely clear water, but it's also a time when storms can sweep in with 15-foot waves. There are no currents and visibility averages 80 feet to 150 feet. Water temperatures range from 82°F to 84°F in summer and 76°F to 78°F in winter.

Because most divers who come here are veterans, Turks and Caicos divemasters take experienced divers on adventurous jaunts. There is plenty of tamer fare for the novice. The pros get the sharks; the novices get the groupers.

Providenciales (or 'Provo,' as it is known) is the most developed and is quite spectacular, but Grand Turk is perhaps the best island for diving. The west (leeward) side of Grand Turk has a remarkable vertical wall running the island's full length as little as 400 yards from shore. The wall begins in just 35 feet of water, making it accessible to novice divers, and plunges 7000 feet in the blink of an eye. Salt Cay and South Caicos are also emerging as major dive sites.

North Atlantic humpback whales cruise the Turks Island Passage off Grand Turk in winter, as do manta rays in summer. Sometimes in winter you can hear the melodic lowing of whales as they cruise to and from their breeding grounds in the Mouchoir Banks (also known as the Silver Banks) southeast of Grand Turk. (The *ping…ping* that you might hear is said to be the deepwater sonar of Russian submarines. Remember *The Hunt for Red October?*) Schools of dolphins abound and placid whale sharks, the largest of all fish, are occasionally seen. Even sperm whales are a rare but possible sighting.

See the Activities sections, as well as the related boxed texts, in the island chapters for detailed information on key dive and snorkel sites and local operators.

Blue Holes

Many of the caves in The Bahamas are underwater, accessed either by large 'blue holes,' circular water-filled pits that look like bomb craters (see Geology in the Facts about The Bahamas chapter) or by their egresses in the limestone walls of the Bahama Banks. Most islands have blue holes.

Many commercial dive operators offer blue-hole dives for certified scuba divers. The visibility is astonishing, the sensations exhilarating. But diving blue holes is not for novices! Diving is legally restricted to an 80-foot depth for holes and 150-foot penetration in walls, and you must remain within sight of the exit. For deeper dives, you need to be cave-dive certified. It can be a dangerous business. The insurgence and resurgence of current can be colossal: 'high to low, suck to blow.' And the waters deep down can be terribly cold.

Organizations

The following organizations are good to know:

Divers Alert Network
(DAN; in the US ☎ 919-684-2948, 800-446-2671, fax 919-490-6630, dan@diversalertnetwork.org; 24-hour emergency line ☎ 919-684-8111) The Peter B Bennett Center, 6 W Colony Place, Durham, NC 27705, USA, offering divers' health insurance, covering evacuation and treatment in emergencies
Web site: www.diversalertnetwork.org

National Association of Underwater Instructors
(NAUI; in the US ☎ 813-628-6284, 800-553-6284, fax 813-628-8253, nauihq@nauiww.org) 9942 Currie Davis Drive, suite H, Tampa, FL 33619-2667, USA
Web site: www.naui.org

Professional Association of Diving Instructors
(PADI; in the US ☎ 949-858-7234, 800-729-7234, fax 949-858-7264) 30151 Tomas St, Rancho Santa Margarita, CA 92688-2125, USA
Web site: www.padi.com

Recompression Chambers

There are two recompression chambers in The Bahamas. One is operated by the Underwater Explorers Society (UNEXSO; ☎ 242-373-1244; in the US ☎ 800-922-3483) at Port Lucaya Marina in Freeport (Grand Bahama). The second is at the Club Med Columbus Isle resort (☎ 242-331-2000, fax

242-331-2222; in North America ☎ 800-932-2582, fax 602-443-2086) on San Salvador.

In Turks and Caicos, there is a recompression chamber at the Associated Medical Practices clinic (☎ 649-946-4242) on Provo.

Operators

There are dozens of licensed dive operators. Many hotels also offer dive facilities.

Resort courses (also called 'Discover Scuba' or 'Intro to Scuba') for beginners are offered by most dive operators. They usually last a few hours. You also can take certification courses lasting several days. Licensed dive operators are required to adhere to strict safety standards. *Never* go diving with one of the freelance guides that solicit business on beaches.

Costs average about US$35 to US$60 for a one-tank dive or US$50 to US$80 for a two-tank dive. Introductory half-day resort courses normally cost about US$50 and a full PADI certification course will cost US$299 to US$399. Certified divers should bring their PADI or NAUI certificate.

The Bahamas Diving Association (in the US ☎ 954-932-0051, 800-866-3483, info@bahamasdiving.com), PO Box 21707, Fort Lauderdale, FL 33335-1707, USA, publishes a free *Bahamas Dive Guide*, *Dive Guide Video*, and *CD-ROM Dive Guide*. The Web site is www.bahamasdiving.com.

The Travelin' Diver's Chapbook (Elephant Socks Publishing) is a compendium of opinions on and recommendations of dive resorts and live-aboard boats written by people who've partaken. It has a 12-page section on The Bahamas. It's a handy reference for comparing resorts and making your choice based on unbiased critiques. Contact the publisher at PO Box 1658, Sausalito, CA 94966, USA.

Another good resource is *Undercurrent*, which also offers unbiased reviews of dive locations and equipment. The Web site is www.undercurrent.org.

Many dive package tours are available from specialist dive-tour operators in North America. Package tours can offer considerable savings.

The Scuba Bimini Dive Centre (see the South Bimini section) offers tours that leave from Florida; guests stay at the Bimini Yacht Club in Alice Town, North Bimini. Scuba Bimini (☎ 954-359-2705, 800-848-4073, fax 954-462-4100, info@scubabimini.com), PO Box 21766, Fort Lauderdale, FL 33335, has scuba packages based here, too, if you don't want the air transport. The Web site is www.scubabimini.com.

Other reputable companies include the following:

Caribbean Adventures (in the US ☎ 800-433-3483, fax 954-467-3335, sales@worlddive.com) 1525 S Andrews Ave, suite 227, Fort Lauderdale, FL 33316, USA
Web site: www.worlddive.com

Neal Watson's Undersea Adventures (in the US ☎ 954-462-3400, 800-327-8150, fax 954-462-4100, info@nealwatson.com) PO Box 21766, Fort Lauderdale, FL 33335, USA
Web site: www.nealwatson.com

Tropical Adventures Travel (in the US ☎ 206-441-3483, 888-250-1799, fax 206-441-5431, dive@divetropical.com)
Web site: www.divetropical.com

See the Diving sections in the island chapters for individual dive operators and specifics on the best dive sites.

Live-Aboard Dive Boats

These boats are designed specifically for divers, with onboard meals and accommodations, and often with E-6 film processing labs. They roam from site to site on year-round, usually weeklong, itineraries. Package dive-tour operators (see above) offer charters.

Nekton Diving Cruises (in the US ☎ 954-463-9324, 800-899-6753, fax 954-463-8938, nekton1@aol.com), 520 SE 32nd St, Fort Lauderdale, FL 33316, USA, offers weeklong diving vacations aboard the deluxe, twin-hulled *Nekton Pilot*, a state-of-the-art catamaran with an elevated dive platform as wide as its 40-foot-wide stern. The company offers free 'Learn to Dive' lessons for novice trip members. The Web site is www.nektoncruises.com.

Cat Ppalu is a catamaran that operates from Nassau on six-night dive cruises. Likewise, *Morning Star*, *Pirates' Lady*, and *Sea Explorer* are three sister sailboats that depart Miami and Nassau on three- to nine-day cruises. For information, email linde@smallshipcruises.com or visit its Web site at www.smallshipcruises.com.

Other live-aboard operators include the following:

Blackbeard's Cruises (in the US ☎ 305-888-1226, 800-327-9600, fax 305-884-4214, capthook@ blackbeard-cruises.com)
Web site: www.blackbeard-cruises.com

Bottom Time Adventures (in the US ☎ 954-921-7798, 800-234-8464, fax 954-920-5578, info@bottomtimeadventures.com)
Web site: www.bottomtimeadventures.com

The Dream Team (in the US ☎ 561-848-5375, 888-277-8181, fax 561-840-7946, dream2@gate.net)
Web site: www.dolphindreamteam.com

Sea Fever Diving Cruises (in the US ☎ 800-443-3837, fax 305-531-3127, seafever@seafever.com)
Web site: www.seafever.com

In the Turks and Caicos, there are three live-aboards:

Tao is a 56-foot trimaran offering weeklong dive excursions; contact Tao Charters (☎ 649-231-6767, fax 649-941-5510, tao@provo.net).

Sea Dancer is a deluxe 110-foot dive boat sleeping 18 divers and offering five dives daily in weeklong packages from Caicos Marina on Provo (☎/ fax 649-946-5276; in the US ☎ 612-953-4124, fax 612-431-5023, divetrip@bitstream.net).

Turks & Caicos Aggressor is a 100-foot dive boat with an E-6 photo lab and hot tub. It sleeps 14 divers; contact Aggressor Fleet (in the US ☎ 504-385-2628, 800-348-2628, fax 504-384-0817, info@ aggressor.com).
Web site: www.aggressor.com

Shark Dives

Perhaps the most exhilarating experience you can have is staring eye-to-eye with a shark. Divers rarely see a shark in the wild – the critters are wary of humans and usually give divers a wide berth – unless there's food about. But as several commercial dive operators know, *feed* the sharks and you – yes, *you* – can be there as the toothy horde circles and rips.

Shark-feeding dives are offered by Coral Divers, on New Providence; UNEXSO, on Grand Bahama; Stella Maris Resort, on Long Island; Walker's Cay, in the northern Abacos; and Dive Abaco, in Marsh Harbour (Abacos). See the Activities or Diving & Snorkeling sections of the island chapters for details.

Shark Research At Walker's Cay in the Abacos, Oceanographic Expeditions (in tandem with the National Marine Fisheries Service, the University of Miami, and the Aquarium of the Americas) conducts research into shark behavior. Volunteer divers are needed to help with the work (see the Abacos chapter for contact information and details).

Whale Dives

Bottom Time Adventures and the dive boat *Turks & Caicos Aggressor* (see above) offer a special treat: diving trips with humpback whales in the Silver Banks marine park. See the Turks Islands chapter for details.

SNORKELING

If you can swim, you can snorkel, which means donning a swim mask (for better viewing), flippers (for easier movement in water), and a breathing tube that lets you keep your face in the water full time. Snorkel equipment can be rented at most beach hotels, resorts, and dive centers for about US$10 a day.

All the dive operators mentioned earlier in this chapter also rent gear and offer snorkel trips.

Out Island Snorkeling Adventures

In The Bahamas, Jean-Michel Cousteau (son of the late Jacques Cousteau, the world-famous diver and explorer) has designed Out Island Snorkeling Adventures with an emphasis on education and a focus on families.

Over 25 resorts participate in the program, which is designed for a minimum four-day stay and costs US$240 for snorkel instruction, three guided excursions, a snorkel guidebook, and your own mask, fins, snorkel, and gear bag. (The program costs US$97 without the personal gear.) Cousteau has also designed 'get your feet wet' adventures for beginners. Contact the company through the Bahamas Out Islands Promotion Board (in the US ☎ 305-931-6612, 800-688-4752, fax 305-931-6867, info@bahama-out-islands.com), 19495 Biscayne Blvd, No 809, Aventura, FL 33180, USA.

Dolphin Encounters

A specialty of The Bahamas is swimming with dolphins. Who can resist their inimitable smiles as they cavort around you, while their gleeful high-pitched songs and staccato clicking ring through the water?

The animals are far more approachable with snorkels than with noisy scuba gear. But dolphins, despite their cheery smiles, are unpredictable wild creatures. Heed the following advice:

- Remain passive if a dolphin approaches.
- Do not swim or chase after dolphins. They may perceive you as a threat and bite you.
- Never touch a dolphin, for the same reasons.
- Do not lie or swim on your back, as this can make dolphins unpredictable.
- If a dolphin becomes aggressive or unpredictable, exit the water slowly.

On New Providence, cruise excursions depart Paradise Island for Blue Lagoon Island, where you can swim with dolphins or wade out to meet them in a protected lagoon. On Grand Bahama, UNEXSO offers a variety of dolphin experiences. On North Bimini, Bimini Undersea Adventures and Bottom Time Adventures can take you out to meet wild dolphins. See the Biminis chapter for details.

The protected inshore waters of the Sea of Abaco immediately southeast of Marsh Harbour are also home to a resident population of about 100 bottle-nosed dolphins.

Bottom Time Adventures (in the US ☎ 800-234-8464, fax 954-920-5578, info@bottomtimeadventures.com) offers dolphin swims in summer (US$1395). The trips leave from Ft Lauderdale. Travelers live abord ship for 3 to 5 days, and shore time is in West End, Grand Bahama.

Natural Habitat Adventures (in the US ☎ 303-449-3711, 800-543-8917, fax 303-449-3712, nathab@worldnet.att.net), 2945 Center Green Court, Boulder, CO 80301, USA, offers a summertime 'Dolphin Watch' program that allows you to join a weeklong expedition on the open ocean aboard *Jennifer Marie*, a 70-foot schooner that accommodates eight guests. The center of action is White Sand Ridge, northwest of Grand Bahama, where Atlantic spotted dolphins are common. You don't need to be an expert swimmer. The Web site is www.nathab.com.

Oceanic Society Expeditions (in the US ☎ 415-441-1106, 800-326-7491, fax 415-474-3395), Fort Mason, Building E, San Francisco, CA 94123, USA, invites divers to participate in research trips to learn more about dolphin behavior in Bahamian waters. Weeklong trips are offered only in the summer, with accommodations aboard a 70-foot research vessel. The Web site is www.oceanic-society.org.

OTHER WATER SPORTS

Most resorts offer water sports, often included in the hotel price. At other locales you may pay extra, usually by the hour. However, motorized water sports, such as water-skiing, jet skiing, and parasailing, are almost exclusively the domain of private

Cousteau's legacy lives on in the Bahamas.

concessionaires (the hotels don't want the liability issues) who rent equipment on the beaches near resorts.

In the Family Islands water-sports facilities are mostly limited to whatever individual resorts and hotels may offer.

See the island chapters' Activities and Places to Stay listings for details on local water-sports options.

GOLF

One of The Bahamas' strengths is golf, predominantly on New Providence and Grand Bahama. The nation boasts nine courses, open to visitors for a daily green fee or to guests for free. Additional courses were in the works on Exuma.

See the New Providence and Grand Bahama chapters, as well as the Treasure Cay section in the Abacos chapter, the Cotton Bay section in the Eleuthera chapter, and the Great Exuma section in the Exumas chapter for details on new and existing golf courses.

The Bahamas hosts several leading international golf tournaments; see the Special Events section of the Facts for the Visitor chapter for a few of the more popular ones.

The Turks and Caicos' sole golf course is at the state-of-the-art Provo Golf Club.

TENNIS

There's no shortage of tennis courts. Most upscale resorts have at least one and nonguests are usually permitted for a fee.

The largest concentration by far is on New Providence, with over 80 courts. Club Med has clinics with professional instruction at its properties on Paradise Island and San Salvador. You'll also find plenty of tennis courts on Grand Bahama, on Harbour Island, and in Marsh Harbour. Many courts belonging to older properties, however, are run down, especially on the Family Islands.

Turks and Caicos' resorts feature tennis courts, notably Club Med's facility on Providenciales.

KAYAKING

Miles and miles of creeks and flats provide wonderful entrances to the redolent world of the mangroves and wetlands of Grand Bahamas and the Family Islands.

Many hotels and resorts rent kayaks or provide free use for guests. And kayaking is now being introduced as an organized activity by several tour operators. Sea kayaks are stable, safe, and perfect for novices. They are light and easily maneuverable...and silent, allowing you to glide into areas rich in birdlife.

Guided excursions are offered in the Abacos and on Grand Bahama. See the island chapters for contact information. The Exuma Land & Sea Park is a particularly good destination for kayaking. If you want a total immersion kayaking trip, the following companies can set you up.

Ibis Tours (in the US ☎ 800-525-9411, fax 914-738-1605, info@ibistours.com), PO Box 208, Pelham, NY 10803, USA, offers week-long kayaking trips from Nassau through the Exuma Cays using 20-foot-long, two-person sea kayaks fitted with sails, paddles, and a foot-operated rudder. No experience is required. Each day involves about two hours of kayaking in the morning and afternoon. You camp out at night on lonesome beaches, with comfy mattresses and tents (should you choose). The Web site is www.ibistours.com.

Ecosummer Expeditions (in Canada ☎ 250-674-0102, fax 250-674-2197; in the US ☎ 800-465-8884, trips@ecosummer.com) has similar trips. Its mailing address in Canada is PO Box 1765, Clearwater, BC, Canada V0E 1N0; in the USA write 936 Peace Portal Drive, No 240, Blaine, WA 98231, USA . The Web site is www.ecosummer.com.

Mountain Travel*Sobek (in the US ☎ 510-527-8100, 888-687-6235, info@mtsobek.com), 6420 Fairmount Ave, El Cerrito, CA 94530, USA, offers eight-day kayaking trips in winter for US$1690. The Web site is www.mtsobek.com.

Nature Quest (☎ 949-499-9561, 800-369-3033, fax 949-499-0812, natureqst@aol.com) also offers kayaking trips. Its mailing address is 30872 S Coast Hwy, PMB185, Laguna Beach, CA 92651, USA. The Web site is www.naturequesttours.com.

Bring aquasocks and snorkel fins!

CAVING

The Bahamas has spelunkers salivating. The islands are honeycombed with dozens of limestone caverns, many only partially explored and mapped.

In some, Lucayan Indian petroglyphs add to the allure. Many caves are also roosts for harmless bats.

Use extreme caution if you're exploring without a guide. Take a powerful flashlight and spare bulb and batteries.

The Turks and Caicos also have plenty of caves, notably Conch Bar Caves National Park on Middle Caicos, a 15-mile-long system full of stalactites and stalagmites. A few tour operators offer daylong cave excursions here (see the Caicos Islands chapter), but spelunkers are otherwise on their own.

Also see Blue Holes, under Diving earlier in this chapter, for a different type of caving.

HORSEBACK RIDING

Although there are plenty of wild horses and donkeys on the southern islands, horseback riding hasn't taken off as a sport or pastime. The most impressive stable is the New Columbus Horse-Riding Ranch near Cockburn Town (San Salvador), where beach and trail rides are offered and individual and group lessons are available. There are also stables on New Providence and Grand Bahama.

BICYCLING

Relatively few people explore the islands by bicycle, and few locals use them, though the relative flatness of the islands would seem to be ideal for biking.

Many hotels and concessions rent bicycles (US$8 to US$20 a day). A few places offer mountain bikes. Most, however, offer heavy single-gear pachyderms called beach cruisers, definitely *not* built for touring. The single gear is fine on the flat, but you can't build up much speed, and the slightest hill or patch of sand will stump you. Often the wheels are bent or the seat coil-springs have given way; even if they haven't, you're sure to have a sore behind after a few miles.

It is far better to bring your own mountain bike. See Bicycles, in the Getting Around chapter, for advice.

The three Club Med properties offer guided cycling excursions, as do a handful of other resorts. Few tour operators offer guided cycling trips. In Nassau, Pedal & Paddle Ecoadventures has a half-day bike ride.

Grand Bahama hosts the Tour de Freeport 100-mile road race in spring.

BIRD WATCHING

The Bahamas is heaven to bird watchers (see Flora & Fauna in the Facts about The Bahamas chapter). More than two dozen reserves protect over 230 bird species, including West Indian flamingos and Bahama parrots. Virtually any island is good, though the southern islands are best, especially Great Inagua.

In the field all you need is a good pair of binoculars and a guide to the birds of the Caribbean (see recommendations in Books in the Facts for the Visitor chapter). The Ministry of Tourism and the Bahamas National Trust (BNT) cosponsor four-day introductory bird courses on a regular basis, based at the BNT's headquarters at The Retreat in New Providence, and the BNT's reserve and museum, the Rand Memorial Nature Centre, in Freeport. See the New Providence and Grand Bahama chapters for contact information; the Bahamas Tourist Office can also provide details.

In the Abacos, Sand Dollar Tours has bird-watching trips.

In the Turks and Caicos, the best sites are the wetlands along the south shores of North and Middle Caicos. The main attraction is Flamingo Pond on North Caicos, one of several lakes on the island where flamingos and other waterfowl gather in large numbers. Another good spot is Vine Point & Ocean Hole Nature Reserve, an offshore frigatebird breeding colony near Middle Caicos. Flamingos also inhabit South Caicos and can be seen at the edge of Cockburn Harbour.

In Provo head to Northwest Point Marine National Park, where saline ponds and wetlands attract breeding and migrant waterfowl.

Grand Turk boasts the wetlands of South Creek National Park, good for spotting migrating shorebirds and waders. For rare seabirds, hire a boat and guide to take you to Grand Turk Cays Land & Sea Park, a series of tiny cays east of Grand Turk that are important nesting sites for gulls, sooty terns, frigate birds, and boobies.

HIKING

As an organized activity, hiking is embryonic in the islands. Mostly you're on your own. Trails are limited, although a few wildlife reserves have tracks. Several islands have tracks originally cut by lumber companies (others, associated with cotton plantations, were cut two centuries ago).

Many trails are overgrown. You may find hiking even a short way demanding: The oppressive heat can turn what seems like an easy stroll into a trudge.

Travel light. Always carry plenty of water. Don't attempt to hike farther than your physical health will allow. Take plenty of insect repellent, especially in summer, plus a small first-aid kit when hiking in out-of-the-way places.

Rarely will you be far from a settlement. However, it's easy to become complacent. The limestone terrain is too treacherous to permit you to wander off the track safely, as thick vegetation hides sinkholes and crevasses. It's easy to injure yourself, and phones and first aid may not be close at hand. Be especially wary of clifftops, which are often undercut and can give way easily.

Lucayan National Park (Grand Bahama) has particularly good hiking, with short trails leading to caverns and winding through mangroves and woodlands. In the Abacos, Abaco Outback and Sand Dollar Tours offer guided hiking in Abaco National Park.

The backcountry of Great Abaco and Andros is popular with hunters seeking wild boar...*beware* boars and hunters alike! Consider hiring a hunter as a guide.

Cat Island has some of the best hiking. The Fernandez Bay Village resort is a good starting point; the owners can provide maps and even a guide, if required.

On Great Inagua, trails lead into Inagua National Park, a semiarid, rugged landscape with fabulous bird watching.

In the Turks and Caicos, the Middle Caicos Reserve & Trail System has 10 miles of trails along the north coast: an entrance into the shoreline ecosystems, freshwater lakes, and pine forests. The trail system is to be extended along the entire north coast. On Provo you can follow dirt tracks along the east and west shores to Northwest Point Marine National Park.

SURFING & WINDSURFING

If you're seeking the ultimate wave, look elsewhere. There are a few spots on The Bahamas' east coasts, however, where surfers can find decent Atlantic waves, notably Surfer's Beach on Eleuthera and, most importantly, Garbanzo Reef off Elbow Cay (Abacos). Winter months are best.

Virtually the entire east side of the chain is fringed by an offshore barrier reef onto which the waves break, making surfing dangerous far out. The trade winds, however, continue to blow inside the barrier reef, so the placid stretches inside the reef are perfect for windsurfing (in the absence of other coral).

Resorts and concessionaires rent equipment on the main beaches of New Providence and Grand Bahama. Many hotels provide free sailboard use for guests. The Romora Bay Club on Harbour Island (Eleuthera) is another good bet for windsurfing.

The Bahamas Windsurfing Championship is held in January in Freeport.

The Turks and Caicos islands are virgin territory for surfers but superbly suited to windsurfing. On Provo, Grace Bay is a fabulous location for windsurfing, with the consistent trade winds behind you.

On Grand Turk you'll often see windsurfers whizzing along the waters of North Creek.

VOLUNTEER RESEARCH

Several scientific organizations offer trips in which participants engage in field research on the natural environment of The Bahamas.

Earthwatch (in the US ☎ 978-461-0081, 800-776-0188, fax 978-461-2332, info@earthwatch.org; in the UK ☎ 1865-311600, fax 1865-311383; in Australia 03-9682-6828, fax 03-9686-3652), 3 Clock Tower Place, suite 100, Maynard, MA 01754, USA, needs participants for its studies of marine environments on San Salvador, the blue holes of Andros, marine mammals, and lemon sharks. Projects, which change from year to year, have included caving and archeological digs. The Web site is www.earthwatch.org

Getting There & Away

AIR

The Bahamas is well served by flights from North America and Europe, and abundant direct and connecting airline service puts it within easy reach of anywhere in the world. Its proximity to Florida means regular, relatively inexpensive flights from Miami, Fort Lauderdale, and Orlando, as well as other East Coast gateways. Nassau is less than three hours' flying time from the northeast USA and about 30 minutes by jet from Miami.

General information about travel between islands is provided in the Getting Around chapter.

Airports & Airlines

The Bahamas has six international airports, including the two major hubs: Nassau International Airport (New Providence) and Freeport International Airport (Grand Bahama). Some flights also land at Marsh Harbour (Abacos), North Eleuthera and Governor's Harbour (Eleuthera), and George Town (Exumas).

Bahamasair, 'commuter' charters, and private planes deliver passengers to other airfields throughout the archipelago.

The following major airlines have offices in Nassau and Freeport:

Air Canada
☎ 242-377-7035, ☎ 242-377-8411

Air Jamaica
☎ 800-523-5585

American Airlines/American Eagle
☎ 800-433-7300, ☎ 242-352-5415

Bahamasair
☎ 242-377-5505, ☎ 242-352-8341

British Airways
☎ 800-247-9297, 242-377-8886

Chalk's Ocean Airways
☎ 242-363-1687, 800-424-2557

Continental Connection/Gulfstream International
☎ 242-394-6019 or 800-231-0856, ☎ 242-352-6447

Delta Air Lines/Comair
☎ 242-377-7774, 800-354-9822

LB Ltd
☎ 242-352-3389

The first number given in the list above is for the Nassau office; the second is for the Freeport office. Most airline offices in Nassau are in Norfolk House, on Frederick St.

Buying Tickets

Plane tickets probably will be the most expensive items in your budget, and buying them can be an intimidating business. There is likely to be a multitude of airlines and travel agents hoping to separate you from your money, and it is always worth putting aside a few hours to research the current state of the market. Start early. Some of the cheapest tickets must be bought months in advance, and some popular flights sell out early.

Schedules and fares are subject to change, especially in the transition from winter to summer seasons. Most airlines charge differ-

---

Warning

The information in this chapter is particularly vulnerable to change: Prices for international travel are volatile, routes are introduced and canceled, schedules change, special deals come and go, and rules and visa requirements are amended. Airlines and governments seem to take a perverse pleasure in making price structures and regulations as complicated as possible. You should check directly with the airline or a travel agent to make sure you understand how a fare (and any ticket you may buy) works. In addition, the travel industry is highly competitive, and there are many lurks and perks.

The upshot of this is that you should get opinions, quotes, and advice from as many airlines and travel agents as possible before you part with your hard-earned cash. The details given in this chapter should be regarded as pointers and are not a substitute for your own careful, up-to-date research.

ent fares according to the season (highest fares are normally mid-December through mid-April, the peak season). Fares are reduced up to 30% in low season (usually mid-April to mid-December) and shoulder seasons (between peak and low seasons). Traveling on a weekday (Monday through Thursday) may also reduce the cost. Booking early is the key to the best deals.

Use the fares quoted in this book only as guides. They are approximate and based on the rates advertised by travel agents at press time. A quoted airfare does not necessarily constitute a recommendation for the carrier.

Once you have your ticket, write down its number, together with the flight number and other details, and keep the information separate from the ticket. If the ticket is lost or stolen, this will help you get a replacement.

It's sensible to buy travel insurance as early as possible (see Visas & Documents in the Facts for the Visitor chapter). If you buy it the week before you fly, you may find, for example, that you're not covered for delays to your flight caused by strikes or other industrial action.

Some airlines offer a special email discount service. You can subscribe to receive regular updates of discounted fares at short notice. They usually apply only to weekend getaways. Visit the airlines' Web sites for information.

Departure Tax
Each individual aged six years or older must pay a US$15 departure tax upon leaving The Bahamas by air (US$18 from Freeport).

The USA
You have plenty of options. Most major US carriers, including American Airlines/American Eagle, Continental Airlines/Continental Connection, and US Airways Express, fly to The Bahamas. This allows you to use frequent-flyer and other discount promotions. The most popular routings are via Miami and New York, but The Bahamas also is served by direct flights from a dozen or so other cities.

Some airlines offer special rates at select hotels in conjunction with the purchase of a

Travelers with Special Needs

If you have special needs of any sort – you've broken a leg, you're vegetarian, traveling in a wheelchair, taking the baby, terrified of flying – you should let the airline know as soon as possible so that they can make arrangements accordingly. You should remind them when you reconfirm your booking (at least 72 hours before departure) and again when you check in at the airport.

Airports and airlines can be surprisingly helpful, but they do need advance warning. Most international airports will provide escorts from check-in desk to plane when needed, and there should be ramps, lifts, and reachable phones. Aircraft toilets, on the other hand, are likely to present a problem; travelers should discuss this with the airline at an early stage.

Hearing impaired travelers can ask that airport and in-flight announcements be written down for them.

Guide dogs for the blind will often have to travel in a specially pressurized baggage compartment with other animals, away from their owner, though smaller guide dogs are sometimes admitted to the cabin. All guide dogs will be subject to the same quarantine laws (six months in isolation, etc) as any other animal when entering or returning to countries currently free of rabies, such as Britain or Australia.

Children younger than two years of age travel for 10% of the standard fare (free on some airlines), as long as they don't occupy a seat. They don't get a luggage allowance either. 'Skycots' should be provided by the airline if they're requested in advance; these will hold a child weighing up to about 22lb. Children between two and 12 can usually occupy a seat for one-half to two-thirds of the full fare and do get a luggage allowance. Strollers (pushchairs) can often be taken as hand luggage.

ticket. For example, guests at Sandals (a leading resort chain) who are members of American Airlines' AAdvantage frequent-flyer program are awarded 1000 miles for a stay of three or more nights.

American Airlines/American Eagle (☎ 800-433-7300 for information and reservations in the USA, Canada, Mexico, or the Caribbean) has by far the most frequent service to Nassau. It has 22 hour-long flights daily from Miami (US$180 roundtrip) using American Eagle turboprops, plus four flights from Fort Lauderdale. American also flies from Miami to Freeport (US$120 roundtrip), Governor's Harbour (US$246 roundtrip), and Rock Sound, Eleuthera.

Bahamasair (☎ 800-222-4262), the national airline, flies jets several times daily to Nassau from Miami (40 minutes, US$185 roundtrip), Fort Lauderdale, Orlando, and West Palm Beach. It also offers direct flights from Miami to Freeport (US$110 roundtrip), and from West Palm Beach to Marsh Harbour (US$215 roundtrip).

Continental Airlines (in the US ☎ 305-871-1200, 800-231-0856) flies daily from Newark, New Jersey, to Nassau (US$457 roundtrip). Its subsidiary, Continental Connection, has flights to Nassau, Freeport, North Eleuthera, and Marsh Harbour and Treasure Cay, Abacos (starting at about $US200 roundtrip) from Miami and Fort Lauderdale, plus 10 other Florida cities, Atlanta, and Mobile, Alabama. The flights are operated by Gulfstream International.

Delta Air Lines (☎ 800-241-4141, 800-221-1212) has daily jet service to Nassau from Atlanta (US$369 roundtrip); New York City – La Guardia (US$355 roundtrip); and Orlando. Its commuter airline Comair (☎ 800-354-9822) flies turboprops to Nassau and Freeport (US$357) from Orlando and Fort Lauderdale.

TWA (☎ 800-221-2000) serves Nassau from New York's JFK Airport six days a week via Florida using Gulfstream International (US$182 one-way), and serves Freeport (US$493 roundtrip) five days a week from New York's La Guardia, in conjunction with Nassau/Paradise Island Express. It also operates from Florida to Marsh Harbour, Treasure Cay, and North Eleuthera using Gulfstream International.

US Airways Express (☎ 800-622-1015) flies to Nassau from Charlotte, North Carolina (US$416), and Philadelphia (US$407). It also flies from Miami to North Eleuthera or Governor's Harbour (US$289); and from Miami and Orlando to Treasure Cay (US$327) and Marsh Harbour (US$302).

To Freeport the lowest fares are offered by LB Ltd (formerly Laker Airways; in the US ☎ 800-422-7466, 800-545-1300), which flies from Baltimore, Cincinnati, Cleveland, Raleigh, and Richmond (all from US$285 plus US$62 tax), and Fort Lauderdale. It also offers air-land packages.

Chalk's Ocean Airways (formerly Pan-Am Air Bridge; ☎ 305-371-8628, 800-424-2557, fax 305-359-5240, info@chalksoceanairways.com) offers scheduled daily seaplane flights (US$222 roundtrip) to the Biminis and Paradise Island from Miami's Watson Island and Fort Lauderdale's Jet Center (☎ 954-359-0329). It also serves Walker's Cay (Abacos) from Fort Lauderdale.

Charter Flights There are two types of charter flights to The Bahamas. The first, utilizing large-body jets, is chartered by large tour operators and normally sold as air-land packages that include accommodations. Typically, three-, five-, and seven-night packages are offered in conjunction with flights. These flights generally offer the lowest fares for confirmed reservations (sometimes more than one-third less than regular airlines' prices), and can be booked through most travel agencies. You sometimes can book one-way tickets with charter airlines for less than half of their roundtrip fares. These flights are usually direct, without the hub stop common on ordinary airline flights. Few charters are listed in airline computer reservations systems, as they're operated by wholesale tour operators with whom you or your travel agent will have to deal directly.

There are drawbacks. Although you can buy the ticket without an advance-purchase requirement, you do have to fix your departure and return dates well in advance; a

Air Travel Glossary

Cancellation Penalties If you have to cancel or change a discounted ticket, heavy penalties are often involved; insurance can sometimes be taken out against these penalties. Some airlines impose penalties on regular tickets as well, particularly against 'no-show' passengers.

Courier Fares Businesses often need to send urgent documents or freight securely and quickly. Courier companies hire people to accompany the package through customs and, in return, offer a discount ticket that is sometimes a phenomenal bargain. However, you may have to surrender all your baggage allowance and take only carry-on luggage.

Full Fares Airlines traditionally offer 1st-class (coded F), business-class (coded J) and economy-class (coded Y) tickets. These days, so many promotional and discounted fares are available that few passengers pay full economy fare.

Lost Tickets If you lose your airline ticket, an airline will usually treat it like a traveler's check and, after inquiries, issue you another one. Legally, however, an airline is entitled to treat it like cash: if you lose it, it's gone forever. Take good care of your tickets.

Onward Tickets An entry requirement for many countries is a ticket out of the country. If you're unsure of your next move, the easiest solution is to buy the cheapest onward ticket to a neighboring country or a ticket from a reliable airline that can later be refunded if you do not use it.

Open-Jaw Tickets These are return tickets that permit you to fly into one place but return from another. If available, these tickets can save you backtracking to your arrival point.

Overbooking Because almost every flight has some passengers who fail to show up, airlines often book more passengers than they have seats. Usually excess passengers make up for the no-shows, but occasionally somebody gets 'bumped' onto the next available flight. Guess who it is most likely to be? The passengers who check in late.

Promotional Fares These are officially discounted fares, available from travel agencies or direct from the airline.

Reconfirmation If you don't reconfirm your flight at least 72 hours prior to departure, the airline may delete your name from the passenger list. You should call to find out if your airline requires reconfirmation.

Restrictions Discounted tickets often have various restrictions – for example, they may need to be paid for in advance, or altering them may incur a penalty. Other restrictions include minimum and maximum periods you must be away.

Round-the-World Tickets RTW tickets give you a limited period (usually a year) in which to circumnavigate the globe. You can go anywhere the carrying airlines go as long as you don't backtrack. The number of stopovers or total number of separate flights is decided before you set off, and these tickets usually cost a bit more than a basic return flight.

Transferred Tickets Airline tickets cannot be transferred from one person to another. Travelers sometimes try to sell the return half of a ticket, but officials can ask you to prove that you are the person named on the ticket. On an international flight, tickets are compared with passports.

Travel Periods Ticket prices vary with the time of year. There is a low (off-peak) season and a high (peak) season, and often a low-shoulder season and a high-shoulder season as well. Usually the fare depends on your outward flight – if you depart in the high season and return in the low season, you pay the high-season fare.

substantial fee may apply for any changes or cancellations (you should consider cancellation insurance in the event of illness, etc). Seating may be more cramped, planes are usually full, and flight times often are at inconvenient hours. And though US charter operators are bonded with the US government, if the tour operator or airline defaults, you may have problems getting your money back. Also, charter flights are often less organized than those of major scheduled carriers, and processing at airline counters often is more confused and time-consuming.

Check the Sunday travel sections of major city newspapers. Your travel agent also should be able to provide a listing.

Key charter companies serving The Bahamas include Apple Vacations (on the East Coast ☎ 800-727-3400, on the West Coast ☎ 800-365-2775), the largest operator, flying to Nassau from Baltimore/Washington, DC; Pittsburgh; and Philadelphia. It also flies to Freeport. You must book through a travel agent. Apple will not quote prices directly over the phone.

GoGo Worldwide Vacations (☎ 800-333-3454) has charters to Nassau from Newark and other destinations. TNT Vacations (☎ 617-262-9200, 800-225-7678) serves Nassau and Freeport from Boston and Pittsburgh.

See the Organized Tours section at the end of this chapter for a list of tour companies that also offer charters.

The other type of charter airlines often is called 'commuter' airlines; it utilizes small planes, usually carrying only about 10 passengers, though larger craft sometimes are used. Individual seats are sold, but small groups also can charter the planes. Fares are generally considerably lower than on larger carriers but are nonrefundable (nor can you get a credit if you miss a flight). Rarely are scheduled departures offered. Flights are also more subject to cancellation in the event that not enough people buy seats.

The following airlines offer charter service from major Florida airports:

Abaco Air
☎ 242-367-2266

Air Charter One
☎ 561-750-6200, 800-538-3548, fax 561-750-6111

Air Sunshine
☎ 954-434-8900

Bel Air
☎ 954-524-0115

Bimini Island Air
☎ 954-938-8991, fax 954-938-9524

Cherokee Air
☎ 242-367-2089, fax 242-367-2530

Dolphin Atlantic Airlines
☎ 954-359-9919, 800-353-8010, fax 954-359-9939

Island Air Charters
☎ 954-359-9942, 800-444-9904, fax 954-524-0115

Island Express
☎ 954-359-0380

Long Island Wings
☎ 242-357-1013

Lynx Air International
☎ 888-596-9247, fax 954-772-1141

Major Air Services
☎/fax 242-352-5778

Nassau/Paradise Island Express
☎ 201-467-4670, 800-722-4262

Sandpiper Air
☎ 242-328-7591, fax 242-328-5069

Trans-Caribbean Air
☎ 954-434-5271, 888-239-2929, fax 954-434-2171

Tropical Diversions Air
☎ 954-921-9084

Walker's International
☎ 954-359-1400, 800-432-2092, fax 954-359-1414

Several Family Island hotels offer charter services from Florida. (See Hotel Charters in the Getting Around chapter for details.)

Courier Flights There are very few courier flights to the Caribbean region. However, the leading booking agency for courier companies, NOW Voyager (☎ 212-431-1616), 74 Varick St, No 307, New York, NY 10013, does have courier flights to the Caribbean. You must pay a one-time US$50 registration fee. The Web site is www.nowvoyagertravel.com.

Discount Tickets Many discount-ticket agencies sell reduced-rate tickets to The Bahamas and the Caribbean.

The *New York Times*, *Los Angeles Times*, and most other major city newspapers all have weekly travel sections in which you'll find any number of ads quoting low airfares.

Numerous Web sites can help you find the cheapest airfares. Good starting points are www.travelocity.com and www.expedia.com. You'll find other discount travel sites on the Web by searching for 'discount airfares.'

Council Travel (CIEE; ☎ 212-822-2600, 800-226-8624, info@ciee.org) and STA Travel (STA; ☎ 410-859-4200, 800-777-0112) have offices in major cities nationwide. Visit

their Web sites at www.ciee.org and www
.sta.com for information.

One of the leading discount brokers is Pan
Express Travel (☎ 212-719-9292, 800-518-
7726), 55 W 39th St, New York, NY 10018,
USA. Also try Discount Airfares, with a Web
site at www.discount-airfares.com; and Airfares for Less (☎ 954-565-8667), with a Web
site at www.airfares-for-less.com.

Standby & Last Minute If you can fly on
very short notice (usually within seven days
of travel), consider buying a ticket from a
'last-minute' ticket broker. These companies buy surplus seats from charter airlines
(and sometimes from scheduled carriers)
at hugely discounted prices. The airlines
would rather fill the seats than fly empty,
and you reap the reward. Discounts can be
as great as 40% for a confirmed seat.

Most last-minute ticket agencies require
that you become a member of their club;
annual fees cost about US$40, for which you
receive regular updates.

Check out Moment's Notice (☎ 212-486-
0500), 7301 New Utrecht, Brooklyn, NY
11204. The Web site is www.moments-notice
.com.

Canada

The only scheduled carrier operating from
Canada is Air Canada (☎ 888-247-2262, 800-
869-9000), which serves Nassau (C$517
roundtrip) and Freeport from Toronto.

Leading city newspapers such as the
Toronto Globe & Mail and the *Vancouver
Sun* carry travel agents' ads. The magazine
Great Expeditions, PO Box 8000-411, Ab-
botsford, BC V2S 6H1, is also useful.

Charter Flights Canada 3000 (☎ 416-674-
2661, 877-359-2263) also flies from Toronto
to Nassau (C$389 roundtrip). The Web site
is www.canada3000.ca.

One of the leading brokers is Last
Minute Travel Club (☎ 416-449-5400, 877-
970-3500), which specializes in air/hotel
packages to the Caribbean. The Web site is
www.lastminuteclub.com.

Regent Holidays (☎ 905-673-3343, 800-263-
8776) offers charter flights and air/hotel pack-

ages using Air Transat. Its Web site is www
.regentholidays.com. Conquest Tours (☎ 416-
665-9255, 800-268-1925, fax 416-665-6811) flies
from Toronto, Winnipeg, and Halifax to
Nassau; from Toronto and Ottawa to Freeport;
and from Halifax to Freeport. Signature Vacations (☎ 416-967-1510, fax 416-967-7154) operates twice-weekly flights to Nassau year-round
from Toronto for as low as C$399. The Web
site is www.signature.ca.

Canadian Universities Travel Service
(Travel CUTS; ☎ 416-979-2406) has offices
in all major cities. It sells discount airfares
to the general public as well as to students.

Australia & New Zealand

There is no direct service to The Bahamas;
travelers from Australia or New Zealand must
fly via the USA or the UK. Direct service
between Australia, New Zealand, and the
USA is provided by the following airlines:

Air New Zealand
  ☎ 02-9223-4666 in Sydney
  ☎ 09-366-2400 in Auckland
Delta Airlines
  ☎ 02-9262-1777 in Sydney
  ☎ 09-379-3370 in Auckland
Qantas
  ☎ 02-9957-0111 in Sydney
  ☎ 09-357-8900 in Auckland
United Airlines
  ☎ 02-9237-8888 in Sydney
  ☎ 09-307-9500 in Auckland

You also can fly via Santiago, Chile, or
Buenos Aires, Argentina.

Consider a round-the-world (RTW)
ticket, which offers the option of several additional stop-overs at marginal cost.

In Australia, STA Travel (in Sydney ☎ 800-
63-7444) and Flight Centres International
(☎ 13-1600) are major dealers in cheap airfares. Other good sources for discount tickets
include Anywhere Travel (☎ 63-0411) and
Thomas Cook (☎ 13-1771, 800-06-4824).

In New Zealand try the following for discount airfares:

Brisbane Discount Travel
  ☎ 09-366-0061, 800-808040
Destinations Unlimited
  ☎ 09-373-4033

Flight Centre
☎ 09-309-6171
STA Travel
☎ 09-309-0458
Thomas Cook
☎ 09-379-3920

Check the travel agents' ads in the yellow pages and phone around.

The UK

The Bahamas is well served by direct flights from the UK. Several airlines also feed Miami, Orlando, and Fort Lauderdale from the UK, including American Airlines, Delta Air Lines, and Virgin Atlantic. American Airlines and Delta have connecting service to The Bahamas.

British Airways (☎ 020-8897-4000) offers direct service to Nassau and Freeport from Heathrow, plus daily flights to Miami. It also operates a charter service to Nassau (£358 roundtrip) from Gatwick. It's advisable to check seasonal variations in schedules, before you decide on the dates for your trip.

Bahamasair (☎ 020-7437-8766, fax 020-7734-6460), 79 Dean St, London W1V 6HY, has a sales office, but does not offer direct flights between the UK and The Bahamas.

Most British travel agents are registered with the Association of British Travel Agents (ABTA). If you have paid an ABTA-registered agent for a flight and the agent then goes out of business, ABTA will guarantee a refund or alternative. Unregistered bucket shops are riskier but also sometimes cheaper.

Two of the leading air-only travel specialists are Caribbean Gold (☎ 020-8741-8491) and Caribbean Travel (☎ 020-8969-6230).

For discount tickets, try the following travel agencies:

Council Travel
(☎ 020-7437-7767) 29a Poland St, London W1V
London Flight Centre
(☎ 020-7244-6411) 131 Earls Court Rd, London SW5
STA Travel
(☎ 020-7361-6262) 86 Old Brompton Rd, London SW7
Trailfinders
(☎ 020-7937-5400) 194 Kensington High St, London W8 7RG

Look in the listings magazine *Time Out*, plus the Sunday papers and *Exchange & Mart* for ads.

Charter Flights The Bahamas is a major charter destination from the UK. Many tour operators have contracted seats with airlines. You should be able to find fares as low as £250 in low season, and £550 in high season.

Thomson Holidays (☎ 020-7387-9321, 0990-502555, fax 020-7387-8451), Greater London House, Hampstead Rd, London NW1 7SD, flies to Nassau from Gatwick and Manchester using Britannia Airways. Other leading charter operators include the following:

Airtours	☎ 01706-260000
British Airways Holidays	☎ 01293-617000
Caribbean Connection	☎ 01244-341131
Caribtours	☎ 02075-813517
Cosmos	☎ 01614-805799
Harlequin Worldwide	☎ 01708-852780
Jetlife Holidays	☎ 01322-614801
Kuoni	☎ 01306-742222
Simply Caribbean	☎ 01423-526887
Thomas Cook	☎ 01733-332255
Unijet Travel	☎ 01444-459191
Virgin Holidays	☎ 01293-617181

Continental Europe

There are no direct scheduled flights to The Bahamas from Europe. Your best option is to fly to Miami and connect with a flight to The Bahamas.

From Milan, Italy, Ventaclub (☎ 39-2-467-541, fax 4675-4999) has weekly charter flights on Lauda Air to Eleuthera year-round.

Also in Italy, Hotelplan Italia (☎ 39-2-721-361, fax 2-877-558), Corso Italia 1, Milano 20129 and Viaggidea SRL (☎ 39-2-895-291, fax 2-846-771), Caribbean, via Biondelli 1, Milano 20141 have discount fares to The Bahamas.

In Denmark, Cruise & Travel (☎ 45-33-11-95-00, fax 45-33-11-95-01), Bredgade 35C, Copenhagen DK1260 K, specializes in travel to the Caribbean.

In France contact Alternative Travel (☎ 01-42-89-42-46, fax 42-89-80-73), 8 ave de Messine, Paris 75008, or Austral, 29 rue Dupuits Mauger, Rennes 35000.

Asia

There are no direct flights: Travelers fly via London or Florida. Hong Kong is the discount plane-ticket capital of the region. Its bucket shops are at least as reliable as those of other cities. If you can, ask the advice of other travelers before buying a ticket (perhaps on www.lonelyplanet.com's Thorn Tree discussion board).

STA Travel has branches in Hong Kong, Tokyo, Singapore, Bangkok, and Kuala Lumpur.

In Japan you might try one of the following agencies:

Alize Corporation
(☎ 3-3407-4272, fax 3-3407-8400) Aoyama Kyodo Bldg, No 803, 3-6-18 Kita Aoyama, Minato-ku, Tokyo 107

All Nippon Airways World Tours
(☎ 3-3581-7231, fax 3-3580-0361) Kasumigaseki Bldg, 3-2-5 Kasumigaseki, Chiyoda-ku, Tokyo 100

Island International
(☎ 3-3401-4096, fax 3-3401-1629) 4-11-14-204 Jingumae, Shibuya-ku, Tokyo 150

L&A Tours
(☎ 3-5474-7723, fax 3-3746-2478) No 608, 3-1-19 Nishi Azabu, Minato-ku, Tokyo 106

The Caribbean

Air Jamaica (☎ 800-523-5585) flies from Montego Bay to Nassau four times weekly, with connecting flights via Mo' Bay from several eastern Caribbean islands (fares start at US$244 roundtrip for a seven-day excursion). Cubana (☎ 53-7-78-4961, 53-7-33-4949) flies from Havana to Nassau (US$99 one-way). Also see the Organized Tours section later in this chapter.

Private Plane

About 45,000 private pilots fly to The Bahamas annually. An aircraft is an ideal way to get there and around, giving you the flexibility and freedom to flit between islands in a jiff. Distances between islands are short and the chain boasts dozens of airstrips, ranging from ex-US military facilities with 4500-foot-plus asphalt runways to short patches of crushed coral. Many of the strips are private, so check before putting down. Most have tie-downs. Some do not have fuel. Landing fees and per-day parking fees each average US$6.

Your first destination in The Bahamas must be an official port of entry (there's at least one for each island; the island chapters will tell you where it is), where you must clear customs and immigration.

Your first step in planning your trip is to contact the Bahamas Pilot Briefing Center via the Bahamas Tourist Office (☎ 800-327-7678) for the latest information.

Step two should be to purchase Betty and Tom Jones' superb *The Pilot's Guide to The Bahamas and Caribbean* (Pilot Publishing). For more on this and other books about flying small planes in The Bahamas, see the Guidebooks section of the Facts for the Visitor chapter.

The Bahamas Aeronautical Authorities (☎ 242-377-7281), Dept of Civil Aviation, PO Box N-975, Nassau, The Bahamas, oversees all flights and airports. It has an aeronautical information service (☎ 242-377-7116). Be sure to call US customs (☎ 305-526-7155) in advance, too, to ensure compliance with regulations, as improper procedures can result in whopping fines.

For weather and flight information, contact Weather & Flight Info, Miami FSS/IPSS (☎ 305-233-2600).

Should things go wrong, you can contact the Bahamas Air-Sea Rescue Association (BASRA; ☎242-322-3877, VHF channel 16) or the US Coast Guard's 24-hour Search & Rescue operations center (☎ 757-398-6231, 2182 SSB). Also see the Emergency section in the Facts for the Visitor chapter.

Air Journey (☎ 561-841-1551, 888-554-3774, fax 561-839-4441, Thierry@AirJourney.com), 4411 Beach Circle, suite 1A, West Palm Beach, FL 33407, USA, offers group tours to The Bahamas for pilots flying their own planes.

SEA
Cruise Ship

If all you want is a short taste of The Bahamas, consider visiting by cruise ship.

The Bahamas is by far the most popular port of call in the Caribbean region.

Almost two dozen cruise companies include Nassau or Freeport on their itineraries. A few also call at their own private Bahamian cays, where passengers alight for beach- and water-based fun. The rest of the Bahamian islands are usually bypassed.

Each day is usually spent at a different port of call; most travel between ports takes place at night. Ashore the cruise companies offer various tour options. Be aware that shore excursions cost extra and can add considerably to the price of a cruise. Or you can sightsee on your own. You're not going to have enough time to get a real feel for the islands.

Cruise experiences vary vastly according to the cruise company and individual ship you choose. *Caveat emptor!* One person's sugar may be another's poison. Fortunately, there's something for everyone.

The Cruise Line International Association (CLIA; ☎ 212-921-0066, fax 212-921-0549, info@cruising.org), 500 Fifth Ave, No 1407, New York, NY 10110, USA, is a handy resource. The Web site is www.cruising.org.

Most cruises that call in The Bahamas depart from Florida, and, less frequently, from New York.

Immigration and customs formalities are handled by the cruise companies upon arrival in port.

Major cruise lines include the following:

Cape Canaveral Cruise Line
☎ 321-783-4052, 800-910-7447

Carnival Cruise Lines
☎ 305-599-2200, 800-327-9501

Celebrity Cruises
☎ 305-358-7325, 800-437-3111

Costa Cruises
☎ 305-358-7325, 800-462-6782

Crystal Cruises
☎ 310-785-9300, 800-446-6620

Discovery Cruises
☎ 800-866-8687, 800-937-4477

Disney Cruise Line
☎ 407-566-3500, 800-511-8444

Dolphin Cruise Lines
☎ 305-358-5122

Holland America Line
☎ 206-281-3535, 800-426-0327

Norwegian Cruise Line (NCL)
☎ 305-436-4000, 800-327-7030

Premier Cruises
☎ 305-358-5122, 800-990-7770

Princess Cruises
☎ 310-553-1770, 800-421-0522

Royal Caribbean Cruise Lines
☎ 305-379-4731, 800-327-6700

Cruising *from* The Bahamas is generally more offbeat, offering a chance to explore some of the Bahamian islands and other Caribbean locales.

American Canadian Caribbean Line (☎ 401-247-0955, 800-556-7450, fax 401-247-2350, info@accl-smallships.com) traditionally has offered 12-day mid-winter trips from Nassau to Providenciales (Turks and Caicos), stopping at five Exuma cays, George Town, Long Island, Acklins Island, the Plana Cays, and Mayaguana aboard its 92-passenger vessels. The trips were discontinued in 1999 but the company planned to reintroduce them in 2001, with February and March departures. Write to PO Box 368, Warren, RI 02885, USA.

Catering to divers, Out Island Voyages (☎ 242-394-0951, 800-241-4591, fax 242-394-0948, ballymena@bahamas.net.bs) has the sleek 20-passenger *Ballymena*, offering deluxe cruises to the Exumas and farther afield, beginning at about US$1125 for a three-day cruise, including diving. Write them at 13 Shirley St Plaza, PO Box N-7775, Nassau, The Bahamas.

World Explorer Cruises' (☎ 415-820-9200) 739-passenger *Universe Explorer* retraces the route of Spanish galleons around the Caribbean rim, calling at places steeped in the allure of the old Spanish Main. The itinerary slates 25 hours of informal lectures and educational videos, and there's a plush library with 15,000 volumes. Each winter the vessel departs Nassau for eight- and 14-day voyages. Write to 555 Montgomery St, suite 1400, San Francisco, CA 94111, USA.

Ferry

SeaJets (☎ 954-384-8977, 877-273-2538, fax 561-844-1994, bahamas@seajets.com) operates a 250-passenger Boeing 929 hydrofoil, departing Palm Beach, Florida, at 9 am and 3:30 pm; returning at noon and 6:15 pm. The roundtrip journey costs US$99 adult, US$50 children. Return trips depart Grand Bahama at 11:30 am and 6:50 pm.

A 300-foot-long, high-speed catamaran, *The Cat*, that briefly operated between Miami and Nassau was discontinued in 2000, but may be resurrected. The old fare was US$119 roundtrip.

Private Yacht

The sheltered waters of the 750-mile-long archipelago attract thousands of yachters each year. Winds and currents favor the passage south. Sailing conditions are at their best in summer, though you should keep fully abreast of weather reports, as summer is hurricane season.

Upon arrival in The Bahamas, you *must* clear customs and immigration. Specified marinas on each island are designated ports of entry (you may not enter at any other place):

Abacos – Green Turtle Cay, Marsh Harbour, Spanish Cay, Walker's Cay

Andros – Congo Town, Fresh Creek, Mangrove Cay, Morgan's Bluff

Berry Islands – Chub Cay, Great Harbour Cay

Biminis – Alice Town, North Cat Cay

Cat Island – Smith's Bay, New Bight

Eleuthera – Governor's Harbour, Harbour Island, Hatchett Bay, Rock Sound, Spanish Wells, Powell Point

Exumas – George Town

Grand Bahama – Freeport Harbour, Lucaya Marina, Port Lucaya Marina, Old Bahamas Bay Marina (West End), Xanadu Marina

Great Inagua – Matthew Town

Long Island – Stella Maris

Mayaguana – Abraham's Bay

New Providence – Nassau (any yacht basin)

Ragged Island – Duncan Town

San Salvador – Cockburn Town

See details on each port's marinas in the island chapters.

You'll require the regular documentation for foreign travel (see the Visas & Documents section in the Facts for the Visitor chapter), including a cruising permit (US$10), which is issued at your first port of entry in The Bahamas and is good for 12 months. Ask for a fishing permit (US$20, good for three months) for your boat if you're planning on baiting a hook. Permits can be renewed annually. Your crew and guests all will need either a passport or birth certificate (a driver's license is not proof of citizenship). Depending on your time of arrival, there may be customs and immigration charges.

You'll need to clear customs again upon arrival at *each* island. It's a hassle, but The Bahamas' drug problem is such that you should be sympathetic to this policy. Anticipate the possibility of being boarded and searched by the US or Bahamian coast guard.

A full description of official requirements is given in the *Yachtsman's Guide to The Bahamas and Turks & Caicos* (see the Books section of the Facts for the Visitor chapter).

You must have a separate import permit for any pets on board. Write the Director of the Dept of Agriculture, PO Box N-3704, Nassau, The Bahamas (☎ 242-325-7413, fax 242-325-3960).

The Bahamas Out Islands Promotion Board (see Tourist Offices in the Facts for the Visitor chapter) publishes a booklet of marina information, including rates and facilities. For information about sailing guidebooks, see the Guidebooks section in the Facts for the Visitor chapter.

Maps & Charts You'll need accurate maps and charts for any voyage through the region's reef-infested waters. British Admiralty charts, US Defense Mapping Agency charts, and Imray yachting charts are all accurate. You can order them in advance from Bluewater Books & Charts (☎ 954-763-6533, 800-942-2583), 1481 SE 17th St, Fort Lauderdale, FL 33316, USA. The Web site is www.bluewaterweb.com.

The *Yachtsman's Guide to The Bahamas and Turks & Caicos* has small sketch charts, but they are *not* intended for use in navigation. Larger-scale (11 by 17-inch) versions of the charts can be ordered for US$3.50 each; they're highly detailed and durable. A complete set of 72 charts covering The Bahamas as well as the Turks and Caicos costs US$195. Contact Tropic Isle Publishers (see the Books section of the Facts for the Visitor chapter).

Waterproof Charts (☎ 800-423-9026), 320 Cross St, Punta Gorda, FL 33950, USA, publishes a series of large-scale waterproof sectional charts of The Bahamas. They mostly show physical features and are of limited use as travel maps.

US government charts of the region can be ordered through most marine stores, as can detailed National Oceanic & Atmospheric Administration (NOAA) charts. Contact NOAA (☎ 301-436-6829, distribution@noaa.gov), NOAA Distribution Division, National Ocean Services, Riverdale, MD 20737-1199, USA, or Better Boating Association, PO Box 407, Needham, MA 02192. The NOAA has a Web site at www.nws.noaa.gov.

Crewing Crewing aboard a yacht destined for The Bahamas from North America or the Caribbean is a popular way of getting to the islands. You can ask around in ports or yacht marinas for any irregular passenger services by yacht or cargo boat between Caribbean islands and The Bahamas. Check the bulletin boards of marinas: often you'll find a note advertising for crew or you can leave one of your own.

Yacht charter companies may be able to assist you.

Bahamas Boating Flings In summer the Bahamas Ministry of Tourism and the South Florida Marine Industries Association cosponsor 'Bahamas Boating Flings,' organized flotillas that cross to the Biminis from Fort Lauderdale in groups of no more than 30 vessels; participation costs US$65. For information, call the Bahamas Tourist Office (☎ 800-327-7678).

Freighter

Gone are the good ol' days when travelers could buy passage aboard the banana freighters that plied between the Caribbean and North America and Europe.

The one guaranteed option is the *Amazing Grace*. Windjammer Barefoot Cruises (☎ 305-672-6453, 800-327-2601, fax 305-674-1219, windbc@windjammer.com) offers a down-home experience on a 13-day cruise from Freeport to Trinidad aboard the *Amazing Grace*, a 'workhorse' vessel supplying the company's clipper ships in the Caribbean (none of which sail to The Bahamas). It has elegant cabins and heaps of charm. It stops at Nassau, Little San Salvador, Conception Island, Little Inagua, and the Plana Cays, plus Grand Turk and Providenciales. Its mailing address is PO Box 190120, Miami Beach, FL 33119-0120, USA.

Ford's Freighter Travel Guide (☎ 818-449-3106, 800-531-7774), 180 South Lake Ave, suite 3335, Pasadena, CA 91101, USA, and *TravelTips* (☎ 718-939-2400, 800-872-8584, info@travltips.com), PO Box 580218, Flushing, NY 11358, USA, list freight ships that take passengers. The Web site is www.travltips.com.

ORGANIZED TOURS

There are dozens of organized tours to The Bahamas. The vast majority are sun-and-sand package tours, usually using charter flights (see Charter Flights earlier in this chapter) and including roundtrip airfare, airport transfers, hotel accommodations, and breakfasts and certain other meals, all for a guaranteed price.

Most per-person prices quoted by tour operators are based on double occupancy (two people sharing a room). An additional charge ('single supplement') applies to anyone wishing to room alone. If you want a package that is specific to some activity, such as fishing, kayaking, or diving, please see the Outdoor Activities chapter.

The USA

Several tour companies specialize in The Bahamas.

The biggest charter operator is Apple Vacations, with flights from several major US cities. American Fly AAway Vacations also has packages.

Bahamas Travel Network (☎ 305-438-4222, 800-513-5535, fax 305-438-4220, info@maduro.net), 1043 SE 17th St, Fort Lauderdale, FL 33316, specializes in the Family Islands. For further information, the Web site is www.bahamastravelnet.com

Grand Bahama Vacations (☎ 800-545-1300), 1170 Lee Wagener Blvd, suite 200, Fort Lauderdale, FL 33315, a collective sales arm of 12 Grand Bahama hotels, has all-inclusive air-hotel packages with direct service from 13 cities throughout the eastern and southern US. Rates begin as low as US$299. For full information and rates, visit its Web site at www.gbvac.com.

The following tour operators also are active in The Bahamas market:

American Airlines Fly AAway
☎ 800-433-7300

Apple Vacations
☎ 610-359-6500;
East Coast 800-727-3400;
West Coast 800-365-2775

Bahamas Travel Network
☎ 305-438-4222, 800-513-5535

Caribbean Concepts
☎ 516-496-9800, 800-423-4433

Caribbean Vacation Network
☎ 305-673-8822, 800-423-4095

Changes In L'Attitude
☎ 800-330-8272

Delta Dream Vacations
☎ 800-233-7260

Flyaway Vacations
☎ 800-832-8383

Friendly Holidays
☎ 516-358-1320, 800-221-9748

Funjet Vacations
☎ 414-351-3553, 800-558-3050

Globetrotters
☎ 617-621-9911, 800-999-9696

GoGo Worldwide Vacations
☎ 800-821-3731

Grand Bahama Vacations
☎ 800-545-1300

Inter-Island Tours
☎ 212-686-4868, 800-245-3434

Island Flight Vacations
☎ 800-786-2877

Nassau Paradise Island Express
☎ 800-722-4262

Paradise Island Vacations
☎ 800-722-7466

Sun Splash Tours
☎ 212-366-4922, 800-426-7710

Travel Impressions
☎ 516-845-8000, 800-284-0044

US Airways Vacations
☎ 800-455-0123

Canada
The following tour operators specialize in The Bahamas and the Caribbean. Most offer charter flights:

Air Canada Vacations
☎ 514-876-0704, fax 514-876-3699
Web site: www.adavacations.com

Air Transat Holidays
☎ 514-987-1616, fax 514-987-8029
Web site: www.airtransatholidays.com

Albatours
☎ 416-485-1700, 800-665-2522, fax 416-746-0397, info@albatours, com
Web site: www.albatours.com

Conquest Tours
☎ 416-665-9255, 800-268-1925, fax 416-665-6811
Web site:www.travelconquest.com

Regent Holidays
☎ 905-673-3343, fax 905-673-1717
Web site: www.regentholidays.com

Signature Vacation
☎ 416-967-1510, fax 416-967-7154
Web site: www.signature.ca

Sunquest Vacations
☎ 416-485-1700, 877-485-6060, fax 416-485-9479
Web site: www.sunquest.com

Australia & New Zealand
Contours Travel (☎ 03-9329-5211, fax 03-9329-6314), 466 Victoria St, N Melbourne, Victoria 3051, is Australia's largest tour operator/wholesaler to the Caribbean and The Bahamas.

In New Zealand contact Innovative Travel (☎ 3-365-3910, fax 3-365-5755), PO Box 21, 247 Edgeware, Christchurch, which is about the only tour operator with an emerging Caribbean/Bahamian specialty.

The UK
The Caribbean Centre (☎ 020-8940-3399, fax 020-8940-7424), 3 The Green, Richmond,

Surrey TW9 1PL, offers packages to The Bahamas.

Also see Charter Flights in the Air section earlier in this chapter.

Asia

Island International (☎ 03-3401-4096, fax 3-3401-1629), 4-11-14-204 Jingumae, Shibuya-ku, Tokyo 150, specializes in travel to the Caribbean and The Bahamas.

Specialty Tours

Aside from those offering activity-related tours, very few companies offer specialty tours to The Bahamas.

An excellent resource is *Specialty Travel Index* (☎ 415-459-4900, 800-442-4922, fax 415-459-4974, info@specialtytravel.com), 305 San Anselmo Ave, suite 313, San Anselmo, CA 94960, USA, or visit their Web site at www.specialtytravel.com. It offers tours from operators ranging from Earthwatch to Sportours to Gorp Travel. The *Island Vacation Guide* (☎ 203-655-8091, 800-962-2080, fax 203-655-6689), PO Box 2367, Darien, CT 06820, USA, also lists tours to The Bahamas and Turks and Caicos.

Specialty tours are listed by activity in the Outdoor Activities chapter.

Getting Around

Perusing a map, you may be tempted to think that island-hopping down the chain is easy. It ain't, unless you have your own boat or plane. Interisland air is centered on Nassau. Getting between the islands without constantly backtracking is a bit of a feat. Even the mail boats are Nassau-centric.

Details – including fare and schedule information – can be found in the island chapters.

AIR

Interisland flights offer the only quick and convenient way to travel within The Bahamas, and islanders ride airplanes like Londoners use buses.

The scene is dominated by Bahamasair (in Nassau ☎ 242-377-5505; in Freeport 242-

352-8341; in the US ☎ 800-222-4262, fax 305-593-6246), the government-owned airline that has preciously guarded its quasimonopoly on scheduled interisland flights. Onboard service is good, the standard of piloting exemplary, there is just one class, and only rarely is seating assigned. There's even a Web site at www.bahamasair.com. The airline has been beset with mismanagement, though things have improved in the past few years.

Bahamasair serves New Providence, Grand Bahama, and all the main Family Islands with regular flights, using little 36-passenger Shorts and Dash-8 turboprop planes and small jets. Schedules change frequently and with little notice (no attempt is

Bahamasair Schedule

Schedules change frequently. At press time Bahamasair offered flights from Nassau to the following destinations:

Destination	Frequency	Fares
Abraham Bay(Mayaguana)	Monday, Wednesday, Friday	US$84
Andros Town (Andros)	Daily	US$42
Arthur's Town (Cat Island)	Tuesday, Friday, Sunday	US$60
Colonel Hill (Crooked Island)	Wednesday, Saturday	US$84
Congo Town (South Andros)	Daily	US$42
Deadman's Cay (Long Island)	Daily	US$64
Freeport (Grand Bahama)	Daily	US$64
George Town (Exumas)	Daily	US$60
Governor's Harbour (Eleuthera)	Daily	US$48
Mangrove Cay (South Andros)	Daily	US$42
Marsh Harbour (Abacos)	Daily	US$60
Matthew Town (Great Inagua)	Monday, Wednesday, Friday	US$90
New Bight (Cat Island)	Monday, Thursday, Saturday	US$60
North Eleuthera (Eleuthera)	Daily	US$48
Rock Sound (Eleuthera)	Daily	US$48
San Andros (Central Andros)	Daily	US$42
San Salvador (San Salvador)	Daily	US$64
Spring Point (Acklins Island)	Tuesday, Saturday	US$94
Stella Maris (Long Island)	Daily	US$64
Treasure Cay (Abacos)	Daily	US$60

made to notify passengers who have advance reservations). *Always double-check flight times on the day prior to departure!*

The airline operates on a hub-and-spoke system, with Nassau as its hub. Even if you want to fly between adjacent islands, such as Cat Island and Long Island, you will have to first return to Nassau. If you do a lot of island-hopping, you'll begin to feel like a yo-yo and may need to overnight in Nassau between flights. Budget accordingly.

Some flights, such as the one to Freeport, go more often than once a day; full flight details can be found in the island chapters. If possible, allow several hours' leeway for connecting flights. Flights are consistently late – often by several hours – or canceled. Occasionally they take off early! You'll often be told that flights are sold out, but don't believe it. Get yourself waitlisted, then hang up and call again: often a seat will have magically appeared. Bahamians tend to book the next available flight, then get themselves on the standby list for the flight they really want. You should do the same, calling on the day you wish to fly.

In Nassau anticipate a long wait at the Bahamasair check-in counter. Many locals will be laden with a gross excess of luggage and boxes. This is where Bahamians are at their worst. Line-jumping is common, and your complaints may be met with an aggressive, in-your-face response.

The luggage limit is 70 lbs per person. Ensure that your bags are tagged with the correct destination.

When flights are turbulent, Bahamian passengers take to calling out as if they were in church: *'Oh, Lord! Oh, Lord Jesus!'* On a *really* bumpy flight, it can get pretty loud!

Air Passes

Bahamasair occasionally offers discount passes. A reader reports that it has a 'Discover the Bahamas Airpass' for travelers arriving from Miami or Orlando, but I was unable to confirm this with sales and reservation staff.

Bahamasair also offers a frequent-flyer discount: Book 10 full-fare legs and you'll get the 11th free.

Charter Flights

Each of the Family Islands are served by commuter airlines and charter flights. Most are based in Nassau, but their itineraries often hop from airstrip to airstrip and may include several islands. Some airlines have carved out their own turf. Congo Air, for example, is the main commuter carrier to Andros.

You can also charter a small aircraft, usually carrying up to six people, from these companies. Typically, expect to pay US$200 to US$600 one-way for the plane, depending on distance. If there are several people sharing the flight, this option becomes cost-effective. This is especially true if you wish to do some island-hopping and want to save time and avoid the cost of repeatedly returning to Nassau with Bahamasair.

Charter and commuter companies offering interisland service include the following:

Cat Island Air ☎ 242-377-3318
Congo Air ☎ 242-377-5382, fax 242-377-7413
Falcon Air ☎ 242-377-1703
Flamingo Air ☎/fax 242-377-0354
Island Express in the US ☎ 954-359-0380, fax 954-359-7944
Major's Air Services ☎ 242-352-5778
Sandpiper Air ☎ 242-377-5751
Sky Unlimited ☎ 242-377-8993, 242-377-8777
Southern Air ☎ 242-377-2014, fax 242-377-1066
Taino Air ☎ 242-352-8885, fax 242-352-5175
Trans-Island Air ☎ 242-327-5979

Hotel Charters Several hotels offer charter service, including the following:

Andros
   Small Hope Bay Lodge
     (☎ 242-368-2014, 800-223-6961, fax 242-368-2015)

Cat Island
   Fernandez Bay Village
     (☎ 242-342-3043, fax 242-342-3051; in the US
     ☎ 954-474-4821, 800-940-1905, fax 954-474-4864)
   Greenwood Beach Resort (☎/fax 242-342-3053)

Grand Bahama
   Deep Water Cay Club (☎ 242-353-3073; in the
   US 954-359-0488, fax 954-359-9488)

Long Island
  Stella Maris Resort (☎ 242-338-2051, fax 242-338-2052; in the US ☎ 954-359-8236, 800-426-0466, fax 954-359-8238)

San Salvador
  Club Med Columbus Isle (☎ 242-331-2000, fax 242-331-2222; in North America ☎ 800-453-2582, fax 602-443-2086)
  Riding Rock Inn Resort (☎ 242-331-2631, fax 242-331-2020; in the US ☎ 954-359-8353, 800-272-1492, fax 954-359-8254)

A few resorts also offer charter service to and from Florida. See the island chapters for fare information.

Helicopter

Paradise Island Helicopters (☎ 242-363-4016, pager 242-340-2744) offers transportation between Nassau/Paradise Island and the Family Islands, as well as Grand Bahama. The company also offers sightseeing tours. See the New Providence chapter for times and prices.

BUS

Traveling by bus is a bomb except in Nassau and Freeport, where dozens of private jitneys (minibuses) are licensed to operate around the city on pre-established routes.

Alas, there is no public transportation on any of the Family Islands. Some enterprising individuals operate infrequent minibus service on a few islands (see island chapters).

There are no public buses at airports. The local taxi drivers' union (which has called a general strike over the issue in past years) is too powerful. Likewise, no hotels are permitted to operate their own transfer service for guests. A few larger resorts include airport-hotel transfers in their room rates, although they must defer to local taxis, which provide the service. See the Taxi section in this chapter for information on getting to and from the airports.

CAR

Driving in the islands is a no-brainer. A paved highway circles New Providence, which is also crisscrossed by a small number of main roads. A single highway runs the length of most other inhabited islands and

cays, with side roads leading to settlements a short distance away. The islands' main highways are usually called 'Queen's Hwy' or 'King's Hwy.'

Conditions vary from excellent to awful. The main roads are usually in good condition. Many have recently been repaved. Those that await their turn are often indented with deep potholes. Minor, unpaved roads are often corrugated and sometimes rutted by rain; these are best tackled with a 4WD vehicle. Believe any Bahamian who tells you that a road is bad.

Bahamians are generally cautious and civilized drivers. Traffic jams frequently occur in Nassau, but most drivers accept things in good grace, though there will often be some arrogant SOB trying to squeeze down the center divide.

As a whole they drive faster than do US drivers and far too fast for local conditions. Too many drivers can't stand being behind another car. On New Providence, be prepared for cars overtaking you with harrowing, daredevil folly. Use extreme caution and drive defensively, especially at night.

On New Providence and Grand Bahama streets are well-signed, as they are in most major settlements. Distances may seem minor, but what appears on a map to be a 30-minute journey will usually take longer.

Road Rules

Always drive on the *left*. Remember: 'Keep left and you'll always be right.' Another saying worth remembering is: 'De left side is de right side; de right side is suicide!' (However, most vehicles have the steering wheel on the left-hand side also.) Speed limits are 30mph in settlements and 50mph on main highways. Observe them.

At traffic circles (roundabouts), remember to circle in a clockwise direction, entering to the left. You must give way to traffic already in the circle. *Be cautious!* Not all Bahamians agree on who has right of way, which leads to frequent collisions.

The Bahamas has no compulsory seatbelt law, but it *is* compulsory to wear a helmet when riding a motorcycle or scooter.

Gasoline

Esso, Shell, and Texaco maintain gas (petrol) stations on most islands. Gas stations are usually open from 8 am to about 7 pm. Some close on Sunday. In Nassau and Freeport you'll find stations open 24 hours a day. Gasoline costs US$2.65 to US$3.75 per US gallon.

Credit cards are accepted in major settlements. Elsewhere, it's cash only, please!

Security

You don't need to be paranoid, especially in the Family Islands, where theft is a minor problem. Still, it's always best to park in an established parking lot when possible, especially in Nassau. Always remove any belongings from the car, or at the very least, keep them locked in the trunk.

Women can feel comfortable driving alone in the Family Islands or in Nassau. At night, avoid Nassau's Over-the-Hill area, if possible; lock your doors.

Picking Up Passengers

In the Family Islands, where income levels are low and few people own cars, filling the empty seat in your car will go a long way toward easing the burden of Bahamians forced to rely on passing vehicles. You'll often see people waving you down with a lackadaisical sweep of an outstretched hand. You can feel secure offering rides to virtually anyone in the Family Islands, but use common sense and caution when giving rides, especially in Nassau.

Mechanical Problems

There is no national roadside service organization to phone when you have car trouble. The larger rental agencies in Nassau and Freeport have a 24-hour service number in case of breakdown or other emergencies. In the Family Islands, where most car-rental agencies are mom-and-pop operations, you may or may not be given a telephone number to call.

If you do break down and must use a local mechanic, you should do so only for minor work; otherwise the rental agency may balk at reimbursing you for work they haven't authorized.

Accidents

Hopefully you won't have one, but if you "mash up," there are a few rules to obey. First, don't move the vehicles, and don't let anyone else move them, including the other driver. Have someone call the police, and remain at the scene until a police officer arrives (this may take a while). Make sure to get the name and address of anyone involved in the accident, as well as their license number and details of their vehicle. Take photos of the scene if possible, and get the names and addresses of any witnesses. Don't get drawn into an argument. Call the rental company as soon as possible.

Rental

Several major international car-rental companies have outlets in Nassau and Freeport, along with smaller local firms (see the Getting Around sections in the New Providence and Grand Bahama chapters). In the Family Islands there aren't many established agencies. Usually a few locals earn extra income by renting their private cars.

You usually rent for a 24-hour period. In Nassau and Freeport modern US-model cars are available at rates starting at US$50, but rates go as high as about US$125 for large 4WD vehicles. Elsewhere rates begin at about US$60 per day, even for a beat-up old jalopy. You can save as much as 25% by booking in advance through the larger US companies *before* your arrival in The Bahamas:

Avis	☎ 800-331-1212
Budget	☎ 800-527-0770
Dollar	☎ 800-800-4000
Hertz	☎ 800-654-3131
National	☎ 800-227-7368

In peak season you may find that vehicles are not available. It's wise to reconfirm before arrival. Usually your car will be delivered to your hotel. Allow for some flexibility in the Family Islands, where a cash deposit – up to US$500 – may be requested to cover the owner's deductible (a similar deposit, payable by credit card, is required by the major companies in Nassau and on Grand Bahama).

There is rarely a difference in rates between low and peak seasons. Most companies include unlimited mileage; a few others set a limit and charge a fee for excess miles.

Keep copies of any paperwork. Mom-and-pop operators usually don't give you any paperwork, however; they simply hand you the keys.

Before signing any paperwork or driving away, go over the vehicle very carefully to identify any dents or problems. Make sure they are all marked up or pointed out to the owner before you drive away. Otherwise you're likely to be charged for the slightest scrape. Don't forget to check the cigarette lighter and interior switches, which often are missing. Make sure there's a spare tire.

Your hotel or the rental company can usually arrange a driver for an extra fee.

Insurance Check in advance to see whether your current insurance or credit card covers you for driving while abroad. In Nassau and Freeport the major rental agencies will recommend damage-waiver insurance, which limits your liability in the event of an accident or damage. It should cost about US$12 a day – a valuable investment. American Express cardholders can waive this requirement: Most car-rental companies recognize its policy, which covers car insurance. Mom-and-pop operations don't offer insurance coverage; your deposit covers the owner's deductible, but you may be asked to accept *full* liability!

Driver's License Renters must be 21 (some companies rent only to those 25 or older). You can drive on your foreign license for up to three months. For details on longer stays, see Driver's Licenses & Permits in the Facts for the Visitor chapter.

MOTORCYCLE & SCOOTER
There's a special thrill to exploring on two wheels, and it's a good option for compact resort areas, where a car may be overkill.

Scooters are available at major tourist areas. A few companies also rent motorcy-

cles. These companies are far more lax than the major car-rental companies, though you usually still have to show a driver's license. Scooters cost about US$30 to US$45 daily, including insurance; hourly rental is sometimes offered. A US$100 deposit is typically required.

Wearing a helmet is mandatory. Count yourself lucky to be given one that fits!

Ride cautiously! Road conditions are extremely hazardous, especially away from developed areas. You'll encounter potholes, loose gravel, fast drivers, narrow roads, free-roaming goats, and kamikaze chickens. See the Car section in this chapter for more information about road rules and conditions.

BICYCLE
Cycling is a cheap, convenient, healthy, environmentally sound, and above all *fun* way to travel. Major resort hotels rent bicycles. Typical costs are US$7 to US$20 daily. Unfortunately, the bikes are beach cruisers: They're heavy, have only one gear, and the pedal also acts as the brake. They are not designed for long-distance touring and are virtually guaranteed to give you a sore bum. Mountain bikes seldom are available.

If you take your own bicycle, go over it with a fine-tooth comb and augment your repair kit with every imaginable spare. You won't be able to buy that crucial gizmo when your bicycle breaks down in the back of beyond.

Most international airlines will let you ship a bicycle at no extra charge. Bahamasair and charter airlines, however, disdain bicycles, so transporting your bike between islands might be a problem. You can ship your bicycle between islands by mail boat. (See Mail Boat, later in this chapter, for information about mail-boat travel.) You can take it to pieces and put it in a bike bag or box, but it's much easier to simply wheel your bike to the check-in desk, where it should be treated as a piece of luggage. You may have to remove the pedals and turn the handlebars sideways so that the bike takes up less space in the aircraft's hold. Check all this with the airline well in advance, preferably before you buy your ticket.

Mail-Boat Schedule

Contact the Dockmaster's Office (☎ 242-393-1064) at Potter's Cay, Nassau, for the latest itineraries and fares.

The following schedule and one-way fares applied at press time:

Destination	Boat	Depart Nassau	Duration	Fare
Abacos (Sandy Point, Moore's Island)	Captain Gurth Dean	Friday	6 hours	Call dockmaster for time and fare
Abacos (Marsh Harbour, Green Turtle Cay)	Captain Gurth Dean	6 pm Tuesday	5½ hours	Call dockmaster for fare
Abacos (Sandy Point, Moore's Island, Bullock's Harbour)	Champion II	8 pm Friday	11 hours	US$25
Andros (Mangrove Cay, Cargill Creek, Bowen Sound)	Lady Gloria	9:30 am Tuesday	5 hours	US$30
Andros (Drigg's Hill, Congo Town, The Bluff, Kemp's Bay)	Captain Moxey	11 pm Monday	7½ hours	US$30
Andros (Mangrove Cay, Lisbon Creek)	Mangrove Cay Express	6 pm Wednesday	5½ hours	US$30
Andros (Mastic Point, Nicholls Town, Morgan's Bluff)	Lisa J II	3:30 pm Wednesday	5 hours	US$30
Andros (North)	Lady Margo	4 pm Tuesday	7½ hours	US$30
Andros (North)	Challenger	Call dockmaster for time and fare		
Andros (South)	Delmar L	10 pm Thursday	7½ hours	US$30
Andros (Stafford Creek, Blanket Sound, Staniard Creek, Fresh Creek, Behring Point)	Lady D	Noon Tuesday	5 hours	US$30
Biminis & North Cat Cay	Bimini Mack	Call dockmaster for time	12 hours	US$45
Cat Island (New Bight, Bennett's Harbour, Arthur's Town)	North Cat Island Special	1 pm Wednesday	14 hours	US$40
Cat Island (New Bight, Old Bight, Smith Bay)	Sea Hauler	3 pm Tuesday	17 hours	US$40

Mail-Boat Schedule

Destination	Boat	Depart Nassau	Duration	Fare
Crooked Island, Acklins Island & Mayaguana (Landrail Point, Spring Point, Betsy Bay)	*Lady Mathilda*	Call dockmaster for time and duration		US$70
Eleuthera (Current, The Bluff, Hatchet Bay)	*Current Pride*	7 am Thursday	5½ hours	US$30
Eleuthera (Governor's Harbour)	*Eleuthera Express*	5 pm Monday	5½ hours	US$30
Eleuthera (Governor's Harbour, Hatchet Bay)	*Captain Fox*	1 pm Friday	6 hours	US$30
Eleuthera (Rock Sound, Davis Harbour, South Eleuthera)	*Bahamas Daybreak III*	5 pm Monday	5 hours	US$30
Eleuthera (Spanish Wells)	*Eleuthera Express*	7 am Thursday	5 hours	US$20
Eleuthera (Spanish Wells)	*Spanish Rose*	7 am Thursday	5 hours	US$20
Exumas (George Town)	*Grand Master*	2 pm Tuesday	12 hours	US$35
Exumas & Ragged Island (Staniel Cay, Black Point, Little Farmer's Cay, Barreterre)	*Ettienne & Cephas*	2 pm Tuesday	21 hours	US$30
Grand Bahama (Freeport)	*Marcella III*	4 pm Wednesday	12 hours	US$45
Long Island (Seymours, Salt Pond, Deadman's Cay)	*Sherice M*	1 pm Tuesday	17 hours	US$45
Long Island & Great Inagua (Clarence Town, Matthew Town)	*Abilin*	Noon Tuesday	17 hours	US$45
San Salvador & Rum Cay (Cockburn Town, United Estates, Port Nelson)	*Lady Francis*	6 pm Tuesday	Call dockmaster for duration	US$40

Mail-boat service between islands is limited to the routes shown. You cannot, for example, catch a mail boat from Cat Island to the Inaguas. Thus, if you plan on island-hopping, you may have to return to Nassau repeatedly.

HITCHHIKING

Technically, hitchhiking is illegal in The Bahamas. Still, locals (including women and children) without cars rely on it. In the Family Islands, everyone hitchhikes or gives rides as a matter of course. Many Bahamians may offer to give you a ride or a tour. Often this is done from the goodness of their hearts; at other times it becomes clear that a monetary donation would be appreciated.

While hitchhiking is never entirely safe and Lonely Planet recommends against it, hitchhiking in The Bahamas (outside Nassau) is as safe as it is anywhere. Travelers who decide to hitchhike should understand that they are taking a small but potentially serious risk. Let someone know where you are planning to go.

BOAT
Ferry & Water Taxi

The only ferry in the islands is Bahamas FastFerries (☎ 242-323-2166/8, fax 242-322-8185, info@bahamasferries.com), a high-speed ferry linking Nassau and Eleuthera.

Water taxis ply between Nassau and Paradise Island. Several other offshore islands are served by private water taxis. For example, Harbour Island and Spanish Wells are linked to North Eleuthera; Green Turtle Cay (Abacos) is served from the dock a few miles north of Treasure Cay; and water taxis run to Great Guana, Man O' War, and Elbow Cays (Abacos) from Marsh Harbour.

Government-run water taxis link islands that are a short distance apart, such as North Bimini and South Bimini; Mangrove Cay and South Andros; and Crooked and Acklins Islands. Passage is usually twice daily and usually free.

See island chapters for details; water taxi docks are on the maps.

Mail Boat

The mail-boat schedule is on the preceding pages.

About 29 mail boats under government contract serve all the inhabited islands from Potter's Cay in Nassau. They traditionally sail overnight for journeys lasting five to 24 hours, carrying passengers going 'down home' and others wishing to get a taste of Family Island life.

Mail boats have etched their names – along with those of skippers such as Edgar Moxey of the *Captain Moxey* – in the maritime history of The Bahamas. Introduction of mail-boat service was first proposed in the House of Assembly in 1819. The first service began in 1832. The principal station was on Crooked Island, where vessels carrying mail between England and the US via the Crooked Island Passage called. Packages were distributed from Crooked Island to other islands. Soon the boats were carrying other cargo. The government-subsidized, steel-hulled vessels today carry everything from vehicles and groceries to furniture and passengers.

It all sounds so Conradian and romantic, hopping aboard a beaten-up vessel – most are small general-cargo freighters, long on durability and short on luxury and, sometimes, seaworthiness – steered by a cheroot-smoking skipper surrounded by bales of bananas and sacks of letters. (Most mail travels by air these fast-paced days, leaving the hold and every conceivable inch of deck space free for beer and other cargo.)

A mail-boat trip does provide a unique sense of adventure and puts you close to Bahamians. But be prepared to have your carefully made plans shredded. All the vessels are slow and notoriously unreliable. You'll need to be flexible.

Mail-boat travel can also be arduous. Many of the passages, such as the Crooked Island Passage and the crosscurrents in the New Providence Passage, are quite treacherous. Occasional (OK, make that frequent) rough seas and the smell of diesel can induce seasickness.

Note that a 2nd-class ticket guarantees only passage; you'll have to pay extra (usually US$5) for 1st class to secure a coveted bunk about the size of a stretcher. Accommodations vary from Spartan to ultra-Spartan. Often the only sleeping spaces are on wooden benches lining the narrow corridors...and you'll have to scramble for *your* spot before the savvy islanders.

The losers get to sleep on the greasy floor. Sleeping on deck is usually better than suffering the fetid conditions below. This is not the *Love Boat!*

You may be handed some fruit, a soda, and perhaps a tin of Spam upon boarding, but don't count on it. Take eats and drinks – especially a bottle of rum – to share with locals. A pack of cards comes in handy.

Private Yacht

If you plan on boating around, refer to the information about sailing The Bahamas in the Outdoor Activities and Getting There & Away chapters.

Boat Excursions

As you'd expect in an archipelago of 700 islands and almost countless cays, boat excursions are a mainstay of exploring. Several travel companies in Nassau/Paradise Island and Grand Bahama offer excursions to other islands. See the New Providence and Grand Bahama chapters. See the Getting There & Away chapter for a few options for taking a cruise through The Bahamas.

In the Family Islands, you can arrange your own excursions with local boatowners. Prices are negotiable and range from US$50 for a two-hour excursion by small speedboat to US$300 or so for a daylong excursion on a larger vessel with skipper.

TAXI

There's no shortage of licensed taxis in Nassau and Freeport, where they can be hailed on the streets. Taxis are also the main local transportation in the Family Islands, where they must be summoned by radio or telephone. Some taxis are modern US-made minivans. Others are old US-model jalopies ready for the scrap heap. The seat belts have usually and inexplicably been removed.

All taxi operators are licensed. Taxi fares are fixed by the government according to

distance: US$2 for the first quarter-mile and US30¢ for each additional quarter-mile. Rates are usually for two people. Each additional person is charged a flat-rate US$2. Fixed rates have been established from airports and cruise terminals to specific hotels and major destinations. These rates should be displayed in the taxi. Tipping is discretionary and not automatically expected.

Few taxi drivers use their meters. Most taxi drivers are entirely reliable, especially in the Family Islands. However, you should beware some crafty scams in Nassau and Freeport, where an unscrupulous driver may attempt to charge additional people the same rate as the first and second person.

You can use taxis for long-distance touring at government-fixed rates of US$25 per hour and US$10 per additional half-hour. Minivans can charge more. In some cases rates may be negotiable. A half-day tour may cost about US$100. Expect to pay at least US$150 for a full-day tour. Whatever you choose, agree on a fare *before* setting out.

On New Providence and Grand Bahama, and even in the more remote Family Islands, taxis usually show up to meet incoming flights (if not, someone at the airport will radio for a taxi on your behalf).

Local islanders may offer to guide you around in their cars. Some do this for free; others expect payment. They may be too proud to ask you directly for money, so you must judge the mood and act accordingly.

ORGANIZED TOURS

There are plenty of organized tours in Nassau and on Grand Bahama. See the New Providence and Grand Bahama chapters for complete details on these and other tours.

Companies also offer many nature tours and activity-oriented trips on the islands and on the water. See the Outdoor Activities chapter and island chapters for details.

New Providence

- **pop 171,542**

New Providence is the most important island in the Bahamian chain. Nearly two-thirds of the nation's population lives here, overwhelmingly in Nassau, the capital, which sprawls over much of eastern New Providence. More than 70% of all visitors to The Bahamas land in Nassau.

The ovoid island is 21 miles east to west and 7 miles north to south at its widest. The

Highlights

- Lively Bay St and Rawson Square, brimming with historic buildings and bustle
- Paradise Island's Cabbage Beach. And you thought Cable Beach was cool!
- Colorful Potter's Cay, where locals buy fresh fruit and fish
- Atlantis for its incredible themed water-park...and don't forget the Casino at Atlantis!
- Compass Point – if you can't stay here, at least treat yourself to a meal
- Blue Lagoon Island, a fabulous cay where you can snorkel with dolphins
- The dive sites north of Paradise Island and southwest of New Providence

resort zones are limited to Paradise Island, just north of Nassau; downtown Nassau; and Cable Beach, 3 miles west of central Nassau. Paradise Island boasts two of The Bahamas' longest and most stunning beaches, the Casino at Atlantis, and luxury resorts highlighted by the incredible Atlantis complex. Cable Beach offers long, curving sands lined with hotels, and the Crystal Palace Casino.

Very few foreign visitors break out of the established tourist routine to engage with the locals or discover what the island is like away from the narrow touristy corridor from Cable Beach to Paradise Island. Nassau is so overwhelmingly geared to the tourist that the 'real' island takes some seeking out. Yet it lies close at hand, albeit in modern (and motley) fishing villages along the south shore, and at fishing wharves where locals gather to chat over conch salads. Beyond sprawling Nassau, however, the island is humdrum and sparsely populated. There are few sites of interest. Most of the interior is marshy, with large lakes and dense scrub forest favored by locals as impromptu garbage dumps. Bird watchers might do well here, and canoeing is offered on Lake Nancy. The diving is superb off the south shore.

A boom in hotel construction and renovation has swept Nassau and Paradise Island in the past few years as properties attempt to cash in on the islands' rebirth, with a 25% increase in hotel rooms since 1997. The sidewalks are cleaner, public services have been enhanced, and even the locals (who developed a reputation in the 1980s for surliness) are friendlier.

Nassau

- **pop 170,000**

Nassau, on the island's northeast shore, exudes a special charm lent by a blend of Old World architecture and contemporary vitality. Modern Nassau is a far cry from the rustic yet rowdy village that once harbored pirates, prostitutes, and ragamuffins. The city is steeped in modern US ways, which meld well with a quasi-Caribbean flavor. The historic downtown core – some 10 blocks long and four blocks wide – is replete with colonial edifices. Some are grand neocolonial government buildings; others are quaint wooden and limestone homes and office buildings in vernacular style. A recent renovation of the main thoroughfare – Bay St – in the heart of downtown has added sparkle, and the renovation is slated to extend eastward.

But downtown is more than a pretty snapshot. It is also the center of commerce and government, policed by officers in immaculately starched white jackets and black pants or skirts trimmed with a red line (some wear white pith helmets to beat back the sun). The city is world renowned as a lively financial center where Brits in pinstriped shirts manage billions of dollars of wealthy folks' assets.

The heart of touristic affairs extends along the waterfront and along Bay St, one block inland. It's a beehive of activity when the cruise ships disgorge their hordes and cash registers tinkle to the sound of the tourists' silver dollars. Wherever you are in downtown Nassau, the ships loom over you; when in port, their presence is overwhelming. A half-dozen ships at a time often berth, their white hulls sleekly reflected in the turquoise waters.

The low-income and middle-class suburbs extend inland for miles. The government ministries, modern shopping malls, and colleges also lie south of downtown along Thompson Blvd in areas where few tourists venture. There are few sights of interest in this area. An exception might be Over-the-Hill, an African-Bahamian enclave of colorful wooden houses just south of downtown…but it's an area requiring caution.

HISTORY

Nassau's colorful history is steeped in rum-running and roguery. It all began in 1648, when William Sayle and his party of Eleutheran Adventurers briefly landed. The island became known as Sayle's Island, but the party didn't settle. Buccaneers did, establishing a base beyond the reach of any authority. (See History in the Facts about The Bahamas chapter for details on this period.)

The first settlement, established in 1666, was named Charles Town. There was little formal structure. The dirt streets were lined by brothels and taverns for 'common cheats, thieves, and lewd persons.' In 1684 virtually the entire population fled to the American colonies when the Spaniards sacked the town as retribution for relentless attacks by Charles Town's pirates. The town was rebuilt and renamed Nassau in 1695, with Fort Nassau on the site now occupied by the British Colonial Hilton hotel. Nassau was attacked again in 1703 by a combined Spanish and French force that destroyed the fort.

In 1718 Governor Woodes Rogers arrived to establish order and an administration answerable to the English crown. Piracy was suppressed. Still, by the middle of the 18th century the public buildings comprised merely a church, along with a jail, courthouse, and Assembly House in a single, ruinous building at the northeast corner of Bay St – then known as 'The Strand' – and today's Market St. In the 1760s Governor William Shirley, former governor of Massachusetts, brought a Yankee sense of order and ingenuity to the creation of a *real* city. The swamps were drained, the land was surveyed, and tidy new streets were laid.

The American Revolution boosted the city's fortunes, as citizens took to running the English blockade. Meanwhile a flood of Loyalist refugees – many quite wealthy or entrepreneurial – began arriving, lending new vigor to the city. In 1787 the haughty and inept Earl of Dunmore arrived as governor of the Bahamas, despite disgracing himself in the posts of governor of New York and Virginia in events before and during the American Revolution. His critics – there were many – accused him of a reprehensible private life, while bemoaning appointments to office of 'bankrupts, beggars, blackguards, and the husbands of his whores.'

His legacy is evident today in several fine buildings, including the two batteries he

NEW PROVIDENCE

77°25'W

PLACES TO STAY
1 Compass Point
4 Orange Hill Beach Inn
25 Clarion Resort South Ocean
34 Coral Harbour Beach House & Villas

PLACES TO EAT
2 Traveller's Rest
6 Nesbit's
19 Corner Hotel
20 KFC; Domino's Pizza; Wendy's; Golden Gates Shopping Center
27 Honeycomb Beach Club
28 Avery's Restaurant & Bar

OTHER
3 Police Station
5 Canoeing
7 Shell Gas Station
8 BaTelCo
9 Lyford Cay Club

10 Lyford Cay Centre
11 Entrance Gate to Lyford Cay
12 Lyford Cay Hospital
13 Bahamasair Headquarters
14 General Aviation Terminal (Private Charters)
15 Towne Centre Mall
16 The Mall at Marathon; Galleria Cinema
17 Prince Charles Shopping Centre; RND Cinemas
18 Blackbeard's Tower
21 Esso Station
22 Her Majesty's Prison (Fox Hill)
23 Clifton Pier Power Station
24 Commonwealth Brewery
26 Stuart's Cove Dive South Ocean
29 Happy Trail Stables
30 Royal Bahamas Defence Force Base
31 Nassau Scuba Centre
32 Sunskiff Divers
33 Dive Dive Dive
35 Bacardi Rum Factory

◿ Dive Site

Sandyport Bay

Orange Hill Beach
Love Beach
Northwest Point
Gambier Village
⌂ The Caves
Blake Rd
🏝 5
John F. Kennedy Dr
Lake Nancy

Old Fort Point
Tropical Garden Rd
3
☆

Windsor Field Rd
13 🛬 14
Nassau International Airport
Lake Killarney

10
Western Rd
Lyford Cay Drive
9
11
12 **Mt Pleasant**

WWII Bomber
Goulding Cay
Lyford Cay
Golf Course
Western Rd
Clifton Point
Willaurie Wreck
S Ocean Rd
South Ocean Golf Course
Never Say Never Again Wreck
23
24
25
Southwest Rd
26
Coral Harbour Rd
Adelaide Rd
Adelaide
Adelaide Beach
27
28
29
Corry Sound
Millars Sound

Southwest Bay
20,000 Leagues
Coral Harbour
32
30
31
33
34
Ranfurly Drive
Bacardi Rd
35

25°00'N

77°30'W   77°25'W

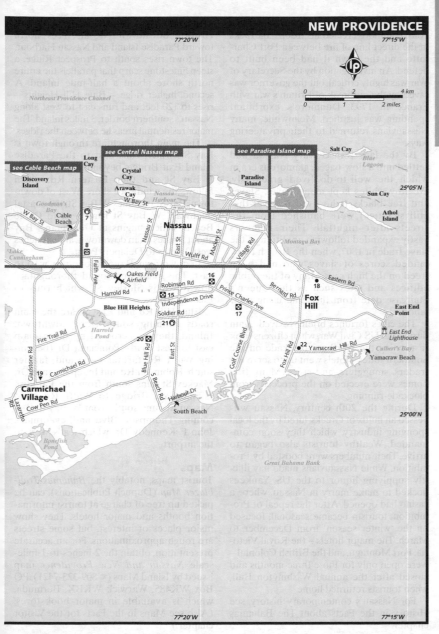

erected: Fort Charlotte and Fort Fincastle. Alas, Dunmore erected his troops' barracks in the direct line of fire between Fort Charlotte and the town it had been built to defend. An investigation by the Secretary of War was highly critical, but the governor was saved by the outbreak of Britain's war with France in 1793. Dunmore's exorbitant spending was justified. Meanwhile, many Nassauvians returned to their privateering ways.

By the late 18th century Nassau had settled into a slow-paced, glamorous era in which the well-to-do lived graciously. Wealthy whites kept many slaves. Slaves and free blacks (who lived in Over-the-Hill shanties) were banished from the streets after nightfall. Their numbers vastly expanded following abolition of the slave trade in 1807, when the British Navy landed scores of slaves who had been freed on the high seas. Many of the public edifices and sites such as the Queen's Staircase date from this time using their labor.

The city's fortunes briefly revived again during the US Civil War, when citizens took to running the Northern blockade on the Southern states. Hotels went up to serve the traders, smugglers, and spies. Many fine homes were erected on the proceeds from blockade-running.

During the 20th century, Nassau witnessed an influx of Greeks, lured by the local sponging industry, which they soon commanded. Wealthy tourists also began to arrive. Their numbers were boosted by Prohibition. While Nassauvians made hay illicitly supplying liquor to the US, Yankees flocked to make merry in Nassau, where a casino had opened. After the repeal of Prohibition, tourism became seasonal, focused on the 'winter season' from December to March. The major hotels – the Royal Victoria, Fort Montagu, and the British Colonial – were open only for those three months and closed after the annual Washington Ball, when tourists returned home.

For Nassau's contemporary history, see History in the Facts about The Bahamas chapter.

ORIENTATION

Historic downtown Nassau faces north toward Paradise Island and Nassau Harbour. The town rises south to Prospect Ridge, a steep limestone scarp that parallels the entire north shore about a half-mile inland. A second, higher ridge – Blue Hill Heights – rises to 120 feet and runs east to west along Nassau's southern border, 3 miles inland. The major residential areas lie between the ridges.

The main thoroughfare through town is Bay St, which runs east to the Paradise Island Exit Bridge; beyond, it continues as E Bay St and then Eastern Rd, which follows the windward shore. West of downtown, Bay St becomes W Bay St, the coastal 'highway.' W Bay St runs west to Cable Beach, which begins at Goodman's Bay about 3 miles from downtown, and stretches west 2 miles to Delaport Point.

In downtown, Bay St is one-way west to east. The main westbound thoroughfare downtown is Shirley St, which runs to Eastern Rd.

Blue Hill Rd and East St are the main roads running south from downtown. Inland, they are crossed by three main east-to-west roads: Poinciana Dr (becoming Wulff Rd farther east) and, farther south, Robinson Rd and Independence Dr. Mackey St runs south from the Paradise Island Exit Bridge to Wulff Rd. And Nassau St runs south from W Bay St, becoming Thompson Blvd and, eventually, John F Kennedy Dr, which leads west to the airport.

Maps

Tourist maps, notably the *Bahamas Trailblazer Map* (Dupuch Publications), can be picked up free of charge at tourist information booths and major hotels. They show major places of interest, but some streets are rough approximations. For an accurate presentation, obtain the 2-inches-to-1-mile-scale *Nassau and New Providence* map issued by Island Maps (☎ 809-323-7421), PO Box WK485, Warwick WKBX, Bermuda, which is available in major bookstores. (Also see Maps in the Facts for the Visitor chapter.)

INFORMATION
Tourist Offices
The Bahamas Tourist Office has an information office (☎ 242-377-6806) in the airport arrivals terminal. The main information office (☎ 242-326-9781), on the north side of Rawson Square, is open 8:30 am to 6 pm Monday to Friday, 8:30 am to 5 pm Saturday, and 8:30 am to 3 pm Sunday. There's also a tourist information bureau (☎ 242-302-2062) beside the Straw Market on Bay St; it's open the same hours.

The Ministry of Tourism headquarters (☎ 242-356-7591, 242-322-7501) is on Frederick St, off Bay St; it's open 9 am to 5 pm weekdays.

The Nassau/Paradise Island Promotion Board (☎ 242-322-8383/4, fax 242-326-5346) is at Hotel's House on Deans Lane.

Embassies & Consulates
The British High Commission (☎ 242-325-7471, fax 242-323-3871) is in the Bitco Bldg on East St at Shirley St. The Canadian Consulate (☎ 242-393-2123/4, fax 242-393-1305) is in Shirley St Plaza; the US Embassy & Consulate (☎ 242-322-1181, fax 242-328-7838) is in the Mosmar Bldg on Queen St near Marlborough St; the German Honorary Consul (☎ 242-322-8032) is on W Bay St; and the Japanese Honorary Consul (☎ 242-322-8560) is on Elizabeth Ave.

A few other consulates are listed in the New Providence section of the phone book under the listing 'Diplomatic and Consular Representation.'

Money
There are plenty of banks clustered around Rawson Square (good for passengers off the cruise ships) and Bay St. Some banks have ATMs, notably Scotiabank on Rawson Square and Barclays on Bay St, which have 24-hour machines accepting Visa, MasterCard, and Discover cards. They dispense US dollars. Additional ATMs dispense Bahamian dollars, including those at Royal Bank of Canada branches (there's one on E Hill St, one on Bay St, and another in Cable Beach) and at the Esso stations at Village and Wulff Rds, and East St and Soldier Rd.

In Cable Beach you'll find a Scotiabank in the Cecil Wallace Whitfield Centre opposite the Nassau Beach Hotel, and the Commonwealth Bank and British American Bank immediately west, where there's also a Western Union. Western Union also has an office downtown on Frederick St. A CIBC banking center is opposite Sandals Royal Bahamian in Cable Beach.

American Express is represented by Playtours (☎ 242-322-2931) at 303 Shirley St between Charlotte and Parliament Sts, downtown.

Discounts
The free *Tourist News* and *What's On* newspapers (see the Publications section, later in this chapter) each have coupons inside for discounts on restaurants, entertainment, sightseeing excursions, and shopping.

Post & Communications
The main post office (☎ 242-322-3025), on E Hill St at Parliament Sts, is open 8:30 am to 5:30 pm weekdays and 8:30 am to 12:30 pm Saturday. There is also a post office at Cable Beach.

Federal Express (☎ 242-322-5656) has an office downtown on Frederick St. DHL (☎ 242-394-4040) has an office behind Hooters' on E Bay St.

BaTelCo has an office (☎ 242-323-6414) on East St a half-block south of Bay St, with public phone booths for international calls. It's open 7 am to 10 pm daily. BaTelCo's headquarters (☎ 242-323-4911) is on John F Kennedy Dr.

See Post & Communications in the Facts for the Visitor chapter for details on other services available in Nassau.

Internet Resources
The Bahamas Internet Café, on Bay St, offers Internet access, as do Chippie's Wall St Café, and Tobacco & Coffee Bar (☎ 242-356-2087), both on Bay St. The latter is open 9 am to 11 pm daily.

The Internet Lounge (☎ 242-356-2217, internetlounge@bahamas.net.bs), also on Bay St just east of Elizabeth Ave, charges US20¢ per minute for Internet time. And Computers

CENTRAL NASSAU

PLACES TO STAY
2 Crystal Cay Marine
  Park & Villas
7 Arawak Inn
15 Dillet's Guest House
31 City Lodge Hotel
39 Nassau Harbour Club;
  Tony Cheng's
40 Red Carpet Inn
46 Montagu Beach Inn
51 Orchard Hotel

PLACES TO EAT
4 The Zoo Café; The Zoo
5 Burger King; Cafe Aroma
8 Outdoor Conch Market
16 Chinese Kitchen

17 Silver Dollar
27 Dunkin' Donuts; Domino's Pizza
29 Hooter's; DHL
30 Outback Steak Restaurant
35 Pink Pearl Cafe
41 Mantagu Gardens
45 East Villa
48 Sun And...
49 Tamarind Hill

OTHER
1 Underwater Observatory (Closed)
3 Crystal Cay Marine Park (Closed)
6 Texaco Gas Station
9 Police Station
10 Clifford Park; Cricket Club
11 Ardastra Gardens & Zoo

12 Botanical Garden
13 Fort Charlotte
14 Nassau/Paradise Island
  Promotion Board
18 Nassau Guardian
19 College of The Bahamas Library
20 Clarence A Bain Bldg; Road
  Traffic Department
21 Queen Elizabeth Sports Centre
22 FastFerries Dock
23 Potter's Cay Market
24 Police Station
25 Mail Boats; Dockmaster's Office
26 East Bay Yacht Basin;
  Coral Reef Charters
28 Gold's Gym; Double Dragon
32 Shirley Street Theatre

33 Canadian Consulate
34 Divers Haven
36 Nassau Yacht Haven
37 German Consul
38 Harbour Bay Shopping Center
42 Nassau Harbour Club & Marina
43 Fort Montagu
44 Club Waterloo
47 Montagu Ramp
50 Doongalik Studios
52 Palmdale Shopping Centre
53 Dundas Centre for the
  Performing Arts
54 The Retreat
55 Village Lanes (Bowling)
56 Esso Station
57 Village Squash Club

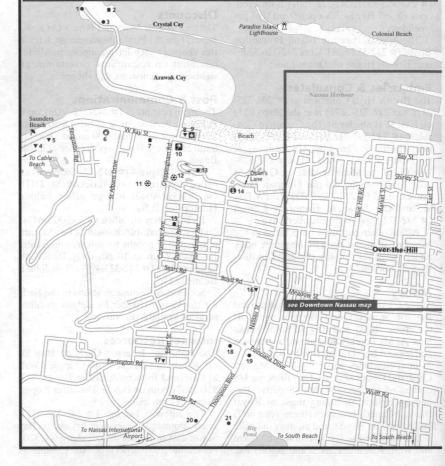

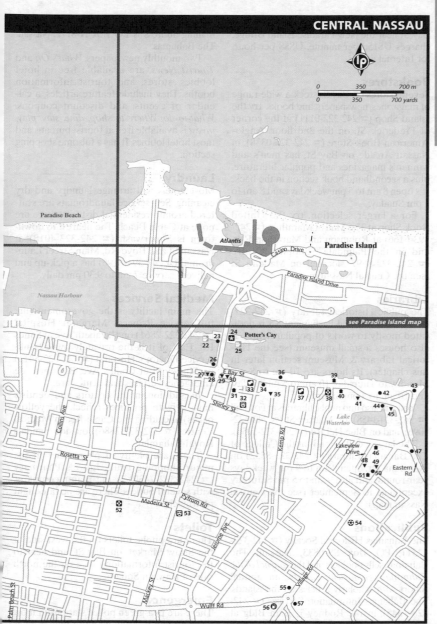

CENTRAL NASSAU

Paradise Beach

Atlantis

Paradise Island

Nassau Harbour

Casino Drive

Paradise Island Drive

see Paradise Island map

Potter's Cay

E Bay St

Shirley St

Lake Waterloo

Collins Ave

Rosetta St

Kemp Rd

Lakeview Drive

Eastern Rd

Madeira St

Pyfrom Rd

Jerome Ave

Mackey St

Village Rd

Wulff Rd

Palm Beach St

& Software Unlimited (☎ 242-334-3444), on Bay St near the New Paradise Island Bridge, charges US15¢ per minute, US$8 per hour, for Internet access.

Bookstores

Several stores on Bay St stock a wide range of magazines, newspapers, and books. Try the Island Shop (☎ 242-322-0111) at the corner of Frederick St, on the 2nd floor. Anglo-American Book Store (☎ 242-325-0338), in Nassau Arcade on Bay St, has men's and women's magazines and popular literature, plus a secondhand book section in the back. It's open 8 am to 5 pm weekdays and 8 am to 1 pm Sunday.

For a larger selection, try the United Book Shop at The Mall at Marathon (☎ 242-393-6166) at Robinson and Marathon Rds, and in the Palmdale Shopping Centre (☎ 242-322-8597), located on Madeira St (see the Central Nassau map).

Libraries

The public Historical Library (☎ 242-322-4907) at Shirley and Parliament Sts is dedicated mostly to works of popular fiction. It also houses a small museum (see the Historical Library & Museum section later in this chapter). Its hours are 10 am to 8 pm Monday to Thursday, 10 am to 5 pm Friday, and 10 am to 4 pm Saturday.

You will also find public libraries at Fox Hill (☎ 242-324-1458), on Mackey St (☎ 242-322-1096), and on Blue Hill Rd (☎ 242-322-1056).

The largest collection is at the College of The Bahamas Library (☎ 242-323-8552) on Poinciana Dr, open 8 am to 9 pm weekdays year-round, and also 9 am to 5 pm Saturday except July to September (see the Central Nassau map).

Publications

The Bahamas Historical Society (☎ 242-322-4231), PO Box SS-6833, Nassau, The Bahamas, sells booklets and the *Journal of the Bahamian Historical Society*, an annual report with scholarly articles on the islands. The Bahamas Information Services (☎ 242-328-1345), in the Rodney E Bain Bldg at Shirley and Parliament Sts, publishes a monthly newsletter called *Infoserve*; the mailing address is PO Box N-8172, Nassau, The Bahamas.

Two monthly newspapers, *What's On* and *Tourist News*, are available free in hotel lobbies, stores, and tourist information booths. They include feature articles, a calendar of events, and discount coupons. *What-to-do: Where to shop, dine, stay, play, invest* is available free at tourist bureaus and most hotel lobbies. It has a fulsome shopping section.

Laundry

Most hotels will arrange laundry and dry cleaning. Self-service laundromats are scattered around residential districts; there are none at Cable Beach. The nearest to downtown is Superwash (☎ 242-323-4018) at Nassau St and Boyd Rd. Main Street Laundromat (☎ 242-394-8196) has a pick-up and delivery service 7 am to 9:30 pm daily.

Medical Services

The main facility is the government-run, full-service Princess Margaret Hospital (☎ 242-322-2861) on Elizabeth Ave at Sands Rd. East of it is the privately owned, full-service Doctor's Hospital (☎ 242-322-8411) on Shirley St at Collins Ave. Both provide emergency services and acute care.

In addition, many doctors and dentists have private practices (check the yellow pages), including the Cable Beach Medical Centre (☎ 242-327-2886), outside Sandals Royal Bahamian.

There are plenty of pharmacies in the major shopping malls. Lowe's Pharmacy (☎ 242-322-7430) is the major company, with several outlets. There are no late-night pharmacies.

Toilets

There are public toilets on the west side of the Straw Market, on Bay St, and next to the tourist information office on the north side of Rawson Square.

Emergency

There are pea-green police stations in most districts; you'll rarely be more than 2 miles from one. For emergencies, call ☎ 911. The main police station is on East St (☎ 242-322-1647/8) between Sands Rd and Prison Lane, about 500 yards south of Bay St; another is on Bay St, 300 yards east of Rawson Square. In Cable Beach, call ☎ 242-327-8800.

You can also reach the police at ☎ 242-322-4444, an ambulance at ☎ 242-322-2221, or the Red Cross at ☎ 242-323-7370.

Dangers & Annoyances

A few hustlers hang out around Bay St, surreptitiously offering drugs. Some of the vendors around the Straw Market can be a bit too pushy, as can one or two of the hair-braiders at Prince George Wharf. Most usually take your 'No, thanks' in good grace.

Occasionally a hotel doorman or other individual may hint subtly that drugs or a nighttime partner can be made available, but these are offered in an offhand way. At night a few hookers hang around downtown, hoping to snare the amorous sailor or tourist, but their presence will hardly be noticed.

Many locals bemoan Nassau's 'soaring' crime rate, which includes muggings, murders, and drug-related violence, relegated mostly to the Over-the-Hill area (Bains Town and Grants Town neighborhoods). This area should be avoided at night. Use caution by day, as this area's down-at-the-heels quality is aggravated by the presence of 'Joneses' (drug users). You should also avoid walking alone downtown at night; stick to well-lit main streets.

Most thefts occur from hotel rooms or at the beaches or swimming pools. Also be wary of friendly strangers wanting to assist you by carrying your bags or belongings.

DOWNTOWN NASSAU

The heart of downtown Nassau is a compact historic district whose many well-preserved 18th- and 19th-century buildings evoke a colorful past.

Before setting out on a walking tour of downtown, obtain a copy of *Nassau's Historic Buildings* by C Sieghbert Russell (Bahamas National Trust), available at the Bahamas Historical Society Museum. If the heat is oppressive, hop aboard a canopied surrey, the picturesque horse-drawn coaches available for hire at Prince George Wharf.

Marlborough Street & W Bay Street

Marlborough St is a busy three-block-long street that leads east to Bay St and west to W Bay St and thence to Cable Beach. Much of the north side of Marlborough St, once occupied by Fort Nassau, is taken up by the **British Colonial Hilton**, fronted by a statue dedicated to Governor Woodes Rogers, plus a rusty anchor and cannon. Remnants of the old walls can be seen on the hotel grounds.

Marlborough St runs east into King St, which parallels Bay St for two blocks. This is the heart of financial affairs, concentrated between Cumberland and Market Sts. Several old cut-stone buildings here are now fine restaurants.

Queen St, which ascends south from Marlborough St, is lined with fine balconied colonial homes, notably the **Devonshire House** at No 11. Two blocks east, Cumberland St boasts **Cumberland House** and **The Deanery**, described as 'the quintessential trademark of colonial Bahamian architecture.'

At Marlborough St's west end, it becomes Virginia St. Prim **St Mary's Church** is found on Virginia St; it was built in 1868 and could have fallen out of a postcard depicting the English countryside. The junction of Marlborough and West Sts has several fine old balconied houses.

Greek Orthodox Church Nassau has a large Greek community served by the Kurikon, also called the Greek Orthodox Church of the Annunciation, erected in 1932 one block south of the Marlborough and West Sts junction. It's intimate and beautiful within, with an exquisite gilt chandelier. Most mornings a small congregation can be found here, chanting you back in time and place to Mykonos or Crete. *Marvelous!* About 70 local families religiously attend (pardon the pun).

Pirates of Nassau This world-class interactive museum (☎ 242-356-3759, fax 242-356-3951, pirates@bahamas.net.bs), on King St,

DOWNTOWN NASSAU

Nassau Harbour

Prince George Wharf

Private Beach

To Arawak Cay
& Cable Beach

0   150   300 m
0   150   300 yards

W Bay St

Cunningham Lane

Virginia St

Nassau St

Heathfield St

Chesterfield St

West St

Queen St

Augusta St

Delancy St

Petticoat Ln

Meeting St

Dillet St

South St

Adderley St

Wilkinson St

Cambridge Lane

Cockburn St

Blue Hill Rd

Market St

Goat Alley

Prison Lane

North St

Anderson St

Over-the-Hill

Prospect Ridge

School Lane

Marlborough St

King St

Cumberland St

George St

Duke St

Prince's St

W Hill St

Hospital Lane

Frederick St

Charlotte St

Trinity Pl

Shirley St

E Hill St

Parliament St

East St

Sands Rd

Bennet's Hill

Navy Lion Rd

Bay St

Woodes Rogers Walk

Straw Market

Rawson Square

Parliament Square

St Francis Xavier Cathedral

Nassau Harbour

PLACES TO STAY		
7	Holiday Inn Junkanoo Beach Hotel	
9	El Greco	
11	Ocean Spray Hotel	
15	West Bay Hotel	
19	British Colonial Hilton Nassau; Portofino Restaurant	
35	Grand Central Hotel	
47	Harbour Moon Hotel	
58	Sunshine Guesthouse	
68	Towne Hotel	
71	Mignon Guest House	
91	Graycliff Hotel & Restaurant	
104	The Diplomat Inn	

105 Buena Vista Restaurant & Hotel
106 International Traveller's Rest
107 Park Manor Guesthouse

PLACES TO EAT
12 Europa Restaurant
13 Chez Willie
16 House of Wong
23 Chippie's Wall St Cafe
27 Sbarro's
28 Café Skan's
31 Dockside Bar & Grill; Iguana; Prince George Plaza
38 Planet Hollywood

42 Burger King; Seaworld Explorer Office
48 VIP Chinese Restaurant
49 Lady J's; Drop Zone
51 Crocodile's Waterfront Bar & Grill; Last Quarter
54 Hammerhead Bar & Grill; Computers & Software Unlimited
59 McDonald's
61 Imperial Take-Away
62 Conch Fritters Bar & Grill
63 Dunkin' Donuts
66 Billabong's
73 Bahamian Kitchen
77 The Cellar
83 Café Matisse
87 Gaylord's

90 Humidor Restaurant; Graycliff Cigar Co
98 Green Shutters Inn
102 King Alpha Ital Restaurant

OTHER
1 Ferries to Paradise Island
2 Water Taxi to Paradise Island
3 Surreys
4 Junkanoo Expo
5 Hair-Braiders
6 Seaworld Explorer
8 Police Station
10 Charlie's Bar
14 Avis Rent-a-Car
17 Knowles Scooter & Bike Rental
18 Dollar Rent-a-Car

DOWNTOWN NASSAU

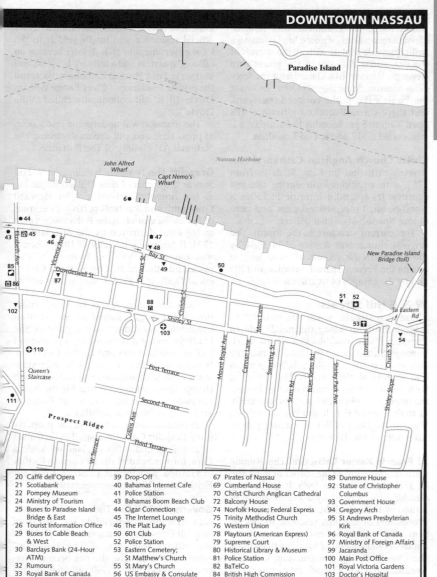

Paradise Island

Nassau Harbour

Ferry

John Alfred Wharf

Capt Nemo's Wharf

6

New Paradise Island Bridge (toll)

To Eastern Rd

Elizabeth Ave

43
45
44
46
85
86
87

Victoria Ave

Dowdeswell St

Bay St

Devaux St

Christie St

47
48
49
50

51 52
53
54

Moss Lane

Lovers Ln

Church St

102

Shirley St

103

Mount Royal Ave

Caman Lane

Sweeting St

Sears Rd

Buen Retiro Rd

Shirley Park Ave

Shirley Slope

110

Queen's Staircase

First Terrace

Second Terrace

111

Prospect Ridge

Collins Ave

W Terrace

Third Terrace

20 Caffè dell'Opera	39 Drop-Off	67 Pirates of Nassau	89 Dunmore House
21 Scotiabank	40 Bahamas Internet Cafe	69 Cumberland House	92 Statue of Christopher Columbus
22 Pompey Museum	41 Police Station	70 Christ Church Anglican Cathedral	
24 Ministry of Tourism	43 Bahamas Boom Beach Club	72 Balcony House	93 Government House
25 Buses to Paradise Island Bridge & East	44 Cigar Connection	74 Norfolk House; Federal Express	94 Gregory Arch
	45 The Internet Lounge	75 Trinity Methodist Church	95 St Andrews Presbyterian Kirk
26 Tourist Information Office	46 The Plait Lady	76 Western Union	
29 Buses to Cable Beach & West	50 601 Club	78 Playtours (American Express)	96 Royal Bank of Canada
	52 Police Station	79 Supreme Court	97 Ministry of Foreign Affairs
30 Barclays Bank (24-Hour ATM)	53 Eastern Cemetery; St Matthew's Church	80 Historical Library & Museum	99 Jacaranda
32 Rumours	55 St Mary's Church	81 Police Station	100 Main Post Office
33 Royal Bank of Canada	56 US Embassy & Consulate	82 BaTelCo	101 Royal Victoria Gardens
34 Masonic Temple	57 Greek Orthodox Church	84 British High Commission	103 Doctor's Hospital
36 Scotiabank (24-Hour ATM)	60 Devonshire House	85 Japanese Consulate	108 Police Headquarters
37 Tourist Information; ATM; Public Toilets	64 Majestic Tours	86 Bahamas Historical Society Museum	109 Fort Fincastle
	65 The Deanery	88 Collins House	110 Princess Margaret Hospital
			111 Water Tower

50 yards east of George St, offers exciting walk-through entertainment, with realistic life-size recreations of pirate life including a twilit quayside replete with all the sounds of the era, and a cutaway of the pirate ship *Revenge*. Beware Blackbeard and his ferocious amazon, Anne Bonney! You can sup at the Pirate's Bar in the enclosed courtyard, and there's a well-stocked gift store. It's open 9 am to 5 pm Monday to Saturday; admission is US$12 adults, US$7 children.

Christ Church Anglican Cathedral This striking cathedral on King St dates from 1753, with additions built during the last century. Its splendid interior includes a wood-beamed roof, stained glass, and pendulous Spanish-style chandeliers.

The current structure is the fourth. The original church was destroyed in 1684 by the Spaniards. Its successors were leveled during the French-Spanish invasion in 1703 and by the ravages of weather and termites.

W & E Hill Streets

These two streets, which run parallel to Nassau Harbour along the north side of Prospect Ridge, one block south of Marlborough St, are joined by Duke St, running east to west for one block between them and slightly to their north. They're lined with important historical buildings, including impressive old homes such as **Jacaranda**, at the corner of E Hill and Parliament Sts, home to the Duke of Windsor during part of his tenure in The Bahamas.

St Francis Xavier Cathedral This Roman Catholic cathedral, at the corner of West and W Hill Sts, dates from 1885. It has a long, slender nave topped by a bell tower, illumined within at night. Many prominent Protestants of the time resented the incursion of the Catholics and ascribed to the hands of God the bolt of lightning that struck the church during construction, killing a workman and doing significant damage.

Dunmore House The huge three-story balconied mansion, across from the cathedral on W Hill St, was erected by Lord Dunmore

after his arrival as governor in 1787. Dunmore leased it to the government as his official residence and finally sold it to the local government in 1801. It later became an officers' quarters and a military hospital, and also served as a Roman Catholic mission and the private residence of Chief Justice William Doyle (it is still colloquially called 'Villa Doyle').

The mansion was undergoing restoration at press time and will eventually house the National Art Gallery of The Bahamas.

Graycliff This beautiful building, on W Hill St near the corner of Blue Hill Rd, began life as the home of privateer John Howard Graysmith and was built partly on the ruins of the oldest church in the Bahamas, erected in 1694 but destroyed by the Spaniards in 1703. It became a hostelry in 1844, when it was known as 'Victoria House'; it later passed into the hands of the Earl and Countess of Dudley; in 1974 it once again became a hotel.

Over the years it has received many prominent guests, including Sir Winston Churchill, who lodged as the guest of the Dudleys. Today it is owned by a prominent Italian couple, Anna and Enrico Garzaroli. It is one of the city's finest hotels and restaurants, flush with antiques and redolent with charm and a splendid venue for the host's renowned cigar dinners. (See the Places to Stay section for more details.)

Two doors down and part of the property is the **Graycliff Cigar Co**, staffed by 20 Cuban cigar rollers under the tutelage of Avelino Lara, former head of the El Laguito factory in Havana, and former personal roller for Fidel Castro. Visitors are welcome.

Government House The conch-pink Georgian structure commanding the city from atop Mt Fitzwilliam, just south of W Hill St, is the official residence of The Bahamas' governor-general. The site has been in government hands since 1799 although governors lived there prior to that time; the original home was built in 1737 by Governor Fitzwilliam (1733–38). A new structure was built in 1806. Additional wings were added during the 20th century, but the entire house was swiftly destroyed by a hurricane in 1929. The current building was completed in 1932. The lavish decorations date from 1940, when the Duke of Windsor arrived as governor.

Visitors can walk the grounds for a close look at the building but you'll have to request permission from the guards, who must accompany you. *One two! One two!* Twice a month, you can 'have a cuppa' with the governor-general's wife (see the 'People to People' boxed text in the Facts for the Visitor chapter) or watch the changing of the guard. This tradition of pomp and ceremony includes a performance of the Royal Bahamas Police Force Band. It occurs twice a month at 10 am; call ☎ 242-322-2020 to confirm date and time.

Check out the **statue of Christopher Columbus**, depicting him in a rather jaunty outfit on the steps overlooking Duke St. It was designed by US writer Washington Irving – who dressed the 15th-century Genoese explorer in the garb of Irving's day – and presented to Governor Smythe in 1830. At night Columbus is suffused by the glow of colored spotlights.

A stone arch topped with iron railings – **Gregory Arch** – spans Market St (cutting through Prospect Ridge) at the east end of Government House grounds.

St Andrews Presbyterian Kirk 'The Kirk,' below Government House on Prince's and Market Sts, is a handsome crenellated church that owes its existence to a Loyalist who settled in Nassau at the end of the American Revolution. In 1798 he established the St Andrew's Society, comprising 55 Scots, to 'cultivate good understanding and social intercourse.' The Freemasons laid the cornerstone in 1810, and the church has since undergone many architectural changes. Its ministers traditionally were culled from the Presbyterian clergy of Edinburgh and Glasgow.

Follow the curling road uphill past Gregory Arch to continue along E Hill St.

Ministry of Foreign Affairs East of Gregory Arch, on E Hill St at the corner of Glinton St and boasting a fine view over the city, is a beautiful pink Georgian edifice fronted by cannon. The government's foreign affairs are handled within. Outside you'll see a modern purple sculpture – *El Vigía (The Lookout)* – by Mexican sculptor Sebastian. It was a gift from the Mexican government for the 1992 quincentennial of Columbus' landing.

Bay Street

This is the heart of the duty-free shopping district. Bay St heads east from the highrise, colonial-era **British Colonial Hilton** at the junction with Marlborough St and Navy Lion Rd. It runs about 2 miles to the Paradise Island Exit Bridge (see the East of Downtown section later in this chapter for things to see on E Bay St).

The most imposing of the many impressive buildings is the **Royal Bank of Canada**, which has done business in this grandiose stone structure since 1919. Opposite is another notable edifice: the **Masonic Temple**, dedicated in 1885.

Pompey Museum The Bahamas' history is told through displays at this small museum (☎ 242-326-2566) in Vendue House, 50 yards east of Navy Lion Rd. The building was once a slave-auction site, and the museum is named in memory of a slave who led a rebellion in 1830 on Exuma. The exhibits include artifacts, straw-work, historical documents, and drawings tracing events from the Lucayan period to the bootlegging era. The upstairs room features a permanent exhibit of naive paintings by noted artist Amos Ferguson. It's open 10 am to 4:30 pm Monday to Friday and 10 am to 1 pm Saturday; admission is US$1/US50¢ adults/children.

Straw Market Life at the west end of Bay St is dominated by what is said to be the world's largest straw market. Some 160 vendors set up stalls daily to sell everything from straw-work to T-shirts, woodcarvings, shell souvenirs, and other island handicrafts. You can watch craftspeople whittling wood or weaving straw. The undisputed matriarch is Diana Thompson, fondly called 'Aunt Di.' She has been selling straw since the early 1930s (from the age of 10).

Balcony House This beautiful two-story cedar structure – a restored 18th-century merchant's house that was named for its prominent balcony supported by wooden knee braces – is on Market St a few blocks off Bay St. The original slave kitchen remains, as does the staircase, taken from a sailing ship. It is now a local history museum, open 10 am to 1 pm and 2 to 4 pm Monday, Wednesday, and Friday; donations are accepted. Call the Pompey Museum (see above) for more information.

Rawson Square

The heart of town, the zero milestone for tourists, is Rawson Square, on the south side of Bay St five blocks east of Marlborough St. It's a natural place to begin a walking tour, particularly for cruise-ship passengers, as the square lies immediately south of Prince George Wharf, within two or three minutes' walk from the cruise-ship gangplanks.

On the north side of the square is the main tourist information office, where you can pick up free maps and information. Guided walking tours also begin here. Nearby, note the patinated life-size bronze statue **Bahamian Woman**, which honors women's role during 'years of adversity.' She holds a small child. In the center of the square is a **bust of Sir Milo Butler**, the first governor-general of the independent nation, and a fountain pool with leaping bronze dolphins.

Parliament Square

The area immediately south of Rawson Square on Bay St is known as Parliament Square for its conclave of all-important public buildings. On three sides of the square, they are the office of the Lead of the Opposition (on the left), the House of Assembly (right), and the Senate (facing Bay St). It's amazing to think that these three twee buildings are the center of government! The pink-and-white Georgian neo-classical buildings were built between 1805 and 1813. In their midst, facing north over Bay St, is the **Queen Victoria Statue**, un-

veiled in 1905 yet portraying the monarch as a young woman. She gleams alabaster-white in the sunlight but looks decidedly unamused as she peers down on passersby.

You can peek inside the House of Assembly to watch proceedings when it's in session. Arrangements can be made at the House Office of the Clerk of Courts (☎ 242-322-7500). Note its green carpet, symbolizing the English meadow where King John was forced to sign the Magna Carta in 1215. The Senate also has a visitors' gallery, with tickets given out free on a first-come, first-served basis.

Immediately south of Parliament Square is the **Supreme Court**, a Georgian edifice between Parliament St and Bank Lane. Here bewigged and begowned judges perform their duties.

A few yards farther north is the small **Garden of Remembrance**, with a cenotaph honoring Bahamian soldiers who died in the two world wars (note the plaque to four members of the Royal Bahamas Defence Force killed in 1980 when their patrol vessel, *Flamingo*, was attacked by Cuban MiGs).

Prince George Wharf

The historic cruise-ship wharf, north of Rawson Square and Bay St, is the gateway to Nassau for 1.7 million visitors a year!

The wharf is fronted by bustling **Woodes Rogers Walk**, lined with souvenir stalls, fast-food outlets, and a canopied stand where **horse-drawn surreys** await customers. Ferries to Paradise Island also leave from Woodes Rogers Walk (see the Getting There & Away section).

The old wharfside customs building today houses the **Junkanoo Expo** (☎ 242-356-2731), which tells of the history and cultural importance of the annual Junkanoo festival held each Boxing Day (December 26) and New Year's Eve throughout the islands. The museum displays some of the elaborate winning costumes and floats, plus goatskin drums, cowbells, and other paraphernalia that make Junkanoo the colorful highlight of the social calendar. It's open 9 am to 5 pm Monday to Saturday, and 3 to 5 pm Sunday; admission is US$1/US50¢ adults/children.

Hair Braids

If your hair is more than an inch long, you won't get 5 yards along the beach or Prince George Wharf before someone will approach you and ask if you'd like your hair braided. Braiders even have their own braiding booth outside the wharf.

Some people choose to get a token braid or two, while others have all their locks braided and laced with colored beads. Braiding costs US$2 per braid or about US$20 for a headful.

Once you're braided, you may need to apply sunscreen to protect newly exposed scalp.

Shirley Street

At the foot of Prospect Ridge, Shirley St parallels Bay St. Its attractions include historic buildings, museums, and gardens.

Trinity Methodist Church This delightful church, at the west end of Shirley St on Frederick St at Trinity Place, was originally planned for a congregation of 800 people. Alas, the four carpenters sent from Scotland all succumbed to yellow fever, and a more modest church was built in 1861. It had been open only a year when it was blown down by a hurricane. The current church dates from 1869 and was significantly repaired following damage in the 1928 hurricane.

Historical Library & Museum The Nassau Public Library (☎ 242-322-4907), between Parliament St and Bank Lane one block south of Rawson Square, is housed in an unusual octagonal building erected in the 1790s as a jail (the dungeon still exists below ground). Convicts gave way to books in 1873. Note the model of the *Arethusa*, the rumrunning schooner of Captain Bill McCoy.

A museum on the 2nd floor, dedicated to the peaceful Lucayan Indians, has a motley collection of artifacts, including bones, a few old maps, engravings, photographs, shells, stamps, and old parchments.

Both are open 10 am to 8 pm Monday to Thursday, 10 am to 5 pm Friday, and 10 am to 4 pm Saturday; admission is free.

Royal Victoria Gardens This opulent garden, across from the library on the ridge to the south of Shirley St, is on the site of the sprawling Royal Victoria Hotel (now partly in ruins). Pathways lead past more than 300 species of tropical plants, many sown when the resplendent three-story Royal Vic opened in 1861 – a true relic of the US Civil War. Overnight the hotel established itself as a popular rendezvous for blockade-runners, Confederate officers, Union spies, and other colorful characters. After the war, the hotel went through lean times. Alas, she breathed her last as a hotel in 1971, when she was consumed by flames. Parts of the extant remains house government ministries.

Bahamas Historical Society Museum This impressive little place (☎ 242-322-4231), on Shirley St at Elizabeth Ave, has a modest miscellany of artifacts and documents tracing the islands' history from Lucayan times to the contemporary era. It's worth the admission merely to admire the beautiful model of the Spanish galleon *Santa Luceno*. A free history lecture is offered at 6 pm every last Thursday of the month. The mailing address is PO Box SS-6833, Nassau, The Bahamas. It's open 10 am to 4 pm weekdays and 10 am to noon Saturday; admission costs US$1/US50¢ adults/children.

Collins House Continue east to Collins Ave and you'll come upon this imposing neoclassical building, built in 1929 by the Honorable Ralph Gregory Collins to replace the family home destroyed in a hurricane the prior year. The beautiful two-story property was later used as a school and in 1971 took on its present role as the government's Ministry of Education and Culture.

Bennet's Hill

Elizabeth Ave slopes south past Princess Margaret Hospital, uphill to Bennet's Hill (part of Prospect Ridge).

Queen's Staircase At the south end of Elizabeth Ave, a passage and 90-foot-deep gorge in Prospect Ridge lead to Fort Fincastle and a water tower (see below). The passageway was cut from solid limestone by slaves, beginning in the 1790s, with the intent of constructing a roadway through Prospect Ridge. Emancipation was proclaimed before it could be finished.

The box canyon is cool and shady, and it has been beautified with towering palms. Rainwater oozes from the walls, feeding prolific epiphytes. The passageway is also lined with souvenir stalls. At its end, the Queen's Staircase (also known as the '66 Steps') leads up to the fort. Freelance guides may hustle you at the top. They'll immediately launch into the staircase's history. If you don't want their services, say so at this stage and they'll accept in good grace, but the guides can provide some intriguing anecdotes to liven up your viewing. They'll expect a tip (what you pay is up to you, depending on the length and quality of the spiel).

Fort Fincastle This tiny fortress was built in 1793 by Lord Dunmore. Why it was whimsically built in the shape of a paddle-wheel steamer isn't clear. The fort faces east and was intended to guard 'all the Town and the Road to the Eastward.' It was never put to the test and later served as a lighthouse and signal station. It lies partly in ruins but retains intriguing old cannons.

Water Tower The tall tower (☎ 242-322-2442) behind the fort was erected in 1928 to maintain water pressure on the island. It is 126 feet tall and provides a marvelous panoramic view of Nassau. You can walk up the narrow, winding staircase – there are 216 steps – or take the elevator. Tours are offered 8 am to 5 pm daily except Thursday for US50¢.

Over-the-Hill

This middle- and low-income area – bounded by East St and Blue Hill Rd to the east and west, and Prospect and Blue Hill Ridges to the north and south – is the heart and soul of African-Bahamian life in Nassau and the source of its most passionate politics.

The area began as a settlement for free blacks and slaves liberated from slave ships after 1807 by the British Navy. After emancipation in 1834, the area – comprising the villages of Grants Town and Bains Town and, farther east, Fox Hill – expanded. Most inhabitants were destitute and lived in squalor.

Over-the-Hill is still Nassau's seedy side, although the worst shanties are gone and there are pleasant middle-class pockets amid the potholed roads lined with wood-and-tin huts and renovated cottages gaily painted in prime Caribbean colors. This is where you'll find lively traditional culture. Games of *warri* – an African board game – are played beneath shade trees. Many locals paint or make handicrafts. The local bars have rake 'n' scrape bands, and the churches here are among the more lively on New Providence. Worth visiting are **Wesley Methodist Church** (dating from 1847) and the **St Agnes Anglican Church** (one year younger), both at Market and Cockburn Sts.

Caution is needed, as Nassau's ruffians and drug users and pushers are concentrated here.

EAST OF DOWNTOWN
Eastern Cemetery

Near the juncture of Bay and Dowdeswell Sts, this grassy cemetery holds the remains of pirates and other rascals executed during the past three centuries. The tumbledown tombs are above ground.

Behind is **St Matthew's Church**, a handsome, tall-steepled edifice dating from 1802. The cemetery to the west of the churchyard is called the 'Jew's Cemetery.'

Potter's Cay

The liveliest market in town takes place daily beneath the Paradise Island Exit Bridge (see the Central Nassau map) on a manmade cay where fishing boats arrive each day from other islands, carrying conch, crab, jack, mackerel, spiny lobster, fruit, and vegetables. Locals sell the harvest – alive, dead, dried, filleted – from stalls. You can watch them dicing vegetables, chopping up turtles, and preparing conch.

It gets boisterous on Friday, payday, when males congregate to spend their money on booze and conch.

The mail boats serving the Family Islands also berth here. It's a great place to hang out and watch the pandemonium whenever a boat arrives or prepares to embark.

The Retreat

This 11-acre garden, 200 yards south of Shirley St on Village Rd, is the headquarters of the Bahamas National Trust (BNT; ☎ 242-393-1317, fax 242-393-4978), housed in a 150-year-old building. It claims one of the largest private collections of palms in the world (176 species, many quite rare, representing more than half of all known genera of palms), begun in 1925 by original property owners Arthur and Margaret Langlois. The star of the show was a rare and awesome Ceylonese talipot palm that expended all its energy in 1986 on a once-in-a-lifetime bloom and then died.

Other specimens include hardwoods such as mahogany. Native orchids grace the trunks, and splendid ferns nestle in the limestone holes in which the palms are planted.

It's open 9 am to 5 pm Monday to Friday. Half-hour tours are offered, beginning at noon on Tuesday, Wednesday, and Thursday; admission is US$2. The mailing address is PO Box N-4105, Nassau, The Bahamas.

Doongalik Studios

For a look at Junkanoo items being created, check out this splendid communal art studio (☎ 242-394-1886, fax 242-394-0717, email: dstudios@bahamas.net.bs), at 18 Village Rd. The papaya-hued main building serves as a gallery for Bahamian fine art and showcases Junkanoo crafts, fine art, T-shirts, and rainbow-hued furniture. To the rear, you can watch a dedicated group of artists conjuring Junkanoo masks and other fanciful pieces. The entrance is guarded by three larger than life statues. There's a bush garden to the rear featuring many native trees and plants.

Fort Montagu

There's not much to draw you to this diminutive fort, though the place is intact and the cannon *in situ*. The oldest of Nassau's remaining strongholds, it was built in 1741 to guard the eastern approach to Nassau Harbour. It never fired its cannon in anger. It's closed to the public and is merely a curiosity in passing.

Eastern Road

A shoreline park south of Fort Montagu is lined with palms and casuarina trees. Two hundred yards from the fort, at the junction of Shirley St and Eastern Rd, is **Montagu Ramp**, a wharf where locals bring fish and conch ashore to clean and sell. You'll smell it well before you see it!

Eastern Rd skirts Montagu Bay through the subdivision of Blair (see the New Providence map). This windward shore is quite scenic as far as the **East End Lighthouse** on McPherson's Bend, at the easternmost point of New Providence. Just south is **Yamacraw Beach**, where the road turns west and heads inland through a middle-class residential area, ending at **Her Majesty's Prison**.

Eastern Rd is paralleled by a slope lined with upscale villas that are festooned in bougainvillea and framed by lush lawns. Sitting atop the ridge 2 miles south of Fort Montagu is **Blackbeard's Tower**, a semi-derelict cut-stone tower that, according to local lore, was built by Edward Teach – 'Blackbeard' – as a lookout tower. Historians point out that it was actually built in the late 18th century, long after the infamous pirate had been killed. The view is good but the place isn't worth the journey in its own right.

To reach it, you go up an unmarked path next to a green-and-white house called 'Tower Leigh,' 400 yards south of Fox Hill Rd.

Fox Hill

Fox Hill Rd leads half a mile south from Eastern Rd, over the hill to the village of Fox Hill (also known as Sandilands), which has a simple, rural charm drawn from its many old wood-and-limestone houses set amid copses. It began life in the 18th century as a free-slave settlement named Creek Village. During the 1900s, Robert

Sandilands, Chief Justice of the Bahamas, bought much of the area and distributed land grants to blacks for £10 or the equivalent in labor. The recipients named their settlement after their benefactor.

Freedom Park, at the juncture of Fox Hill Rd and Bernard Rd, is the center of town and the setting each year for Emancipation Day celebrations in the first week of August.

Other highlights include **St Anne's Anglican Church** on Fox Hill Rd, dating from 1867, and fortresslike **St Augustine's Monastery** (☎ 242-364-1331), atop a rocky perch on Bernard Rd. This working monastery was designed by Father Jerome, the itinerant architect-cleric who blessed Cat and Long Islands with beautiful churches (see the boxed text, 'Father Jerome,' in the Cat Island chapter). The imposing building dates from 1947 and is still used by Benedictine monks, who give guided tours (donations are appreciated)…a fascinating glimpse of monastic life. A college run by the monks is attached.

WEST OF DOWNTOWN

W Bay St leads westward along Nassau Harbour. About a half-mile from the British Colonial Hilton, you'll see remains of a battery of cannon on the harbor side, immediately next to the road. A cricket ground, **Clifford Park** (also called 'Haynes' Oval'), is to the south; it's the site of the annual Independence Day festivities on July 10.

Fort Charlotte

This fort (☎ 242-322-7500), the largest in The Bahamas, was built between 1787 and 1790 to guard the west entrance to Nassau Harbour. Sitting on the ridge above Clifford Park, it is intact and today is painted white. The deep moat and exterior walls were cut from solid rock and the walls buttressed by cedars. Lord Dunmore estimated its cost as a 'trifling' £4000, and to ensure the approval of the crown, proposed to name it Charlotte, after the consort of King George III. Within a year Dunmore had exceeded all resources. Reluctantly the English War Office forwarded the extra £17,846 required to complete the fort. Dunmore's folly was

ill-conceived, with the troops' barracks erected directly in the line of fire!

Today its moat, dungeon, underground tunnels, and bombproof chambers make an intriguing excursion, enhanced by a re-creation of a torture chamber, much like Madame Toussaud's house of horrors. Tours, led by guides in period costume, including Sam the 'Dungeon Man,' are offered every half-hour from 9 am to 4:30 pm daily. Entrance is free but the guides expect a tip.

Botanical Garden

Immediately west of the fort is the botanical garden (☎ 242-323-5975), on Chippingham Rd 200 yards south of W Bay St. It was constructed in 1951 on the site of an old rock quarry (known as 'the pit') that once supplied stones for construction during colonial times. The lush but poorly maintained 26-acre *Fantasia* has more than 600 species of tropical plants – many indigenous to The Bahamas – plus lily ponds, grottoes, and a waterfall fountain donated by the government of China. A re-creation of a Lucayan village with thatched *bohios* has seen better days. The gardens slope uphill to the east, offering fine views. It is open 8 am to 4 pm weekdays and 9 am to 4 pm weekends; admission is US$1/US50¢ adults/children.

Ardastra Gardens & Zoo

The privately run 6-acre garden-cum-zoo (☎ 242-323-5806, fax 242-323-7232), near the junction where Columbus Ave meets Chippingham Rd, 100 yards southwest of the Botanical Garden, features about 50 species of animals, birds, and reptiles from around the world. Indigenous species of flora and fauna include agoutis, hutias, snakes, and the endangered Bahama parrot, which, uniquely, is bred in captivity here. The zoo also has a large collection of nonnative species, including monkeys, caimans, and sleek cats such as jaguars and ocelots. The undisputed highlight, however, is the gang of West Indian flamingos trained to strut their stuff on voice command at 11 am and 2 and 4 pm daily. The birds get Sunday off.

Facilities include a snack bar and toilets. It's open 9 am to 4:30 pm daily. It is closed

Christmas Day. Admission costs US$12/6 adults/children.

Arawak Cay

This manmade 'island' lies north of W Bay St in front of Fort Charlotte. It serves as a commercial dock and water-storage area for the barges that bring Nassau's water supply from Andros. The entrance to the cay gets lively at lunchtime and on weekends, when locals gather for conch and fresh fish sold from fancifully decorated wooden stalls.

Crystal Cay Marine Park

One of Nassau's renowned landmarks is a white spaceship-shaped structure hovering above the ocean immediately north of Arawak Cay, to which it is attached by a bridge. The structure – the entrance to an underwater marine observatory – is the showpiece of the Crystal Cay Marine Park (☎ 242-328-1036, 800-328-8814, fax 242-323-3202), reached by following the access road that loops west around Crystal Cay. Alas, the facility, which included shark tanks, turtle pools, marine gardens, a stingray pool, and other attractions, closed in spring 2000, ostensibly for a complete remake, and it was uncertain when and if it would reopen.

CABLE BEACH

Cable Beach is a self-contained resort 3 miles west of downtown Nassau, linked by W Bay St. The beach is named for the telegraphic cable laid from Florida in 1892 that came ashore here. Nassau's major resort hotels are here, hovering over a seemingly endless sliver of pure-white sand shelving into turquoise shallows. Dominating the scene is the garish, purple Nassau Marriott, even more garish at night, when a rainbow assortment of neon lights rims the exterior of its three towers. There are water sports and restaurants aplenty, plus golf, tennis, and the Crystal Palace Casino, but no *sites* of interest.

Cable Beach lines Goodman's (east) and Sandyport (west) Bays, encircled by Delaport Point to the west and Brown's Point to the east. Near Brown's Point, the beach is

Which Beach?

Cable Beach – The most beautiful beach on the main island is about 2 miles long and has plenty of water sports and activity. Hotels, restaurants, and bars line the beach.

Love Beach – This small, little-used beach near Gambier Village is about 12 miles west of downtown. There's good snorkeling, and Compass Point is at hand.

Orange Hill Beach – About 8 miles west of downtown, this small, narrow beach is popular with local families. There are a few restaurants and bars nearby.

Saunders Beach – Between Cable Beach and downtown, this small beach is favored by local families. It has no facilities.

South Ocean Beach – On the southwest side of the island, this beach is narrow, secluded, several miles long, and trodden by very few people. You'll find great scuba diving offshore.

Western Esplanade Beach – On W Bay St, downtown Nassau's only beach stretches west from the British Colonial Hilton Hotel (which has its own private beach). It has limited attractions and no facilities, but is within minutes of downtown restaurants and hotels. It's popular with local men.

Paradise Island has its own beautiful beaches:

Cabbage Beach – This stunner stretches 2 miles along the north shore, with plenty of activity and water sports. Several resorts have facilities at the west end.

Paradise Beach – This beautiful beach curves gently along the northwest shore of the island; it is very lonesome to the west. The resorts have their own facilities, but nonguests can pay for privileges.

Pirate's Cove – This well-protected beauty nestles in its own cove west of Atlantis. It has no facilities.

Snorkeler's Cove Beach – Another beauty, this beach is east of Cabbage Beach. It is favored by day-trippers on picnicking and snorkeling excursions from Nassau.

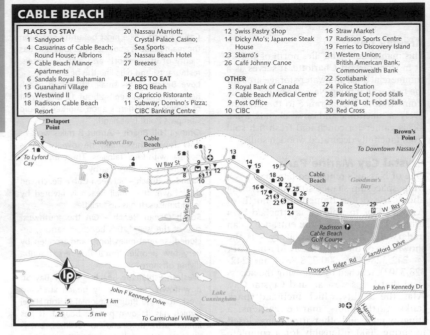

CABLE BEACH

PLACES TO STAY
1 Sandyport
4 Casuarinas of Cable Beach;
  Round House; Albrions
5 Cable Beach Manor
  Apartments
6 Sandals Royal Bahamian
13 Guanahani Village
15 Westwind II
18 Radisson Cable Beach
  Resort
20 Nassau Marriott;
  Crystal Palace Casino;
  Sea Sports
25 Nassau Beach Hotel
27 Breezes

PLACES TO EAT
2 BBQ Beach
8 Capriccio Ristorante
11 Subway; Domino's Pizza;
  CIBC Banking Centre

12 Swiss Pastry Shop
14 Dicky Mo's; Japanese Steak
  House
23 Sbarro's
26 Café Johnny Canoe

OTHER
3 Royal Bank of Canada
7 Cable Beach Medical Centre
9 Post Office
10 CIBC

16 Straw Market
17 Radisson Sports Centre
19 Ferries to Discovery Island
21 Western Union;
  British American Bank;
  Commonwealth Bank
22 Scotiabank
24 Police Station
28 Parking Lot; Food Stalls
29 Parking Lot; Food Stalls
30 Red Cross

called Goodman's Beach; it's popular with locals, who flock there on weekends and leave Cable Beach proper to tourists.

One mile east of Cable Beach is tiny **Saunders Beach**, popular with locals at lunchtime (they sit in their cars, munching cracked conch) and on weekends. At Delaport Point there's a massive 144-acre, waterfront residential and resort development named Sandyport.

At Cable Beach, W Bay St becomes a wide boulevard (two lanes in each direction) with a landscaped central median complete with jogging track – the Tropical Walkway. Labels set in the walkway describe the flora.

Discovery Island

For a break, you can head out to this small cay – formerly Balmoral Island – about a mile offshore from Cable Beach (see the New Providence map). It is now leased by the Sandals chain but is open to nonguests. It has its own beach, an atmospheric restau-

rant, and a lively bar with swim-up pool and Jacuzzi. Trails lead to quiet nooks.

Free ferries run regularly from Sandals Royal Bahamian (for guests only). Ferries also operate from the pier between the Radisson and Marriott hotels on a regular basis, charging US$10 roundtrip.

ACTIVITIES
Diving & Snorkeling

New Providence offers superb diving close to its shores, including fantastic wall and wreck dives. The most noted sites lie off the southwest coast between Coral Harbour and Lyford Cay. You'll find most of the marinas mapped on the Central Nassau map.

Bahama Divers (☎ 242-393-1466, fax 242-393-6078, bahdiver@bahamas.net.bs; in the US ☎ 954-351-9533, 800-398-3483), at Nassau Yacht Haven on E Bay St, offers a variety of dive trips, including the Lost Blue Hole (famous for its sharks and schools of stingrays) and wrecks. It has a three-hour learn-to-dive course as well as PADI certification courses (US$399). A single dive costs US$45; a two-tank dive costs US$70; a night dive is US$50. It rents out equipment.

Coral Divers (☎ 242-362-1263, fax 242-362-2407) offers several dives, including a 'shark dive' for US$110 in which you watch sharks being hand-fed at Bull Shark Wall or Shark Buoy. A two-tank dive costs US$65; a night dive costs US$100. Snorkel trips cost US$25. It rents snorkel and scuba gear. The company will certify you. Write to Coral Divers at PO Box CB-11961, Nassau, The Bahamas.

Other companies include Divers Haven (☎ 242-393-0869) on E Bay St, Diving Safaris (☎ 242-393-2522), and Sun Divers (☎ 242-325-8927), in the Bayshore Marina.

Most upscale hotels also offer diving.

All dive operators also offer snorkeling, as do tour companies, which have trips to offshore cays. You can even go snorkeling with dolphins at Blue Lagoon or Salt Cay; see Dolphin Encounters in the Paradise Island section for details.

See the West New Providence and South New Providence sections in this chapter for details on operators elsewhere on the island. For a list of prime sites, see the Dive & Snorkel Sites boxed text, and for more information about diving and snorkeling in The Bahamas, see the Outdoor Activities chapter.

Boating & Sailing

You can charter boats from any of the following marinas on E Bay St:

Brown's Boat Basin ☎ 242-393-3331, fax 242-393-1868

East Bay Yacht Basin ☎/fax 242-394-1816

Nassau Harbour Club & Marina ☎ 242-393-0771, fax 242-393-5393

Nassau Yacht Haven ☎ 242-393-8173

See the Outdoor Activities chapter for general information about sailing and chartering boats.

You can rent your own little speedboat from Coral Reef Charters (☎ 242-362-2058)

at the East Bay Yacht Basin wharf, immediately south of Potter's Cay. A six-seater Excel costs US$175/350 half/full day. Hotel transfers cost US$3.50 to downtown; US$7 to Cable Beach. It sounds like a pretty cool way to take yourself to an offshore cay.

Larger vessels can also be chartered, including the *King Fisher* (☎ 242-393-3739) and the *Chubasco* (☎ 242-322-8148, fax 242-326-4140, chubasco@nsn.com), which charters for US$300/500 half/full day. Both are based at the wharf beneath the Paradise Island Bridge.

Dive & Snorkel Sites

New Providence has many excellent sites for diving and snorkeling:

Anchor – A coral head pokes out of a wall 60 feet below the surface, teeming with fish life.

Lost Ocean Blue Hole – This vertical cavern gapes in 30 feet of water on a sand bottom frequented by nurse sharks and stingrays. The cave bells out to 200 feet and deeper. There's a lobster-filled cavern at 80 feet.

Oasis Wall – This deep dive just off Old Fort Beach is known for reef corals all the way down to 200 feet. There's plenty of lobster and pelagics, too.

Razorback – It's named for the arcing ridge of coral-covered limestone that rises from a sand bottom before plummeting into the Tongue of the Ocean. The reef is a menagerie of fish. The wall attracts hammerhead sharks.

School House – This site features endless varieties of coral at depths rarely exceeding 20 feet. Fish life ranges from blennies and gobies to schooling yellowtail.

The Valley – Says *Skin Diving* magazine: 'Into the valley of death swam the 600 groupers. Coral to the left of them, coral to the right, and the Tongue of the Ocean just over the ridge. They spawned like there was no tomorrow.' Imagine...just you and the sharks watching the yearly group(er) sex.

Sport Fishing

Nassau is a good base for sport fishing, with superb sites just 20 minutes away. Charters can be arranged at most major hotels or by calling any of the marinas listed under Boating & Sailing, above. Try the following:

Born Free Charter Service	☎ 242-393-4144
Brown's Charter	☎ 242-324-2061
Chubasco Charters	☎ 242-322-8148
Kingfisher Charters	☎ 242-393-3739

Also see the Paradise Island section, later in this chapter.

Boat Excursions

Dozens of day trips are offered, with options for snorkeling, diving, beach time, island visits, partying, sunset and dinner cruises, and other activities. A few vessels depart the Nassau waterfront; most depart the dock immediately west of the Paradise Island Bridge. See the Paradise Island section for details.

Bahamas Fastferries (☎ 242-323-2166, fax 242-322-8185) offers a 'Harbour Island Day Away' excursion to Eleuthera from Potter's Cay, including a tour of Harbour Island and lunch on Pink Sands Beach (US$139, or US$89 for children).

Topsail Yacht Charters (☎ 242-393-0820) offers full-day cruises to Rose Island aboard the *Liberty Call*, *Riding High*, and *Wind Dance* sailboats. Half-day trips cost US$35, with picnic lunch and snorkeling. Full-day trips, a champagne-and-cocktail cruise, and a private dinner cruise are also offered.

The Booze&Cruise Co Ltd (☎ 242-393-3722) has four-hour cruises aboard *Lucayan Queen*, departing Nassau Yacht Haven on E Bay St at 1:30 pm daily, for US$30 with free drinks. A full-day excursion costs US$50. It also has sunset cruises. Hotel transfers are provided.

Barefoot Sailing Cruises (☎ 242-393-0820, fax 242-393-5817, barefoot@bahamas.net.bs) offers half- and full-day sailing and snorkel cruises to the outlying cays, plus a champagne sunset cruise. Private charters are also offered.

Half- and full-day excursions to Blackbeard's Cay (☎ 242-323-5519) are also offered. And Captain TJ (☎ 242-323-7770) offers day (US$39) and evening (US$59) cruises aboard his three-masted schooner.

Hartley's Undersea Walk (☎ 242-393-8234/7569) offers a four-hour cruise that includes an escorted undersea adventure with a difference. You'll don a roomy brass helmet with large glass windows for all-around viewing. The half-day trip begins with a cruise aboard the *Pied Piper*, a 57-foot catamaran with a sun deck and lounge. Trips depart at 9:30 am and 1:30 pm daily from Nassau Yacht Haven. The trip costs US$39.

Submarine *Seaworld Explorer* (☎ 242-356-2548) is a 45-passenger semisubmarine with an air-con hull lined with large windows below water level. The 90-minute excursion takes in the coral reefs of the Sea Gardens Marine Park off the north shore, and costs U$29, US$19 for children. Its office is in the Moses Shopping Plaza on Bay St.

You can even pilot your own 'Underwater Bubble' with Sub Bahamas (☎ 242-362-4171). Imagine a seahorse-shaped scooter with an air tank in lieu of wheels, and a giant plastic bubble that envelops your shoulders and head (US$89).

Undersea Walk: You're under water but your hair stays dry!

Other Water Sports

Cable Beach offers every kind of beach and water activity, including parasailing, water-skiing, and windsurfing. Most resort hotels either include water sports in their rates or offer them as optional extras. However, few resorts offer *motorized* water sports, which are the domain of local entrepreneurs such as Sea Sports (☎ 242-327-6200) at the Nassau Marriott, which also offers sea kayaks, Hobie Cats, Sunfish, and sailboards.

Surf Watersports (☎ 242-327-7711 ext 6590) rents sailboards, small sailboats, and kayaks.

Golf

New Providence has two championship golf courses, both open to the public. The challenging Radisson Cable Beach Golf Course (☎ 242-327-6000, 800-777-7800) in Cable Beach charges a US$105 green fee (US$85 for nine holes). The oldest course in The Bahamas, it is managed by Arnold Palmer...the very same! Its well-maintained greens and fairways, particularly the back nine, are dotted with water traps. Its vital statistics: 72-par, 7040 yards, 13 lakes and 50 sand traps.

Another excellent course, the South Ocean Golf Course, is at New Providence's western tip; see the West New Providence section for details. Also see the Paradise Island section later in this chapter for more golfing options.

Tennis, Racquetball & Squash

Dozens of hotels have tennis courts, most notably the British Colonial Hilton (☎ 242-322-3301) on Marlborough St; and the Radisson Cable Beach Golf Course (☎ 242-327-6000). Nonguests are charged a fee, typically US$5 per person. Night play costs US$10.

The Radisson Sports Centre, opposite the Radisson Cable Beach, has racquetball courts and charges US$15 per hour for nonguests (free to guests). You'll find squash courts at the Village Squash Club (☎ 242-323-1580) on Village Rd; it charges US$12 per hour (plus US$4 for nonguests). The facility includes swimming pool and sauna.

Bird Watching

The Bahamas National Trust (☎ 242-393-1317) offers guided bird-watching walks every month.

Bicycling

Pedal & Paddle Ecoventures (☎ 242-362-2772, fax 242-362-2044), PO Box CB-12564, Nassau, The Bahamas, has a half-day, 3-mile bicycle ride for US$49. You'll cycle through the pine forests and mangrove creeks of New Providence and paddle in two-person kayaks to a shallow reef for snorkeling. You must be at least 4 feet 6 inches tall to participate.

Spas & Gyms

Gold's Gym (☎ 242-394-6975), on Mackey St at Bay St (see the Central Nassau map), charges nonmembers US$5. A Gold's Gym was under construction at Sandyport.

The gym at the Radisson Sports Centre in Cable Beach is free to everyone. All the upscale resorts have gyms or spas. Sandals Royal Bahamian has a top-notch full-service spa offering everything from mud baths to Swedish massage and reflexology.

Fitness fanatics can run the shaded jogging trail that snakes along the central median of W Bay St, a 1½-mile-long path from Sandals Royal Bahamian to the Cable Beach Golf Course. The Nassau Hash House Harriers have an organized run each Monday (April to October) or Sunday (October to April). Contact Ewan Tough (☎ 242-323-4966, 242-362-4654).

Other Activities

Village Lanes (☎ 242-393-2427), at Village and Wulff Rds, has a 20-lane bowling alley. It's open 9:30 am to midnight daily and charges US$2.50 to US$3 per game.

Canoeing trips (☎ 242-356-4283) are offered on Lake Nancy, a shallow lake fringed by marshes near the airport. You can nip through a canal to Lake Killarney, a much larger neighbor. Access is off John F Kennedy Dr near Blake Rd.

ORGANIZED TOURS
City Tours

Forty-five-minute walking tours are offered by independent BahamaHost guides from the tourist information office (☎ 242-326-9772, 328-7810) or from the Ministry of Tourism's Tour Unit (☎ 242-322-8634) in Rawson Square. Tours depart every 90 minutes between 10 am and 4 pm, Tuesday, Wednesday, Friday, and Sunday, and cost US$5 per person. They're supposedly offered twice an hour, but times are flexi-

---

¡Cuba Sí!

You won't be long in The Bahamas (or the Turks and Caicos) before you notice advertisements for excursions to Cuba, which lies a mere 100 miles from Nassau. Despite its hardships and faults, Cuba offers a profound experience that far exceeds most visitors' expectations.

In 1999 more than 1.6 million foreigners visited Cuba, including about 160,000 US citizens, mostly through Mexico and Nassau. For US citizens, the temptation to visit an island that Washington, DC, has dubbed off-limits holds a compelling allure (see What Uncle Sam Says, below).

All you need to fly from Nassau is your passport and a tourist visa issued on the spot by Cubana Airlines or any of the Bahamian or Turks and Caicos companies that specialize in excursions to this intriguing island of socialism and sensuality. Havana is about one hour from Nassau and about 90 minutes from the Turks and Caicos.

Foreign visitors can travel freely and mingle with Cubans, usually without restraint.

I recommend a visit to Havana. I *love* this city of tropical charms! Walking Havana's streets is otherworldly. The Spanish colonial buildings hard up against the Atlantic are handsome indeed. Old Havana (proclaimed a World Heritage Site by UNESCO in 1982 and currently being restored to haughty grandeur) is an exhilarating 350-acre repository of castles, churches, and columned mansions dating back centuries. Bohemian cafes spill onto colonial plazas, and at bars such as La Bodeguita and El Floridita you can sit with Ernest Hemingway's ghost and savor the proletarian fusion of dialectics and rum.

And Cuban communism doesn't mean you can't have fun. Cuba blends Caribbean rhythms with Latin sensuality. Music – salsa, rumba, and hip-swiveling *despolete* – is everywhere. Dance clubs throb to the latest sounds: world beat, hip-hop, and soca. And the Cuban people are incredibly gifted, generous, courteous, and intellectual – they will steal your heart!

What Uncle Sam Says The US Government's Trading with the Enemy Act, while not actually barring its citizens from traveling to Cuba, prohibits them from spending money there or otherwise engaging in financial transactions with Cuba. To spend even a cent, US citizens have to obtain a Treasury Dept license, which is granted only to journalists, academic researchers, and Cuban-Americans with family in Cuba. (However, if you purchase a cruise or an all-inclusive package in The Bahamas or the Turks and Caicos and don't actually spend any money in Cuba, your visit is entirely legal!)

The Clinton administration has gradually eased travel restrictions. Few transgressions are ever prosecuted.

The Cuban government has an open-door policy and welcomes US tourists. Savvy to the complications faced by US tourists, Cuban immigration officials don't stamp passports.

Getting There & Away Several Bahamian tour companies offer weekend and longer excursions using Cubana Airline charters from Nassau. Several airline charter companies in the Turks and Caicos offer their own flights from Providenciales. Most include airfare, transfers, city tours, some meals and entertainment, and accommodations for overnight trips. You can pay for your tour with a US credit card. However, with a few exceptions, US credit cards cannot be used in Cuba.

The trips are open – *legally* – to US citizens as long as they don't spend money in Cuba.

ble. The itinerary incorporates all the main downtown sites between Prince George Wharf and Fort Fincastle. The maximum group size is 10.

Henry's Mobile Tours (☎ 242-380-1081 beeper) offers one-hour guided walking tours, as well as 'mobile tours' into local communities.

Bahamas Experience (☎ 242-356-2985, fax 242-356-7118) and Majestic Tours (☎ 242-322-2606, fax 242-326-5785), at Hillside Manor on Cumberland St, also offer city tours, as do Happy Tours (☎ 242-323-4555) on Nassau St, and Tropical Tours (☎ 242-322-5791) at Palmdale Ave and Mackey St.

Flightseeing
Safari Seaplanes (☎ 242-393-2522/1179) offers flightseeing tours to the Exumas, including three stops, a picnic lunch at Warderick Wells, and snorkeling in Thunderball Grotto. Its mailing address is PO Box N-9067, Nassau, The Bahamas.

SPECIAL EVENTS
Nassau hosts the country's largest annual Junkanoo celebrations, beginning before dawn on Boxing Day (December 26) and New Year's Day. There's also the Goombay Summer Festival, a midyear Junkanoo that is held every June.

Opening of Parliament
This colorful formal occasion features the Royal Bahamas Police Force Band marching in pith helmets, starched white tunics, and leopard-skin shawls. The governor-general delivers a speech on behalf of Her Majesty, to whom the gathered officials swear allegiance.

Opening of the Supreme Court Sessions
Pageantry also marks the start of Supreme Court sessions in January, April, July, and October. Lawyers and judges in full regalia march to Christ Church Anglican Cathedral for a service followed by an inspection of the Guard-of-Honor. Music and even more pageantry are provided by the police force band.

Classic Cars Race
You don't expect to see vintage race cars tearing down Bay St. But lo! Racing is an island tradition dating back to the 1950s, when Porsches, MGs, Lotuses, and even Formula Ones, driven by the great names of motor sports, challenged the Nassau circuit on an old airstrip that is now the international airport. The annual race was discontinued in 1989 but was resurrected in January 1997 with Cable Beach as its venue. It now takes place every January. Contact the Ministry of Tourism (☎ 242-302-2006) for more information.

Bahamas Atlantis Superboat Challenge
The world's fastest powerboats tear it up off the shores of New Providence in this world-class race held each September. The winner's *average* lap speed over the 12½-mile course typically exceeds 115mph! The event is the last in the year's championship calendar, adding to the feverish excitement. You can watch it from the shore as the race passes through Nassau Harbour and under the Paradise Island Bridge; for information, call the Ministry of Tourism (☎ 242-322-7500).

Other Happenings
The BTO (see the Information section) provides complete lists of special events. Dates vary from year to year.

January
Ebony Fashion Fair Held at the end of the month at the Super Club Breezes (sponsored by *Ebony* magazine); attracts socialites and aspiring models and showcases the latest designs; call Pilot Club of Nassau (☎ 242-325-6006) for details

February
International Food Fair Features cookouts and contests

People of the Bahamas Annual Archives Exhibition Highlights the contributions of various ethnic groups to the nation

April
Snipe Winter Sailing Championship Draws home-made boats to race one another in Montagu

Bay; contact Royal Nassau Sailing Club (☎ 242-393-0145) for details

June

Caribbean Muzik Fest Weeklong festival features a range of music, from reggae to soca to dance hall, at the Queen Elizabeth Sports Centre; 8 pm until dawn; US$30; for details, call the Ministry of Tourism (☎ 242-322-7500)

August

Emancipation Day Celebrated on the first Monday of the month; Fox Hill features an early-morning 'Junkanoo Rush' and holds its own emancipation celebration a week later

Miss Bahamas Contest Features contestants vying for the title of Miss Bahamas; the winner represents the country in the Miss World contest; for details, call ☎ 242-393-4041

October

Great Bahamas Seafood Festival Held on Arawak Cay, with live entertainment (including Junkanoo) and a cooking competition

International Cultural Weekend Bahamians of all shades and cultural backgrounds come together to celebrate their unity; features arts and crafts displays, food fests, float parades, and live music; for information call ☎ 242-302-2076

Guy Fawkes Night Gunpowder Plot villain is recalled in Nassau's nighttime parade on November 5

December

Police Band Annual Christmas & Classical Concert Royal Bahamas Police Force Band performs at the Atlantis resort on Paradise Island

PLACES TO STAY

Nassau isn't cheap or getting cheaper. Many hotels are outrageously overpriced, but there are a few bargains. In general, downtown hotels tend to be smaller, quainter, and cheaper than those in Cable Beach, where the more urbane resorts are concentrated.

There's a notice board with information on small hotels in the immigration lounge of Nassau International Airport. *Caveat emptor!* Brochures tell you little and are often more misleading than illuminating. Pay particular attention to my comments on ambiance.

Budget

The *Diplomat Inn* (☎ 242-325-2688, 4 Delancy St) has nine simple rooms with ceiling fans and shared bathrooms for US$25 single or double. It serves mostly locals and is poorly managed.

The Bahamas only hostel, the *International Travellers Lodge & Youth Hostel* (☎ 242-325-4147, internationaltravellerslodge@yahoo.com, 23 Delancy St) has 20 simply yet pleasantly appointed air-con rooms, each with two single or queen beds, a dresser, and ceiling fan. Some have shared baths. There's also a dorm with shared bathroom. There's a small restaurant serving creole food, and an open-air bar out back. The place is lovingly tended by Geoffrey Collie. It's part of the International Youth Hostel Association. A space in the dorm costs US$26 per person, including breakfast. Private rooms run from US$45/68 single/double in summer to US$65/76 in winter. A US$25 key and linen deposit is required. Credit cards can be used for reservations only. Airport transfers cost US$12 one-way. The postal address is PO Box CB-13558, Nassau, The Bahamas.

The *Mignon Guest House* (☎ 242-322-4771, 12 Market St) is favored by budget travelers. It is splendidly situated in the heart of downtown and a veritable bargain at US$40/45 single/double year-round, including tax. There are six small rooms, clean and quaint, with fans and central air-con, but with shared toilet and bathroom. All have a TV. Guests have access to a small kitchen. The Greek resident-owners, Steve and Mary Antonas, run a tight ship: strictly no non-guests! The mailing address is PO Box N-786, Nassau, The Bahamas.

Mid-Range

Downtown The modest *Park Manor Guesthouse* (☎ 242-356-5471, fax 242-325-3554), on Market St uphill from Government House, isn't a true guesthouse. It has a range of offerings. 'Efficiencies' for two people cost US$48; studio apartments for up to four people cost US$60. Deluxe apartments for six cost US$83, and a small cottage costs US$55. Most rooms have king-size beds; all have kitchenette, fans, and air-con. There's an amoeba-shaped pool in the forecourt. The postal address is PO Box N-4164, Nassau, The Bahamas.

The uninspired *Sunshine Guesthouse* (☎ 242-322-3888, *15 West St*), has rooms in a two-story home for US$50. The mailing address is PO Box N-535, Nassau, The Bahamas.

An alternative is the equally unre-markable but adequate *Ocean Spray Hotel* (☎ 242-322-8032, *fax 242-325-5731, information@oceansprayhotel.com*) on W Bay St, with 28 air-con rooms, all with TV, refrigerator, and in-room safe, and the Europa Restaurant. Rates are US$60/70 single/double low season, US$75/85 high season.

The basic *Harbour Moon Hotel* (☎ 242-323-8120, *fax 242-328-0374*), at the corner of Bay and Devaux Sts, has small, simple rooms for US$50/60 single/double, with air-con, color TV, telephone, and a private bath-room with hot water. The beds are oversize. It's nothing inspirational, just a place to rest your head, though it's well placed for a stroll into town. Its postal address is PO Box N-646, Nassau, The Bahamas.

If you're not fussy, try the *Grand Central Hotel* (☎ 242-322-8356, *fax 242-325-2018*) at Bay and Parliament Sts, with 35 small rooms in a dowdy orange-and-brown decor. Each has a TV, air-con, and phone; there's no pool or restaurant. Singles cost US$65, doubles US$70. A room in the small guesthouse across the road costs US$56. The mailing address is PO Box N-4084, Nassau, The Bahamas.

The ho-hum *Buena Vista Restaurant & Hotel* (☎ 242-322-2811, *fax 242-322-5881*) is on Delancy St. This grand old mansion, which is acclaimed for its restaurant, has six rooms, all upstairs, each with air-con, TV, radio, and direct-line phones. However, the accommodations aren't all they're often cracked up to be. Rates begin at US$60.

El Greco (☎ 242-325-1121, *fax 242-325-1124*), at the corner of W Bay and Augusta Sts at the west end of downtown, is a compact family-run hotel, enhanced by Spanish decor; the friendly owners are Greek. The clean,

spacious rooms surround a small courtyard with a pool, and bougainvillea adds color. The rooms upstairs are larger and offer more light, with balconies over the courtyard. Take a suite in the main building if possible; some of them are huge. Rooms cost about US$87/97; the postal address is PO Box N-4187, Nassau, The Bahamas.

The *Towne Hotel* (☎ 242-322-8450, *fax 242-328-1512, townehotel@bahamaweb .com, 40 George St*) offers 46 small, dingy air-con rooms, each with fans, king-size bed, and a TV past its prime. Rates are US$70 to US$85 in summer, US$84 to US$104 in winter, including continental breakfast. The mailing address is PO Box N-4804, Nassau, The Bahamas.

A more expensive, albeit soulless option is the *Holiday Inn Junkanoo Beach Hotel* (☎ 242-356-0000, 800-465-4329, *fax 242-323-1408*), formerly the Astoria, on W Bay St at Nassau St. The 117 recently remodeled rooms are clean and decorated in bright tropical pastels, and each has a balcony, TV, and king-size bed or two doubles. Standard rooms cost US$70 single or double, deluxe rooms cost US$100. The restoration was ongoing at press time. The postal address is PO Box N-3236, Nassau, The Bahamas.

Nearby, also on West Bay St, is the West Bay Hotel, due to open in late 2000.

Farther Afield West of downtown, a basic option is the simple, family-run *Arawak Inn* (☎/*fax 242-322-2638; ask for Lloyd Gay*) on W Bay St near Chippingham Rd. It has six small, simple, self-contained, air-con rooms with kitchenette, TV, and ceiling fans. Sizes vary. It's basic but fine. No children under 12 are accepted. Rates are US$45 to US$70 per night single or double based on two night minimum; US$50 to US$75 for one night. The postal address is PO Box N-3222, Nassau, The Bahamas.

Dillet's Guest House (☎ 242-325-1133, 800-742-4276, *fax 242-325-7183*), on Dunmore Ave at Strachan St (see the Central Nassau map), is one of Nassau's true gems, overflow-ing with homey hospitality. A row of tall palms guides you up the path to the 1920s-era home, with rocking chairs on the veranda.

The huge lounge features an Old World fire-place, wicker furniture, and squawking para-keets. The house is festooned with original art. Each of the seven simple yet graciously decorated air-con rooms has cable TV (all but two have a kitchenette). Six rooms are planned in a new extension, plus a small dipping pool. There are hammocks slung between trees. Rates – US$85 single/double in summer, US$125 in winter, and US$25 for a third person – include continental break-fast. Dinners are available on request for US$20. A small gift shop sells quality crafts. The mailing address is PO Box N-204, Nassau, The Bahamas.

The 34-room *City Lodge Hotel* (☎ 242-394-2591, fax 242-394-3636), just off E Bay St, is clean and adequate but dingy. Air-con rooms have TV and phone and cost US$45 mid-week and US$60 Thursday to Satur-day. There's a pool and small store. Secu-rity may be an issue: The front desk is hidden behind thick glass. The hotel's postal address is PO Box SS-6275, Nassau, The Bahamas.

Other hotels east of town include the charmless *Montagu Beach Inn* (☎ 242-393-0475, fax 242-393-6061) on E Shirley St, whose 33 large, pleasantly furnished rooms cost US$63 single or double year-round. The inn has a pool and a nightclub. The postal address is PO Box N-1411, Nassau, The Bahamas. Nearby and more appealing is the *Orchard Hotel* (☎ 242-393-1297, fax 242-394-3562) on Village Rd, with 14 cot-tages set in quiet, lush grounds centered on a small pool. Each is pleasantly furnished and has air-con, TV, and a small kitchen. There's a small bar. Studios cost US$70 to US$90; cottages cost US$105 standard, US$120 superior. The postal address is PO Box N-1514, Nassau, The Bahamas.

The *Red Carpet Inn* (☎ 242-393-8681, fax 242-393-9055), on E Bay St, is a contempo-rary 40-room hotel with adequate but charmless rooms. They're clean, with double beds, air-con and fan, TV, and phone. Some have a kitchenette. Rates range from US$94 standard to US$99 deluxe, including taxes. The postal address is PO Box SS-6233, Nassau, The Bahamas.

A more upscale option, popular with yachters, is the *Nassau Harbour Club* (☎ 242-393-0771, fax 242-393-5393) on E Bay St, which overlooks the marina and has a pool and sun deck suspended over the water. The decor – tropical prints against stark-white walls – is appealing. The 50 air-con rooms and suites are clean, albeit mod-estly furnished (some are rather dimly lit). Each has a TV and phone. Winter rates run from US$90 single or double for a standard room to US$130 for a deluxe minisuite. Its postal address is PO Box SS-5755, Nassau, The Bahamas.

Top End

Downtown Dominating the west end of downtown Bay St is the *British Colonial Hilton Nassau* (☎ 242-322-3301, 800-445-8667, fax 242-322-2286), a massive grande dame of a hotel built in 1922 and the loca-tion shoot for two James Bond movies. It re-opened in January 1999 after a thorough renovation that shrank its 510 rooms to 291 expanded rooms, including 21 executive and junior suites. The rooms boast exquisite and elegant contemporary decor and modern amenities, with superb marble-lined bath-rooms and a surfeit of mahogany. Three floors are designated as business and execu-tive room floors. The newly landscaped grounds open onto the hotel's private beach, plus a small marina. There are two restau-rants (one a gourmet offering), a swimming pool, tennis courts, and some water sports. A dive operation was to be added. Rates range from US$103 with a 'Value Pass' or US$189 standard or US$285 king. The 'Double-O Suite,' stocked with James Bond movies and Bond posters on the walls, starts at US$350. The postal address is PO Box N-7148, Nassau, The Bahamas.

Nassau's most venerable hotel is the 250-year-old *Graycliff Hotel & Restaurant* (☎ 242-322-2796, fax 242-326-6110), a Geor-gian home built by a wealthy pirate and loftily situated above town on W Hill St. It is the only *Relais et Chateaux* establishment in the West Indies. Run by live-in proprietors Enrico and Anna Garzaroli and their son Paolo, Graycliff is a veritable museum of period antiques and fine prints. The nine lofty-ceilinged rooms and five romantic cottage suites in the garden have windows on all sides. Each has air-con, king bed, cable TV, plump robes, and other luxe extras; several have whirlpool baths. Bathrooms are exquisite. Feeling opulent? Check out (or into) the Mandarino Suite, done up in an Asian motif with an oversize bathroom and bed. Rates range from US$250 to US$400 in summer; US$310 to US$550 in winter. The hotel features a beautiful garden, a saltwater Olympic-length pool – one of three pools – in a stone courtyard, and a well-stocked humidor from which to choose a select torpedo to puff on with a cognac chosen from the hotel's vast cellar. The restaurant is acclaimed. Guests are met at the airport and whisked to Graycliff in a Mercedes limo. The mailing address is PO Box N-10246, Nassau, The Bahamas.

An equally luxe extension, the *Graycliff Cigar Co* (☎ 242-328-7050), two doors down, caters to cigar lovers with six guest rooms, a two-bedroom villa with antique furnishings, its own restaurant/bar called Humidor, a walk-in humidor, and a small cigar factory and store. Cigar dinners are hosted. It shares the pools and other facilities with its venerable neighbor.

Farther Afield Seeking an upscale villa? Consider *Crystal Cay Marine Park & Villas* (☎ 242-328-1036, 888-662-7728, fax 242-323-3202, coral@bahamas.net.bs) on Crystal Cay off W Bay St. These 22 secluded and handsome one-bedroom villas are lavishly adorned with elegant contemporary decor and offer a breezy setting atop the coral shore. Each has a fully stocked kitchen, minibar, satellite TV, and VCR, plus a private courtyard with a deep plunge pool. You can sit with a sundowner cocktail and watch the cruise ships go by at what seems like fingertip distance. There's a private beach two minutes' stroll away. Villa rates begin at US$125/225 single/double in low season and rise to US$250/350 in peak season.

Cable Beach Near the west end of Cable Beach, *Casuarinas of Cable Beach* (☎ 242-

327-8153, fax 242-327-8152) spans W Bay St. The rooms are nice enough, with pleasing furnishings, but the public areas are dowdy. Some are timeworn; others are more attractive, especially room No 15, the graciously appointed 'suite.' In-room cable TV offers pay-per-view programs, including adult movies. Telephones are not direct dial. There are two swimming pools, one on each side of the road. It boasts two restaurants. There's access to a tiny beach. Rates begin at US$95 single or double and run to US$195 for a two-bedroom suite. The mailing address is PO Box CB-13225, Nassau, The Bahamas.

The vast *Radisson Cable Beach Resort* (☎ 242-327-6000, 800-333-3333, fax 242-327-6987, radcblebch@aol.com; in the US ☎ 800-432-0221, fax 305-932-0023) has 669 ocean-view rooms, all with a balcony, overlooking an exquisitely landscaped, 25,000-sq-foot courtyard with three large pools, cascading falls, whirlpool spas, and shady palms. The spacious, air-con rooms have king-size beds. The resort offers 'Camp Junkanoo,' an extensive supervised program for kids. Activities include tennis, golf on a championship 18-hole course, racquetball, squash, and water sports. There are six restaurants. One night of hosted off-property dining is included for guests staying four or more nights. It also has a shopping arcade and direct access to the Marriott's Crystal Palace Casino. Rates begin at US$185 single or double in low season for SuperSaver rooms, rising to US$245 in high season, and range from US$220 to US$280 for deluxe rooms. All-inclusive packages are offered. The postal address is PO Box N-4914, Nassau, The Bahamas.

I also like the *Nassau Beach Hotel* (☎ 242-327-7711, fax 242-327-8829; in the US ☎ 888-627-7282), an intimate and traditional hotel that was featured in two James Bond movies before it lost its luster. A US$12 million refurbishment that added a pool and lavish landscaping was completed in spring 1999, elevating the property from a two- to three-star hotel. All the rooms are admirable, but those in the East Wing are splendid – they're spacious and have beautiful Edwardian mahogany furniture. Cable

TV with optional pay-per-view channels is standard. There's a small shopping arcade and several dining options, including Café Johnny Canoe. Water sports are offered. The hotel has a fiercely loyal clientele. Rates range from US$135 single or double in summer to US$235 winter for standard rooms, and run to US$370 to US$500 for two-bedroom suites. You can also choose an all-inclusive package. The hotel's postal address is PO Box N-7756, Nassau, The Bahamas.

Just west, in garish counterpoint, is the **Nassau Marriott** (☎ 242-327-6200, 800-333-3333, fax 242-327-6801), a purple-and-neon futuristic hotel straight out of a Flash Gordon movie. This megahotel (it has 867 rooms and suites in five towers) is run to high standards, despite exuding a Las Vegas gaudiness. The rooms are tastefully done in subdued contemporary decor. The Galaxy Suite is said to be the most expensive hotel room in the world...a paltry US$25,000 a night! Facilities include the Crystal Palace Casino, a cabaret nightclub, a shopping plaza, and several bars and restaurants. The Sportsbook Sports Bar & Deli offers a splendid buffet. The hotel also has a 'Kids Club,' with supervised activities and theme days, costing US$10 per child per hour. Babysitting costs US$15 per hour. The landscaped beachfront courtyard has a 100-foot waterslide. Low season rates began at US$169 standard, US$189 deluxe ocean-view. The hotel's postal address is PO Box N-8306, Nassau, The Bahamas.

Immediately west of the Radisson is **Westwind II** (☎ 242-327-7211; in the US ☎ 616-942-5555, fax 616-942-0974). This resort boasts upscale, self-contained, two-bedroom air-con villas in lush grounds centered on two swimming pools, and features a clubhouse with bar and grill. Each unit has satellite TV and a fully furnished kitchen. Winter rates range from US$150 to US$230 low season for up to four guests, and US$225 to US$320 high season. The local mailing address is PO Box CB-11006, Nassau, The Bahamas; in the US write 3200 Broadmoor St, Grand Rapids, MI 49508.

Near the east end of the beach is **Breezes** (☎ 242-327-5356, fax 242-327-5356, info@ superclubs.com; in the US ☎ 800-330-8272; in the UK ☎ 208-390-7652), part of the SuperClubs all-inclusive chain. The resort is noisy and a bit crass, drawing an unsophisticated clientele. All the public arenas are gaudily painted: The dining room is like a refectory decorated by David Hockney. The 391 spacious rooms are modestly decorated. The courtyard boasts five pools, including a huge Jacuzzi and a misting pool. It's perfect for gregarious sorts who don't mind the rattle of Ping-Pong balls, pajama parties, Mr & Mrs Bikini Contests, talent shows, Junkanoos, sailing lessons, outdoor games, trampoline clinics on the beach, and even a Friday-night outdoor circus show. There's an inline skating and jogging track, the Hurricane dance club, and a Queen Anne–style piano bar. All-inclusive room rates began at US$240 double in low season, US$295 in peak season. The resort was adding 92 junior suites. The mailing address is PO Box CB-13049, Nassau, The Bahamas.

Guanahani Village (☎ 242-327-7568, fax 242-327-8311) has oceanfront rental units in tree-story townhouses from US$300 nightly. You can also try **Cable Beach Manor Apartments** (☎ 242-327-7785), which offers long-term rentals, as does **Sandyport** (☎ 242-327-4641, fax 242-327-3663), the snazzy new residential-resort complex and marina at the west end of Cable Beach. Sandyport's postal address is PO Box N-8585, Nassau, The Bahamas.

The most sophisticated place – for (hetero-sexual) couples only – is **Sandals Royal Bahamian** (☎ 242-327-6400, fax 242-327-6961, info@sandals.com; in the US ☎ 888-726-3257). The flagship of the renowned Sandals hotel chain – voted 'World's Best All-Inclusive Resorts' and 'Top Caribbean Hotel Group' three years in a row at the World Travel Awards – is the most elegant all-inclusive resort in the region. Stay here and you'll feel it truly is 'better in The Bahamas.' Beyond the marble-sheathed lobby are 406 air-con rooms, from beachfront rooms and villas to suites, including 210 voluminous concierge suites (five designed for handicapped travelers). All feature regal handcrafted mahogany furniture and king-size beds. Suites have their own concierge. Sandals has eight restaurants (including gourmet Italian and Japanese restaurants), a nightclub, and various bars, including an authentic pub brought over from England. The property extends over 13 landscaped acres, including a private beach with water sports; there are also four whirlpools, a misting pool, and two vast swimming pools, each a centerpiece of opulent architectural fantasy with statues and stately columns. A third pool, Jacuzzi, and the atmospheric Café Goombay are on Sandals' private island, Discovery, with its own beach. The resort is also a full-service spa (voted one of the Top 10 in the world by *Condé Nast Traveler*). Golf at the Radisson Cable Beach Golf Club and scuba diving are included at no extra cost. Per-person rates range from US$315 to US$610, March 30 to December 19 (US$645 to US$925 the rest of the year). Week-long packages provide discounts. Once inside the doors, you pay nothing extra. The mailing address is PO Box CB-13005, Cable Beach, Nassau, The Bahamas.

PLACES TO EAT

Nassau's eateries run the gamut from colorful local establishments serving down-home dishes to chic restaurants offering world-class gourmet fare. Also consider Paradise Island, which offers several fine restaurants, and additional eateries to the west and south of Nassau. See the other Places to Eat sections in this chapter for details.

Budget

Downtown Vegetarians should head to the *King Alpha Ital Restaurant*, on Elizabeth Ave near Shirley St, a genuine and duly colorful Rastafarian eatery festooned with inscriptions honoring Jah. It serves such fare as fried snapper for US$6, a 'veggie plate' for US$5, and patties for US$2, washed down with sorrel and other natural drinks.

I recommend the *Bahamian Kitchen* (☎ 242-325-0702) on Trinity Place, a local favorite specializing in seafood dishes from US$7, but also serving salads and sandwiches from US$4, plus okra soup, curried chicken, boil' fish, and hashed beef and grits. It's a great value! It has takeout service.

Conch Fritters Bar & Grill (☎ 242-323-8778), on Marlborough St, is a fast-food–style joint specializing in conch dishes that's handy for a quick snack downtown. It's open 11:30 am to midnight.

A good place for breakfast or lunch is *Café Skan's* (☎ 242-322-2486) on Bay St at Frederick St. It's clean and offers a large US-style breakfast menu, including pancakes and omelets from US$5 and steak and eggs for US$11. Locals eat here, too. There's often a wait. Likewise try *Chippie's Wall St Café*, one block west, next to the Pompey Museum, with an upstairs veranda where local and international artists perform.

The cutesy roadside *Lady J's*, a tiny shack on Bay St near Christie St, offers cheap Indian and Caribbean dishes.

You can also stroll to Over-the-Hill and dine with locals at *Royal Castle*, about half a mile south of Government House on Blue Hill Rd. It's full of offbeat ambiance. It advertises breakfasts for US$1.25, befitting the income level of the region. Take care hereabouts at night!

Fast-food junkies will find a *McDonald's* on Marlborough St, a block away from a splendid fast-food Chinese takeout – *Imperial Take-Away* – opposite the British Colonial Hotel. *Burger King* has an outlet overlooking the water in the Moses Shopping Plaza on E Bay St, as well as several other locations around town. Likewise, *Domino's Pizza* has more outlets than you can shake a stick at.

Nassau has a handful of cafes including *Jitter's Coffee House*, downtown on Bay St above The Girls from Brazil swimwear store. *Café Aroma*, at Saunders Point, midway between downtown and Cable Beach, sells excellent pastries, as does *Bahamas Internet Cafe*, on Bay St at Elizabeth, one block east of Rawson Square.

Dunkin' Donuts has an outlet on the corner of Marlborough St and Cumberland St. And *Planet Hollywood*, at the corner of Bay and East Sts, has a juice bar.

Need a frozen-yogurt antidote to the heat? *TCBY* has an outlet on Nassau St near Poinciana Dr.

Farther Afield West of downtown, the undisputed place to be as one with local residents is the *Outdoor Conch Market* between Arawak Cay and W Bay St. Locals, who call it 'Fish Fry,' flock here on weekends to the two dozen or so restaurants and stalls with names like 'The House of Love.' Typically, six conch fritters cost US$1 and a platter of cracked conch with fries costs US$6. You'll also find early morning breakfasts of stewed conch (US$3) or corned beef with sardines (US$2). You can wash your conch down with fresh fruit drinks or coconut juice ('sky juice') bought at the Daiquiri Bar. The Great Bahamas Seafood Festival is held here each October.

A sign at the entrance to the cay reminds you that conch is an aphrodisiac:

First the conch

Then the love

What? Not without the glove!

A glove, of course, is a condom!

Farther west is *The Zoo Café* (☎ 242-322-7195), a sports bar and grill serving burgers, curry shrimp, barbecued chicken and the like. It's open noon to 2 am daily.

East of downtown, an alternative is *Montagu Ramp* at the east end of Shirley St, where conch is landed and cleaned. A couple of small stalls also sell pineapple, coconut, and raisin cake for US$1 a slice. You can get a grouper dinner for US$7.

Nearby, *Hooters* (☎ 242-394-8926), on E Bay St at the foot of Paradise Island Exit Bridge, offers burgers, salads, and sandwiches for less than US$10, plus crab legs (US$15), oysters, etc. It's open 11 am to midnight Monday to Thursday, 11 am to 1 am Friday and Saturday, and 1 pm to 11 pm Sunday.

The 'big car, big cigar crowd' heads to *Mr T's Sporting Lounge*, on Mackey St, for boil' fish on Sunday morning, while *Mamma Lyddie's Place*, Over-the-Hill on Market St, is also renowned locally for boil' fish, johnny cakes, and guava duff. Likewise, *Same Ole Place* (☎ 242-322-1311), in the Oakes Field area on Thompson Blvd, serves okra soup, crawfish, and pork chops, drawing locals ranging from the hoi-polloi to The Honorable Prime Minister Hubert Ingraham.

I like the simple *Tamarind Hill* (☎ 242-393-1306), in a gaily painted wooden home on Village Rd (see the Central Nassau map). Fare includes Bahamian dishes, plus sandwiches averaging US$5, quiche for US$6.50, and eclectic entrees washed down with house cocktails such as a Tamarind Hill Smoothie. It has a happy hour from 5 to 7:30 pm.

Roscoe's (☎ 242-322-2810), on Bay St, is a delicatessen selling international cheeses, crabmeat, smoked salmon, etc, perfect for putting together a picnic.

Burger King has an outlet at Saunders Beach between downtown and Cable Beach.

Cable Beach One of the few places to find cheap beef patties (for US$1) is the *Swiss Pastry Shop* on W Bay St near Sandals Royal Bahamian; it also serves fresh-baked pastries and desserts.

Sbarro's (☎ 242-327-3076) has a fast-food outlet outside the Nassau Beach Hotel. You can fill up on pizzas, calzones, salads, or American-Italian fare for less than US$6 with a drink. Sbarro's also offers daily Italian and Bahamian specials.

Other options include *Subway* and *Domino's Pizza*, both in the shopping strip opposite Sandals. Here, too, is *Caripelago Restaurant & Bar* (☎ 242-327-4749), in the West Bay Shopping Centre; it serves iced coffee for US$1.50.

Mid-Range

Downtown The *Portofino Restaurant* in the British Colonial Hilton is an elegant option for buffet breakfast; the all-you-can-eat Sunday brunch (US$18.50) draws locals.

For Greek food, check out the *Athena Café* on Bay St, with an open-air balcony where you can enjoy souvlaki, Greek salad, and the like while watching the street life below.

You'd swear you were in an old inn in Surrey upon entering the **Green Shutters Inn** (☎ 242-322-3701, 48 Parliament St). Its beamed ceiling, leather chairs, and tartan carpet are matched by a menu that includes a ploughman's platter, calf's liver, and bangers and mash…all less than US$10 and washed down with a pint of English ale. It has a three-course dinner for US$24. It's open daily 11:30 am to midnight; closed Sunday evening.

The Cellar (☎ 242-322-8877, 11 Charlotte St) is another agreeable, oak-beamed, English-style pub. It's elegant and intimate and serves some of the best continental cuisine in Nassau, including superb pastas and a tasty steak and mushroom pie. Entrees cost US$10 and upward.

Billabong's (☎ 242-326-7774, 20 Cumberland St) has a warm ambiance and a snug, 'down-under' feel. This pub is housed in a 200-year-old building with rough-hewn whitewashed walls and a black ceiling scribbled with chalk marks like the aboriginal drawings of Australia. Its eclectic menu includes lasagna for US$10, and pies and fries.

If you're browsing the Rawson Square area, try **Parliament Café** (☎ 242-322-2836) on Parliament St. Simple fare includes burgers, salads, and Bahamian food, but you'll also find creations such as smoked mahi-mahi, beer-battered shrimp with honey mustard sauce, and green rice loaf with cheese. Most dishes cost less than US$10.

On Bay St try the **Dockside Bar & Grill**, upstairs in Prince George Plaza. It finds inspiration from Greece in such dishes as spicy chicken in pita for US$8. Also here is **Iguana**, serving Bahamian and continental fare. And **Sbarro's**, serving Italian fast-food, has an outlet opposite the Straw Market on Bay St.

For Chinese food, I recommend the **House of Wong** (☎ 242-326-0045) on West St at the west end of Marlborough St. It's clean and airy and serves filling and tasty dishes prepared by a chef from Hong Kong. Lunch specials cost US$6.95. Dinner entrees begin at US$12. The egg rolls, costing US$4, are a meal in themselves. It's open 11:30 am to 3 pm and 6 to 11 pm. The **VIP Chinese Restaurant**

(☎ 242-322-1599), at the corner of Bay and Devaux Sts, offers Szechwan and Cantonese cuisine. Entrees cost upward of US$8.

Care for a sonata with your pasta? Then head to the **Caffé dell'Opera** (☎ 242-356-6118), on the 2nd floor of an old church on Marlborough St, serving regional Italian dishes amid suitably Sicilian decor.

The Indian cuisine at **Gaylord's** (☎ 242-356-3004), on Dowdeswell St, is excellent. Chicken masala costs US$9.50 and tandooris begin at US$13, but the rice is a whopping US$4. Budget a minimum of US$25. The restaurant is part of the acclaimed Gaylord's chain, with outlets in New Delhi, Bombay, London, New York, and San Francisco.

German visitors with a longing for home cooking should head to the **Europa Restaurant** on W Bay St. It serves Bavarian knockwurst for US$9.50 and wiener schnitzel for US$12, plus Bahamian fare and Italian pastas starting at US$13.

Nearby, **Chez Willie** (☎ 242-322-5364), also on W Bay St, offers French and Bahamian gourmet cuisine such as pumpkin soup for US$5 and blackened swordfish for US$15.

Farther Afield An option for Chinese west of downtown is the **Chinese Kitchen** near the junction of Nassau St and Boyd Rd.

Crocodile's Waterfront Bar & Grill (☎ 242-323-3341), on Bay St, is a totally casual affair serving Bahamian fare, steaks, and seafood under thatched huts over Nassau Harbour.

The best Chinese restaurant in town is **East Villa** (☎ 242-393-3377), an elegant and popular Chinese-run eatery on E Bay St. Its wide menu runs from US$12 for entrees. The cuisine is excellent, but if you like it hot you'd better specify extra hot, as it caters to mild Bahamian tastes. Also east of downtown is the **Double Dragon** (☎ 242-393-5718) on Mackey St at the foot of the Paradise Island Exit Bridge. No menu item is more than US$14 (for lobster chop suey). Alternately, try **Tony Cheng's** (☎ 242-393-8175) at Nassau Harbour Club on E Bay St, specializing in seafood with a Chinese twist.

The *Outback Steak Restaurant* (☎ 242-394-8145), on Bay St at the foot of Paradise Island Exit Bridge, offers all manner of steak dishes plus pastas and seafood, served in an Australian atmosphere with surfboards, boomerangs, and other Aussie paraphernalia.

Cable Beach I like *Dicky Mo's* (☎ 242-327-7854), a seafood restaurant in the heart of the Cable Beach strip. The place is atmospheric, done up in a rustic wharflike motif, and the servers wear captains' uniforms. The wide-ranging menu is reasonably priced. It has daily specials such as pan-fried snapper for US$9 and minced lobster for US$14. Try the black bean and onion soup for US$5. There's an English-style pub inside.

Another of my favorites is *Café Johnny Canoe* (☎ 242-327-3373), adjoining the Nassau Beach Hotel. You can sit on the rustic yet atmospheric outside deck (lit up at night by Christmas lights), or in the brightly colored air-con interior. The wide breakfast menu includes US or Bahamian fare for US$6 or less, plus burgers, sandwiches and local favorites for lunch and dinner. Try the spiced tuna-salad sandwich. The cocktails are bucket-size! It's open 7:30 am to midnight and there's a Junkanoo performance on Friday evening.

The *Japanese Steak House* (☎ 242-327-7781), adjoining Dicky Mo's, boasts genuine Asian decor. The sushi, for US$20, is excellent, though portions are small. The various hibachi dishes are cooked at your table and are pricey, beginning at US$20. You can ring up US$80 for two with no problem.

For Italian, head to the small, cozy, family-run *Capriccio Ristorante* (☎ 242-327-8547) at the junction of W Bay St and Skyline Dr. Its romantic ambiance is enhanced by classical music. The dishes are superb – you're sure to find your Italian favorite – and reasonably priced, from US$5 to US$25. *Mama mia!*...there's *real* espresso, too.

Don't forget the hotel restaurants. The Radisson Cable Beach offers the atmospheric *Tequila Pepe's* for Mexican food; *Avocado's* for nouveau California cuisine; *Amici* for Italian; and *The Forge*, where

grilled meats are prepared at your table. The all-you-can-eat buffet breakfast in the *Bimini Restaurant* is a bargain at US$13.

Also praiseworthy are the expensive *Black Angus Grill* in the Nassau Marriott and the more moderately priced *Beef Cellar* in the Nassau Beach Hotel, serving various types of steaks. The Marriott's *Sole Mare* Italian restaurant is also good and serves through midnight.

The *Round House* (☎ 242-327-8153), in a historic structure at the Casuarinas hotel, serves Chinese; it's open noon to 3 pm and 6 to 10 pm. Entrees cost US$10 to US$25.

Top End
Downtown If your budget allows it, head to *Graycliff Hotel & Restaurant* (☎ 242-322-2796 ext 307) on W Hill St, whose restaurant fills the glass-enclosed wraparound balcony of an exquisite colonial mansion. Lace tablecloths, gilt porcelain, and silverware add a regal note to The Bahamas' only five-star restaurant. Its beautifully rendered, French-inspired cuisine will burn a hole in your pocket, though: The cheapest soup costs US$9! Typical entrees include rack of lamb for US$42 and filet mignon for US$34. The signature dish is lobster. Steep, yes, but it has been rated among the world's 10 best restaurants by *Lifestyles of the Rich and Famous*. The wine cellar claims the largest collection – supposedly 180,000 bottles – in the Caribbean region, and there is no better selection of fine Cuban cigars with which to end the evening. Understandably, jacket and tie are required.

Next door is the Graycliff's equally noble *Humidor Restaurant* (☎ 242-322-2796 ext 301), a Grand Award Winner in *Wine Spectator*. This elegant bistro serves California-Caribbean fare under the baton of master chef Philip Bethel. Typical dishes include seafood in scallop shell (US$11) and pasta in saffron cream sauce with mussels and roasted bell peppers (US$20). The adjacent lounge is awash in Cuban art.

The *Wedgewood Room* (☎ 242-322-3301 ext 4045) in the British Colonial Hilton offers exquisite decor and gourmet seafood plus fine cuts of beef. Typical dishes include a rum- and honey-cured smoked salmon (US$13) and dover sole in nut brown butter (US$38). It's open 6 to 10:30 pm Monday to Saturday.

Even better is chic **Café Matisse** (☎ 242-356-7012) on Bank Lane, the local in-spot blending contemporary and classical elements such as leopard fabrics, rich hardwoods, bare limestone walls, and Matisse prints. You can dine outside beneath huge shade trees on the patio. The menu boasts an Italian flair at relatively bargain prices: homemade pastas and pizzas for less than US$10 and seafood from US$12. Dinner entrees include such winners as shrimp in red curry sauce for US$22. The service is exemplary.

The **Buena Vista Hotel & Restaurant** (☎ 242-322-2811) on Delancy St also has elegant (albeit jaded) silver-and-crystal dining in a period setting. You can also dine on a patio. The creative menu has strong French and Italian influences. Entrees begin at US$27; it's open 7 to 11 pm.

Farther Afield For surf 'n' turf, head to **Montagu Gardens** (☎ 242-394-6347) on E Bay St. This casually elegant place serves a wide range of continental fare alongside steaks, seafood, ribs, lamb dishes, and burgers. Prices run US$10 to US$37 for entrees.

Another top-notch find in the same price bracket is **Pink Pearl Café** (☎ 242-394-6413), in a two-story house on E Bay St (see the Central Nassau map), with a wraparound, breeze-swept deck. It boasts modern decor and serves such appetizers as roasted peppers, spinach and cho-cho, plus pizzas, sandwiches, and such mouthwatering entrees as ginger chicken and guava-glazed pork.

An acclaimed option is the oddly named **Sun And...** (☎ 242-393-1205), in a converted home on Lakeview Dr, a cul-de-sac off the east end of Shirley St (see the Central Nassau map). Its homey yet elegant ambiance matches its highly acclaimed menu, offering superb French cuisine as well as Bahamian dishes with a French

twist. The rack of lamb will set you back a staggering US$74, but the veal sweetbreads will cost you just US$32. The desserts are equally renowned. It's open 6:30 to 9:30 pm only, daily except Monday. Reservations are recommended.

BBQ Beach (☎ 242-327-3088), at Sandyport, serves such treats as butternut squash soup, roasted Cornish game hen, and banana and Nassau Royale parfait...all under the creative genius of Chef Neale Jones, formerly of Gleneagles, in Scotland. Appetizers begin at around US$5; entrees run from US$12 to US$35.

ENTERTAINMENT

Downtown Nassau is virtually dead at night, even when cruise ships are in port. The night scene is concentrated in Cable Beach and on Paradise Island (see the Paradise Island section later in this chapter).

The earthy nightlife that is a feature of other countries in the region is absent here. Unlike neighboring islands (such as Jamaica) where go-go clubs are a staple, The Bahamas' nocturnal scene is held in tight rein by the overriding influence of the Christian community, including the Bahamas Christian Council.

At the other end of the spectrum, afternoon tea parties are held regularly at Government House as part of the People-to-People program, designed to put tourists in closer contact with locals (see the 'People to People' boxed text in the Facts for the Visitor chapter).

Dance Clubs

The dance club of choice is **The Zoo** (☎ 242-322-7195), near Saunders Beach on W Bay St. This ultramodern club has the de rigueur laser-light show and piped fog, plus house, techno, R&B, and reggae music. Five bars boast individual decor. It gets packed with a youngish crowd. Eats are available, and there's an open 'VIP Lounge.' Admission costs a whopping US$40 Thursday to Saturday (US$20 Sunday to Wednesday) but is free to guests of Sandals Royal Bahamian, Breezes, and Club Med (you'll need your ID). You can also get in free if you dine at

The Zoo Café or Café Johnny Canoe (see the Places to Eat section earlier in this chapter), which have the same owner. Look for coupons (found, for example, on the back of the *What-to-do* tourist guide), good for US$5 admission. A cocktail can set you back US$6 or more. It has a Ladies' Night.

The snazziest place is the *601 Club* (☎ 242-322-3041, 601 Bay St), on the east end of downtown. The club's dress code forbids sneakers, and jackets are standard for men. No one under 25 is admitted. It has live music. Thursday is Ladies' Night, with free entry for women until 11 pm (US$5 thereafter). Admission otherwise costs US$15 (US$5 for Happy Hour, 5 to 8 pm Friday; US$20 after 8 pm), but tourists with a pass from a taxi driver can get in for US$5. It's open Thursday through Sunday.

A new and popular downtown option is the *Bahamas Boom Beach Club* (☎ 242-325-7733), on Elizabeth Ave at Bay St, with a state-of-the-art sound and light system and three bars. Entrance costs US$20, but visitors can get in free with discount coupons from tourist newspapers. Take a taxi or go as a group if walking on Bay St.

Several resort hotels have their own dance clubs, too, including *Sandals Royal Bahamian*, which is private. Nonguests can buy an evening pass to *Breezes*, and the *Fanta-Z Disco* at the Radisson Cable Beach is open to all comers.

Casinos & Floorshows

The *Crystal Palace Casino* (☎ 242-327-6200), at the Nassau Marriott in Cable Beach, boasts 800 slot machines, 51 blackjack tables, nine roulette wheels, and other games. It's open to anyone over 21 years of age. (Bahamian residents, however, may not gamble.) It's open 10 am to 4 am daily, but a video slot-machine section operates 24 hours. A second casino is located on Paradise Island (see the Paradise Island section later in this chapter).

The 800-seat *Rainforest Theatre* (☎ 242-327-6200 ext 6861), at the Crystal Palace Casino, hosts the 'Magical Voyage' show nightly except Monday (times vary). This Las Vegas–style revue blends comedy and a

fantastic magician act with sexy routines by leggy showgirls and male dance troupes. The show costs US$39, including a drink. No photos are allowed. The show changes themes regularly.

The *King & Knights Club* (☎ 242-327-5321, fax 242-327-0741, kingeric@batelnet .bs), at the Nassau Beach Hotel in Cable Beach, offers a native dance show that includes traditional rake 'n' scrape music, limbo, a fire dance, and Junkanoo music. Shows are at 8:30 nightly except Sunday and cost US$25 per person, including one drink.

McClure's Comedy Club & Humidor (☎ 242-361-7484), also in the Nassau Beach Hotel, has a comedy show Friday through Sunday nights. Entry costs US$15.

Pubs & Bars

Most bars in Nassau bill themselves either as English-style pubs or US-style sports bars (or 'satellite lounges'). Many are hybrids.

Most resort hotels have at least one bar, ranging from the traditionally English motif of the *Out Island Bar* in the Nassau Beach Hotel to more lively options at the *Nassau Marriott*, *Breezes* (nonguests can purchase evening passes for US$60), and *Sandals Royal Bahamian*, which is closed to nonguests. Quieter bars are represented by the lounge bar in the British Colonial Hilton on Marlborough St, which also has *Blackbeard's*, an atmospheric English-style pub, and the ritzy *Wedgewood Bar* for the martini crowd.

Other English pubs are represented by *Green Shutters Inn*, *Billabong's*, *The Cellar*, and the *Europa* (see the Places to Eat section). Also check out the bar at *Compass Point* (see the West New Providence section).

The only wine bar is *Rumours* (☎ 242-323-2925), on Charlotte St N.

The *Drop-Off* (☎ 242-322-3444), on Bay St near East St, is a popular basement bar and dance club that attracts a mix of locals and staff from the cruise ships (plus an occasional working girl hoping to snare a randy seaman). It has a suitably international flavor, plus cool, hip music and occasional live bands. Dig the walls, lined with faux aquariums – the water is real, but the fish are fake. Its eclectic selection includes Boddington's draft ale for US$5. It starts to jam after midnight, especially on weekends when the ships are in port.

Want to check out the football game? Then head to *Hooters* (☎ 242-394-8926), on E Bay St at the foot of Paradise Island Exit Bridge. You can watch the game on ESPN while being attended by waitresses in Hooters' trademark orange hot-pants and body-hugging white tank tops. The juke box plays Motown. Alternately, try the *Dockside Sports Bar & Grill*, upstairs in Prince George Plaza near Bay and Frederick Sts, or *Hammerhead Bar & Grill* (☎ 242-393-3625), on E Bay St near the New Paradise Island Bridge.

Charlie's Bar, at W Bay and Augusta Sts, attracts expats and locals for darts and pool.

The wild side of things is represented by the Shooters Bar at *Club Waterloo* (☎ 242-393-7324), near Fort Montagu on E Bay St. It's popular with the younger college crowd, which flocks to do shooters and leap from the bungee tower. The club has a separate dance club and a quieter, more sober lounge popular with locals. There's live music Tuesday to Saturday. It's open 9 pm to 4 am nightly; admission costs US$20.

In the same wild vein, try *Cuda Bay*, on the waterfront at the Nassau Harbour Club on E Bay St, which is open 4 pm to 7 pm and has shots for US$1. You are advised to 'get screwed' (with vodka and orange juice). *Crocodile's Waterfront Bar & Grill*, on Bay St, is likewise a popular party place with great views over the harbor to boot. Adjoining *Last Quarter* (☎ 242-323-3341), overlooking the harbor on E Bay St, 100 yards west of the New Paradise Island Exit Bridge, plays soft rock and blues, Tuesday to Saturday; entry costs US$10 on Friday and Saturday.

You won't experience local color by playing the tourist, however. For that, you need to hang out at satellite lounges (so named for their satellite TVs). Although middle-class locals tend toward the same places as out-of-towners, there are plenty of funky watering holes where the non-monied classes down beers and play dominoes. Most have a TV and pool table.

On Bay St downtown, try the quiet *Pacific Bar*, just west of Victoria Ave; or *Millie's Place*, just west of Devaux St.

Farther afield, try the *Silver Dollar* at Farrington Rd and Eden St, and *The Outback*, opposite the Esso station on Thompson Blvd, a street that offers true local color at a clutch of local bars. *Whip Sea Lounge* on Potter's Cay is a small, funky bar popular with the Bahamian underclass; it hosts live music on Friday, Saturday, and Sunday.

Cinemas

Choose the *RND Cinemas* in the Prince Charles Shopping Centre on Prince Charles Ave, or *Galleria Cinema*, in the Mall at Marathon, at Prince Charles Ave and Marathon Rd. Both are southeast of downtown (see the New Providence map).

Theater

The most important venue is the *Dundas Centre for the Performing Arts* (☎ 242-393-3728) on Mackey St. Plays, dance, and (occasionally) ballets are held here. The season runs February through September (US$10 to US$15). Watch for 'Summer Madness,' when popular local theatrical troupes such as James Catalyn & Friends use humor to address contemporary issues in Bahamian society. The National Youth Choir holds an annual concert in late April or early May.

The *Shirley Street Theatre* (☎ 242-393-2884) on Shirley St, was due to be converted to a performing arts center.

Look for performances by the Nassau Amateur Operatic Society, Chamber Singers, and Diocesan Chorale.

Jazz

The *Last Quarter*, in Crocodile's Waterfront Bar & Grill on E Bay St, offers live jazz. *Chippie's Wall St Cafe*, on Bay St, has live jazz and R&B on Saturday night, and also hosts a Latin Night on Friday, with salsa and merengue. *Pink Pearl Café*, on Bay St, does jazz and R&B, draws headliner names, and hosts jam sessions.

Folk & Traditional Music

For rake 'n' scrape music on Sunday evenings, check out the *Same Ole Place* (☎ *242-322-1311*), in the Oakes Field area on Thompson Blvd. This earthy Over-the-Hill spot is the domain of less-monied locals and guarantees a warm welcome and a richly rewarding experience.

SPECTATOR SPORTS

Cricket is played on weekends from March to December at Clifford Park (☎ 242-322-1875/3622), below Fort Charlotte on W Bay St. There's no charge to watch.

Baseball games are hosted at the Queen Elizabeth Sports Centre (☎ 242-323-5163) off Thompson Blvd (see the Central Nassau map).

Also see Special Events and Spectator Sports in the Facts for the Visitor chapter.

SHOPPING

Bay St is lined with arcades (such as Prince George Plaza) and duty-free stores selling everything from Swiss watches and Colombian emeralds to Milanese fashions and lacy lingerie (savings are not guaranteed; it pays to check out prices at home before visiting The Bahamas). Dozens of stores sell T-shirts and kitschy souvenirs. The side streets are favored by stores selling leather goods, artwork, and collectibles. Most of the stores close at night and on Sunday, even when the cruise ships are in port.

Upscale resorts also have jewelry and gift stores. The largest are the 'malls' in the Radisson Cable Beach and Nassau Marriott.

Before going on a mad spending spree, obtain a copy of *What-to-do: Where to shop, dine, stay, play, invest* from one of the visitors' centers.

Most Bahamians do their shopping in Miami, but they are also served by major shopping malls in the residential areas south of downtown (see the New Providence map). The largest, with 70 stores, is The Mall at Marathon (☎ 242-393-4043) at Marathon and Robinson Rds (you can take the shuttle that leaves from outside KFC on Woodes Rogers Walk for US$1 one-way).

The Towne Centre Mall (☎ 242-326-6992), at Blue Hill Rd and Independence Dr, is another multilevel mall.

Duty-Free Goods & Collectibles

Jewelry is the big-ticket item, including watches. The largest chain is Colombian Emeralds (☎ 800-666-3889), with several outlets, followed by The Colombian (☎ 242-325-4083). John Bull (☎ 242-322-4252) and Little Switzerland (☎ 242-322-8324) also have several outlets, including on Bay St, with a vast selection of jewelry, perfumes, leather goods, and accessories.

For perfumes try The Perfume Shop at Bay and Frederick Sts, or Lightbourn's Perfume Centre at Bay and George Sts.

For porcelain and crystal, check out Treasure Traders (☎ 242-322-8521) at Bay and Market Sts. For linens, head to The Linen Shop at Bay and Frederick Sts. The best places for leather goods are Fendi at Bay and Charlotte Sts, The Brass & Leather Shop on Charlotte St off Bay St, and The Leather Shop on Bank Lane off Bay St.

You can buy rare coins and postage stamps at Coin of the Realm (☎ 242-322-4497) on Charlotte St. The main post office has a philatelic bureau (☎ 242-322-3344) at E Hill and Parliament Sts.

See the Facts for the Visitor chapter for general information on buying duty-free goods.

Straw-Work & Native Items

The Straw Market at the west end of Bay St near Prince George Wharf is a veritable Bahamian souk, bustling with vendors selling T-shirts, wood carvings, and straw baskets, mats, dolls, hats, and other items. Many of the straw items are imported from Asia. The vendors expect you to bargain – it's part of the fun. Don't hesitate to beat the price down a little (10% is about normal). However, many of the vendors are relatively poor, so don't be too miserly! Prices for straw pieces range from about US$5 for a minipurse to US$25 for a large handbag.

The best place for genuine locally made woven items is The Plait Lady (☎ 242-356-

5584) at Bay St and Victoria Ave, with everything from straw-work to conch-shell mats made on-site.

You'll also find a large straw and crafts market across from the Radisson Cable Beach, and another in the gorge leading to the Queen's Staircase on Elizabeth Ave.

A diverse range of island-made items is offered at the Green Lizard (☎ 242-356-5103) on W Bay St, with everything from straw goods, hand-printed Androsia batiks, and sarongs, to guava jams, pepper sauces, and even Haitian artworks and hammocks. Likewise, Doongalik Studios (☎ 242-394-1886), at 18 Village Rd, offers an excellent range of Bahamian art and craft products, including Junkanoo masks.

Artwork

You can admire – or purchase – originals by leading contemporary artists such as Eddie Minnis and Chan Pratt at Unique Gifts (☎ 242-326-0522) on Charlotte St. Nearby, also exhibiting original works, is Charlotte's Gallery (☎ 242-322-6310). On W Bay St, Caripelago Café (☎ 242-326-3568) features an exhibit by a different artist each month. Also check out the Kennedy Gallery (☎ 242-325-7662) on Parliament St, the Nassau Art Gallery (☎ 242-393-1482) in the East Bay Shopping Centre just east of the Paradise Island Exit Bridge, and the Andrew Aitken Art Gallery (☎ 242-328-7065) on Madeira St in the Palmdale district.

Clothing

You'll find T-shirts and resortwear at all the resort boutiques and in dozens of stores downtown. Several stores also sell simple casualwear made from Androsia batiks.

There are few bargains on high-fashion clothing. Try Coles of Nassau (☎ 242-322-8393) on Parliament St, selling designer fashions such as Calvin Klein, Vittadini, and Mondi. The Bay (☎ 242-356-3918) and, for men, Bonneville Bones (☎ 242-328-0804), both on Bay St, also sell elegant designer duds, as does Gucci (☎ 242-325-0561) on Saffrey Square off Bay St.

To pick up some designer leathers, head over to Leather Masters (☎ 242-322-7597) on Parliament St.

Women seeking something *totally* sexy for the beach should head to The Girls from Brazil (☎ 242-323-5966) on Bay St at Parliament St, selling a wide assortment of Brazilian-made bikinis…you know, the dental-floss kind your momma wouldn't want you to wear. Tell her you also bought one of their beautiful cover-ups. A good selection of beachwear is also sold at Mademoiselle (☎ 242-322-5130) at Bay and Frederick Sts.

Cigars

Now that *everyone's* smoking stogies, you may want to take home a box of premium Cuban cigars, which you can buy for a song in Nassau. The Pipe of Peace (☎ 242-325-2022), at Bay and Charlotte Sts, has a fine selection, as do the Havana Humidor (☎ 242-363-5809), opposite Barclays Bank on Bay St, and Cigar Connection, at Bay St and Elizabeth Ave.

Best of all is to watch your smokes being hand-rolled at the Graycliff Cigar Co (☎ 242-322-2796) on W Hill St. Here, Cuban rollers make the award-winning Graycliff brand of five-star cigars, plus the lesser but still noble Bahiba brand.

Remember, Uncle Sam prohibits US citizens from buying Cuban cigars – *that's* 'trading with the enemy' – and US Customs agents will confiscate 'em if they find 'em. See Shopping in the Facts for the Visitor chapter.

Antiques

Seeking island antiques? Then head to Marlborough Antiques (☎ 242-328-0502) at the west end of Marlborough St. It has a wide range, including many items on a nautical theme. Prices are high! For antique maps and etchings, try Balmain Antiques (☎ 242-323-7421) at Bay and

Charlotte Sts, on the 2nd floor of the Mason's Bldg.

Music

If you're serious about music, head to Cody's Music & Video Centre (☎ 242-323-8215) at E Bay and Armstrong Sts. It carries a large stock of native and Caribbean music. The owner, Cody Carter, can guide you.

Want to take a Junkanoo drum home? Head to Pyfroms (☎ 242-322-2603) on Bay St, which sells drums and other musical instruments.

Sex Potents

If you want to put some pep in your love life, buy some Ginseng ('The Sexy Thing') Golden Tonic, an herbal medicine made from ginseng and bee-pollen tonic. Please let me know if it adds a sting to your love life. Many stores sell it, or you can call Luden Ltd (☎ 242-322-2117) on Dowdeswell St.

Alternately, look for 'strongback,' a local herb used by practitioners of bush medicine as an alternative to Viagra. There *are* other potents, but many of them are aimed at the libido, which is an abiding Bahamian interest.

Photographic Equipment

Nassau has few professional photo stores and equally few camera stores. One of the best selections is at John Bull (☎ 242-322-4252) on Bay St. Also try Mr Photo on Frederick St off Bay St, which has one-hour developing.

Cameras are often advertised as, say, '20% below manufacturer's suggested retail price.' But that 'retail price' may be much higher than what you'd actually pay for the same item at home. Check prices at home beforehand.

GETTING THERE & AWAY
Air

Nassau is served by direct flights from numerous US cities, Canada, the UK, Jamaica, Cuba, and the Turks and Caicos. See the Getting There & Away chapter for airlines' and charter companies' international and Nassau telephone numbers, as well as some representative routes and fares.

The vast majority of visitors to The Bahamas arrive at Nassau International Airport (☎ 242-377-7281), about 8 miles west of downtown Nassau. Nassau serves as the hub for air service to all the other islands.

Immigrations and customs are usually a breeze, although there may be a lengthy wait if there are several flights arriving from Miami at once, full of Bahamian nationals. Customs officials tend to go through their baggage with a fine-tooth comb. Fortunately, there's an express lane for foreign visitors.

You'll find a tourist information desk with maps and pamphlets beyond Immigration. The car-rental agencies are located just beyond Customs. The corridor straight ahead, which leads to the domestic departure terminal, has a post office, open 9:30 am to 1 pm and 2 pm to 4:30 pm weekdays; and a bank, open from 9:30 am to 3 pm Monday to Thursday and 9:30 am to 5 pm Friday. The bank has an outside ATM linked to Cirrus. There's also a telephone exchange. See the Getting Around section later in this chapter for information on local transportation to and from the airport.

Services in the airport's domestic departures lounge include a restaurant, snack shop, telephones, and TV. All flights to the US depart from a separate terminal 100 yards west of the arrivals terminal.

Some interisland private charter planes arrive at and depart the General Aviation Terminal on Coral Harbour Rd, a half-mile east of the main terminal. There's a snack bar, restrooms, taxis, and telephone, plus an Immigration and Customs office. Porters will charge you US$3.

To/From Elsewhere in The Bahamas Service to neighboring islands is offered by Bahamasair and local charter airlines. Nassau is Bahamasair's hub, and its service to all other Bahamian islands is centered here. See the Getting Around chapter and the island chapters' Getting There & Away sections for details on flights, times, and fares.

Boat

More than a dozen cruise lines offer cruises from Florida to Nassau or include Nassau on their Caribbean itineraries. All berth at Prince George Wharf. See the Getting There & Away chapter for details.

At Prince George Wharf, there is no terminal building. There's a tourist information and ATM booth opposite the wharf, where the surreys (horse-drawn cabs) also park.

Mail Boat Mail boats regularly depart Potter's Cay for Grand Bahama and all the Family Islands. See the Mail Boat section in the Getting Around chapter for a complete schedule of departures. You can call the Dockmaster's Office (☎ 242-393-1064) for the latest information.

Private Yacht Nassau has several marinas, including the following:

East Bay Yacht Basin (☎/fax 242-394-1816)

Lightbourne Marina (☎ 242-393-5285, fax 242-393-6236), PO Box N-4849, Nassau

Nassau Harbour Club & Marina (☎ 242-393-0771, fax 242-393-5393), PO Box SS-5755, Nassau

Nassau Yacht Haven (☎ 242-393-8173)

All are east of the Paradise Island Exit Bridge (see the Central Nassau map). Moorings are at a premium. Reservations are advised. All vessels must clear themselves with Nassau Harbour Control (VHF channel 16) when entering or departing Nassau.

Paradise Island also has marinas; see the Paradise Island section for details, as well as information on water taxis to Paradise Island.

GETTING AROUND
To/From the Airport

There are no buses to or from the airport. The taxi-drivers' union has things sewn up. Only a handful of leading hotels provide shuttle services. If you're prebooked into one of the major hotels, you'll be steered to minibuses operated by the bigger tour operators. They're parked to the left as you exit the arrivals hall.

Taxis are available immediately outside the arrivals lounge. There's an official dispatcher (☎ 242-323-5111) and no hustlers. Rates are fixed by the government. A taxi for two people to Cable Beach costs US$15; to downtown and Prince George Wharf, US$20; to Paradise Island, US$24 (plus US$2 bridge toll). Each additional person costs US$3. Some taxi drivers may try to charge the third or fourth person the same rate as for two people. Don't fall for this rip-off!

There's a telephone desk for limousine services immediately beyond Immigration.

Bus

Nassau is well served by minibuses, called 'jitneys,' operated by private companies (about 40 companies in all). Jitneys run throughout the day, 6 am to 8 pm. There are no fixed schedules.

Buses No 10 and 10A serve Cable Beach and downtown along Bay St, running as far east as Sandy Point. They stop in front of each hotel in Cable Beach, and you'll rarely have to wait more than five minutes for a bus. Bus No 38 also links Cable Beach and downtown, although eastbound the bus turns inland at Goodman's Bay and takes a circuitous route through town, passing through Over-the-Hill and eventually depositing you at Prince George Wharf.

Buses Nos 24 and 30 run to the New Paradise Island Bridge but *not* to the island.

All buses depart downtown from Frederick St at Bay St.

Bus stops are well marked, but you can also wave the jitneys down or request a stop anywhere along their routes. To request a stop when you're onboard, simply shout, 'Bus stop!'

The standard fare is US75¢ (children US50¢). No change is given for dollar bills, although the drivers will change US$5 bills (you receive US$4 back). You pay the driver upon exiting the bus.

Car & Scooter

Most downtown streets are one-way and they are often congested. Traffic moves only eastbound along Bay St and westbound along Shirley St.

Parking downtown is at a premium. It's easiest to head for the public parking lot on Charlotte St (there are several others nearby), where you can park all day for US$7.50 maximum (US$2.50 the first hour). You'll also find parking lots on Elizabeth Ave, which charge US$3 per day.

You really don't need a car to explore Nassau. If you intend to explore farther afield, the following US companies have rental booths at the airport:

Avis	☎ 242-377-7121
Budget	☎ 242-377-7405
Dollar	☎ 242-377-7301
Hertz	☎ 242-377-8684

Avis' rates begin at US$70 for a subcompact automatic (Geo Metro or Suzuki Swift) and run up to US$115 for a Ford Taurus. It also has offices at Cable Beach (☎ 242-322-2889) and downtown (☎ 242-326-6380) on W Bay St. Call ☎ 800-228-0668 for international reservations.

Dollar (☎ 242-325-3716) has an office at the British Colonial Hilton Hotel and offers slightly lower rates.

Budget has a toll free number – ☎ 800-457-6526 – for international reservations, as does Hertz (☎ 800-654-3131).

Several local companies also rent cars. Try Orange Creek Rentals (☎ 242-323-4967, 800-891-7655, fax 242-356-5005, serenity@ bahamas.net.bs), which has cars from US$39 daily. Also try Elite Car Rentals (☎ 242-394-1737). Bahamas Jeep Rentals (☎ 242-322-5377) rents Wrangler Jeeps.

Insurance policies vary, so check the costs and details carefully before making a commitment. Usually, collision damage waiver insurance costs US$12 a day, with a small deductible that you'll be required to pay in the event of an accident.

Scooters are widely available and can be found outside most major hotels. Downtown, try Knowles Scooter & Bike Rental (☎ 242-356-0741), outside the British Colonial Hilton Hotel. It rents scooters for US$30 half-day, and US$50 for a full day.

You'll also find scooters for rent opposite the resorts on the south side of W Bay St in Cable Beach.

Taxi

Cabs wait outside all major hotels. Rarely, you may be able to flag down a taxi passing on the road. Usually taxis are radio-dispatched. Summon a taxi by calling Meter Cabs (☎ 242-323-5111) on Davis St or the Bahamas Taxi Cab Union (☎ 242-323-4555) on Nassau St.

Taxis are metered; most drivers use them. Fares are pre-determined by the government. Short rides cost US$2 for the first quarter-mile and US30¢ for each additional mile for two people (additional passengers are charged a flat-rate US$2 each). If you cross the New Paradise Island Bridge, you must pay the US$2 bridge toll.

The fare from Cable Beach to downtown is about US$9 to US$12, depending on where you're dropped off. A trip between Cable Beach and Paradise Island costs about US$18 (plus bridge toll). A ride from downtown to Paradise Island costs about US$10.

You can negotiate with a driver for a guided tour of the island. The legal maximum charge for a tour is US$20 per hour for a five-passenger cab, plus US$10 per extra half-hour; minivans cost US$25 per hour.

Bicycle

Ask if your hotel rents bicycles. Few do, but most places that rent scooters also rent bicycles. Knowles (see Car & Scooter, above) charges US$20 per day. The bicycles are beach cruisers, single-gear bikes on which the pedal functions as the brake.

Surrey

Nassau's quaint horse-drawn surreys are a great way to explore downtown Nassau at an easy pace. They begin and end from Woodes Rogers Walk at Prince George Wharf. Rates are negotiable. A 30-minute ride costs approximately US$10 per person. Negotiate a price before climbing aboard if you want to hire a surrey for longer touring. They're available 9 am to 4:30 pm daily, except 1 to 2 pm (November to April) and 1 to 3 pm (May to October), when the horses are rested.

Walking

You can walk anywhere downtown: Note that the land rises incrementally inland, and on a hot day it can be a stiff and sweaty, albeit short, hike. The bridges linking Nassau to Paradise Island have pedestrian walkways.

Organized Tours

Several reputable companies offer guided excursions to leading attractions, everything from free guided walking tours of historic Nassau led by Ministry of Tourism guides (☎ 242-322-8634) to a nightclub tour offered by Majestic Tours (☎ 242-322-2606, fax 242-326-5785), which also has half-day guided tours of Nassau and New Providence.

Paradise Island

Part of Nassau or separate from it? Paradise Island lies almost shouting distance across the harbor from Nassau, to which it is linked by two great arcing bridges. Despite its proximity, its level of sophistication and markedly contemporary development make it distinct, with a mood wholly different from the city across the 'bay.'

The island is entirely a resort entity and boasts many ritzy hotels, the nation's most sophisticated casino, and gorgeous white beaches that outclass all others on New Providence. In general, it attracts a more monied crowd than does Nassau's Cable Beach, which is a sort of Reno to Paradise Island's Las Vegas.

In prior centuries it was used for raising pigs and became known as Hog Island. Early in the 20th century, a few wealthy socialites – they formed the Porcupine Club, for *multi*millionaires only – built homes. In 1939 Dr Axel Wenner-Gren, a wealthy Swedish industrialist, bought much of the island. After the war he developed a hideaway, which he called 'Shangri-La,' with a terraced garden modeled on Versailles. Wenner-Gren later sold the property to

wealthy scion Huntington Hartford II. The playboy millionaire built a 52-room hotel – the Ocean Club – on the estate, convinced the Bahamian legislature to rename the island 'Paradise Island,' and then added a marina, an 18-hole golf course, and even a 14th-century cloister that he purchased from newspaper magnate William Randolph Hearst.

No bridge existed back then and the island boasted super-snob appeal: 'There will be no automobiles, no roulette wheels, no honky-tonks on Hog Island,' Hartford proclaimed. The Ocean Club became the home-away-from-home for the Shah of Iran while in residence in the Bahamas. But the club did not fare well, and the island was sold to the Mary Carter Paint Company. As Resorts International, the company built the magnificent bridge in 1967 and set up the Paradise Island Casino before falling into the hands of Donald Trump and Merv Griffin, who built other resorts nearby, as well as the airport. After a brief construction surge, when dozens of expensive homes went up, the island felt the effects of a worldwide economic recession.

In 1994 billionaire Sol Kerzner's Sun International, a South African company that now owns 70% of the island (and is the largest employer in The Bahamas after the Bahamian government), scooped up three resorts, demolished two, and built an amazing hotel, casino, and entertainment complex – Atlantis – that has inspired other hoteliers to invest. Thus the island has regained immense vigor. The Atlantis project includes massive private home development for the super-rich (Oprah Winfrey and Michael Jordan are reputed to have bought homes carved into the woodlands behind Cabbage Beach). A second bridge was built in 1998 to handle the increased traffic.

Despite this, and despite its small size, there are plenty of sequestered coves along the sand-lined shores and plenty of lonesome spots away from the hordes.

Orientation

The island is 4 miles long and a half-mile wide, tapering to the west. It is divided in

PARADISE ISLAND

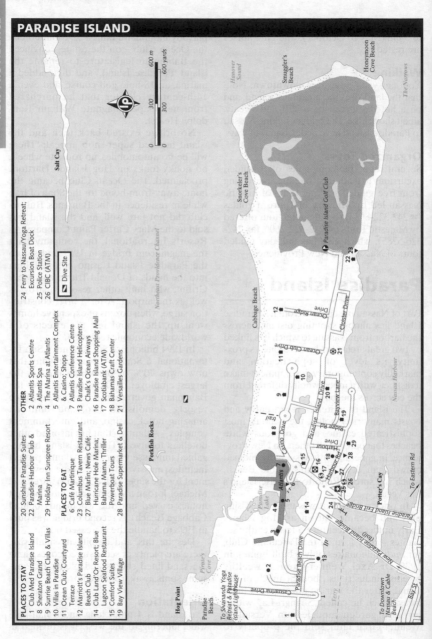

PLACES TO STAY
1 Club Med Paradise Island
8 Sheraton Grand
9 Sunrise Beach Club & Villas
10 Villas in Paradise
11 Ocean Club; Courtyard
   Terrace
12 Marriott's Paradise Island
   Beach Club
14 Club Land'Or Resort; Blue
   Lagoon Seafood Restaurant
15 Comfort Suites
19 Bay View Village
20 Sunshine Paradise Suites
22 Paradise Harbour Club &
   Marina
29 Holiday Inn Sunspree Resort

PLACES TO EAT
6 Café Martinique
23 Columbus Tavern Restaurant
27 Blue Marlin; News Café;
   Hurricane Hole Marina;
   Bahama Mama; Thriller
   Powerboat Tours
28 Paradise Supermarket & Deli

OTHER
2 Atlantis Sports Centre
3 Atlantis Spa
4 The Marina at Atlantis
5 Atlantis Entertainment Complex
   & Casino; Shops
7 Atlantis Conference Centre
13 Paradise Island Helicopters;
   Chalk's Ocean Airways
16 Paradise Island Shopping Mall
17 Scotiabank (ATM)
18 Bahamas Craft Center
21 Versailles Gardens
24 Ferry to Nassau/Yoga Retreat;
   Excursion Boat Dock
25 Police Station
26 CIBC (ATM)

■ Dive Site

two by a narrow manmade waterway linking Nassau Harbour to the Atlantis marina.

Two road bridges (one to enter and the other to exit the island) link Paradise Island to New Providence. The entry bridge runs from Bay St at Church St (by St Mathews Church) and descends to a tollbooth and Paradise Beach Dr on the island. To the left, Paradise Beach Dr descends through a tunnel and leads to the entrances for Chalk's Ocean Airways, the Atlantis Sports Centre, Club Med, and the Great Hall of Waters and Royal Towers at Atlantis; to the right it leads to a roundabout (traffic circle), from where Casino Dr leads north to the Atlantis Casino and Convention Center, Coral Towers at Atlantis, the Sheraton Grand, and 2-mile-long Cabbage Beach.

Paradise Island Dr, a block north of the roundabout, leads east from Casino Dr to the Ocean Club and Paradise Island Golf Course. Immediately south of the roundabout is Paradise Island Exit Bridge, which connects to Mackey St at Bay St in Nassau.

From the entrance to Club Med, Casuarina Dr runs north to Pirate's Cove. The cove is separated by a small peninsula – Hog Point – from 2-mile-long Paradise Beach, with sand as white and fine as pulverized sugar. It curls west to the red-and-white-striped Paradise Island Lighthouse at the tip of the island.

East of Cabbage Beach and separated by a small headland is Snorkeler's Cove Beach, another stunner that is usually deserted except for the few hours midday when excursion boats disgorge passengers for snorkeling and picnics. Virtually deserted Smuggler's Beach lines the east shore.

Both bridges have pedestrian walkways.

Information

There is no tourist information booth on the island. *Paradise Islander* is a slick full-color tourist magazine. Most hotel rooms stock a free copy for guests.

Scotiabank has a branch by the roundabout on the north side of the Exit Bridge. CIBC has a branch at Hurricane Hole Marina. Both have outdoor ATMs.

Atlantis

No trip would be complete without a visit to Atlantis' 14-acre waterscape, the source of the hotel's slogan: 'An ocean runs through it.' Here the world's largest open-air aquarium teems with over 100 species of tropical fish. The facility is dominated by the soaring rose-pink structures topped by spired cupolas and leaping sailfish, sparking images of Indiana Jones and the Temple of Doom.

Sun International remade the Paradise Island Resort & Casino as the Atlantis at a cost of US$850 million. It now has waterfalls and the quarter-mile 'Lazy River Ride' for tubing, plus six exhibit lagoons filled with live coral, more than 14,000 fish, and heaps of other sea life. It's best viewed from a 100-foot-long underwater Plexiglas walkway or from other subaqueous tunnels surrounded by massive aquariums through which 3 million gallons of ocean water are recycled four times each day. In all the facility has 8.1 million gallons of fresh and saltwater pools and lagoons, including a seven-acre snorkeling lagoon.

The waterscape is centered on The Dig, a full-size depiction of the ruins of Atlantis, linked by interconnecting passageways; and a Mayan Temple with six water slides, one of which – the Leap of Faith – sends brave vacationers through a Plexiglas tube that plummets down through the Predator Lagoon full of sharks.

The best time to check it out is the 10 am feeding on Tuesday, Thursday, and weekends. At noon or 4 pm, head to the Seagrapes Lagoon to watch the 9-foot-long sawfish being fed.

Guided walking tours (US$25 to nonguests) are offered from the Coral Towers Lobby at 10 am and at 1 and 4 pm. For details, call ☎ 242-363-3000 and ask for Guest Services, ext 28.

The complex also includes the Discovery Channel Camp, an interactive educational experience designed and run in association with the Discovery Channel. From 'Base Camp' (a remake of a sunken Spanish galleon) to a state-of-the-art technology lab, the camp is a wholesome learning experience. Activities cost US$35 per half-day, and US$45 at night.

Versailles Gardens

Dr Axel Wenner-Gren's ostentatious binge resulted in the creation of this sweeping 35-acre garden, stepped in tiers and lined with classical statues depicting the millionaire's heroes. They span the ages: Hercules, Napoleon Bonaparte, and Franklin D Roosevelt to name a few.

Paradise Island Dr runs through the gardens, which fall away on both sides. At the crest is a classical gazebo of columned arches – **The Cloisters** – where weddings are often held. This genuine 600-year-old structure was originally part of an Augustine estate in France.

Activities

Water sports are available at all the resorts along Paradise and Cabbage Beaches. Most of the motorized sports are operated by local entrepreneurs. Typical prices include

US$35 for 30 minutes' Jet Skiing; US$15 per person for a 15-minute banana boat ride, and US$25 for 10 minutes' parasailing. The main outlet is Sea & Ski Ocean Sports (☎ 242-363-3370) at the Sheraton Grand on Cabbage Beach; it also offers snorkeling for US$25 and scuba diving for US$35 per single-tank dive.

The Paradise Island Golf Club (☎ 242-363-300, 800-321-3000) is for the exclusive use of guests of Atlantis and the Ocean Club (see the Places to Stay section). It has been redesigned by Tom Weiskopf, and was closed and still being revamped at press time. Its 14th hole is legendary for its splendid vistas. Green fees had not been announced.

Sport fishing is available from charter boats at The Marina at Atlantis and Hurricane Hole Marina.

All the resorts have tennis courts. The main venue, however, is Club Med Paradise

Wedding Bells

The Bahamas is a popular destination for honeymooners, many of whom tie the knot in the islands. The requirements are easily met. The Bahamas now allows nonresidents to marry with just a 24-hour wait.

The license costs US$40 and can be obtained from the Registrar General's Office (☎ 242-326-5371, 242-328-7810) in the Rodney E Bain Bldg on Parliament St in Nassau. You'll need photo identification, proof of citizenship, proof of status if divorced or widowed, and an 'Affidavit of Competency to Marry' from the US Embassy & Consulate (it costs US$10). No blood test is required. Anyone under 18 years of age requires notarized parental consent.

The Ministry of Tourism (☎ 242-322-7500) has a 'Weddings in Paradise' service that will put you in touch with local consultants who can plan a wedding. Most major hotels and tour operators can also make arrangements; they usually ask couples to send notarized copies of required documents at least one month in advance. Major resorts have special honeymoon packages and can arrange a wedding with a minister.

You can even get married underwater (provided you and your spouse-to-be are certified divers) in Grand Bahama with the Underwater Explorers Society (UNEXSO; ☎ 242-373-1244; in the US ☎ 800-992-DIVE, 954-351-9889).

For a pre-planned wedding package, call the US-based company The Islands of the Bahamas (☎ 888-NUPTIALS).

Island (☎ 242-363-2640), with 20 courts, professional instructors, and special tennis clinics with one-on-one teaching by seeded professionals. The Ocean Club (☎ 242-363-3000) also has a major tennis program and it hosts tennis championships.

The Atlantis resort offers a complete Sports Center, including six Decturf and four Hydroturf tennis courts, a four-lane lap pool, a full-size basketball and volleyball court, and an Astro-turf golf course. And the 25,000-sq-foot Spa at Atlantis has complete facilities and services for spiritual and physical rejuvenation.

Boat Excursions Most cruises depart Paradise Island from the dock immediately west of the Paradise Island Exit Bridge.

Several uninhabited cays are sprinkled northeast of New Providence, most enticingly, Blue Lagoon on Salt Cay, which is featured on several day cruises (also see Dolphin Encounters, later in this section). It's a 30-minute ride. Here you can create your own desert-island fantasy. Choose among snorkeling, parasailing, volleyball, or even a dolphin encounter. A live band plays. There's a craft center; the Stingray City Marine Park (☎ 242-363-3179), where you can swim with the rays; and helicopter tours. There are nature walks, changing rooms, restrooms, showers, and 250 hammocks slung between palms.

A half-day excursion to Blue Lagoon with Nassau Cruises (☎ 242-353-3577, fax 242-363-1657) costs US$20 per person; a six-hour trip costs US$35; a full day costs US$45, including hotel transfers, unlimited water sports, and lunch. The company operates the 100-foot-long, three-deck *Calypso I* and *Calypso II*, taking up to 125 people at a time. Each boat has a bar and dancing, and dinners are offered. Departures are at 10 and 11:30 am daily, returning to Paradise Island at 1:30, 3, and 4 pm. Its mailing address is PO Box N-7366, Nassau, The Bahamas.

The same company also offers a 'Historical Harbour Cruise' around Paradise Island, passing the lighthouse, Arawak Cay, pirate homes, and other sites, tracing The Bahamas' colorful past. The trips depart at

9:30 am daily; they take about 90 minutes and cost US$25.

Flying Cloud Catamaran Cruises (☎ 242-363-4430) offers similar cruises aboard the *Flying Cloud*, a 57-foot catamaran that departs Paradise Island. It sails daily except Thursday and Sunday. A half-day cruise costs US$35; a dinner cruise costs US$55. Out Island Voyages (☎ 242-394-0951) offers excursion cruises from the same dock.

Sea Island Adventures (☎ 242-325-3910, fax 242-328-2581, seaisle@bahamas.net.bs) offers trips to Rose Island aboard a canopied catamaran. The Web site is www.seaisl.com.

For adventures farther afield, Island World Adventures (☎ 242-394-8960, fax 242-363-1657, cruise@bahamas.net.bs) offers daylong excursions to Saddleback Cay (Exumas), speeding you there aboard the 45-foot, high-powered *EcoTime*. You can skinny-dip on any of six beaches, take guided hikes, snorkel, etc. The trips depart Paradise Island daily from the ferry terminal beneath Paradise Island Exit Bridge and include a stop at Leaf Cay to commune with iguanas. The mailing address is PO Box N-7366, Paradise Island, The Bahamas.

Another day-trip opertor, Powerboat Adventures (☎ 242-327-5385, fax 242-393-7029, info@powerboatadventures.com), also whisks you out to the Exumas at breakneck speed aboard 900-hp boats. The excursion includes shark feeding, snorkeling with stingrays, a barbecue lunch, and plenty of rum swizzles. Its postal address is PO Box CB-13315, Nassau, The Bahamas.

Thriller Powerboat Tours (☎ 242-363-4685) offers 30-minute hair-raisers from The Marina at Atlantis using a super-charged race-boat. The Web site is www.thrillerboat.com.

Dolphin Encounters Wow! Kids (regardless of age) can swim with trained Atlantic bottle-nosed dolphins in a protected lagoon – Blue Lagoon – on Salt Cay. Trips are offered by Nassau Cruises (☎ 242-363-3577, fax 242-363-1657, cruise@bahamas.net.bs), PO Box N-7366, Nassau, The Bahamas; the ride costs US$20 (US$10 children), or US$50 (US$25 children) including lunch, rum drinks, and some watersports. The movies *Zeus & Roxanne*, *Splash*, and *Flipper* were filmed at this 2-sq-mile private cay and featured the aquatic stars Jake, MacGyver, and Fatman.

You can take a half-day trip to Blue Lagoon with Dolphin Encounters (☎ 242-327-5066, 242-363-1653, fax 242-327-5059, stm@bahamas.net.bs) from Paradise Island. It includes a 30-minute swim with these clever mammals; the trip costs from US$75 for a basic trip to US$145 including the swim. The animals will swim around you and even let you touch them. Nonswimmers and toddlers can opt for the less-expensive, more sedate option, standing in a shallow lagoon where the dolphins will also let you touch them. A 'Stingray Snorkel' is also offered at Blue Lagoon for US$45. The trips depart the ferry terminal at the base of Paradise Island Exit Bridge. The Web site is www.dolphinswims.com.

Helicopter Tours Paradise Island Helicopters (☎ 242-363-4016) has breathtaking whirlybird tours over Nassau and Paradise Island and out to Blue Lagoon on Salt Cay. The 10-minute 'The Native' tour, which costs US$45 to US$90 depending on the number of people, is a good way to get your bearings…and some spectacular photos. Longer tours are offered. Trips are offered 9 am to 6 pm daily from the Paradise Island Heliport on Paradise Beach Dr.

Places to Stay

Paradise Island is not a budget-traveler's haven. Nonetheless, there are a few gems.

Budget & Mid-Range *Sivananda Yoga Retreat (☎ 242-363-2902, 800-783-9642, fax 242-363-3783, nassau@sivananda.org)* is a reclusive gem amid lush, tranquil grounds on the slender western peninsula of Paradise Island. The place – also known as 'Club Meditation' – is the epitome of calm simplicity. It has dozens of tent sites beneath shady palms (watch out for falling coconuts), where you can camp for US$50. Dormitory rooms in the main building cost US$59. Other accommodations are in rustic

yet cozy cabins in the Oriental garden or facing the beach; double occupancy rates are US$69 garden-view, US$79 oceanfront (US$10 extra for air-con), including two buffet-style lacto-vegetarian meals plus meditation and yoga workshops and classes. Reservations are essential. Bring your own towel. Families with children are welcome. You can reach it by walking along Paradise Beach. A free water taxi will take you from the ferry terminal just west of the Paradise Island Exit Bridge. The retreat's postal address is PO Box N-7550, Nassau, The Bahamas.

Another gem, 400 yards west of the Yoga Retreat, is *Chaplin House (☎/fax 242-363-2918, chaphse@batelnet.bs)*, a delightfully funky old home lived in by Ronnie and Joan Carol, who rent four charming and romantic (albeit simple) cottages of whitewashed rough-hewn hardwoods. The cottages vary in size. Each has a kitchen, air-con, and fan. Verandahs look out over lush grounds where macaws hang out freely in fruit trees. The Carols prefer long-term rentals. Studio apartments cost US$95/105 summer/winter; two-bedroom cottages cost US$110 to US$120 summer, US$120 to US$140 winter. A third person sharing costs US$20. No credit cards are accepted. The postal address is PO Box SS-6034, Nassau, The Bahamas.

The *Howelton Rose House (☎ 242-363-3363, fax 242-377-3383)*, a B&B also known as the Pink House, is a Georgian-style inn that operates like a family-owned manor. It dates from 1927, when it was owned by the Sears (as in Sears-Roebuck) family, and was featured in the 1994 movie *My Father, the Hero*, in which a father (Gerard Depardieu) and daughter take a Caribbean vacation. It nestles amid 15 acres of tropical gardens toward the west end of the island. Each of the four bedrooms opens onto its own balcony or patio. The lounge and other public arenas are jammed with antiques, wicker furniture, blue-and-white chintz sofas, and other faded mementos of genteel grandeur, lending the home a charming French-chateaux feel. Gracious owner Minni Winn oversees your comfort. Access is via Club Med. Rooms rent for US$100/120 in summer/winter. A bargain! Its mailing address is PO Box SS-19157, Paradise Island, The Bahamas.

Top End The *Paradise Harbour Club & Marina* (☎ 242-363-2992, 800-742-4276, fax 242-363-2840, phclub@gmx.net), at the east end of Paradise Island Dr, is a small, attractive, Swiss-run property in a marina setting. It's popular with German tour groups. Recently renovated rooms are spacious and clean, with large kitchens and contemporary decor. There's no beach at hand, but the splendid Columbus Tavern Restaurant is here, and the small pool has a water cascade. Hotel room rates are US$120 single or double in summer, US$150 in winter. Junior suites cost US$180/210; apartments cost US$250/275 one/two-bedroom in summer, and US$350/410 in winter. Its postal address is PO Box SS-5804, Nassau, The Bahamas.

Bay View Village (☎ 242-363-2555, fax 242-363-2370, bayview@batelnet.bs), in a leafy, upscale residential area, has cozy and pleasing recently refurbished air-con rooms that feature TVs, microwaves, hair dryers, and in-room safes (extra charge). Rates range from US$140/190 summer/winter for one-bedroom suites through US$355/485 for deluxe six-person villas. Bay View's postal address is PO Box SS-6308, Nassau, The Bahamas. It's also popular with German charter groups, as is *Sunshine Paradise Suites* (☎ 242-363-3955, 800-813-6847, fax 242-363-3840, sunshine@bahamas.net.bs), a similar property farther north on Paradise Island Dr, which has 16 self-catering apartment suites for daily, weekly, and monthly rental. Rates are US$135/165 for one/two bedrooms in summer; US$165/195 in winter. There's a small pool in the front courtyard. Its mailing address is PO Box SS-5206, Paradise Island, Nassau, The Bahamas.

Soulless *Comfort Suites* (☎ 242-363-3680, 800-228-5150, fax 242-363-2588, comsuite@batelnet.bs) is a US-motel–style option on Casino Dr. It recently completed a renovation to its 150 junior suites, which are nicely furnished with king-size beds, sofa bed,

cable TV, minibar, hairdryer, and safe. The pool and sun deck areas are attractive. Kids under 18 stay free with parents. Guests have free access to all Atlantis facilities and can make charges directly to their rooms. Superior suites with island views begin at US$150 single or double in low-season; deluxe suites with garden views start at US$170. Luxury suites begin at US$195. The postal address is PO Box SS-6202, Nassau, The Bahamas.

In a decidedly French vein is *Club Med Paradise Island* (☎ 242-363-2640, 800-258-2633, fax 242-363-3496). The resort, spanning the island from Paradise Beach to Nassau Harbour, was created from three turn-of-the-century estates on 23 beautifully landscaped acres. It now has 41 single-occupancy rooms added to its 320 air-con doubles, all decorated in soft earth tones and exotic art. At its heart is the main dining room, theater, and nightclub. Dining is family-style. There are also two open-air restaurants. The club boasts an Olympic-size pool, 19 tennis courts, and an intensive tennis program each spring. Excursions, water sports, and recreational activities are offered. Club Med is for gregarious folks – if you're reclusive, it could be a banana peel waiting to happen. Per-person rates are US$158/161 summer/winter for a standard double room. One-week packages cost US$1106/1127. Deluxe rooms cost 10% more. Single rooms cost 20% to 100% more than the standard rates, depending on season. Honeymooners can choose the exquisite 'House in the Woods,' a two-story, Bermudan-style private villa with gingerbread trim, housekeeping service, and wraparound porches on both levels, plus a wrought-iron bed with a plump down duvet as soft as a cloud. It costs US$220 per person or US$395 during holiday periods. Its postal address is PO Box N-7137, Nassau, The Bahamas.

I like the cozy *Club Land'Or Resort* (☎ 242-363-2400, fax 242-363-3403, info@clublandor.com; in the US ☎ 804-346-8200, 800-552-2839), which faces onto Paradise Lake and has a contemporary Mediterranean feel. It's centered on a small pool.

The one-bedroom 'villas' (rooms) are romantically furnished, with French lace curtains; they sleep up to six people and have splendid kitchens. It boasts the fine Blue Lagoon Restaurant and has entertainment and guided excursions. A shuttle runs to Paradise Beach twice daily. Rates begin at US$165 garden-view, US$195 water-view single or double in summer; US$225 and US$250, respectively, in winter. Each additional person costs US$25. The mailing address is PO Box SS-6429, Paradise Island, Nassau, The Bahamas.

The **Holiday Inn Sunspree Resort** (☎ 242-363-2561, fax 242-363-3803; in the US ☎ 800-331-6471) opened in 2000 as a classy remake of the former Paradise Island Fun Club, with 250 rooms overlooking Nassau Harbour. There are two elegant air-con restaurants, a whirlpool, gym, two tennis courts, plus a free-form pool with rocky islands and water cascade, a sun deck and a small beach with volleyball. The rooms are nicely furnished and have necessary conveniences. Room rates are US$180 to US$229 in winter. The postal address is PO Box SS-6249, Paradise Island, Nassau, The Bahamas.

Villas in Paradise (☎ 242-363-2998, fax 242-363-2703) on Casino Dr offers one- to four-bedroom villas with private pool, full kitchen, and options for king-size beds. Summer rates range from US$210 to US$395; winter rates range from US$289 to US$495. A minimum seven-night stay is required at Christmas, New Year's, and Easter. The mailing address is PO Box SS-6379, Paradise Island, Nassau, The Bahamas.

A high-rise option is the **Sheraton Grand** (☎ 242-363-3500, 800-782-9488, fax 242-363-3900, paradise@sheratongrand.com) on Casino Dr. This former Radisson reopened in early 2000 after its second multimillion-dollar remake in two years. It's very contemporary, with 340 spacious air-con rooms and suites – all in fresh, calming decor – that overlook the spectacular beach and a huge triangular pool and sun deck. Each has cable TV with pay-per-view movies, modems, direct-dial phone, coffee-maker, hair-dryer, in-room safe, and mini-bar. There's a choice of restaurants, plus night-lit tennis courts, watersports, and a nightclub. Room rates range from US$220 to US$250 in summer, US$305 to US$335 in winter; suites cost US$270 to US$640 in summer, US$365 to US$900 in winter. The mailing address is PO Box SS-6307, Paradise Island, Nassau, The Bahamas.

Lushly landscaped **Sunrise Beach Club & Villas** (☎ 242-363-250, 888-387-2875, fax 242-363-2308, info@sunrisebeachvillas.com), on Casino Dr, is an Italianate complex of reclusive, upscale villas, beautifully furnished and highlighted within by two-person marble tubs. Other romantic touches include bathrooms with stained-glass windows and a tiny garden with burbling waterfall in each lounge. Some villas have mezzanine bedrooms. There are two small, exquisitely landscaped swimming pools. Daily rates range from US$234 to US$822 in summer; US$315 to US$912 in winter, depending on villa size. The mailing address is PO Box SS-6519, Nassau, The Bahamas.

Two-bedroom villas – good for up to six people – can be found at **Marriott's Paradise Island Beach Club** (☎ 242-363-2523, 800-845-5279, fax 242-363-2130), a handsome complex on Ocean Ridge Dr, right on Cabbage Beach. Each has a fully equipped kitchen, whirlpool bath, plus patio. Facilities include a swimming pool with swim-up bar. Winter rates average US$375/2500 daily/ weekly. It has no restaurant. The postal address is PO Box N-10600, Nassau, The Bahamas.

Merge Disneyland, Las Vegas, and Sea World and you have **Atlantis** (☎ 242-363-3000, fax 242-363-3524; in the US ☎ 800-281-3000), a bustling mega-resort unlike any hotel this side of Vegas. This 23-story resort has an appropriately mammoth lobby – the Great Hall of Waters, plus 2345 rooms and suites in the Royal Towers, Coral Towers, Beach Tower, and villas. Spanning the two Royal Towers is a 5000-sq-ft Bridge Suite suspended 16 stories above ground, with 360 degree vistas. Rooms come in several categories, including queen and king rooms, and junior, executive, grand, presidential, and royal suites…all boasting balcony, TV with in-room movies, phones, safe, minibar,

Breezy beach in Nassau

Big Red Boat

Atlantis Resort

Packed beach in Paradise Island

Paradise Island water sports

Heads up: Grand Bahama's Dolphin Experience

Grand Bahama's Shark Junction

Diving the Willaurie wreck off New Providence

and either soft yellow decor blending with rattan and light wood furniture or, in the Royal Towers, regal furnishings with supremely comfortable king-size beds, cavernous bathrooms with lots of marble, plus large-screen TVs with Spectravision. The highlight is the resort's theme waterpark (see the Atlantis section earlier in this chapter). Atlantis also has nine swimming pools, 40 specialty restaurants, numerous bars, and an entertainment complex with a 50,000-sq-foot casino, cabaret, and shows. Needless to say, it has all watersports and exercise facilities, plus a full-service spa, a shopping plaza, and a Discovery Channel Camp guaranteed to keep kids entertained for days. Winter rates begin at US$300/350 standard/deluxe, single or double. Summer rates are 50% lower. The resort offers special package rates. A MAP (breakfast and dinner plan) package costs US$43 per person per day, and a 'Gourmet Dining Plan' costs US$72. Its postal address is PO Box N-4777, Nassau, The Bahamas.

You'll know you've arrived if you can afford to stay at the **Ocean Club** (☎ 242-363-3000, fax 242-363-2424), a snooty extension of the Atlantis complex. This exquisite colonial property exudes European elegance, with exclusive touches such as complimentary shoe shines. The 103 rooms and suites (including 50 new rooms in construction at press time) plus five two-bedroom villas are capacious, with large his-and-her bathrooms done up in marble, elegant bygone-era decor, and state-of-the-art amenities like a 27-inch TV. Crystal and silver sparkle on linen-draped tables around the courtyard dining area, one of three upscale eateries (a beachfront restaurant was being added as part of a US$50 million expansion). The resort abuts a splendid section of beach, has a Bermudan-style bar, and boasts nine tennis courts plus the nearby Paradise Island Golf Course. Guests have access to Atlantis' facilities. Rates range from US$400 to US$700 for rooms, US$715 to US$780 for suites, and US$810 for two-bedroom villas. The club's postal address is PO Box N-4777, Nassau, The Bahamas.

Places to Eat

There are few budget options. One of the best is the **News Café** (☎ 242-363-4684) in Hurricane Hole Plaza. This delightful deli has air-con or patio dining, and offers salads and sandwiches for around US$6, coffees, espressos, cappuccinos, etc, plus desserts, including ice creams. It has free international newspapers to read, and sells magazines.

The **Blue Marlin** (☎ 242-363-2660), also at Hurricane Hole, has lunch specials for US$5; its sunset dinner specials for US$14 include limbo dancing and Junkanoo.

The **Blue Lagoon Seafood Restaurant** (☎ 242-363-2400), at Club Land'Or Resort, offers a US$8 American breakfast special, and a US$25 dinner special (try the lobster fettuccini). The restaurant has splendid decor: Tiffany lamps, plentiful hardwood, and plate-glass windows with views of the gardens below. Or choose burgers and sandwiches at the poolside bar; the chicken-filet burger for US$5 is excellent.

About 1 mile east is the **Columbus Tavern Restaurant** (☎ 242-363-2534), at Paradise Harbour Club's marina and exuding a maritime air. It offers French and Swiss specialties, such as stuffed escargots in shells, roast duck à l'orange, and sirloin steak. Entrees range from US$10 to US$34.

The Atlantis boasts 40 eateries and bars, including **Atlas Bar & Grill**, a high-energy video cafe reminiscent of the Roman Forum, with views of the casino action and an American menu; the posh **Five Twins**, with a sushi bar and cigar bar plus dancing; **The Marketplace**, the mainstay restaurant with an international menu in an 'Old World' setting; and **Fathoms**, an elegant, romantic seafood restaurant surrounded by the Plexiglas walls of the shark tanks. There's something for every taste here: a deli, a Bahamian fast-food joint, **Murray's** for Italian, and **Voyagers** for desserts and gourmet coffees served into the wee hours. Reservations are essential, as places such as **Café Martinique**, featured in the James Bond movie *Thunderball*, are often booked solid two days in advance.

The Ocean Club's **Courtyard Terrace** (☎ 242-363-3000) is favored by monied locals. The setting is splendid (see the Places to Stay section), with a live band playing easy-listening and jazz tunes. The continental cuisine – heavily leaning to seafood – has been acclaimed, but I was disappointed. Expect to pay US$50 per person and up for dinner. Jacket and tie are required for men. The dress code in the Ocean Club's other two eateries is casually elegant. Reservations are recommended.

Club Med opens its doors to outsiders on Friday and Saturday nights for the finest buffet spread on the island; it costs US$60, including entertainment.

You can buy groceries at the *Paradise Supermarket & Deli* on Harbour Rd.

Entertainment

Casinos & Floorshows The 30,000-sq-foot *Atlantis Casino* (☎ 242-363-3000) is the largest in the Caribbean and the centerpiece of a gigantic entertainment complex featuring thematic visions celebrating ancient mythology and the Atlantis legend. It has 980 slot machines and 78 gaming tables. It's not Monte Carlo, but casually elegant dress is appreciated.

Atlantis' multi-faceted entertainment complex includes a theater where a Las Vegas–style revue featuring befeathered women in G-strings and high heels dancing alongside besequined, leotard-clad male counterparts was planned. Comedy and a magician's act are also featured.

A steel band, flaming limbo, and Junkanoo are offered at the *Blue Marlin* (☎ 242-363-2660) at 8:30 pm Tuesday to Sunday for US$15 (see Places to Eat, above).

Nightclubs & Bars Most hotels have bars, including a fistful of options at *Atlantis*, including *Plato's Lounge*, with candlelight and a pianist, and the *Piranha Club*, below ground in The Dig and where you can watch the eponymous fish through Plexiglas. A crooner sings nightly at the *Oasis Lounge* of Club Land'Or. And live musicians perform at *Bahama Mama Mia* in Hurricane Hole Marina.

Dragons is Atlantis' hot, high-tech nightclub, hugely popular with locals as well as tourists. It opens to the casino. Entry is free to hotel guests; US$30 to others.

Club Med has its own disco.

Comedy For giggles, check out the stand-up comedy at *Joker's Wild* (☎ 242-363-2222) in Atlantis. The cocktail show is at 9:30 pm Tuesday to Sunday and costs US$20.

Shopping

Duty-free items and resortwear are sold at boutiques in major hotels and at the small Paradise Island Shopping Mall, just north of the roundabout. The Atlantis complex features the Crystal Court shopping complex with several dozen designer stores combining a taste of Fifth Avenue with Rodeo Dr...from Gucci and Ferragamo to Greenfire Emeralds, John Bull, and even a cigar store.

Solomon's Mines has a jewelry outlet at Hurricane Hole Marina.

Dozens of vendors display at Bahamas Craft Centre, on Harbour Rd. Bargaining is expected.

Getting There & Away

Air The Paradise Island Airport closed permanently in 1999 to make way for an expansion of the golf course.

Chalk's Ocean Airways (formerly Pan-Am Air Bridge) flies seaplanes from Miami's Watson Island twice daily using clipper planes; fares begin at US$88/195 one-way/roundtrip. It also flies daily from Fort Lauderdale's Jet Center. You'll drone along at 180mph in a Grumman-built Mallard. The flying boats arrive and depart the Paradise Island Seaplane Terminal, adjacent to the channel entrance for The Marina at Atlantis. They take off and land right in Nassau Harbour, like speedboats, with water splashing against their windows. *Way to go!*

Chalk's also flies from Paradise Island to the Biminis once daily.

Paradise Island Helicopters (☎ 242-363-4016) offers transportation between Nassau/Paradise Island and the Family Islands, as well as Grand Bahama. Charter rates are US$750 per hour and include the return trip, with or without passengers (thus, you pay for the return trip even if you're traveling only in one direction). The company also offers sightseeing 'helitours.' The Web site is www.bahamasnet.com/helicopter.

Bus There's no bus service to Paradise Island. However, you can catch Bus Nos 24 or 30 from Frederick St in downtown Nassau to the New Paradise Island Bridge for US75¢, and then walk over to the island.

Boat The Marina at Atlantis (☎ 242-363-6068) is a luxury marina with 63 mega-yacht slips for vessels from 40 feet to 220 feet in length, and offers boaters access to all the resort complex facilities.

The Hurricane Hole Marina (☎ 242-363-3600, fax 242-363-3604), PO Box SS-6317, Paradise Island, The Bahamas, is just east of the Paradise Island Bridge.

Paradise Harbour Club & Marina (☎ 242-363-2992, fax 242-363-2840) charges US$1.25 per foot daily.

A two-level ferry departs Nassau for Paradise Island from the cruise dock (US$3 per person) every 30 minutes, 9:30 am to 6 pm, departing when full. It deposits passengers at the ferry terminal just west of the Paradise Island Exit Bridge, where ferries for Nassau depart on a regular basis. You'll see the signs or be hustled aboard by touts.

Water taxis also ply the same route, but leave Nassau from Woodes Rogers Walk. They will drop you at Club Med or any of the Paradise Island wharves by request, including Yoga Retreat.

Getting Around

There are no jitneys. However, the 'Casino Express' operated by Atlantis runs a clockwise route throughout the day and early evening, picking up and dropping off passengers at major hotels; the fare is US$1.

Taxis Fares are fixed. A taxi for two people from Paradise Island to Nassau costs US$10; to Cable Beach, US$18; and to Paradise Island hotels, US$5 to US$6, plus extra for each additional person.

Car & Scooter Avis (☎ 242-363-2061) has an office between the Exit Bridge and Comfort Suites Hotel. Dollar (☎ 242-363-3500 ext 6182) has an outlet at the Sheraton Grand.

You can rent scooters from outside the Sheraton Grand for US$40 daily.

Mopeds cost US$30 daily from Club Land'Or and from rental agencies at Pirate's Cove.

Bicycle You can rent bicycles from Club Land'Or (US$6 for four hours, US$10 daily) and at Pirate's Cove (US$20 per day). They're single-gear beach cruisers with back-pedal brakes, but the island is flat and bicycling should prove no hardship given the short distances.

Club Land'Or offers a midwinter coupon for 50% discount on rentals.

West New Providence

Running west from Cable Beach on the island's north shore, W Bay St offers a beautiful drive. A narrow and forested limestone ridge south of the road parallels the shore. The area is favored by the wealthy, who have their upscale homes atop the ridge.

One-and-a-half miles west of Delaport Point you'll pass The Caves, just east of Blake Rd. This large cavern system once sheltered Lucayan Indians. You can peer into the entrance and maybe go farther with a flashlight and guide.

Just west of The Caves is Orange Hill Beach, shaded by sea grapes and palms. It is undeveloped (except for the Orange Hill Beach Inn, hidden on the bluff overlooking the beach) and very popular with locals on weekends. The owners of the hotel caused a storm in 1997 when they cut down the casuarinas (the trees drop pine needles onto the sands).

Other pocket-size slivers of white sand lie along the shoreline farther west. There is little development, except for Gambier Village, a small settlement that was founded for liberated slaves shortly after 1807. At the foot of the village, by the shore, is Compass Point, one of the country's most intimate resorts. It's worth a stop for lunch or dinner.

West of Compass Point is Love Beach, beyond which the road turns inland and curls past the small settlement of Mt Pleasant and around **Lyford Cay**, a sprawling estate of manicured, tree-lined streets and canals framed by glorious multimillion dollar mansions. Only a lucky few who receive a personal invitation from one of the residents will ever see beyond the walls of Lyford Cay, one of the world's most exclusive residential retreats, the 'Beverly Hills of The Bahamas.' Mere residence alone, however, does not automatically ensure your acceptance as a member of the prestigious Lyford Cay Club, which offers golf, tennis, and boating.

Although nicknamed 'Lifeless Cay' (because as a winter residence or second home for the rich and famous it was relatively dead except around Christmas and Easter), this exclusive hot property is experiencing a second wind.

The main road – now called Western Rd – continues around the perimeter of Lyford Cay. At the extreme west end you can follow an unmarked turnoff to a little wooden wharf and sheltered beach where you can look over the iridescent waters to some of the ritzy homes.

Beyond, the road curves around the island's westernmost apex, Clifton Point (the site of old plantation ruins), bringing you to the Clifton Pier Power Station, which supplies the island's electricity. Petroleum is unloaded here to supply the island's gas stations; fire-red miniature oil tankers bob dramatically at anchor in channels cut into the limestone cliff face. The **Commonwealth Brewery** is here, too.

A proposal to build a luxury gated community – Clifton Cay – that calls for canals to be cut into the limestone has outraged Bahamian citizens who fear that it will destroy or harm the wetlands, tropical hardwood forests and valuable reefs and dive sites in the adjacent marine system, which

are feeding grounds for green, hawksbill, and giant loggerhead turtles. (There is also significant evidence of Lucayan occupation.) The Clifton Park Committee (☎ 242-393-7604), a coalition of environmental and social activists, is working to create a nature park to protect the area.

Beyond the brewery you'll pass the South Ocean Golf Course and a 5-mile-long beach lining Southwest Bay.

Information
There's a shopping center – Lyford Cay Centre – outside Lyford Cay's gates, with a bank, police station, gas station, supermarket, art gallery, and liquor store. Lyford Cay also has a hospital (☎ 242-362-4025).

Diving & Snorkeling
The island's finest dive sites lie immediately off Clifton Point, where the coral wall drops away into the deep. There are also several wrecks, including a WWII bomber in the shallows west of Lyford Cay. Scenes from *Thunderball* were shot here.

Stuart's Cove Dive South Ocean (☎/fax 242-362-4171, 800-879-9832, info@stuart-cove.com) is based in South Ocean. A two-tank dive costs US$75, an introductory dive costs US$89, and a full PADI certification course costs US$350. The company's highlight is a rendezvous with sharks in a feeding frenzy on a 'Shark Awareness Program' that is preceded by a separate free dive with sharks. It has a professional photo center. Its mailing address is PO Box CB-13137, Nassau, The Bahamas. The Web site is www.stuartcove.com.

Stuart's Cove also offers snorkeling trips for US$35.

Golf
The Clarion Resort South Ocean (see Places to Stay, below) boasts the PGA-championship–rated South Ocean Golf Course (☎ 242-363-4391, 877-766-2326) amid rolling uplands that offer fine seascapes. The green fee is US$90, including cart; US$65 for resort guests. Vital statistics: 72-par, 6707 yards. Reservations are advised.

Places to Stay

The family-run *Orange Hill Beach Inn* (☎ 242-327-7157, 800-805-5485, fax 242-327-5186, *orangehil@batelnet.bs*), on the bluff overlooking Orange Hill Beach, just off W Bay St less than 2 miles from the airport, is preferred for overnights in transit between islands; it's also one of the few hotels to offer airport drop-offs (US$3; a taxi costs US$10). The entrance sign reads 'Fawlty Towers,' but I think that's just Danny and Judy Lowe's idea of a joke! They run their no-frills place with a casual familiarity that particularly appeals to Europeans. There's a small pool. The bar runs on the honor system, and the games room has about every board game. The 32 rooms, in modern, albeit soulless units, have contemporary furniture, refrigerators, microwaves, and toasters. There are also studios and apartments with kitchens. Summer rates are US$81 single, US$91 to US$111 double; winter rates are US$98 single, US$108 to US$138 double. It's overpriced. The inn's mailing address is PO Box N-8583, Nassau, The Bahamas.

I think the brightest star in the island's hotel galaxy is *Compass Point* (☎ 242-327-4500, fax 242-327-3299, *compasspoint@islandoutpost.com; in the US* ☎ 305-534-2135, 800-688-7678, fax 305-672-2881) in Gambier Village, beloved by musicians recording at Compass Point Studios across the road, as well as celebs like Naomi Campbell and Cindy Crawford. It's impossible to not fall in love with Island Outpost's creation, done up in Junkanoo colors: purples, teal blues, canary yellows, blood-reds, sea-greens, and pinks-turning-to-cherry when fired by the setting sun. No stone or tile or furnishing went unpainted in the decorative abandon. It perches over a coral shore, with 13 huts and cottages and five cozy cabañas edging up to the turquoise water. The octagonal clapboard cottages (some on stilts) boast large windows, cute porches, conical beamed ceilings, and rustic yet tasteful furnishings, as well as rocking chairs, fluffy bathrobes, potpourri bowls, mosquito coils, a CD player with hip CDs, VCR, and an oversize bedstead mirror to give lovers a thrill. Mid-April through mid-December, rates are at US$200 for cabañas, US$255 to US$280 for one-bedroom cottages, US$330 for a two-bedroom cottage, and US$625 for a penthouse cottage. In peak season rates are US$215, US$315 to US$355, US$425, and US$800, respectively. The restaurant attracts locals in the know, as does the bar. Compass Point offers water sports. Its mailing address is Island Outpost, 1320 Ocean Dr, Miami Beach, FL 33139, USA.

The *Clarion Resort South Ocean* (☎ 242-362-4391, 800-252-7466, fax 242-362-4810, *clarion@batelnet.bs; elsewhere in the world* ☎ 877-766-2326) is an upscale, self-contained, all-inclusive property with a country-club feel and a splendid aesthetic in its public arenas and 250 spacious air-con rooms: 109 'moderate' garden-view rooms in the 'Club House'; and 129 'premier' rooms in the colonial-style Great House with ocean-views. Each has tiled floors, private balcony, telephone, cable TV, and ceiling fan; 'premier' rooms have Jacuzzi-style bathtubs, ceiling fans and mini-refrigerators. A thorough remake was completed in 1999, with the addition of an entertainment complex (a casino was also planned). There are three restaurants and three bars, plus two swimming pools, tennis

courts, and a jogging trail. Water sports are offered. 'Camp Jama' offers fully supervised activities for kids. Garden-view rooms cost US$115/195 summer/winter; ocean-view rooms cost US$165/295. Golf packages are sold. It has its own straw market, plus scooter rental. The resort's mailing address is PO Box N-8191, South Ocean, New Providence, The Bahamas.

Places to Eat

Nesbit's, an unpretentious eatery 400 yards west of Sandyport on the road to Lyford Cay, serves Bahamian fare and is very popular with locals.

The *Orange Hill Beach Inn* has a restaurant that serves home-style fare. The simple dinner menu changes daily; prices range from US$12 to US$23. No fruits are offered for breakfast. The lunch menu includes salads and sandwiches for US$4. Dinner service stops promptly at 8:30 pm.

The Traveller's Rest (☎ 242-327-7633), 1 mile west of Orange Hill Beach, offers colorful, Hockneyesque ambiance (it's full of Caribbean artwork) and an eclectic menu, including a seafood platter for US$18.

Some of the finest cuisine on the island – and surely the best value – is found at the exquisite restaurant at *Compass Point*. Here chef Stephen Bastian has evolved a fine fusion of Californian, Mediterranean, Pacific Rim, and Caribbean cuisine, such as pizza with jerk chicken and roasted sweet potatoes; Bahamian sushi rolls with conch, mango, and cucumber; and smoked mahi-mahi on a sweet potato pancake. Entrees typically cost US$10 to US$30 – a steal by Bahamian standards. Imagine fried oysters for just US$10. Equally creative breakfasts cost about US$12. Full-bodied specialty drinks cost US$8.50. You can dine indoors or on the breezy waterfront terrace. The fashionable bar is a favorite of locals, including such reclusive residents as Sean Connery, plus waifish models, local parliamentarians, and Hollywood stars and starlets.

Getting There & Away

Western Transportation operates hourly bus service to the Clarion Resort South Ocean from Bay and George Sts in Nassau between 7:30 am and midnight. Service runs via Cable Beach and Compass Point. The fare from Compass Point is US$1.75. Other buses include Coastline Nos 10 and 38. You have to flag down the bus.

A shuttle runs to downtown Nassau from the Clarion Resort South Ocean every two hours and costs US$2 one-way.

A taxi from Orange Hill to Cable Beach costs U$10, and US$15 to downtown.

The Clarion Resort South Ocean also rents scooters.

South New Providence

From the South Ocean area, Adelaide Rd runs east, about 2 miles inland and parallel to the shore, which is accessed by side roads. East of Coral Harbour Rd, which runs north to the airport, Adelaide Rd becomes Carmichael Rd, passing east to west through Carmichael Village (a lower-income residential area founded in the 1800s as a settlement for free slaves) to Blue Hill Rd, which runs north to central Nassau and south to South Beach.

There's little along this shore to lure you. Most of it is backed by mangroves, swampy wetlands, and brine pools, parts of which have been used for years as impromptu rubbish dumps. Curiously, dozens of minor Christian bodies have erected their little churches along these roads.

Adelaide

Seventeen miles southwest of Nassau, Adelaide is a quiet village whose nostalgic lifestyle revolves around fishing. Visually it isn't noteworthy, but it is about as close as you can get to traditional life on the island. The village dates back to 1832, when it was founded for slaves freed from a Portuguese slavetrader, on a spit of land jutting into a navigable creek rich in conch, fish, and lobster.

A hurricane in 1926 wrecked the harbor and a heavily laden lumber ship was sunk at the mouth of Adelaide Creek, leaving a meager conduit at the east end of the wetlands. Tidal flow diminished, and eventually the free-flowing creek began silting up. A causeway, built across the creek in 1946 to link the village to the beach, cut off the remaining flow. In ensuing years more causeways were built, and houses were erected along the beach and on subdivided plots. Tidal flow was entirely restricted. The mangroves began to die and the wetlands system – an important fish-breeding area – stagnated. The area became a garbage dump.

In 1990 the Bahamas National Trust initiated a plan to restore Adelaide Creek. An army of volunteers and schoolchildren was gathered, and as news of the project spread, people from all over New Providence showed up to lend a hand. Donations flooded in to replace the causeways with bridges. On Earth Day the creek's mouth was reopened and a tidal creek was reborn. Almost immediately marine life returned: crabs, shads, and even bonefish. Today baby tiger sharks, barracudas, snappers, lobsters, and vast armadas of other young fish journey in and out.

The village is fronted by narrow, white-sand **Adelaide Beach**, extending between South Ocean and the village. Fishing boats are drawn up on the beach.

Coral Harbour

Coral Harbour Rd leads south to this residential marina community. Several dive and sport-fishing operators are based here, and there's a small beach.

Coral Harbour Rd turns west along the shore, becoming Ranfurly Dr, and dead-ends at the base of the Royal Bahamas Defence Force.

Bacardi Rum Factory

After Fidel Castro's expropriation of the Bacardi family's rum factories during the Cuban Revolution, the family set up its business in other locales, including a site on the south shore of New Providence. The plant, which is at the end of Bacardi Rd, east of Coral Harbour and southwest of Carmichael Village, produces Bacardi rum (the family successfully sued the Castro

regime for the Bacardi title) from sugar imported from other Caribbean islands.

Free 30-minute guided tours (☎ 242-362-1412) are offered at 11 am and 2 pm Monday to Thursday and 11 am Friday. Tours are for eight people or more, but you can hang around in the Pavilion, sampling free drinks in the hope that other visitors achieve a quorum.

Activities

Three dive operators are based at Coral Harbour: Dive Dive Dive (☎ 242-362-1401), Sunskiff Divers (☎ 242-362-1979), and the Nassau Scuba Centre (☎ 242-362-1964, nealwatson@aol.com; in North America ☎ 888-962-7728). Nassau Scuba Centre's Web site is www.nassau-scuba-centre.com.

Happy Trail Stables (☎ 242-362-1820), off Coral Harbour Rd, offers horseback rides daily except Sunday by reservation (US$50 for 90 minutes, including hotel transfers).

Places to Stay & Eat

Coral Harbour Beach House & Villas *(☎ 242-362-2210, fax 242-361-6514)* is a lonesome eight-unit beachfront property in Coral Harbour that's good for those seeking a reclusive, breezy escape. Rooms are dowdily furnished, and have air-con and fan. Take an upstairs room with a balcony and more light, plus a shower (downstairs rooms have a tub only). There's a barbecue pit and hammocks stretched between palms. The beach is tiny. Rooms cost US$83; large units sleeping four cost US$100. The mailing address is PO Box N-9750, Nassau, The Bahamas.

Family Islanders check into the ***Corner Hotel*** *(☎ 242-361-7445)*, a dreary institutional hotel on Carmichael Rd in Carmichael Village. Rooms cost US$55. The restaurant is appealing, however, with a large, eclectic menu featuring huge portions of local favorites such as tuna and grits for US$4, sheep's-tongue souse for US$7.50, and fried grouper and chips for US$7.

There are two options for eats in Adelaide, though no place to rest your head. The first, ***Avery's Restaurant & Bar*** *(☎ 242-362-1547)*, is an unassuming place serving such Bahamian dishes as curried chicken, and mutton. It has live entertainment on weekends.

One of the island's offbeat gems is – or was – the **Honeycomb Beach Club** (☎ 242-362-1417), a delightfully funky place to cool your feet and enjoy cracked conch and pork chops until Hurricane Floyd knocked the stuffing out of it. It was closed at press time, but may open again.

If you need a fast-food fix, **Wendy's**, **KFC**, and **Domino's Pizza** have outlets at the Golden Gates Shopping Centre, at the east end of Carmichael Rd.

Getting There & Away

To get to south New Providence from Nassau, catch Bus No 6 downtown. This bus runs along Blue Hill Rd, Carmichael Rd, and Adelaide Rd.

Grand Bahama

• pop 42,000

Grand Bahama, an ox-jaw–shaped island 110 miles northwest of New Providence, is the second most popular tourist destination in The Bahamas. It boasts sugar-white beaches, beautiful waters, and a panoply of lodgings, casinos, excellent golf courses, and water sports concentrated in Freeport and its contiguous, distinctly tourist-oriented suburb, Lucaya (normally written 'Freeport/ Lucaya').

Grand Bahama takes its name from *gran baja mar*, the Spanish name for the 'great shallow sea.' It is 85 miles long, 17 miles across at its widest, and flat as a pancake. Its south shore is lined with startlingly beautiful beaches. The north shore comprises

Highlights

- Diving with dolphins and/or sharks – a thrill a minute, courtesy of UNEXSO
- Sea kayaking in Lucayan National Park
- Picnicking at Gold Rock Beach
- Golfing at the Lucaya Golf & Country Club
- Sunning at Peterson Cay National Park
- Bonefishing at Deep Water Cay

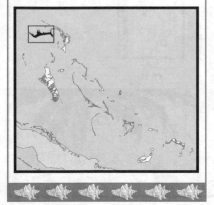

mangroves and wetlands with plenty of birdlife. The cays to the east boast good bonefishing.

Most of the island is smothered by great stands of Cuban pines, with an understory of dwarf palms (mostly thatch, palmetto, and cabbage). Plump curly-tailed lizards are everywhere, scurrying across the sands or through the undergrowth. There are raccoons and nonpoisonous snakes. And green and loggerhead turtles (and, infrequently, hawksbills) emerge from the sea to nest at Gold Rock Creek, Hawksbill Creek, and at High Rock (near Freetown). Development and tourist visitation, however, have vastly reduced the turtle population.

Scuba diving is splendid, with options for swimming with dolphins or sharks. Several companies cater to ecotourists with kayak trips, hikes, and jeep safaris. One of the island's most attractive features is Lucayan National Park, east of Freeport/Lucaya. Beyond Freeport/Lucaya settlements are limited to dour fishing villages.

Juan Ponce de León visited the island in 1513 while searching for the Fountain of Youth, and pirates had bases here during the 17th and 18th centuries. The island had a brief boom as a supply depot for the Confederacy during the US Civil War and as a staging post for rumrunners during Prohibition. When Sir Billy Butlins (of English holiday-camp fame) opened a resort at the western tip of the island in 1948, it looked like Grand Bahama might experience a tourism coup. Alas, the project fizzled. The island's economy continued to limp along based on lumbering, fishing, and diving for sponges – ways of life that died out only a decade ago.

Grand Bahama has been described as 'a culturally antiseptic mecca for fast-lane vacationers.' The island has typically attracted a less sophisticated clientele than have Nassau and the Family Islands; Floridians and folks from New Jersey come for a few days of inexpensive fun. Freeport/Lucaya is

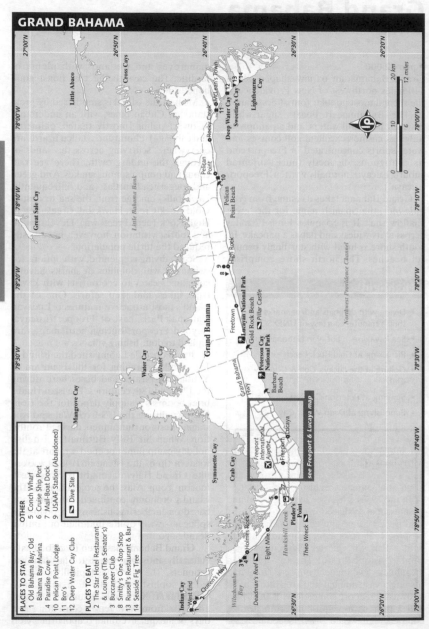

GRAND BAHAMA

PLACES TO STAY
1 Old Bahama Bay; Old
   Bahama Bay Marina
4 Paradise Cove
10 Pelican Point Lodge
11 Bro's
12 Deep Water Cay Club

PLACES TO EAT
2 The Star Hotel Restaurant
   & Lounge (The Senator's)
3 Buccaneer Club
8 Smitty's One Stop Shop
13 Russell's Restaurant & Bar
14 Seaside Fig Tree

OTHER
5 Conch Wharf
6 Cruise Ship Port
7 Mail-Boat Dock
9 USAAF Station (Abandoned)

⚓ Dive Site

also popular with day-trippers arriving on cruise ships from Florida and with college students at spring break (when copious amounts of alcohol are consumed, resulting in rowdiness that is an embarrassment to the island). The tourism board does *not* promote spring break.

Today the island is enjoying a renaissance, part of an eight-year government effort to revitalize the island through tourism. Several hotels have been remade (most were, until recently, owned by the government and reflected the low quality that can come with public ownership), air service has increased, new cruise facilities are being laid out, and a new resort and residential development are planned for the island's West End. The new vitality, however, is focused on the all-new Lucayan resort, a 1350-room, 372-acre integrated resort complex with two championship golf courses, a casino, spa, 40,000 sq feet of meeting space, and complete upscale services.

Freeport & Lucaya

- **pop 33,000**

Grand Bahama is dominated by Freeport and its southeastern extension, Lucaya. Freeport is a planned city with wide, grid-arranged streets and uninspired modern buildings. The strange, sprawling entity lacks both an easily definable character and easily recognizable center. There *is* a center; however, it is lost amid copses of pine and resembles an Australian outback town – with about as much appeal – and comprising half a dozen banks, a few dozen stores, and not a single building of historical interest.

In the 1950s, a Yankee lumber baron and businessman, Wallace Groves, looked at the wild tracts of pine and envisioned a city. He proposed a development plan and signed up with a Brit, Sir Charles Hayward, with a similar vision. Presto! The two pulled a megabuck development out of a straw hat, turning a vast, uninhabited area into a town known as Freeport, complete with an airport and a port with an oil-bunkering storage complex that would prove a bonanza for

The Bahamas (oil is still purchased, stored, and resold at a handsome profit to the US). In 1955 the British crown gave them permission to buy and develop 150,000 acres of the island's midsection in exchange for tax-free status and an exclusive right to grant and administer business licenses until 2015. Vast marina channels were dug and handsome benefits offered to waterfront home-builders. What little there was of West Indian and British architecture was sacrilegiously bulldozed.

Groves then envisioned turning Freeport/Lucaya into a tourist mecca. Following The Bahamas' independence in 1973, however, Prime Minister Lynden Pindling's Nassau-centered administration came to heads with freewheeling, foreign-dominated Freeport. Grand Bahama suffered in the political battle of wills, resulting in an exodus of wealthy white foreign residents. The island began to stagnate – a state of affairs that lasted until the Free National Movement victory of 1992.

The city of Freeport promotes itself rather grandly as an offshore financial center and the nation's high-technology industrial center (both, however, are meager), and as a prime residential community for second-home dwellers. It is still overseen by the Grand Bahama Port Authority, or 'The Port,' set up by Groves, which maintains strict zoning laws, issues (or denies) all business licenses, and has the same defining role in matters of commercial probity as the Christian Council has in Nassau.

In 1996 a development group, Sun & Sea Estates, began a major redevelopment project in Lucaya. The five-year, US$290 million mega-resort project has integrated existing hotels with new hotels, vacation clubs, restaurants, shops, theme parks, a new golf course and golf school, and a marina. Many hope that massive investment will do for Grand Bahama what Sun International's Atlantis resort project did for Paradise Island.

ORIENTATION

The area known as Freeport/Lucaya sprawls over west-central Grand Bahama between

GRAND BAHAMA

FREEPORT & LUCAYA

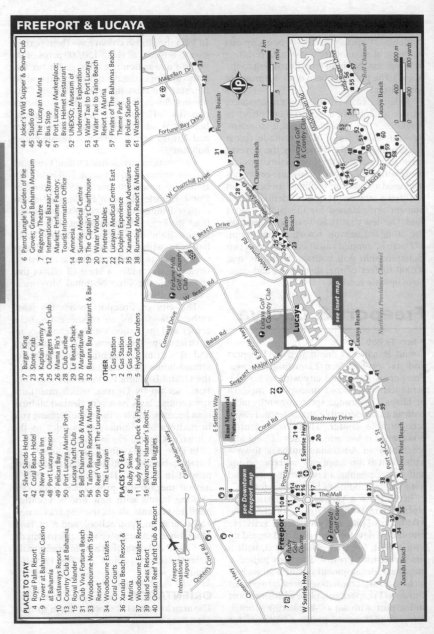

PLACES TO STAY

4 Royal Palm Resort
9 Tower at Bahamia; Casino at Bahamia
10 Castaways Resort
13 Country Club at Bahamia
15 Royal Islander
31 Club Viva Fortuna Beach
33 Woodbourne North Star Resort
34 Woodbourne Estates Coral Courts
36 Xanadu Beach Resort & Marina
37 Woodbourne Estates Resort
39 Island Seas Resort
40 Ocean Reef Yacht Club & Resort
41 Silver Sands Hotel
42 Coral Beach Hotel
43 New Victoria Inn
48 Port Lucaya Resort
49 Pelican Bay
50 Port Lucaya Marina; Port Lucaya Yacht Club
55 Bell Channel Club & Marina
56 Taino Beach Resort & Marina
59 Reef Village at The Lucayan
60 The Lucayan

PLACES TO EAT

8 Ruby Swiss
11 Lady Ruthnell's Deck & Pizzeria
16 Silvano's; Islander's Roost; Bahama Buggies
17 Burger King
23 Stone Crab
24 Kaptain Kenny's
25 Outriggers Beach Club
26 Mama Flo's
28 Club Caribe
29 Le Beach Shack
30 Margaritaville
32 Banana Bay Restaurant & Bar

OTHER

1 Gas Station
2 Gas Station
3 Gas Station
5 Hydroflora Gardens
6 Parrot Jungle's Garden of the Groves; Grand Bahama Museum
7 Regency Theatre
12 International Bazaar; Straw Market; Perfume Factory; Tourist Information Office
14 Sunrise Medical Centre
18 Sunrise Medical Centre
19 The Captain's Charthouse
20 Water World
21 Pinetree Stables
22 Lucayan Medical Centre East
27 Dolphin Experience
35 Xanadu Undersea Adventures
38 Running Mon Resort & Marina
44 Joker's Wild Supper & Show Club
45 Studio 69
46 The Lucayan Marina
47 Bus Stop
51 Port Lucaya Marketplace; Brass Helmet Restaurant
52 UNEXSO; Museum of Underwater Exploration
53 Water Taxi to Port Lucaya
54 Water Taxi to Taino Beach Resort & Marina
57 Pirates of The Bahamas Beach Theme Park
58 Police Station
61 Watersports

two waterways: Hawksbill Creek (also known as the Freeport Harbour Channel) to the west and the 7½-mile-long Grand Lucayan Waterway to the east.

Downtown Freeport, 1 mile south of the airport, takes up eight square blocks west of 'the Mall,' which is E Mall Dr, the main boulevard that leads south from Independence Circle outside the airport to Xanadu Beach on the south shore. The heart of touristy Freeport is 1 mile south of downtown, centered on Ranfurly Circle, the Aladdin-domed Resort at Bahamia (formerly the Bahamian Princess Resort & Casino), and the International Bazaar.

Queen's Hwy runs southwest from the airport to the Cruise Ship Port via an area of petrochemical industries and some of the island's poorest residential sections, Hawksbill and Pinder's Point. W Sunrise Hwy runs west to the Cruise Ship Port from Ranfurly Circle.

E Sunrise Hwy runs east from Ranfurly Circle to the Grand Lucayan Waterway, beyond which it continues as the Grand Bahama Hwy to the eastern end of the island. Sea Horse Rd leads south from E Sunrise Hwy to the Port Lucaya Marina, at the heart of the Lucaya district. Between Port Lucaya and Xanadu Beach is Silver Point Beach, a residential marina community with three hotels.

Taino, Churchill, and Fortune Beaches extend east from Port Lucaya.

Maps
Etienne Dupuch Publications Ltd publishes a *Bahamas Trailblazer Map* for Grand Bahama. You can pick up one in hotel lobbies and at tourist information booths.

INFORMATION
Tourist Offices
The Grand Bahama Island Tourism Board (☎ 242-352-8044, 800-448-3386, fax 242-352-2714) has a tourism information office in the International Bazaar (see the Freeport & Lucaya map). The postal address is PO Box F-40251, Freeport, Grand Bahama, The Bahamas. It also has a US office (☎ 305-935-9461, 800-448-3386, fax 305-935-9464) at 1

Turnberry Place, 19495 Biscayne Blvd, No 809, Aventura, FL 33180, USA.

The Ministry of Tourism (☎ 242-352-8044) has its main office in the Charles Hayward Library on E Mall Dr near Pioneers Way (see the Downtown Freeport map). There are also tourist information booths at Grand Bahama International Airport, the Cruise Ship Port, and near the roundabout at the east end of Port Lucaya Marketplace.

Money
CIBC (☎ 242-352-6651), Scotiabank (☎ 242-352-6774), the Royal Bank of Canada (☎ 242-352-6631), and Barclays Bank (☎ 242-352-8391) have downtown branches (see the Downtown Freeport map), as do the British American Bank (☎ 242-352-6676), on the Mall, and the Bank of the Bahamas (☎ 242-352-7483). Western Union (☎ 242-352-6676) is at the British American Bank.

Post & Communications
The main post office (☎ 242-352-9371) is downtown on Explorers Way midway between W Mall Dr and E Mall Dr; it's open 9 am to 5:30 pm weekdays. You can also buy stamps at most outlets that sell postcards.

Federal Express (☎ 242-352-3402) has an office one block south (see the Downtown Freeport map), open 9 am to 5 pm weekdays.

BaTelCo (☎ 242-352-6731/9352) has offices on Pioneer's Way and one block south at Kipling's Lane, with telephone and fax service.

Internet Resources
Cyber Cafe (☎ 242-351-7283, forbesco@aol.com), in the Regent Centre W, at West Mall and Explorers Way, lets you surf the Web and check your emails while sipping a cool drink or a coffee (see the Downtown Freeport map). Internet access costs US20¢ per minute. It also has fax and photocopying service, and is open 9 am to 10 pm Monday to Saturday, and 11 am to 8 pm Sunday.

Travel Agencies
Tour agencies in hotel lobbies can make travel reservations, or call the Bahamas Travel Agency (☎ 242-352-3141).

GRAND BAHAMA

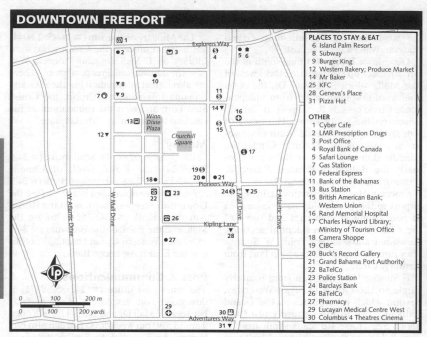

DOWNTOWN FREEPORT

PLACES TO STAY & EAT
6 Island Palm Resort
8 Subway
9 Burger King
12 Western Bakery; Produce Market
14 Mr Baker
25 KFC
28 Geneva's Place
31 Pizza Hut

OTHER
1 Cyber Cafe
2 LMR Prescription Drugs
3 Post Office
4 Royal Bank of Canada
5 Safari Lounge
7 Gas Station
10 Federal Express
11 Bank of the Bahamas
13 Bus Station
15 British American Bank;
   Western Union
16 Rand Memorial Hospital
17 Charles Hayward Library;
   Ministry of Tourism Office
18 Camera Shoppe
19 CIBC
20 Buck's Record Gallery
21 Grand Bahama Port Authority
22 BaTelCo
23 Police Station
24 Barclays Bank
26 BaTelCo
27 Pharmacy
29 Lucayan Medical Centre West
30 Columbus 4 Theatres Cinema

Bookstores & Libraries

Try the Freeport Book Centre (☎ 242-352-3759) at 14 W Mall Dr, downtown.

The Charles Hayward Library (☎ 242-352-7048), on E Mall Dr near Pioneers Way (see the Downtown Freeport map), is open 10 am to 5 pm Monday, Wednesday, and Friday and 10 am to 2 pm Saturday.

Publications

The *Freeport News* is an afternoon daily, published Monday to Saturday. The *Freeport Times* is published monthly.

Dan Beuttner's *Inside Grand Bahamas* is billed as 'the guide to the people, places, and activities of Grand Bahamas,' and so it is, and more. A splendid guide!

What's On, a free monthly tourist newspaper that has discount coupons to a wide variety of restaurants, stores, and excursions, is published by Aberland Publications (☎ 242-351-8051), PO Box F-40517, Freeport, Grand Bahama, The Bahamas. Etienne

Dupuch Publications Ltd (☎ 242-323-5665, fax 242-323-8722) publishes the biannual *What-to-do in Freeport/Lucaya, Grand Bahama*, a small-format tourist guide full of handy information and discount coupons. The similarly sized *Island Magazine* provides information on shopping, dining, and entertainment. All three are available in hotel lobbies and tourist information booths.

Also look for a *Discover Port Lucaya* booklet, which has a map of Port Lucaya and discount coupons.

Laundry

Upscale hotels will arrange for laundry and dry cleaning. You'll also find laundries and dry cleaners listed in the yellow pages.

Medical Services

The main health-care facility is the Rand Memorial Hospital (☎ 242-352-6735) on E Mall Dr between Pioneers Way and Explorers Way (see the Downtown Freeport map).

Other facilities include the Lucayan Medical Centre West (☎ 242-352-7288), downtown on Adventurers Way, and Sunrise Medical Centre (☎ 242-373-3333) and Lucaya Medical Centre East (☎ 242-373-7400), both on E Sunrise Hwy (see the Freeport & Lucaya map).

If that ol' toothache begins to bite, call Dr Larry Bain (☎ 242-352-8492), in the Sun Alliance Bldg on Pioneers Way, downtown. The office is open 8:30 am to 4 pm Monday to Wednesday and 8:30 am to noon Thursday and Friday.

For the Grand Bahama Red Cross, call ☎ 242-352-7163.

There are few pharmacies. Try LMR Prescription Drugs (☎ 242-352-7327) in the mall on 1 W Mall Dr at Explorers Way (see the Downtown Freeport map); it's open 8 am to 9 pm Monday to Saturday.

Emergency
In an emergency call ☎ 911. For air-sea rescue, call ☎ 242-352-2628. For an ambulance, call ☎ 242-352-2689; for the police, call ☎ 242-348-3444.

Dangers & Annoyances
The Freeport/Lucaya area is comprised mostly of sedate, relatively crime-free middle-class suburbs. You should, however, use caution downtown near Winn Dixie Plaza and in the low-income settlements around Pinder's Point and Eight Mile. The usual caution is advised when roaming anywhere at night. Don't leave your belongings unattended.

There is no hustling, but drug trafficking still occurs.

West of Freeport, locals advise against picking up male hitchhikers along the road to Holmes Rock, as there have been many problems.

THINGS TO SEE & DO
Downtown Freeport
The official town center lies 1 mile north of the International Bazaar between W Mall and E Mall Drs. At its heart is **Winn Dixie Plaza**. Downtown, the only noteworthy sightseeing item is a massive bronze bust of

Sir Winston Churchill on a pedestal in the otherwise nondescript Churchill Square.

E Mall Dr is lined with young strangler fig trees and makes for a pleasant walk.

International Bazaar
This compact, hokey, overrated, Disney-style emporium, on the northwest side of Ranfurly Circle (see the Freeport & Lucaya map), is worth a browse for curiosity's sake and for shopping. Beyond the Japanese *torii* gates, a maze of tight-knit lanes lined with restaurants and shops imitate international venues, from Asia to Scandinavia. Most of the approximately 100 shops are dedicated to duty-free items from around the world: The French section is replete with perfumes and a Greek store sells Greek clothing, but jewelry and T-shirt stores outnumber all others. There's a walk-through workshop where you can watch jewelry being made. Most restaurants stay open until 10 pm or so, but stores close at 6 pm.

There's a public bus stop about 200 yards west of the straw market on the north side of the bazaar. You'll find a tourist information booth and small police station 50 yards west of the entrance gate.

Perfume Factory
The 'factory' (☎ 242-352-9391, fax 242-352-9040) is in a plum-and-white replica of an 18th-century mansion at the rear of the International Bazaar, opposite the straw market (see the Freeport & Lucaya map). You're greeted by hostesses in period dress who lead you on a tour showing you how perfumes are made using the six 'Fragrances of the Bahamas,' the name of the factory's tiny company. Every bottle of 'Sand' perfume for men has real Bahamian sand; each bottle of 'Pink Pearl' contains several conch-shell pearls. You can even mix, bottle, and name your own fragrance for US\$20. Bottles of perfume purchased here cost about 50% less than US retail prices. The free five-minute tours are offered 10 am to 5:30 pm weekdays.

You can order Fragrances of the Bahamas perfumes in the US by calling ☎ 305-294-8681 or ☎ 800-628-9033.

GRAND BAHAMA

Rand Memorial Nature Centre

This natural haven is the headquarters of the Bahamas National Trust (BNT; ☎ 242-352-5438) on Grand Bahama. On E Settlers Way about 2 miles east of downtown Freeport (see the Freeport & Lucaya map), the center began in 1969 as a living memorial to Freeport philanthropist James Rand. The nature retreat shows off more than 130 types of native plants, including 21 species of orchids; an open, grassy meadow, highlighted by wildflowers in spring and summer; and a native coppice that has grown here since before the time of Columbus.

A half-mile–long trail winds through many acres of coppice and pine barrens, where a flock of West Indian flamingos stride about in a freshwater pond adorned with water lilies. (A small native fish, the Bahamian gambusia, keeps the water free of mosquito larvae.) Rand is a gathering spot for wild birds, including Cuban emerald hummingbirds, the tiny yet stunning parula, and Antillean peewees peering down from their perches in the pines. There are great blue herons and egrets, and even kingfishers and ospreys fish here. Raccoons and red-eared turtles also call it home, as do tree frogs who often lay their eggs in the birdbaths. Curly-tailed lizards rush down the trails to greet visitors. Butterflies are common, and harmless brown-racer and corn snakes are occasionally seen. There's a replica of a Lucayan village.

Guided walks are offered at 10 am and 2 pm weekdays and 10 am Saturday. They're free with admission: US$5/3 adults/children. It's open weekdays 9 am to 4 pm, and Saturday 9 am to 1 pm. A bird-watcher's tour and a wildflower tour are offered the first and third Saturday of each month, respectively. A gift shop sells quality nature-related items.

Port Lucaya Marketplace

This 12-acre shopping, dining, and entertainment area fronts the Port Lucaya complex (☎ 242-373-8888/8446, fax 242-373-7630, newhope@batelnet.bs), an integrated yacht basin and waterfront tourism project (see the Freeport & Lucaya map). It's more couched in Bahamian culture than is Freeport's International Bazaar, and much

more appealing. Boardwalks lend a Monterey kind of feel. At its heart is Count Basie Square, where local musicians perform. There are cultural activities – everything from church choirs to Junkanoo bands – in the evening and on weekends.

Ye Olde Pirate Bottle House (☎ 242-373-2000) is a quasi-museum and antique store with 250 or so bottles dating back to the 17th century. It's open 9 am to 6 pm daily; US$3/2 adults/children. Its Web site is www.portlucaya.com.

Hydroflora Gardens

This landscaped garden (☎ 242-352-6052), on E Beach Dr at E Sunrise Hwy (see the Freeport & Lucaya map), is another lush world of shrubs, tropical fruit trees, and fragrant foliage. Highlights include a rock garden, a 'chapel of blooms,' and a hydroponics garden. It's open 9 am to 5 pm Monday to Saturday; US$5/3 guided/unguided.

Parrot Jungle's Garden of the Groves

This 11-acre garden (☎ 242-373-5668, bwildlife@batelnet.bs), at the intersection of Midshipman Rd and Magellan Dr (see the Freeport & Lucaya map), is a lush Eden filled with exotic plants and shrubs from around the world – 5000 species in all. There's a 400-foot-long fern gully and a hanging garden, as well as four waterfalls cascading into a placid lake ringed with tropical foliage, and ponds waded by flamingos. For children, the highlight is a petting zoo and lots of parrots in cages.

The gardens contain the **Grand Bahama Museum**, dedicated to the history of the island from the time of the Lucayans. The mailing address is PO Box 43282, Grand Bahama, The Bahamas. The garden and museum are open 9 am to 4 pm daily; admission is US$8/5 adults/children under 10.

Xanadu Beach

This deep but unexciting white-sand beach at the south end of the Mall is the most accessible beach from downtown. It extends westward about a half-mile and is quite adequate for a day of sunning or splashing around in the shallows. There's a crafts market, snack bar, and water sports. Lounge chairs rent for US$2. The beach is dominated by the Xanadu Beach Resort & Marina (see the Places to Stay section), the former private domain of Howard Hughes, who ensconced himself on the 12th and 13th floors for two years until his death in 1976.

A courtesy bus operates between the Resort at Bahamia and Xanadu Beach.

Silver Point Beach
This beach lies due east of Xanadu Beach, from which it is separated by two marina channels. It is accessed off E Sunrise Hwy by Beachway Dr. The new Island Seas Resort stands at the eastern end, beside another harbor channel separating Silver Point Beach from Lucaya Beach. There are watersports.

A courtesy bus operates between the Resort at Bahamia and Island Seas Resort.

Lucaya Beach
This stunner runs east from Silver Sands Hotel to Bell Channel, at the mouth of the Port Lucaya harbor. There are watersports, restaurants, and other facilities at the eastern end, where the three hotels of The Lucayan complex and Port Lucaya cater to tourists. The central, less trammeled part of the beach can also be accessed from various suburban roads.

Taino Beach
East of Bell Channel lies Taino Beach. This miles-long beach has sand as fine as confectioner's sugar, and is the setting for water sports and several popular restaurants. To the north is the waterfront settlement of Smith's Point, a disheveled cluster of tiny houses; most of its occupants are related to the matriarch, Mama Flo.

Churchill, Fortune & Barbary Beaches
Two beautiful beaches, Churchill and Fortune, extend several miles east of Taino Beach, from which they are separated by Sanctuary Bay, a marina complex lined with homes of the well heeled, notably along the

beachfront road, Spanish Main Dr (also called 'New Millionaire's Row'). Fortune Beach has several eateries popular with locals on weekends.

Farther east, beyond the Grand Lucayan Waterway, is secluded and seductive Barbary Beach. Each spring its shoreline bursts into bloom with white spider lilies.

ACTIVITIES
Diving & Snorkeling
Diving is excellent off Grand Bahama. One prime site is the *Theo* wreck, a 240-foot-long sunken freighter with safe swim-throughs in the hold and engine room; the resident moray eels are friendly. Another is East End Paradise, an underwater coral range. Two Spanish galleons – the *Santa Gertrude* and *San Ignacio* – ran aground in 1682 off the south shore near present-day Lucaya. The wrecks remain for you to explore.

Experienced divers can check out Ben's Cave, part of Lucayan National Park, where you can follow permanently installed cable lines through underwater caves for up to 7 miles. The dive is limited to qualified divers, who must obtain a permit from the Underwater Explorers Society (UNEXSO; ☎ 242-373-1244; in the US ☎ 954-351-9889, 800-922-3483, fax 954-351-9740, info@unexso.com), at Port Lucaya Marina (see the Freeport & Lucaya map), which offers a full range of dive programs, from guided reef dives for US$39/72 one/two-tank to a three-tank all-day dive for US$102. It offers a 20-dive card with no expiration date for US$499. It also offers specialty dives, including underwater photo instruction from US$60. Beginners can take the plunge after three hours of professional instruction in training pools for US$99. It has a fully stocked dive shop and a recompression chamber, and rents underwater photo equipment and offers film processing. I've heard several reports of UNEXSO's dives being oversubscribed and rushed. In 2000, it opened a new, 40,000-sq-foot facility with a 14-foot-deep training pool (and a Museum of Underwater Exploration was planned). The local mailing address is PO Box F-42433, Freeport, Grand Bahama, The

GRAND BAHAMA

Bahamas; in the USA write PO Box 22878, Fort Lauderdale, FL 33335.

Other dive operators based here include:

Caribbean Divers, ☎ 242-373-9111, 800-336-0938, in the Bell Channel Inn

Sunn Odyssey Divers, ☎ 242-373-4014, in Silver Palm Court

Xanadu Undersea Adventures, ☎ 242-352-3811, at Xanadu Beach

Typical three-hour 'learn-to-dive' options cost US$80 to US$100. All the dive operators offer snorkel trips that cost US$20 to US$40, including transportation. UNEXSO has a special trip for children for US$18. A good snorkel spot is Paradise Cove, where fish are abundant at Deadman's Reef (see the West of Freeport section, later in this chapter).

A 'SnorkelRama' excursion to Treasure Reef is offered aboard the *Bahama Mama* (☎ 242-373-7863); US$18/14 adults/children. Fantasia Tours (☎ 242-373-8681, patdiane@ grouper.batelnet.bs) also offers snorkeling trips three times daily for US$25 from Port Lucaya. And East End Adventures (☎ 242-351-6250, 242-373-6662, fax 242-352-7676, safari@batelnet.bs; in the US ☎ 800-448-3386), in Port Lucaya, has an all-day snorkeling safari for US$85, visiting various sites by speedboat.

Dolphin Encounters

The Dolphin Experience (☎ 242-373-1250, fax 242-373-3948, dolphexp@batelnet.bs), operated by UNEXSO (see the Freeport & Lucaya map), offers several options for diving with dolphins, including a two-hour trip called 'The Close Encounter' for US$39 for nondivers, who receive an educational lecture and then

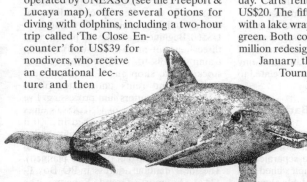

stand waist-deep in a sheltered lagoon, where they meet the semi-wild dolphins. You can swim with the dolphins for US$99. And a full-day 'Dolphin Assistant Trainer' program for US$179 permits you to shadow trainers in the waters at Sanctuary Lagoon. Divers can purchase a two-tank 'Dolphin Dive' add-on to a regular two-dive scuba package for US$109. The dives leave from Taino Beach. Hotel transfers are offered. Reservations are advised.

Shark Dives

You can also swim amid Caribbean reef sharks while a diver wearing a chain-mail suit hand-feeds these predators. Two other divers armed with sticks are on hand to ward off wayward sharks. You'll have to sign a legal release form saying it isn't UNEXSO's fault if the sharks decide you look tastier than the fish. A cameraperson will record your swim on video for an extra fee. This event takes place at Shark Junction. The dive adds US$40 to normal dive rates. Reservations are advised. Contact UNEXSO (see the Diving & Snorkeling section, earlier in this chapter).

Golf

The island has five championship courses (see the Freeport & Lucaya map). Emerald & Ruby Golf Courses (☎ 242-352-6721 ext 4600, ☎ 800-545-1300), part of the Resort at Bahamia complex, are twin, 72-par Dick Wilson creations. Green fees are US$75 per day. Carts rent for US$45; clubs rent for US$20. The fifth is Ruby's signature hole, with a lake wrapped around the fairway and green. Both courses were to receive US$3 million redesigns beginning in late 2000. In January the Bahamia Pro-Am Golf Tournament is held here.

Fortune Hills Golf & Country Club (☎ 242-373-4500), off E Sunrise Hwy, is a Dick Wilson–designed championship nine-hole course good for beginners. Vital statistics: 36-par, 3458 yards.

Games cost US$51. Club rental costs US$10.

Lucaya Golf & Country Club (☎ 242-373-1066, 800-622-6770), at The Lucayan, is a 6800-yard course. It is considered a sedate course, yet it's rated one of the top courses in the Caribbean. There are plenty of water hazards, including a signature 18th hole featuring a lake in front of the two-tiered green that has the Balancing Boulders of Lucaya, a man-made fantasy in stone complete with 20-foot-high waterfall. Fees are US$106 for 18 holes, including cart rental. It hosts the European Golf Weeks each October.

The Reef Golf Course, a new 18-hole, Robert Trent Jones II course, was due to open in Lucaya in 2001, with scenic lakes that come into play on 13 of the 18 holes.

A new 18-hole course is planned at the Old Bahama Bay Resort & Marina at West End (see the West of Freeport section, later in this chapter, for details).

Miniature Golf
There's miniature golf at Pirates of The Bahamas Beach Theme Park (☎ 242-373-8456), on Jolly Roger Dr in Taino Beach, and at the new Water World (☎ 242-373-2197), on E Sunrise Hwy at Britannia Blvd (see the Freeport & Lucaya map). The latter has two 18-hole courses with hazards. It has a small restaurant and ice cream parlor and is open 10 am to 11 pm daily. The cost is US$10/6 adults/children.

Sport Fishing & Bonefishing
The Gulf Stream, off the west coast of Grand Bahama, teems with game fish. The Northwest Providence Channel drops to 2000 feet just 400 yards off the south shore, where snapper and barracuda are prevalent. And bonefishing is superb on the flats of the Little Bahama Bank to the north and east.

Charter vessels include the *Night Hawk*, operated by Night Hawk Fishing (☎ 242-373-7226); half-day fishing trips cost US$35 and depart from Port Lucaya Marina at 9 am and 1:15 pm daily except Friday (see the Freeport & Lucaya map). Nighttime

shark fishing is offered on Tuesday and Thursday for US$40.

Other charter operators include Nautical Adventures (☎ 242-373-7180), at Port Lucaya, and Running Mon Marina (☎ 242-352-6834).

Boat Excursions
Pat & Diane Tours (☎ 242-373-8681, email patdiane@batelnet.bs) offers a 'Reef 'n' Wreck' day cruise and snorkel adventure, with a beach party, for US$40/27 adults/children. It also has a 'Sunset Sailing Cruise' aboard *My-Tri*, a 52-foot trimaran, for US$30. Running Mon Marina (☎ 242-352-6834) offers daily deep-sea fishing charters, and glass-bottomed boat tours on their *Coral Princess*.

Similar cruises are offered aboard the *Bahama Mama* Monday, Wednesday, and Friday. A sunset cruise with limbo show costs US$35; a dinner cruise with show costs US$39. You can book at hotel desks.

Reef Tours (☎ 242-373-5880/5891) offers party cruises for US$35, a nocturnal 'booze cruise' (US$39) and snorkel excursions aboard the *Island Princess*, a 72-foot twin-hulled powerboat, and the smaller *Lucayan Princess*. Kids under five go free.

Several other boats depart Port Lucaya Marina on excursions, including the *Mermaid Kitty*, a massive glass-bottomed boat, and the *Seaworld Explorer* (☎ 242-373-7863), a glass-lined semi-submersible that stays on the surface. It departs from Port Lucaya Marina four times daily for 90-minute tours (US$39 adult, US$25 children).

Other Water Sports
Most resort hotels rent snorkel gear, sea kayaks, Sunfish, Windsurfers, and equipment for other water sports. Independent concessions are also located on most beaches. Jet Skis rent for US$30 to US$50 per half-hour. Paradise Watersports (☎ 242-352-2887), at Xanadu Beach, offers water sports, including parasailing, at beach concessions.

Waverunner Rentals (☎ 242-373-8456) charges US$30 per 15 minutes for Jet Skis. It also offers banana-boat rides (US$10), parasailing (US$30), and windsurfing from several beaches. Ocean Motion (☎ 242-373-2139) offers a similar range of watersports at Reef Village at the Lucayan (see the Freeport & Lucaya map).

Other Activities

Pinetree Stables (☎ 242-373-3600, pinetree@batelnet.bs) offers horseback rides through the pine forests and along the south shore at 9 and 11 am and 2 pm daily except Monday for US$45. Riding lessons are offered by appointment; the mailing address is PO Box F-42915, N Beachway Dr, Freeport, Grand Bahama, The Bahamas (see the Freeport & Lucaya map).

Most resorts have tennis courts, notably the Resort at Bahamia with 12 courts. Typical fees are US$5 to US$10 per hour, US$10 to US$20 for night play.

Sea Surf Lanes (☎ 242-352-5784), on Queen's Hwy, has bowling alleys for US$3 per game.

ORGANIZED TOURS
City Tours

Several companies offer half- and full-day sightseeing tours, taking in most sites in and around Freeport/Lucaya. Some also offer island tours and activities. Typical prices are US$20/14 adults/children for half-day tours and US$30/20 for a full-day tour as far afield as West End. Companies include the following:

Bahamas Travel ☎ 242-352-3141

H Forbes Charters ☎ 242-352-9311, hforbes@grouper.batelnet.bs

Grand Bahama Taxi Union ☎ 242-352-7858/7101

Sunworld Travel & Safari Car Rental ☎ 242-352-3717

For a bird's-eye view, try a flightseeing tour with Taino Air (☎ 242-352-8885) or Major's Air Services (☎ 242-352-5778).

Cultural & Nature Tours

East End Adventures (☎ 242-351-6250, fax 242-352-7676, safari@batelnet.bs; in the US ☎ 800-448-3386) offers three distinct ecology-oriented '4x4 Bush & Sea Eco-Safaris,' including a blue hole snorkeling safari (US$85).

Another tour is to Sweeting's and Lightbourne Cays at the extreme eastern end of the island, with a stop at Lucayan National Park (see the Sweeting's Cay section later in this chapter for information).

Kayak Nature Tours (☎/fax 242-373-2485, kayaknaturetours@aol.com) offers guided sea kayaking tours from Freeport into Lucayan National Park (see the Lucayan National Park section, later in this chapter, for information).

Nautical Adventures (☎ 242-373-7180) has a 'Historic Cave Tour,' taking in Lucayan National Park and Gold Rock Beach. H Forbes Charter & Tours (☎ 242-352-9311, fax 242-352-9313) offers a similar tour for US$30 to the East End.

JC Specialty Tours (☎ 242-557-6505) also offers what it calls an 'island-culture adventure and eco-adventure.'

People to People

The Ministry of Tourism's 'People to People' program puts you in touch with locals who follow a similar lifestyle to visitors interested in meeting them. Call the Grand Bahama Island Tourism Board (☎ 242-352-8044) for information.

SPECIAL EVENTS

The highlight of the social calendar is the New Year's Day Junkanoo Parade that kicks off at 5 am downtown, with costumed revelers and a cacophony of sounds.

The Bahamas Windsurfing Championship is held in Freeport each January. The Xanadu Marina Offshore Fishing Tournament is held each February with two categories: bottom fishing and deep-sea fishing. Call ☎ 242-352-8044 for information.

March traditionally sees the Freeport Rugby Club Annual Easter Rugby Festival, when international teams arrive to compete. Call Bob Davies of the Freeport Rugby Football Club (☎ 242-352-2952) for information. The Grand Bahama 5K Road Race is also held in March. Each spring Grand Bahama also hosts the Tour de Freeport 100-mile bicycle race.

The annual sailing regatta is held in late June at Taino Beach, and July witnesses the

Some of The Bahamas' best windsurfing is here.

annual Grand Bahama Games, a mini-Olympics pitting local sports figures against each other.

Sleepy McLean's Town, at the east end of the island, hosts the Conch Cracking Contest each October. The full-day event features other contests and entertainment

The Annual Grand Bahama Triathlon is usually held in October at the Lucayan Cricket Club; contact Bruce Silvera (☎ 242-373-7460). Athletes compete in November's Annual Grand Bahama Conchman Triathlon; contact John Bradley (☎ 242-373-4521).

PLACES TO STAY

There are no budget accommodations or camping options. Most hotels tack at least a 2% to 5% service charge and a 4% to 8% government tax onto the room rates quoted below.

Mid-Range

Freeport The *Island Palm Resort* (☎ 242-352-6648, fax 242-352-6640), on Explorers Way at E Mall Dr (see the Downtown Freeport map), is a Miami-style property centered on a small pool and landscaped courtyard. It's popular with a local clientele. The 158 modestly furnished rooms cost US$79 single or double; some are dingy, as are the bathrooms, but it's advantageously close to the airport. The mailing address is

PO Box F-402000, Freeport, Grand Bahama, The Bahamas.

The *Royal Palm Resort* (☎ 242-352-3462, 800-315-6054, fax 242-352-5759, royal@batelnet.bs), nearby on E Mall Dr (see the Freeport & Lucaya map), is another motel-style property with modern furnishings. Its 48 rooms have cable TV and surround a pool and sundeck. There's a tennis court and a restaurant, plus free shuttle to the beaches and International Bazaar. Room rates are US$60 standard, US$75 superior. Its mailing address is PO Box F-44900, Freeport, Grand Bahama, The Bahamas.

Castaways Resort (☎ 242-352-6682, 800-545-1300, fax 242-352-5087, castaway@batelnet.bs), a stone's throw from the Resort at Bahamia and International Bazaar on E Mall Dr, was closed and undergoing a complete renovation at press time. It may reopen after January 2001.

A better option is the *Royal Islander* (☎ 242-351-6000, fax 242-351-3546, 800-899-7797, royalisland@hotmail.com), a pleasing two-story property centered on a courtyard with pool and shady palms (see the Freeport & Lucaya map). Rooms are large and nicely furnished, with heaps of light. Standard rooms cost US$92 to US$102 single and US$104 to US$114 double in summer, and US$112 to US$122 single, US$124 to US$134 double in winter. Its postal address is PO Box F-2549, Freeport, Grand Bahama, The Bahamas.

Lucaya In Lucaya, your moderately priced option is the *New Victoria Inn* (☎ 242-373-3040, fax 242-373-3874), a motel-style hotel at Port Lucaya that serves out-of-towners, spring-breakers, and budget-conscious travelers (see the Freeport & Lucaya map). The 40 rooms have modest decor, including phone and TV. There's a pool and Jacuzzi. It's a 15-minute walk from the beach and is overpriced at US$65/75 summer/winter. A meal plan costs US$25 daily. The mailing address is PO Box F-41261, Freeport, Grand Bahama, The Bahamas.

The Beaches The condo-style *Silver Sands Hotel* (☎ 242-373-5700, fax 242-373-1039), at Silver Point Beach (see the Freeport &

GRAND BAHAMA

Lucaya map), boasts 144 studio apartments and 20 one-bedroom luxury suites, all done up in contemporary decor with a full kitchen. Rates are US$74 single, US$84 double year-round. There's a restaurant and a separate snack bar. It has tennis and racquetball courts and two swimming pools. Its postal address is PO Box F-42385, Freeport, Grand Bahma, The Bahamas. An alternative nearby is the beachfront, high-rise condo-style *Coral Beach Hotel* (☎ 242-373-2468, fax 242-373-5140), which rents 10 rooms – the rest are timeshare units – for US$70/75 single/double in summer, US$90/100 in winter. Four units have full kitchens and rent for US$100/125 summer/winter. You can write to PO Box F-42468, Freeport, Grand Bahama, The Bahamas.

The *Running Mon Resort & Marina* (☎ 242-352-6834, 800-315-6054, fax 242-352-6835, 208 Kelly Court) faces the marina at the south end of the Mall (see the Freeport & Lucaya map). It has 32 air-con rooms with contemporary furnishings, plus the Mainsail Restaurant and Compass Lounge, plus an on-site dive shop, deep-sea fishing charters, and a swimming pool. Free transport is offered to Xanadu Beach (a 20-minute walk), the Casino at Bahamia, and Port Lucaya. Rooms cost US$79 to US$89 single or double in summer, US$99 to US$109 in winter. A deluxe suite for US$219 features a Jacuzzi. Its postal address is PO Box F-42663, Freeport, Grand Bahama, The Bahamas.

Top End

Freeport The grande dame of hotels is the *Resort at Bahamia* (☎ 242-352-6721, fax 242-352-2542; in the US ☎ 800-545-1300), formerly the Bahamas Princess Resort & Casino, a landmark with its plump Arabic domes and minarets crowning Freeport like a mirage. It's popular with package vacationers from the northeast US who flock here for the gambling at the casino. The Emerald & Ruby Golf Courses are part of the property. The dual-property, 965-room complex was to receive a US$42 million renovation in 2000. Sometime in 2001, its 10-story Tower at Bahamia will be rebranded as

a Crowne Plaza; the Country Club at Bahamia, across the street, was also to be remodeled and will reopen as a Holiday Inn Sunspree.

The *Tower at Bahamia* complex boasts a massive pool with Jacuzzi and a sun deck landscaped with rocks and a waterfall. There are several restaurants and bars and 12 tennis courts, plus Camp Seashells for children. A much-vaunted refurbishment in 1999 enhanced the rooms with a '60s retro look but did little to enhance the tacky and bilious pink and green decor in public arenas. The self-contained *Country Club at Bahamia* is far more active than the laid-back Tower, though the prices are lower. The 565 rooms in two- and three-story low-rises are tastefully decorated and arranged in a circle around a splendid pool landscaped with waterfalls. It attracts a more upscale crowd.

Rooms in the Tower cost US$118/128 superior/deluxe in low season and rise to US$195/205 in peak season. Rooms in the Country Club cost US$98/108 in low season and rise to US$175/185 in peak season. Suites range from US$180 to US$700 in low season, and US$250 to US$1100 in high season. An all-inclusive option costs US$79 extra. It also has golf and other packages. The postal address is PO Box F-40207, Freeport, Grand Bahama, The Bahamas.

Lucaya An appealing harborside option is the *Port Lucaya Resort* (☎ 242-373-6618, 800-582-2921, fax 242-373-6652, vacation@ batelnet.bs). This 160-room hotel sits on a peninsula adjacent to the Port Lucaya Marketplace and has 10 two-story units encircling lawns and a pool. All rooms have patios or balconies. Facilities include volleyball, shuffleboard, a restaurant, and a full-service marina. Rates are US$80 to US$110 summer, US$100 to US$135 winter. Suites cost US$150 to US$200 in summer, US$175 to US$250 in winter. Its postal address is PO Box F-42452, Freeport, Grand Bahama, The Bahamas.

Another exclusive charmer perfect for scuba divers is *Pelican Bay* (☎ 242-373-9550, 800-600-9192, fax 242-373-9551, pelicanb@

batelnet.bs), next to UNEXSO and Port Lucaya Marketplace. This 'boutique' hotel boasts exquisite contemporary structures built in classical Bermudan style. It recently expanded to 96 spacious air-con rooms at the water's edge, each with satellite TV, phone, safe, refrigerators, coffee machine and minibar, plus private balcony. There's a small pool, hot tub, pool bar, and restaurant. Room rates are US$110/125/140 standard/ superior/deluxe in summer; US$115/135/155 in winter. The mailing address is PO Box F-42654, Freeport, Grand Bahama, The Bahamas.

The *Taino Beach Resort & Marina* (☎ 242-373-4677, 5 Jolly Roger Dr), at the far west end of Taino Beach near Port Lucaya, is popular with families. It has 68 comfortable apartments, a nice ambience, a pleasing restaurant, and an array of water sports. Weekly rates were US$750/1100/1350 one/ two/three-bedroom units. Its postal address is PO Box F-43819, Freeport, Grand Bahama, The Bahamas.

Nearby, also on the east side of Bell Channel and Port Lucaya Marina, is the *Bell Channel Club & Marina* (☎ 242-373-2673, fax 242-373-3802, bellchan@batelnet.bs) on Jolly Roger Dr. It has spacious two-bedroom suites and three-bedroom townhouse condominiums with whirlpool tubs and patios on the water. Facilities include a pool, tennis court, clubhouse, and marina. Call for rates. Its postal address is PO Box F-44053, Freeport, Grand Bahama, The Bahamas. A new resort, the *Ritz Beach Resort*, was under construction in 2000 adjacent to the Bell Channel Club & Marina.

In 1999, the first phase of Lucaya's jewel, *The Lucayan* (☎ 242-373-1333, 800-582-2926, fax 242-373-8804; in the US ☎ 800-582-2926), a 1350-room mega-resort, opened, replacing the Lucayan Beach Resort, Atlantik Beach Resort, and Grand Bahama Beach Hotel. (The Atlantik was demolished to make way for a new property between the other two renovated hotels.) The complex boasts seven acres of oceanfront, plus 14 restaurants, a casino, and a full-service spa (both slated to open in 2001), three swimming pools totaling 50,000 sq feet, kiddies' facilities, the Village Market Promenade of boutiques and shops, and two 18-hole golf courses, all linked by a three-quarter-mile boardwalk.

The resort includes the 500-room *Reef Village at The Lucayan*, the only portion complete at press time. It boasts marvelous contemporary decor throughout, with lively Caribbean colors, exquisite modern furnishings, and an uptempo ambience. Its snazzy Barracuda restaurant and bar opens to a vast sundeck and swimming pool themed on a historic sugar mill with a waterslide. Rates for standard rooms are US$197/227 summer/ winter, including taxes and gratuities.

The 250-room *Lucayan Lighthouse Point*, studded by the hotel's historic red-and-white-striped lighthouse, and the 545-room *Lucayan Breakers* were slated to open by 2001.

The Beaches The high-rise *Xanadu Beach Resort & Marina* (☎ 242-352-6783, fax 242-352-5799, xanadu@batelnet.bs) looks over its eponymous beach (see the Freeport & Lucaya map). It has 186 rooms and suites, all with private balcony. It has tennis courts, water sports, plus an on-site dive shop and a full-service marina. Room rates range from US$94 to US$129 in summer, and US$125 to US$170 in winter. Suites range from US$150 to US$300 in summer and US$200 to US$400 in winter. Meal plans are offered. Contact the resort by mail at PO Box F-42438, Freeport, Grand Bahama, The Bahamas.

For a self-catering option, try *Woodbourne Estates Resort* (☎/fax 242-352-4069), which encompasses three resorts. *Woodbourne Estates Coral Courts*, near Xanadu Beach at the south end of the Mall, has 20 studios for US$100 and one-, two-, and three-bedroom apartments and efficiencies for US$135 to US$195. The much farther west *Woodbourne North Star Resort*, at Fortune Beach, and the *Woodbourne Estates Resort* have 22 and 30 two-bedroom apartments, respectively, sleeping up to six people for US$160. Rates fall for long-term stays. The property serves a mostly Canadian time-share clientele. It rents bicycles for US$10 per day. Its postal address is PO Box F-42453, Freeport, Grand Bahamas, Bahama (see the Freeport & Lucaya map).

Near Silver Point Beach, the *Ocean Reef Yacht Club & Resort* (☎ 242-373-4662, oceanreef@batelnet.bs) offers 64 townhouses and suites with Jacuzzis beside the marina. It has two swimming pools, one with a swim-up bar. Rates range from US$155 to US$310.

The *Island Seas Resort* (☎ 242-373-1271, fax 242-373-1275, iseas@mail.batelnet.bs, 123 Silver Point Dr), nearby, also offers one- and two-bedroom self-catering beachfront units. Facilities include a pool with swim-up bar, plus tennis, shuffleboard court, and watersports. Rates are US$130/155 summer/winter for one-bedroom, US$180/210 for two-bedroom units. One-bedroom beachview units cost US$100 more. Its postal address is PO Box F-44735, Freeport, Grand Bahama, The Bahamas.

The Italian-run *Club Viva Fortuna Beach* (☎ 242-373-4000, 800-898-9968, fax 242-373-5555), on Fortune Beach, is an all-inclusive resort that attempts to copy Club Med with modest success. The sprawling 204-room resort is meagerly landscaped but has a large pool and sun deck and backs a beautiful section of beach. A second restaurant, opened in 1999 as part of a $3 million renovation, has improved the dining standards. Per person rates range from US$154/220 single/double occupancy in low season to US$224/320 in high season, including all meals and beverages, water sports (motorized water sports cost extra), and nightly entertainment presented in the impressive open theater. Its mailing address is PO Box F-42398, Freeport, Grand Bahama, The Bahamas.

PLACES TO EAT

There's no shortage of places to eat, but most serve bland or routine fare, often at New York prices. Unless otherwise noted, these places to eat can be found on the Freeport & Lucaya map.

Freeport & Lucaya

The International Bazaar has more than a dozen places to eat, including an English-style pub. Most serve Bahamian fare. Some have bargain-priced breakfast specials. The restaurants are supposed to serve a free Bahama Mama cocktail with a purchase of lunch or dinner, though none advertise this. *Cafe Michel's* (☎ 242-352-2191) offers romantic patio dining beneath a suitably French-style awning. A US-style breakfast costs around US$5, as does a sandwich lunch. Its eclectic entrees range from steaks to fish and chips. The food is mediocre. Similarly, *Le Rendezvous* has patio dining and breakfast specials as low as US$1.95. The *Japanese Steak House* (☎ 242-352-9521) looks appealing but is overpriced, and canned vegetables don't improve things. For Greek food, try *The Plaka* (☎ 242-352-5932). It has authentic Hellenic cuisine: souvlaki, kebabs, moussaka, and retsina to wash it all down.

A good lunch bargain is *Lady Ruthnell's Deck & Pizzeria*, on the north side of the International Bazaar, serving filling tuna sandwiches and fries for US$3.50 and pizzas from US$4 upwards. For barbecue chicken, head next door to *Le Chicken Shack*, where you can grab a bite for US$3.50.

For Italian fare, try *Silvano's* (☎ 242-352-5110), an elegant restaurant on the northeast side of Ranfurly Circle, suitably Italianate in decor, with a full menu of dishes averaging US$12. It's open evenings only and is closed Monday. It has an ice-cream parlor, *Gelati Silvano's*, selling homemade ice cream; the factory supplies most of The Bahamas.

In the same price range is *Islander's Roost* (☎ 242-352-5110), adjoining Silvano's. One of the few eateries with a Caribbean flavor, it serves Bahamian and US dishes and offers live entertainment nightly. It's open 5 pm to 1 am Monday to Saturday and is closed Sunday.

Some of the best European cuisine is served at *Ruby Swiss* (☎ 242-352-8507), next to Tower at Bahamia, on W Sunrise Hwy at W Atlantic Dr. It has an all-you-can-eat pasta bar for US$10, and a two-for-one dinner special for US$35. The *Crown Room* (☎ 242-352-7811), at the Casino at Bahamia (see the Entertainment section, later in this chapter), claims to serve gourmet continental cuisine; jackets are required.

In the heart of downtown, try *Mr Baker* on E Mall Dr (see the Downtown Freeport map). It's a bakery and fast-food deli serving sandwiches and hot dishes such as barbecued ribs, coleslaw, and rice or potato for US$6 and broccoli and garlic-stuffed potato for US$5. It also has breakfast specials. For lunch, locals head to *Geneva's Place* (☎ 242-352-5085) on E Mall Dr at Kipling Lane, a good place to try Bahamian dishes, including guava duff dessert (dumpling laced with guava purée and drowned in a milky rum sauce). *Pizza Hut*, on E Mall Dr at Adventurers Way, has an all-you-can-eat luncheon buffet for US$7 each Wednesday.

The Beaches

The Port Lucaya Marketplace (see the Freeport & Lucaya map) has about two dozen choices. There are several English-style pubs. Fancy a curry or pizza? Head to *Pisces* (☎ 242-373-5192); plan to spend about US$15. *Domino's Pizza* has an outlet here, too. *Zorba's* (☎ 242-373-6137) offers tasty, reasonably priced Greek cuisine such as chicken souvlaki for US$5 and moussaka and Greek salad for US$8, to be enjoyed alfresco beneath a canopy of grapevines and pink bougainvillea. The *China Cafe* (☎ 242-373-2398) has Chinese lunch specials for US$3.50 and dinner specials for US$8.50, though the cuisine is mediocre. For breakfast specials, try the *Caribbean Cafe* (☎ 242-373-5866), where the menu includes oatmeal and toast for US$3.50, muffins for US$1.75, and pancakes for US$4.50.

The most elegant eatery is *Luciano's* (☎ 242-373-9100), also in the Marketplace, specializing in Italian and French fare. Try the grilled Dover sole with new potatoes, or the superb grouper with almonds. The filling dishes begin at about US$20 and are enjoyed on a breeze-swept balcony.

At last visit, the *Brass Helmet Restaurant* (☎ 242-373-2032), above UNEXSO, was closed and being rebuilt in a new building adjacent. The former outlet boasted divers' helmets as decor, plus a great white shark crashing through the wall, plus a reasonably priced menu heavy on seafood.

Nearby, the floating *Ferry House* (☎ 242-373-1595), in Pelican Bay at Port Lucaya, offers free appetizers plus a seafood and international menu. It's open 7 am to 10 pm daily except Tuesday, when it serves breakfast only.

Dining options at Reef Village at The Lucayan (see Places to Stay, earlier) range from *On Higher Grounds*, a coffee shop serving pastries, and the *Sugar Mill Bar & Grill*, overlooking the sea, to *Barracudas*, with upbeat contemporary decor, for Bahamian and international seafood.

At Churchill Beach, *Club Caribe* (☎ 242-373-6866) bills itself as a Boston-style eatery. It's simple yet homey and a marvelous place to hang out on the wooden deck over the beach. A volleyball net may tempt you from indulgent lazing with a cool pint of Fosters. An omelet breakfast or ham and eggs costs US$3.50. Salads, burgers, and peas 'n' rice are similarly priced. Main dishes begin at US$10. Hotel transfers are provided. Its open 10:30 am to 6 pm daily except Monday. A similar, though less atmospheric, option is *Le Beach Shack*, next door.

For a down-home taste of local color, head to *Mama Flo's* at Taino Beach, alias the White Wave Club Bar & Pool Hall. It's a funky little bar run by a colorful Bahama mama who whips up native fare for a few bucks. The offbeat *Outriggers Beach Club* (☎ 242-373-4811), 400 yards west of Mama Flo's and overlooking the beach, is popular for its Wednesday-night fish fry, when the place gets packed. It's run by Mama Flo's daughter.

The *Surfside Restaurant* (☎ 242-373-1814), at Taino, has a salt-assaulted deck over the beach. Tony is a colorful dude who'll keep you amused while preparing your roast (grilled) conch.

Nearby, *Kaptain Kenny's* (☎ 242-373-8689) is an all-timber beachfront bar and restaurant pervaded by a maritime mood enhanced by nets and driftwood and waitresses in nautical costume. It offers Bahamian fare, salads, and sandwiches, plus a daily special, including all-you-can-drink Bahama Mamas for US$14. Tour buses unload their cargo here. There are water sports. A weekly afternoon beach party for US$30 and a sunset bonfire for US$25 are offered, with limbo and beer-drinking contests. It's open daily from 9 am until way late.

The more upscale **Stone Crab** (☎ 242-373-1442), next to Kaptain Kenny's, serves steak and seafood averaging US$20 (it also has beach parties for US$40).

Nearby is the **Pirates of The Bahamas Beach Theme Park** (☎ 242-373-8456), on Jolly Roger Rd, serving Bahamian dishes. It also offers miniature golf, sea kayaks, paddle boats, and Jet Skis. An all-you-can-eat bonfire buffet is offered nightly except Saturday, with limbo and dancing (US$40). Hotel desks arrange tours.

At Fortune Beach, try the waterfront **Banana Bay Restaurant and Bar**.

ENTERTAINMENT
Casinos & Floorshows

The **Casino at Bahamia** (☎ 242-352-6721), in the Tower at Bahamia on W Sunrise Hwy, has over 400 slots, 40 blackjack tables, eight dice tables, eight roulette wheels, and other games of chance. Admission is free. No beachwear, bare feet, or bare backs are allowed. The casino also has a sports book section where bets may be placed on sports and other major events.

The Casino at Bahamia has a small-scale Las Vegas–style revue, 'Nightlife,' with brief toplessness and dance routines combining classical and contemporary movement. A comedy act is part of the routine. Shows are at 8:30 and 10:45 pm nightly except Monday; they cost US$15, including two drinks. The **Tower at Bahamia** (☎ 242-352-6721) has its own revue, 'The Sultan's Tent,' appealing to patrons who enjoy besequined Liberaces.

You can also try your luck at **The Lucayan Casino**, scheduled to open in 2001.

There are several 'native revues.' One of the best is 'Goombaya' in the Palm Pavilion at **Country Club at Bahamia** (☎ 242-352-7811), with singing, dancing, and Junkanoo. Shows are at 6:30 and 7:30 pm Tuesday and Saturday; they cost US$39 with dinner. The

Tower at Bahamia also has a 'Panache Native Show' at 9 pm nightly except Saturday.

A 'Native Floorshow' with calypso is hosted at **The Captain's Charthouse** (☎ 242-373-3900), on E Sunrise Hwy, at 7 and 9 pm nightly except Monday. The **Yellowbird Show Club** at the International Bazaar has a show with fire-eating and limbo dancing at 9 pm nightly except Sunday; it costs US$20, including two drinks.

For comedy, check out **Joker's Wild Supper & Show Club** (☎ 242-373-7765) on Midshipman Rd in Lucaya, where a dinner show featuring limbo and 'voodoo' dancers is held at 7 pm nightly except Sunday. Comedy is also hosted at **Club Illusions** (☎ 242-373-8576) at Port Lucaya Marina.

Pubs & Bars

A hot spot in the town center is **Lady Ruthnell's Deck & Pizzeria** (☎ 242-351-4759) at the International Bazaar. It's the center of action during spring break, and at any time of year attracts a young, beer-guzzling crowd. The bar has a large-screen TV. Happy hour is 5 to 7 pm daily.

For sports action try the **Red Dog Sports Bar** (☎ 242-352-2700) across the street in the Pub on the Mall, on Ranfurly Circus, and which also has an English pub.

Coconuts (☎ 242-373-1271) at Island Seas Resort (see the Places to Stay section) is a popular poolside bar; it has happy hour nightly at 4 pm. And the beachside **Margaritaville** (☎ 242-373-4525), near Club Viva Fortuna Beach, has golden oldies on the jukebox; it has a beach bonfire on Tuesday night.

Bars in the Port Lucaya Marketplace include *Bahama Mama's Lounge* (☎ 242-373-8514); *Rum Runners* (☎ 242-373-7233); the *Happy Bar & Lounge* (☎ 242-373-6852), a sports bar with TV; and *the* place to watch the game, the *Junkanoo Sports Bar & Grill* (☎ 242-373-6170). Also here is *Shenanigan's Irish Pub* (☎ 242-373-4734), serving Guinness, and *The Pub at Port Lucaya* (☎ 242-373-8450), recreating a touch of jolly old England. Finally, the *Prop Club* at Reef Village at The Lucayan is popular; this sports bar has TV screens and a dance floor, plus glass walls that lift up to expose a sand volleyball court.

At Taino Beach, *Kaptain Kenny's* and *Le Beach Shack* (☎ 242-373-4525) are happenin' spots.

The local bar scene is limited to a few vapid 'satellite lounges.'

Live Music

Little Joe Cartwright performs calypso and soca at *Port Lucaya Marketplace* (☎ 242-373-8446) 7:30 to 10 pm nightly; a roller-skating limbo dancer (!) and fire-eaters are featured. Similar sounds can be heard at the lively *John B Bar* (☎ 242-352-7811) at the Country Club at Bahamia, and at *Becky's Restaurant* (☎ 242-352-8717) in the International Bazaar.

The Ozzy Hall Trio plays Bahamian hits and classics Tuesday, Wednesday, and Thursday in the lobby of *Reef Village at The Lucayan*.

For jazz, try *Illusions Jazz & Comedy Club* (☎ 242-457-5015) in Port Lucaya Marketplace, with live jazz twice weekly; a US$10 cover applies after 10 pm. You can also catch jazz at the piano bar of the *Port Lucaya Yacht Club* (☎ 242-373-6618) nightly except Tuesday.

Also a good spot for sedate listening is *Ruby Swiss* (☎ 242-352-8507), next to the Tower at Bahamia. It stays open until 6 am.

Dance Clubs

Locals head to the *Safari Lounge* (☎ 242-352-2805) on E Mall Dr, or *Club 2000*, at Lady Ruthnell's Deck, with an indoor disco

nightly; entrance is free Monday to Thursday, but US$5 on weekends.

The best place is *Amnesia* (☎ 242-351-2582), opposite the International Bazaar on E Mall Dr. This tropical-themed nightclub has a state-of-the-art light and sound system blending Caribbean, hip-hop, and Top 40. Beautiful female hostesses parade in a lingerie show. It offers hors d'oeuvres on Friday night. Hours vary.

Studio 69 (☎ 242-373-4824), on Midshipman Rd in Lucaya, was popular with the gay crowd until local prejudice forced it back underground. The club still hosts disco for all-comers.

Theater

The Freeport Players Guild (☎ 242-373-8400) puts on plays each September to June at the *Regency Theatre* (☎ 242-352-5533), west of the Ruby Golf Course (see the Freeport & Lucaya map). The Grand Bahama Players (☎ 242-352-7071, 242-373-2299) also perform here. Tickets usually cost US$10. Dinner shows cost US$50, including a bottle of champagne. Also check for performances by the Freeport Friends of the Arts (☎ 242-373-1528).

Cinemas

Freeport has two cinemas: the *Columbus 4 Theatres Cinema* (☎ 242-352-7478) on E Mall Dr at Adventurers Way (see the Downtown Freeport map); and the five-screen *RND Cinemas* (☎ 242-351-3456) on E Atlantic Dr. Admission costs US$5.

SHOPPING

The shopping is unsophisticated except for jewelry and perfumes, and real bargains are hard to find. Locals do their shopping downtown at malls such as The Towne Centre and Churchill Square.

What-to-do in Freeport/Lucaya, Grand Bahama (see Publications under Information earlier in this chapter) lists major stores and has maps of the International Bazaar and Port Lucaya Marketplace, plus a handy perfume price-comparison chart.

The many jewelry stores include The Colombian (☎ 242-352-5380), Colombian

Emeralds International (☎ 800-666-3889), and Jeweler's Warehouse, all with outlets in the International Bazaar and Port Lucaya Marketplace.

For embroidered linens, silk pajamas, and the like, try Far East Traders (in the International Bazaar ☎ 242-352-9280; in the Port Lucaya Marketplace ☎ 242-373-8697).

The International Bazaar has about 100 stores, including Fendi (☎ 242-352-7908) for Italian leather; Freeport Jewelers (☎ 242-352-2004) and John Bull (☎ 242-352-2626) for jewelry; The Gallery (☎ 242-352-2660) and Island Galleria (☎ 242-352-8194), both specializing in crystal and fine porcelain; and Gucci (☎ 242-352-4580) for Italian clothing, leather, and accessories. The Plaka (☎ 242-352-5932) sells items from Greece. The Taj Emporium (☎ 242-373-5099) sells Indian imports, from children's toys to fashionwear.

Several stores in the bazaar sell perfumes. The Perfume Factory (☎ 242-352-9391) is immediately north of the bazaar (see the Perfume Factory section under Freeport & Lucaya, earlier in this chapter). And the Caribbean Sea Treasures Factory (☎ 242-352-5380) is also here; it offers tours demonstrating how jewelry is made out of shells and coral.

The 6-acre Port Lucaya Marketplace shopping complex has 85 stores. It has Gucci (☎ 242-373-2973), Island Galleria (☎ 242-373-8404), The Jewellery Box (☎ 242-373-8319), Linens of Lucaya (☎ 242-352-8697), and Nautique (☎ 242-373-1522), which specializes in resortwear, silk paintings and other artwork, and custom-made crafts with a nautical theme. Samos of Lucaya (☎ 242-373-5846) sells Greek imports.

Cigars

Cuban cigars are a great buy. Most quality gift shops sell Cohibas (the Rolls-Royce of cigars), Montecristos, and other notable brands at 50% or more off black-market prices in the US. The best place is Smoker's World (☎ 242-351-6899) in the Ginza Bldg of the International Bazaar.

US citizens are legally barred from purchasing *any* Cuban products, even if bought in The Bahamas. See the boxed text '¡Cuba

Sí!' in the New Providence chapter for details on US customs regulations. Bahamian retailers sell without distinction.

Straw-Work & Native Items

There are several straw markets, notably behind the International Bazaar, where dozens of stalls sell all manner of woven straw crafts, as well as T-shirts, carvings, and ethnic jewelry. The hustling is light, and it's no gauntlet to browse. You'll find similar markets at the Port Lucaya Marketplace, Xanadu Beach, and Kaptain Kenny's at Taino Beach.

Look for native woodcarvings, especially the simple yet dramatic works by Michael Hoyte, often hewn from ebony driftwood washed ashore from Africa.

For Bahamian sauces and preserves, specialty oils, and other culinary items, head to Solomon's Food Court (☎ 242-352-9681) on Cedar St near the International Bazaar.

Music

Serious music buffs should head to Buck's Record Gallery (☎ 242-352-5170), downtown on Pioneers Way near E Mall Dr, or Intercity Music (☎ 242-352-8820) in Port Lucaya Marketplace.

Photographic Equipment

A few stores in the International Bazaar sell cameras and photographic and video equipment, including film. Also try the Camera Shoppe, 20 Pioneers Way, downtown, and the Photo Specialist (☎ 242-373-7858) in Port Lucaya Marketplace.

GETTING THERE & AWAY
Air

Grand Bahama International Airport (☎ 242-352-6020) is 2 miles north of central Freeport. It recently underwent a US$6 million expansion. There's a tourist board information booth, currency exchange office, and car rental booths across the road from the arrivals hall.

See the Getting There & Away and Getting Around chapters for airlines' and charter companies' international and Freeport telephone numbers.

To/From Elsewhere in The Bahamas Bahamasair (☎ 242-352-8341) flies between Nassau and Freeport eight times daily (US$64 one-way).

Major's Air Services (☎ 242-352-5778, 242-352-5781, majorsair@BahamasVG.com) has flights between Freeport and the Biminis (US$50 each way) plus most other islands in the Bahamas chain. Its terminal is 400 yards east of the main airport terminal and accessed by a separate road from the main highway; if returning a rental car, leave plenty of time for a transfer.

Taino Air (☎ 242-352-8885, fax 242-352-5175) flies between Freeport and Andros, Eleuthera, and Marsh Harbour (Abacos).

Boat
Cruise Ship Several companies offer cruises to Freeport. For details on cruises, see the Getting There & Away chapter.

The three-pier Cruise Ship Port is about 6 miles west of town. The terminal features immigration and customs facilities, duty-free stores, snack bars, and other visitor facilities. Taxis (☎ 242-352-7101) provide service into town and the beaches; rides cost US$12 to US$15 to downtown, US$15 to US$20 to Lucaya.

Mail Boat & Ferry The mail boat *Marcella III* sails at 4 pm Wednesday for Freeport from Nassau (US$45 one-way). It docks half a mile east of the Cruise Ship Port (see the Grand Bahama map). There are no services or facilities, but taxis are available; call the Taxi Union at ☎ 242-352-7101.

SeaJets (☎ 954-384-8977, 877-273-2538, fax 561-844-1994, bahamas@seajets.com) operates a 250-passenger Boeing 929 hydrofoil, departing Palm Beach, Florida, at 9 am and 3:30 pm; returning at noon and 6:15 pm. The roundtrip journey costs US$99 adult, US$50 children. Return trips depart Grand Bahamas at 11:30 am and 6:50 pm.

Private Yacht Xanadu Beach Resort & Marina (☎ 242-352-6782) has 60 slips and charges from US$40 daily dockage.

The modern Port Lucaya Marina & Yacht Club (☎ 242-373-9090, fax 242-373-5884, port@batelnet.bs), off Sea Horse Rd, has 150 slips for boats up to 160 feet in length. Dockage costs US$1 per foot (US$35 minimum). On the north side of Port Lucaya, the Lucayan Marina (☎ 242-373-7616, fax 242-373-7630) has 125 slips and charges US$1 per foot.

Running Mon Marina (☎ 242-352-6834) is a 66-slip marina at the foot of the Mall charging US$1 per foot per day.

You must clear customs and immigration at Lucayan Marina, Port Lucaya Marina, or Xanadu Marina (see the Freeport & Lucaya map).

GETTING AROUND
To/From the Airport
There's no bus service to or from the airport. Taxi rides to/from the Resort at Bahamia cost US$6 to US$8, and US$12 to US$15 to/from Lucaya.

Bus
A handful of private minibuses operate as 'public buses' on assigned routes from the bus depot downtown at Winn Dixie Plaza, traveling as far afield as West End and McLean's Town. Buses tend to leave when the driver decides he has enough passengers. Fares are US75¢ for travel in town, and US$1 to Port Lucaya Marketplace via E Mall Dr and the International Bazaar, E Sunrise Hwy, Coral Rd, and Royal Palm Way. The bus stop in Lucaya is on Seahorse Dr, 400 yards west of the Port Lucaya Market.

The Ministry of Tourism office (☎ 242-352-8044) can provide a list of bus routes.

Free shuttles also run between the Resort at Bahamia and Xanadu Beach and Island Sea Resort (at Silver Point Beach) every 30 minutes.

Car & Scooter
The following companies have car-rental agencies at the airport:

Avis	☎ 242-352-7666
Dollar	☎ 242-352-9325
Hertz	☎ 242-352-3297
Sears Rent-a-Car	☎ 242-352-8841

If you like the wind in your hair, consider a street-worthy dune buggy from Bahama Buggies (☎ 242-352-8750), opposite the International Bazaar on E Mall Dr. It charges US$50 for eight hours, US$65 per day, or US$300 weekly. Insurance costs US$15 daily.

You can rent a scooter in the forecourt of the Towers at Bahamia (☎ 242-352-7035) for US$30/50 half/full day, plus US$100 deposit, including gas and unlimited mileage. Summer specials are offered.

Taxi

You'll find taxis at the airport and major hotels. Fares are fixed by the government for short distances (see the Getting Around chapter). Bonded taxis (with white license plates) can't go outside the tax-free zone. Other taxis can take you anywhere on the island for US$25 to US$35 per hour. Expect to pay US$60 to US$100 to West End.

You can call for a radio-dispatched taxi from Freeport Taxi (☎ 242-352-6666) or Grand Bahama Taxi Union (☎ 242-352-7101).

Boat

A water taxi runs between Port Lucaya and the Taino Beach Resort & Marina every hour. It departs Taino Beach on the hour and departs Lucaya at 10 minutes past (US$2 one-way).

East of Freeport

East of the Grand Lucayan Waterway, the Grand Bahama Hwy runs parallel to the shore to the east end of the island. Side roads lead to the south shore, which boasts white-sand beaches running in endless scallops as pristine and as dazzling as movie creations. The drive itself is ho-hum. Watch out for the dangerous 90° bends between Rocky Creek and McLean's Town. Other side roads lead to the north shore wetlands.

WATER CAY

This tiny, simple settlement is on the cay of that name, 2 miles off the north shore. The community relies on fishing and is as unspoiled as things get on Grand Bahama.

You can catch a boat from Hawksbill Creek or the Grand Lucayan Waterway or drive the dirt road from the Grand Bahama Hwy to the north shore dock, where you might be able to hire a local's boat to Water Cay.

OLD FREE TOWN & OWL HOLE

The settlement of Old Free Town, 3 miles east of the Grand Lucayan Waterway, was forcibly abandoned in the 1960s when the Port Authority acquired the land and relocated the inhabitants to the new city of Freeport. A few derelict buildings remain. More interesting is the surrounding swamp containing several blue holes (subaqueous caves), notably Mermaid's Lair and Owl Hole, with a flask-shaped opening that drops 35 feet to water level. Stalactites dangle from the roof of the bowl. Owls have nested on the sill as long as residents can remember. It's not signed; you'll need a guide – see the Organized Tours section of Freeport & Lucaya, earlier in this chapter.

PETERSON CAY NATIONAL PARK

This 1½-acre park, 1 mile offshore and 15 miles east of Freeport, is the only cay on Grand Bahama's south shore. It is one of the Family Islands' most heavily used getaway spots, popular with locals with boats on weekends. Coral reefs provide splendid snorkeling and diving. You can hire a boat from any marina in Freeport/Lucaya. Take snorkel gear and a picnic.

LUCAYAN NATIONAL PARK

This 40-acre park is Grand Bahama's finest treasure. There are two halves to the park, divided by the Grand Bahama Hwy. On the north side, trails lead from the parking lot onto a limestone plateau riddled with caves that open to the longest known underwater cave system in the world, with over 6 charted miles of tunnels. (Cave diving is allowed only by special permit under the supervision of UNEXSO in Port Lucaya. See the Diving & Snorkeling section of Freeport & Lucaya, earlier in this chapter.)

Two main caves open to the surface, forming blue holes – **Ben's Cave** and **Burial**

Mound Cave – where fresh water floats atop saltwater. Steps lead down to viewing platforms above the water level. Colonies of harmless bats use the cave's cool interior as a nursery in summer. Ben's Cave is also the home of a recently discovered and unique class of opaque, blind crustacean – *Speleonectes lucayensis* – that resembles a swimming centipede. Bring some bread to toss into the jade-colored waters and fish will magically appear. In 1986 four skeletons of indigenous Lucayans were found on the floor of one cave, which is thought to have been a cemetery.

Across the road, the **Creek Trail** (330 yards) and **Mangrove Swamp Trail** (480 yards) form a loop, easily walked in 20 minutes, through three distinct shoreline ecosystems (other ecosystems – including rocky coppice and pineland – exist north of the road). Information signs provide edification. The transition zone is formed of bonsai-like ming, cedar, mahogany, and poisonwood, cinnecord, cabbage palms, and agaves, which produce towering yellow flowers favored by insects and hummingbirds. Their low branches are festooned by orchids and bromeliads.

Between this zone and the shore lies a large mangrove swash dominated by air plants. With fortune you might spot a raccoon and land crabs, or even an osprey. Keen-eyed herons wade the shallows on the lookout for tidbits while waterfowl splash about in the sloughs. The marsh is drained by **Gold Rock Creek**. The waters are a habitat for snapper, barracuda, manta ray, and crab. In fact, passages lead underground between the creek and the Lucayan Caves so that ocean fish are often seen in the blue holes north of the road.

The third zone is the whiteland coppice, which abuts the sandy shore and is dominated by giant poisonwood trees, pigeon plum, and other trees favored by woodpeckers ('peckerwoods' in local parlance).

Both trails spill out onto the secluded and beautiful **Gold Rock Beach**, fringed by dunes fixed by coco plum, sea grape, spider lily, and casuarina (or Australian pine). At low tide the white sand is rippled as far as

Explore mangroves in Lucayan National Park.

the eye can see; the wide beach arcs in a seemingly endless scimitar. It's named for the small rock that lies 200 yards offshore.

There are no facilities. No camping is allowed. Bring a picnic lunch and bug spray (the casuarinas provide a perfect habitat for biting sand fleas). The park is open daily year-round, but Ben's Cave is closed in June and July to protect the bats' nursery.

For more information, contact the Bahamas National Trust (☎ 242-352-5438) in the Rand Memorial Nature Center, PO Box F-43441, Freeport, Grand Bahama, The Bahamas.

Getting There & Away

A minivan ('jitney') from Winn Dixie Plaza, downtown Freeport, passes by the park en route to McLean's Town (about US$5 oneway). A taxi from Freeport will cost about US$30.

Erika Moultrie's Kayak Nature Tours (☎/fax 242-373-2485, kayaknaturetours@aol.com) offers guided sea kayak tours from Freeport into the wetlands for US$59, including hotel transfers and picnic lunch on Gold Rock Beach. Erika acts as guide, pointing out the birdlife, crabs, and other marine life. The company also offers a bird-watching trip (US$49).

East End Adventures includes the park in its 'safari trip' to Sweeting's Cay. See the Sweeting's Cay section later in this chapter for details.

LUCAYAN NATIONAL PARK TO McLEAN'S TOWN

The route is lined with several tiny settlements (see the Grand Bahama map), notably sleepy Freetown, now slowly dying since nearby Gold Rock USAAF Missile Tracking Station – the first tracking station downrange of Cape Canaveral – closed down. Farther east, you'll pass High Rock, a hamlet with several old wooden homes overlooking the sea from a bluff.

About 10 miles east, beyond the Burma Oil Depot (with a harbor facility for the world's largest supertankers), is Pelican Point Beach – *fabulous!* – and Rocky Creek, another hamlet known for its blue hole full of marine life.

The fishing village of McLean's Town is a flyblown place surrounded by mangroves at the eastern tip of the island…literally the end of the road. Locals make a living from conch and lobster fishing and as fishing guides. The village is the jumping-off place for boat rides to Sweeting's, Lightbourne, and Deep Water Cays.

This somnolent hamlet comes alive briefly for the Conch Cracking Contest each October. Contestants compete to crack and clean the most conchs from their shells – an ugly business. The full-day event includes entertainment such as a greasy-pole climb, bingo, swim races, amateur boxing, and live rake 'n' scrape bands.

Bonefishing

Captain Phil & Mel's Bonefishing Guide Service (☎ 242-353-3023, pager 242-340-1971, philmel@batelnet.bs) charges US$250 for a half-day and US$350 per full day, with transport to and from Freeport.

Places to Stay

A homey and reclusive place beside the beach at Pelican Point, *Pelican Point Lodge* (☎ 242-353-6064; in the US ☎ 603-598-8464, PeliPoint@aol.com) is a perfect escape from tourist traps. It's run by Freddie Long, a friendly chap who lives in the blue-and-white house across the road. He has three family-style units resembling a Midwest trailer park. Each has air-con and a kitch-enette. Rates are US$60/70 one/two-bedroom. There's a funky little bar and restaurant – *Breezes* – attached.

Entering McLean's Town, you can't miss the mint-green, three-story building on the left. This is *Bro's* (☎ 242-353-3440), with a choice of clean yet spartan single rooms and two-bedroom apartments, some with kitch-enette. Some have air-con. Rates are US$30 to US$50.

Places to Eat

About 5 miles east of Lucayan National Park, *Smitty's One Stop Shop* offers burgers and basic fare; it also sells gasoline and has a general store. There are several other basic roadside options along the route, at any of which you could be the first out-of-towner all week.

In McLean's Town check out the *East Sunrise Bar & Restaurant*, serving seafood, with dancing at night. You can buy groceries at the *Cooper's Convenience Store*, a tiny hut in the middle of the village. *Maxida's*, adjacent to the wharves, offers fish and chips for US$9, pork chops for US$10, and burgers for US$2. It has a pool table and on weekend nights rises from torpor with music and dancing.

Getting There & Around

A minibus operates daily from Winn Dixie Plaza in downtown Freeport; see the Getting Around section earlier in this chapter for more details.

East End Adventures includes McLean's Town on its day trip to Sweeting's Cay (see the Sweeting's Cay section, below).

Freddie Long has a taxi service at Pelican Point Lodge.

DEEP WATER CAY

Only true isolationists know about this get-away-from-it-all fishing mecca, 1 mile south-east of McLean's Town. Deep Water Cay boasts 250 sq miles of fertile flats and miles-long, crystal-clear creeks darkened by schools of the elusive 'gray ghosts,' or bonefish. The cay is a paradise for anglers hoping to top the record 13½-lb catch. The Deep Water Cay Club (see Places to Stay, below) has a tackle

Hope Town Lighthouse, Abaco

Bonefishing the flats at sunset

Sailing in the Abacos

Mural in Marsh Harbour

The sand really is this pink on Harbour Island.

Colorful clapboard houses in Dunmore Town, Harbour Island

shop and operates a fleet of custom-designed 16-foot Dolphin Super Skiffs.

Bountiful birdlife adds to the allure. If fishing isn't your thing, you can sail, dive, snorkel, play croquet, or lounge by the saltwater pool.

Places to Stay

The *Deep Water Cay Club* (☎ 242-353-3073; in the US ☎ 954-359-0488, fax 954-359-9488, bahamabone@aol.com) sleeps 18 guests in cottage apartments. It's intimate and a tad exclusive, a feeling enhanced by the decor: an amalgam of a Yukon timber lodge and a Kashmiri houseboat. The seven air-con cottages have ceiling fan, refrigerator, and coffeemaker, but no telephone or TV. You can relax in hammocks. The clubhouse – you can walk or take the electric golf cart – features a self-service bar and communal dining. Accommodations are available only in three-, four-, and seven-night packages. Three-night packages cost US$1375/1298/1444 fall/ winter/spring. Reservations are essential. The club is closed mid-July to September, as well as December and January. Its mailing address is 1100 Lee Wagener Blvd, No 352, Ft Lauderdale, FL 33315, USA.

Getting There & Away

The Deep Water Cay Club arranges direct charters from Fort Lauderdale and West Palm Beach to the cay, which has its own tiny airstrip (US$310 roundtrip). A commuter flight from Freeport (4 person minimum) costs US$60 per person each way; the club can arrange it.

Alternately, you can take a boat from McLean's Town for about US$40 roundtrip, but you may be able to negotiate a lower price. It's a 10-minute ride. A taxi/ferry ride from Freeport costs US$125 for up to 4 people, each way.

SWEETING'S CAY

This small cay, 3 miles south of Deep Water Cay, is worth a visit for a reclusive escape. Its few dozen residents still make a living from sponging and conching.

Facilities include a small *motel* with cottages for rent. There's *Russell's Restaurant*

& Bar on the waterfront and *Seaside Fig Tree*, which serves up conch dishes. And Miss Pinne will load you up with freshbaked bread, fried fish, and peas 'n' rice.

You can hire a boat in McLean's Town to get to Sweeting's Cay, but the easiest way to get here is on a full-day 'safari' offered by East End Adventures (☎ 242-351-6250, fax 242-352-7676, safari@batelnet.bs; in the US ☎ 800-448-3386) in Freeport. The trip to the 'Grand Bahamian Outback' is by jeep and includes time for bird watching and a stop at Lucayan National Park, followed by a speedboat ride to the cays, where you get a traditional Bahamian lunch and while away the afternoon sunning, snorkeling, or fishing. The trip costs US$110, including transport from your hotel. East End's postal address is PO Box F-44322, Freeport, Grand Bahama, The Bahamas.

West of Freeport

HAWKSBILL CREEK TO WEST END

West of Freeport, a slender, scrub-covered peninsula, separated from the 'mainland' by Freeport Harbour Channel, extends northwest to West End. The main road, Queen's Hwy, runs inland of the coast. A second road parallels the coast but offers little scenic value. There are few beaches until you reach Deadman's Reef.

The channel opens to Hawksbill Creek, named for the once-common marine turtles that now only infrequently come ashore. Fishermen bring their catch ashore here to the Conch Wharf; huge shell mounds line the road. West of the channel is the sprawling, low-income suburb of Eight Mile, fronted by a rocky, shellstrewn, and grossly littered beach. Nearby are several 'boiling holes' (subterranean water-filled holes that bubble under pressure of the tides).

Eight Mile extends west to Holmes Rock, another charmless village stretched along the road for several miles. Locals advise against picking up male hitchhikers along this road, as there have been many

GRAND BAHAMA

problems. As one old lady to whom I gave a ride said: 'Don't pick up no-one darlin', you don't know who is who. Dem plenty bad men.'

There's good diving offshore, especially at **Paradise Cove**. This private beach operation is perfect for a day of reclusive beach lounging (see the Grand Bahama map). The setting is splendid within the cusp of a protected lagoon sheltered by Deadman's Reef. Beach volleyball and water sports are offered. Kayaks cost US$15 per hour, a float is US$2, and snorkel gear costs US$10. A 'snorkel tour' costs US$25. And you can dine on burgers or hot dogs on a large, shaded wooden deck with camp-style tables. It's open 10 am to sunset daily. Excursions are offered from Freeport/Lucaya. Call ☎ 242-349-2677 for information.

A public bus from Winn Dixie Plaza in Freeport costs US$1 to Eight Mile, and US$2 to Holmes Rock.

Places to Stay & Eat

The *Tasty Pot Shop* is a colorful, funky little place on the main road at Holmes Rock, where you'll find several other modest places to eat with locals.

Paradise Cove (☎ *242-349-2677, pcove@ batelnet.bs*), at Deadman's Reef, is a home-away-from-home run by a friendly Bahamian, Barry Smith. It has five apartments sleeping up to six people; they cost US$75 for a one-bedroom apartment, US$105 for a two-bedroom cottage, and US$195 for a two-bedroom suite. Weekly rates are offered. They're large, clean, and well-furnished in contemporary decor with full kitchens. The snack bar features sandwiches, burgers, grilled chicken (US$4), and conch dishes. A clubhouse and more apartments were planned. The mailing address is PO Box F-42629, Freeport, Grand Bahama, The Bahamas.

Farther up the road is the atmospheric *Buccaneer Club* (☎ *242-349-3794*), centered on a magnificent Old World stone-and-timber restaurant festooned with polished driftwood and nautical regalia. You can also dine outside on a patio shaded by palms. The menu lists native seafood for US$4 to

US$10, Wiener schnitzel for US$19, and steaks, rack of lamb, and broiled lobster for US$25 to US$30. It has a reasonable wine list. It's open 5 to 10:30 pm daily except Monday. Reservations are recommended. Hotel transfers from Freeport/Lucaya are offered.

WEST END

This fishing village, 25 miles west of Freeport, could have fallen from the set of Robin Williams' movie *Popeye*, with its tumbledown shacks, half-sunken boats, and piles of sun-bleached conch shells. Pretty the two-street village is not, but there is no denying its somnolent and somewhat sleazy renegade charm.

West End was once the center of activity on the island…a bustling hive of activity when Prohibition rumrunners ruled the roost and yachters with sterling surnames like Kennedy, DuPont, or Hearst were callers to the Grand Bahama Resort & Country Club. It became a bit of a Wild West town and blossomed until the development of Freeport knocked the wind out of its sails. West End had a brief renaissance two decades ago when the resort reopened as Jack Tar Village. It closed again in 1990 but has arisen like a phoenix as the Old Bahama Bay Resort & Marina, with an 18-hole golf course slated to open in 2002.

Lovers of offbeat lifestyles may enjoy watching fishermen hang their nets to dry, extract conch from their shells, or snooze in the shade, where they take their simple pleasures with a beer and dominoes in hand. Locals warn out-of-towners to stick to the shoreline road and avoid the backroads inland, where there are many 'Joneses'… rascals who hang out smoking marijuana and hassling passers-by.

The village also boasts the 1893 stone-and-wood **Mary Magdalene Church**, complete with three small yet beautiful stained-glass windows in contemporary style.

The flats north of West End are good for **bonefishing**. Bonefish Folley (☎ 242-346-6233) is the area's best-known guide.

The police station, BaTelCo office, and health clinic are next to each other at the far west end of the village.

Places to Stay & Eat

The homey *Harbour Hotel* (☎ /fax 242-346-6495), opposite Mary Magdalene Church, has nine simple air-con rooms with cable TV for US$65 single or double, US$85 for a mini-suite, and US$120 for a suite. It has a small pool and a restaurant.

The former Jack Tar Resort was demolished and a new property, *Old Bahama Bay Resort & Marina* (☎ 242-346-6500, fax 242-346-6546), was due to open in early 2001. The low rise, 170-room resort is centered on the two-story Bahamian-style Customs House. It comprises 47 oceanfront Bahamian-style cottages as part of a 150-acre resort development that includes private homes. Furnishings in the open-suite rooms – no walls separate the living room and bedroom – will include net canopies over the beds, plus sofas, coffee makers, minifridges, telephones, faxes, modem lines, and porches with hammocks. Facilities include a swimming pool, tennis courts, a gym, spa, dive shop, and 72-slip marina, which will grow to be 200 slips in 2001.

The place to groove with the locals is The Senator's, officially *The Star Hotel Restaurant & Lounge* (☎ 242-346-6207), in a weather-worn, two-story clapboard hotel (now defunct). The Bahamian fare is simple and cheap. Mrs Grant cooks up a great conch chowder.

Locals will tell you the best conch salad (minced scorched conch) is served at the *Chicken Nest* (☎ 242-346-6440) on the outskirts of town. *Yvonne's* serves a mean conchburger.

The *Harbour Hotel* restaurant serves lunch poolside and offers dinner in the air-con dining room.

Entertainment

When darkness descends, locals gather at the *Double Deuce Nightclub*, overhanging the water at the east end of town. The *Harbour Hotel* has dancing on Friday, Saturday, and Sunday.

The *Chicken Nest* has a jukebox, dart board, and pool table. Or you can spend a night slapping down dominoes or checkers with the guys (where are the women?) who gather at rickety tables beneath the shady, lopsided eaves of *The Senator's*.

An informal street party called the 'West End Move' is held on the waterfront every Saturday afternoon.

Getting There & Away

A public minibus runs twice daily from the International Bazaar and Port Lucaya Marketplace for US$3 each way. The service runs hourly on Saturday. A taxi from Freeport or Lucaya will cost up to US$100 roundtrip for four people.

The modern Old Bahama Bay Marina (☎ 242-346-6500) has a fuel dock, 72 slips, electricity, water, and telephones. The Harbour Hotel & Marina (☎ 242-346-6432) charges US$20 per day up to 30 feet, and US50¢ per foot over 30 feet.

Several tour operators include West End in their daylong sightseeing excursions from Freeport. See Organized Tours in the Freeport & Lucaya section.

Biminis

• pop 1638

Ernest Hemingway's 'islands in the stream' perch on the edge of the Gulf Stream, just 50 miles east of Miami (the city's glow can be seen at night) and 120 miles northwest of Nassau. The Bimini group – the westernmost of the Bahamian archipelago – is barely 10 sq miles and flat as a flounder. The name is a Lucayan Indian term meaning 'two islands.'

North Bimini (locally referred to as simply 'Bimini') is shaped like an inverted crab's claw, 7 miles long and no more than 400 yards across at the main island's widest point. Below it and separated by only 150 yards of water lies South Bimini, a chunkier and virtually uninhabited plot of land. A sprinkling of small, slender cays lies farther south. Together the islands have fewer than

Highlights

- Dancing to rake 'n' scrape music at the Compleat Angler Hotel
- Hanging your underwear from the rafters of the End of the World Bar
- Fishing Hemingway's 'Deep Blue River'
- Diving the Bimini Road...is it really part of Atlantis?
- Swimming with dolphins

1700 full-time residents, known as Biminites, who like to interact with the world on their own laid-back, sometimes lawless, terms. Most everything happens in Alice Town on Bimini, especially in midsummer, when folks from Florida arrive in flocks to savor a lifestyle that putters along in the slow lane.

Bimini is also favored by college students whooping it up during spring break, a time for wet-T-shirt contests and drunken good times. At other times this is the kind of place to fish, relax, sit around drinking beer, and tell big-fish stories.

The Gulf Stream brings game fish close to shore in quest of baitfish moving off the Bahama Banks. You name it – wahoo, tuna, sailfish, mako shark, barracuda, and, above all, blue marlin and other billfish that put up a bruising battle – they're all waiting for you to cast your lure and notch up a record catch that would make 'Papa' Hemingway jealous. Sport-fishing boats are a mainstay of the local economy. Those who prefer smaller fry look east to the Biminis' flats.

Scuba divers are lured to the islands' crystal-clear waters. Sunken Spanish galleons and the wreck of a WWI freighter lie in the shallows between South Bimini and North Cat Cay. There's the Bimini Road off Bimini, alluringly claimed to be part of the 'lost city' of Atlantis. And there's the famous Bimini Wall, plummeting over 4000 feet. See the 'Dive & Snorkel Sites' boxed text later in this chapter for the Biminis' other underwater highlights.

The Biminis are also famous for dives with wild dolphins. Pods of rare Atlantic spotted dolphins are regularly seen, and they like nothing better than to cavort and swim nose to nose with humans. Unlike the more well-known bottle-nosed dolphins, spotted dolphins seem to seek out human interaction in the wild, though they do not train well in captivity.

At least one islander, Ansil Saunders, a famous boatbuilder, carries on a family tradition that started last century when, as he says, 'four white men from Scotland moved down from Canada, married four black women from Bimini,' and developed the Bimini Bonefisher boat. His boats – handmade of five-ply, quarter-inch mahogany (the wood is quieter than fiberglass, a crucial advantage in the bonefish game) – can glide through salt-water flats that are barely 6 inches deep.

History

In 1513 the Spanish explorer Juan Ponce de León, then governor of Puerto Rico, drifted through the archipelago seeking the Fountain of Youth. He had heard tales from the Lucayans of a miraculous spring in the Biminis that bestowed youthfulness on whomever bathed in the crystalline waters. Ponce de León touched ashore at most of the Bahamian islands but missed the Biminis and found Florida instead.

Later, pirates such as Henry Morgan thought the Biminis a splendid lair in which to lie in wait for treasure fleets making haste homeward via the Gulf Stream. The five founding families who first put down roots here in 1835 did so as licensed wreckers – individuals who 'rescue' ships and their cargoes. The advent of steamships and pilot lights ended the wrecking industry, so Biminites took to sponging – a thriving business that lasted until a blight in the 1930s killed the sponges.

In 1920 the Biminis got a boost from Prohibition. English and Scottish distilleries worked overtime to supply merchant ships that quickly moved whiskey to the Biminis for the illicit 50-mile run to the USA. Alice Town became the export capital and briefly the busiest port in the Bahamas.

Ernest Hemingway made the Biminis famous in his best-selling *Islands in the Stream*, which autobiographically reflects his hard-drinking, hard-fighting, egotistical ways when he briefly made it his summer home during the mid-1930s. The Biminis' popularity was also helped along by other notables, including Kip Farrington, Jr, editor of *Field & Stream*; Howard Hughes; and Adam Clayton Powell, Jr, the outspoken black New York congressman and Harlem preacher who came to be with his mistress and, er,

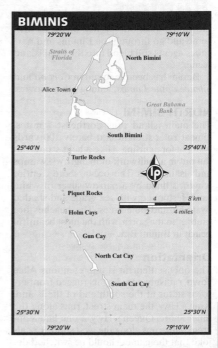

BIMINIS

lash out at hypocrisies from his bar by the sea. (More recently, US presidential contender Gary Hart famously ruined his career here when he was spotted cavorting on a sport-fishing boat – appropriately named *Monkey Business* – with a blonde bombshell who was not his wife.)

In 1936 a chap named Neville Norton Stuart turned a Prohibition-era bar into the Bimini Big Game Fishing Club, building on the tourism boom fostered by the Bimini Bay Rod and Gun Club, begun in the early 1920s. Most guests flew in on 'Poppy' Chalk's seaplanes; the company is still in operation today. The opening of an international airstrip on South Bimini in 1957 boosted the Biminis' fortunes. Rockwell International even built an executive retreat (now the Bimini Bay Hotel) here for its top brass and most important customers.

In ensuing decades the Biminis became a major stopover for drug shipments. Things have definitely quieted since the local drug lords were put out of business in the mid-1980s, but plenty of drugs still come and go through the Biminis and narcotics agents still blend into the local island scene.

Bimini has been featured in *Cocoon* and *Silence of the Lambs*, among other movies.

NORTH BIMINI

The main island runs northeast 7 miles, almost ruler-straight and barely 100 yards wide, before curling – like a bent straw – to fan out in a quiltwork of mangrove swamps and fishing flats. The ocean shore's entire length is lined by a narrow sliver of white sand, festooned with sea grape and shaded by palm and pine trees. The beaches are prettier to the north, with the most beautiful beach in Bimini Bay.

Orientation

The only settlement is unpretentious **Alice Town**, raffishly guarding its rugged frontier-town status at the south end of the island. King's Hwy, the main street, runs along the inner shore. Queen's Hwy, a one-lane concrete path, runs along the west shore. Locals joke that the names should be switched depending on the gender of the British monarch, with the main road honoring the ruler. Queen's Hwy and King's Hwy merge in Bailey Town, an extension of Alice Town, 2 miles north. Bailey Town – where most Biminites live – merges into Porgy Bay (also spelled 'Poggy Bay').

The road terminates at the north end of Porgy Bay at the entrance to the undeveloped Bimini Bay Estate. You can continue north along the dirt road that leads to Bimini Bay. A chain bars your way beyond the Bimini Bay Hotel (now closed), but with permission you can continue all the way around the north along a sandy trail cushioned by pine needles. Mangroves line the east shore: The moment you stop, ravenous mosquitoes descend.

Information

Lamour Rolle runs the local tourist office (☎ 242-347-3529, fax 242-347-3530), in the government offices at the north end of town. It's open 8 am to 5 pm Monday to Friday.

The main immigration office (☎ 242-347-3446) is in the government offices on King's Hwy at the north end of Alice Town; it's open 9 am to 5:30 pm Monday to Friday. The main customs office (☎ 242-347-3100) is beside the mail-boat dock. If you're flying to the island, however, you'll clear immigration and customs at either the Chalk's seaplane port in Bimini or the South Bimini airstrip.

There's a Royal Bank of Canada (☎ 242-347-3031) 50 yards south of the Compleat Angler Hotel, open 9 am to 3 pm Monday and Friday and 9 am to 1 pm Tuesday to Thursday.

The post office (☎ 242-347-3546) is in the government offices at the north end of Alice Town; it's open 9 am to 5:30 pm Monday to Friday. A sign says you must be 'properly attired to enter' (no bare feet or slovenly dress). Despite the Biminis' proximity to Miami, mail to the USA can take several weeks. Consider mailing in the US at the end of your trip. Alternatively, you can drop US-bound mail in the post basket at the check-in counter at the Chalk's Seaplane Terminal (see map North & South Bimini); US stamps are accepted. US stamps, however, are *not* accepted by Bahamian post offices.

There are public telephone booths all along the King's Hwy. Some take phone cards; others are coin-operated. The BaTelCo office (☎ 242-347-3311) in Alice Town sells phone cards.

The small library is opposite the customs building at the mail-boat dock.

You can use the coin-operated laundry (from four US25¢ coins per wash) tucked off King's Hwy about 100 yards north of the government offices. Sparklet Laundromat (☎ 242-347-2451) is beside the Trev Inn in Porgy Bay.

The Bimini Medical Clinic (☎ 242-347-3210) is in the government offices. The Bimini Community Medical Clinic is 100 yards north of the Trev Inn in Porgy Bay.

For emergency assistance call ☎ 919 or for the police, ☎ 242-347-3144.

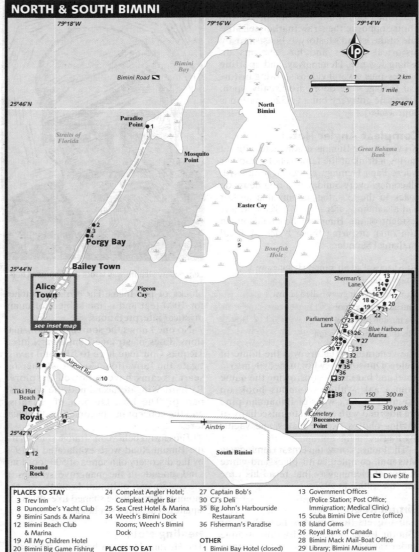

NORTH & SOUTH BIMINI

PLACES TO STAY
3 Trev Inn
8 Duncombe's Yacht Club
9 Bimini Sands & Marina
12 Bimini Beach Club
   & Marina
19 All My Children Hotel
20 Bimini Big Game Fishing
   Club & Marina;
   Gulfstream Restaurant;
   Fisherman's Wharf
23 Bimini Blue Water Resort;
   Anchorage Restaurant
   & Bar

24 Compleat Angler Hotel;
   Compleat Angler Bar
25 Sea Crest Hotel & Marina
34 Weech's Bimini Dock
   Rooms; Weech's Bimini
   Dock

PLACES TO EAT
7 Morgan's Grocery
14 Bimini Breeze
16 Lala's Restaurant
17 Burger Queen
21 Jontra's Food Store
22 Red Lion Pub

27 Captain Bob's
30 CJ's Deli
35 Big John's Harbourside
   Restaurant
36 Fisherman's Paradise

OTHER
1 Bimini Bay Hotel (closed)
2 Spook Hill
4 Sparklet Laundromat
5 Healing Hole
6 Water Taxi to North Bimini
10 Fountain of Youth
11 Shark Laboratory

13 Government Offices
   (Police Station; Post Office;
   Immigration; Medical Clinic)
15 Scuba Bimini Dive Centre (office)
18 Island Gems
26 Royal Bank of Canada
28 Bimini Mack Mail-Boat Office
29 Library; Bimini Museum
31 Customs Building; Mail-Boat Dock
32 Water Taxi to South Bimini
33 Bimini Undersea Adventures;
   Kayak Bimini; Gateway Gallery
37 End of the World Saloon
38 Chalk's Seaplane Terminal

BIMINIS

Bimini Museum

This small one-room museum, above the library opposite the straw market, tells the tale of the island's history. It boasts mostly historical photos and has sections on fishing legends, Hemingway, and sporting figures, plus several videos showing historical footage. The doors are usually open; there's no entry fee but a US$2 donation is appreciated.

Compleat Angler Hotel

No visit to the Biminis is complete without raising a drink at the famous hotel and bar where Papa Hemingway duked it out with all comers every Sunday in a ring he made (back in the '30s, the indomitable author had a standing offer to pay US$100 to any resident of the Biminis who could punch him out), inspiring these lyrics by local Nathaniel Saunders:

Mr Knapp called Mr Ernest Hemingway
A big fat slob.
Mr Ernest Hemingway balled his fist
And gave him a knob.
Big fat slob in Bimini
This the night we have fun.

Lengendary Hemingway wrote and caroused here.

The venerable structure was the home of Helen Duncombe, who turned it into a hotel and bar in 1935, borrowing the name from Izaak Walton's famous book on fishing. The dark walls of Bahamian pine are adorned with an eclectic miscellany of angling photos, license plates, and yachting flags.

The lounge is now the **Ernest Hemingway Museum**, complete with black-and-white photos of Hemingway that recall his time here from 1935 to 1937.

Bimini Road

Scuba divers flock to Moselle's Shoal, or 'Bimini Road' – named for the strange underwater formations resembling paving blocks of a giant aqua-highway – off Paradise Point at the north end of Bimini Bay. The enormous limestone blocks are clearly visible in shallow water, resembling the massive hand-hewn building blocks of the Incas. The 'road' stretches for 1000 feet and is the subject of many mystical interpretations.

No one knows the source of the formations. Tales of strange happenings lured Jacques Cousteau here to film and investigate the formation. Countless other research teams have followed. Explorer Richard Wingate acclaimed the shoal as part of 'The Lost Outpost of Atlantis,' and the concept has become fixed in local lore.

Those who believe in strange sources for the Bimini Road were exhilarated in 1977 by the discovery of a series of 500-foot-long sand mounds in the mangrove swamps in the eastern part of Bimini. From the air, the mounds appear to be shaped like a shark, a square, a cat, and a sea horse.

Healing Hole

The Healing Hole is a bubbling freshwater sulfur spring that's said to possess mystical powers. It's well hidden in a small cove near the Bonefish Hole. The spot, surrounded by mangroves, is just south of Easter Cay and is accessed by a narrow, 200-yard-long meandering cut barely wide enough for extending your arms. You'll need a guide; see Bonefishing & Sport Fishing, later in this section, for likely candidates. The hole is buried deep in the forest. It is canopied by leafy mangroves through which sunlight dapples down magically, sparkling the water like a disco strobe.

When you're wading through the forest, keep to the center, as the slanted edges are slippery. Wear rubber boots for traction and to protect against stubbing your toes on mangrove roots.

Once you're at the hole, ease into the tea-brown water (if only to avoid the mosquitoes). A cool upwelling meets the saline waters, inducing a sudden temperature drop and a nippy surprise for bathers. Fear not crocodiles; the only 'snappers' are juveniles of a nonbiting fish species of that name. The smell is a bit like an unflushed toilet, but it's only natural sulfur. Still, you might want to rinse off at the dock to avoid stares as you head back to your hotel.

During each solstice you may come across bands of visitors standing in the chest-deep water, holding hands and chanting incantations to who knows whom…perhaps the gods of Atlantis? And what of the hole's healing properties? Well, many visitors seem to experience an enigmatic calming sensation. In 1965 Martin Luther King, Jr, came to the Biminis to meditate and draft his acceptance speech for the Nobel Peace Prize. Knowing King's need for solitude, bonefish guide Ansil Saunders took the civil-rights leader to the Healing Hole. Local lore attributes the inspiration for his 'I Have a Dream' speech to the mystical effect of the waters. (Saunders calls the creek 'Dr King's Creek of Peace.')

Other Things to See
Several restaurants, such as Captain Bob's, have **Fishing Halls of Fame** celebrating those who've made the islands' angling heritage an international draw. Dozens of photos and memorabilia recall celebrities and commoners who have pulled prize-winning fish from the drink.

Ask a local to point out **Memory Ledge**. Locals claim that if you lie down here, you'll be flooded with flashbacks.

The ridge above **Spook Hill**, a cemetery at the east end of Porgy Bay, drops to a **beach** popular with locals on weekends for picnics. It's a great spot for enjoying sunsets.

Bonefishing & Sport Fishing
What drew Hemingway more than half a century ago still draws people today – the famous big fish. The catch of the day in winter months is wahoo. All manner of other gamefish is caught year-round. The hot spots are Moselle's Shoal (or Bimini Road) off Paradise Point; just off Bimini Bay's Three Sisters Rock; and off Great Isaac, 15 miles north.

Bimini Big Game Fishing Club & Marina (☎ 242-347-3391, 800-737-1007), Blue Water Marina (☎ 242-347-3166, fax 242-347-3293), at the Bimini Blue Water Resort, and Weech's Bimini Dock (☎ 242-347-3290) all charter boats and skippers and can recommend guides. Typical fees are US$275/400 half/full-day, depending on the size of vessel. Marinas on South Bimini also offer charters; see that section for details.

Big game fishing at its finest

In addition, many Biminites charter boats, including the following:

Frank Hinsey
Nina, a 28-foot Bertram
(☎ 242-347-3072)

Captain Bob Smith
Miss Bonita II, a 51-foot Hatteras
(☎ 242-347-2367)

Captain Jerome Stuart
Miss Bonita, a 32-foot Hatteras
(☎ 242-347-2081)

Captain Tony Stuart
Sir Tones, a 51-foot Hatteras
(☎ 242-347-2656)

Captain Alfred Sweeting
Nutting Honey, a 28-foot Bertram
(☎ 242-347-3447)

For bottom fishing, you need a local guide. The best are talked about reverentially, the way basketball fans talk of Michael Jordan. For snapper, grouper, and grunt, the most highly acclaimed guide is Elvis Saunders (☎ 242-347-3055). For bonefish, try to hire the world champ, Bonefish Ansil Saunders (☎ 242-347-2178), who charges US$150/275 half/full-day. Or try Bonefish Cordell (☎ 242-347-2576), Bonefish Ebbie (☎ 242-347-2053), Bonefish Jackson (☎ 242-347-2315), and Bonefish Tommy (☎ 242-347-3234).

You can rent gear locally. A little store called Bonefish Bill's, opposite the Bimini Big Game Fishing Club, sells bait and tackle.

There are almost a dozen sport-fishing tournaments each year. The Bacardi Rum Billfish Tournament is hosted by the Bimini Big Game Fishing Club in March. The club also hosts the Bimini Break (Blue Marlin) Rendezvous each April. Anglers under age 18 are encouraged to participate in the Big Game Club Family Tournament, hosted in early August, when the Bimini Native Fishing Tournament also pits native skills against those of tourists. The Big Game/Small Boat Tournament is in September. In November anglers fly in for the All Wahoo Fishing Tournament. The Annual Bonefish Willies Tournament and the Adam Clayton Powell, Jr, Memorial Fishing Tournament are held in December. See the Outdoor Activities chapter for additional fishing tournaments.

Diving & Snorkeling

Bimini Undersea Adventures (☎ 242-347-3089, fax 242-347-3079, email: info@biminiundersea.com; in the USA ☎ 305-653-5572, 800-348-4644, fax 305-652-9148), PO Box 693515, Miami, FL 33269, USA, offers dive trips aboard their dive vessels, the 32-foot *Delphine* and 42-foot *Adventurer*. Trips cost US$49/69 for one/two-tank dives, and US$50 for a night dive. An introductory dive costs US$99, including instruction. It offers multiday packages. You

---

Dive & Snorkel Sites

Dive Sites

Bimini Barge – The 270-foot *Sapona* wreck lies close to shore in 90 feet of water, just 75 yards from the Gulf Stream drop-off. The result: a one-two punch of prolific reef life and pelagic big boys.

Bimini Road – Some think these stone monoliths were once part of Atlantis!

Hawksbill Reef – This reef is home to large numbers of lobsters and reef fish. The television series *The Last Frontier* was shot here.

Little Caverns – Mountainous coral formations rise on a sandy bottom at 65 feet.

Off the Wall – The Gulf Stream carries you at this popular drift site at 130 feet along the continental shelf. Beyond, the abyss drops to 2000 feet.

Snorkel Sites

Bimini Shoreline – Coral and rock formations here are smothered by sponges.

Eagle Ray Run – The run is a kind of underwater *Star Wars*, with eagle rays in fighter formation.

LaChance Rocks – Lots of small marine critters hang out near these huge rocks.

Stingray Hole – Friendly stingrays glide around waiting to be hand-fed.

Turtle Rocks – Plenty of coral, fish, and turtles can be found here.

can rent equipment including cylinders for US$10 per day, regulators for US$15, and wet suits for US$10, and get air fills. Underwater camera rentals cost US$25; US$65 for videos. You need to bring your own lights for night dives. Bimini Undersea also maintains permanent moorings at key dive sites. Call VHF channel 06 to find out which are available.

Snorkel trips with Bimini Undersea Adventures cost US$25/15 adults/children; masks, fins, and snorkels go for US$15.

The company also takes divers to swim with dolphins. It offers 'Wild Dolphin Excursions' (US$99/59 adults/children; children under eight free). Interactions usually last about one hour, but the dolphins are in charge. The Web site is www.biminiundersea .com.

Bottom Time Adventures (in the US ☎ 800-234-8464, fax 954-920-5578, info@ bottomtimeadventures.com) offers dolphin swims in summer (US$1395). The Scuba Bimini Dive Centre (see the South Bimini section, later in this chapter; ☎ 242-347-4444) has an office opposite the Bimini Big Game Club.

For getting out on your own, Charlie Weech (☎ 242-347-3290) will rent you a boat at Weech's Bimini Dock.

See the Organized Tours section of the Getting There & Away chapter for trips to the Biminis that leave from Florida.

Kayaking
Sea kayaks are perfect for exploring the shores and mangroves and are easy to use. Take a sun hat and insect repellent.

Bimini Undersea Adventures (see Diving & Snorkeling, above) offers guided kayak tours of the mangrove creeks for US$50/90 half/full-day. It also rents one-person sea kayaks for US$25/45 half/full-day and two-person kayaks for US$40/70. The Web site is www.kayakbimini.com.

Organized Tours
Ashley Saunders, author of *History of Bimini*, leads one-hour guided walking tours of Bimini, beginning at the government offices, for US$10. Call the Bimini Tourist

Office (see Information, earlier in this section).

Special Events
The Biminis' party-hearty islanders put on a Junkanoo extraordinaire each Boxing Day and New Year's Day, and on July 10th in celebration of Bahamian independence. There's also a festive, if early, 5 am Christmas Day parade.

The Bimini Regatta Blast at the end of March features live reggae and other bands. The Bimini Festival in mid-May features a sport-fishing tourney and cookouts.

The Biminis welcome yachters in the annual Bahamas Boating Flings each June through mid-August, when first-time boaters arrive en masse from Fort Lauderdale. See the Sea section in the Getting There & Away chapter for more details.

Places to Stay
All the hotels in Alice Town are strung along King's Hwy. Hotel rooms are usually sold out during big fishing tournaments: *Book early.*

Weech's Bimini Dock (☎ 242-347-3028, fax 242-347-3508, VHF channel 18) has four bay-view rooms overlooking the marina. They're airy and clean with plenty of light, and cost US$75 single or double. An efficiency apartment for four people costs US$150. The postal address is PO Box 613, Bimini, The Bahamas.

The three-story, all-wood-paneled *Compleat Angler Hotel* (☎ 242-347-3122/3185, fax 242-347-3293) has 12 air-con rooms above the venerable bar. The rooms are dowdy, albeit adequate and quaint, with their original pine walls. Bathrooms vary in size; some are tiny. Want to sleep where Hemingway snoozed and penned parts of *To Have and Have Not*? Then take Room No 1. Expect a *lot* of noise at night from the bar downstairs. Rates range from US$65 to US$80. The mailing address is PO Box 601, Bimini, The Bahamas.

The modern *Sea Crest Hotel* (☎ 242-347-3071; marina ☎ 242-347-3477) has 10 modestly furnished air-con rooms, all with both a single and double bed, TV, and patio with marina view. There's no restaurant or pool. Rooms cost US$90; one/two-bedroom suites cost US$200/290. Its postal address is PO Box 654, Bimini, The Bahamas.

The **Bimini Blue Water Resort** (☎ 242-347-3166, fax 242-347-3293) offers full marina facilities. The rooms in the older building are atmospheric; those in the newer extension have a 1960s cheap-motel feel, with wood-veneer walls and faux-bamboo furniture, plus small TV, minifridge, and balcony. Bathrooms have large showers. Rooms cost US$97 single or double year-round. You can also choose a twin-bedroom suite for US$190, the 'Anchorage Cottage' for US$65, or the three-bedroom 'Blue Marlin Cottage' for US$285 (Ernest Hemingway's former home away from home, with a stone fireplace in the wood-paneled lounge). The hotel has a bar and good restaurant – The Anchorage (see Places to Eat, below), plus a pool. A variety of water-based activities are offered, including sport-fishing boats. The mailing address is PO Box 601, Bimini, The Bahamas.

The **All My Children Hotel** (☎ 242-347-3334), named for the late owner's many offspring, has modern yet unremarkable air-con rooms with large, clean bathrooms and small color TVs. They're overpriced at US$95/108/115 double/queen/king. The hotel also has jaded and soulless rooms for US$70 in an older house next door and a cottage with kitchen, plus a huge 'suite' with two double beds for US$220. The hotel was for sale at press time.

The **Bimini Big Game Fishing Club** (☎ 242-347-3391, 800-737-1007, fax 242-347-3392, biggame@janics.com) is a favorite of anglers and yachters and has grounds festooned with bougainvillea and palms. The self-contained hotel has 49 air-con rooms, cottages, and penthouse suites decorated in rattan, with plate-glass sliding doors opening onto patios or balconies. The cottages each have a kitchenette but no cooking is allowed. Room rates start at US$154 moderate, US$170 superior year-round. Cottages cost US$200; suites cost US$310. Facilities include a small pool, two restau-rants, three bars, a gift shop, and tennis courts, plus water sports, excursions, and a large, fully equipped marina. Charter boats are available, as are bonefishing and deep-sea adventures. The mailing address is PO Box 523238, Miami, FL 33152, USA.

In Porgy Bay, the new **Trev Inn** (☎ 242-347-2452, fax 242-347-2498, email sparklet@ batelnet.bs) has seven small rooms, each featuring a full kitchen with stove and mi-crowave, plus cable TV and pleasant, modern furniture. Room rates are US$99 in-cluding tax and continental breakfast. It also has an apartment that rents for US$160.

Others to consider include **Dun's Bay-front Apartments** (☎ 242-347-2093), above Dun's Florist on King's Hwy at the north end of Alice Town; **Sea View Apartments** (☎ 242-347-2444) in Porgy Bay; and **Ellis' Cottage** (☎ 242-347-2483), with three cot-tages in Porgy Bay. The latter's mailing address is PO Box 611, Bimini, The Bahamas.

The Bimini Bay Hotel Marina & Casino (☎/fax 242-347-2171), 3½ miles north of Alice Town, is a proposed remake of the Bimini Bay Hotel, an atmospheric 1950s Miami-deco–style entity atop a rocky head-land at the south end of Bimini Bay. A much-vaunted redevelopment to include condominiums, a golf course, and marina stalled in 2000, and the hotel was closed.

A new hotel under construction south of Weech's Dock was due to open in 2001.

Places to Eat

In the morning everybody rubs their eyes and heads to **Captain Bob's** (☎ 242-347-3260) on the Blue Harbour Marina, south of the Compleat Angler Hotel. Try the excel-lent corned-beef hash with eggs for US$6. It serves the usual seafood dishes, too, and is open at 6:30 am. Also check out **Bimini Breeze** (☎ 242-347-3511), 50 yards north of the Bimini Big Game Fishing Club.

CJ's Deli, opposite the customs building, is a pleasant hole-in-the-wall, serving break-fast and lunch cooked to order. It also sells ice cream and shakes.

The **Anchorage Restaurant & Bar** (☎ 242-347-3166), at the Bimini Blue Water Resort, serves good breakfasts starting at

US$3. Try the Hearty Hemingway with eggs; hash browns or grits; bacon, ham, or sausage; and coffee and juice for US$6.50. Lunchtime sandwiches, burgers, and salads are reasonably priced. Dinners – seafood and steaks – begin at US$14. The grouper with spicy sauce is excellent. (The turkey dinner is, alas, canned.) Box lunches cost US$10.

The elegant *Gulfstream Restaurant* (☎ 242-347-3391), at the Bimini Big Game Fishing Club & Marina, offers seafood, beef, and chicken dishes beginning at US$13. You'll dine to the toe-tapping sounds of Rattee Sweeting playing his acoustic guitar. Try the spicy Bahamian gumbo, pepperpot stew, or smoked game fish. Reservations are recommended. Also here is the *Fisherman's Wharf*, with a large menu of seafood and steaks starting at US$12 and an extensive wine list; the *Barefoot Bar*, serving snacks; and the resort's *Sports Bar & Grill*, which has three satellite TVs and features Bahamian and US dishes, including conchburgers and pizza.

Lala's Restaurant, opposite the Bimini Big Game Fishing Club, is a great place to savor fried chicken, fritters, fish fingers, and other fare with the locals. The intimate *Red Lion Pub* (☎ 242-347-3259), near the Bimini Big Game Fishing Club, specializes in steaks and ribs. Try the braised lamb shanks or the Shrimp Delight (shrimp stuffed with conch, fish, and secret spice), followed with key lime pie or banana cream pie. Entrées begin at about US$10. It's open 6 to 11 pm Tuesday to Sunday.

Snacks are sometimes served at the *Compleat Angler Hotel*, where chef Humphrey Dottin might toss some marlin or other game fish on the grill and offer free sandwiches to all.

At the south end of town is *Fisherman's Paradise* (☎ 242-347-3220), a pleasant place popular with locals. It has indoor and outdoor seating, though the patio catches the stink of nearby conch shells. Try the boil or stew fish breakfast. Pork chops cost US$5; fishpot of the day is US$12. It's open 7 to 11 am, noon to 3 pm, and 6 to 10 pm

daily. A similar, smaller option is *Big John's Harborside Restaurant*, a stone's throw north.

Fast food? You've heard of Burger King, 'Home of the (Big) Whopper'? Well, head to *Burger Queen*, 'Home of the Little Whopper,' across the street from the All Age School at the north end of Alice Town. (The 'Queen' is Ivy Brown.)

In Bailey Town, I recommend *Sandra's Bar & Restaurant* (☎ 242-347-2336) on King's Hwy, a charming little family-style place serving Bahamian favorites. A conch salad or fish snack costs US$6.

Tiger's Den, in Porgy Bay, sells burgers for US$2 and snacks. It also has a convenience store and serves pig or chicken souse for US$5 on Saturday. North of Porgy Bay, the *Bimini Bay Hotel* (☎ 242-347-2171) has an elegant dining room serving lunch and dinner by reservation only.

You can buy Bimini's exquisite, renowned homemade white bread and confections at *roadside shacks* opposite All My Children Hotel and Bimini Big Game Fishing Club. Coconut candy costs US$1, raisin bread is US$2.50, and delicious banana cake is US$5.

For groceries, head to *Jontra's Food Store* or *Manny's Supermarket*, opposite Bimini Big Game Fishing Club, or *Jone's Mini-Supermarket* in Bailey Town.

Entertainment

The larger-than-life *Compleat Angler Bar* (☎ 242-347-2122), where Ernest Hemingway hung his hat, is still the center of action more than 50 years later, drawing colorful, offbeat characters. It's *the* place to be when the calypso band strikes up and the dance floor begins to cook. The band plays three to seven nights a week December to April, and Wednesday night and weekends the rest of the year. One of the rooms holds the original bar, fashioned from Prohibition-era rum kegs. The Angler is open 11 am to 1 am daily.

While Hemingway swigged at the Angler, Adam Clayton Powell, Jr, tippled at the *End of the World Saloon* (☎ 242-347-2094). Locally called the Sand Bar, it's a shack – near Chalk's Seaplane Terminal – about the size of a prison cell, where he kept locals amused with his wit and audacity. The health authorities recently had the original funky shack condemned, and it's been replaced with a modern wooden unit. But the floor is still covered in sand, dogs wander in and out, you can add your scrawl to the graffiti-covered walls, and bras and panties still hang from the rafters and ceiling fans. You still don't have to whip yours off on-site, but many folks do! If the place seems dead, try again after midnight, when the locals stir. It closes at 3 am.

Dancing also takes place on weekends at **Fisherman's Paradise**.

The **Island House Bar** (☎ 242-347-2439), opposite the Red Lion Pub, has a pool table. It's open 11 am to 3 am. Just up the road is **Bimini Breeze** (☎ 242-347-3511). Serious fisherfolk like to gather to tell tall tales at the Harbour Lounge in the Bimini Big Game Fishing Club.

In Bailey Town check out the upstairs bar known as the **Specialty Paris** (there's no sign) opposite the Anglican Church, where an octogenarian named Nathaniel Saunders – alias 'Piccolo Pete' – and his rake 'n' scrape band occasionally put tunes together on a ukulele, conga drum, and spoon and handsaw.

Shopping
For T-shirts and native crafts, check out the Straw Market opposite the library/Bimini Museum, or the Logo Shoppe at Bimini Big Game Fishing Club. Gateway Gallery, next to Bimini Undersea Adventures, sells quality arts and crafts with an island theme.

For duty-free perfumes, head to the Perfume Bar, opposite the customs building. Sue & Joy's Variety Store specializes in jewelry and island-made fragrances; it is open 9 am to 8 pm daily. Island Gems, opposite the Bimini Big Game Fishing Club, sells Cuban cigars and Androsia batik shirts, plus jewelry and perfumes.

The liquor store at Bimini Big Game Fishing Club will deliver to your yacht.

Getting There & Away
Air Chalk's Ocean Airways (☎ 242-347-3024; in the US ☎ 800-424-2557) flies here

from Miami and Fort Lauderdale, Florida; see the Getting There & Away chapter for details. Chalk's seaplanes wing down like swans in the water, then waddle ashore at the south end of Alice Town. An Immigration and Customs office is right there for those arriving from the US. No hand luggage is allowed. All other planes land at the airstrip at the east end of South Bimini (see Getting There & Away under South Bimini, later in this chapter).

Chalk's also operates daily flights from Paradise Island (US$95 one-way, US$175 roundtrip). Locals advise that you also reserve a seat with Sky Unlimited (see Getting There & Away under South Bimini, later in this chapter) if you intend to fly on Chalk's from New Providence or Paradise Island, as Chalk's service is unreliable.

Boat The official port of entry is in Alice Town. Yachters must clear immigration and customs at the Bimini Big Game Fishing Club.

The Bimini Big Game Fishing Club (☎ 242-347-3391, 800-737-1007) is the best-equipped marina and has 100 slips for boats up to 100 feet; it's US$1.25 per foot per day (with a minimum of US$40), plus US$15 for electricity (mandatory). The Bimini Blue Water Marina (☎ 242-347-3166, fax 242-347-3293) has 32 slips and full facilities. Dockage costs US75¢ per foot. Smaller marinas include Weech's Bimini Dock (☎ 242-347-3028), which charges US70¢ per foot per day (US$20 minimum), including water, and Sea Crest Marina (☎ 242-347-3477), which charges US90¢ per foot (US$30 minimum).

The Biminis and North Cat Cay are served from Nassau by the mail boat *Bimini Mack* (12 hours, US$45 one-way). Information and tickets can be had at the mail-boat office in Alice Town on Parliament Lane, 50 yards west of the customs building; its open 9 am to 4 pm Monday to Friday.

Water-taxi service between North and South Bimini is offered by TSL Water Taxi and PHK Water Taxi, departing near the Bimini mail-boat dock; the trip costs US$3.

Getting Around

Golf Cart, Moped & Scooter Most places are within walking distance. However, the fashionable mode of transport is an electric golf cart, which you can rent from the Compleat Angler Hotel (☎ 242-347-3122) or Captain Pat's at the Sea Crest Marina (☎ 242-347-3477). Captain Pat charges US$20 for the first hour, US$10 each additional hour, or US$50/65 half/full-day. You can rent golf carts elsewhere; look for posted signs.

You can rent mopeds and scooters from Bimini Rentals (☎ 242-347-3400) or Sawyer's Scooter Rental (☎ 242-347-2555), both near the Bimini Big Game Fishing Club.

Taxi & Bicycle Bimini Bus Service operates a taxi-van up and down King's Hwy. You can wave it down anywhere. Fares depend on the distance of your trip. A taxi from the seaplane terminal to the Compleat Angler Hotel or Bimini Big Game Fishing Club costs US$3. A tour of the island will cost US$5.

Bimini Undersea Adventures (☎ 242-347-3089, fax 242-347-3079) rents bikes for US$10/15/25 hourly/half day/full day.

SOUTH BIMINI

Less-developed South Bimini has long been favored by US expats, who as early as the 1930s built plush houses on the island. Today the man-made canals of the Port Royal area, to the southwest, are lined with homes used by Yankees who fly or boat in for weekends. The rest of the 5-mile (east to west) by 2-mile (north to south) island is dominated by mangrove, tropical hardwood forest, and brackish pools. Along the south shore, the mangroves surround Duck Lake, full of waterfowl in winter.

A paved road leads from the water-taxi dock, on the northwest tip, to the airport. A dirt road loops around the west and south shores, connecting with Airport Rd.

There's a public phone at Duncombe's Yacht Club and another at the airstrip. For police assistance in South Bimini, call ☎ 242-347-3424.

Fountain of Youth

Ponce de León's mythical Fountain of Youth is said to be 2 miles southeast of the water-taxi berth on Airport Rd. Look for the sign amid the undergrowth to the side of the road. It's actually a natural, 18-inch-wide hole (often dry) in the limestone, surrounded by a crumbling wall...and hardly worth a journey in its own right.

Shipwreck

The remains of the *Sapona*, a concrete ship, lie half-submerged offshore, 4 miles south of South Bimini. It was built by Henry Ford during WWI. During Prohibition it was anchored here and turned into a private club – a favored haunt of the rumrunners. The *Sapona* was wrecked by a hurricane in 1929 and has since been used as a bomber's target and smuggler's cache. Today it sits in 15 feet of water and is favored by divers.

Shark Laboratory

Officially named the Bimini Biological Field Station (VHF channel 88), this education and research center east of Port Royal is affiliated with the University of Miami. Most of the research involves the lemon shark, one of the 13 shark species common hereabouts. Visitors are welcome and the staff is glad to give tours of the facility, time permitting (visiting during bad weather is best, when staff members are on hand). There are no sharks here, however.

Volunteer researchers are needed. Contact Dr Samuel H Gruber (in the US ☎/fax 305-274-0628, sgruber@ rsmas.miami.edu), 9300 SW 99th St, Miami, FL 33176-2050, USA.

Tiki Hut Beach

This lovely 2-mile strip of white sand lines the west shore. The beach is backed by a beautiful stretch of vegetation, including thatch palm, sisal, beach morning glory, and blooming nightshade.

There's a small shade-hut, Tiki Hut, at the island's south end, where snorkeling is best along the rocky shore running south to Corner Reef. Just offshore, 15 feet down, are rock formations similar to the Bimini

BIMINIS

Road, off Bimini. Spotted eagle rays can be seen close to shore.

Buccaneer Point, at the north end of the beach, is also good for snorkeling, especially at high tide. Beware of the strong currents. An airplane forced down by the US Drug Enforcement Administration lies just offshore.

Corner Reef is a small reef protected by rocks and cays half a mile south of Tiki Hut Beach, near the Bimini Beach Club. Its flats are popular with spotted eagle rays, and two large schools of grunts sleep here during the day before going out to feed at night in the beds of grasses. The tiny cave and rocks are home to lobsters, octopuses, and crabs.

Activities

The Bimini Beach Club & Marina (see Places to Stay & Eat, below) charters boats and skippers for sport fishing, and can recommend guides.

Rodney Rolle (VHF channel 68) rents sea kayaks for US$25/40 half/full-day.

See the Getting There & Away chapter for organized tours that leave from the US.

Places to Stay & Eat

Bimini Beach Club & Marina (☎ 242-359-8228, bimini@gate.net; in the USA ☎ 954-725-0919), at the southwest tip of the island, is popular with scuba divers. It has 40 air-con rooms but was closed for restoration at press time, having been taken over by the owners of Bimini Sands & Marina.

Bimini Sands & Marina (☎ 242-347-3500, fax 242-347-3501, fcooney@bimini .com; in the USA ☎ 561-739-9008), half a mile south of Buccaneer Point, is a new development that when completed will have 216 one- and two-bedroom luxury townhouses and 50 boat slips on floating docks. The units are splendid – very spacious and flooded by sunlight – and each has a huge kitchen, large patio, and pleasing decor. The exteriors, which look like they're made of cement and stucco, are actually made of a weatherproof rubber laminate on a steel frame! Rates begin at US$175/1000 daily/weekly for one bedroom; US$300/1750 for

two bedrooms. A two-night minimum applies. Dockage costs from US$30 per night. The mailing address is 6801 Lake Worth Rd, Lake Worth, FL 33463, USA.

Duncombe's Yacht Club (☎ 242-347-3115) is a homey affair with 10 air-con, modestly appointed rooms for US$60. It serves island meals in its pleasing restaurant.

The Petite Conch restaurant at Bimini Sands overlooks the marina, and the resort has a beach grill and Tiki hut.

You can stock up on drinks and snacks at *Morgan's Grocery* or *Morgan's Liquor Store*, the only stores on the island; they're near Duncombe's Yacht Club.

Getting There & Away

Air The airstrip is 3½ miles east of the ferry dock.

Sky Unlimited (☎ 242-347-2301) flies to and from Nassau Friday and Sunday (US$70 each way). Major's Air Services has flights between Freeport and the Biminis (US$50 each way).

Boat TSL Water Taxi and PHK Water Taxi operate water-taxi service between Bimini and South Bimini, departing near the Bimini mail-boat dock; the trip costs US$3.

Bimini Sands Marina charges from US$30 daily for dockage.

Getting Around

TSL or PHK shuttle taxis take you from the airstrip to the Bimini Beach Club or Bimini Sands for US$3, or to the water-taxi berth for US$5 per person, which includes a one-way ferry ride to North Bimini. Minibus taxis wait at the South Bimini wharf for the water taxis.

Rodney Rolle, who runs TSL, rents bicycles at the South Bimini wharf for US$12/15 half/full-day.

TSL Water Taxi offers a tour to the Fountain of Youth and South Bimini for US$5, including bus transfer from your hotel.

NORTH CAT CAY

Ten miles south of South Bimini, North Cat Cay is a private island run as an exclusive, members-only club, beloved by magnates,

Hollywood stars, and the late former US president Nixon. The west shore and top half of the east shore are divided into private lots tucked amid bougainvillea and surrounded by sturdy gumbo limbo, hibiscus, and palm. Only club members and their guests may swim in the pool, sunbathe on the diamond-dust beaches, play a round at the nine-hole Windsor Downs Golf Course, or sleep at the club. Nonmembers are restricted to the marina area. For information on membership, call the Cat Cay Yacht Club (see below).

The medical clinic is open 10 am to noon daily. The staff is available at other times for emergencies.

Places to Stay & Eat
Only members and their sponsored guests are allowed to rent accommodations on the island. The *Cat Cay Yacht Club (☎ 242-347-3565, fax 242-347-3564)* has six hotel rooms with twin beds, TV, and refrigerator for US$150, plus one apartment with a king-size bed, TV, and kitchen for US$250. Some of the 70 privately owned villas are also available.

The *Nauticat* restaurant, overlooking the marina, is open to nonmembers, as is the *Haigh House Bar*. The marina's other facilities are for members and their guests only.

The marina has a *grocery* and a *liquor store*.

Getting There & Away
Air Island Air Charters flies to North Cat Cay from the Fort Lauderdale Jet Center (US$90 one-way). Private charters cost US$375 one-way for the entire plane.

Chalk's Ocean Airways (☎ 242-347-3024) also offers service to North Cat Cay from Florida and Paradise Island.

Private pilots with STOL aircraft can use the 1100-foot-long strip for a landing fee of US$25. There's also a seaplane ramp and helipad.

You can clear immigration and customs here 9:30 am to 4 pm Monday to Friday.

Boat North Cat Cay has an 82-slip marina with commissary (open 10 am to 6 pm Monday to Saturday) and full facilities. Dockage costs US$1.50 per foot per day. 'Transient' boaters are limited to a two-day stay. The *Bimini Mack* mail boat sails here from Nassau weekly (see the North Bimini section, earlier in this chapter).

Getting Around
The island is small enough that you can walk everywhere. Golf carts, however, can be rented at the marina for US$35 daily.

Berry Islands

• **pop 650**

The 30 mostly uninhabited islands and cays of the Berry Islands are strung out north from Chub Cay, 35 miles northwest of Nassau, to Great Stirrup Cay, a span of about 25 miles. The islands sit atop a plateau rising between the Northwest Providence Channel (to the north) and the Tongue of the Ocean (to the south). The largest and most important island is Great Harbour Cay, a 10-mile-long, 1-mile-wide tendon of limestone composed of scrub-covered rolling terrain.

Birds far outnumber humans in the Berries, and it is quite possible to find your own tiny cay where you can cast cares and clothes to the wind.

The islands' history is inconsequential. In the 1830s King William IV of England decided Great Stirrup Cay would make a good home for freed slaves. A settlement – appropriately named Williamstown – was

Highlights

- Shelling on scintillating Shell Beach
- Sport fishing in the Tongue of the Ocean
- Down-home eating in Bullock's Harbour
- Escaping to chic Chub Cay, if money's not a problem

begun, but it failed within a few years, the thin soils yielding no produce. Little else happened until the 1960s, when Douglas Fairbanks, Jr, and others among the US social elite took Great Harbour Cay to their bosoms. The Great Harbour Cay Club was formed, and nine rippling fairways were sculpted on the rises falling down to the sea. Marinas lined with waterfront homes were constructed. Jet-setters briefly flocked, including Brigitte Bardot, Cary Grant, and members of the Rockefeller clan (mobster Meyer Lansky also had a stake). However, the troubled club was closed and ransacked in the mid-'70s.

Several cays are privately owned, such as Bond's Cay, where a private bird sanctuary is maintained, and Cistern Cay, a stone's throw off northwest Great Harbour Cay. Great Stirrup and Little Stirrup (also known as Coco Cay) are the private domains of Norwegian Cruise Line and Royal Caribbean Cruise Lines, which deposit their passengers here for a day of R&R. Passengers are tendered ashore by the *Bahama Rama Mama*, based in Bullock's Harbour on Great Harbour Cay.

GREAT HARBOUR CAY
• **pop 500**

The vast majority of Berry Islanders live on Great Harbour Cay in **Bullock's Harbour**, a small settlement on its own island, connected to Great Harbour Cay by a causeway across the Bay of Five Pirates. The somewhat rundown village is raucous with the crowing of cockerels, which pick at the piles of garbage that are strewn everywhere.

The center of touristy happenings is Great Harbour Marina, built on a narrow channel south of Bullock's Harbour and entered via a slender cut with cliffs to each side.

The island's main attraction is the 8-mile-long white-sand beach along the windward (east) shore, where the shallows run every shade of jade green. The beach is formed by

BERRY ISLANDS

two great scallops: Sugar Beach to the north and Great Harbour Bay to the south. A few dozen expats have houses along the shore. Great Harbour Bay runs south to Shell Beach and a reef (exposed at low tide) that is good for finding sand dollars.

Shark Creek separates Shell Beach and the northern part of Great Harbour Cay from the wild, uninhabited southern part.

The island's west shore comprises mangroves, flats, and brine pools favored by herons and egrets. Most of the interior is smothered in thatch palm, scrub, and casuarinas; snakes and butterflies abound. There are vast flats for bonefishing. A road – Great Harbour Drive – runs the length of the east coast.

The island's annual Homecoming Regatta is held each August, with plenty of home cooking, live music, and fun. Call the local government office (☎ 242-367-8291) to find out exact dates and activities.

Information

Customs (☎ 242-367-8566) and immigration (☎ 242-367-8112) are at the airport.

There's no bank. Public telephone kiosks are found at Great Harbour Marina and at the post office (☎ 242-367-8293) in Bullock's Harbour, which is open 9 am to 5:30 pm weekdays. BaTelCo (☎ 242-367-8199) has an office in Bullock's Harbor. You can buy stamps and drop off mail at Happy People's Gift Shop & Rentals at Great Harbour Marina from 8 am to 5 pm daily.

There's a medical clinic (☎ 242-367-8400) by the post office in Bullock's Harbour, open 9 am to 2 pm weekdays. A doctor makes monthly calls.

The laundromat at Great Harbour Cay Marina takes US$2 in US25¢ coins.

For police assistance, call ☎ 919 or ☎ 242-367-8344. The station is in Bullock's Harbour.

Diving & Snorkeling

There are good dive and snorkel sites northeast of Great Harbour Cay. Great Harbour Marina (☎ 242-367-8005, fax 242-367-8115) offers daily dive excursions. Percy Darville (☎ 242-367-8119), who has an office at the marina, can also guide certified divers.

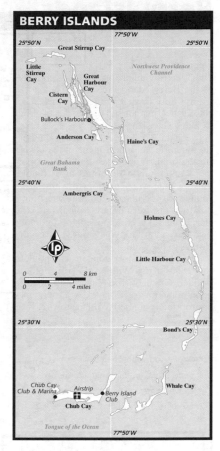

Happy People's Gift Shop & Rentals, at Great Harbour Marina, rents snorkel gear (US$3 for snorkel and fins, US$10 full set). Its postal address is PO Box N-10308, Nassau, The Bahamas.

Bonefishing & Sport Fishing

The Berries are superb for fishing.

The best guide is Percy Darville (see above). He charges US$215/315 half/full-day, including boat charter for bonefishing, and US$350/500 half/full-day for deep-sea fishing.

Happy People's Gift Shop & Rentals (see above) rents a 15-foot bonefishing skiff

BERRY ISLANDS

GREAT HARBOUR CAY

Dive Site
Fishing
Snorkeling

Bay of Five Pirates

BULLOCK'S HARBOUR

Pirates Way Rd

Golf Course

Royal Palm Drive

Causeway

0   250   500 m
0   250   500 yards

PLACES TO STAY
1 Beach Villas
13 Tropical Diversions Resort
   at Great Harbour Cay
18 The Harbour Inn

PLACES TO EAT
2 Mama & Papa T's Beach Club
5 Watergate Bar & Restaurant
8 A&L Grocery
9 Pinder's Grocery
14 Great Harbour Yacht Club
   Restaurant & Bar

15 Tamboo Dinner Club
17 The Wharf

OTHER
3 Government Dock
4 Robert's Lounge & Disco
6 School
7 Police Station
10 Post Office; Medical Clinic
11 BaTelCo
12 Gas Dock
16 Great Harbour Marina; Happy
   People's Gift Shop & Rentals

Northwest Providence Channel

Bullock's Cay

Cistern Cay

Rat Cay

Sugar Beach

Great Harbour Cay

Pirates Way Rd

Highpoint Drive

Fairway Drive

Great Harbour Drive

Little Petit Cay

Petit Cay

Great Harbour Bay

Bullock's Harbour

see inset map

Bamboo Cay

Great Bahama Bank

Royal Palm Dr

Golf Course

Airport

Shell Beach

Shark Creek

Anderson Cay

25°48'W
25°46'W
25°46'W
25°44'W
25°44'W

77°52'W
77°50'W

0   .5   1 km
0   .25   .5 mile

for US$85/105 half/full-day. It also rents fishing rods for US$15 and sells tackle.

Permits are required for visiting sport-fishing boats (US$20). See the Outdoor Activities chapter for details on how to obtain permits.

Golf

There's a nine-hole golf course a half mile southeast of the marina. The clubhouse closed a few years ago, but Happy People's (see above) rents clubs for US$15 a day.

Places to Stay

The Harbour Inn (☎/fax 242-367-8117) offers four rooms on the hill behind Happy People's at the marina. The rooms vary in size, but each is daintily decorated in cool whites with frilly bedspreads. All have a kitchenette, refrigerator, TV, and air-con. Daily rates range from US$75 to US$125; the proprietor's postal address is c/o Happy People's, PO Box N-10308, Nassau, The Bahamas.

Tropical Diversions Resort at Great Harbour Cay (☎ 242-367-8838, fax 242-367-8115, tdbahamas@aol.com; in the US ☎ 954-921-9084, 800-343-7256, fax 954-921-1044) offers two-bedroom, two-story townhouses with patios and decks overlooking the marina, with private docks below, for US$180 to US$300. All are splendidly decorated and have air-con, TV, washing machine, and full kitchen. It also has beach villas.

Paul and Jane Rich (☎ 242-367-8854), who run the Pool Restaurant, have two *Beach Villas* on Great Harbour Bay, with patios facing the ocean. One has a sleeping loft (US$125); the other has two bedrooms (US$300).

Places to Eat

Overlooking the marina, *The Wharf* (☎ 242-367-8762) serves hearty US-style and Bahamian breakfasts from US$5. It also serves salads, soups, and burgers, plus a wide dinner menu with seafood entrées from US$13 and pizzas from US$9. It's open 7 to 11 am and 4 pm to midnight and is closed Tuesday.

The *Great Harbour Yacht Club Restaurant & Bar* (☎ 242-367-8051) is open from noon to 11 pm daily, and offers seafood, grilled meats, and a mouthwatering raisin and rum iced cake.

The elegant *Tamboo Dinner Club* (☎ 242-367-8203), at the marina, is open on Wednesday and Saturday by reservation only (call early). The menu includes boned duck, Bahamian-style spicy chicken, and seafood. Meals cost US$25 to US$30, including soup, salad, entrée, and dessert. When more than 20 people are dining, a buffet is offered, and diners without reservations can sometimes be accommodated. No shorts or hats; jackets are preferred on Saturday night.

In town, *Watergate Bar & Restaurant* (☎ 242-367-8244), opposite the school, serves huge servings of pork chops, peas 'n' rice, and potato salad (US$8). It's a gas at lunchtime, when the school kids in vermilion-and-white uniforms pour in like a storm of sweet peas to order takeout meals.

The cavernous and charmless *Whitewater Restaurant* (☎ 242-367-8050), right opposite the park in Bullock's Harbour, serves the best meals in town, say locals. It's open from 7 am to midnight.

Mama & Papa T's Beach Club offers breakfast and lunch, plus snacks until 3 pm, on the beach facing Great Harbour Bay. Try a burger or Angie's Special Sandwich washed down by a beer or Goombay Smash.

You can buy groceries and general goods at the *Marina Store* (☎ 242-367-8768) in the marina. There are plenty of small grocery stores.

Entertainment

The bar with TV at *The Wharf* is favored by young males from Bullock's Harbour; it's a great place to hear local banter, full of wit and wisdom and innuendo. Nearby, *Tamboo Dinner Club* welcomes drop-in guests. It's open Wednesday and Saturday, with an elegant bar, a library, backgammon boards, and a giant TV with VCR. There's a dress code. Local expat homeowners gather here.

In Bullock's Harbour you can sup with locals at *Watergate*, adorned with signs such as 'No swearing during school hours,' and 'Keep off the grass; take her to a motel.' The *Whitewater Restaurant* has a 'satellite lounge' with large-screen TV that shows imported sports over the bar. To boogie down, check out *Robert's Lounge & Disco*, next to the grocery at the north end of town.

Shopping

For souvenirs, check out Happy People's or Lilly's Boutique at the airport. (Many locals make a killing importing Taiwanese straw hats and selling them on the Stirrup cays to the cruise-ship passengers.)

Getting There & Away

Air Tropical Diversions Air (in the US ☎ 954-921-9084) flies guests in from Fort Lauderdale on charter. Bel Air (☎ 954-524-0115) also flies from Fort Lauderdale on Fridays and Sundays (US$199).

Cat Island Air (☎ 242-361-8021; in Nassau ☎ 242-377-3318) flies from Nassau twice daily (US$50 one-way). Departure times are tentative; leave plenty of time for connecting flights, especially since the return flight goes via Sandy Point (Abacos).

Major's Air Services (in Freeport ☎ 242-552-5778/81, fax 242-352-5788) flies from Freeport to Great Harbour on Monday.

Private pilots must clear entry into The Bahamas on Great Harbour, even if they're heading to Chub Cay.

Boat Boaters and pilots arriving from abroad must clear immigration (☎ 242-367-8112) and customs (☎ 242-367-8566) at Great Harbour Marina (☎ 242-367-8005, fax 242-367-8115, VHF channels 16 and 68), which has 86 slips and full services. It charges US80¢ a foot March to September, US65¢ September through February.

Getting Around

Transportation Unlimited (☎ 242-367-8466/8711) provides a taxi service. Reginald Farrington (☎ 242-367-8089, VHF channel 16) will also taxi you around Great Harbour.

Happy People's rents bicycles (US$2 per hour, US$15 full-day, US$90 weekly with eighth day free) and scooters (US$30/40 half/full-day), as well as Suzuki jeeps (US$40/50 half/full-day or US$300 weekly with the eighth day free). Deposits are required.

Happy People's also rents boats, including 15-foot skiffs from US$100 per day, and 20-foot Welcraft from US$125.

CHUB CAY

The southernmost isle in the chain is virtually the private domain of the Chub Cay Club & Marina, and the most visited of the Berry Islands due to its location midway between Nassau and Bimini. Once the exclusive territory of a small group of wealthy Texans, today it's a favorite of such moneyed folks as Quincy Jones and Bill Cosby, though it's open to daytime visitors and nonmembers. The cay is also favored for itinerant boats and for sport fishing. It has a full-service marina and two beaches.

Chub Cay is shaped like an ox's jawbone. The 4-mile-long island curls north at its east end; this peninsula is Frazer's Hog Cay, where hogs were once raised. A small beach lines the shore.

Chub Cay hosts the annual Bahamas Billfish Championship in March, the Chub Cay Championship fishing tourney each April, and the Chub Cay All Billfish Classic and the Blue Marlin Tournament in July.

Diving

Chub Cay sits at the edge of the Tongue of the Ocean and offers fabulous wall diving. One of the best sites is Mama Rhoda Rock, protected by the Bahamas National Trust and known for its moray eels, lobsters, and yellow trumpetfish, as well as healthy staghorn and elkhorn coral. There's a shipwreck with cannon nearby.

The Scuba Center at the Chub Cay Club (☎ 242-323-2412, info@scubachub.com) offers dive packages, including transport and lodging, if you wish.

Places to Stay & Eat

The tranquil *Chub Cay Club & Marina* (☎ 242-325-1490, fax 242-322-5199, chub@ chubcay.com; in the US ☎ 800-662-8555), at the west end of Chub Cay, looks out onto a splendid horseshoe-shaped beach and has eight recently redecorated rooms facing the freshwater swimming pool. Each has cable TV, refrigerator, and coffeemaker, plus either a king-size bed or two twin beds. It also has nine two- and three-bedroom beachfront villas. The club offers tennis and water sports, including scuba diving and sport fishing. Room rates begin at US$175 year-round; villas begin at US$450. The mailing address is PO Box 661067, Miami Springs, FL 33266-1067, USA.

Berry Island Club (VHF channel 16; in the US ☎ 800-933-3533), a historic two-story building on Frazer's Hog Cay, has three nicely appointed air-con rooms over the stone-and-timber club house; one room has a four-poster bed. The restaurant has a fine reputation among passing sailors (the Cajun dishes – the owners are from Louisiana – are served with veggies from the back garden), and the charming little bar draws mariners. Rates are US$75 to US$125. Its postal address is PO Box 500955, Marathon, FL 33050, USA.

The Chub Cay Club's *Harbour House Restaurant* serves Bahamian and US dishes; it's open 7 am to 9 pm, though only a small adjunct is open to nonmembers. Try the fish in coconut served with mango chutney.

Getting There & Away

The only flights in are from the US. Bel Air (in the US ☎ 954-524-0115) flies from Fort Lauderdale on Friday and Sunday. Island Express (in the US ☎ 954-359-0380) flies from Fort Lauderdale daily except Wednesday and Thursday. Bimini Island Air (in the US ☎ 954-938-8991, fax 954-938-9524, andrea@flybia.com) serves Chub Cay with charters.

The Chub Cay Club provides taxi transfers to and from the airport. The Club's marina (☎ 242-325-1490, VHF channel 18) has 96 slips and charges US$1 per foot per day. Berry Island Club (VHF channel 16; in the US ☎ 800-933-3533) has dockage for boats up to 120 feet.

Abacos

• pop 12,000

The Abacos – at 649 sq miles, the second-largest land mass in the country – lie at the northernmost end of The Bahamas. The boomerang-shaped chain comprises Abaco (the main island) and the Abaco Cays, a necklace of dozens of smaller cays; most lie 2 to 4 miles off Abaco's east shore and stretch 200 miles from Walker's Cay in the northwest to Cherokee Sound in the southeast. The Sea of Abaco, the protected waters in the cays' lee, is favored by yachters. Indeed, the Abacos and yachting go together like wind and sail, earning the chain the nickname 'The Sailing Capital of the World.' The

Highlights

- Strolling through picture-perfect Hope Town on Elbow Cay
- Sailing the Sea of Abaco
- Hiking and bird watching around Hole-in-the-Wall Lighthouse
- Celebrating Christmas and New Year's Junkanoo
- Watching Joe Albury handcraft a wooden boat on Man O' War Cay
- Sport fishing at Walker's Cay and the Shark Rodeo

southernmost island is 106 miles north of Nassau.

The main island, Abaco, technically consists of Great Abaco, the lower part of the island, and Little Abaco, its northwestern extension. Inhabitants of the cays often refer to Abaco simply as 'the mainland.' Abaco is 130 miles long yet rarely more than 4 miles wide.

Most folks live in Marsh Harbour (the largest town in the Abacos) or on the Loyalist Cays (the name comes from these cays' early settlers, who arrived here after fleeing persecution during and after the American Revolution). There are four Loyalist Cays: Elbow, Man O' War, and Great Guana Cays flank Marsh Harbour; Green Turtle Cay lies farther north.

Spanish explorers, after decimating the Indian population on the island they called 'Habacoa' (a Lucayan word), moved on. The French attempted a settlement – Lucayonique – in 1625, but it quickly failed and no remains of it have been found.

After the American Revolution, numerous Loyalists who left the newly independent USA settled in the Abacos. Many of the first to arrive were blacks who departed New York in August 1783 aboard the *Nautilus* and *William*, arriving in 'Abbico' near today's Treasure Cay. They founded the village of Carleton (commemorated today by Carleton Point), named for Sir Guy Carleton, commander-in-chief of the British forces in North America. Another group of Loyalists settled an area known as Cherokee Sound.

Some Carleton settlers left to found Marsh Harbour and settle the cays, each of which started with only one or two families (the Alburys on Man O' War, the Lowes and Sawyers on Green Turtle, the Malones and Bethels on Elbow). Their names linger on today in quaint communities whose residents cherish their past and independence. (On the eve of Bahamian independence in 1972, Loyalist Abaconians petitioned the

Dive & Snorkel Sites

Dive Sites

Adirondack Wreck – Forty feet below the surface near Man O' War Cay lies this fascinating wreck, with cannon still exposed.

Barge – This WWII landing craft lies 40 feet down and is now home to myriad fish species.

Bonita Wreck – Another WWII wreck, this one is a freighter at 60 feet below the surface, populated by groupers that like to be hand-fed.

Old Wreck – Encrusted by coral and undulating sea whips, this wreck has an octopus that lives in the anchor winch.

Pirate's Cathedral – This swim-through cavern off Walker's Cay offers a religious experience, with rays, parrotfish, and groupers.

Queen's II – Schools of dolphin frequent this spot at the outer edge of the Little Bahama Bank.

Sandy Cay – This cay claims one of the largest stands of elkhorn coral in the world.

San Jacinto Wreck – This Civil War–era steamship sits at 40 feet below the surface, guarded by a friendly moray eel.

Shark Rodeo – One of the Abacos' premier sites: You kneel on the seabed in 35 feet of water off Walker's Cay and watch sharks swirl around you as they feed.

Sue's Reef – WWII relics are scattered 30 feet below the surface; damsels, snappers, and grunts guard the ledges and canyons.

Tarpon Dive – Named for the game fish that swim along this wall, which drops 50 feet off Green Turtle Cay. You can hand-feed a moray eel here. And Big Ben, the oversize grouper, says 'Hi!'

Snorkel Sites

Angelfish Reef – Want to be one with swarms of angelfish? Head here.

Blue Strip Reef – A fish-spawning area with lots of tropical fish.

Crawfish Shallows – This is the best place to find lobster…and sleeping nurse sharks.

Elkhorn Park – Octopi favor this site, which has acres of elkhorn coral.

Fowl Cay Reef – 'Gillie,' a friendly grouper, guards this reef.

Hope Town Reef – This reef has elkhorn and brain coral, plus schooling fish.

Meghan's Mesa – You'll find corals of every species here.

Mermaid Reef – No, there are no mermaids…but there are plenty of big green moray eels and schools of snapper.

Pelican Park – Eagle rays patrol this area, where sea turtles carouse.

The Pillars – Huge coral pillars are found here.

Sandy Cay Reef – This reef is known for spotted eagle rays and huge stingrays.

Sanka Shoal – This is the place to see puffer fish, which inflate like spiked basketballs.

Smuggler's Rest – An upright plane wreck where porcupine fish have taken the controls.

Spanish Cannon – A Spanish galleon hangs on the reef, with cannon scattered about.

White Hole – Grottoes and caverns surround a protected coral basin.

Wrecker's Reef – Once favored by pirates plundering treasures, today it's preferred by sea turtles.

Queen to be separated from The Bahamas as a British crown colony; when they were denied, the most radical elements even contemplated a revolution.)

The Loyalist settlers were mostly merchants and craftspeople. After a brief and unsuccessful tenure as farmers, many moved on. Of the 2000 settlers, only 400 stayed, equally divided between blacks and whites. Those that remained resorted to what they knew best – trading, boatbuilding, and salvaging shipwrecks – and became relatively wealthy. The cays even evolved a vernacular New England–style architecture, called 'Abaco style,' notable for its high-pitched roofs and wide clapboarding. The form became so popular that in the 1860s many prefabricated houses were made and shipped to Florida.

The Abacos' gaily painted, gingerbread clapboard houses are still framed by white picket fences and set along narrow streets bordered by hibiscus, vivid pink oleander, and bougainvillea as red as bright lipstick. And the dour Protestantism of the Loyalists also lives on. Each cay has followed its own church (Gospel Church on Man O' War, the Church of God on Green Turtle) with its own traditions. When the preacher speaks on Green Turtle, the devout shout, *'Hallelujah, brother!'* On Man O' War they mumble, *'Mmmmm-mm.'* Abaconians even talk with a quaint Elizabethan lilt, nurtured by the isolation of island life.

There are no large, showy hotels. Instead the Abacos boast homey cottages and inns on talcum-fine beaches or alongside the many marinas. Walker's Cay, sitting on the edge of the Gulf Stream in the far northwest, is one of The Bahamas' prime sportfishing sites. Coral reef gardens fringing the Atlantic beckon divers and snorkelers. See the Dive & Snorkel Sites sidebar for details on the Abacos' best sites.

Ashore, most of Abaco is smothered with scrub and pine forest, good for bird watching and nature hikes (access is via a web of logging roads) and popular with locals hunting wild boar.

The Abacos boast four national parks, notably Pelican Cays Land & Sea Park, preserving the barrier islands and coral reefs

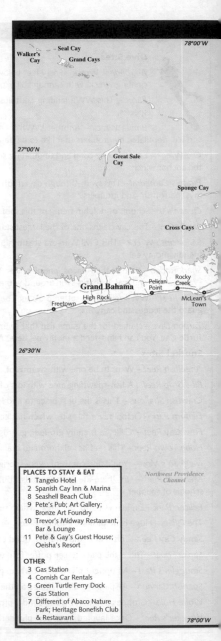

PLACES TO STAY & EAT
1 Tangelo Hotel
2 Spanish Cay Inn & Marina
8 Seashell Beach Club
9 Pete's Pub; Art Gallery;
    Bronze Art Foundry
10 Trevor's Midway Restaurant,
    Bar & Lounge
11 Pete & Gay's Guest House;
    Oeisha's Resort

OTHER
3 Gas Station
4 Cornish Car Rentals
5 Green Turtle Ferry Dock
6 Gas Station
7 Different of Abaco Nature
    Park; Heritage Bonefish Club
    & Restaurant

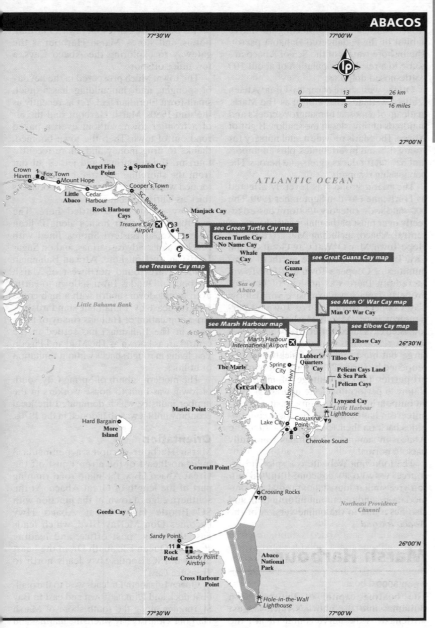

ABACOS

ATLANTIC OCEAN

Crown Haven
Fox Town
Mount Hope
Little Abaco
Cedar Harbour
Angel Fish Point
Spanish Cay
Cooper's Town
SC Bootle Hwy
Rock Harbour Cays
Treasure Cay Airport
Manjack Cay
see Green Turtle Cay map
Green Turtle Cay
No Name Cay
see Treasure Cay map
Whale Cay
Great Guana Cay
see Great Guana Cay map
Sea of Abaco
Little Bahama Bank
see Man O' War Cay map
Man O' War Cay
see Marsh Harbour map
Marsh Harbour International Airport
The Marls
Spring City
Lubber's Quarters Cay
see Elbow Cay map
Elbow Cay
Tilloo Cay
Pelican Cays Land & Sea Park
Pelican Cays
Mastic Point
Great Abaco
Great Abaco Hwy
Lake City
Casuarina Point
Lynyard Cay
Little Harbour Lighthouse
Hard Bargain
More Island
Cherokee Sound
Cornwall Point
Crossing Rocks
Northeast Providence Channel
Gorda Cay
Sandy Point
Rock Point
Sandy Point Airstrip
Abaco National Park
Cross Harbour Point
Hole-in-the-Wall Lighthouse

0   13   26 km
0   8   16 miles

77°30'W
77°00'W
27°00'N
26°30'N
26°00'N
77°30'W
77°00'W

south of Tilloo Cay; and, in the far south, Abaco National Park, protecting the native habitat of the endangered Bahama parrot. The inshore waters of the Sea of Abaco are home to a resident population of about 100 bottle-nosed dolphins.

Off the west shore of central Great Abaco is a vast wetlands area known as The Marls, made up of a mosaic of mangrove creeks and hundreds of tiny isles in the shallow Bight of Abaco. The Marls provide a vital nursery for young fish and invertebrates, plus an important habitat for ducks, egrets, and herons. The bonefishing is superb.

The island group was severely affected by Hurricane Floyd in September 1999. The 600-mile-wide, category 4/5 storm passed directly over most of the major settlements of central Abaco, including Marsh Harbour, Hope Town, Man O' War Cay, Great Guana Cay, Treasure Cay and the northern communities of Cooper's Town and Fox Town. Incredibly, there was no loss of life, but property damage was extensive, with Elbow Cay, Cooper's Town, and Fox Town hit particularly hard. Marsh Harbour and the touristed cays fared better. Many hotels and seaside rental units were damaged by storm surge, but most renovated quickly and had reopened by spring 2000 (fortunately, many properties took advantage of insurance claims to perform overdue upgrades). And an outpouring of community spirit and volunteerism has helped get the local communities back on their feet. When I visited the Abacos in summer 2000, things were fully back to normal.

The following Web site is a splendid resource: www.go-abacos.com; http://oii.net/ can give similar tourist, boat rental, accommodations, and restaurant information, and also has a link to the online version of the *Abaco Journal*.

Marsh Harbour

• **pop 5000**
The boating capital of the northern Bahamas and the nation's third-largest settlement is the nerve center (if not the soul) of the Abacos, with most of the area's businesses, dive operators, marinas, hotels, and stores. Marsh Harbour is the gateway to exploring the Abaco Cays, a few miles offshore.

The town, which prospered in the heyday of sponging and shipbuilding, has a quiet, small-town Floridian feel. Yet as recently as the mid-1980s, Marsh Harbour had the air of a frontier town, without even a paved road out of town. Then the town boomed, thanks to drug money and, more recently, tourism. Today marinas and jetties jut out from the shoreline like tree branches, festooned with sleek yachts and motorboats as thick as Christmas baubles.

Many expats have settled here. The wealthiest have their homes along Pelican Shores Rd; at Eastern Shores, lined with beaches and shady casuarinas; and on Sugar Loaf Cay, just offshore. African-Bahamian residents are found northwest of Marsh Harbour in Dundas Town, a down-to-earth, even tumbledown suburb with a high crime rate (at least by Bahamian standards). A large population of Haitians (many of them born in The Bahamas) has settled in the central areas known as The Mud and Pigeon Pea, living in rough shacks without sanitation or utilities.

The modern suburb of Spring City, south of town, was built to house workers in the lumber industry, which dominated the local economy until it was abandoned in the 1970s.

Orientation
Marsh Harbour occupies a peninsula 3 miles northeast of the airport, just off the Great Abaco Hwy, the main road running part of the length of Great Abaco. At the southern edge of town, at the junction with SC Bootle Hwy, Great Abaco Hwy becomes Don McKay Blvd, which leads past the clinic, post office, and leading stores to Queen Elizabeth Dr, in the heart of town. (SC Bootle Hwy leads north to Treasure Cay.)

Queen Elizabeth Dr leads west to the mailboat dock and Dundas Town and east to Bay St, running along the south shore of Marsh Harbour's touristy bay, where the marinas and

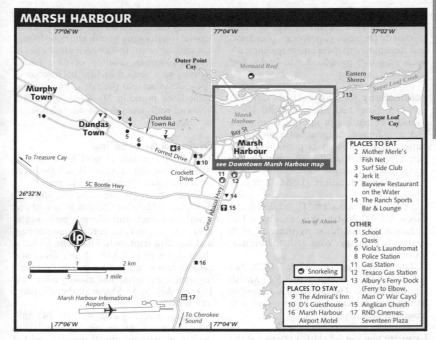

MARSH HARBOUR

PLACES TO EAT
2 Mother Merle's Fish Net
3 Surf Side Club
4 Jerk It
7 Bayview Restaurant on the Water
14 The Ranch Sports Bar & Lounge

OTHER
1 School
5 Oasis
6 Viola's Laundromat
8 Police Station
11 Gas Station
12 Texaco Gas Station
13 Albury's Ferry Dock (Ferry to Elbow, Man O' War Cays)
15 Anglican Church
17 RND Cinemas; Seventeen Plaza

PLACES TO STAY
9 The Admiral's Inn
10 D's Guesthouse
16 Marsh Harbour Airport Motel

hotels are concentrated. Bay St leads past the Abaco Beach Resort and ends at Albury's Ferry Dock; it continues as a dirt road along Eastern Shore, ending at Parrot Point.

From Bay St, Pelican Shores Rd leads north around a second peninsula – Pelican Shore – that curls around the northern side of Marsh Harbour to form the bay.

Information

Tourist Offices Don Cornish and Wynsome Ferguson run the Abaco Tourist Office (☎ 242-367-3067, fax 242-367-3068) in Memorial Plaza on Queen Elizabeth Dr.

Immigration The immigration office (☎ 242-367-2536) is in the upper level of Dove Plaza, along with the post office, on Don McKay Blvd.

Money Barclays Bank (☎ 242-367-2152) has an office at Don McKay Blvd and Queen Elizabeth Dr. CIBC Bank (☎ 242-

367-2166), one block south, has a drive-through teller. Scotiabank (☎ 242-367-2142) and Royal Bank of Canada (☎ 242-367-2420) have nearby branches. Banks are open 9:30 am to 3 pm Monday to Thursday and 9:30 am to 5 pm Friday.

The ATM at Scotiabank operates 24 hours and accepts VISA, MasterCard, and any bank card on the Plus or Cirrus network.

Post & Communications The post office (☎ 242-367-2571) is on Don McKay Blvd.

Public telephone booths are prominently located. BaTelCo's main office is on the south side of Queen Elizabeth Dr.

Radio Abaco offers the latest news, plus music and chat shows on 93.5FM.

Travel Agencies Try the Travel Spot (☎ 242-367-2817) in Memorial Plaza on Queen Elizabeth Dr, or A&W Travel Service (☎ 242-367-2806) off Don McKay Blvd near the Abaco Shopping Centre.

Bookstores The Loyalist Shoppe (☎ 242-367-2701), at Don McKay Blvd and Queen Elizabeth Dr, sells paperbacks plus local and foreign newspapers and magazines; it's open 9 am to 5 pm Monday to Friday and until noon Saturday.

Publications The glossy *Abaco Life*, PO Box 1366, Fort Lauderdale, FL 33302, USA, focuses on matters of interest to tourists. Pick it up free of charge at hotels and other outlets in the Abacos. It publishes a detailed foldout map of the Abacos with separate maps of major settlements, which costs US$3 at retailers (US$5 including postage).

The *Abaco Journal* (☎ 242-367-2580), PO Box AB-20642, Marsh Harbour, Abaco, The Bahamas, is a monthly news journal; US$20 yearly. It's on the Web at http://oii.net/Journal/.

The Abaconian (☎ 242-367-2677, fax 242-367-3677), PO Box AB-20551, Marsh Harbour, Abaco, The Bahamas, is a monthly newspaper dedicated to local issues and news; US$2 yearly.

Laundry You can get clothes washed at the coin-op Harbour View Marina Laundromat, on Bay St, or at Viola's Laundromat out near Dundas Town.

Medical Services The government-run Marsh Harbour Clinic (☎ 242-367-4010) is just off Don McKay Blvd. The nearby private Abaco Medical Clinic (☎ 242-367-4240, emergencies outside hours ☎ 242-367-3159) is open 9 am to noon and 2 to 4 pm Monday to Thursday and 9 am to 2 pm Friday. And Abaco Family Medicine (☎ 242-367-2295) has a clinic in the south of town just off Don McKay Blvd. Toothache? Head to the Greater Abaco Dental Clinic (☎ 242-367-4070) on Don McKay Blvd.

For pharmaceuticals, try The Chemist Shoppe (☎ 242-367-3106) on Don McKay Blvd.

Emergency The police station (☎ 242-367-2560) is west of downtown on Dundas Town Rd. In an emergency call ☎ 919.

Seaview Castle

The only site of interest is the canary-yellow 'castle' overlooking Marsh Harbour from a hill east of town. It was once the home of Evans Cottman, author of *Out Island Doctor*, who settled in Marsh Harbour in 1944. Cottman told the tale of building his crenellated home in *My Castle in the Air*. You can walk from downtown in about 20 minutes.

Diving & Snorkeling

The Abaco Beach Resort Dive Centre (☎ 242-367-4649), at Abaco Beach Resort & Boat Harbour, offers dive packages.

Dive Abaco (☎ 242-367-2787, 800-247-5338, fax 242-367-4779, dive@dive-abaco.com), at Conch Inn Marina, rents scuba gear, offers resort and certification courses, and has dive trips daily. The menu includes shark dives from US$80. Night dives and camera rental can be arranged and snorkeling trips are offered. The mailing address is PO Box AB-20555, Marsh Harbour, Abaco, The Bahamas.

Logan 'Skeet' LaChance (☎ 242-367-2014), a famous marine-life expert and divemaster, offers educational two-day snorkel trips that teach various aspects of fish and coral interaction. Trips for up to six people are preceded by a slide presentation.

Abaco Outback offers a variety of snorkel trips on its tours; see the Organized Tours section, below.

Snorkeling is good at Mermaid Reef on the north side of Marsh Harbour.

Boating & Sailing

Sailboats and motorboats can be rented at most marinas. Demand often exceeds supply, so make reservations early.

The Moorings (☎ 242-367-4000, fax 242-367-4004; in the US ☎ 727-535-1446, 888-952-8420, fax 727-530-9747), at Conch Inn Marina, has seven types of vessel, including sailboats from 35 feet to 46 feet and catamarans, all fully equipped, with CD/stereo, snorkel gear, and dinghy. Rates vary according to season, beginning at US$270/1860 daily/weekly for the cheapest vessel. Three-day weekend specials are offered. Skippers,

DOWNTOWN MARSH HARBOUR

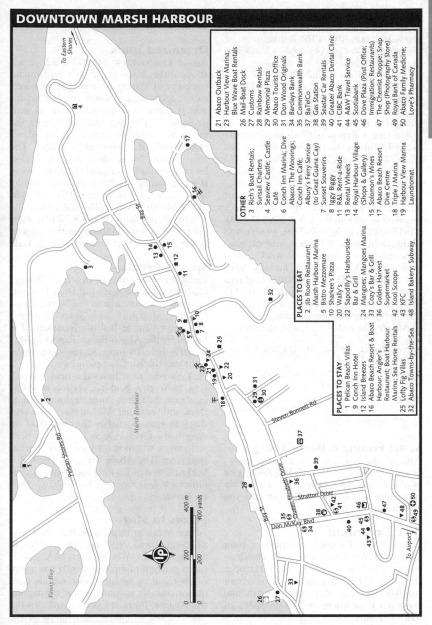

PLACES TO STAY
1 Pelican Beach Villas
9 Conch Inn Hotel
12 Island Breezes
16 Abaco Beach Resort & Boat Harbour; Angler's Restaurant; Boat Harbour Marina; Sea Horse Rentals
25 Lofty Fig Villas
32 Abaco Towns-by-the-Sea

PLACES TO EAT
2 Jib Room Restaurant; Marsh Harbour Marina
5 Bistro Mezzomare
10 Sharkee's Pizza
20 Wally's
22 Sapodilly's Harbourside Bar & Grill
24 Mangoes; Mangoes Marina
33 Cozy's Bar & Grill
36 Golden Harvest Supermarket
42 Kool Scoops
43 KFC
48 Island Bakery; Subway

OTHER
3 Rich's Boat Rentals; Sunsail Charters
4 Seaview Castle; Castle Café
6 Conch Inn Marina; Dive Abaco; The Moorings; Conch Inn Café; Albury's Ferry Service (to Great Guana Cay)
7 Sunset Souvenirs
8 Iggy Biggy
11 R&L Rent-a-Ride
13 Rental Wheels
14 Royal Harbour Village (Shops & Gallery)
15 Solomon's Mines
17 Abaco Beach Resort Dive Centre
18 Triple J Marina
19 Harbour View Marina Laundromat
21 Abaco Outback
23 Harbour View Marina; Blue Wave Boat Rentals
26 Mail-Boat Dock
27 Customs
28 Rainbow Rentals
29 Memorial Plaza
30 Abaco Tourist Office
31 Don Wood Originals
34 Barclays Bank
35 Commonwealth Bank
37 BaTelCo
38 Gas Station
39 Seastar Car Rentals
40 Greater Abaco Dental Clinic
41 CIBC Bank
44 A&W Travel Service
45 Scotiabank
46 Dove Plaza (Post Office; Immigration; Restaurants)
47 The Chemist Shoppe; Snap Shop (Photography Store)
49 Royal Bank of Canada
50 Abaco Family Medicine; Love's Pharmacy

cooks, sailboards, and kayaks are available. In The Bahamas write PO Box AB-20469, Marsh Harbour, Abaco, The Bahamas; in the US write 19345 US Hwy 19 N, Clearwater FL 33764.

Blue Wave Boat Rentals (☎ 242-367-3910, fax 242-367-3911), at Harbour View Marina, charges US$95 to US$140 daily; US$350 to US$370 for three days; and US$575 to US$840 weekly.

Sea Horse Rentals (☎ 242-367-2513, fax 242-367-2516), at Boat Harbour Marina, has 18- to 24-foot boats. Its postal address is PO Box AB-20013, Marsh Harbour, Abaco, The Bahamas.

The Abaco Beach Resort & Boat Harbour hosts Florida Yacht Charters (☎ 242-367-4853, fax 242-367-4854; in the US ☎ 305-532-8600, 800-537-0050, fax 305-535-3179, go-abacos@floridayacht.com), with sailboats, catamarans, and power cruisers, and weekly rates from US$1650 to US$6000. The local mailing address is PO Box AB-20511, Marsh Harbour, Abaco, The Bahamas; in the US write 1290 5th St, Miami Beach, FL 33139. The Web site is www.floridayacht.com.

Also try the following rental agencies:

Laysue Rentals (☎ 242-367-4414, fax 242-367-4356), Triple J Marina

Rainbow Rentals (☎ 242-367-4602, fax 242-367-4601), Union Jack Dock

Rich's Boat Rentals (☎ 242-367-2742, fax 242-367-2682, richsrentals@oii.net), between Sunsail Charters and Fish House

Sport Fishing & Bonefishing

Any of the marinas can arrange sport fishing. Jay Sawyer (☎ 242-367-3941), one of the best guides around, and Captain Justin Sands (☎ 242-367-3526) can take you bonefishing.

Boat Excursions

The *William H Albury*, a schooner built on Man O' War Cay in 1963, sails weeklong and weekend passages from Marsh Harbour to Green Turtle Cay and Little Harbour for US$150 per day. Call Out-Island Schooner Expeditions (☎ 242-367-3386), or write PO Box AB21013, Marsh Harbour,

Abaco, The Bahamas. The Web site is www.heritageschooner/albury.com.

Organized Tours

Abaco Outback (☎ 242-477-5682, email: abacooutback@oii.net), an ecotourism company at Harbour View Marina, offers nature tours exploring the Abacos' wilder side. It offers a full-day guided 'safari tour' to Snake Cay, with kayaking through the mangrove systems, lunch on an island beach, and a drift snorkel for US$65. The trip is good for birding and for orchid lovers (orchids thrive amid the mangroves). It was planning to offer overnight camping trips. Its mailing address is PO Box AB-21013, Marsh Harbour, The Bahamas.

Sand Dollar Tours (☎ 242-367-2189) offers guided bird watching and nature trips to Abaco National Park and Hole-in-the-Wall.

Special Events

The Abacos are home to an array of fishing-related events. In April the Boat Harbour All Fish Tournament and the North Abaco Championship are held in Marsh Harbour. The Penny Turtle Billfish Tournament is hosted by the Abaco Beach Resort in May or early June. In June the resort hosts the Bahamas Billfish Championships.

A Native Crafts Festival is held in April. Regatta Week is held in early July in Marsh Harbour and other towns, featuring sailing races and festivities. Mid-summer also sees the Bahamas Goombay Summer Fest. In August the Great Abaco Triathlon is held, including a triathlon for kids and a 'Sprintman' race. The Abaco Heritage Festival is held in October. Contact the Abaco Tourist Office (☎ 242-367-3067, fax 242-367-3068) for details.

Places to Stay

Abaco Vacation Rentals (in the US ☎ 978-874-5995, 800-633-9197, fax 978-874-6308, 40 Stone Hill Rd, Westminster, MA 01473) offers many rental properties. It has a free 64-page catalog listing private rentals, from quaint cottages to luxury villas, throughout the Abacos. There are photos and descriptions of the properties and maps of the islands showing their locations on its Web site, www.abacovacations.com.

Bahamians tend to lay their heads at less touristed properties, such as *The Admiral's Inn* (☎ 242-367-2022), a modest property on the way to Dundas Town, with six simple rooms for US$55 each.

Another option is *D's Guesthouse* (☎/fax 242-367-3980, pager 357-6944), at the corner of Crockett and Forrest Drs on the west edge of town. It has four one-bedroom units and two two-bedroom units in a modern home. Albeit soulless, they offer simple yet pleasant furnishings, air-con, TV, refrigerator, microwave oven, and coffeepot. It's a 20-minute walk to the nearest restaurant, but there is a small grocery store and a food stall serving meals to each side. The office closes at 5 pm; if you're checking in after that, be sure to make appropriate arrangements. Rates are US$70 to US$85 low-season, US$80 to US$95 high-season, including tax. Its mailing address is PO Box AB-20655, Marsh Harbour, Abaco, The Bahamas.

If all you want is a bed near the airport, check into the soulless *Marsh Harbour Airport Motel* (☎ 242-367-4402, fax 242-367-4401), with seven air-con rooms, plus laundry. The spacious, modestly furnished rooms each have a TV and phone and cost a steep US$78 single or double.

Island Breezes (☎ 242-367-3776), on Bay St, is a small roadside property with eight modestly furnished, air-con rooms for US$84 single or double. There's no pool or restaurant; the mailing address is PO Box AB-20453, Marsh Harbour, Abaco, The Bahamas.

I like the *Lofty Fig Villas* (☎/fax 242-367-2681; in North America ☎ 800-688-4752), on Bay St, comprising six spacious, canary-yellow, air-con efficiency cottages in a serene setting centered on a small pool. Each has a queen-size bed, sofa bed, bright tropical colors, heaps of light, and a screened patio opening onto the lush lawn. Rates for one or two people are US$94/611 nightly/weekly in summer; US$114/737 winter. Its postal address is PO Box AB-20437, Marsh Harbour, Abaco, The Bahamas.

The *Conch Inn Hotel* (☎ 242-367-4000, fax 242-367-4004, moorings_conchinn@ oii.net; in the US ☎ 800-688-4752), on Bay St, has nine spacious, recently refurbished air-con rooms, each with a queen-size and a double bed, cable TV, and tiny patio opening to a sand garden with kiddies' playground. There's a 75-slip marina, excellent restaurant and bar, and a small freshwater pool. It's operated by The Moorings yacht charter company. Rooms cost US$90/120 double low/high season; each extra person costs US$10. The postal address is PO Box AB-20469, Abaco, The Bahamas.

Abaco Towns-by-the-Sea (☎ 242-367-2287, for reservations ☎ 800-247-5338, fax 242-367-4779, abacotowns@dive-abaco.com) sustained severe damage during Hurricane Floyd but was swiftly renovated and now offers 68 tastefully appointed, sparkling white, two-bedroom self-catering units – billed as 'villas' – nestled in rolling terrain and facing the Sea of Abaco. There's a large pool, tennis courts, and organized activities. Some rooms are a bit dark, but the property is quiet. Units cost US$699/899 garden-view/ ocean-view weekly. The postal address is PO Box AB-20486, Marsh Harbour, Abaco, The Bahamas.

Pelican Beach Villas (☎ 242-367-3600, 800-642-7268, pelican@g-net.net; in the US fax 912-654-3300), nestled amid casuarinas off Pelican Shores Rd at the head of the harbor, has six air-con, two-bedroom cottage villas with ceiling fans, kitchen, phones, and TVs, plus private decks with sliding glass doors. Rattan furnishings are enhanced by a tropical motif and sloped wooden ceilings. Housekeeping is available. Hammocks are slung outside. There's an 87-foot dock. Mermaid Reef lies offshore. Rates begin at US$185/195 single/double nightly, US$1245/ 1295 weekly. The postal address is PO Box AB-20304, Abaco, The Bahamas.

The *Abaco Beach Resort & Boat Harbour* (☎ 242-367-2158, 800-468-4799, fax 242-367-4154, abrandbh@oii.net) boasts a Hawaiian feel, with tall palms and lush lawns sloping down to a small beach and the Sea of Abaco. It was battered by Floyd but has received a full makeover. The 72 overlarge, handsomely appointed rooms (20 were added in 2000) have limestone tile floors, gracious contemporary furnishings, kitchenettes, and private patios. It also has six two-bedroom cottage-bungalows with kitchens and private decks. All have air-con, phone, and satellite TV. There are also four suites, costing US$350 single or double. Rooms cost US$195 to US$225 single or double; deluxe rooms cost US$265. Cottages cost US$550. There's an attractive octagonal pool with swim-up bar, a kiddies' pool, tennis courts, dive shop, and a gift shop and laundry, plus the Angler's Restaurant overlooking the marina. Its mailing address is PO Box AB-20511, Marsh Harbour, Abaco, The Bahamas.

Places to Eat

My favorite place to breakfast is the *Bistro Mezzomare* (☎ 242-367-2319) at Conch Inn Marina. It's also open daily for lunch and dinner (except Tuesday). It serves burgers, Caesar salad (US$8), sandwiches, pastas, plus island specialties such as seafood soup (seafood sautéed in garlic and white wine and stewed in light tomato sauce (US$18). Entrees cost US$18 to US$28. Try the tasty grouper calypso. The bar is famous for its Conch Killer.

Also try *Cozy's Bar & Grill* (☎ 242-367-5090) on Queen Elizabeth Dr, 100 yards west of a CIBC Bank. This modestly elegant eatery serves island dishes and is very popular with locals for lunch and dinner. It's open 7 am to midnight and has a bar.

At *Castle Café* (☎ 242-367-2315), atop the hill on the east side of Marsh Harbour, sandwiches cost US$3 to US$7, and Gail Cottman's home creations, such as chicken-rice soup for US$4, should be washed down by the house drink, the Castle Creeper, for US$3.50. It's open 11 am to 5 pm Monday to Friday.

To be one with locals, head to *Mother Merle's Fish Net* (☎ 242-367-2770), a down-to-earth spot in Dundas Town. It serves moderately priced native dishes; it's open for dinner only. Several funky little snack shops line the road in Dundas Town: Try *Jerk It*, selling spicy jerked chicken, pork,

and fish, and *Surf Side Club* (☎ 242-367-2762) at Dundas Point.

Craving your favorite regional cuisine? Head to the *Golden Grouper* (☎ 242-367-2301) in Dove Plaza. It serves regional specialties on specific nights, such as Chinese on Wednesday. It's open 7 am to 3 pm and 6 to 9 pm, except Sunday, 7 am to 3 pm only.

Want to try wild boar? Check out *The Ranch Sports Bar & Lounge* (☎ 242-367-2733), south of downtown on Don McKay Blvd, a satellite lounge that also serves wild boar souse.

The Abaco Beach Resort's elegant *Angler's Restaurant* (☎ 242-367-2158) serves some of the finest and most creative cuisine in town. Appetizers such as lime grouper with wasabi sauce begin at US$4; entrees such as curried shrimp madras begin at US$20. Breakfasts start at US$7. It's open 7 am to 10 pm.

The lovely and popular *Mangoes* (☎ 242-367-2366), on Bay St, serves dinner specials – usually international dishes with a Bahamian twist – on a shaded deck. It also serves snacks such as popcorn shrimp and steak fajitas. Prices for main dishes are in the mid-US$20s range. Happy hour is 5 to 7 pm. Wednesday is margarita night.

For romantic, candlelit ambience, try *Wally's* (☎ 242-367-2074), in a two-story house on Bay St with terrace and indoor dining. Entrees such as coconut shrimp begin at US$20. It also serves soups, salads, and sandwiches. It's open 11:30 am to 3 pm and 6 to 9 pm Tuesday to Saturday. Reservations are suggested.

For colorful, down-to-earth ambience, try nearby *Sapodilly's Harbourside Bar & Grill* (☎ 242-367-3498), which serves native dishes on a deck with shade trees. It also has burgers and sandwiches, plus a catch-of-the-day for US$19. It's open 11:30 am to 3 pm and 6:30 to 9:30 pm Tuesday to Saturday and 1 to 3 pm Sunday.

The *Jib Room Restaurant* (☎ 242-367-2700), at Marsh Harbour Marina on the north side of the marina, has barbecue specials at 7 pm on Wednesday and Sunday nights, with live island music. Take your pick of chicken or lobster plus ribs (Wednesday) or steak (Sunday). The set price is US$20. It also has snacks and lunch Wednesday to Monday.

Bayview Restaurant on the Water (☎ 242-367-3738), on Dundas Town Rd, specializes in Bahamian seafood. It has a Sunday champagne brunch and a Saturday-night prime rib special; it's open 11 am to 11 pm daily.

For fast food, try *Subway* (☎ 242-367-2798) on Don McKay Blvd. *Sharkee's Pizza* (☎ 242-367-3535), opposite the Conch Inn Hotel, will deliver.

Kool Scoops, next to CIBC Bank in town, has a zillion flavors of ice cream.

For fresh-baked breads and pastries, head to *Flour House Bakery* (☎ 242-367-4233) on Bay St, open 7 am to 6:30 pm Monday to Saturday; or *Island Bakery* in B&V Plaza across from the Abaco Shopping Centre.

You can buy meats, canned goods, and produce at *Golden Harvest Supermarket*, on Queen Elizabeth Dr.

Entertainment

Mariners gather at the *Sand Bar* (☎ 242-367-2871) at the Abaco Beach Resort, where there's live music nightly except Tuesday. There's live music on Saturday evening at *Wally's*, with dancing helped along by Wally's Special, the lethal house drink guaranteed to wipe out your motor skills. Several other restaurants also have live music (see the Places to Eat section, above).

Other touristed favorites are *Sapodilly's*, with a pool table and two-for-one cocktails during happy hour (6:30 pm Friday), plus live calypso on Friday and Saturday nights, and Monday night football on the TV; and *Mangoes* (☎ 242-367-2366), which has live music on Tuesday and Thursday evenings. The latter's house drink is named Hurricane Libby after Libby Roberts, the lady of the house.

The Ranch Sports Bar & Lounge (☎ 242-367-2733), on Don McKay Blvd, has dart boards, plus pool tables and satellite TV. There's live music on Sunday evening. It has disco on Friday and Saturday nights; as does *Disco 404*, where the cover is US$10.

In Dundas Town, the *Oasis* and *Surf Side Club* are earthy satellite lounges that double as dance clubs on weekends (see the Marsh Harbour map).

The *RND Cinemas* (☎ 242-367-4382), at Seventeen Plaza near the airport, shows first-run movies.

Shopping

For duty-free watches, jewelry, china, and crystal, try Solomon's Mines (☎ 242-367-3191), outside the entrance to the Abaco Beach Resort, or the John Bull shop (☎ 242-367-2473) on Bay St.

Royal Harbour Village, opposite the entrance to the Abaco Beach Resort, features handcrafted jewelry at Sand Dollar-Abaco Gold (☎ 242-367-4405) and a fabulous array of art at the Juliette Art Gallery, with originals and prints by leading Bahamian artists. Cultural Illusions, downstairs, sells island-made batiks, dolls, and candles.

Don Wood – self-proclaimed 'Carver, Sailor, Rum Barrel Bailer' – sculpts wood, gold, and other metals into stunning creations, from earrings to desktop ornaments such as turtles and swordfish. His studio, Don Wood Originals (☎/fax 242-367-3681), is the blue shack on the east side of Memorial Plaza fronted by a swordfish.

Sunset Souvenirs (☎ 242-367-2658), across from the Conch Inn Hotel, sell beautiful resortwear and jewelry, as does Island Gallery (☎ 242-366-0354). Mangoes has a large selection of T-shirts and resortwear. Iggy Biggy (☎ 242-367-3596), on Bay St across from the Conch Inn Marina, sells resort clothing, T-shirts, gifts, jewelry, and island music.

Look for the vibrant watercolors on silk by Marjolein Scott, carried by Cultural Illusions in Memorial Plaza on Elizabeth Dr.

You can buy photographic equipment at Snap Shop (☎ 242-367-3020) on Don McKay Blvd on the way out of town.

Getting There & Away

Air Marsh Harbour's airport has restrooms, telephones, and a small snack bar. There's no gift shop or rental-car service. See airlines' international routes and numbers in the Getting There & Away chapter.

Bahamasair (in Marsh Harbour ☎ 242-367-2095) flies from West Palm Beach daily

(US$215 roundtrip), and from Nassau several times daily (US$60 one-way).

Taino Air (in Marsh Harbour ☎ 242-367-3193) flies between Freeport and Marsh Harbour via Treasure Cay (US$99). Abaco Air (☎ 242-367-2266) offers charter service from Marsh Harbour, as does Cherokee Air (☎ 242-367-2089).

Island Express (in Marsh Harbour ☎ 242-367-3597) flies from Fort Lauderdale, West Palm Beach, and Miami.

Boat Albury's Ferry Service (☎ 242-367-3147, fax 242-365-6487) operates scheduled water taxis to Elbow, Man O' War, and Great Guana Cays (see those cays' sections in this chapter for details). The dock for Elbow and Man O' War is at the east end of Bay St; that for Great Guana Cay is at The Conch Inn Marina. The ferry has its schedule online at http://oii.net/alburysferry.

The mail boat *Captain Gurth Dean* departs Nassau for Marsh Harbour at 6 pm Tuesday, returning to Nassau at 7 pm Thursday (12 hours, US$45 one-way) from the mail-boat dock near the customs building on W Bay St. The vessel also stops at Hope Town, Treasure Cay, and Green Turtle Cay. Call ☎ 242-393-1064 to inquire about or confirm the schedule.

The Boat Harbour Marina (☎ 242-367-2736, fax 242-367-2819) at Abaco Beach Resort has 165 slips for yachts up to 150 feet and complete facilities. Dockage costs US$1.50 per foot. The Conch Inn Marina (☎ 242-367-4000, fax 242-367-4004), another full-service facility, charges US60¢ per foot.

Mangoes Marina (☎ 242-367-4255, fax 242-367-3336) charges US65¢ a foot. Farther west is Triple J Marina (☎ 242-367-2163). Marsh Harbour Marina (☎ 242-367-2700), on the north side of the bay, has 50 slips and a wide range of services.

Getting Around
Car, Moped & Motorcycle Seastar Car Rentals (☎ 242-367-2840, fax 242-367-4356), 100 yards south of Golden Harvest Supermarket, rents economy- to full-size US cars from US$70/350 daily/weekly, with free airport transfers. It's open 7 am to 6 pm Monday

to Saturday. Sunday pickup and drop-off can be arranged. Its mailing address is PO Box AB-20438, Marsh Harbour, Abaco, The Bahamas.

A&P Auto Rental (☎ 242-367-2655) is located in K&S Auto on Don McKay Blvd.

Rental Wheels (☎ 242-367-4643), on Bay St, offers mopeds for US$10 per hour, US$25 to US$35 daily, plus cars for US$75 to US$85 daily.

Taxi Fares are pre-established. Taxis run up and down Marsh Harbour. A ride between Marsh Harbour's airport and most hotels costs US$10 for two. A ride between Albury's Ferry Dock in Eastern Shores and points in Marsh Harbour range from US$2 for the hotels to US$12 for the airport.

Bicycle Rental Wheels (☎ 242-367-4643), on Bay St, charges US$2 per hour, US$5 half-day, US$8 full-day, and US$35 per week for beach cruisers. R&L Rent-a-Ride (☎ 242-367-4289) rents adults' and kids' bicycles for US$5/8/35 half-day/full day/weekly.

Sea Horse Rentals (☎ 242-367-2513, fax 242-367-2516), at Boat Harbour Marina, has bicycles for US$10 the first day, US$5 per extra day, and US$35 weekly.

Loyalist Cays

East of Marsh Harbour lie three Loyalist Cays: Elbow, Man O' War, and Great Guana. (The fourth Loyalist Cay, Green Turtle, lies many miles to their northwest, accessed from its own dock; see the Northwest of Marsh Harbour section.)

ELBOW CAY
Six miles east of Marsh Harbour is Elbow Cay. **Hope Town**, anchored in a well-protected harbor at the north end of the 5-mile-long island, is one of the quaintest of all Caribbean villages, boasting about 100 superbly preserved and gaily painted old homes.

The picturesque hamlet (pop 450) was founded in 1785 by Loyalists from South Carolina (their 300 or so blond, blue-eyed descendants are still here, interacting – but not intermarrying – with a black population). Originally called 'Great Harbour,' the Lilliputian place has a quaintness that you may imagine only Hollywood could create.

The town, pickled in aspic on the east slope of a splendid harbor, is pinned by a 120-foot red-and-white–ringed lighthouse. Two narrow lanes encircle the village; the streets are called 'Up Along' and 'Down Along' (formally, 'Back St' and 'Bay St'). Most cottages and churches are painted white, with gingerbread trim and shutters of rich pastels, and fronted by gardens full of bougainvillea and hibiscus spilling their blossoms over picket fences and walls.

A few locals still make a living by fishing or boatbuilding, but most rely on the tourist trade. A town council maintains strict building and business codes. No cars are allowed in the village. The only sounds are the thrum of motorboats, chimes of church bells, echoes of hammers on wood, coos of doves, and the rustle of the breeze in the palms.

The town has seen several periods of boom, beginning with the US Civil War, when the island prospered as a base for blockade-runners carrying English goods to and from the Southern states. By 1887 Abaconian pineapples were Hope Town's primary export, shipped to Jacksonville, Florida, aboard a fleet of locally built schooners. By 1897 the trade had been replaced by sponging, plus exports of turtles' shells, oranges, and sisal. In 1938 a blight wiped out the sponge beds and the industry, too.

In the early 20th century – the zenith of the sponging industry – Hope Town was home port to more than 200 two- and three-masted schooners. Sponging fostered a local shipbuilding industry that reached its peak in the 1920s.

Winer Malone, the last of a great generation of Hope Town boatbuilders, still crafts traditional Abaco dinghies entirely from memory, with no power tools whatsoever, from trees he cuts himself on Great Abaco. (He no longer accepts callers or gives interviews unless you're interested in having a boat built.)

Elbow Cay sustained considerable damage from Hurricane Floyd, although the town itself fared not too badly and the famed Hope Town Lighthouse, although damaged, was left standing. The boatbuilding skills were put to good use in the clean-up and rebuilding, which included restructuring the sand dunes that Floyd washed away on the white-sand beaches that rim the Atlantic shore.

North of Hope Town, a dirt road leads past Cook's Cove to Hope Town Point, the northern tip of the island. Queen's Hwy leads south from Hope Town past White Sound, a large flask-shaped bay opening to the leeward shore. There has been considerable private development here in recent years. The White Sound area sustained massive destruction during Hurricane Floyd: the road was washed away, cutting Elbow Cay in half, and most of the homes in the White Sound area were completely destroyed.

The intriguing history of the island is related in *A Guide & History of Hope Town* by Steve Dodge and Vernon Malone; it's available at Vernon's Grocery & Upper Crust Bakery (see the Places to Eat section).

Hope Town hosts Regatta Week in July, featuring sailing races and festivities.

Information

There's a meager visitors' information bureau in the peppermint-green building facing the government dock on Bay St. It's not staffed. You can pick up leaflets here and glean information from the bulletin boards.

The police station (☎ 242-366-0108) and post office (☎ 242-366-0098) are upstairs in the same building. BaTelCo is at the south end of town. Many businesses and homes communicate by VHF channel 16. Malone Estates (☎ 242-366-0060, fax 242-366-0157), on Back St, has an 'Out Island Internet Computer Suite' that charges US$5 for the first 15 minutes of Internet access, US50¢ per minute thereafter. It's open 10 am to 4 pm Monday to Saturday.

CIBC (☎ 242-366-0296), on Fig Tree Lane, is open 10 am to 2 pm Tuesday, and 10 am to 1 pm Friday.

Ida Albury at the Suds Away Laundry, on Back St near Hope Town Temptations,

ELBOW CAY

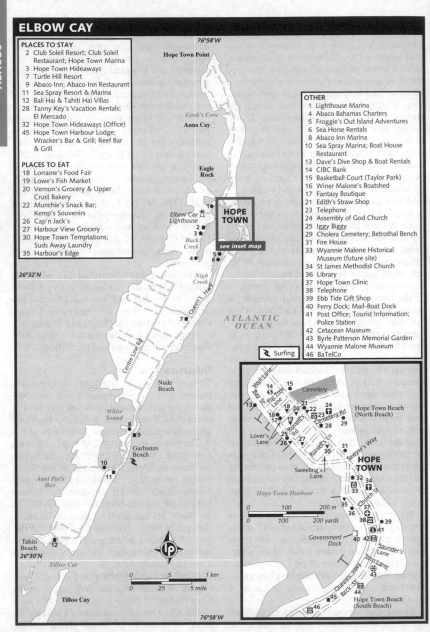

PLACES TO STAY

2 Club Soleil Resort; Club Soleil Restaurant; Hope Town Marina
3 Hope Town Hideaways
7 Turtle Hill Resort
9 Abaco Inn; Abaco Inn Restaurant
11 Sea Spray Resort & Marina
12 Bali Hai & Tahiti Hai Villas
28 Tanny Key's Vacation Rentals; El Mercado
32 Hope Town Hideaways (Office)
45 Hope Town Harbour Lodge; Wracker's Bar & Grill; Reef Bar & Grill

PLACES TO EAT

18 Lorraine's Food Fair
19 Lowe's Fish Market
20 Vernon's Grocery & Upper Crust Bakery
22 Munchie's Snack Bar; Kemp's Souvenirs
26 Cap'n Jack's
27 Harbour View Grocery
30 Hope Town Temptations; Suds Away Laundry
35 Harbour's Edge

OTHER

1 Lighthouse Marina
4 Abaco Bahamas Charters
5 Froggie's Out Island Adventures
6 Sea Horse Rentals
8 Abaco Inn Marina
10 Sea Spray Marina; Boat House Restaurant
13 Dave's Dive Shop & Boat Rentals
14 CIBC Bank
15 Basketball Court (Taylor Park)
16 Winer Malone's Boatshed
17 Fantasy Boutique
21 Edith's Straw Shop
23 Telephone
24 Assembly of God Church
25 Iggy Biggy
29 Cholera Cemetery; Betrothal Bench
31 Fire House
33 Wyannie Malone Historical Museum (future site)
34 St James Methodist Church
36 Library
37 Hope Town Clinic
38 Telephone
39 Ebb Tide Gift Shop
40 Ferry Dock; Mail-Boat Dock
41 Post Office; Tourist Information; Police Station
42 Cetacean Museum
43 Byrle Patterson Memorial Garden
44 Wyannie Malone Museum
46 BaTelCo

Hope Town Point

Cook's Cove

Anna Cay

Eagle Rock

Elbow Cay Lighthouse

HOPE TOWN

see inset map

Back Creek

Nigh Creek

ATLANTIC OCEAN

Surfing

Centre Line Rd

Queen's Hwy

Nude Beach

White Sound

Garbanzo Beach

Aunt Pat's Bay

Tahiti Beach

Tilloo Cut

Tilloo Cay

76°58'W

26°32'N

26°30'N

HOPE TOWN

Cemetery

Hope Town Beach (North Beach)

Lover's Lane

Sweeting's Lane

Hope Town Harbour

Government Dock

Saunder's Lane

Hope Town Beach (South Beach)

Queens Hwy

Back St

Church St

Sawyer's Way

0   100   200 m
0   100   200 yards

0   .25   .5   1 km
0   .25   .5 mile

charges US$2/lb for washing, drying, and folding. It's open daily except Wednesday and Sunday.

The Hope Town Clinic (☎ 242-366-0108), also by the government dock, has an emergency room and pharmacy.

Hope Town has a volunteer fire and rescue brigade. If you need emergency assistance, call VHF channel 16, then channel 76; alternately, you can reach the individual volunteers at ☎ 242-366-0087/0363/0023/4044/0143.

There's a kiddies' playground on Bay St. Hilary Albury (☎ 242-366-0290) acts as a babysitter.

Elbow Cay Lighthouse

Hope Town is dominated by the historic, candy-striped Elbow Cay Lighthouse on the harbor's west shore. You can ascend the 100 steps for a picture-perfect view. Construction was begun in 1838 and completed in 1863 after lengthy delays caused by local wreckers fearful of the lighthouse's effects on their profiteering. They vandalized the structure and cut off water supplies to the laborers. It still shines today through a revolving Fresnel lens that magnifies light from a kerosene mantle.

Wyannie Malone Museum

This splendid little museum on Back St is a repository for an eclectic miscellany of artifacts and exhibits, including a unique collection of genealogical information pertaining to Loyalist settlers and Lucayan Indians. The kitchen and bedrooms are maintained as they would have looked two centuries ago. Even the outhouse is still in place.

The museum is staffed by volunteers from 10:30 am to 12:30 pm Monday to Saturday (hours are curtailed May to September); US$1. You can call ☎ 242-366-0033 to request a special opening. At last visit, it was due to move to a new, purpose-built location on Bay St in traditional style.

Byrle Patterson Memorial Garden

This tiny garden, just northeast of the museum, has two bronze sculptures of dolphins and a seagull shaded by pine trees. It slopes to the ocean where steps lead onto Hope Town Beach. There's a gazebo for admiring the view.

Cholera Cemetery

These mildewed graves, on a thread-thin lane named Cemetery Rd off Back St, recall the cholera epidemic that swept through Hope Town in 1850, claiming one-third of the population. Note the weathered Betrothal Bench at the crest of the hill.

Cetacean Museum

This tiny museum, in the old peppermint-green building facing the government dock on Bay St, has a few whale bones, charts, a fine mural, and a map showing sightings of whales in Bahamian waters. Eleven species have been sighted in recent years in and around Elbow Cay. Admission is free.

South of Hope Town

South of Hope Town, Queen's Hwy swings inland then turns south as Centre Line Rd, emerging again on the dramatic, wave-pounded Atlantic shore. Nudism is tolerated along a portion of the beautiful beach. The road continues south along a narrow peninsula between the ocean and White Sound, a shallow, mangrove-lined bay with the Sea Spray Resort & Marina at its southern end.

The road around White Sound was washed away during Hurricane Floyd, as were most of the houses between the Abaco Inn and Sea Spray Resort, and much of the Nude Beach was stripped of sand…all since restored.

The road continues to Tahiti Beach at the southwestern tip of the cay. It extends as a sandbar along the peninsula and is backed by an extensive palm grove. Marine turtles still come ashore to nest on the champagne-colored beach. Floyd took much of the gloss away, but it still draws boaters who come to lie on the sand or wade in the shallows.

Diving & Snorkeling

The reefs off the Atlantic side are excellent for diving and snorkeling. The waters near Hope Town and the northern tip of the cay offer calmer waters and are easily reached by swimming from shore. Staghorn, elkhorn, star, and brain coral are abundant.

Dave's Dive Shop & Boat Rentals (☎ 242-366-0029, fax 242-366-0420) offers daily dive trips (US$50/65 one/two-tank) and snorkel trips (US$30). It rents equipment. Hope Town Harbour Lodge (see Places to Stay, below) offers snorkel trips and rents snorkel gear.

Sea Spray Marina (☎ 242-366-0065) offers snorkel trips and rents snorkel gear for US$8 per day.

Bonefishing & Sport Fishing

Bonefishing guides include Dave Malone (☎ 242-366-0029) and Truman Major (☎ 242-366-0101).

Sea Spray Marina (see Diving & Snorkeling, above) arranges reef fishing and bonefishing for US$100 half-day in your boat; it also arranges deep-sea fishing for up to four people for US$350/500 half/full day, including the boat.

Elbow Cay's weeklong, family-oriented Abaco Anglers Tournament in mid-April requires little gear and costs just US$70/25 adults/kids. If you enter the bonefishing category, note that Maitland Lowe has won every year since 1972! The Lighthouse Marina (☎ 242-366-0004) can give you specific dates and more information.

Surfing

The offshore waters boast at least six good surfing breaks on the south Atlantic shore, especially in winter months. The Bahamas' top surfing is at the reef off Garbanzo Beach, 2 miles south of Hope Town. Bring your own gear.

Boat Excursions

Froggie's Out Island Adventures (☎ 242-365-6494, froggies@mail.batelnet.bs), down the narrow cove south of the harbor, offers full-day excursions to Great Guana Cay with snorkeling at Fowl Cay; and to Little Harbour with snorkeling at Sandy Cay. Both cost US$45. It also offers half-day snorkeling (US$35) and scuba (US$50/60 one/two-tank) trips.

Albury's Ferry Service (in Marsh Harbour ☎ 242-367-3147) offers sightseeing excursions for US$390 for up to 10 people.

Places to Stay

Hope Town The *Hope Town Harbour Lodge* (☎ 242-366-0095, 800-316-7844, fax 242-366-0286, info@hopetownlodge.com), atop a bluff at the south end of Hope Town, is lovingly tended by owners Raymond and Catherine Ketay. It has 20 simply furnished yet brightly decorated and thoroughly renovated rooms, many overlooking the harbor. Cottages spill down the garden toward the beach. Some have air-con; others have ceiling fans. All have picture-postcard views and lively tropical fabrics. Facilities include a splendid restaurant and bar, a small pool and sun deck, and water sports. Bicycle and boat rentals – including powerboats – are offered, plus snorkel gear. Year-round rates range from US$110/120 single/double harbor-view to US$140/160 oceanfront. An old two-story house, sleeping six, costs from US$300 daily, US$1500 weekly. The staff are super-friendly and efficient. They will prepare a picnic basket on request.

Club Soleil Resort (☎ 242-366-0003, fax 242-366-0254, info@clubsoleil.com; in the US ☎ 800-688-4752), on the west side of the harbor, offers a taste of the Mediterranean. It has six air-con rooms, each with TV/VCR, refrigerator, and coffeemaker, plus a balcony facing the harbor. There's a restaurant, freshwater pool, and bar where you can sip the house special, the Tropical Shock. The resort has diving, snorkeling, and a complimentary boat service. Access is by boat. Rooms cost US$115/120 double summer/winter, US$125/130 triple.

Nearby, *Hope Town Hideaways* (☎ 242-366-0224, 800-688-4752, fax 242-366-0434, enquiries@hopetown.com, 1 Purple Porpoise Place, Hope Town) has more than 20 villas in an 11-acre complex south of the lighthouse. The views are fabulous! All have central air-con, kitchen, housekeeper, cathedral ceiling, gazebos with porch swings, TV/VCR, and exquisite furnishings; many also have a private swimming pool. There's a marina and a sandy harborfront. Visit its Web site at www.hopetown.com for details and rates; they are rented by the week only. The Web site can link you with a map and information on rental villas all over Elbow Cay.

There are dozens of other cottages for rent, such as *Hope Town Villas* (☎ 242-366-0030, 800-688-4752, fax 242-366-0377, htvillas@batelnet.bs), comprising two beautifully restored air-con Loyalist cottages; nightly rates are US$175/225 single/double, US$200/250 three or four people; weekly rates are US$1050/1350 and US$1200/1500. Two-story 'Cozy Villa' overlooks a small park 50 yards from the beach; it has three bedrooms and one bathroom. The two-bedroom 'Harbour Villa' faces the harbor and lighthouse and has its own dock. A 50% prepayment is required. Write to Patte and Michael Myers, General Delivery, Hope Town, Abaco, The Bahamas.

Also try *Sunrise Beach House* (☎ 242-366-0224, fax 242-366-0434), a three-bedroom cottage with exquisite decor in West Indian style and with net-draped four-poster bed. Peggy and Chris Thompson rent out this charming house for US$900 to US$3500 per week depending on the number of people.

Other house rentals are represented by agents such as *Tanny Key's Vacation Rentals* (☎ 242-366-0053, fax 242-366-0051), which offers 17 houses in Hope Town and 13 elsewhere on the island. The houses range in size and price, beginning at about $650 per week for one or two people at Los Pinos, a one bedroom, one bath apartment downtown. Tanny has an office at El Mercado on Back St. Her Web site is www.tannykey.com.

South of Hope Town The intimate, unpretentious *Abaco Inn* (☎ 242-366-0133, 800-468-8799, fax 242-366-0113, abacoinn@batelnet.bs), about 2 miles southwest of Hope Town, crowns a bluff between two beaches at the narrowest point of the island. Hurricane Floyd socked the hotel full on the snout and the older parts of the inn were washed out to sea. Fully rebuilt and refurbished, it has 12 air-con, wood-shingled cabins surrounded by silver buttonwood, sea grape, and palm. Each has ceiling fans, porches with chaise longues and beach chairs, and hammocks slung between palms. There's a lively bar in the stone-and-wood lodge. Year-round rates are US$110/125 single/double harbor-view,

US$125/140 ocean-view, US$195 to US$235 suites.

Turtle Hill Resort (☎/fax 242-366-0557, 800-339-2124, amy@turtlehill.com) has three beautiful cottage-style villas around a swimming pool poised over the Atlantic on the outskirts of town on Queen's Hwy. Each handsomely appointed, air-con two-bedroom villa sleeps six people and has cable TV/VCR, ceiling fans, and fully equipped kitchen. Rates, ranging from US$190 to US$270 nightly low season, US$280 to US$380 high season; US$1100 to US$1500 weekly low season, US$1650 to US$2050 high season, include use of a golf cart.

The villagelike, pink-and-green *Sea Spray Resort & Marina* (☎ 242-366-0065, fax 242-366-0383, seasprayres@oii.net) has four one-bedroom and four two-bedroom villas, all 'cottage-style,' with air-con, full kitchen, king-size beds, and sofa beds. The ocean-front villa was destroyed by Hurricane Floyd, which also badly damaged the marina, but it, too, had been repaired when I last visited. One/two-bedroom harbor-view villas cost US$159 to US$220 nightly, US$95 to US$1325 weekly; ocean-view two-bedroom villas cost US$291/1750 nightly/weekly. A three-night minimum applies; rates are for one to four people. There's a new pool and the clubhouse has a pool table and TV. Free Sunfish sailing is offered and surfboards, sailboards, bicycles, and snorkel gear are available for rent. There's a free shuttle to Hope Town; water taxis take 20 minutes.

Abaco Vacation Rentals (see Places to Stay in the Marsh Harbour section, earlier in this chapter) represents over 30 villas and cottages on the cay, from the deluxe, four-bedroom *Bali Hai* on Tahiti Beach (US$6687 to US$9187 weekly depending on the number of guests) and the 200-year-old *Parliament Hill House* (from US$1275 weekly), to *Bill-n-Coo*, an exquisite cottage overlooking Parrot Cay (US$575 weekly). Most properties require a three- or seven-day minimum stay. Bali Hai, *Tahiti-Hai*, and *Tip-o-Tahiti* are also represented by Hope Town Hideaways, based in the exquisite pink-and-white cottage on Bay St.

You can view Bali Hai (in the US ☎970-925-5519, fax 970-948-2850, batchelor@aspeninfo.com) and other properties at the following Web sites: www.10kvacationrentals.com or www.hopetown.com.

Places to Eat
Hope Town The Hope Town Harbour Lodge's waterfront *Reef Bar & Grill* (☎ 242-366-0095) is a good place to savor conch burgers, island nachos with conch salsa, or grouper fritters; meals average US$5. The Caesar salad is excellent. Free fritters and veggies are served during happy hour (4 to 5 pm).

The fanciest place in town is the hotel's *Wracker's Bar & Grill*, in the upper dining terrace, where you can dine in or out. Breakfast is served Monday to Saturday, with daily specials (such as huevos rancheros on Friday) for US$6.50. A Sunday champagne brunch costs US$20 (US$10 for children under 12); reservations are required. Dinner is served 6:30 to 9:30 pm Tuesday to Saturday. Try the grouper and vegetable spring rolls for US$9.50, followed by a pizette, starting at US$12. Typical dishes include grilled lamb chops, and pepper fillet (both US$26). Nightly specials include such treats as coconut-battered lobster. The chocolate brownie and ice cream dessert, for US$4.50, is divine.

Similarly down-home and upscale dining, from burgers to seafood platters, are offered at *Club Soleil Restaurant*. The owners will dispatch a water taxi to pick you up and drop you off.

Another favorite for Bahamian seafood is *Cap'n Jack's* (☎ 242-366-0247) on the harborfront; it's open 8:30 to 10:30 am and 11 am to 9 pm. Free hotel transfers are offered. In a similar vein, try *Harbour's Edge* (☎ 242-366-0087), a popular waterside eatery with salads and burgers, including a veggie burger (US$8) and a snapper burger, plus a Saturday-night pizza special. Prices at both places start at US$4 for snacks and about US$18 for dinner entrees.

The simple *Main Street Grill* (☎ 242-366-4993) is a good place for burgers and sandwiches, as is *Munchie's Snack Bar*, serving pizzas, burgers, etc, in a little shaded patio with rough-hewn furniture.

Harbour View Grocery sells fresh produce and groceries, as does *Lorraine's Food Fair* and *Vernon's Grocery & Upper Crust Bakery*; and *Hope Town Temptations*, next door, sells coffees, salads, sandwiches, and locally made ice cream.

Robert Lowe has a *fish market* (☎ 242-366-0266) at his house on Russell's Rd.

South of Hope Town The *Abaco Inn Restaurant* (☎ 242-366-0133) offers an eclectic menu including vegetarian meals, but has a heavy slant toward Bahamian seafood. Reservations are required. The *Boat House Restaurant*, at Sea Spray Marina, serves breakfasts from US$5, plus lunch and dinner, featuring Caesar salad for US$8 and entrees (from filet mignon to seafood primavera) starting at US$18. It also has a Sunday brunch for US$20. Reservations are required.

Entertainment
Elbow Cay is kinda sleepy. The two happenin' spots are *Harbour's Edge* and *Cap'n Jack's*. The former, favored by locals, has a pool table and satellite TV, plus live music on weekends. Its Over the Edge drink (Matusalem and banana rums and fruit juices) is the result of a three-week taste-testing. Cap'n Jack's, which has a live band on Wednesday and Friday, is famed for its Jack Hammer, combining copious rum, vodka, and Tía María, and guaranteed to get you jiving.

The *Sea Spray Resort* has a BBQ with live DJ on Monday, and hosts live music on Wednesday evening.

Shopping
Several stores sell quality crafts, jewelry, and artwork. On Back St try Edith's Straw Shop or Ebb Tide Gift Shop, which has Androsia batiks, locally made spices and preserves, and beautiful artwork. You can buy magazines here. Edith also does hair braiding.

Kemp's Souvenirs, on Back St, has pottery, batiks, and spiced coffees. El Mercado, also on Back St, sells jewelry and a wide range of resortwear and batiks, as does Iggy Biggy (☎ 242-366-0354) on Bay St. For Cuban cigars, try Fantasy Boutique on Bay St.

Getting There & Away

You have to get here by boat, usually from Marsh Harbour. Albury's Ferry Service (in Marsh Harbour ☎ 242-367-3147, fax 242-365-6487) has water taxis from Marsh Harbour to Elbow Cay at 7:15, 9 and 10:30 am and 12:15, 2, 4 and 5:30 pm daily (the 7:15 am ferry doesn't operate on weekends), returning at 8, 9:45, and 11:30 am and 1:30, 3, 4, and 5 pm (the 5 pm ferry doesn't operate on Sunday); 20 minutes, US$8 per person one-way or US$12 roundtrip same day, children half-price. The ferry will stop at all the docks and marinas on Elbow Cay, including many hotels and the government dock. A charter costs US$50 for up to five people, US$10 for each extra person. You can also charter the Albury's Ferry to Green Turtle Cay for US$240 for up to 10 people.

A water taxi runs from Man O' War Cay to Hope Town at 7:30 am daily, returning at 4:30 pm. The taxi pilot will drop you off and pick you up at specific docks as requested.

The mail boat *Captain Gurth Dean* sails to Hope Town from Nassau on Tuesday. See the Marsh Harbour section for information.

Lighthouse Marina (☎ 242-366-0154, fax 242-366-0171, Lighthse@batelnet.bs), with the only fuel dock, charges US75¢ per foot. Hope Town Marina (☎ 242-366-0003), at Club Soleil Resort, charges US65¢ per foot. The marina at Hope Town Hideaways (☎ 242-366-0224, fax 242-366-0434) has 12 slips with metered water and electricity.

At White Sound, Sea Spray Marina (☎ 242-366-0065) has a 24-slip, full-service marina exclusively for the use of guests at the Sea Spray Resort. It charges US85¢ per foot; boats shorter than 22 feet may stay free.

Getting Around

You can walk or bicycle everywhere in Hope Town. Vehicular traffic is banned along Bay St. There's no road on the west side of the harbor. To get there, you can hitch a boat ride from any of the docks along Bay St.

Island Cart Rentals (☎ 242-366-0448), Hope Town Cart Rentals (☎ 242-366-0064), and T&N (☎ 242-366-0069) rent golf carts for US$35/210 daily/weekly. They'll deliver free of charge to your hotel.

Harbour's Edge restaurant rents bicycles for US$10 daily.

Abaco Bahamas Charters (☎/fax 242-366-0151, 800-626-5690, info@abacocharters .com) rents boats from their base here. Its Web site is www.abacocharters.com.

You can also rent boats from Island Marine Boat Rentals (☎ 242-366-0282, fax 242-366-0281, info@islandmarine.com), located in the Parrot Cays and with free boat delivery; Club Soleil Boat Rentals (☎ 242-366-0003); Sea Horse Rentals (☎ 242-366-0023); and Dave's Dive Shop & Boat Rentals (☎ 242-366-0029, fax 242-366-0420), which charges US$75 to US$110 daily, US$385 to US$600 weekly.

LUBBER'S QUARTERS CAY

This 300-acre private island lies between Marsh Harbour and Elbow Cay. A few scattered cottages and villas peek from between the trees. It's a good place for reclusive escapades or prowling the flats for bonefish. There are secluded beaches and short nature trails.

Places to Stay & Eat

There are no hotels or stores.

Villa Poincianna (in the US ☎ 970-667-8160, paradise@poincianna.com) is a modern, spacious waterfront house with two air-con bedrooms and its own dock. It rents for US$950 to US$1250 depending on the number of guests. You can view it at www.poincianna.com.

Abaco Vacation Rentals (see Places to Stay in the Marsh Harbour section) offers six properties, including *Refuge* and *Retreat*, two charming cottages on the undeveloped northwest side of the island. Each has solar electricity, propane refrigerator and stove, VHF radio, and cellular phones. Rates – US$400 to US$620 weekly – depend on the number of people.

Yahoe's Sand Bar & Grill (☎ 242-366-3110) offers seafood and burgers for lunch and dinner daily except Monday. Dinner reservations are requested. *Cracker P's* also serves burgers and grilled chicken and veggies; it's closed on Wednesday and Thursday. It has a floating dock and sand volleyball court.

TILLOO CAY

This 5-mile-long cay, a spitting distance south of Elbow Cay, is renowned for its bonefishing flats and as a nesting site for seabirds, including the rare and beautiful tropicbird.

One of the handful of residents is Brigitte Bowyer, a German-born artist famous for her beautiful watercolors of local scenes. She welcomes visitors to her studio. You can reach her on VHF channel 16 (her call name is 'Honka Loo') or write her c/o Postmistress, Hope Town, Abaco, The Bahamas.

PELICAN CAYS LAND & SEA PARK

This 2100-acre park protects the half-dozen tiny Pelican Cays, south of Tilloo, and their surrounding waters and fringing reef, centered around **Sandy Cay Underwater National Sea Park**, which has great snorkeling. The cays are nesting sites for bridled, sooty, and least terns. The park also boasts shallow coral gardens and underwater caves abounding with marine life.

MAN O' WAR CAY
• pop 250

Fishhook-shaped Man O' War, 3 miles northwest of Elbow Cay, is as different from Elbow as chalk is from cheese. Tourism has barely touched this diminutive, tendril-thin isle and its sole namesake village. A fistful of New England–style homes line the narrow concrete lanes that creep up the slope. But most houses are modern bungalows, fronted by prim lawns and hedges, with plastic fishing balls hanging from trees.

Man O' War is an 'industrial boat-building center.' The shore is crowded with marinas and boat sheds that resonate with the thud of hammers and buzz of electrical tools. Virtually the entire population lives off the sea, sailing homemade fiberglass boats or 12-foot wooden crawfish boats. Dozens of Man O' War sailing

dinghies dating back half a century are still being used and are still in perfect condition, fun to sail and fast as the wind.

Shipbuilding on Man O' War goes back almost 200 years, anchored on Schooner's Landing. Fifty years ago there were about a dozen boatbuilders on Man O' War Cay. Each evolved their own distinct designs – you could tell who built a boat just by looking at it. You can still watch the shipbuilders at work, diligently scraping bottoms, painting hulls, and in one case holding fast to traditional methods of carpentry. The majority, less concerned for their craft, fashion their boats from fiberglass to meet the demand for faster, motorized boats. Today fiberglass is the lifeblood of Man O' War's boatbuilding industry.

The boatyards employ black laborers, mostly 'Bahaitians' (Haitians born in The Bahamas) who are also employed as domestic help and are obliged to leave the lily-white island by nightfall. They live on the mainland (Great Abaco) and commute to Man O' War. The cay's all-white population is renowned for graciousness and industriousness, the product of a Bible-steeped lifestyle that prohibits the sale of liquor. (There are no bars, but you can bring your own booze.) And if you go around wearing skimpy clothing, passing citizens may offer an indignant reminder of their unwritten rules of decorum. You'll even find religious fliers outside homes for passersby to pick up.

For a history of the cay, read *Man O' War: My Island Home* by Haziel Albury (Holly Press).

Two narrow concrete lanes run parallel to the harbor (the uppermost, Queen's Hwy, continues as a dirt road to the north and south ends of the island). You can walk from one end of the village to the other in 10 minutes, but most locals get around by golf cart or moped (the young men zip around on motorcycles). No one walks; the men get their exercise at work but a dietician and aerobic instructor would find plenty of business among the local women.

Calm turquoise waters wash up to the white beach that stretches lazily along the windward shore. The wreck of the USS

MAN O' WAR CAY

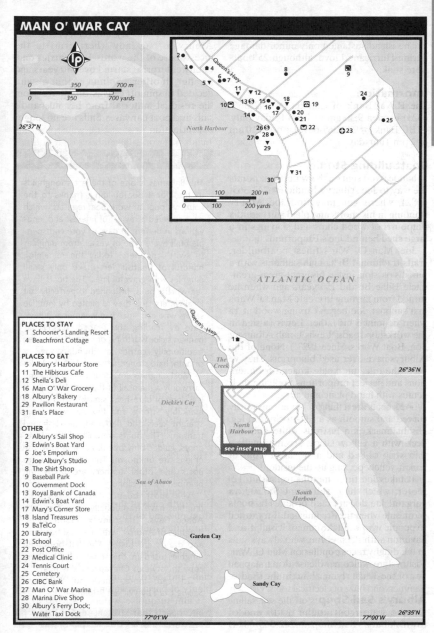

PLACES TO STAY
1 Schooner's Landing Resort
4 Beachfront Cottage

PLACES TO EAT
5 Albury's Harbour Store
11 The Hibiscus Cafe
12 Sheila's Deli
16 Man O' War Grocery
18 Albury's Bakery
29 Pavilion Restaurant
31 Ena's Place

OTHER
2 Albury's Sail Shop
3 Edwin's Boat Yard
6 Joe's Emporium
7 Joe Albury's Studio
8 The Shirt Shop
9 Baseball Park
10 Government Dock
13 Royal Bank of Canada
14 Edwin's Boat Yard
15 Mary's Corner Store
18 Island Treasures
19 BaTelCo
20 Library
21 School
22 Post Office
23 Medical Clinic
24 Tennis Court
25 Cemetery
26 CIBC Bank
27 Man O' War Marina
28 Marina Dive Shop
30 Albury's Ferry Dock;
    Water Taxi Dock

ATLANTIC OCEAN

North Harbour

Queen's Hwy

The Creek

Dickie's Cay

North Harbour

see inset map

Sea of Abaco

South Harbour

Garden Cay

Sandy Cay

26°37'N

26°36'N

26°35'N

77°01'W

77°00'W

ABACOS

Adirondack, which went down in 1862, lies offshore in 40 feet of water.

The island sustained only minor damage during Hurricane Floyd, although 25 boats were sunk.

Information
The Royal Bank of Canada (☎ 242-365-6323) is open 9:30 am to 1 pm Friday only. CIBC Bank (☎ 242-365-6098) is open 10 am to 2 pm Thursday.

Boatbuilding Studio
A handcarved sign on the waterfront points the way to Joe Albury's Studio (☎ 242-365-6082), where you may find Joe Albury standing in his shorts and plaid shirt amid a potpourri of wood chips and shavings in a large shed behind Joe's Emporium.

Joe, Man O' War's finest boatbuilder, crafts traditional Bahamian sailboats with a purist's passion, just as his great-great-great-uncle Billie Bo did 150 years ago when he turned from farming to create Man O' War's first sailboat. Joe began carving wood at 15 when he joined his father, Lewis (a sign in the workshop reads: 'Lewis Uriah Albury & Son, Boat Works, Since 1927'). None of the Alburys have ever used blueprints. They've used 'the rule,' an innate knack for dimensions and perfect proportions, applying their genius with hand plane and adz.

Joe's boats are a thing of joy: as sensuously curved and smooth as a silk-stockinged leg. His hallmark is a lustrous white hull and deck with a yellow stripe, accented with a thin strip of red and a signature coat of lemon-yellow perking up the inside.

It takes Joe three months to finish a 12-footer, which he'll sell for US$7500...a bargain! Joe doesn't take orders. His boats go on sale when they're finished. 'I try to sell to people who will take care of it, sail it, and have fun with it,' says Joe, who always sails in the dinghy races popular on Man O' War. Visitors are welcome. Please don't step on any of the 30 cats lying about in the shade.

Albury's Sail Shop
On the waterfront at the north end of town, Albury's Sail Shop (☎ 242-365-6014) is abuzz with the whir of sewing machines. The hive of activity is overseen by Lois Albury, a 'bag lady' (her term) in the nicest sense of the words. Lois carries on a family enterprise started over 40 years ago by her mother, Selima Albury, who decided to spin off canvas 'ditty bags' from the residual material from her husband's sails and boat canvases. Sails are no longer in production.

Bahamian Sailing Craft

The Bahamas is one of the last strongholds of traditional boatbuilding, thanks to the country's popular work-boat regattas, which have fostered a revival of interest and innovations in design. In days of yore craftspeople built every type of vessel, from dinghies to swift schooners. Today the remaining handful of boatbuilders make only small dinghies with graceful lines. The boats have sea-worthy hulls, fashioned to perfectly suit local waters, and they're piloted by intuitive sailors who can smell bad weather and navigate by reading the seabed. (Every Bahamian sailor worth his or her salt, however, traditionally carries a 'thunderstone,' a smooth, hard stone that is said to bring luck.)

Most dinghies are about 15 feet long and carry only a mainsail (if the boat has a jib, it is a sloop or bare-head smack). They are remarkably strong and flexible, with long, straight keels and flattened, heart-shaped transoms. The boats are built without blueprints, guided only by rules of thumb whose origins are unknown. The stem and stern posts and other timbers are rakes and plumbed by eye alone.

The most beautiful and seaworthy dinghies have traditionally come from the Abaco Cays. The convex 'moon sheer' dinghies of Andros, with minimal transoms and drags, are faster. The flat-bottomed dinghies used in the shoals off Eleuthera copy the style of Chesapeake Bay boats.

To learn more, check out *Bahamian Sailing Craft* by William R Johnson, Jr.

The 30-plus types of bags, duffels, totes, and cosmetic cases made at the Sail Shop – and sold nowhere else – all have their roots in the ditty bag that Lois' mum sewed to hold her little boy's marbles more than 50 years ago. Today Lois is assisted by numerous other family members, who also fashion items using Androsia batiks.

It's open 8 am to 5 pm weekdays and 8 am to 4 pm Saturday.

Outdoor Activities

The Marina Dive Shop (☎ 242-365-6013) rents equipment (except regulators) and provides air fills but does not offer dives. You can rent snorkel gear for US$10 per day. It also offers kayak and bicycle rentals.

Maitland 'Bonefish Dundee' Lowe (☎ 242-366-0234), the local expert bonefishing guide, charges US$200/300 half/full day for up to four people.

Places to Stay

Northeast of town off Queen's Hwy, **Schooner's Landing Resort** (☎ 242-365-6072, 800-633-9197, fax 242-365-6285, info@ SchoonersLanding.com) has four modern air-con townhouses with full kitchen. Each two-bedroom, two-story house is roofed with red tile and tastefully decorated with crisp white linens and lace in the bedrooms, plus a TV/VCR, separate dining room, and private patio. There's private dockage, plus a bar and gazebo with barbecue pit and hammocks over the coral shore. Beaches lie a stone's throw in either direction. Rates are US$175/995 nightly/weekly (three nights minimum).

David Albury (☎ 242-365-6059) rents two **houses** in town. An idyllic **beachfront cottage** is offered for rent by CTL (☎ 317-849-5308, 6929 Creekside Lane, Indianapolis, IN 46220, USA).

Another one-bedroom, gingerbread-trimmed cottage – **Port Deck** – is available on Dickie's Cay, a sliver of land west of Man O' War. It's furnished in nautical decor and done up in light-finished pine. A dinghy is included in the US$850 weekly rental fee. Contact Abaco Vacation Rentals (see Places to Stay in the Marsh Harbour section, earlier in this chapter) for rental or reservations.

Places to Eat

Getting breakfast is difficult. No eatery opens before 10:30 am, although you can get fresh bread and pastries at **Albury's Bakery**.

The most popular spot is **The Hibiscus Cafe**, where you'll dine indoors in a chilled room. It serves filling salads and sandwiches for US$7 to US$10, plus ice cream.

The **Pavilion Restaurant**, on the waterfront, sells burgers and sandwiches for US$3 and upward. It has barbecue specials on Friday and Saturday for US$9 and upward. **Ena's Place** (☎ 242-365-6187) also sells burgers, sandwiches, conch fritters, and homemade pies, along with Bahamian fare enjoyed al fresco on a shady raised porch; it's open 10 am to 9:30 pm daily and has a Wednesday and Saturday BBQ, plus dinner by reservation only on Friday.

Sheila's Deli (☎ 242-365-6118) offers a different dish each night. For US$10, I had steamed pork chops, mashed potatoes, coleslaw, and corn. It opens at 5:30 pm and serves until the food is gone. Don't be late. Locals arrive for takeout, but you can dine in Sheila's home or on the patio.

Albury's Harbour Store is a fully stocked grocery. You can also pick up groceries at **Man O' War Grocery** and **Mary's Corner Store.**

Entertainment

There are no bars or social clubs. The village is still as death after nightfall. Every Thursday a 'social hour' is held at 5 pm at the Man O' War Marina. Bring food to share.

Shopping

Albury's Sail Shop (see that section, above) has a wide array of cotton tote bags, purses, and hats for as little as US$20. T-shirts cost about US$16. It once made water-resistant jackets that were considered a bit of a highbrow fashion statement among boaters and entertainers, from Paul Newman to Perry Como; I was told that the jackets might be re-introduced.

ABACOS

Joe's Emporium, in front of Joe Albury's Studio, is an Aladdin's Cave of crafts, arts, souvenirs, books, wind chimes, sponges, and Joe's wooden jewelry boxes, cutting boards, and famous half-ribbed model boats (US$475, or US$680 including crating and shipping). Joe's brother custom makes furniture.

The Shirt Shop (☎ 242-365-6077) sells scores of designs relating to Man O' War and The Bahamas.

Island Treasures (☎ 242-365-6072, fax 242-565-6285) is a trove of T-shirts, blown-glass figurines, and jewelry.

Getting There & Away

Albury's Ferry Service (☎ 242-367-3147, fax 242-365-6487) operates scheduled water taxis from Marsh Harbour at 10:30 am and 12:15, 2:30, 4, and 5:30 pm daily (the 12:15 and 2:30 pm ferries don't operate on Sunday); US$8 one-way, US$12 roundtrip the same day, children half-price. Return service departs Man O' War at 8 and 11:30 am and 1:30 and 3:15 pm (there is no 11:30 am or 3:15 pm service on Sunday). Charters cost US$50 one-way for up to six people and US$10 for each extra person. Albury's Ferry Service also has sightseeing trips and charters to outlying cays.

A water taxi also runs to Great Guana Cay at 7:30 am and 3:30 pm Friday; and from Man O' War to Elbow Cay at 7:30 am, returning at 4:30 pm. It leaves from the same dock as the ferry to Marsh Harbour.

Facilities for boaters include the 60-slip Man O' War Marina (☎ 242-365-6008), complete with kiddies' playground, and Edwin's Boat Yard (☎ 242-365-6006), with two locations.

Getting Around

You can rent golf carts at Carts-R-Us (☎ 242-365-6072) and Island Treasures (☎ 242-365-6072, fax 242-565-6285).

GREAT GUANA CAY
• pop 150

Six-mile-long Great Guana Cay, 8 miles north of Marsh Harbour and 5 miles north-west of Man O' War Cay, is the least devel-oped of the Loyalist Cays, with a tiny, unso-phisticated fishing village that curls around palm-fringed Kidd's Cove. The islanders earn most of their income from lobstering, although tourism is evolving apace. Just southeast of Great Guana Cay, 6 miles north of Marsh Harbour, lies **Fowl Cay Reef Preserve**, a national underwater sea park. It protects a stunning coral reef and, ashore, the nesting sites of sea birds.

Most visitors are day-trippers from Marsh Harbour come to sup at Nipper's Beach Bar & Grill (see Places to Eat, later in this chapter), which draws folks from near and far for its weekend feasts. The Ritz-Carlton hotel chain reportedly is con-sidering erecting a deluxe 150-room hotel and golf course. And there has been a bit of a boom in home construction to the north during recent years, including a 215-acre tract where million-dollar homes are rising like mushrooms on a damp log.

The only noteworthy site is the ceme-tery on a rise behind the village, which con-sists of two dozen houses, an Anglican church, and a one-room schoolhouse. The island's claim to fame is a spectacular, seamless, 5-mile-long beach of white sand that runs the length of the Atlantic shore.

Lobster Fishermen

With luck, you may still see fishermen in 'smacks' up to 40 feet long, catching lobster in time-tested tradition: One man rows while the other looks through a glass-bottomed bucket held in the water. When a lobster's antennae are spotted waving from under a ledge, an L-shaped pole, or 'tickler,' is lowered to entice the creature into the open. It's then snagged in a 'bully' net attached to another pole. A large iron ring, about 4 feet across and spanned by a loose rope netting, is used to catch turtles.

Lobster, fish, and conch are kept alive in a well filled with seawater that circulates through holes in the bottom when the boat's under sail.

Several little beaches lie tucked into coves on the leeward shore; a reef runs the length of the cay, 50 feet offshore; and several uninhabited islands lie close at hand. Wild dolphins occasionally call in to frolic in Kidd's Cove.

A weathered old sign reads: 'It's Better in the Bahamas, but…It's Gooder in Guana.' Alas, the famous skull hanging on a deck opposite Tom's Gift Store on the waterfront was stolen in 2000; it uttered things like: 'I see you!' and 'Where are you going?'

A rugged sand-and-rock road cuts north through the scrubby undergrowth.

July's Regatta Week features sailing races and festivities on Great Guana and other towns and cays.

Information

There's a public telephone on the waterfront across from Tom's Gift Store. It takes only phonecards, which you can buy at the BaTelCo office next to the school in the village, open 9 am to 5:30 pm Monday to Friday. The post office is next door.

For laundry, the Guana Beach Resort (see Places to Stay, below) charges US$5 per wash and US$5 per dry.

Activities

Great Guana has superb snorkeling inside the reef along its windward shore; you can rent gear from Tom's Gift Store (see the Shopping section) for US$5 per day. You can rent fishing gear at Kidd's Cove Rentals (☎ 242-365-5046) or from Guana Seaside Village, which also rents boats. Local bonefishing expert Henry Sands (☎ 242-365-5140) will guide you.

The Guana Beach Resort offers day trips (with lunch) to Marsh Harbour and dinner cruises from 5:30 pm to midnight.

Froggie's Out Island Adventures (☎ 242-365-6494), at Dolphin Beach Resort, offers diving and snorkeling trips to Fowl Cay and Sandy Cay.

Places to Stay

Fancy a Canadian-style, air-con log cabin on the beach? *Ocean Frontier Hideaways* (☎ 242-365-5143, info@oceanfrontier.com; in

North America ☎ 519-389-4846, fax 519-389-3027), next to Nipper's Beach Bar & Grill (see Places to Eat, below), offers six of the same, with the advantage of the famous bar facilities at hand. Rates are US$1200 per week for up to four people. They're homespun within.

Guana Seaside Village (☎ 242-365-5106, 800-242-0942, fax 242-365-5146, info@GuanaSeaside.com; in the US ☎ 877-681-3091), on a lonesome beachfront north of the village at Crossing Bay, has eight nonsmoking rooms, including two ill-lit suites with kitchenette. Cottages were to be added. The two oceanfront rooms have marvelous vistas through plate-glass doors. You can dine on the grassy patio or in the simple restaurant. There's a small bar, plus a poolside bar and grill, and a restaurant. The resort has a small dock and a separate bar and grill for 'cruise-by' dining. Sport-fishing boats, motorboats, and tackle are available for rent, and there's bonefishing right off the dock. Rates range from US$90 to US$110 April to December, and US$135 to US$160 December to April. Its postal address is PO Box AB-20756, Marsh Harbour, Abacos, The Bahamas.

The *Guana Beach Resort* (☎ 242-365-5133, 800-227-3366, fax 242-365-5134, guanabeach@guanabeach.com; in the US ☎ 954-747-9130) nestles in a coconut grove adjacent to the public dock. The eight beachfront rooms (some with king-size beds and kitchenette) and seven two-bedroom suites are spacious and have been completely refurbished since Hurricane Floyd. There's a pool, sun deck, hammocks, volleyball, and water sports. Boats up to 150 feet can berth at the dock. A renovation has livened up the previously dull restaurant, destroyed by Hurricane Floyd. Summertime rates range from US$150 for a beachfront room to US$220 for a two-bedroom suite; they rise to US$165 and US$240 in winter. Rates include water sports, snorkel gear, and water-taxi transfer from Marsh Harbour. Air-inclusive packages are offered from Florida. Its mailing address is PO Box AB-20474, Marsh Harbor, The Bahamas.

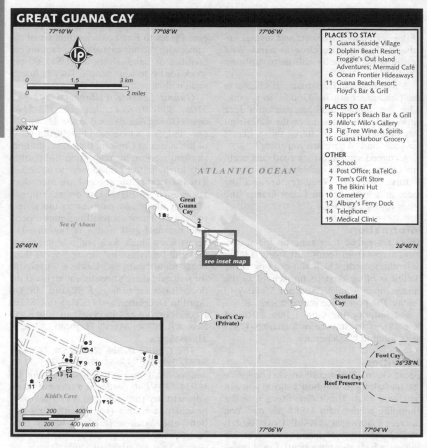

GREAT GUANA CAY

PLACES TO STAY
1 Guana Seaside Village
2 Dolphin Beach Resort;
  Froggie's Out Island
  Adventures; Mermaid Café
6 Ocean Frontier Hideaways
11 Guana Beach Resort;
  Floyd's Bar & Grill

PLACES TO EAT
5 Nipper's Beach Bar & Grill
9 Milo's; Milo's Gallery
13 Fig Tree Wine & Spirits
16 Guana Harbour Grocery

OTHER
3 School
4 Post Office; BaTelCo
7 Tom's Gift Store
8 The Bikini Hut
10 Cemetery
12 Albury's Ferry Dock
14 Telephone
15 Medical Clinic

I love the **Dolphin Beach Resort** (☎/fax 242-365-5137, relax@dolphinbeachresort.com; in the US ☎ 800-222-2646, fax 800-678-7479), a secluded, cozy, romantic option that operates like a B&B and offers four efficiency rooms in the main lodge, plus eight cottages in traditional clapboard style, and a three-bedroom beachhouse. All are exquisitely and individually decorated in lively tropical pastels and come with air-con, kitchen facilities, and balconies or decks. The woodsy 10-acre site has nature trails, plus there's a small swimming pool, and bicycles and kayaks are available. Rates are US$115 to US$130 low-season,

US$155 to US$170 high-season for rooms; US$140 to US$225 low-season, and US$190 to US$275 high-season for the cottages. The house and two larger cottages rent by the week only, beginning at US$1050.

Coco Paradise (☎ 242-365-5197, 877-464-7272, fax 242-365-5179, info@cocoparadise .com; in the US ☎ 321-725-1971, fax 321-725-3986) has island-style, one-bedroom, air-con cottages amid the sand dunes, each with ceiling fans, a mini-bar, fridge, microwave and coffee maker, plus patio. Sleeper couches in the living room accommodate two extra people. Facilities include a beach bar, restaurant, and gift shop. Rates are US$100/120 summer/winter.

Several homes and villas are for rent, including **Penury Hall South** *(in the US ☎ 207-244-7102, fax 207-244-5651, tstrong@ acadia.net)*, a three-bedroom property with a wrap-around deck that rents for US$850 (US$950 for five or six people). Its mailing address is Box 68, Southwest Harbor, ME 04678, USA. You can view it online at www. 10kvacationrentals.com.

Abaco Vacation Rentals (see Places to Stay in the Marsh Harbour section) rents villas and cottages, as does Bahama Vacations (in the US ☎ 603-659-8312).

A new 54-room hotel was planned at the **Orchid Bay Yacht Club & Marina**, south of the harbor.

Places to Eat
The 'in' spot drawing folks from all over the Abacos is **Nipper's Beach Bar & Grill** *(☎ 242-365-5143, johnny@nippersbar.com)*, a timber-frame bar and grill on a bluff overlooking the beach behind the village. It has a large deck with tables and benches painted in tropical pastels, shaded by even more flamboyant umbrellas. There's a two-tier pool with water cascade and swim-up bar. The menu includes salads, burgers for US$7, and a seafood dinner for US$14. A roast wild boar buffet is offered on Sunday afternoon for US$15. It gets lively at night, when the music is cranked up. Nipper's has an annual Easter-egg hunt in the coral reef, plus regatta parties in July. The bar opens at 10 am; lunch is served 11 am to 3:30 pm; and dinner is served 6 to 10 pm. Nipper's even has a Web site at www.nippersbar.com.

Floyd's Bar & Grill, in the Guana Beach Resort, offers poolside dining and the usual menu, from seafood to steaks. Mexican food is served on Monday. The house drink – the Guana Grabber – should help get you under the limbo bar...or try the Hurricane Floyd, which is sure to knock you over!

The **Guana Seaside Village** has a romantic restaurant serving seafood, steaks, pastas, and scrumptious desserts. It also hosts an island-style, hickory-smoked barbecue buffet from 12:30 to 9 pm on Saturday for

US$14. The **Mermaid Café**, in the Dolphin Beach Resort, is another excellent option.

Coco Paradise has a beach bar and grill; it offers a Wednesday night 'conch out,' a Friday night BBQ, and a Saturday scampi special. It also serves mouthwatering treats such as garlic shrimp and crabmeat quiche. It serves free coffee to all comers.

For groceries, try **Guana Harbour Grocery**. **Fig Tree Wine & Spirits** caters to imbibers. A crusty local named Milo sells fresh fruit and vegetables from a harborfront stall by the dock.

Entertainment
Stone McEwan plays calypso at Nipper's on Sunday afternoon. Coco Paradise has Monday Night Football; the beach bar is open nightly.

Shopping
Tom's Gift Store (☎ 242-365-5021) sells T-shirts, postcards, souvenirs, and bargain-priced Cuban cigars. The gift shop in the Guana Beach Resort has postcards and resortwear, as does Milo's Gift Shop, and The Bikini Hut, selling all manner of sexy swimwear.

Getting There & Around
Albury's Ferry Service (☎ 242-367-3147, fax 242-365-6487) operates water taxis from The Conch Inn Marina in Marsh Harbour at 7:15 and 10:15 am and 1:15, 3:30, and 5:30 pm weekdays, returning at 9 and 11:30 am and 2:30 and 5:30 pm; US$5 each way. A charter costs US$80 for up to six people, US$12 for each extra person. It will drop off or pick up at the Guana Seaside Village and other locations upon request.

The Guana Beach Resort has a deep-water marina. More significant is the new, top-end Orchid Bay Yacht Club & Marina (☎ 242-365-5175, fax 365-5166, orchidbay@ yahoo.com), at the southern end of the cove, with 64 slips and all facilities.

Donna's Golf Cart & Bike Rentals (☎ 242-365-5195) rents golf carts for US$35 daily, and bicycles. Guana Beach Resort also has bicycles (free for its guests) and rents golf carts for US$35/200 daily/weekly.

South of Marsh Harbour

The Great Abaco Hwy runs from Marsh Harbour to Sandy Point, at the southwestern end of the island (see the Abacos map at the beginning of this chapter). The area suffered extensive flood and wind damage during Hurricane Floyd but was beginning to bounce back at last visit in summer 2000.

LITTLE HARBOUR

I adore this tiny bay, 20 miles south of Marsh Harbour. The perfectly sheltered crescent bay is held in the cusp of crumbling limestone cliffs topped by wild lilies and plums. The spectacular setting is enhanced by a scimitar-shaped beach along the south shore, where Atlantic rollers crash ashore on the lee side of a narrow peninsula. A kerosene-lantern lighthouse looms over the bay. You can climb to the top for a view of the waves running in toward the reef and the wreck of the *Anne Bonney*.

A few expats have built their houses here, and the bay is popular with yachters and turtles, which swim around the anchorage. The area is protected by the Bahamas National Trust.

There is no truth to the news items on the Internet claiming that the foundry and Pete's Pub (see Places to Stay & Eat, below) had been destroyed, although two yachts were washed up into a cave and left hanging high and dry.

Bronze Art Foundry

The bay is famous for Randolph Johnston's bronze foundry (☎ 242-367-2720) at the north end of the beach. Johnston, a Canadian, began casting bronze in his teens. In 1952 he settled at Little Harbour with his wife, Margot Broxton (an accomplished ceramist), and three sons. For the first few years, they lived in a cave. Johnston built his own electricity-generating plant and a foundry and furnace to cast pieces weighing up to 600 lbs. Today his work adorns many Bahamian public spaces, including Rawson Square in Nassau. He died in 1992 after

writing his autobiography, *An Artist on His Island*.

His son Peter took over the foundry, where he creates marine sculptures and gold jewelry. You can take a guided tour; note *Nine Ages of Man*, a bronze piece showing figures from crawling infancy to the grave. The foundry (which was flooded by Hurricane Floyd but quickly restored) is open 10 am to noon and 2 to 4 pm Monday to Saturday.

Johnston's works are sold in the adjacent gallery (☎ 242-366-2250), a repository for works by other leading jewelers, sculptors, and painters. It's open 11 am to 4 pm Monday to Saturday and Sunday by appointment. The mailing address is c/o Cherokee Radio, PO Box AB-20282, Marsh Harbour, Abaco, The Bahamas.

Places to Stay & Eat

'Funky and fun' describes *Pete's Pub (no phone, fax c/o Cherokee Radio 242-366-2250)*, a beachside bar and grill knocked together from driftwood, with sand for a floor and T-shirts and ships' pendants for decor. You can sip grog at a bar shaped like a ship's prow and order burgers or barbecue from the open grill. Don't miss the famous 'Pete's Pub Pig & Pea Party' every Saturday. A full kitchen was being added and guest chefs were to be invited to prepare dinners available by reservation only (by radio, VHF channel 16).

Pete's hosts a four-day Dolphin Festival each May, featuring tennis, fishing, the Pirates' Ball (costumes a must), and cocktails. It costs US$30. And the Mad Hatter's Party, which venued in May 2000, was scheduled to become an annual event…with silly dress from the 'adult-themed' to the Hope Town Fairy (ferry – get it?).

Pete planned to build a half dozen or so rental villas.

Getting There & Away

The turnoff from Great Abaco Hwy is 15 miles south of Marsh Harbour and leads to Cherokee Sound; 2 miles before Cherokee Sound, a turnoff leads to Little Harbour via a rough dirt road; 4WD is recommended.

A taxi from Marsh Harbour will cost about US$70 one-way.

On Sunday, a minibus (US$10) leaves from outside Sharkee's and from Sapodilly's in Marsh Harbour to the pig roast at Pete's Pub. The minibus from Sapodilly's also runs on Wednesday.

Froggie's Out Island Adventures (see Boat Excursions in the Elbow Cay section, earlier in this chapter) offers excursions to Little Harbour.

Albury's Ferry Service (☎ 242-365-6010) will take you from Marsh Harbour.

CHEROKEE SOUND
• pop 150

The small, pin-neat village of Cherokee Sound, 25 miles south of Marsh Harbour, sits at the end of a peninsula jutting out into its namesake sound, surrounded by mangrove shores and miles of turquoise flats. The locals are descendants of Loyalists who arrived in 1783 and passed their genes down in splendid isolation for the next two centuries (note the short triangular noses typical of these parts). Little over a decade ago, the only way to reach this remote fishing village was by boat. Electricity arrived only in 1996!

The clapboard and cement houses are raised off the ground…a fortunate thing, as Cherokee Sound experienced severe flooding (wild pigs were seen swimming to safety) during Hurricane Floyd, which ripped away the docks. Most houses are painted gleaming-white, with pastel shutters and trim, and separated by neatly clipped lawns. The only sites of interest are a marble memorial to sailors of past days, outside the BaTelCo office; the Methodist Church, with its varnished wood ceiling; and the Pentecostal churches, from which hymns waft on almost any night.

Most of the local men make a living diving for lobsters and are often gone for weeks at a time. The younger lads – they'll get their turn lobstering in due course – go out at night sharking, looking for jaws to sell to the tourist trade in Marsh Harbour, or hunt foot-long *tiniki* crabs. The men still hunt pigeon and wild boar, too, in the pinelands. The town is famous for its quilts.

The best time to visit is Cherokee Day, when a large tent goes up outside the schoolhouse, homegrown food is passed around, and everyone participates in quilt auctions and tugs of war.

Places to Stay & Eat
Seaview Cottage (☎/fax 242-366-2053, seaview@oii.net; in the US ☎ 305-261-0566) is a fully furnished, air-con cottage with a microwave oven, TV/VCR (but no local television reception). A cook can be arranged. It rents for US$100 nightly (3-night minimum).

There is no restaurant and there's only one grocery store: the *Cherokee Food Fair* (☎ 242-366-2022), where Miss Lorraine can arrange cottage rentals. You can buy homemade bread from Diane – that's 'Dy-yanne' – Sawyer (☎ 242-366-2022), who will also cook meals in her home on request.

Getting There & Around
A taxi from Marsh Harbour will cost about US$70 one-way. See Getting There & Away in the Little Harbour section, above, for driving information.

Locals such as Tommy and Trevor Sawyer take visitors boating for about US$75 per half-day. Noel Lowe (☎ 242-366-2107) will take you out for US$125 for a full day.

CASUARINA POINT
This small fishing village lies on the west side of Cherokee Sound, with a beautiful beach shelving into fabulous jade-colored boeflats.

Different of Abaco Nature Park
Immediately west of Casuarina Point, Different of Abaco Nature Park (☎ 242-366-2150, fax 242-327-8152) is a kind of little-visited and somewhat run-down natural adventure park where you can go bird watching and hiking in the extensive mangroves and pine forests. It bills itself as an 'eco-resort,' boasting a bird sanctuary, flamingo park, and nature trails. You can rent canoes, and guides

will take you bonefishing on the extensive flats. There are telescopes for stargazing, and you can commune with wild boar, Laro the donkey, and myriad wildlife, and explore the replica Lucayan Village. Sportfishing is offered. The Web site is www.differentofabaco.com.

Places to Stay & Eat

Rustic, eccentric *Heritage Bonefish Club & Restaurant* (☎ 242-366-2150, fax 242-327-8152, different@oii.net; in the US ☎ 800-688-4752), at Different of Abaco, has eight basic furnished rooms with hardwood floors, two double beds, air-con, and screened patios overlooking the swamps. Rooms are US$125 nightly, including all meals; no credit cards are accepted; all-inclusive packages begin at US$699 per person for four nights. You can also choose among 14 rustic thatched huts with shared bathroom. There's a small gift shop. The property has an all-timber restaurant serving the likes of sautéed grouper and wild boar; meals cost US$16 to US$20. You can also buy bush teas (US$3). Its postal address is PO Box AB-20092, Marsh Harbour, Abaco, The Bahamas.

Different of Abaco also has a full-service 10-suite *Seashell Beach Club* on the miles-long beach (contact information same as above). The modest, meagerly appointed rooms have high ceilings with fans, plus oceanfront verandas. The atmospheric dining room and bar are made of hardwoods. There's a whirlpool, and skiffs are

Frigate birds over Different of Abaco Nature Park

available to take you bonefishing. Rooms cost US$200, or US$800 per person for four nights, all-inclusive.

Getting There & Away

Casuarina Point is 1 mile east of the Great Abaco Hwy (the turnoff is 2 miles south of the turnoff for Cherokee Sound).

Sand Dollar Tours (☎ 242-367-2189, fax 242-367-3296), PO Box AB-20538, Marsh Harbour, Abaco, The Bahamas, offers guided tours to Different of Abaco, including swimming and shelling at Casuarina Point, for US$20 per person. It also has excursions to Little Harbour and Cherokee Sound and to remote Abaco settlements.

CROSSING ROCKS

This forlorn fishing village, 40 miles south of Marsh Harbour, lines the grassy shores of 2-mile-long Long Beach. The white-sand beach has rocks for tidepooling. The residents of the funky, fly-blown hamlet seem to barely eke a living from the sea. Most of the out-of-kilter shacks disappeared courtesy of Hurricane Floyd.

Crossing Rocks is named for the isthmus where Great Abaco narrows to its most slender point.

Trevor's Midway Restaurant, Bar & Lounge (☎ 242-366-2199), on the Great Abaco Hwy at the turnoff for Crossing Rocks, sells native dishes.

SANDY POINT

South of Crossing Rocks, the Great Abaco Hwy sweeps southwest through vast acres of pineland and ends at Sandy Point, a picturesque fishing community backed by a coconut palm plantation, 60 miles south of Marsh Harbour. Fishing smacks are drawn up on the beach and nets are lain out to dry.

The Walt Disney Company owns Gorda Cay, 8 miles offshore, which it uses as a private island stopover for its *Disney Magic* and *Disney Wonder* cruise ships.

There's a post office and BaTelCo station in Sandy Point, as well as a government clinic (☎ 242-366-4010), open 9 am to 1 pm weekdays.

Marine Mammal Research

Diane Claridge (☎ 242-366-4155), a marine biologist, conducts research on whales and dolphins from her base at Sandy Point. She is funded by a research grant from Earthwatch (in the US ☎ 800-776-0188, fax 617-926-8532, info@earthwatch.org), 680 Mt Auburn St, Watertown, MA 02272, USA. Earthwatch groups spend 10 days here learning about the Abacos' marine mammals and assisting with research, often using kayaks to see eye-to-eye with beaked whales and dolphins.

Places to Stay & Eat

Oeisha's Resort (☎ 242-366-4139, fax 242-365-6285), between the airstrip and settlement, has air-con rooms for about US$60 and a restaurant that doubles as a dance club. *Pete & Gay's Guest House* (☎ 242-366-4119, fax 242-366-4007), at the head of the dock, has air-con rooms with TV. It charges about US$60 and also serves meals.

The other eatery of choice is *Nancy's Seaside Inn Restaurant & Bar* (☎ 242-366-4120).

Getting There & Away

Cat Island Air flies from Nassau to Sandy Point on Wednesday, Friday, and Sunday (US$60 one-way). Bahamasair has irregular, seasonal service to Sandy Point.

The *Captain Gurth Dean* mail boat sails from Nassau to Sandy Point on Friday, also stopping at More Island (11 hours, US$25 one-way). Call ☎ 242-393-1064 for departure time.

Sand Dollar Tours (see contact information under Casuarina Point, above) offers a guided tour to Sandy Point and Crossing Rocks, including a visit to Different of Abaco, for US$30.

MORE ISLAND

Twenty miles northwest of Sandy Point, More Island is the only inhabited island off the west coast of the Abaco mainland. The settlements of **Hard Bargain** and **The Bight** have a long fishing tradition and a wild, rustic spirit.

There's a medical clinic (☎ 242-366-6105).

Tom's Inn, near the airstrip, and *Gator's Inn*, in The Bight, have no-frills rooms. A couple of local eateries serve native dishes and there's a grocery.

Cat Island Air flies from Nassau to More Island on Wednesday, Friday, and Sunday (US$60 one-way).

ABACO NATIONAL PARK

The pendulous udder of Great Abaco is smothered in native Caribbean pine and hardwood forest (part of Sandy Point Forest Preserve), much of it within 32-sq-mile Abaco National Park, established in 1994 to protect the major habitat of the endangered Bahama parrot. About 1100 parrots survive here.

There's also an extensive limestone cave system to explore (the local parrot population is unique – the birds nest in holes in the limestone rocks), plus hiking trails, lonesome beaches, and incredibly wild and spectacular scenery along the Atlantic shore.

Hole-in-the-Wall Lighthouse

The dramatic headland at the southern tip of the island is dominated by this red-and-white-hooped lighthouse, looming over the scrubby shore and reached by a horrendously potholed and tortuous road that adds to the sense of separation from civilization. The whistling wind emphasizes the wild beauty. You can climb to the top of the lighthouse for even more stupendous views.

Organized Tours

Sand Dollar Tours (☎ 242-367-2189) includes Abaco National Park, Hole-in-the-Wall, and the surrounding area on guided nature trips from Marsh Harbour.

Getting There & Away

A turnoff for the park is signed 10 miles south of Crossing Rocks. The road runs south, straight and treacherously potholed, for about 15 miles, then gives way to a dirt-and-rock track that snakes through scrubland for another 5 miles.

Northwest of Marsh Harbour

TREASURE CAY
• pop 1200

Treasure Cay, 17 miles north of Marsh Harbour, is not a true cay but a narrow peninsula jutting from the mainland like a sea horse's snout. Its north shore flaunts a 4-mile-long, crescent-shaped white-sand beach shelving gently into a vast expanse of turquoise waters extending almost to the horizon. The beach is named in sections from west to east: Casuarina, Banyan, Buckingham, Brigantine, Sandpiper, and Leeward.

Treasure Cay boasts a large residential and resort complex and is popular with yachters, who call in at the marina.

The Abacos' first Loyalist settlement was founded in 1783 at Carleton Point, at the northwestern end of Treasure Cay; it was later abandoned and only overgrown ruins remain. In the 1950s the first tourist development in the Abacos arose here (thanks to Leonard Thompson, a colorful character 'born in a hurricane under a coconut tree' who was instrumental in the birth of Bahamian tourism). An 18-hole championship golf course was conjured. The original hotel burned down in 1961 and was demolished in 2000. The cay now features a handsome modern complex of condos, villas, and hotel-style rooms.

Treasure Cay suffered extensive damage during Hurricane Floyd, including to the marina and boats docked there: an eight-foot storm surge flooded the bottom floors of condos around the marina. But all was well by summer 2000.

In May the Annual Bahamian Arts & Crafts Show is held here as part of the Treasure Cay Fishing Tournament.

Information
The Royal Bank of Canada (☎ 242-365-8119) is open 10:30 am to 3 pm Tuesday and Thursday. The post office is open 9 am to noon and 2 to 5 pm weekdays. There's a BaTelCo office (☎ 242-365-8000) on Treasure Cay Rd, and one southwest of town.

For the police, call ☎ 242-365-8048.

Annie's Laundry charges US$3 per load for a wash and US$3 for drying.

For medical attention, call Treasure Cay Clinic (☎ 242-367-3350) or the Corbett Medical Centre (☎ 242-365-8288).

Golf & Tennis
The Abacos' sole 18-hole golf course, the Treasure Cay Golf Course (☎ 242-365-8045, 800-327-1584) is known for its narrow fairways. Vital statistics: 72-par, 6985 yards. In 1999, *Golf Digest* voted it the premier golf course in the Bahamas. Games cost US$60, or US$50 for hotel or marina guests; a golf cart costs US$25. Tennis courts, also here, cost US$14 per hour. These discount rates apply only to guests of the Treasure Cay Hotel Resort & Marina; nonguests will pay more.

Bonefishing & Sport Fishing
There's good bonefishing in the shallow waters on the south side of the peninsula. The marina has sport-fishing charters and guides and hosts tournaments, including the Treasure Cay Fishing Tournament in May. Try Kingfish Charters (☎ 242-365-0104). Mark Carroll (☎ 242-365-8582) acts as a fishing guide.

Diving, Snorkeling & Other Water Sports
Divers Down (☎ 242-365-8465, fax 242-365-8508, VHF channel 16 or 79), at the marina, rents scuba equipment and offers dives (US$60/80 one/two-tank) and certification. It has snorkel trips for US$35. You can rent a mask, snorkel, and fins for US$10. Its postal address is PO Box AB-22212, Treasure Cay, Abaco, The Bahamas.

Rich's Rentals (☎ 242-365-8582) offers a snorkel-and-scuba picnic trip with a seafood lunch served on the beach. Likewise, JIC Boat Rentals (☎ 242-365-8465, fax 242-365-8508) offers half-day excursions to Shell Island and Great Guana Cay and to New Plymouth and Green Turtle Cay. And Abaco Adventures (☎ 242-365-8749) offers excursions to Great Guana Cay and Man O' War Cay.

Sunfish sailboats, kayaks, and sailboards can be rented on Buckingham Beach.

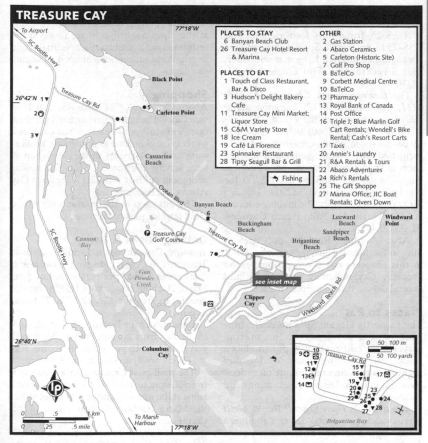

TREASURE CAY

PLACES TO STAY
6 Banyan Beach Club
26 Treasure Cay Hotel Resort & Marina

PLACES TO EAT
1 Touch of Class Restaurant, Bar & Disco
3 Hudson's Delight Bakery Cafe
11 Treasure Cay Mini Market; Liquor Store
15 C&M Variety Store
18 Ice Cream
19 Café La Florence
23 Spinnaker Restaurant
28 Tipsy Seagull Bar & Grill

OTHER
2 Gas Station
4 Abaco Ceramics
5 Carleton (Historic Site)
7 Golf Pro Shop
8 BaTelCo
9 Corbett Medical Centre
10 BaTelCo
12 Pharmacy
13 Royal Bank of Canada
14 Post Office
16 Triple J; Blue Marlin Golf Cart Rentals; Wendell's Bike Rental; Cash's Resort Carts
17 Taxis
20 Annie's Laundry
21 R&A Rentals & Tours
22 Abaco Adventures
24 Rich's Rentals
25 The Gift Shoppe
27 Marina Office; JIC Boat Rentals; Divers Down

Places to Stay

Treasure Cay Hotel Resort & Marina *(☎ 242-365-8578, fax 242-365-8362, info@ treasurecay.com; in the US ☎ 954-525-7711, 800-327-1584, fax 954-525-1699)* has hotel rooms, villas, condo units, and two-bedroom homes – 'Treasure Houses' – with decks and stunning interior decor. Standard rooms face the marina. All rooms are air-con and have cable TV, mini-fridge, coffeemaker, ironing board and iron, hairdryer, and patio. Slightly larger deluxe rooms have microwave ovens. Suites have loft bedrooms and are more luxuriously appointed. Standard rooms cost US$90/100 single/double low season, US$125/155 peak season. Deluxe rooms cost US$140/170 low season, US$190/225 peak season. Suites cost US$275 to US$315, depending on season and occupancy.

The complex includes ***Treasure Houses Villas***, luxurious beachfront air-con two-bedroom villas with kitchens, living rooms, decks, cable TV, washer and dryer, and bicycles. Some have a colonial era look…quite exquisite. The villas surround a freshwater lagoon complete with foot bridges, waterfalls, and grottos. The houses sleep up to six people and are set in carefully landscaped grounds with freshwater pools; rates begin at US$325 for up to four people and US$425 for six people. Special golf and dive packages are offered. Its postal address is 2301 S Federal Hwy, Fort Lauderdale, FL 33316, USA.

The *Banyan Beach Club* (☎ 242-365-8111, fax 242-365-8112, banyanbeach@banyanbeach.com; in the US ☎ 888-625-3060, fax 561-625-3060) offers two- and three-bedroom condos, each beautifully furnished with rattan chairs and leather sofas and boasting a fully equipped kitchen. Nightly rates are US$120 to US$200 for one-bedroom units, and US$200 to US$275 for two-bedroom units. The mailing address is 2720 Biarritz Dr, Palm Beach Gardens, FL 33410, USA.

Abaco Vacation Rentals (see Places to Stay in the Marsh Harbour section, earlier in this chapter) has seven properties on Treasure Cay, including two condos and several deluxe three-bedroom homes.

Places to Eat

The modestly elegant *Spinnaker Restaurant* (☎ 242-365-8569) at the marina serves from 7:30 am to 9:30 pm and has a theme night buffet each Wednesday night. You can dine indoors or on a deck over the marina. Dinner reservations are requested.

The marina's *Tipsy Seagull Bar & Grill* serves salads, pizzas, and desserts and has a Friday night barbecue. There's also a place for *ice cream* near the marina.

Locals frequent *Touch of Class Restaurant, Bar & Disco* (☎ 242-365-8195), on the highway 100 yards south of the turnoff for Treasure Cay. It serves native dishes. *Hudson's Delight Bakery Cafe* (☎ 242-365-8648), 100 yards farther south, offers coffees and baked goods.

Café La Florence sells home-baked cookies, fresh bread, pies, and cakes. It has a patio.

The *C&M Variety Store* stocks a large supply of groceries, although there's a larger grocery – *Treasure Cay Mini Market* – 50 yards west, with a liquor store adjacent.

Entertainment

A cocktail party is hosted on Friday evening at the *Tipsy Seagull*, a huge, all-wood bar festooned with nautical paraphernalia and overlooking an amoeba-shaped pool and sun deck.

Shopping

Abaco Ceramics (☎ 242-365-8489), on Treasure Cay Rd near the highway, has a gift shop, open 9 am to 3 pm weekdays. You can watch workers hand-making and -painting kitchenware and adornments in the workshop. A huge serving plate costs US$60. The mailing address is PO Box AB-22117, Treasure Cay, Abaco, The Bahamas.

The gift shop at the marina sells Abaco Gold jewelry, plus resortwear.

Getting There & Away

Treasure Cay Airport is 15 miles north of Treasure Cay. A taxi between the two points costs about US$12 per person. A taxi from Marsh Harbour costs about US$55 (for two people) to Treasure Cay and US$75 to the airport.

Bahamasair (in Treasure Cay ☎ 242-365-8600) flies from Nassau daily (US$60 each way). Island Express (in Treasure Cay ☎ 242-354-8697) flies from Fort Lauderdale.

The mail boat *Captain Gurth Dean* sails from Nassau to Treasure Cay on Tuesday; it stops at the marina, among other places. See the Marsh Harbour section earlier in this chapter for details.

The 150-slip full-service marina (☎ 242-365-8250; in the US ☎ 800-327-1584) accommodates yachts up to 140 feet. Dockage costs US85¢ per foot per day (less in low season), including cable TV.

Getting Around

Triple J (☎ 242-365-0161) rents cars for US$75 daily. Rich's Rentals (☎ 242-365-8582) rents scooters for US$45 for 24 hours, as does R&A Rentals & Tours. Wendell's Bike Rental (☎ 242-365-8687) rents bicycles for US$5/7 half/full day.

You can rent golf carts from Cash's Resort Carts (☎ 242-365-8465, VHF channel 16 and 79) for US$40/245 daily/weekly; or from Blue Marlin Golf Cart Rentals at the marina.

Rich's Rentals (☎ 242-365-8582) has a wide range of boats, from 17-foot Bone Fishers for US$70/380 daily/weekly to 26-foot Novas for US$135/700.

You can also rent 20- to 26-foot boats from JIC Boat Rentals (☎ 242-365-8465, fax 242-365-8508) from US$130 daily.

GREEN TURTLE CAY

Eight miles north of Treasure Cay, Green Turtle is the northernmost of the four Loyalist Cays. The town of **New Plymouth** (pop 450) is a time capsule and living museum redolent with Loyalist history. It was declared a historic district in 1999 and many buildings are being restored. The effort has been redoubled since Hurricane Floyd struck.

The town lies on the shore of Settlement Creek, at the westernmost end of a hooked peninsula formed by Black Sound at the south end of the island. The three-masted schooner that sailed into these sun-dappled waters in 1783 carried 500 New Yorkers (mostly Irish Protestants whose property had been confiscated by the victorious colonials). During the 19th century, the town they founded grew to be the second-largest city in the Bahamas. Today's sleepy storybook village has lost none of its venerable charm, thanks to its pastel-painted, clapboarded, gingerbread-trimmed houses and its lively churches (the daffodil-yellow Gospel Chapel, at New Plymouth and Parliament Sts, is renowned for its rousing revival meetings).

The rest of the island is the domain of wealthy expats, but none of them own land in town. Loyalist descendants won't sell town property to out-of-towners; they prefer to keep it in the family, undeeded. Many locals live by conching and lobstering.

The Atlantic shore is lined with fabulous white-sand beaches and reefs. Loggerhead turtles still crawl ashore to nest.

Information

Barclays Bank (☎ 242-365-4144), at the far end of Parliament St, is open 10 am to 1 pm Tuesday and Thursday.

The tiny police station (☎ 242-365-4450) and post office are adjacent in the historic pink-and-white building on Parliament St at King St.

There are phone booths in several locales, including outside the library (direct-dial), by the ferry dock (phonecard operated), and at the BaTelCo office (☎ 242-365-4113) at the east end of town (it also has fax service).

Sid's Grocery offers Internet and email access for US$2 connection, and US$1 per minute thereafter.

The library, adjoining the post office, has a good collection of novels and general reference. Books are borrowed on the honor system.

The government's Green Turtle Cay Clinic (☎ 242-365-4028), one block west of the New Plymouth Club & Inn, has a nurse on duty; a doctor is available on Tuesday and Thursday. The Sunlight Medical Centre (☎ 242-365-4409) has a doctor.

Albert Lowe Museum

This exquisite museum (☎ 242-365-1494), at Parliament and King Sts, is housed in a building dating from 1826 that has served as headquarters for the US consul and as home to Neville Chamberlain before he became prime minister of England. The museum was founded in 1976 by the nation's most prominent artist, Alton Roland Lowe, who has dedicated most of his adult life to preserving the long-neglected history of his native Abacos. A separate gallery honors his work, as well as those of artist James Mastin, who produced the busts in the nearby sculpture garden. The more than 100 Lowe family members on the island contributed the model sailing ships, historical items, and documents that tell the various chapters of local history. The Lowes are descended from Gideon Lowe, who was on that first boat in 1783. It's open 9 am to 11:45 am and 1 to 4:30 pm Monday to Saturday. Admission costs US$1.

Alton Lowe Studio

Homegrown artist Alton Roland Lowe is the nation's artist laureate and certainly its most successful (his works are sought after

ABACOS

GREEN TURTLE CAY

PLACES TO STAY
1 Coco Bay Cottages
2 Green Turtle Club & Marina
4 Bluff House Beach Hotel
7 Villa Pasha
8 Other Shore Club & Marina
10 Linton's Beach & Harbour Cottages
16 Pelican Cove Guest Cottage
41 New Plymouth Club & Inn

PLACES TO EAT
6 Bluff House Marina Restaurant
14 Rooster Restaurant & Pub; Rooster's Rest
18 Plymouth Rock Café; Ocean Blue Gallery
20 Sid's Groceries
21 Old Tyme Sweet Shoppe
22 Lowe's Food Store; Island Deli & Bake Shoppe; Lowe Gift Shoppe
26 Gerry's Food Store & Gift Shop
29 Laura's Kitchen
35 Wrecking Tree
36 McIntosh Restaurant & Bakery
37 Clara & Ruth's Barbecue
38 Mike's Bar & Restaurant

OTHER
3 Brendal's Dive Shop
5 Bluff House Marina
9 Abaco Yacht Services
11 Black Sound Marina
12 Robert's Dock
13 BaTelCo
15 Alton Lowe Studio; Garden Theatre
17 Mail-Boat Dock
19 Barclays Bank
23 Golden Reef Souvenirs
24 Loyalist Memorial Sculpture Garden
25 Vert Lowe's Model Ship Shoppe
27 Sunlight Medical Centre
28 Public Dock; Telephone
30 Shell Hut; New Plymouth Golf Carts
31 Curtis Bike Rental
32 Ferry Dock

33 Ferry Office
34 Miss Emily's Blue Bee Bar
39 Gospel Chapel
40 Green Turtle Cay Clinic
42 Loyalist Rose Shoppe
43 Albert Lowe Museum
44 Post Office; Library; Telephone
45 Police Station
46 Cemetery

77°20'W

0   .5   1 km
0   .25   .5 mile

26°48'N

Sea of Abaco

Coco Bay

1

Bluff Cay

2
3

White Sound

4
25
6

White Sound

Long Bay Cay

Loyalist Rd

Long Bay

7

26°46'N

9
10

8

11
12
Black Sound

NEW PLYMOUTH
see inset map

13
14

15
16
Gillam Bay

Gillam Bay Rd

0   100   200 m
0   100   200 yards

17

18
19
Charles St
Bay St
22
20
26
27
28
21
23
25
32
39
24
31
40
41 42
43
30
38
44
45
New Plymouth St
Crown St
King St
Mission St
Parliament St
York St
Hill St
35
34
37
36
Victoria St
46
Query Rd
Walters St

Settlement Creek

77°20'W

by monarchs, prime ministers, and others with heaps of cash to spare). He inherited his artistic skills from his father, Albert, a noted sea captain, inventor, musician, artist, and historian. Alton has built a permanent exhibition hall and cultural center about a half-mile outside town at the head of Black Sound. There's no sign. Look for the tall white gates set back from the road and the white, pink, and peppermint-green house amid trees on the hill above. July and December are open months; otherwise it's by appointment only (☎ 242-365-4264).

Vert Lowe's Model Ship Shoppe

Vert, Alton's brother, makes intricate model sailing ships, a genius he also picked up from his father, a master model-boat builder. When his father died, leaving a presold three-master only partially finished, Vert (☎ 242-365-4170) thought the decent thing to do would be to complete the project. Vert works on commission for a hefty fee but hasn't moved out of his dinky garage, up an alley off Bay St, where you are welcome to watch him conjuring miniature sailing vessels from redwood, spruce, and fir.

Loyalist Memorial Sculpture Garden

This splendid garden, on Parliament St at New Plymouth St, features 25 bronze busts of notable Loyalists and slaves from all the Bahamian islands, arranged in the shape of the Union Jack. Two Loyalist women – one black, one white – stand as the centerpiece atop a coral platform, with a bronze plaque written by author Sandra Riley. She movingly describes the abuse of Americans loyal to King George during the American Revolution and their plight, which led to the settlement of the Abacos. This moving testament to the indomitable spirit of the Loyalists gives equal emphasis to the often forgotten role of slaves and other blacks who fled behind British lines and were guaranteed liberty and protection.

Cemetery

The 200-year-old bones of Loyalist ancestors lie in this twee cemetery at the east end of Parliament St. Many of the graves are so old that they've crumbled and sunk. Even so, descendants of the long-deceased still pretty the graves with flowers and wreaths.

Gillam Bay Beach

This handsome beach lies a half-mile east of town. The 2-mile-wide bay shelves into countless acres of limpid turquoise shallows. The large sandbar is good for shelling.

White Sound & Coco Bay

Touristy White Sound, 2 miles north of New Plymouth, is a deep bay protected by a bluff-faced peninsula – the setting for a notably wealthy expat community that other islanders term the 'White Sound Society' for its aloof ways. Pre-Columbian Lucayan artifacts have been found on the bluff.

Dirt roads lead north from White Sound to the wild Atlantic shore and Coco Bay, with a lovely crescent of powder-soft sand. A more recent, less aloof crop of expats have homes north of Coco Bay, hidden along the shores amid wild brush. They are very welcoming and can relate marvelous tales of the island…like the time a huge section of a US Air Force Titan missile washed ashore from the Atlantic! The Air Force neglected to claim it, until one day a helicopter whirred in, dispatching a military squad and scaring the dickens out of locals (many of whom were involved in drug trafficking). The squad hauled off some top-secret components, leaving folks to display parts of the missile in their gardens.

Diving & Snorkeling

Near the Green Turtle Club & Marina in White Sound, Brendal's Dive Shop (☎ 242-365-4411, brendals@grouper.batelnet.bs; in the US ☎ 954-467-1133, 800-780-9941) has dive packages. A two-day, four-tank package costs US$130; 10 one-tank dives cost US$350. Its certification course costs US$450. Beginners can take the plunge for US$85. Snorkel trips cost US$30. You can rent equipment, including snorkel and underwater camera and video gear.

Sport Fishing & Bonefishing

Rick Sawyer's Playmate Charter Fishing (☎ 242-365-4261) can take you fishing for US$140/230 half/full-day. Ronnie Sawyer (☎ 242-365-4070) also guides.

The Green Turtle Club & Marina hosts the annual billfishing tournament in May.

Boat Excursions

The Green Turtle Club & Marina offers island cruises to guests aboard the 42-foot *Amorosa*.

Brendal Stevens (see the Diving & Snorkeling section, above) offers daylong sailing cruises with beach cookout and punch on Manjack or No Name Cays for US$75. Options include snorkeling, hand-feeding stingrays, diving for lobster, hiking, and shelling. He offers glass-bottomed boat trips for US$40, sunset cruises, and excursions to Nipper's on Great Guana Cay.

Special Events

Green Turtle Cay's traditional Junkanoo parades, held on Boxing Day and New Year's Day, attract scores of visitors. New Plymouth's narrow streets are thronged in an extravaganza of clanging cowbells and blasting conch shells. The partying begins before dawn, the formal parade at 2 pm.

Green Turtle's paraders are followed by the Bunce, a bogeyman who lives in the forest, covered in a sheet and propelled down the street in a wheelbarrow, terrifying the kids. (Many islanders firmly believe in the Bunce – or 'Boonce,' as the locals pronounce it – and sleep with a light on at night to keep him away.) The evil spirit is ceremoniously 'captured' and buried during Junkanoo celebrations.

In the weeks leading up to Junkanoo, call in on Corporal Hubert James Smith – Corporal 'Smitty' – the undisputed king of costuming, and watch him make his magical suits. You can find him at Miss Emily's Blue Bee Bar. (See the Entertainment section later in this chapter.)

The annual highlight is Regatta Week, held each July beginning with sailing races and festivities at Green Turtle Cay, followed by the same at Great Guana Cay, Marsh

Harbour, Man O' War Cay, Elbow Cay, and, again, Marsh Harbour.

During the last week in December, the Christmas Concert Under the Stars is held at the Garden Theatre (see the Entertainment section). An Evening of Music and Comedy is traditionally held here in January. Call Ivy Roberts (☎ 242-365-4094) or Alton Lowe (☎ 242-365-4264).

Also in December, during Plymouth Historical Weekend, Green Turtle residents celebrate their Loyalist heritage with cultural events and barbecues.

Places to Stay

New Plymouth The only hotel in town is the marvelously romantic *New Plymouth Club & Inn* (☎ 242-365-4161, fax 242-365-4138; in the US ☎ 800-688-4752), a painstakingly restored colonial inn set amid cloistered gardens replete with cast-iron lampposts and benches. This charmer has nine small air-con rooms with private bathroom and ceiling fan, furnished in period fashion with all the comforts of home, for US$100 single, US$130 double year-round. Facilities include a pool and sun deck with hammock in the compact courtyard, a cozy lounge filled with Toulouse-Lautrec prints, and an elegant restaurant serving gourmet fare.

Linton's Beach & Harbour Cottages (☎ 242-365-4003, fax 242-365-4002; in North America ☎ 615-269-5682, 800-688-4752, fax 615-353-1882) comprise two charmers – Seagrape and Palmetto – on Long Bay Beach, 1 mile north of New Plymouth, set amid 22 acres. Each has a living room and dining area, plus twin bedrooms, fully equipped kitchen, and patio-garden, but no air-con; ceiling fans and breezes do the trick. Rented together, the cottages accommodate up to 10 people. Each rents for US$150/1000 nightly/ weekly single or double mid-September to mid-December. The rest of the year, you'll be charged US$190/1250 single or double and US$220/1450 for three or four people. Bikes are included and there's a private dock. Credit cards are not accepted.

The *Other Shore Club & Marina* (☎ 242-365-4195/4226), on the shore of Black Sound just north of town, has rooms and cottages, plus a swimming pool. Rates range from US$90 to US$130 for two to six people.

Abaco Vacation Rentals (see Places to Stay in the Marsh Harbour section) rents the one-bedroom *Pelican Cove Guest Cottage*, on Gillam Bay Beach, for US$650 weekly.

White Sound & Coco Bay The upscale *Bluff House Beach Hotel* (☎ 242-365-4200/4247, fax 242-365-4248, BluffHouse@ oii.net) is centered on a wooden deck, with rooms cascading down toward the Sea of Abaco. Options include air-con rooms, one-to three-bedroom villas, a range of suites, and even 'treehouses' with kitchenette and stove. The rooms – which were recently renovated and upgraded – all have a refrigerator, coffee-maker, hair dryer, sofabed, and private balcony with marvelous views. The former restaurant was being converted into suites at press time. The four 'Upper Suites' have king-size beds, beautiful decor, and a tremendous setting over the water. Rooms cost US$115/135/145 low/high/peak season. Deluxe rooms cost US$145/180/199. Suites cost US$175/225/250. Villas range from US$210 to US$399 in low season, US$440 to US$550 in peak season. The hotel boasts a pool, plus its own private beach, tennis court, boats, fishing tackle, and golf-cart rentals. The resort has lots of steps and is unsuited to people who have trouble with stairs. The Web site is www.bluffhouse.com.

The *Green Turtle Club & Marina* (☎ 242-365-4271, fax 242-365-4272, info@ greenturtleclub.com; in the USA ☎ 800-688-4752), cradled in the cusp of White Sound Harbor, exudes Cape Cod charm. It sustained considerable damage during Hurricane Floyd but things have been fixed up. It has 26 air-con rooms and cottages and eight villas. Deluxe cottage rooms and harborfront villas are exquisitely decorated, with hardwood floors, throw rugs, period mahogany furniture, and TV/VCR. Ordinary rooms are simpler. Deluxe (lowest-tier) rooms begin at US$150 in low-season and US$185 in high-season. Suites cost US$195 to US$225. One-and two-bedroom villas begin at US$265 and rise to US$395. Facilities include a pool, English-pub–style lounge, and a restaurant

offering candlelit dining. Activities include fishing and diving. Excursions are offered. The mailing address is PO Box AB-22792, Green Turtle Cay, Abaco, The Bahamas.

Coco Bay Cottages (☎ 242-365-5464, fax 242-365-5465, cocobay@oii.net; in North America ☎ 800-752-0166) nestles at the narrowest point of the island, where barely 100 yards of land divide the beaches of Coco Bay from the sandy Atlantic shore. This 5-acre hideaway, with four two-bedroom cottages surrounded by fruit trees, is perfect for an unpretentious, no-frills escape. 'Jamaica' faces the ocean and costs US$200/270 single/double year-round; 'Tahiti' faces the bay and costs US$150/180; 'Pink' and 'Bali Hai' take in the best of both worlds for US$150/210. Each is adorned with rattan furniture and has a cathedral ceiling, a spacious and fully equipped kitchen, wrap-around deck, ceiling fans, and phone. The mailing address is PO Box AB-22759, Green Turtle Cay, Abaco, The Bahamas.

The *Treehouse by the Sea* (☎ /fax 242-365-4258, 800-942-9304 ext 20510, treehouse@ oii.net) has octagonal two-bedroom 'treehouses' with living room and full kitchen, each for up to six people, with air-con, ceiling fans, handsome modern furnishings, and decks. Rates are US$135/850 nightly/weekly. Contact Janet Curtis, Green Turtle Cay, Abaco, The Bahamas.

Long Bay House (☎ 242-365-4294, longbayhouse@grouper.batelnet.bs) is a large oceanfront home on seven acres along Long Bay Beach. It has a screened in porch, decks, and a gazebo with hammocks, plus pool, bicycles, dock, and boat, and an observation tower with 360° views of the island. You can view it and other rental properties online at the following Web site: www .10kvacationrentals.com.

Abaco Vacation Rentals (see the Places to Stay section of the Marsh Harbour section, earlier in this chapter) also rents high-end properties by the week, including *Villa Pasha*, a traditional Caribbean-style villa on the Atlantic shore, luxuriously decorated in period style. It even has a library and master bedroom suite with whirlpool tub, four bathrooms, marble floors, and five TVs. The Web site, www.abacovacations.com, lists other properties as well.

Places to Eat

New Plymouth US breakfasts and local fare for lunch and dinner are served at *McIntosh Restaurant & Bakery*, where you also can buy carrot cake and homemade desserts.

The *Plymouth Rock Café* (☎ 242-365-4234) has counter dining, including a light breakfast and a luncheon sandwich board. It makes omelets on Wednesday. Another good deli option is *Ole B's*, a US-style diner and ice cream parlor on the Bay St waterfront.

Mike's Bar & Restaurant (☎ 242-365-4219) specializes in conch dishes; it's open Monday to Saturday, 11 am to 2 pm only, and for dinner by reservation.

Laura's Kitchen (☎ 242-365-4287), on King St, is lauded by locals. The fare is simple but excellent. The lunch menu includes a tuna sandwich for US$3.50, Bahamian platters for US$8, and a rib-burger special for US$8. The dinner menu changes daily.

The *Island Deli & Bake Shoppe* (☎ 242-365-4082), upstairs from the Lowe Gift Shoppe, specializes in conch dishes. Two other Bahamian-style favorites include *Rooster Restaurant & Pub* (☎ 242-365-4066) and the *Wrecking Tree* (☎ 242-365-4263); it's open 10 am to 9 pm daily.

To really be one with the locals, check out *Clara & Ruth's barbecue* on Saturday in the backyard of their home on Hill St.

For more refined fare, try the *New Plymouth Club & Inn* (☎ 242-365-4161) which has one sitting at 7:30 pm and a choice among three entrees, preceded by hors d'oeuvres at 6:30 pm, served in the cozy lounge-cum-dining room, with jazz and classical music and soft candlelight adding to the romance. Dinner costs US$25 to US$28. Reservations are due by 5 pm. It also serves breakfast 8 to 9 am and lunch (and Sunday brunch) 11:30 am to 1:30 pm.

For ice cream, head to *Olde Tyme Sweet Shoppe* on the waterfront. It has seating under shade umbrellas on the beach.

You can buy groceries at *Lowe's Food Store*, *Gerry's Food Store & Gift Shop*, or *Sid's Groceries*.

White Sound & Coco Bay The elegant, oceanfront Old-English–style *Bluff House Marina Restaurant* (☎ 242-365-4247) was being replaced at press time with an equally elegant new restaurant on White Sound.

The *Green Turtle Club* (☎ 242-365-4271), a member of the Chaine des Rotisseurs gourmet society, offers breakfast and lunch on the patio and gourmet dinners in its exquisite Queen-Anne–style dining room. You choose among three entrees. Reservations must be made before 5 pm.

Entertainment

Miss Emily's Blue Bee Bar is the legendary watering hole that originated the widely copied Goombay Smash. Miss Emily, a teetotaler who died in March 1997, came up with the bar's trademark drink when she was 'fooling around' with mixes about 20 years ago. The place is now run by her son, Corporal Smith ('Smitty' when out of uniform), and her daughter, Violet, who still brews the secret recipe at home in plastic jugs. The simple wooden hut has only rustic seating, and decor is provided by business cards festooning the walls, T-shirts and underwear hanging from the ceiling, and salutations scribbled by happy customers. The mood is rum-thick when the music gets going. The record number of Goombay Smashes drunk by one man in one night is a whopping 23; he had to be taken home in a wheelbarrow. It closes at 10 pm.

You can play pool next door at *Bert's Sea Garden Club*, where Bert Reckley serves a house concoction of coconut rum and milk.

The Gully Roosters perform rake 'n' scrape calypso and soca music at the *Roosters Rest* on Friday and Saturday nights, when the locals get down and dirty. They also play at *Bluff House* on Thursday night; and at the *Green Turtle Club* on Wednesday night.

On Thursday night there's a beach barbecue with live bands and Junkanoo at *Bluff House*. Live music is also offered on Tuesday.

The open-air *Garden Theatre*, adjacent to the Alton Lowe Studio at Black Sound, hosts comedy, musical, and theatrical concerts throughout the year.

Shopping

One visit to Vert Lowe's Model Ship Shoppe (☎ 242-365-4170) will have you reaching for your wallet. Models begin at US$300. A 26-inch one-master costs about US$600. For two- or three-masted ships up to 5 feet long, expect to pay US$1200 to US$2500.

Also look for paintings by Alton Lowe, sold at the gallery next to the Albert Lowe Museum. You might see some of his works displayed at the Ocean Blue Gallery in the Plymouth Rock Café, where over 50 artists are represented by prints, oils, and watercolors. Other gems include stained-glasswork by Rome Heyer.

The Sand Dollar-Abaco Gold sells hand-made gold jewelry, resortwear, plus other souvenirs, as does Golden Reef Souvenirs.

The Loyalist Rose Shoppe sells jewelry and T-shirts. And you should be able to find any odds and ends that you need (plus books, postcards, and kitschy souvenirs) at the Shell Hut variety store.

Bluff House has an upscale boutique. The Green Turtle Club boutique has a wide range of swimwear and casual clothing. The more fashion-conscious might browse the high-class imported ladies wear at Rebecca's, also at the Green Turtle Club.

Getting There & Away

AIT (☎ 242-365-4166) ferries run from the Green Turtle Dock, 2 miles south of Treasure Cay airport, at 8, 9, and 11 am and 12:15, 1:30, 3, and 4:30 pm daily, returning at 8:30, 10:30, and 11:30 am and 1:30, 2:30, 3:30, 4:30, and 5:30 pm (10 minutes, US$8 one-way). The skipper will drop you off at the dock nearest your hotel. If you rented a villa, your skipper will radio ahead so that the caretaker will be waiting for you. Ferries also operate on demand for people with flights; call ahead.

A taxi from Treasure Cay Airport to the ferry dock costs US$3 per person, US$5 minimum; from Marsh Harbour, it's about US$75 for two people.

The mail boat *Captain Gurth Dean* calls in once a week from Nassau; see the Marsh Harbour Getting There & Away section for information.

The Black Sound Marina (☎ 242-365-4531) has slips, gas, water, electricity, showers, laundry, and wet storage. The Other Shore Club & Marina (☎ 242-365-4338), also at Black Sound, also has a full-service marina, as does Robert's Dock (☎ 242-365-4249). Black Sound is considered a hurricane shelter.

Green Turtle Club & Marina (☎ 242-365-4271) has a full-service marina accommodating boats up to 150 feet; US70¢ per foot. The shoreside Bluff House Marina was still open at press time, but an all-new, full-service marina was in the works.

Green Turtle Cay is a Port of Entry for The Bahamas; customs and immigration (☎ 242-365-4077) is on Parliament St, in New Plymouth.

Getting Around

The preferred mode of transportation is the golf cart, available through New Plymouth Golf Carts, at the Shell Hut, and D&P Rentals (☎ 242-365-4125), which also rents scooters for US$35 daily.

There are two taxi services: OMRI's Taxis and McIntosh Taxis (to reach either call ☎ 242-365-4309, VHF channel 06). A ride between New Plymouth and Coco Bay or White Sound costs about US$10 for two people.

Curtis Bike Rental, at the town dock, charges US$6/10 half/full-day. Brendal Stevens of Brendal's Dive Shop (☎ 242-365-4411) also rents bicycles. You also can rent boats from Brendal's for US$15/60 hourly/daily.

You can rent boats from Donny's Boat Rental (☎ 242-365-4271) at the Green Turtle Club.

COOPER'S TOWN

This small settlement, the *only* settlement in the 30 miles between Treasure Cay and the northern tip of Great Abaco, is a center for commercial citrus farms, hidden away from the road amid the pine forests that dominate the island. Most of the residents earn their livings working in Treasure Cay or conching and lobstering, which is honored at the funky **Albert Bootle Museum**. The main street is one block east of SC Bootle Hwy.

ABACOS

The prime minister and FNM leader, Hubert A Ingraham, is the homegrown representative for Cooper's Town.

There's a clinic (☎ 242-365-0300) and a laundromat and general store. The Shell gas station, destroyed by Hurricane Floyd, was being rebuilt at last visit.

You can take rooms at the *M&M Guest House* (☎ *242-365-0142*), which has a restaurant.

The delightful *Conch Crawl Inn & Shipwreck Bar* (☎ *242-365-0423*), a weathered-wood restaurant on the waterfront, serves seafood and native dishes amid a motley yet endearing decor of turtle shells and fishing nets. At night it becomes a lively spot and has sports on TV.

SPANISH CAY

This 3-mile-long sliver, once owned by Queen Elizabeth II, is 3 miles off the northern tip of Great Abaco. Most of its 185 acres are covered in palm groves and tropical forest, with a few homes of the international gentry hidden in their midst. Four beautiful beaches line the east shore.

Places to Stay & Eat

Spanish Cay Inn & Marina (☎ *242-365-0083, fax 242-365-0466*) is a small luxury resort whose original owner used to host the Dallas Cowboys. It has five 'villa-suites' from US$150 year-round, as well as seven one- and two-bedroom apartment bungalows starting at US$200. There are two waterfront restaurants (rebuilt since Hurricane Floyd) and a tennis court, plus a swimming pool and whirlpool with a nearby bar. Golf carts are available, as are boats for fishing or diving. The mailing address is PO Box AB-882, Cooper's Town, Abaco, The Bahamas.

The *Point House* (☎ *242-359-6622*) restaurant, at the marina, serves breakfast and lunch, but it's very expensive. The *Wrecker's Bar*, sitting atop stilts over the ocean, serves snacks.

Getting There & Away

Spanish Cay has a 5000-foot airstrip for guests arriving by private plane, plus a new full-service 70-slip marina (☎/fax 242-365-

0083), rebuilt since Hurricane Floyd, with full services. It charges US$1 per foot.

A free water taxi runs from the government dock at Cooper's Town. A taxi from Treasure Cay Airport to the dock will cost US$30 for two people, US$5 per additional person.

LITTLE ABACO

Great Abaco ends 5 miles northwest of Cooper's Town at Angel Fish Point, where SC Bootle Hwy swings west over a bridge onto Little Abaco island.

The population lives in four small and relatively poor settlements: Cedar Harbour, Mount Hope, Fox Town, and Crown Haven. Together they bill themselves as 'The Pride of Abaco,' though the few middle-class homes mingle with more numerous tumble-down hovels and shacks, many of which were destroyed by Hurricane Floyd. Most of the locals live by conching and lobstering.

There's a post office and police station in Fox Town.

There are a few modest beaches and the bonefishing on the south side of Little Abaco is said to be excellent. In Crown Haven the road fizzles out at a rickety wharf where in late afternoon you may watch lobster being landed and the day's conch catch being gutted.

Many Abaconians literally live off lobster.

The Little Abaco Homecoming is held in early June.

A taxi from Treasure Cay Airport will cost about US$60 for two. The Tangelo Hotel will pick you up at the airport for US$10 for two. Sand Dollar Tours (☎ 242-367-2189) offers tours to Crown Haven from Marsh Harbour.

Places to Stay & Eat
The *Tangelo Hotel* (☎ 242-365-2222), on the fringe of Fox Town, describes itself as the 'best hotel in Little Abaco.' Indeed, it's practically the only one. Congenially run by Gladys Saunders, this otherwise soulless hotel has 12 modestly furnished air-con rooms, each with TV, ceiling fans, plenty of hot water, and either one double or two twin beds; US$65 single or double year-round. Transfers are offered to and from Treasure Cay Airport. Gladys prepares excellent grouper lunches and dinners for US$8.

In Fox Town, Merline and Millie McIntosh have a small hotel – *Millie's Guesthouse* (☎ 242-365-2046) – with four air-con rooms for US$45, plus an efficiency for US$55. It's next to the Shell gas station.

The *Valley Restaurant*, also beside the gas station, serves seafood; it has a pool table and TV. Here, too, you can buy groceries at *M&M Grocery Store*.

Several local restaurants serve native dishes and double as nightspots.

Northwest Cays

GRAND CAY
• pop 400
Near the top of the Abacos chain, Grand Cay is as offbeat as things get in The Bahamas. Most of the staff of the Walker's Cay Hotel & Marina live here (see Walker's Cay, below), traveling back and forth by boat, but very few visitors call. You can hop a ride for about US$10 one-way.

Grand Cay is divided into the larger, box-shaped, virtually uninhabited isle of that name and, to its east, Little Grand Cay and Mermaid Cay, with small settlements. There are several beaches; the most spec-

tacular is Wells Bay, which runs the 2-mile west shore of Grand Cay. The bonefishing here is superb; ask Gerald Rolle or Willard Munnings to guide you; anyone in town can direct you to them.

There's a medical clinic on Grand Cay.

Places to Stay & Eat
Rosie Curry runs the *Island Bay Restaurant & Motel* (☎ 242-353-1200). The 20 air-con rooms, for US$50, are modest but each has a TV; some have a kitchenette. The motel has a launderette. Meals are served if pre-ordered.

There are several other eateries, including Eddie Cooper's *Hilltop View Restaurant & Lounge*. You can buy fresh bread at *Ena's Bakery* and groceries at *Father & Son Grocery*.

Entertainment
On weekends the *Island Bay* and *Seaside Bar* get in the groove with dance clubs, and the bar at Island Bay also has a pool table.

Getting There & Away
Island Bay Restaurant & Motel has a marina with 15 slips, with water, gas, and diesel.

Roosevelt Curry operates a water taxi between Walker's Cay and Grand Cay. There's no charge if you're going to eat at the Island Bay (six passengers minimum; otherwise there's a fee). You can call him there from the marina. Any local boater will run you between the cays for about US$5.

WALKER'S CAY
Tiny Walker's Cay, the 'Top of The Bahamas,' is a craggy coral outcrop rising to 50 feet at the uppermost end of the Abacos chain, on the outer edge of the Little Bahama Bank. The isle is dominated by a single marina and hotel, high on the eastern bluff. There's no settlement, and the population is limited to plump curly-tailed lizards and a flock of sooty terns, caterwauling and honking. Frigate birds also wing overhead.

Walker's Cay is acclaimed for diving and sport fishing (it claims 'more International Game Fishing Association – IGFA – records than any other resort').

By following the airstrip (stay to the margins, as the strip is very active), you'll reach a slender, scimitar-shaped white-sand beach; another teeny beach is tucked away at the westernmost end of the airstrip.

Walker's Cay is surrounded by even tinier cays, to which Walker's Cay Hotel & Marina staff will run you and strand you for an hour or day (after preparing you a box lunch).

All visitors from overseas must clear immigration (☎ 242-353-1215) and customs (☎ 242-353-1211) at the airstrip; the office is open 9 am to 5 pm daily.

Diving & Snorkeling

Walker's Cay is fringed by a barrier reef that offers spectacular diving, often in less than 30 feet of water. Highlights include old wrecks, including a WWII relic; Jeanette's Reef, boasting a large population of eels; caverns populated by silver minnows; and Travel Agent Reef, a beautiful coral garden ideal for snorkelers and novice divers.

The Sea Below Dive Shop (☎ 242-353-1252, 800-925-5377, fax 242-353-1339), in the Walker's Cay Hotel & Marina, has full equipment rental, including 35mm cameras. It offers instruction for PADI certification for US$300. Two dive trips are offered daily (US$50/75 one/two-tank; US$55 night dives). Snorkel trips are offered for US$20.

For a real hoot, you can kneel on the sea bottom, 35 feet down, while hungry sharks swirl around you. The island's famous Shark Rodeo (US$65/85 one/two-tank) often attracts dozens of blacktip and Caribbean reef sharks at a time. They'll swim up close to check you out, but they're more interested in the 'chumsicle' – a plastic trash can filled with stinking fish tails, heads, and entrails – that acts to ravenous sharks as a subaqueous dinner bell. As soon as the bucket hits the water, they rip into the fish. The noise of crunching bones – the water amplifies sound – can be unsettling. All will be fine. Just keep your eyes on the chumsicle and stay clear of sharks fighting for food. And please don't wave your hands, swim erratically, or otherwise act like food.

Sport Fishing & Bonefishing

Charter boats are available at the marina from US$225/350 half/full day, including guide, tackle, and bait. Bonefishing costs US$325 (full day only) for an 18-foot skiff. Reservations are recommended.

The North Abaco Sportfishing Championship is held on Walker's Cay each April. In May the cay hosts the Walker's Cay Billfish Tournament and the Bertram-Hatteras Shootout.

Volunteer Research

Researchers from the Aquarium of the Americas in New Orleans, along with the National Marine Fisheries Service, the University of Miami, Walker's Cay National Park, and Oceanographic Expeditions, are involved in a long-term effort to study shark behavior around Walker's Cay. Hollywood couldn't have come up with a better name: the 'Apex Predator Project.'

Volunteer divers are needed to study and photograph sharks during monthly, week-long trips. To qualify, you must have completed at least 25 logged dives and three night dives in the past five years. Contact Oceanographic Expeditions (in the US ☎/ fax 504-488-1573, seascience@aol.com), 4418 St Ann St, New Orleans, LA 70119-3608, USA.

Oceanographic Expeditions also needs volunteers for its 'Project Reef Spawn' at Walker's Cay. The study seeks to unravel the mystery of coral spawning, when zillions of egg bundles are released simultaneously, like a storm of Alka Seltzer bubbles, on the one night a year that many coral species throughout the hemisphere reproduce. This amazing event occurs predictably in late August. Again, to qualify you must have completed at least 25 logged dives and three night dives in the past five years.

Places to Stay & Eat

Walker's Cay Hotel & Marina (☎ 242-353-1252, fax 242-353-1339, walkerscay@ mindspring.com; in the US ☎ 954-359-1400, 800-925-5377, fax 954-359-1414) nestles over the marina. It has 62 air-con rooms that have been renovated since Hurricane Floyd. Each has private bathroom and terrace, but no TVs, radios, or telephones. The resort has two swimming pools (one fresh water, the other saltwater) and a Jacuzzi, plus stores, two bars, a volleyball court, tennis, and water sports. 'Coral' rooms cost US$110 mid-September through March, US$140 in summer – the reverse of normal seasonal rates. Pool-view 'Hibiscus' rooms are slightly better and cost US$120/160. Two-bedroom octagonal 'villas' over the ocean cost from US$225/325. A MAP (breakfast and dinner) plan costs US$38 per person. Special rates are offered for divers and private pilots. A three-day/two-night package for US$399 double includes airfare from Fort Lauderdale. The resort's mailing address is 700 SW 34th St, Fort Lauderdale, FL 33315, USA.

The resort also rents the three-bedroom Harbour House, which boasts a pool table and has a Jacuzzi on a deck with views over the marina, for US$450/575.

The *Conch Pearl* restaurant specializes in seafood and continental favorites of variable quality, with entrees from US$13 upward (my seafood pasta was bland). It's open for breakfast and dinner only. Service is friendly but unsure.

The *Lobster Trap* (☎ 242-352-5252), at the marina, serves Bahamian seafood (including a seafood pizza), plus burgers and sandwiches. It has a pool table and is open 11 am to 3 pm during summer and 11 am to 11 pm in winter.

Getting There & Away

Air Chalk's Ocean Airways operates to Walker's Cay from Fort Lauderdale three times daily except Tuesday (US$250 round-trip). The seaplanes depart from the Jet Center on N Perimeter Rd, on the north side of Fort Lauderdale's international airport. No hand luggage is allowed on board, and luggage is strictly limited to 30 lbs. Contact Walker's Cay Hotel for information and reservations.

Major's Air Service (☎ 242-352-5778, 242-352-5781, majorsair@BahamasVG.com) flies to Walker's Cay from Freeport.

Private planes are charged a US$42 airport fee. Jet fuel is available.

Boat The marina has 75 slips, plus a bar, commissary, and other services. Dockage costs from US$1.35 per foot daily, including electricity. Free winter dockage is provided September to March, when there's a special '50/50' room/dockage program.

Andros

• pop 8500

One hundred miles long and up to 45 miles wide, Andros is the largest island in The Bahamas. It has escaped the commercial development of Nassau, just 25 miles away; in fact, its 2300 sq miles represent one of the largest tracts of unexplored land in the Western Hemisphere.

Andros actually comprises three main islands separated by enormous bights, or sounds, up to 25 miles wide and full of innumerable cays (there are four regional airports; be sure to fly to the correct one for wherever you intend to stay). It is further divided by countless creeks that cut its low surface into a fragmented jigsaw puzzle and either meander tortuously from coast to coast, open to lakes, or meld into endless mangrove swamps. Even at high tide – when the 'muds' are flooded and the island shrinks considerably – Andros is almost as large as all the other Bahamian islands combined.

Most of Andros is covered with acres of palm savannas and eerie primal forests – mahogany, pine, and palmetto – and by vast mangrove wetlands that form a huge and vital nursery for multitudes of fish and invertebrates.

The forests are home to wild boar, dove, duck, quail, and white-crowned pigeon (each spring a traditional pigeon hunt is held). During late spring and early summer, giant land crabs cross the road en masse for a paroxysm of mating and egg laying. All are trophies for locals eager to add to their kitchen pots. The skies are patrolled by turkey buzzards (the 'aerial surveillance squadron,' as they are called). And the shrieks of ospreys are commonly heard. Or is that the screech of chickcharnies?…red-eyed, three-fingered, owl-like elves with beards and feathered scalps who hang by their tails from cottonwood trees. They wreak mayhem on whomever disturbs them. To you or me, the cheeky chickcharnie is a product of local imagination. But to the Androsians, the devil-in-disguise is as real as the nose on your face (the failure of Neville Chamberlain's sisal plantation in the 1890s is blamed on chickcharnies). One thing that *is* real is the fierce horsefly, locally called the 'doctor fly' because its bite hurts like a syringe.

Andros is bounded on one side by the Great Bahama Bank, an underwater plateau that is about as shallow as the island is high. A 140-mile-long coral reef lies a few hundred yards to 2 miles off the east shore (surpassed in length only by Australia's Great Barrier Reef and the reef off the Caribbean coast of Central America). Beyond it and barely 2 miles from shore, the plateau drops off to a very dark 6000 feet in the Tongue of the Ocean canyon.

The wild island became a refuge for both Seminole Indians and runaway slaves fleeing

Highlights

- Diving the wall of the third-longest coral reef in the world
- Plunging into an Androsian blue hole
- Bonefishing with Charlie Smith or 'Jolly Boy' Forbes
- Going sponging with a local guide
- Learning about the weaving and lives of Seminole descendants in Red Bay

Florida during colonial days. A community of their descendants still exists in Red Bay on the northwest coast. A string of other small settlements dots the eastern seaboard. Nicely kept modern houses are interspersed with scruffy shacks surrounded by front-lawn furniture such as rusty cars, discarded refrigerators, and other garbage. The settlements sprawl along the one main road and are separated by a flat immensity of scrub, marsh, and pine forest that you might believe really *does* harbor chickcharnies. This is no place for a flat tire!

From above you can make out numerous doughnut-shaped blue holes amid the forests and scrub. The blue holes' levels rise and fall with the tides, alternately pouring water over the surrounding land or draining the brackish streamlets into the underground world to percolate and emerge much, much later from ocean holes inside the fringing reef on the east shore. Androsian blue holes are said to be inhabited by a monstrous octopus called Lusca. Many locals still believe in the creature, although scuba divers have turned up only lobster, shrimp, shark, and smaller fry.

Andros is also renowned for the sponge beds west of the island, which supported much of the population in the late 19th and early 20th centuries until a mysterious blight killed off 99% of the sponges in 1938. The sponges lie in water, or muds, so shallow that they can be pried from the coral with rods. (Some people believe that the island was named by Greek spongers for the Mediterranean island of Andros.) A few locals still make a living sponging, but most earn a living from fishing. The famous Androsian sloops, however, have been replaced by fiberglass outboards. For more on sponging, see the boxed text, 'Sponging,' later in this chapter.

Resort-based tourism has yet to catch on: There are a few homey guesthouses and apartments (dour by Western standards and relying almost exclusively on the Bahamian trade, especially during homecomings) and a fistful of quiet hotels, including a couple of noted scuba resorts and several bonefishing camps.

Dive & Snorkel Sites

Dive Sites

Alex & Cara Caverns – Expert divers can descend to 90 feet to enter these caverns on the edge of the Tongue of the Ocean.

The Barge – This wreck lies 70 feet below the surface and is now a home to large groupers.

The Black Forest – A crop of three dozen black coral trees appears at 70 feet.

The Blue Hole – Large rays and sharks often gather at this tame blue hole with depths down to 100 feet.

Over the Wall – This dive begins at 80 feet and plunges another 100 feet at the edge of the Tongue of the Ocean wall, which itself drops another 6000 feet.

Potomac – This 345-foot British tanker sank in 1929 off Andros' northeast coast.

Snorkel Sites

Central Park – Acres of corals, including elkhorn, are found here.

China Point – Huge fish populations, including blue tangs and sergeant majors, swim here.

The Compressor – Yes…a compressor has metamorphosed into a reef!

Davis Creek – This fascinating tidal flat extends into the mangroves.

Goat Cay – These turtle-grass flats are good for hunting sand dollars.

Liben's Point – This is a vast region with tall elkhorn and star coral.

Red Shoal – Schooling grunts frequent this lone patch of elkhorn reef.

Solarium – Lobsters and stingrays favor these shallow flats.

Trumpet Reef – This reef is known for invertebrates such as brittle stars and spiny urchins.

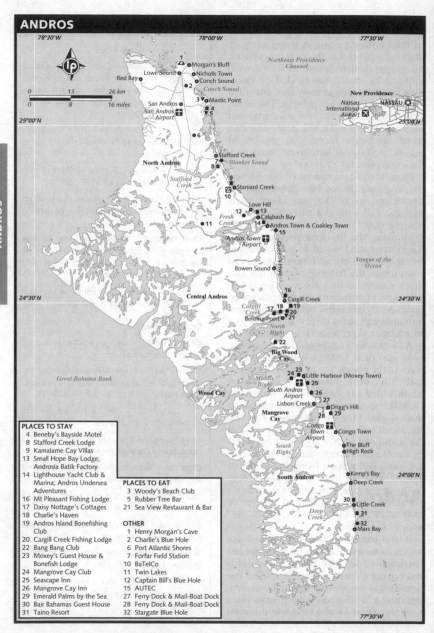

ANDROS

PLACES TO STAY
4   Beneby's Bayside Motel
8   Stafford Creek Lodge
9   Kamalame Cay Villas
13 Small Hope Bay Lodge;
    Androsia Batik Factory
14 Lighthouse Yacht Club &
    Marina; Andros Undersea
    Adventures
16 Mt Pleasant Fishing Lodge
17 Daisy Nottage's Cottages
18 Charlie's Haven
19 Andros Island Bonefishing
    Club
20 Cargill Creek Fishing Lodge
22 Bang Bang Club
23 Moxey's Guest House &
    Bonefish Lodge
24 Mangrove Cay Club
25 Seascape Inn
26 Mangrove Cay Inn
29 Emerald Palms by the Sea
30 Bair Bahamas Guest House
31 Taino Resort

PLACES TO EAT
3   Woody's Beach Club
5   Rubber Tree Bar
21 Sea View Restaurant & Bar

OTHER
1   Henry Morgan's Cave
2   Charlie's Blue Hole
6   Port Atlantic Shores
7   Forfar Field Station
10 BaTelCo
11 Twin Lakes
12 Captain Bill's Blue Hole
15 AUTEC
27 Ferry Dock & Mail-Boat Dock
28 Ferry Dock & Mail-Boat Dock
32 Stargate Blue Hole

Inside the reef's shallows, divers can gambol in an infinite variety of sites. Outside it they can dive the Andros wall, which plunges precipitously to the base of the Tongue of the Ocean.

There are plentiful deep coral canyons, many of which connect to inland blue holes. Gigantic stalactites fill the holes, many of which are entered at depths below 100 feet. There are 178 blue holes inland and another 50 offshore. Blue-hole diving is a specialty of Small Hope Bay Lodge (see the Fresh Creek Area section).

Andros bills itself as the 'Bonefishing Capital of the World.' Several lodges are dedicated to bonefishing, and bonefishing guides can be hired in any community. The Andros Bonefishing Guides Association can provide a recommendation; call Arthur Russell (☎ 242-329-2484) or Andy Smith (☎ 242-368-4261) at Behring Point. In general, you should come with all equipment. Several tour operators in North America offer fishing package tours (see the Outdoor Activities chapter for contact information).

Andros also boasts some good hiking spots. However, the island is popular with hunters seeking wild boar, so you should hike with caution. The Andros Conservation Trust was working on a major conservation effort to protect the coral reefs, woodlands, and bonefish flats at press time; contact Peter Douglas (☎ 242-368-2286, fax 242-368-2285, pgdouglas@batelnet.bs) for information.

North & Central Andros

North and Central Andros form the largest of the three Androsian islands ('North' and 'Central' Andros are one island; the former lies north of Stafford Creek, and Central Andros lies to the south). It has some fine beaches and boneflats. Much of the island is smothered in pine forests that have twice been logged – first to provide pit-props for English coal mines and later for Chicago newspapers. The island's exotic hardwoods, mahogany and lignum vitae (sometimes called 'sailor's cure' because its sap provided a cure for syphilis in the 19th century), for example, are long gone, but the logging tracks remain.

The island hosts the North Andros Thanksgiving Bonefish Tournament each November.

NICHOLLS TOWN AREA

This coastal settlement, housing the majority of Andros' governmental facilities, lies at the extreme north end of the island and is one of the quaintest settlements in the entire island chain. Palms fringe the beach behind which the town spreads in a checkered grid, with quaint modern homes and weatherbeaten wooden shacks scattered along the roads, fishing boats out of kilter along the shore, and US-model cars in various stages of rust on front lawns. It boasts a few small stores, a supermarket, and a gas station, plus a beautiful, modern, Georgian-style **government building** (two miles west, on the entrance road into town) and equally endearing, more venerable colonial era buildings at its heart.

Conch Sound Rd leads south from the heart of town to **Conch Sound**, where old sailing boats lie rotting on the beach. The little fishing village of **Lowe Sound**, two miles west of Nicholls Town, also has fishing boats and nets along the beach. Here you can watch Arthur Russell carve model ships that he fits with Androsia batik sails.

Mastic Point is a small commercial harbor that lies 3 miles east of Queen's Hwy; the turnoff is at San Andros Airport, five miles south of Nicholls Town. Much of the land around San Andros is intensively farmed for citrus, potatoes, tomatoes, and other produce. Ground had been broken on an upscale residential and vacation rental resort development – Port Atlantic Shores – 5 miles south of San Andros, at last visit.

Information

The CIBC bank (☎ 242-329-2382) in Nicholls Town is open Wednesday only, 10 am to

2 pm. There's a Canadian Imperial Bank (☎ 242-329-2382), open 10:30 am to 2:30 pm Wednesday only.

The post office (☎ 242-329-2034), in the government complex on the entrance road to Nicholls Town, is open 9 am to 5:30 pm weekdays. The police station (☎ 919, 242-329-2353) and BaTelCo telephone office (☎ 242-329-2131) are also here, as is the Andromed Medical Centre (☎ 242-329-2171), open 6 am to 8 pm Monday and Wednesday, and 3 pm to 8 pm on Saturday.

There are also clinics in San Andros (☎ 242-329-2055) and Mastic Point (☎ 242-329-1849).

Morgan's Bluff

Two miles north of town the road dead-ends at the tip of the island. There's a nice beach west of the bluff and a wharf where the massive *Titas* tanker and barges take on 6 million gallons of water daily for New Providence. The water is drawn from a massive reservoir north of San Andros that is fed by a vast underground aquifer.

If you believe local lore, Henry Morgan, the wily Welsh pirate, hid his treasure in a cave – **Henry Morgan's Cave** – about 30 yards from the road (it's well signed). Like all good pirates, Morgan ravaged throughout the Caribbean, and Andros was not spared. Tree roots wriggle down into the entrance gallery, where the cave slants down just below head height then opens to a vast Gothic gallery. It would seem from the inscriptions on the walls that the caves are popular trysting spots (not least for bats squirming in the cool shade). Bring a flashlight.

Charlie's Blue Hole

This hole, 3 miles south of Nicholls Town, is renowned for its 'boil,' a whirlpool caused by a rapid egress of water during the change of tidal flow, when water is sucked out to sea through the subterranean passages and any boats that happen to be on the surface can be pulled underwater. Several boats have been lost this way, adding to the local legend of the monstrous octopus, Lusca, in residence here (*'Mon, dawn't go down der. Nobody go down*

der!'). Scuba divers who first explored the hole in the 1970s were quite surprised to find sharks swimming in the narrow caverns. It's signed off Queen's Hwy.

Another hole, **Benjamin's Blue Hole**, has fabulous stalactites and stalagmites gloriously suspended underwater, as if preserved in formaldehyde.

Fishing

At Lowe Sound, Arthur Russell (☎ 242-329-7372) is a recommended bonefishing guide, and Neville 'Uncle JT' Dean can take you out sponging, conching, or lobstering (every morning he leaves at dawn and returns at about 1 pm).

Bonefishing packages, based at the Green Windows Inn (☎ 242-329-2515, fax 242-329-2016), cost from US$700 per person for three-night packages to US$2100 for week-long packages. Visit its Web site at www.bonefishandros.com for more information.

Special Events

The North Andros Regatta is held at Morgan's Bluff in June. The All Andros & Berry Islands Independence Regatta is held in mid-July, kicked off by a bonefishing tournament; it features sailboat races, volleyball, boatbuilding demonstrations, crab cracking, and dominoes.

September sees the Annual Bahamas Free Diving Competition at Nicholls Town. The North Andros Bonefishing Tourna-

Dinghy races highlight Andros homecomings.

ment is held at Thanksgiving, at the end of November.

During the Goombay Summer Festival, major settlements have outdoor festivities each weekend, mid-July through mid-September.

Places to Stay

The *Green Windows Inn* (☎ 242-329-2194, fax 242-329-2016), next to the Texaco gas station in Nicholls Town and a 10-minute walk from the beach, has six air-con rooms with shared bathroom and four suites with private bath, all with satellite TV. The garden has orchids and peacocks. Bicycle rentals and scuba diving are offered and bonefishing trips can be arranged. Room rates are US$75 to US$110. The postal address is PO Box 23076, Nicholls Town, Andros, The Bahamas.

The *Dayshell Motel* (☎ 242-329-2183), behind the beach in the heart of Nicholls Town, is a modest affair with simply furnished rooms for US$63 single or double. It has a small restaurant and gift shop and nightclub.

GJ's Resort Hotel & Restaurant (☎/fax 242-329-2005), on the entrance road to Nicholls Town, has 32 modern, albeit modest, air-con units for US$75/85 single/double. It's overpriced and uninspired.

The motel-style *Conch Sound Resort Inn* (☎ 242-329-2060), at Conch Sound, has seven large, air-con rooms with modestly pleasant furnishings and satellite TV. There are also six concrete cottages with kitchens, a relaxing restaurant and bar, and a swimming pool. The motel is surrounded by pine forests (good for hiking), with the beach a five-minute walk away. Fishing and other activities can be arranged. The rates are US$85 for rooms, US$200 for 'villa-suites,' including airport transfers. Credit cards are not accepted. Its mailing address is PO Box 23029, Nicholls Town, Andros, The Bahamas.

Beneby's Bayside Motel (☎ 242-329-3074), just south of Mastic Point, has simple rooms.

Places to Eat

One of the cleanest spots is *Zelda's*, 200 yards east of the government buildings on the entrance road to Nicholls Town. *Grizzly's Cabin*, nearby, also serves native dishes, as does *Rumours Restaurant & Disco* (☎ 242-329-2398). *Lori's Cornucopia Deli*, behind the bank, serves sandwiches and snacks and has a pool table.

In Nicholls Town, the restaurant at *Green Windows Inn* is modestly elegant, as is the restaurant at *Conch Sound Resort Hotel*. For real atmosphere, however, enjoy fresh fish and a rum cocktail or Kalik beer at one of the funky stalls and bars on the beach.

Hunter's Restaurant & Bar, on Conch Sound Rd, draws locals who play dominoes under the shade of an old wooden sailboat.

In Mastic Point, head to *Woody's Beach Club* or the *Rubber Tree Bar*, where locals play dominoes. The *Bayside Ice Cream & Confectionary* is 200 yards farther south.

You can stock up at the *Pineyard Shopping Centre*, on the main road south of Nicholls Town, next to which a stall called *Brinka's Hallelujah Corner* serves real native fare at its finest.

In Lowe Sound, *Big J's on the Bay Restaurant & Bar* (☎ 242-369-1954) conjures up home-style native dishes and seafood; it's open 7 to 11 am and 1 to 11 pm daily.

Entertainment

A lively rake 'n' scrape band plays at the restaurant in the *Dayshell Motel* in Nicholls Town. *Rumours* also has live bands, plus a disco on weekends, as does the *Late Night Spot* in the Conch Sound Resort Inn.

In Lowe Sound, *Big Josh's* (☎ 242-329-7517) has a satellite lounge, as does the *Twilight Zone* (☎ 242-329-2432), open from 9 pm until late.

Getting There & Away

This area is served by the San Andros Airport, about 10 miles south of Nicholls Town.

Bahamasair (in San Andros ☎ 242-329-2273) offers twice-daily service between Nassau and San Andros (US$45 one-way). Island Express (in the US ☎ 954-359-0380) flies from Fort Lauderdale.

The mail boat *Lisa J II* departs Nassau for Mastic Point at 3:30 pm Wednesday (five

ANDROS

hours, US$30 one-way), with stops at Nicholls Town and Morgan's Bluff.

The Mastic Town harbor is clogged by sunken boats and is not recommended for private boaters.

Getting Around

You can rent cars at Mastic Point from either Basil Martin (☎ 242-329-3169) or Cecil Gaitor (☎ 242-329-3043) for US$65 per day.

There's a gas station at the entrance to Nicholls Town.

RED BAY
* pop 200

This is a down-at-the-heels hamlet in the heart of forest and on the edge of swamp, 15 miles northwest of San Andros. It's the only settlement on the west coast of Andros. Many of the inhabitants are descendants of Seminole Indians and runaway slaves who fled Florida in the 17th and 18th centuries. A few locals earn an income from weaving, for which they are famed. Using practices passed down from Seminole forebears, they hand-weave watertight straw baskets that sell for US$5 and up. Many are interwoven with locally made batik fabrics.

Other locals are known for their wood carvings, notably Henry Wallace, a colorful Rasta character who has exhibited work at the Smithsonian Institute in Washington, DC. But they earn an income mostly from sponging. The creatures are landed at the wharf a mile west of town…a stinky place where flies congregate to make hay on the odiferous, freshly culled sponges. Notice the bamboo crawls offshore used for filtering sponges to clean them.

There are no accommodations or restaurants, but you can get snacks at bars such as *Fred Russell's* and the *Marshall Bar*.

STAFFORD CREEK AREA

The road from Nicholls Town cuts inland (due south) through pine forest, then turns east and leaps over the mouth of Stafford Creek. The settlement, north of the creek, is primitive.

On the other side, a mile south of the creek, is the Forfar Field Station (☎ 242-368-

6129), a privately run research station. It's operated by International Field Studies (in the US ☎ 614-235-4646, 800-962-3805), 709 College Ave, Columbus, OH 43209, USA, and is used mostly by North American high school and college students for field studies in geology, marine biology, and ornithology. The main lodge was built as a dive resort by Archie Forfar, who was killed along with his wife while attempting to set the world's deep-diving record.

Queen's Hwy continues south through Staniard Creek, a dispersed, scruffy settlement on a cay at the south end of Blanket Sound, 30 miles south of San Andros. The place has a backwoods southern US feel – lots of junked cars rusting outside pastel-colored wooden cabins and mildewed homes. The 2-mile-long beach rimming its east shore is indisputably lovely. The Bahamas Environmental Research Station is here.

There's a BaTelCo office just off Queen's Hwy, at the entrance to Staniard Creek. The Central Andros Clinic (☎ 242-368-2626) is here.

Places to Stay & Eat

The *Forfar Field Station* has basic accommodations and may be able to take in visitors on an ad hoc basis. *Ellen's Overnight Rest* (☎ 242-329-6111, fax 242-329-6121), in Blanket Sound, has seven rooms in a basic guesthouse for about US$50. And the 'Dickie Brothers' run the modest *Quality Inn Motel* (☎ 242-368-6217) in Staniard Creek, with 11 rooms for about US$60, plus a restaurant.

Kamalame Cay Villas (☎ 242-368-6281, fax 242-368-6279, kamalame@batelnet.bs), at the north end of Staniard Creek, has luxurious rental villas that rent from US$375 per night including meals. It offers tennis, a swimming pool, marina, and watersports. Its Web site is www.kamalame.com.

Stafford Creek Lodge (☎ /fax 242-368-6259; in the US c/o Pan-Angling ☎ 317-240-3474, 800-533-4353, fax 317-227-6803, mbutzow@ panangling.com), on Stafford Creek about 400 yards inland, is a family-run fishing lodge with spacious air-con cottages with pine furniture, ceiling fans, and decks overlooking the Stafford Creek…good in early mornings for watching dolphins swim up the creek to feed! Package rates begin at US$1410/1880 single/double for three nights, including two days of fishing and meals. Its Web site is www.staffordlodge.com.

Getting There & Away
The *Lady D* mail boat sails to Stafford Creek and Blanket Sound from Nassau at noon Tuesday (five hours, US$30 one-way). It also stops at Staniard Creek, Andros and Coakley Towns (Fresh Creek), and Behring Point.

FRESH CREEK AREA
The contiguous communities that make up the Fresh Creek Township form the node of Central Andros and lie, mostly, north of the watercourse of Fresh Creek. The creek extends inland into the depths of Andros, and since 1995 a wild dolphin has returned seasonally (between forays to sea for mating) to live in the creek. You can snorkel with the dolphin, which seems to enjoy human company (see Small Hope Bay Lodge's listing in the Places to Stay section, below). This is an area popular with divers.

Information
Peter Douglas runs The Bahamas Ministry of Tourism office (☎ 242-368-2286, fax 242-368-2285, pgdouglas@batelnet.bs), beside the Lighthouse Yacht Club & Marina in Andros Town.

The Royal Bank of Canada (☎ 242-368-2071), next door, is open 9:30 am to 3:30 pm Wednesday.

There's a laundromat on Thompson 15th St in Coakley Town, and another next to the gas station in Love Hill.

The Ragnabash Medical Clinic (☎ 242-368-2051) is on Thompson 15th St. The government health center (☎ 242-368-2038) is on the north side of the Fresh Creek Bridge.

The post office and police station (☎ 919, 242-368-2626) adjoin each other on Queen's Hwy, on the north side of Coakley Town.

Andros Town & Coakley Town
The two main settlements – formally referred to as Andros Town – on Central Andros straddle Fresh Creek. The larger is Coakley Town, on the north side of the creek; the hamlet of Andros Town is on the south side. A giant plastic crab greets visitors at the entrance to Coakley Town.

The joint US-UK navies' AUTEC (Atlantic Undersea Test & Evaluation Center) antisubmarine warfare testing facility is 1 mile south of town. The area is strictly off-limits; the same goes for the waters up to 2 miles offshore.

Somerset Beach is 2 miles south of town. There's not much of a beach at high tide, but when the tide recedes, the miles-long beach is extremely deep and splendid. Wading birds patrol the shore, and you can admire the sand dollars at low tide.

Androsia Batik Factory
Be sure to visit this renowned textile factory (☎ 242-368-2080, fax 242-368-2027, Androsia@Androsia.com) where the famous Androsia batiks are made. The factory, which employs 45 islanders, is a Birch-family cottage enterprise that exports fashions and fabrics throughout The Bahamas. Melding age-old wax techniques and island motifs, workers create a wide range of fashionwear out of four types of natural fabrics.

First plain white fabric is stamped with sponge cutouts of shells and other shapes dipped in hot wax and pressed onto the cloth. Then the fabric is steeped in tubs of orange, turquoise, sea-blue, blood-red, pink, or lime-green dye. The waxed surface repels the dye, leaving the desired pattern as plain white. The fabric is then soaked in tubs of extremely hot water that melts and dissolves the wax. The cloth is then hung to dry in the sun before it goes to the cutting and sewing room. You can visit 8 am to 4 pm Monday to Friday, and 8 am to 1 pm Saturday. A guide will show you around. It also has a factory outlet. Its Web site is www.androsia.com.

Calabash Bay & Small Hope Bay
This small coastal settlement, at a crook in the road about 2 miles north of Andros Town, is lent a certain charm by its several churches and the flats, which are picked at

ANDROS

by herons when the tide is out. The bay is also known as **Small Hope Bay**, the name of a hamlet immediately north of Calabash Bay settlement. Why the name? 'I'll tell you the same bullshit everybody else does,' says Jeff Birch, owner of Small Hope Bay Lodge, carrying on his father Dick's tall tale (Dick died in 1996). It seems Henry Morgan and Blackbeard got together here with a cache of treasure. The two rogues rowed ashore with six sailors, buried the loot, then killed the witnesses. As they were rowing back, one said to the other, 'There's small hope that'll ever be found.'

Small Hope Bay settlement merges into the settlement of **Love Hill**, where a side road just north of the gas station leads to pleasant **Love Hill Beach**. Nearby, **Captain Bill's Blue Hole**, hidden amid pine forests, is a popular spot with divers. There's a ladder and a rope swing for would-be Tarzans. Ducks inhabit the pond. To get there, turn left at the white house with statues of lions on its fence just north of Love Hill, then turn right at the crossroads; Desouzas Fruit Farm is to the left.

Twin Lakes

At the end of the 19th century, when sisal growers were thriving, young Neville Chamberlain (British prime minister 1937–40) and his father ran a 4000-acre sisal plantation, Twin Lakes Farm, 16 miles inland up Fresh Creek (see the Andros map). But the enterprise failed. Locals firmly believe that the Chamberlains' effort failed because they disturbed the chickcharnies, who caused Neville no end of grief – not least the scorn of the Munich Pact. Twin Lakes now lies in ruins, but the two blue holes that lent the plantation its name can still be accessed by a rough, overgrown track.

Diving & Snorkeling

Andros Undersea Adventures (☎ 242-368-2795, fax 242-368-2796, androsmm@aol.com; in the US ☎ 800-327-8150) at the Lighthouse Yacht Club & Marina (see Places to Stay, below) offers dives for US$45/70 one/two-tank, blue hole dives, and certification courses, plus snorkel trips for US$25. The

Web site www.divebahamas.com has full informatin.

Small Hope Bay Lodge (see Places to Stay & Eat, below), highly acclaimed by divers, has twice-daily dives for US$45/55 one/two-tank. It specializes in custom-tailored dives, including blue-hole dives and wall dives to 185 feet. The lodge doesn't have the same restrictions as most resorts do on novice divers; even beginners can dive the wall (free introductory lessons are offered). Custom dives cost US$85. PADI certification courses cost US$310. Snorkel trips cost US$15. The lodge rents equipment and fills tanks. A safari snorkel into the interior is offered on request.

Bonefishing & Sport Fishing

Small Hope Bay Lodge and Coakley House (see below) offer bonefishing for US$200/325 half/full day (add US$40 for fishing North Bight or Stafford Creek). They also have reef fishing for US$220/380 half/full day and deep-sea fishing for US$275/480 half/full day. A 36-foot luxury yacht is available for full-day charter for US$800.

The Lighthouse Club & Marina offers bonefishing for US$150/275 half/full day.

Organized Tours

Small Hope Bay Lodge (see Places to Stay, below) offers a 7-night 'Birding & Ecology Adventure' twice-yearly led by ornithologist Dr Mike Baltz (US$1250 all-inclusive).

Places to Stay

In Coakley Town, the laid-back, no-frills *Skinny's Landmark Motel* (☎ 242-368-2082) has 15 simply furnished, modestly priced, pine-walled, air-con rooms above a lively restaurant and bar. The rooms have TVs, roomy closets, and balconies overlooking the village. Room rates are US$55/70 low/peak season; it does not accept credit cards.

Alternately, try Charlie Gay's characterless *Chickcharnie's Hotel* (☎ 242-368-2026, fax 242-368-2492, relax@androslighthouse .com), on the north side of Fresh Creek. It has 16 air-con rooms with TV for US$45 with fan and shared bathroom; US$60 to

US$80 with air-con and private bathroom. Bahamian dishes are served in the dining room, which overlooks the creek.

Across the creek, the government-run **Lighthouse Yacht Club & Marina** (☎ 242-368-2305, fax 242-368-2300; in North America ☎ 800-688-4752) is a modern remake of the old Andros Yacht Club and has 12 air-con rooms, eight with king-size beds, for US$110 to US$120 single or double, and eight two-bedroom cottages for US$130 to US$170 for up to four people. All are nicely furnished in Regency reproductions, with TV, air-con, ceiling fan, and tile floors. There is a spacious, elegant restaurant and bar, a games room, bicycle rentals, a swimming pool, two tennis courts, scuba diving with Andros Undersea Adventures, and fishing charters. The Web site is www.androslighthouse.com.

The Birch family – which also runs Small Hope Bay Lodge near Calabash Bay – has a luxury three-bedroom villa, **Coakley House** (see Small Hope Bay Lodge, below; coakleyhouse@smallhope.com), at the mouth of Fresh Creek in Coakley Town. This beautiful 2100-sq-foot home, amid landscaped grounds, has two large master bedrooms and a third bedroom, all with private bathroom. There's a lounge with TV/VCR, dining room, and full kitchen, plus a patio, 120-foot dock, and bicycles. Boat rental can be arranged. It's a bargain at US$250/1500 daily/weekly in low season (May to October) without housekeeper, US$300/1750 peak season (November to April). Cook and maid service costs US$95 daily. An all-inclusive plan is offered.

The family-run **Small Hope Bay Lodge** (☎ 242-368-2014, 800-223-6961, fax 242-368-2015, shbinfo@smallhope.com), just north of Calabash Bay, is a dedicated dive resort and diamond in the rough. Jeff Birch runs the place like one long house party. The large, all-wood lounge with library, games room, large CD collection, and fireplace is a splendid place to relax. There's a bar hewn from half a boat. The 20 large yet spartan pinewood cabins line the beach amid coconut palms; each has a king-size or double bed, fans, screened windows, and

Androsia batik fabrics. There are four two-bedroom cottages for families (babysitting is offered) and a 'honeymoon' cottage. Rates are US$160/175 per person summer/winter, including airport transfers, three meals daily, all beverages, taxes, service charges, and an introductory scuba or snorkel lesson. Divers on packages pay US$225/235. The lodge offers self-guided nature walks, plus bird watching and biking tours. A 'Safari to Fresh Creek' offers a chance for you to go snorkeling with a wild dolphin. And what say you to an alfresco hot tub, or a massage for US$30/50 half/full hour in the thatched solarium intended for all-over tanning? The lodge has its own charter flights from Fort Lauderdale for US$110 one-way. Its local mailing address is PO Box N-1131, Nassau, The Bahamas; in the USA you can write to PO Box 21667, Fort Lauderdale, FL 33335.

Point of View Villas (☎ 242-368-2750, fax 242-368-2761, info@pointofviewbahamas.com), between Coakley Town and Calabash Bay, is modestly elegant. Looking like a little suburban village complex, it has 14 two-bedroom cottages surrounded by lawns behind the beach. There's a fish-shaped pool and sundeck, whirlpool, bar, tennis courts, and tackle-shop. Air-con rooms have wicker furniture, satellite TVs, and phones. It has an excellent restaurant. Rates are US$250 villa, US$300 ocean- and pool-front, including the use of bicycles.

Places to Eat

In Coakley Town, Charlie Gay makes a mean conch steak at **Chickcharnie's Hotel**, which also has a grocery store. Skinny's wife, Carmetta, brews up a mean hot-pepper sauce to enliven her native dishes at **Skinny's Landmark Restaurant & Satellite Lounge**, which also has a store. The **Square Deal Restaurant** (☎ 242-368-2593), next door, also serves simple Bahamian fare.

However, the most popular spot is **Hank's** (☎ 242-368-2447), with a deck overhanging the creek. It serves from 11 am to 10 pm and has a wild boar and fish fry on Sunday, washed down with the house drink: a Hanky Panky. Monday to Saturday, entrees range from US$7 to US$18. Nearby, *Gaitor's Variety Store & Deli* sells sandwiches, quiches, and the like.

The elegant restaurant at *Lighthouse Yacht Club & Marina* also serves seafood and native dishes, and is good for bargain breakfasts, including omelets, pancakes, and Bahamian specials.

The restaurant at *Point of View Villas* gets thumbs up for its food…everything from pizza and a lobster club sandwich to snapper almondine.

Small Hope Bay Lodge (☎ 242-368-2014, 800-223-6961, fax 242-368-2015) has a fine US-style breakfast daily, plus a buffet lunch featuring a cold-cuts bar and delicious guava duff for dessert. Dinner is served family-style from 7 to 8:30 pm with a choice of entrees; on fine nights, buffet meals are served on a tree-shaded patio by the beach. Reservations are essential for nonguests.

To be one with the locals in Calabash Bay, try *Sampson's Restaurant* (☎ 242-368-2615) or *Captain Crunch Fish Fry*.

You can buy groceries at Chickcharnie's Hotel or at *Adderley's Bargain Mart*. Magnolia sells fruits and veggies from her pick-up truck parked outside the Lighthouse Yacht Club.

Entertainment

The *Rhythm's Entertainment Center & Sports Bar*, on Queen's Hwy north of Coakley Town, is the happenin' place for entertainment. It's lively any night, with live music some weekends when students from the Forfar Field Station (see the Stafford Creek Area section) come into town. Likewise, *Donny's Sugar Sweet Lounge* (☎ 242-368-2080) gets the locals winin'.

Getting There & Away

The Andros Town Airport is 3 miles south of town.

Island Express (in the US ☎ 954-359-0380) flies from Fort Lauderdale. Bahamasair (in Andros Town ☎ 242-368-2560) offers twice-daily service between Nassau and Andros Town (US$45 one-way). Major's Air (in Andros Town ☎ 242-368-2766) links Andros Town and Freeport.

Bahamas Sea Road (☎ 242-323-2166) operates a car-and-passenger ferry service from Nassau to Fresh Creek four times weekly (2½ hours; US$30 each way for passengers).

The *Lady D* mail boat calls here from Nassau on Tuesday; see the Stafford Creek Area section for details.

The Lighthouse Yacht Club & Marina (☎ 242-368-2305) has 18 slips for vessels up to 50 feet. It charges US85¢ per foot.

Getting Around

You can rent a car for US$65 to US$85 per day (plus US$200 deposit) from several places. Try Bill's Rent-a-Car (☎ 242-368-2560, cellular 242-357-2149) or Tropical Car Rental (☎ 242-369-2515) and D&E Car Rental (☎ 242-368-2454), both in Love Hill. Reliable Scooter Rentals (☎ 242-368-2156), in Calabash Bay, rents scooters.

A taxi ride from the Andros Town Airport to Small Hope Bay Lodge costs about US$20 for two. For a taxi, call ☎ 242-329-2273 or ☎ 242-329-2140.

There's an Esso gas station in Love Hill, and gas pumps on Edgecomb's St in Calabash Bay.

CARGILL CREEK AREA

Barely anyone resides between Andros Town and the settlement of **Cargill Creek**, beside its namesake creek about 20 miles south of Fresh Creek. Cargill Creek opens westward into the vast flats of the North and Middle Bights. You are now in bonefishing territory supreme; bonefishing is the sole reason to visit.

Queen's Hwy continues south about two miles to **Behring Point**, a pinprick of a hamlet where the road curls east and fizzles out. The settlement sits atop a bluff overlooking the mouth of North Bight, separating the island from Mangrove Cay.

The *Lady Gloria* mail boat sails from Nassau to Cargill Creek (and Mangrove Cay and Bowen Sound) at 10 pm Tuesday (five hours, US$30 one-way).

Places to Stay

Mt Pleasant Fishing Lodge (☎ 242-368-5171), 2 miles north of Cargill Creek and reached by a winding dirt and mud road, is a rudimentary place to stay, with four rooms and minimal facilities.

A far better option is *Cargill Creek Fishing Lodge* (☎ 242-368-5129, fax 242-329-5046). On the southern outskirts of Cargill Creek village, beside the creek that offers up prize-winning bonefish, it has 11 simple whitewashed rooms. They're clean, well lit, and tile-floored, with lofty wooden ceilings, air-con, ceiling fan, and hot water. There's also a two-bedroom, two-bathroom cottage. The lodge has a small swimming pool and a lively all-wooden bar and restaurant where fisherfolk swap big-fish stories. Daily rates are US$165/300 single/double (meals are included). Guided fishing costs US$300 daily for two people. Packages are offered. A taxi to/from the San Andros Airport costs US$30 for one or two people.

Next door is the *Andros Island Bonefishing Club* (☎ 242-368-5167, fax 242-368-5235; in the US ☎ 619-275-7884, 800-545-5917, fax 619-275-7888, info@worldwidefishing.com), of a similar scale and standard. Most of the 12 spacious cabins are all wood; some are concrete. All have private bathroom, refrigerator, two queen-size beds, and ceiling fans. A restaurant serves native seafood and a bar has a satellite TV. Four-night packages cost US$1730 single, US$1185 per person double, including all meals, transfers, and guided fishing; seven-night packages are US$3290/2205, respectively.

At Behring Point, the small, no-frills *Tranquility Hill* (☎/fax 242-368-4132, email: tranquil@grouper.batelnet.bs) has 10 air-con rooms with lofty wooden ceilings and tile floors. Seven have double beds; three larger, attractive units upstairs have king-size beds and more light. All have TV and fans. Rooms cost US$135/259 single/double in summer, US$167/313 in winter, including three meals daily. Fishing packages are offered. A small dining room serves native dishes. There's a small bar with satellite TV. The hotel has five boats; bonefishing costs US$300 per full day for two people.

A half-mile farther west is *Charlie's Haven* (☎ 242-368-4087, 888-262-0700), a handsome property of stone and varnished wood, with a lively lounge bar where locals and guests hang out with proprietor Charlie Smith, alias Bonefish Charlie, an eccentric and outspoken old character. His place has 10 sparsely furnished air-con rooms with ceiling fans and beds covered in tartan blankets for US$130 per person, including three meals daily. Charlie charges US$300 per day for guided fishing. No credit cards are accepted.

At last visit, Charlie Smith was still working on the *Bang Bang Club*, a fishing club on Port Cay, off Big Wood Cay in North Bight. It was due to open by the end of 2000 with 10 rooms and a four-bedroom cottage, plus dock, pool, kitchen, and dining room.

At the end of the road, a half-mile west of Charlie's Haven, is *Daisy Nottage's Cottages* (☎ 242-368-4293). Daisy – another animated character who also practices bush medicine – rents 10 modest yet appealing modern rooms, plus five two-bedroom cottages with kitchen and living room. Ya gotta like cats…two dozen live on-site! There's a restaurant and bar where Daisy serves conch and other seafood, served with mashed potatoes and fries. She charges US$75 single or double.

Places to Eat

You can dine at any of the fishing lodges. Locals tend to head to *Sea View Restaurant & Bar* (☎ 242-368-4005), 100 yards south of the Cargill Creek Bridge.

You can buy groceries at the *Cargill Creek Convenience Store*.

Entertainment

Leadon's Creek Side Lounge & Disco Center (☎ 242-368-4167) and the *Cribside Lounge* are the happenin' spots hereabouts; the latter is open 9 am to 11 pm weekdays and 9 am to 3 am weekends. Leading Bahamian artists perform at least once monthly. A rake 'n' scrape band named Kelly & the Boys often perform, and 'sexiest female' contests are a staple.

South Andros

South Andros is virtually bypassed by tourists, although the bonefishing is superb and there are some beautiful beaches. Sir Lynden Pindling (former Bahamian prime minister) hails from here, and the local citizenry, uniquely among Bahamians these days, remains partisan in his favor. Despite two decades of favoritism under Pindling's tenure (a government commission found Pindling guilty of 'improper conduct' in accounting for US$3.9 million deposited to his account in transactions involving the government-run Emerald Palms Hotel and other local enterprises), the island is even less developed than North and Central Andros, and there are many pockets of poverty. Most locals make an income from lobstering, crabbing, or sponging.

South Andros is home to a few Androsian iguanas, which can grow to 5 feet in length; they dwell in scattered coppices where people rarely venture.

MANGROVE CAY

The northern part of South Andros is formed by Mangrove Cay, from which it is separated by South Bight. A narrow beach lines almost the entire east shore, and at least 23 blue holes await exploration. **Little Harbour** is the only concentrated settlement, stretching 2 miles south from the north tip of the cay; it's often referred to as Moxey Town, which is actually the northern division of Little Harbour. Electricity came to Mangrove Cay only in 1989, when everybody gathered under its welcome glow as if hot showers had arrived. Lynward Saunders (☎ 242-369-0414) will show you around his processing shed, where sponges are cleaned and dried and made ready for export.

Mangrove Cay is served by South Andros Airport.

Information

The BaTelCo office (☎ 242-369-0131) on Mangrove Cay is a half-mile south of Dorset.

The Mangrove Cay Clinic (☎ 242-369-0089) is in Dorset. You can buy pharmaceu-

Sponging

The sponge is a marine animal composed mainly of microscopic calcareous rods, stars, and hooks held in place by elastic fibers. Nourishment is extracted from water via a vast network of pores and canals. Although they don't have hearts or brains, sponges produce sperm and eggs. There are various species, including the super-soft 'velvet' or wool sponge, and the 'hardhead,' so durable that it has many industrial uses.

Sponging in The Bahamas began in earnest in 1841 after a Frenchman, Gustave Renouard, was shipwrecked here. 'Ooh, la la! Zeez sponges are better zan ze sponges of ze Méditerranée,' said French merchants of the sponges Renouard shipped back to Paris. Greek deep-sea sponge divers left their homeland to make their money from the Bahamian seabed.

Schooners sailed from throughout The Bahamas to gather the prolific wool sponge. Each schooner carried a crew of 20 men, plus six to eight dinghies which were put overboard daily with a crew of two. While one man sculled, the other looked through a glass-bottomed bucket and ripped the sponges from the seabed with a hooked pole. (Today spongers dive with snorkel or scuba gear. They also slice the sponges at the base, leaving the root to regenerate.) Ashore, the sponges were beaten to death and put in shallow-water 'kraals' to allow the flesh to rot and decompose. Then they were rinsed, pounded to a pleasing fluffiness, and strung up to dry before being shipped for sale at the Greek Sponge Exchange in Nassau.

At the close of the 19th century, 500 schooners and sloops and 2800 smaller vessels were working the sponge beds, and in the peak year of 1917, 1½ million pounds of sponges were exported. 'The Mud,' an extensive 140-mile-long, 40-mile-wide shoal off Andros, was a major source of income for sponge divers. Sponging was the chief source of livelihood on all the Bahamian islands until 1938, when a fungal blight killed the sponges overnight.

ticals at Saunder's Drugs, across the road from the White Sand Beach Hotel.

Activities

There is no shortage of bonefishing guides. On Mangrove Cay, try Ralph Moxey (☎ 242-369-0218) or 'Bonefish' John (ask around, everyone knows him), who charges US$250 daily for two people.

Seascape Divers (☎ 242-369-0342) at Seascape Inn, on Mangrove Cay, rents scuba equipment and offers PADI instruction.

Special Events

Little Harbour hosts the three-day August Monday Regatta, when Bahamian skippers congregate to outpace each other. The highlight of the social calendar is the Annual Regatta, also in August, in Lisbon Creek.

Places to Stay

The atmospheric *Moxey's Guest House & Bonefish Lodge* (☎ 242-369-0023, fax 242-369-0726), on the shore in Little Harbour, has six rooms and two suites, the latter with four double beds and kitchen. All have air-con and fans and are modestly yet attractively furnished. There's a delightful dining room, plus a splendid and popular bar with a separate pool room. Four-night packages cost US$1920 single, US$1420 per person double occupancy. It's open mid-September to June.

Hellen's Motel Complex (☎ 242-369-0033), facing a beach about 1 mile south of Little Harbour, is a small, modern complex with 14 rooms. They're clean, tiled, and have a kitchenette and small TV; US$50/65 without/with air-con. There are also air-con cottage mini-suites for US$75. The hotel has a tiny restaurant and bar with TV, popular with Bahamians.

The older *White Sand Beach Hotel* (☎ 242-369-0159), about 400 yards south of Hellen's, has 25 large, carpeted rooms, each capable of sleeping six. They have air-con and fans but are rather dour and dingy. The rooms open to a rundown patio facing the narrow beach, with bonefish flats in front. Newer self-catering units are slightly better and rent for about US$75.

The snazziest place hereabouts is the *Seascape Inn* (☎/fax 242-369-0342, relax@seascapeinn.com), 2 miles south of Little Harbour, on the beachfront amid palms and run by Americans Micky and Joan McGowan. It has five small, simple cabins raised off the ground. They're delightfully decorated, with high wooden ceilings, fans, heaps of light, and wooden patios. Three have single beds; two have queen-size beds. There's a lofty all-timber restaurant and bar on tall stilts, with a TV, dart board, and stereo. On Sunday a fish fry is hosted. There's a dive center; bicycles and kayaks are free to guests. A guided kayak trip explores the bight and there's a small swampland nearby, good for bird watching. The US$110 rate (US$120 superior) includes continental breakfast. The mailing address is PO Box 023824, Mangrove Cay, Andros, The Bahamas.

Another attractive option is the modern yet homey *Mangrove Cay Inn* (☎ 242-369-0069, fax 242-369-0014; in the US ☎ 800-688-4752 ext 431), run by gracious hosts Elliot and Pat Greene (he's from the island, she's from New York). It's set amid lawns about 200 yards from a beach, with three blue holes nearby. The 12 air-con, dimly lit rooms are carpeted, with wooden ceiling, pink decor, ceiling fan, and a little bathroom; they cost US$70 standard, US$75 garden-view. Bike and snorkel-gear rentals are offered. There's a laundry and a bar with an electric piano. No credit cards are accepted.

Bonefishing fans with money to spend should consider the *Mangrove Cay Club* (in the US ☎ 800-626-3526, fax 406-585-3526, info@destinations-ltd.com), which opened in 2000 on the south shore of Middle Bight. This dedicated sportfishing lodge is run by a US company, Destinations Ltd. A four-night minimum stay is required. Packages begin at US$2500 single, US$1680 per person double occupancy for four-nights, all-inclusive. A 20% discount is offered July to mid-August.

There is also the eight-room *Mangrove Cay Beach Hotel & Resort* (☎ 242-369-0004) at the small community of Pinders, plus at least three other basic guesthouses: *Cool Breeze Cottage* (☎ 242-369-0465), the spartan *Bannister Guest House* (☎ 242-369-0188); and *Longley's Guest House* (☎ 242-369-0311); the latter two, with four rooms apiece, are in Lisbon Creek.

Places to Eat
The place to sup is the *Angler's Bar & Grill* at Moxey's Guest House. *Hellen's* has a restaurant and lounge serving native dishes such as stew conch, fish and grits, and fish and chips. Similar dishes are served at *Stacey's Restaurant & Lounge*, about 100 yards to the south. The restaurant at *Mangrove Cay Inn* has a large menu of salads and sandwiches, plus seafood and meat dishes for US$8 to US$16.

Diane Cash (☎ 242-369-0430) will cook you native dishes such as peas 'n' rice; she has a small place about 1 mile south of the Seascape Inn. If you're staying at Mangrove Cay Inn, you might stray down the road to *Auntie B's Restaurant* for simple native dishes.

In Lisbon Creek try the *Aqua-Marine Club*, where Sylvia Bannister cooks up tasty seafood for less than US$10.

You can buy groceries at *McPhee's Food & Variety Store*, opposite Seascape Inn.

Entertainment
The *Seaman's Club*, on the waterfront in Burnt Rock, 2 miles south of Little Harbour, is a colorful place frequented by locals.

You can learn some sexy moves at the *Happy Three Soca Club* (☎ 242-369-0030), the liveliest place on Mangrove Cay, with live soca music, dancing, and a pool table. It's in Grants, south of Little Harbour.

Shopping
The Hibiscus Gift Shop, opposite the Mangrove Cay Inn, sells painted T-shirts, locally made baskets and straw-work, jewelry, and other island-made items.

Getting There & Away
Bahamasair flies twice daily from Nassau to Mangrove Cay (US$50). Congo Air (on Mangrove Cay ☎ 242-369-0021) flies from Nassau to Mangrove Cay twice daily, continuing to Congo Town (South Andros).

A small, government-run passenger ferry runs from Lisbon Creek to Drigg's Hill (South Andros) at 8 am and 4 pm daily. It's free. Mr Moxey, the skipper, will run you across at other times for a fee.

The *Mangrove Cay Express* mail boat sails to Mangrove Cay/Lisbon Creek from Nassau at 6 pm Wednesday (5½ hours, US$30 one-way).

Getting Around
There are two taxis run by Sister B ('B' for Bertha) and Rodam Greene. A ride from the South Andros Airport to Moxey's Guest House costs about US$7; from the airport to the South Andros ferry costs US$18.

DRIGG'S HILL TO CONGO TOWN
Visitors to South Andros proper will land at the Congo Town airport, 3 miles south of Drigg's Hill, a scrawny hamlet facing Mangrove Cay across South Bight at the north tip of the island. The equally diminutive settlement of Congo Town, also known as Long Bay, is 2 miles south of the airport. There are no sites of interest.

There's a BaTelCo office by the ferry terminal at the end of the road in Drigg's Hill.

Activities
Stanley 'Jolly Boy' Forbes (☎ 242-369-4767), a good-humored, roly-poly fella, will take you bonefishing for US$300 daily for two people.

Gibson McKenzie leads a walking tour to a blue hole and the swampland. It takes about two hours. Make arrangements at Emerald Palms by the Sea (see below).

Places to Stay
The government-owned *Emerald Palms by the Sea* (☎ 242-369-2661, fax 242-369-2667) is 3 miles north of the airport, and the only true beach resort on Andros. The 20 air-con rooms all have ceiling fans, TV/VCR, and refrigerator. They're small and stuffy, but have handsome teak reproduction antique furniture; some rooms have king-size four-poster beds. The elegant dining room opens to the pool and beach, where buffets are hosted. There's

a tennis court, shuffleboard, Hobie Cats, and Aqua-Views (surfboards that you lie on to marvel at the marine world through a small glass window). Hammocks hang between palms. Bonefishing, diving, snorkeling, and excursions are offered. The staff are friendly and eager and the mood is relaxed. Free transfers are offered. Rooms cost US$80/90 single/double low season, US$100/110 high season; the Lanai suite costs US$135/150 low season, US$160/190 high season. A MAP (breakfast and dinner) plan costs US$40 daily. The mailing address is PO Box 800, Drigg's Hill, Andros, The Bahamas.

Stuart's Cove Apartments (☎ 242-369-1891) has two modest apartments beside the road 2 miles south of the airport.

Places to Eat
The *Emerald Palms* serves good meals, including glazed conch, crepes Suzettes, stingray, and sea urchin. US or native breakfasts cost US$5 to US$10; dinners are double that. For a more down-to-earth experience, try the *Square Deal*, a native eatery on the roadside 400 yards south of the hotel, or there's the *Bluebird Club* and *Flamingo Club* (☎ 242-369-2671) in Drigg's Hill, offering native dishes. Both clubs have pool tables and are good spots to get a taste of local nightlife.

Shopping
Try Gibson's Straw Market in Congo Town. You can buy homemade jewelry crafted from shells at Wendy's Craft Center, opposite the BaTelCo office in Drigg's Hill.

Getting There & Away
Bahamasair (on South Andros ☎ 242-369-2806) flies twice daily from Nassau to Congo Town (US$50 one-way). Congo Air (in Congo Town ☎ 242-369-2632) flies from Nassau via Mangrove Cay twice daily, and from Congo Town to Freeport on Friday and Saturday.

A minibus runs continually between Drigg's Hill and Mars Bay at the southern end of South Andros. The fare from Drigg's Hill to Kemp's Bay is US$2; US$5 for destinations farther south.

A small, passengers-only government ferry runs from Lisbon Creek on Mangrove Cay (see the Mangrove Cay section, earlier in this chapter).

The mail boat *Captain Moxey* sails to Drigg's Hill and Congo Town from Nassau at 11 pm Monday (7½ hours, US$30 one-way), stopping at The Bluff and Kemp's Bay as well.

Getting Around
You can arrange car rentals from any local willing to give up his or her car through Emerald Palms (see Places to Stay, above). It's a lackadaisical affair, and your car may not be delivered until midday; if so, bargain for a rate other than the standard US$65 per day (a US$100 deposit is normal).

THE BLUFF & HIGH ROCK
Three miles south of Congo Town, The Bluff is the largest and most orderly settlement on the island. The village extends south to the suburb of High Rock, a disorderly place atop a limestone bluff overlooking fabulously blue flats. Two narrow yet beautiful beaches run north and south.

The Government Administrative Office, at the south end of The Bluff, contains the post office, BaTelCo, and police offices. There's a tiny library at the south end of The Bluff; it's open 10:30 am to 5:30 pm weekdays.

Places to Stay & Eat
If you're looking for simple accommodations, try *Lewis' Guest House* (☎ 242-329-4672) atop the bluff, with fine views of the ocean from its 16 rooms, each with private bathroom, TV, and fan for about US$50.

In the same price range, *Kemp's Guest House* (☎ 242-369-3796) has six tiny and dingy rooms next to the Ocean Club restaurant in High Rock. They're scantily furnished but have ceiling fan, TV, and surprisingly large and well-lit bathrooms. Four rooms share a bathroom.

Haylean's Restaurant (☎ 242-369-3505), in High Rock, is recommended for chicken 'n' souse and other native dishes. Here, too, is the *Ocean Club*, serving breakfasts for

ANDROS

about US$6 and dinners for US$8, and *Big J's*, serving breakfasts such as sheep's-tongue souse and grits, sausage, and eggs for US$5, as well as lunch and dinner.

Getting There & Around
The mail boat *Captain Moxey* calls weekly from Nassau; see the Drigg's Hill to Congo Town section for details.

Orthniel Lewis offers car rentals in The Bluff, where there's a gas station.

KEMP'S BAY
Five miles south of High Rock, Kemp's Bay is a small yet lively center of action, with the island's high school and a concentration of services. The settlement seems to be run by Norman Rahming, the local *padrone,* who owns the grocery, marina, boatyard (where Rahming Bonefishing skiffs are made), sport-fishing camp, small guesthouse, and car-rental agency.

The local fishermen look toward Tinker's Rock, which is 1 mile offshore. It's favored by schooling groupers on their annual run. In season, hire a boatsman such as Nathaniel Adams (ask any local to direct you to him) and join the other skiffs and sailless yawls running handlines and traps for the big fish, which have been described as 'stacked in countless layers, thick as sand.' The schooling is a major source of local income, and the fishermen's wives wait on shore with bloodstained aprons and machetes, ready to clean the daily catch, which will be shipped aboard the weekly mail boat to the Nassau market.

The Bank of The Bahamas has an office here; it's open 10 am to 2:45 pm Wednesday. For the police, call ☎ 919 or ☎ 242-369-4733.

Places to Stay & Eat
One mile north of Kemp's Bay, *Rolle's Enterprises* (☎/fax 242-369-1723) rents apartments in Smith Hill. A wash house, restaurant, and bar are attached. *Rehring's Food Store* (☎ 242-369-1608, fax 242-369-1934), in Kemp's Bay, also has modest apartments for rent.

Royal Palm Beach Lodge (☎ 242-369-1608, fax 242-369-1934; in the US ☎ 800-688-

4752), formerly a fishing lodge, has 10 carpeted air-con rooms with TV and mini-fridge. Some rooms are a bit dowdy, with raggedy furniture; others are brighter and better furnished. You can also rent a handsome little two-bedroom cottage made of conch shells! It has a full kitchen and sleeps four people. There's a small restaurant and a swimming pool. Rooms cost US$45 single, US$55 double.

Many locals sup at the *Ocean Club Restaurant & Bar* (☎ 242-369-4796) and at *Big J's on the Bay* (☎ 242-369-1954) in Kemp's Bay.

There's a *grocery* and *general goods store* next to Lewis' Guest House, where *Lewis' Restaurant & Bar* offers barbecues on weekends. In Kemp's Bay you can buy groceries at *Rehring's Food Store*.

Entertainment
On weekend nights head just north of town to Smith Hill, where the beachfront *Cabana Beach Bar* hosts dancing. It has picnic tables and chairs under the palms. *Lewis' Bar* has a dance hall on weekends, when it gets lively.

Getting There & Around
A minibus from Drigg's Hill occasionally stops here; see the Drigg's Hill to Congo Town section for information.

The *Captain Moxey* mail boat calls here weekly from Nassau; see the Drigg's Hill to Congo Town section, earlier in this chapter, for details.

You can rent cars for US$65 at Rahming's Car Rental (☎ 242-369-1608, fax 242-369-1934) at the gas station.

KEMP'S BAY TO MARS BAY
The road continues south, with bridges skipping over Deep Creek and Little Creek via the settlements of those names, then runs through the tiny settlement of Pleasant Bay before arriving in Mars Bay. Here the road comes to an abrupt halt.

Mars Bay is a colorful seaside settlement with quaint wooden and Emancipation-era stone houses painted in bright pastels. You may see old ladies weaving straw, and the fishermen scaling their catch down by the wharf, where a grand old Androsian schooner lies beached.

A minibus from Drigg's Hill runs throughout the day to Mars Bay; see the Drigg's Hill to Congo Town section, earlier in this chapter, for more information.

Stargate Blue Hole
This limpidly azure blue hole, looking like a country pond, is actually the local harbor! It descends to about 300 feet, with galleries of stalactites and stalagmites.

Places to Stay & Eat
Four hundred yards north of the bridge over Deep Creek, *Glato's Bonefish Lodge* (☎ 242-369-4669, fax 242-369-4670) is a rather basic facility with six family apartments for US$65. They sit amid lawns within yards of the ocean and are fully furnished but a bit dour.

For a more intimate experience, head to Little Creek and check in at the beachside *Bair Bahamas Guest House* (☎/fax 242-369-4518; in the US ☎ 800-211-8530, fax 307-672-3920, angling@wavecom.net), where Americans Stanley and Andy Bair play host at their charming, strawberry-pink three-bedroom guesthouse with three air-con rooms with private baths. Imagine, no more than five other anglers at any given time! There's a TV lounge, and meals – including fabulous key-lime pie – are served at a banquet table. A covered porch to the rear overlooks the beach. Local guides take you out on the 17-foot Bonefisher and 18-foot Rahming craft. Three-night packages begin at US$990 single, US$1390 per person double occupancy.

A new bonefishing lodge, *Taino Resort*, was slated to open in 2001.

The place to grab a snack in Mars Bay is *Fisherman's Paradise*, serving native fare.

Eleuthera

• pop 11,000

Eleuthera, a slender wisp of an island about 100 miles long yet barely a bowshot wide, arcs on a radius about 50 miles east of Nassau. It has traditionally been the destination of choice for hobnobbing socialites, drawn here by chic club resorts and by sands the delicate hue of Cristal Rosé champagne.

The name 'Eleuthera' comes from the Greek word *eleutheros*, meaning freedom (the Lucayans who originally settled the island called their home 'Cigatoo'). In 1648 the majority of the 70 Eleutheran Adventur-

ers (see History in the Facts about The Bahamas chapter), who fled religious persecution in Bermuda during the English Civil War era, put ashore on the island's north coast where they holed up in Preacher's Cave. Actually, the island – or rather the Devil's Backbone, an extensive coral reef – found *them*, ripping open the bottom of their boats and forestalling further travel. Thus began English settlement in the Bahamas. They were later joined by Loyalists, who brought their slaves and founded new settlements.

Throughout the 18th century, pineapple production blossomed, and a local variety – the Eleutheran sugar loaf – earned recognition as an especially succulent fruit. In 1900 production peaked, and 7 million pineapples were exported. Alas, they were eventually supplanted by fruit from Cuba, Jamaica, and Hawaii. Eleuthera's pineapple farmers are now a dying breed. Raising pineapples is labor-intensive, requiring backbreaking work that has little appeal for young people.

Locals blame the policies of the Pindling government, which chased foreign investment away. Abandoned silos recall the thriving cattle and chicken industries that evolved in the 1950s, concentrated near Hatchet Bay. Alas, following independence the government bought out the farmers, and within a short span the farms were derelict. Since independence, with the exception of Harbour Island, tourism on Eleuthera has also withered and many once-fashionable resort hotels are now closed.

Development is concentrated on two cays off the coast of North Eleuthera: Harbour Island, with Dunmore Town, and St Georges Island, with Spanish Wells. Both are booming, the former from tourism, the latter from lobstering.

Hurricane Andrew knocked the socks off much of North Eleuthera in 1992, and Hurricane Floyd hit Eleuthera with a right hook in 1999: Governor's Harbour and Harbour Island both sustained severe damage and telephone lines remained down months later. The

Glass Window Bridge was damaged, halting road traffic between the north and south halves of Eleuthera. And Harbour Island's famous pink-sand beach was radically altered…in places, the hurricane created a 40-foot drop-off to the beach, which it enlarged.

The island is famous for its stunning blush-pink sands washed by Atlantic rollers. On the east coast dramatic cliffs, sheltered coves, and offshore coral reefs add to the picture. The Devil's Backbone is still there and in the intervening years has claimed several other ill-fated ships, whose remains await exploration. Divers who 'collect' wrecks will even find a US Civil War–era locomotive submerged at 20 feet. And the Bight of Eleuthera, to the west, is a vast expanse of shallow pavonine waters where bonefish await.

The island was put within easy reach of Nassau in 1999 when a high-speed ferry service was introduced.

A paved road – Queen's Hwy – runs the length of the island, making exploration simple.

Tarbox Geographix publishes four superb sectional tourist maps of Eleuthera, available through Charlie Moore at the Rainbow Inn (☎/fax 242-335-0294, 800-688-0047) at Hatchet Bay; its mailing address is PO Box EL-25053, Governor's Harbour, Eleuthera, The Bahamas.

North Eleuthera

Eleuthera is neatly divided by a tendril-thin isthmus called 'The Glass Window,' one-quarter of the way down the island. Southward, the island dangles like an umbilical cord. Immediately north, the isle broadens out in a rough triangle shaped like a woodpecker's head, with Current Island to the west forming the long beak. To the east, Harbour Island and neighboring cays enclose a vast harbor.

North Eleuthera lies north of, and includes, Governor's Harbour.

HARBOUR ISLAND

This island, 2 miles off the mainland and barely 3 miles long by a quarter-mile wide,

has been rated by *Travel & Leisure* magazine as the prettiest island in the Caribbean. That's a tall order, but no one can argue that 'Briland,' as it is known to the cognoscenti, *is* picture-perfect. It boasts one of The Bahamas' quaintest villages and an indescribably lovely coral-pink beach running the length of the windward shore, where breakers rolling in from Africa are stopped by offshore coral reefs, guaranteeing superb bathing.

Briland (so-named because the locals have trouble pronouncing the letters 'H' and 'R') blends old and new, highlighted by topnotch resorts, among them Pink Sands, the finest resort in The Bahamas.

Quaint **Dunmore Town** (pop 1500), on the harbor side, harks back 300 years. The town was laid out in 1791 by Lord Dunmore, governor of the Bahamas from 1787 to 1796, who had a summer residence here. This time-warp village could have fallen from an artist's canvas, with its pastel-painted clapboard cottages decorated with filigree and surrounded by bougainvillea, hibiscus, and oleander. The clip-clop of hooves has been replaced with the whir of golf carts, but the daily pace is characteristically Bahamian, underscored by the charm and friendliness of the Brilanders.

Dunmore Town was once a noted shipyard and a sugar-refining center from which a rum-making tradition evolved. Today many adults are employed at the dozen or so hotels, while others fish.

Renowned artist Eddie Minnis lives here, representing his beloved island on canvas. And singer Jimmy Buffett is a regular visitor (piloting his Albatross seaplane), as are many Hollywood stars and supermodels.

Golf carts are the main type of island transport.

ELEUTHERA

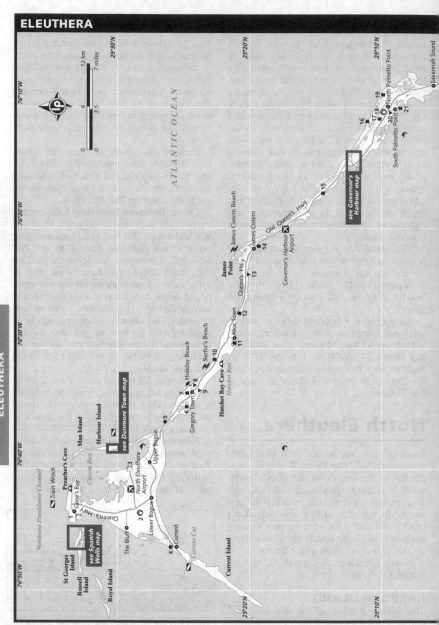

ELEUTHERA

ATLANTIC OCEAN

Northeast Providence Channel

Savannah Sound

North Palmetto Point

South Palmetto Point

see Governor's Harbour map

James Cistern Beach

James Cistern

Governor's Harbour Airport

Old Queen's Hwy

James Point

Queen's Hwy

Alice Town

Surfer's Beach

Holiday Beach

Gregory Town

Hatchet Bay Cave

Hatchet Bay

see Dunmore Town map

Harbour Island

Man Island

Cistern Bay

Preacher's Cave

Gene's Bay

Train Wreck

St Georges Island

Russell Island

Royal Island

see Spanish Wells map

North Eleuthera Airport

Upper Bogue

Lower Bogue

The Bluff

Current

Current Island

Current Cut

Queen's Hwy

ELEUTHERA

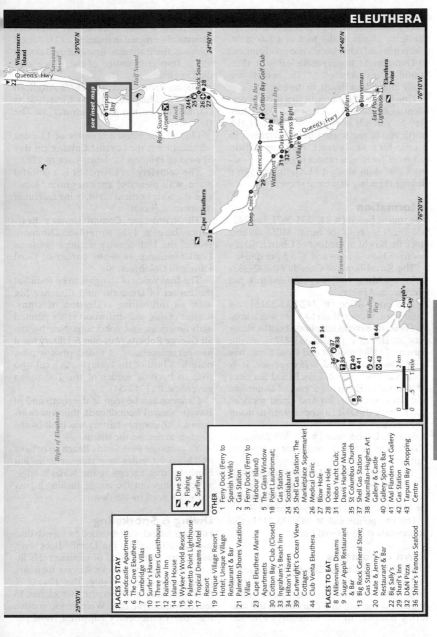

PLACES TO STAY
- 4 Sandcastle Apartments
- 6 The Cove Eleuthera
- 7 Cambridge Villas
- 10 Surfer's Haven
- 11 Three Sisters Guesthouse
- 12 Rainbow Inn
- 14 Island House
- 15 Wykee's World Resort
- 16 Palmetto Point Lighthouse
- 17 Tropical Dreams Motel
- 19 Unique Village Resort
  Hotel; Unique Village
  Restaurant & Bar
- 21 Palmetto Shores Vacation
  Villas
- 23 Cape Eleuthera Marina
  Apartments
- 30 Cotton Bay Club (Closed)
- 33 Ingraham's Beach Inn
- 34 Hilton's Haven
- 39 Cartwright's Ocean View
  Cottages
- 44 Club Venta Eleuthera

PLACES TO EAT
- 8 Millennium Dreams
- 9 Sugar Apple Restaurant
  & Bar
- 13 Big Rock General Store;
  Gas Station
- 20 Mate & Jenny's
  Restaurant & Bar
- 22 Big Sally's
- 29 Sharil's Inn
- 32 D&N Pizza
- 36 Shine's Famous Seafood

OTHER
- 1 Ferry Dock (Ferry to
  Spanish Wells)
- 2 Gas Station
- 3 Ferry Dock (Ferry to
  Harbour Island)
- 5 The Glass Window
- 18 Point Laundromat;
  Gas Station
- 24 Scotiabank
- 25 Shell Gas Station; The
  Marketplace Supermarket
- 26 Medical Clinic
- 27 Blow Hole
- 28 Ocean Hole
- 31 Hobo Yacht Club;
  Davis Harbour Marina
- 35 St Columbus Church
- 37 Shell Gas Station
- 38 Macmillan-Hughes Art
  Gallery & Castle
- 40 Gallery Sports Bar
- 41 Mal Flanders Art Gallery
- 42 Gas Station
- 43 Tarpum Bay Shopping
  Centre

Legend:
- ⚑ Dive Site
- ⚓ Fishing
- Surfing

Orientation

Bay St curls along the harborfront, where the ferry alights at the foot of Church St. Church St and other streets rise gently inland to Dunmore St, which parallels Bay St, then continue to Colebrook St. The resorts are along Pink Sands Beach, to the east.

Colebrook St runs south to a private residential estate and the Romora Bay Club. Bay St extends north to Nesbit St at the north end of the town, where it narrows to a mile-long sandy track (the vegetation closes in, forming a tunnel favored by swallows that skim along it like jetfighters in a dogfight) ending at a coral shore.

Information

The tourist board (☎ 242-333-2621, fax 242-333-2622) is above the Sugar Mill souvenir store on Bay St at the foot of Church St; it's open 9:30 am to 1 pm and 3 to 5 pm daily.

The Royal Bank of Canada (☎ 242-333-2250), on Murray St, is open 9 am to 1 pm Monday and Friday.

The post office (☎ 242-333-2215), on Goal Lane, is open 9 am to 5 pm weekdays.

There are several telephone booths along Bay St. BaTelCo (☎ 242-333-2375), at the corner of Colebrook St and Goal Lane, has telephone booths and a fax service; it is open 8 am to 5:30 pm daily. Island Services (☎ 242-333-3032), at the corner of Dunmore and King Sts, offers fax and email services and represents DHL; it's open 9 am to noon weekdays.

Seaside Laundromat (☎ 242-333-2066), on Bay St near Pitt St, is open 6 am to 6:30 pm daily except Sunday.

The Harbour Island Medical Clinic (☎ 242-333-2182), on Church St, is open 9 am to noon weekdays. The Harbour Pharmacy (☎ 242-333-2178) is on Bay St near Pitt St.

For the police, call ☎ 242-333-3111; the police station is on Goal Lane.

Town Landmarks

The **Wesley Methodist Church**, at the corner of Dunmore and Chapel Sts, was built in 1843 with beautiful hardwood pews and a huge model sailing ship that honors the seafaring tradition of the Brilanders. Outside the church, at the corner of Dunmore and King Sts, is a small obelisk – **Dr Johnson's Memorial** – erected in memory of Dr Albert Johnson, the Bahamas' first qualified doctor and a respected justice of the peace who died in 1895.

Dating from 1768, **St John's Anglican Church**, on Dunmore St near Church St, is claimed to be the oldest church in The Bahamas.

One of the finest examples of Loyalist architecture is the **Loyalist Cottage**, on Bay St west of Princess St, dating back to 1797.

The **cemetery** on Chapel St is a colorful place, with plenty of ancient graves; locals give it a wide berth at night, being fearful of 'sparrots'…ghosts!

The handsome **Commissioner's Residence**, built in 1913 to replace Dunmore House, the 18th-century summer house of Lord Dunmore, is at the corner of Goal Lane and Colebrook St.

The funky side of things is to be found at the corner of Dunmore and Clarence Sts, with an interesting collection of **signs**, license plates, and driftwood relics painted with limericks and aphorisms. Nearby, the **Sir George Roberts Museum & Library** has a meager miscellany of faded photos plus, outside, a bust of the eponymous local who rose to become leader of the Bahamian government (1949–54).

Cannons can be seen at the south end of Bay St. Named **Roundheads**, this now overgrown 17th-century battery was built by the English to defend the island.

Ya gotta see **Pink Sands Beach** to believe it! This deep, miles-long stunner is a faint blush by day, except at the water's edge, which brings out the rouge, turning a rosy red when fired by the dawn.

Diving & Snorkeling

Harbour Island is surrounded by superb dive sites, highlighted by the Devil's Backbone, with more than 3 miles of pristine reefs littered with ancient wrecks. Among them are *Cienfuegos*, a cruise ship; the *Potato & Onion*, a massive 19th-century wreck just 15 feet down; and the Train Wreck, a locomotive that the Confederacy captured from the

DUNMORE TOWN

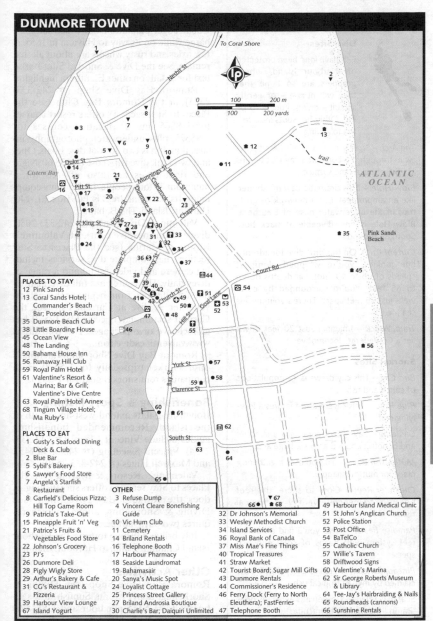

To Coral Shore

Nesbit St
Duke St
Pitt St
King St
Munnings St
Barrack St
Colebrook St
Chapel St
Crown St
Murray St
Church St
Coal Lane
Hill St
York St
Clarence St
South St
Bay St
Princess St
Dunmore St

Cistern Bay

ATLANTIC OCEAN

trail

Pink Sands Beach

Court Rd

0   100   200 m
0   100   200 yards

ELEUTHERA

PLACES TO STAY
12 Pink Sands
13 Coral Sands Hotel;
   Commander's Beach
   Bar; Poseidon Restaurant
35 Dunmore Beach Club
38 Little Boarding House
45 Ocean View
48 The Landing
50 Bahama House Inn
56 Runaway Hill Club
59 Royal Palm Hotel
61 Valentine's Resort &
   Marina; Bar & Grill;
   Valentine's Dive Centre
63 Royal Palm Hotel Annex
68 Tingum Village Hotel;
   Ma Ruby's

PLACES TO EAT
1 Gusty's Seafood Dining
   Deck & Club
2 Blue Bar
5 Sybil's Bakery
6 Sawyer's Food Store
7 Angela's Starfish
   Restaurant
8 Garfield's Delicious Pizza;
   Hill Top Game Room
9 Patricia's Take-Out
18 Pineapple Fruit 'n' Veg
21 Patrice's Fruits &
   Vegetables Food Store
22 Johnson's Grocery
23 PJ's
26 Dunmore Deli
28 Pigly Wigly Store
31 Arthur's Bakery & Cafe
31 CG's Restaurant &
   Pizzeria
39 Harbour View Lounge
67 Island Yogurt

OTHER
3 Refuse Dump
4 Vincent Cleare Bonefishing
   Guide
10 Vic Hum Club
11 Cemetery
14 Briland Rentals
16 Telephone Booth
17 Harbour Pharmacy
18 Seaside Laundromat
19 Bahamasair
20 Sanya's Music Spot
24 Loyalist Cottage
25 Princess Street Gallery
27 Briland Androsia Boutique
30 Charlie's Bar; Daiquiri Unlimited
32 Dr Johnson's Memorial
33 Wesley Methodist Church
34 Island Services
36 Royal Bank of Canada
37 Miss Mae's Fine Things
40 Tropical Treasures
41 Straw Market
42 Tourist Board; Sugar Mill Gifts
43 Dunmore Rentals
44 Commissioner's Residence
46 Ferry Dock (Ferry to North
   Eleuthera); FastFerries
47 Telephone Booth
49 Harbour Island Medical Clinic
51 St John's Anglican Church
52 Police Station
53 Post Office
54 BaTelCo
55 Catholic Church
57 Willie's Tavern
58 Driftwood Signs
60 Valentine's Marina
62 Sir George Roberts Museum
   & Library
64 Tee-Jay's Hairbraiding & Nails
65 Roundheads (cannons)
66 Sunshine Rentals

Dive & Snorkel Sites

Dive Sites

Fish have long been protected off Harbour Island, where groupers are so tame that they will nuzzle – or gently assault – divers, hoping to be fed. Other hot spots include the following:

The Arch – Sharks, rays, and schools of jacks swim through this coral archway that begins at 75 feet below the surface.

Blow Hole – This dramatic cavern, shaped like an amphitheater, is a network of grottoes in the underwater base of Eleuthera. Blow Hole is only diveable at slack tide. Sponges abound.

Current Cut – On this drift dive for adrenaline junkies, you're whipped along at speeds of up to 10 knots, in depths down to 65 feet. You're surrounded by coral walls just 75 feet apart. There's voluminous sea life.

Train Wreck – Imagine! Just 20 feet down lies a Confederate locomotive.

Snorkel Sites

Bird Cay – This cay draws large populations of conch and fish.

Blue Hole – This cavern also features a low-lying reef.

Gaulding's Cay – Soft coral, sea anemone, and bonefish abound across a large area.

Muttonfish Point – This point is a gathering place for mutton snapper.

Oleander Reef – Close to shore, this reef boasts a tremendous variety of tropical fish.

Paradise Beach – Here you'll find a barrier-reef system with heaps of coral and fish species.

Pineapple Rock – Here lies a shipwreck, now claimed by myriad tropical fish.

Seafan Gardens – Gorgonians await, as does 'Baron,' the friendly barracuda.

Union during the US Civil War and sold to a Cuban sugar plantation, but which fell off a barge while on its way to Havana in 1865. A few axles and rusty wheels are about all that remain. See the Dive & Snorkel Sites boxed text for details on other Eleuthera highlights.

Romora Bay Dive Shop (☎ 242-333-2323), at the Romora Bay Club (see the Places to Stay section), offers resort courses for US$65 and certification courses for US$375, plus underwater photography instruction. It has two 30-foot dive boats. One- and two-tank dive trips cost US$35/60. Night and drift dives are also offered for a minimum of four people. It also rents equipment. Its postal address is PO Box EL-146, Harbour Island, The Bahamas.

Valentine's Dive Centre (☎ 242-333-2080, dive@valentinesdive.com), at Valentine's Resort & Marina (see the Places to Stay section), has complete dive services, including camera and video rental and a range of dives daily. The center has full dive instruction for all levels, from beginner through divemaster. A dive at Current Cut (see the Current section, later) costs US$125. It has all-inclusive dive packages. The Web site is www.valventinesdive.com.

Romora Bay Dive Shop and Valentine's offer snorkel trips daily for US$30. Both companies rent snorkel gear for US$10.

Bonefishing & Sport Fishing

Bonefishing flats extend west and south of the island. Recommended bonefishing guides include Vincent Cleare (☎ 242-333-2154), Vincent Sweeting (☎ 242-333-2145), and Maxwell Higgs (☎ 242-333-2530).

Valentine's Resort & Marina (see the Places to Stay section) offers sportfishing, as does the Romora Bay Dive Shop (see Diving & Snorkeling, above), which requires two days' notice.

July brings a fishing tournie, the Harbour Island Championship, to Harbour Island.

Other Activities

Romora Bay Dive Shop (see Diving & Snorkeling, above) rents Sunfish and sailboards for US$15 per hour and US$45/60 half/full day. A local Rastafarian called Martinez rents horses on the beach for US$20 per hour. You also can rent horses by calling ☎ 242-333-2317.

Organized Excursions

For a little 'X-rated' fun *(their* description), Romora Bay Club (see the Places to Stay section, below) will whisk you and the one you love to a secluded cay and maroon you for a while with a picnic hamper and drinks.

Places to Stay

A rental agency, *Island Real Estate* (☎ 242-333-2278, fax 242-333-2354), represents about three dozen rental properties, from quaint one-bedroom cottages to deluxe four-bedroom villas. Rates range from about US$500 to US$2500 weekly; its mailing address is PO Box EL-27045, Harbour Island, The Bahamas.

Edmund Sweeting (☎ 242-333-2145) has a small, slightly unkempt, red-and-white *cottage* with kitchen on Princess St for US$45 a day. The *Little Boarding House*, on Bay St at Murray St, is an old gingerbread house for rent; call the tourist board for information (see the Information section, above).

Ma Ruby has 15 well-lit, air-con rooms in delightful cottages at the casual *Tingum Village Hotel* (☎/fax 242-333-2161) at the south end of town on Colebrook St. The rooms have stone walls, ceiling fan, and tile floors. Three 'suites' have kitchens and whirlpool tubs. There's an outdoor restaurant and a bar. Four additional units were to be added. Rooms cost US$75/95 single/double year-round. 'Suites' cost US$175/250. A cottage with 10 beds in three bedrooms costs US$250.

The modern but charmless *Royal Palm Hotel* (☎ 242-333-2738, fax 242-333-2528, brilandboy@batelnet.bs), at Dunmore and Clarence Sts, has eight air-con rooms, plus six rooms with kitchenette, plus additional rooms and apartments in an annex a block away. All are clean, carpeted, and modestly furnished, including king-size bed, ceiling fan, and TV. Rates are US$79 standard, US$147 deluxe, US$124 for an apartment 'cottage.' The mailing address is PO Box EL-27059, Harbour Island, The Bahamas.

Aqua enthusiasts should head to *Valentine's Resort & Marina* (☎ 242-333-2142, 800-383-6480, fax 242-333-2135, email: info@valentinesresort.com), on Bay St, with 26 air-con rooms, each with pleasing decor and sliding glass doors opening to shady patios. It has a full-service dive shop and marina, lively waterfront bar, attractive freshwater pool and Jacuzzi on a wooden deck, tennis court, and atmospheric restaurant. A shuttle runs to the beach. Summer rates are US$80/95 single/double garden-view, US$90/120 pool-view; winter rates are US$110/120 and US$115/130, respectively. Its postal address is PO Box EL-1, Harbour Island, The Bahamas.

An exquisite in-town option is *The Landing* (☎ 242-333-2707, fax 242-333-2650, landinghi@aol.com), a colonial-era mansion overlooking the harbor near the ferry dock. This recently refurbished 200-year-old charmer has seven gracious air-con rooms, including three honeymoon suites, each with ceiling fan and endearing decor of cool whites, old hardwood floors, antique furniture (including planters. chairs, and four-poster king-size beds with Ralph Lauren linens and drapes), and gleaming white bathrooms. The hotel has a splendid restaurant and an upstairs library and TV lounge with deep sofa. Tracy and Toby are congenial hosts. Rates are US$155 single or double, US$230 suites. The postal address is PO Box EL-190, Harbour Island, The Bahamas. *Recommended!*

In a similar vein is *Bahama House Inn* (☎ 242-333-2201, fax 242-333-2850, bahamhs@batelnet.bs), another restored colonial home at the corner of Dunmore and Hill Sts. It functions as a B&B, with five charming air-con rooms, each with ceiling fans, delightful decor, and a private bath. Some have four-poster beds with drapes. There's a library lounge with TV, and a large garden and patio deck. A studio apartment is also offered. No children under 12 are allowed. Rates are US$85 to US$100 single, US$95 to US$120 double in summer; US$110 to US$125 single, and US$125 to US$145 double in winter, including full breakfast.

ELEUTHERA

Coral Sands Hotel (☎ 242-333-2350, 800-468-2799, fax 242-333-2368, coralsan@batelnet .bs), long a legend among sybarites and socialites, is a 33-room beach resort extending over 14 acres. It was purchased in 1998 and given a much-needed facelift. The carpeted rooms blend Caribbean colors, wicker furniture, and artwork to create a homey feel; oceanfront rooms have French doors opening to balconies. There are also one- to three-bedroom apartments. You can dine at the beach bar or on the patio at the Poseidon Restaurant, overseen by a gourmet chef. There's live entertainment, plus a library, game room with pool table and satellite TV, tennis, and water sports, all included in the rates. You can rent bicycles, scooters, or golf carts. Room rates are US$155/195/260 garden-view/ocean-view/family suite in summer, US$210/260/335 in winter. The apartments cost US$305 to US$615 in summer; US$380 to US$800 in winter.

The equally elegant *Dunmore Beach Club* (☎ 242-333-2200, fax 242-333-2429), due south, has 12 cozy, nicely furnished and recently renovated cottages amid landscaped lawns. Enlarged bathrooms now boast oversize showers and whirlpool tubs. There's a handsome clubhouse with bar and lounge complete with fireplace, and a highly rated restaurant requiring that men wear jackets and ties at dinner. Rates are US$345/445 summer/winter, suites cost US$375/475 (closed September and October). The postal address is PO Box EL-27122, Harbour Island, The Bahamas.

Next south along the beach is *Ocean View* (☎ 242-333-2276, fax 242-333-2459), whose notably irksome owner, 'Pip' Simmons, runs her beautifully yet eclectically decorated nine-bedroom mansion as an upscale home-cum-house-party to which guests are invited. She has a staunch, predominantly European clientele…but the word is that if she doesn't like you, you're out! Rooms cost US$325 year-round, including breakfast and dinner. The mailing address is PO Box EL-134, Harbour Island, The Bahamas.

The *Runaway Hill Club* (☎ 242-333-2150, fax 242-333-2420), next door, is a contemporary, New England–style hotel amid 7 acres of palm-studded gardens. The 10 voluminous air-con rooms face the sea and have a private patio or balcony, ceiling fans, and decor combining tile floors, rattan furniture, and tropical floral prints. Some are in the main building, others in a villa on the hill. There's a freshwater pool. Choose to dine alfresco on a veranda or in the cozy dining room, with gourmet meals and a dress code. Rates are US$200/215 single/double in summer; US$220/240 in winter. The villa costs US$215/220 and US$230/250, respectively. The mailing address is PO Box EL-27031, Harbour Island, The Bahamas.

The *Romora Bay Club* (☎ 242-333-2325, fax 242-333-2500, info@romorabay.com) faces west, with self-catering cottages spilling down through riotously colorful gardens to wooden sun decks and a Jacuzzi. There are also 33 air-con rooms, plus cottages with kitchenettes, and villas. All have a splendid aesthetic, plus fans, cable TVs/ VCRs, CD players, and private patios or balcony views. Sloppy Joe's and the Parrot Bar offer views over the harbor. There's a fine restaurant, plus a clubhouse with lounge and library. It has its own dive facility, plus water sports and tennis, and bicycles can be rented. Summer rates range from US$190 to US$380, including airport transfers, breakfast, lunch, and water sports, plus one scuba dive. Winter rates range from US$280 to US$500. A MAP plan, which includes dinner as well, costs US$38. Seven-night specials are offered, including dive packages. The mailing address is PO Box 7026, Boca Raton, FL 33431, USA.

Outclassing all contenders, however, is *Pink Sands* (☎ 242-333-2030, fax 242-333-2060; in the US ☎ 305-534-2135, 800-688-7678, fax 305-672-2881; in the UK ☎ 800-614790, fax 020-7431-7920), one of the most unpretentiously chic resort hotels in the world, categorically The Bahamas' finest, and a favorite of shutterbug-shy celebs like Christie Brinkley and Ed Bradley. There are 29 rooms in 21 exquisite one-bedroom and four two-bedroom cottages, each secluded amid 16 magnificently landscaped acres spilling down to the beach. Each cottage comes with a golf cart. Decor is sublime: throw rugs on rough-cut marble-like floors, lofty mansard ceilings, and oversize Adirondack chairs with batik fabrics set against a mellow wash of pastels. Each room has a singular color theme – eggshell blue, lavender, and the same blush pink as the namesake beach. Each has central air-con, ceiling fan, satellite TV, CD stereo system with CDs, two-line telephone, wet bar, private patio, and exotic bathrooms with kimono bathrobes. Facilities include three tennis courts, a gym, freshwater pool, and library with audio-visual setup, bar-lounge with Indonesian and Indian motif, plus diving and water sports. Dining is gourmet (see the Places to Eat section for a description of the restaurant), and service is impeccable and relaxed. Room rates range from US$475 to US$1225 from mid-April to mid-December and US$625 to US$2000 mid-December to mid-April, including breakfast and dinner. Find a lover…and go! The postal address is PO Box EL-87, Harbour Island, The Bahamas.

Places to Eat

When the roosters crow, head to **Dunmore Deli** (☎ 242-333-2644), on Princess St at King St, for a breakfast of eggs and muffins. The deli also sells gourmet foods, served on a shady deck. **CG's Restaurant & Pizzeria**, on Dunmore St, is open only for breakfast from 7 am to noon. **Garfield's Delicious Pizza** (☎ 242-333-2889) also offers pizza; it's open noon to 11 pm.

For Bahamian home cooking, head to **Angela's Starfish Restaurant** (☎ 242-333-2253) on Nesbit St, serving breakfast at 7:30 am and closing at 8:30 pm, when a bell signals last orders (reservations are needed for breakfast). **PJ's** offers native dishes in a down-home setting, as does **Patricia's Take-Out**, serving chicken souse, fish and chips, and the like, though the most popular seafood restaurant with locals is **Gusty's Seafood Dining Deck & Club**. You can buy conch ceviche from **Queen Conch**, on Bay St at the foot of Duke St.

The cozy, pink-and-mint-green **Harbour View Lounge** (☎ 242-333-2031), on King St, serves such treats as curried pumpkin soup for US$5 and grilled marinated dolphin fish

for US$26. It has an outside terrace and is closed Monday.

Valentine's Bar & Grill (☎ 242-333-2142) at Valentine's Hotel & Marina, and **Ma Ruby's** (☎ 242-333-2161) at the Tingum Village Hotel, also serve native dishes such as grouper fritter; the former offers outdoor seating and the latter has daily specials in a bright and airy eatery with upbeat decor. This is the proud home of 'Cheeseburgers in Paradise,' featured in Jimmy Buffett's *Parrot Head Handbook*. It's open from 8 am to midnight.

For creative nouvelle cuisine, head to the restaurant in **The Landing** (☎ 242-333-2707), which serves specialty pastas, the likes of capellini with lobster, chile, and lime; and cornish game hen chargrilled with caramelized plantain and tomato cilantro salad. The desserts are to die for, and Cuban cigars are offered for post-prandial pleasure. Dishes cost US$18 and up. It serves espressos and cappuccinos; it's open for breakfast, lunch, and dinner, but is closed Wednesday.

Even more sublime is the restaurant in **Pink Sands**, where Chef Stuart Betteridge conjures up such recherché miracles as Bahamian sushi roll with mango, cucumber, and conch, and cornmeal-dusted game hen on spinach with tamarind honey vinaigrette. The fare is superb and the setting sublime. Nonguests are welcome. The prix fixe four-course dinners cost US$70, with a different menu nightly offering a choice of meat, fish, or pasta. It's open 7 to 10 pm. Pink Sands' beachfront **Blue Bar** serves à la carte lunches to all-comers, with equally mouth-watering fare, including chicken tikka spring rolls (US$8.50) and jerked chicken Caesar salad (US$16.50), washed down with whopping cocktails; it's open noon to 3 pm daily.

Similarly upscale is the **Runaway Hill Club** restaurant, where reservations – and jackets for gentlemen – are required. It's open to the public for dinner only (at 8 pm) and has a set menu for US$40. Likewise, Ludocic Jarland, the acclaimed chef at the **Romora Bay Club**, serves fixed-menu dinners at one seating at 7:30 pm. It also has a dress code.

Commander's Beach Bar, a sun-deck bar and lounge at Coral Sands, earns rave reviews for its grilled lobster-salad sandwich. The hotel's *Poseidon Restaurant* offers alfresco gourmet dining at night, backed by a huge wine list; reservations are required.

Tea parties are occasionally hosted at 3:30 pm at the Commissioner's Residence (see Town Landmarks, earlier in this chapter).

To stock up the larder, try *Patricie's Fruits & Vegetables Food Store* (☎ 242-333-2289), on Pitt St just north of the village center; *Sawyer's Food Store* (☎ 242-333-2356) on Dunmore St; *Pigly Wigly Store* (☎ 242-333-2120) on King St; and *Pineapple Fruit 'n' Veg* (☎ 242-333-2454) on Bay St. There's also *Johnson's Grocery* (☎ 242-333-2279) on Dunmore St.

You can buy fresh herb bread, scrumptious pastries, croissants, and pies at *Arthur's Bakery & Cafe* (☎ 242-333-2285), which serves breakfast and lunch specials, and *Sybil's Bakery*, at the corner of Duke and Dunmore Sts. *Island Yogurt*, at the south end of Colebrook St, serves frozen yogurts.

Entertainment

Humphrey Percentie, Jr, runs a 'museum,' basketball court, and rough-around-the-edges dance hall named *Vic Hum Club* (☎ 242-333-2161) at Barrack and Munnings Sts. This funky locale is as popular for international model shoots as with locals, who dribble on the checkerboard court that doubles as a dance floor. There's also a pool table. Museum? The banana-yellow walls are decorated with 1960s album covers, Junkanoo costume pieces, vintage posters, and fading photos of US athletes. Inevitably, there'll be a basketball game on the TV and a raw, over-the-rim reggae beat guaranteeing action beneath the full moon. The place also hosts performers from Maxi Priest to the bar's own Paddy 'Big Bird' Lewis. The world's largest coconut sits behind the bar. The place can get rowdy, fights often break out, and the owner has a running battle with locals who don't like the noise.

Then there's *Gusty's Seafood Dining Deck & Club*, in the north end of town, which claims to be Jimmy Buffett's original 'Margaritaville' and where the musician has been known to jam. Nearby, *Garfield's Hill Top Game Room* has video game machines.

Willie's Tavern (☎ 242-333-2121), on Dunmore St, is another popular, down-to-earth bar with a lofty ceiling festooned with fishing nets. It has a pool table and sports on TV. *Charlie's Bar*, on Dunmore St, is a calm spot to sup and has a patio where the *Daiquiri Unlimited* stall serves US$3 daiquiries.

The bar at *Pink Sands* offers superb upscale ambiance, with Cuban cigars and riffs off the Island Records label on the sound system. Splendid!

The *Harbour View Lounge* has live music and a dance club on weekends.

Shopping

About 20 top artists, most of them Bahamian, are represented at the Princess Street Gallery (☎ 242-333-2788), where a 24-inch original painting by Eddie Minnis sells for US$7500. Prices begin at US$100. Ceramics are also sold.

Colorful Androsia batiks are on sale at Briland Androsia Boutique (☎ 242-333-2342). Miss Mae's Fine Things, on Dunmore St, sells quality prints, batiks, throw rugs, and other souvenirs, as does Sugar Mill Gifts, on Bay St, facing the ferry dock. For chic casualwear, check out the store at Pink Sands.

There's a waterfront straw market facing Sugar Mill Gifts.

You can buy newspapers, batteries, and Cuban cigars at Tropical Treasures on the waterfront. And Sanya's Music Spot sells tapes and CDs of island music.

Getting There & Away

Air Flights arrive at North Eleuthera Airport (☎ 242-335-1241), 2 miles inland of the harbor on the mainland. See the Getting There & Away chapter for information on flights from the US.

Bahamasair flies daily from Nassau (US$50 one-way); its office on Bay St in Dunmore Town (☎ 242-333-3007) is open 9 am to 1 pm and 2:30 to 5 pm weekdays.

Charter operators in Nassau also fly to North Eleuthera; see the Getting Around chapter for full details.

If you fly in, you'll have to catch a ferry to Harbour Island. The dock for ferries *to* Harbour Island is 2 miles east of North Eleuthera Airport. A taxi to the North Eleuthera dock from the airport costs US$4 per person. The 45-minute taxi ride from Governor's Harbour Airport will cost about US$50. The 10-minute boat ride to Harbour Island costs US$8 solo, US$4 if shared.

Boat Bahamas Fastferries (☎ 242-323-2166, fax 242-322-8185, info@bahamasferries.com) operates a high-speed, luxury 117-passenger catamaran, the *Bo Hengy*, from Potter's Cay, Nassau, on a daily basis, with different schedules for winter and summer. You'll zip along at 35 knots (40mph); the journey takes one hour, 40 minutes and costs US$90 roundtrip (US$139 for an excursion rate with lunch, historical tour, and beach time). The ferry stops briefly at Spanish Wells on both the outbound and return legs.

The Harbour Island ferry dock is at the foot of Church St.

The Harbour Island Marina (☎ 242-333-2427, 'Jolly Roger' VHF channel 16) has 31 deep-water slips and charges US$1 per foot daily. There's also a deck and pool, plus a pleasant restaurant and bar (closed Monday).

Valentine's Marina (☎ 242-333-2142) is an all-new full-service marina for yachts up to 165 feet; it charges US$1 per foot per day.

You also can charter a water taxi between Spanish Wells and Harbour Island (US$50 one-way); there is no scheduled mail-boat service between Nassau and Harbour Island. See the Spanish Wells section for options.

Getting Around

Most everyone walks or uses a bicycle or golf cart, which you can rent from Briland Rentals (☎ 242-333-2243, 242-333-2584 evenings), at Daniel's Den on Bay St. It charges US$40 per day for golf carts, as does Dunmore Rentals (☎ 242-333-2372) on Bay and Church Sts; Royal Palm Golf Cart Rentals (☎ 242-333-2738); and Sunshine Rentals (☎ 242-333-2509), which also rents minivans and jeeps.

Taxis cost US$4 to US$6 between any two points in town. Taxi tours are available from Big M Taxi (☎ 242-333-2043), or with Reggie's (☎ 242-333-2116), or Hen's (☎ 242-333-2116).

On Harbour Island, water taxis operate from the Government Dock.

Ross' Garage (☎ 242-333-2122) rents boats. You also can rent boats from Valentine's; US$400/650 half/full-day.

SPANISH WELLS
• pop 800

Two miles west of North Eleuthera Airport, the road meets Queen's Hwy (there's a gas station at the T-junction), which runs north about 7 miles to Gene's Bay at the north tip of Eleuthera. The road ends at a ferry dock. St Georges Island – dominated by the town of Spanish Wells – lies 1 mile offshore.

Spanish Wells is named for the Spanish galleons that once drew water here before attempting to return home across the Atlantic Ocean. The village dates back to the days of the Eleutheran Adventurers. The deeply religious, somewhat reticent, lily-white population follows a Midwestern US lifestyle, with Swiss-clean orderliness. Generations of isolation have concentrated the gene pool, reflected in traits much of the population shares. Half the island is named Pinder: 'We wor Pinders b'fore we married, an' we're Pinders now.'

The place has been called the 'Island of the Worker Bees.' Tourism is minimal. Lobstering is its major trade and the source of phenomenal incomes (the locals are among the wealthiest of all Bahamians). Fishermen operate from state-of-the-art trawlers and go out as far as 250 miles for a month at a time. Adolescents tend to leave school (to the frustration of local teachers) by the age of 16 to make the most of their years. When the 'boys' are away the town is deathly still, with nary a soul on the starkly lit streets. Weird! Another note of surrealism comes from watching the Mexican-style *paseo* of motor cars cruising the tight circuit at night as locals kill time displaying their status symbols.

A beautiful beach rims the north shore.

Orientation

Spanish Wells is at the eastern end of St Georges Island. The main street runs along

ELEUTHERA

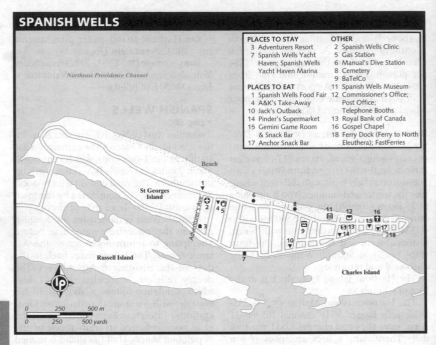

SPANISH WELLS

PLACES TO STAY	OTHER
3 Adventurers Resort	2 Spanish Wells Clinic
7 Spanish Wells Yacht	5 Gas Station
Haven; Spanish Wells	6 Manual's Dive Station
Yacht Haven Marina	8 Cemetery
	9 BaTelCo
PLACES TO EAT	11 Spanish Wells Museum
1 Spanish Wells Food Fair	12 Commissioner's Office;
4 A&K's Take-Away	Post Office;
10 Jack's Outback	Telephone Booths
14 Pinder's Supermarket	13 Royal Bank of Canada
15 Gemini Game Room	16 Gospel Chapel
& Snack Bar	18 Ferry Dock (Ferry to North
17 Anchor Snack Bar	Eleuthera); FastFerries

Northeast Providence Channel

Beach

St Georges
Island

Adventurer's Ave

Russell Island

Charles Island

0   250   500 m
0   250   500 yards

ELEUTHERA

the oceanside, while a second street runs
parallel to it along the harborfront to the
south. Charles Island lies off to the southeast, forming the 100-yard-wide harbor
channel. Russell Island lies to the southwest
and is linked by a bridge (a small community of Haitians lives here in starkly poorer
conditions).

Information
The Royal Bank of Canada (☎ 242-333-
4131) is open 9 am to 3 pm Monday, 9 am to
1 pm Tuesday to Thursday, and 9 am to 5 pm
Friday.

The post office and telephone booths are
in the commissioner's office on the main
street. The BaTelCo office (☎ 242-333-4053)
is four blocks to the west of the Commissioner's Office.

The Spanish Wells clinic (☎ 242-333-
4064) is on the main street at Adventurer's
Ave. Alternately, Dr Stephen Bailey (☎ 242-
333-4868) practices from home. The Spanish

Wells Pharmacy (☎ 242-333-4677) is open
from 8 am to 5 pm Friday to Monday and
8 am to noon Tuesday and Wednesday.

You can reach the police at ☎ 242-333-4030.

Spanish Wells Museum
The island's history is told in this small
museum (☎ 242-333-4710), containing a
motley collection of photos and bric-a-brac,
in a venerable home next to the Islander
Shop (the owner will open up for you; closed
Sunday) on the main street; it's open 10 am
to noon and 1 to 3 pm Monday to Saturday.

Diving & Fishing
Manual's Dive Station (☎ 242-333-4495), on
the main street, is a full-service dive shop. Al
Broadstead (☎ 242-333-4427) will take you
fishing for US$350 a day.

Places to Stay
The *Adventurers Resort* (☎ *242-333-4883, fax
242-333-5073, mapeleaf@batelnet.bs*) is set

back off the harbor channel on Adventurer's Ave. It has nine modestly yet nicely furnished air-con rooms for US$75/465 nightly/weekly. It also has seven apartments for US$100/506 one-bedroom, US$165/715 two-bedroom. All have ceiling fans. The resort has a tiny beach with thatched cabañas and a barbecue pit. The mailing address is PO Box EL-27498, Spanish Wells, Eleuthera, The Bahamas.

Spanish Wells Yacht Haven (☎ 242-333-4255, fax 242-333-4649), on the harborside, charges US$75/85 summer/winter for its three air-con rooms, US$95/105 for its two apartments. There's a modest restaurant and bar, plus a small swimming pool. Rooms have satellite TV. The mailing address is PO Box EL-27427, Spanish Wells, Eleuthera, The Bahamas.

You can rent a two-bedroom, air-con beach cottage with a phone, TV/VCR, stereo, and bikes for US$800 weekly. For details, call ☎ 352-394-4172 (in the US) and ask for information on the Bahama House.

Places to Eat
A&K's Take-Away, on the main street, offers turtle steak in season, alongside fish or turkey burgers. It has grilled tuna and prime-rib specials on Friday night and cream layer cake on Saturday night.

My favorite place is *Jack's Outback* (☎ 242-333-4219), a harborfront eatery done up in mid-American '50s diner style. It serves native fare, including a lobster dinner for US$20 and burgers as well as house specialties. Be sure to check out the hot fudge sundae! A T-bone special is offered on Friday night for US$12.

Other options in Spanish Wells include *Anchor Snack Bar* (open 9 am to 10 pm) and *Gemini Game Room & Snack Bar*, both on the dockside.

For baked goods, try *Dawson's Bakery*; for groceries, try *Pinder's Supermarket*, on the harborfront, and *Spanish Wells Food Fair*, at the west end of Central St.

Getting There & Away
For information on air travel to North Eleuthera, see Getting There & Away under the Harbour Island section, earlier in this chapter.

Bahamas Fastferries' (☎ 242-323-2166, fax 242-322-8185, info@bahamasferries.com) high-speed, luxury 117-passenger catamarans operate from Potter's Cay, Nassau daily with continuing service to Harbour Island. The journey takes 90 minutes and costs US$90.

Water taxis run all day between Spanish Wells and the ferry dock at Gene's Bay (US$5 per person or US$10 solo for the five-minute journey). Lloyd Higgs (☎ 242-333-4101) offers charters for sightseeing trips. You can also charter a water taxi between Harbour Island and Spanish Wells for US$50 one-way.

A taxi (☎ 242-333-4068) ride from the North Eleuthera Airport to Gene's Bay costs US$20, or US$4 per person if shared. In Gene's Bay there's parking, a café, a gift shop, a duty-free liquor store, and a phone booth.

Two mail boats call here: The *Spanish Rose* departs Nassau at 7 am Thursday (five hours, US$20 one-way); the *Eleuthera Express* also departs Nassau at 7 am Thursday (five hours, US$20).

Spanish Wells Yacht Haven Marina (☎ 242-333-4255) has 40 slips; it charges US85¢ a foot.

Getting Around
Most of the locals, from grannies to youngsters, zip around on mopeds (with hardhats for helmets); the rest use golf carts, which can be rented from M&M Car Rentals (☎ 242-333-4585) for US$35/50 half/full-day.

For a taxi or taxi guide, call ☎ 242-333-4222.

You can rent bicycles at Spanish Wells Yacht Haven for US$6/10 half/full-day.

PREACHER'S CAVE
This large cave, at Eleuthera's far northern end, is said to be where the Eleutheran Adventurers found shelter after foundering in 1648. They made an altar here and surely prayed to be rescued. The cavern, which is laced with Swiss-cheese holes, is more a historical curiosity than an engaging site. Light pours down from a large hole in the roof. The cave is fronted by a glorious beach, one of several beaches along the north coast.

ELEUTHERA

Preacher's Cave, which is located about 2 miles east of Gene's Bay, can be reached by traveling down a rough dirt road that leads a half-mile through scrub from Queen's Hwy.

CURRENT

About 5 miles west of the Queen's Hwy (the junction is at Lower Bogue), Current is another white community. Its two narrow, parallel concrete lanes are crisscrossed by three others and lined with clapboard houses and concrete bungalows. It is claimed to be the 'Oldest Settlement on the Island.' The townsfolk – some of whom claim to be descendants of Native Americans exiled here after a massacre at Cape Cod – are known for their basketware.

There's a beautiful beach on the west side of town.

Current Cut

This half-mile-long channel separates North Eleuthera from Current Island, a 10-mile-long continuation of the peninsula. The 'cut' narrows down to a mere 100 yards, and during tidal changes the deep waters run at a swift 6 knots, rippling and swirling, creating eddies that stream in the opposite direction close to shore. It is a popular dive and snorkel spot for strong swimmers who want to 'ride' the current.

Everett Griffin (☎ 242-335-3244) can take you fishing; trips cost US$80/150 half/full day.

Places to Stay & Eat

Monica's Curio Shop, which sells postcards, T-shirts, and souvenirs, also has one- and two-bedroom apartments for US$45/50 daily without/with air-con. Monica also rents a two-bedroom Loyalist cottage for US$45 and a two-bedroom air-con beach house for US$100.

Sandcastle Apartments (☎ 242-335-1264) rents two beachfront cottages a quarter-mile east of town for US$75. Each has a kitchen and sleeps three people.

The only places to eat are *Griffin's Snack Bar* and *Lim's Take-Away & Bakery*.

Getting There & Away

A taxi from North Eleuthera Airport will cost US$22 one-way.

Bahamas Sea Road (☎ 242-323-2166) operates a car-and-passenger ferry service from Nassau to Current six times weekly (US$30 each way for passengers).

The mail boat *Current Pride* sails here from Nassau at 7 am Thursday (5½ hours, US$30 one-way), also stopping at Hatchet Bay and The Bluff. The dockmaster can be reached at ☎ 242-393-1064 for sailing confirmation.

THE GLASS WINDOW

Here, about 7 miles east of Lower Bogue, Eleuthera narrows down to a pencil-thin isthmus that separates the deep blue of the thunderous ocean from the placid, teal-green shoals of the Bight of Eleuthera. Atlantic rollers smash against the rocky headlands, throwing spray hundreds of feet in the air, while a mere 20 yards away the bight waters are still as a pond. The arch that formed the 'window' collapsed a few years ago. Queen's Hwy spans the gap by a solid concrete bridge that was heaved askew by Hurricane Floyd in 1999, halting traffic.

Stop and admire the weathered yet barren moonscape of craggy limestone. Be cautious when you're strolling around here. The cliffs are unstable and the pocked terrain is treacherous underfoot.

GREGORY TOWN

This large settlement, 5 miles south of The Glass Window, nestles dramatically – like a Cornish village – within a steep-sided cove. Onions, peppers, cabbage, watermelons, and other vegetables are grown locally. Gregory Town is most famous as the center of pineapple farming, though the industry is so atrophied that local farmers have difficulty mustering a respectable supply of their usually large and succulent fruits to display at the annual Pineapple Festival. Gregory Town's young men have turned to lobstering, where the big bucks reside.

Gauldings Cay, 4 miles north of Gregory Town, is a splendid stretch of pure-white sand. The Cove Eleuthera (see Places to Stay, below) offers a daily complimentary shuttle to Gauldings Cay for its guests.

The post office and BaTelCo office are down by the harbor, as is a medical clinic.

On the main street, Jay's Laundromat charges US$1.75 per wash.

Activities
Captain 2 (☎ 242-335-5185) offers deep-sea fishing charters from US$100 for three hours, and bonefishing for US$200 for five hours.

Special Events
In early June the town hosts the Annual Eleuthera Pineapple Festival, highlighted by the 'Miss Teen Pineapple Princess Pageant' and the 'Pineathelon,' which is a swim-bike-run competition. There's also the 'Pineapple-on-a-Rope Eating Contest' in which participants with hands tied behind their backs attempt to nibble a dangling pineapple; a basketball shootout; a kayak race; and the Saturday-night 'Junkanoo Rush,' a street party sure to get you in the groove. You can find nonalcoholic pineapple smoothies at the Corner Bar and pineapple tarts at Monica's Bakery, but that's about it. You should contact the Eleuthera Tourism Office (☎ 242-332-2142, fax 242-332-2480) for more detailed information.

Places to Stay
The Cove Eleuthera (☎ 242-335-5142, fax 242-335-5338, ann@thecoveeleuthera.com; in the US ☎ 800-552-5960), about a mile north of town, is perfect for independent-minded travelers who don't want organized activities. It's aptly named, with views over two coves and its own beach where the snorkeling is splendid (snorkel gear is provided). It has 26 air-con rooms in six cottages – since Hurricane Floyd, delightfully refurbished and upgraded in cool pastel colors – fringed by 28 acres of vegetation. Each is furnished in white rattan, with tile floors and private porch or deck. One of the four suites is a honeymoon suite perched on a bluff, with a whirlpool tub and kitchenette. There's also a restaurant with ocean view, a lounge and game room with TV and VCR, a gift store, plus tennis, volleyball, badminton, a freshwater pool with partially shaded deck, and hammocks for alfresco snoozing, which your amiable hosts Ann and George Mullin encourage. Diving can be arranged, and there are bicycles and kayaks. Summer rates range from US$79 to US$109 single, US$89 to US$119 double for garden-view; winter rates are US$99 to US$129 single, US$109 to US$139 double. It closes for September. The mailing address is PO Box EL-1548, Gregory Town, Eleuthera, The Bahamas.

Cambridge Villas (☎ 242-335-5080, fax 242-335-5308; in the US ☎ 800-688-4752), beside the road on the edge of town, has modest, fully equipped air-con apartments, plus a choice of rooms and units sleeping two to eight people. Room rates range from US$60 for twin beds to US$115 for a two-bedroom unit. A MAP plan costs US$30 per person. There's a swimming pool and a pool table, and live calypso bands sometimes entertain. Diving, snorkeling, and fishing trips can be arranged. Its mailing address is PO Box EL-1548, Gregory Town, Eleuthera, The Bahamas.

Places to Eat
The restaurant at *The Cove Eleuthera* serves three filling meals daily, including specials every night. There's a steamed grouper and roast beef buffet on Saurday night. A guitar soloist sometimes plays, and slide shows of underwater life are given during dinner.

The *Sugar Apple Restaurant & Bar* and *Millennium Dreams*, both on the Queen's Hwy atop the hill 1 mile south of town, offer ocean views by which to enjoy Bahamian dishes. The latter has a disco at night.

In town, *Millie's Souse Bowl* specializes in conch souse for US$2. It's a cool place to play dominoes with locals.

For fresh bread, try *Thompson's Bakery* on Queen's Hwy.

Shopping
Cartwright's Straw Market makes and sells baskets, hats, and other straw-work. Terrence Wood sells sponges for US$3 to US$8 at a

store opposite Island Made Gift Shop, a splendid little trove run by Pamela Thompson, who handpaints island scenes on shells and driftwood. She also sells jewelry, resortwear, books, and artwork; guests at The Cove Eleuthera get a 10% discount.

Getting There & Around

Gregory Town is midway between the North Eleuthera and Governor's Harbour Airports. A taxi from North Eleuthera will cost about US$25 for two people or US$40 from Governor's Harbour.

Several locals rent their cars for US$60 daily. Try Hilltop Garage (☎ 242-335-5028).

Albury's Taxi (☎ 242-335-1370) and Wendell's Taxi Service (☎ 242-333-0165) both offer guided island tours.

GREGORY TOWN TO GOVERNOR'S HARBOUR

In the 25 miles between Gregory Town and Governor's Harbour – Eleuthera's main settlement – there are only two towns of any size: **Alice Town**, 7 miles south of Gregory Town and just south of Hatchet Bay, the former center of an Angus cattle enterprise; and **James Cistern**, a picturesque albeit wind-battered waterfront hamlet 8 miles farther south.

Waves kicked up by Hurricane Floyd ravaged the road between Gregory Town and Governor's Harbor in 1999, particularly south of James Cistern; many parts remained washed out (albeit passable) in summer 2000.

The Hatchet Bay Fest in Alice Town each August features dinghy races and partying. Hatchet Bay's harbor was destroyed by Hurricane Floyd, which launched at least one boat 200 feet inland.

There's a post office and BaTelCo station in James Cistern.

Surfer's Beach

This 2-mile-long, lonesome, sugary beach lives up to its name, especially with southwest winds at low tide, when the surf rolls in nicely. The beach is backed by scrub-covered hills and is reached by a horrendously potholed and rocky track from Queen's Hwy, about 2 miles south of Gregory Town.

A Yankee from New Hampshire, Surfer Pete, came to this area, stayed, and married a local woman. He rents surfboards for US$2 and does surfboard repairs. His wife operates Rebecca's Beach Shop.

Hatchet Bay Cave

Spelunkers might enjoy this half-mile-long cave meandering down into the hillside, 5 miles south of Gregory Town (turn south onto the dirt road near the three old silos). From the narrow entrance, a trail connects several chambers, which bear charcoal signatures dating back to the mid-19th century. Some harmless yet fearsome-looking leaf-nosed bats reside within, and deep in the cave stalactites and stalagmites add a touch of romance. No touching! Bring a flashlight and rubber-soled shoes, as the going is slippery. There's a ladder to climb at one stage. You can hire a guide locally.

James Cistern Beach

A bone-jarring dirt road leads north from James Cistern to a 4-mile-long beach good for surfing, where waves sometimes reach 10 feet with a brisk south wind. There's a shipwreck offshore, which is a good spot for snorkeling when the water is calm. The overgrown and arduous Old Queen's Hwy runs the length of the shore, leading north to **James Point**, a lonesome and beautiful setting; 4WD is a must!

Places to Stay

A Bahamian couple, Gilbert and Katherine Kemp, run a quaint guesthouse named **Surfer's Haven** (☎ 242-332-2181, evenings 242-335-0349) on the hillside a half-mile from Surfer's Beach. It has three quaint rooms, each whitewashed, tiled, and simply yet nicely furnished. Katherine cooks native meals or you can use the kitchen. It's a bargain at about US$50 single or double. They have a surfboard for rent.

In Alice Town, Rose Wood operates the **Three Sisters Guesthouse** (☎ 242-335-0482), which has five rooms for about US$45 per night. In James Cistern, Hilton and Elsie Johnson run *Island House* (☎ 242-335-6241, fax 242-335-6356), with four modestly yet nicely furnished air-con apartment units with kitchen and lounge for about US$90.

The *Rainbow Inn* (☎/fax 242-335-0294, 800-688-0047, vacation@rainbowinn.com; in the UK ☎ 020-8876-1296), on a bluff 2 miles south of Alice Town, offers octagonal villas with one, two, or three air-con rooms surrounded by casuarinas and hibiscus. All have kitchenettes, ceiling fans, and private decks facing onto a beach. The hotel has an excellent restaurant, plus tennis courts, a small saltwater lap pool, snorkeling, fishing, and bicycles for hire. Rates are US$115 single or double in summer, US$140 in winter. Larger villas cost US$175/200. The postal address is PO Box EL-25053, Governor's Harbour, Eleuthera, The Bahamas.

Wykee's World Resort (☎ 242-332-2701, fax 242-332-2123, cwweiche@usa.net; in the US ☎ 864-964-9210, fax 864-964-9025), between James Cistern and Governor's Harbour, offers rental villas. Its mailing address is PO Box EL-25176, Governor's Harbour, Eleuthera, The Bahamas.

Places to Eat
The English-pub–style restaurant at the *Rainbow Inn* is furnished with varnished, rough-hewn tables and captain's chairs, and serves Bahamian and continental dishes, from lobster to seafood crepes to homemade key lime pie; it's open 6:30 to 9 pm Wednesday to Saturday. 'Dr Seabreeze' plays on Wednesday and Friday nights.

In Alice Town try the local hangout, *Forget Me Not Club*, a funky little bar and restaurant. There's a grocery store next door, plus the *Red Dirt Game Room & Snack Shack*. And *Red Rolle's Harbour View Restaurant* gets lively on weekends.

Craving pizza? Try *Juneek's Savoury Snacks* in James Cistern, where outdoor clay ovens are still used. It also sells meat patties and ice cream.

For groceries, stop at *Big Rock General Store*, 2 miles west of James Cistern.

Getting There & Away
The Governor's Harbour Airport is 3 miles south of James Cistern.

Bahamas Sea Road (☎ 242-323-2166) operates a car-and-passenger ferry service from Nassau to Hatchet Bay three times weekly (four hours; US$30 each way for passengers).

The mail boat *Current Pride* sails to Hatchet Bay weekly from Nassau, also stopping at The Bluff and Current; see the Current section for details. The *Captain Fox* mail boat departs from Nassau at 1 pm on Friday for Hatchet Bay (six hours, US$30 one-way); call ☎ 242-393-1064 for information. Taxis can take you to Gregory Town or Governor's Harbour (about US$25).

The Hatchet Bay Yacht Club and Marine Service of Eleuthera (☎ 242-335-0186, VHF channel 16) have slips in Alice Town.

GOVERNOR'S HARBOUR
The island 'capital,' midway down Eleuthera, overlooks a broad harbor that runs west along a peninsula to Cupid's Cay, claiming to be the original settlement of the Eleutheran Adventurers; ruins of an old pineapple plantation dating back centuries mark the site, and there are several old homes in a semi-derelict state. Governor's Harbour is also known as Colebrook Town.

During the 19th century, the harbor was filled with schooners shipping pineapples and citrus to New York and New England, or unloading fineries for the wealthy merchants and their wives. The merchants' well-preserved old white clapboard houses, many with ornate gingerbread gable trims, nestle on the hillside east of Queen's Hwy, where royal poincianas blaze vermilion in spring.

A stroll along the bayfront passes **St Patrick's Anglican Church** and cemetery; the historic, pink **Commissioner's Office**; and the 1897 **Haynes Library**.

The beach on the south side of the peninsula is a good spot for shelling. The nicest beaches are over the hill on the Atlantic shore.

Information
Jackie Gibson runs the Bahamas Tourist Office (☎ 242-332-2122, fax 242-332-2480) at Queen's Hwy and Haynes Ave.

ELEUTHERA

GOVERNOR'S HARBOUR

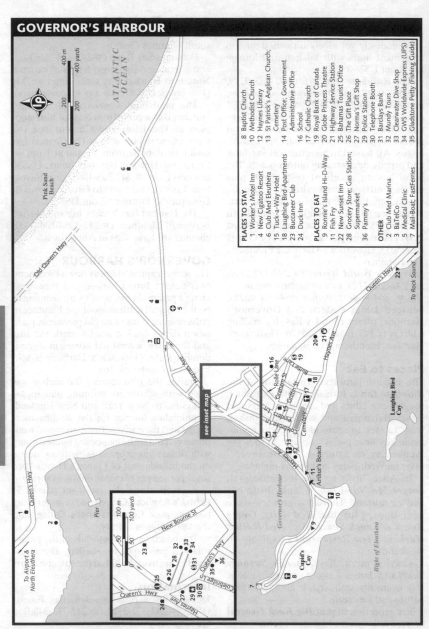

ATLANTIC OCEAN

Pink Sand Beach

Old Queen's Hwy

Queen's Hwy

To Airport &
North Eleuthera

To Rock Sound

Governor's Harbour

Bight of Eleuthera

Laughing Bird
Cay

Cupid's
Cay

Arthur's Beach

Haynes Ave

Haynes Ave

Rolle Lane

Graham St

Griffin St

Bridge Lane

Chapel St

Cemetery

New Bourne St

Colebrook Ln

Pier

see inset map

400 m
400 yards
200
200

100 m
100 yards
50
50

PLACES TO STAY
1 Worker's Motel Inn
4 New Cigatoo Resort
6 Club Med Eleuthera
15 Tuck-a-Way Hotel
18 Laughing Bird Apartments
23 Buccaneer Club
24 Duck Inn

PLACES TO EAT
9 Ronnie's Island Hi-D-Way
11 Fish Fry
22 New Sunset Inn
28 Grocery Store; Gas Station;
    Supermarket
36 Pammy's

OTHER
2 Club Med Marina
3 BaTelCo
5 Medical Clinic
7 Mail-Boat; FastFerries
8 Baptist Church
10 Methodist Church
12 Haynes Library
14 St Patrick's Anglican Church;
    Cemetery
14 Post Office; Government
    Administrative Office
16 School
17 Catholic Church
19 Royal Bank of Canada
20 Globe Princess Theatre
21 Highway Service Station
25 Bahamas Tourist Office
26 The Gift Place
27 Norma's Gift Shop
29 Police Station
30 Telephone Booth
31 Barclays Bank
32 Mundy Tours
33 Clearwater Dive Shop
34 GWS Worldwide Express (UPS)
35 Gladstone Petty (Fishing Guide)

ELEUTHERA

Barclays Bank (☎ 242-332-2300) has a branch in the town's center. Royal Bank of Canada (☎ 242-332-2856) is on Queen's Hwy at the south end of town. Both are open 9:30 am to 3 pm Monday to Thursday and 9:30 am to 5 pm Friday.

The post office (☎ 242-332-2060) is on the harborfront; it's open 9 am to 4:30 pm weekdays. GWS Worldwide Express, in the town center, acts as a UPS agent; it also has fax service (US$3 per page local, US$5 long distance). There's a telephone booth on Queen's Hwy and at BaTelCo (☎ 242-332-2476), atop the hill on Haynes Ave.

Mundy Tours (☎ 242-332-2720) provides full travel service.

The medical clinic (☎ 242-332-2774), at the top of Haynes Ave, is open 9 am to 5 pm Monday to Friday.

The police station (☎ 242-332-2111) is on Queen's Hwy in the town center.

Activities

Clearwater Dive Shop (☎ 242-332-2146, fax 242-332-2546), in the town center, offers dive and snorkel trips. Gladstone Petty (☎ 242-332-2280) will take you reef- and bonefishing. He has an office on Queen's Hwy, downtown.

Places to Stay

The *Tuck-a-Way Hotel* (☎ 242-322-2005, fax 242-322-2775), at Graham St and Rolle Lane, has 12 small, dark, air-con units, all with TV. Rooms cost US$50 to US$60 in summer; US$65 with a kitchen. The mailing address is PO Box EL-45, Governor's Harbour, Eleuthera, The Bahamas.

Laughing Bird Apartments (☎ 242-332-2012, fax 242-332-2358, ddavies@batelnet.bs; in the US ☎ 800-688-4752), on Birdie Lane near Haynes Ave, has cozy one-bedroom studio apartments amid grounds full of hibiscus and palms. Each has a lounge-cum-bedroom and separate kitchen. Some have king-size beds. You can combine rental units to sleep up to six people. The place is run by a delightful English couple, Jean and Dan Davies. A gift shop sells sarongs. Studio apartments cost US$80/90 single/double year-round. Larger apartments closer to

town cost US$95/105/115/125 single/double/triple/quad. Ask about weekly rates. The mailing address is PO Box EL-25076, Governor's Harbour, Eleuthera, The Bahamas.

Buccaneer Club (☎ 242-332-2000, fax 242-332-2888, inquiries@buccaneerclub.com), on the north side of town, is a handsome remake of an historic three-story farmhouse. It has five small yet tastefully appointed air-con rooms with sliding glass doors opening onto a wide balcony. Each has two double beds and a satellite TV. There's a small pool and a well-tended lawn. Rooms cost US$90/101 single/double in summer; US$100/110 winter. The mailing address is PO Box EL-86, Governor's Harbour, Eleuthera, The Bahamas, and the Web site is www.buccaneerclub.com.

The *Duck Inn* (☎ 242-332-2608, fax 242-332-2160, duckin@batelnet.bs), on Queen's Hwy, is a quaint colonial complex set amid an orchid garden. A one-bedroom efficiency – Hunnie Pot Cottage – costs US$110, as does Cupid's Cottage, sleeping two people. The main cottage – Flora – sleeps eight people and costs US$220. The three cottages are decked with orchids and fruit trees, and each features air-con, ceiling fans, wood floors, antiques, plus fully equipped kitchen, dining room, and veranda.

It may surprise you, being greeted most likely by a blond beach bum in nothing more than a loincloth and mirrored sunglasses, to learn that *Club Med Eleuthera* (☎ 242-332-2270, 800-258-2633, fax 242-332-2222) is a family resort. Couples and singles are also welcome. It is designed for gregarious folks, not clams, and has a large French following. The staff are mostly European. Dining is communal. The club offers special kids' programs, plus excursions. There's also a water-sports center. The resort was walloped by Hurricane Floyd and at press time had no definite reopen date or set room rates. Call for more current information.

The *New Cigatoo Resort* (☎ 242-332-3060), at the top of the hill on Haynes Ave, was in final stages of construction at press time. It will feature an Italian restaurant, bar, tea room, swimming pool, and tennis.

ELEUTHERA

Its postal address is PO Box EL-2568, Governor's Harbour, Eleuthera.

The **Worker's Motel Inn** (☎ 242-332-3075), in the Workers Credit Union Plaza, north of town, offers modern air-con rooms.

Places to Eat
To be one with the locals on Friday and Saturday, head to Arthur's Beach for the weekly **fish fry**, when barbecued fish and chicken meals (US$7) are served.

For budget meals, try **Pammy's**, a hole-in-the-wall take-away on Queen's Hwy.

The air-con **Buccaneer Club** (☎ 242-332-2000) serves up native dishes, with dinner entrees from US$12. It has live music some nights; it's closed Wednesday. The **New Sunset Inn**, 1 mile south of town on Queen's Hwy, also serves breakfast, including filling omelets.

On Cupid's Cay, **Ronnie's Island Hi-D-Way** satellite lounge serves native dinners, plus a special of macaroni, peas 'n' rice, and potato salad for US$6.

Entertainment
Everyone heads to Arthur's Beach on Friday and Saturday afternoons and evenings for a fish fry and **jive**, with a deejay providing the sound.

Otherwise, **Ronnie's Island Hi-D-Way** satellite lounge has a virtual monopoly on nightlife. It has a lively sports bar with pool table and wide-screen TV, plus dancing on Friday and Saturday; don't even think of arriving before 10 pm.

The **Globe Princess Theatre**, on Queen's Hwy, shows movies at 8 pm nightly (except Thursday) for US$5.

Shopping
Several stores sell resortwear and jewelry, including Jean Davies at Laughing Bird Apartments. Also try The Gift Place, downtown on Queen's Hwy, which has a large T-shirt gallery; Norma's Gift Shop, across the road; or Brenda's Boutique, on Haynes Ave.

Getting There & Away
Governor's Harbour is served by the Governor's Harbour Airport, about 10 miles north of town. See the Getting There & Away chapter for information on flights from the US. Bahamasair flies daily from Nassau (US$60 each way).

When open, Club Med has charter flights for guests.

Bahamas Fastferries (☎ 242-323-2166, fax 242-322-8185, info@bahamasferries.com) operates high-speed, luxury 117-passenger catamarans from Potter's Cay, Nassau, twice a week. The journey takes two hours and costs US$90 roundtrip.

The **Eleuthera Express** mail boat sails here from Nassau at 5 pm Monday (5½ hours, US$30 one-way). The **Captain Fox** sails at 1 pm Friday (six hours, US$30).

Getting Around
There are no buses to or from the airport; a taxi will cost about US$25 for two.

To hire a taxi or rent a car, call Edgar Gardiner (☎ 242-332-2665), Tommy Pinder (☎ 242-332-2568), Winsett Cooper (☎ 242-332-1592), Dewitt Johnson (☎ 242-335-0211), or Hilton Johnson (☎ 242-335-6341).

NORTH & SOUTH PALMETTO POINT
This modern settlement, 4 miles south of Governor's Harbour, is popular with North American retirees. It is divided between North and South Palmetto by Queen's Hwy. The former backs a stunning 5-mile-long pinkish beach; the latter backs a smaller beach and rocky shore with good bonefishing.

There's a post office, clinic, pharmacy, grocery store, and gas station.

Asa Bethel, owner of Palmetto Shores Vacation Villas (see Places to Stay, below), rents cars, scooters, and boats. Arthur's Taxi (☎ 242-332-2006) also rents cars.

Places to Stay
The modern **Unique Village Resort Hotel** (☎ 242-332-1830, fax 242-332-1838, uniqvill@ mail.batelnet.bs; in the US ☎ 800-223-6510), in North Palmetto Point, enjoys an exquisite setting behind a beautiful beach. It has 10 attractively furnished rooms, two two-bedroom villas, and a one-bedroom apart-

ment, all with ocean view, full kitchen, satellite TV, and radio. There's a swimming pool, a pleasant restaurant and bar with panoramic windows and outside deck, plus grassy lawns with hammocks slung between palm trees. Rates run US$90 to US$110 in summer, US$120 to US$140 winter. The apartment costs US$130 and US$160; villas cost US$160 and US$190 (US$25 per extra person). Children under 12 stay free in winter; kids under 18 stay free in summer. A MAP plan costs US$35. Its mailing address is PO Box EL-187, Governor's Harbour, Eleuthera, The Bahamas.

Heron Hill (in the US ☎ 301-320-2809, fax 703-476-3650), a 10-room colonial-era home, sits atop a coastal bluff overlooking the pink beach. The house has been modernized and has air-con and king-size beds in its four bedrooms. Three separate wings each have their own bath, patio, and sitting area. There's a library and 'gourmet kitchen.' Rates are US$2400 to US$2600 for up to six people. A self-contained apartment below can be rented separately for US$880 year-round.

Palmetto Shores Vacation Villas (☎/fax 242-332-1305), in South Palmetto Point, has modest one-, two-, and three-bedroom air-con villas for US$90/100/110 in summer (US$10 more in winter). Money to blow? Take a 'super deluxe' villa for US$180. Children under 12 are half-price. There's tennis and fishing, and other activities can be arranged. Rental cars are available. Its mailing address is PO Box EL-25131, South Palmetto Point, Eleuthera, The Bahamas.

Tropical Dreams Motel Resort (☎ 242-332-1632) is a modern no-frills, six-unit complex on Dry Hill Rd, 1 mile north of Queen's Hwy and 1 mile from the beach.

You can even rent the *Palmetto Point Lighthouse* (in the US ☎/fax 561-395-0483, info@pinksandbeach.net), a fully-appointed three-bedroom home with king-size bed in the master bedroom that has a sliding glass door to a patio with whirlpool. It rents for US$1400 weekly low-season, US$1680 high-season for four people.

Places to Eat

I like the warm ambiance of *Mate & Jenny's Restaurant & Bar* (☎ 242-332-1504) in South Palmetto Point, serving tasty pizzas from US$7, as well as broiled grouper for US$16 and other native dishes.

For beachfront dining with a view, head to *Unique Village Restaurant & Lounge* (☎ 242-332-1830) serving filling omelettes and fruit plates for breakfast, native dishes, plus steaks and fresh seafood at lunch and dinner. There's a bar.

Fish stalls line South Palmetto beach, where there's a beach bar.

You can buy bread and baked goods at *Meryl's Bakery*, opposite the post office and police station in North Palmetto.

South Eleuthera

SAVANNAH SOUND

This near-destitute hamlet dates back to the 18th century. Goats and chickens roam among tumbledown shacks and collapsed colonial-era buildings. The down-at-the-heels settlement slopes down to a half-mile-wide channel – Savannah Sound – that separates Windermere Island from the mainland. The channel is good for bonefishing.

Big Sally's, just south of town, serves native dishes and doubles as a bar and dance club.

WINDERMERE ISLAND

Secluded, broom-thin Windermere Island boasts a pristine blush-hued beach running the 4-mile Atlantic shore. It is speckled with snazzy homes reflecting its long-standing status as one of the most exclusive hideaways for the rich and famous. The chic Windermere Island Club, once The Bahamas' most fashionable resort, was a favorite of Lord Mountbatten and, later, Prince Charles and Princess Diana. Then it hit hard times and closed.

The island is reached by a small bridge straddling Savannah Sound (the turnoff from Queen's Hwy is 2 miles south of the village).

Places to Stay & Eat

The *Windermere Island Resort* (☎/fax 242-359-7643, windresort@aol.com; in the US

☎ 888-257-2510) offers three-, four-, and five-bedroom villas for rent. Guests are served by a modern clubhouse with a restaurant, pool, and tennis court, and fishing and watersports can be arranged. Rates begin at US$200/250 summer/winter for a suite, US$300/350 apartment, US$375/475 cottage, and US$500/750 villa.

Windermere Island Homes (in the US ☎ 321-725-9790, 888-881-2867, info@ windermereislandhomes.com) rents deluxe villas and cottages. The mailing address is Bahamas Home Rentals, 2722 Riverview Dr, Melbourne, FL 32901, USA.

TARPUM BAY

The road south from Savannah Sound runs along the Bight of Eleuthera, an uninspired drive until you arrive at this delightful seaside fishing village 5 miles north of Rock Sound Airport. It's named for the feisty tarpons that frequent the offshore shallows. The former pineapple-trading port is now a somnolent place comprising quaint old stone buildings, including **St Columbus Church**, and clapboard houses, whitewashed and painted in pretty pastels. This is a perfect spot to cool your heels for a few days, sipping rum cocktails and watching locals cleaning conch on the wharf.

Bonefishing is good in Half Sound, a flask-shaped cove south of beach-lined, crescent-shaped Winding Bay, 1 mile southeast of the town's center.

A taxi from Rock Sound (see below) to Tarpum Bay will cost about US$20 for two. There's a gas station on Queen's Hwy in town, and another 1 mile south of town.

Macmillan-Hughes Art Gallery & Castle

What, you may wonder, is a long-haired Irishman with a bushy white beard, an Oxford-English accent, and fine whistle doing building a 'castle' of limestone just northeast of the town center (☎ 242-334-4091)? This eccentric, self-promotional fella (he bills himself unabashedly as 'Lord of the Scales Demesne Artist Extraordinaire') offers guided tours of his castle-cum-gallery complete with turret and a 3-D relief of King Neptune – allegorically Macmillan – embracing a mermaid. Here he paints and sculpts in bronze; he has works in the Royal Collection. Macmillan also holds an annual flag-raising ceremony. Admission costs US$1.

Mal Flanders Art Gallery

Another, less brash artist has a studio atop the hill south of the town's center. Flanders, a portly American with thick glasses and jet-black hair in a Ronald Reagan style, works at a happy, slothful pace in his bright and airy studio. Flanders, once a columnist for the *Miami Herald*, has lived here since 1972 without a car, TV, radio, or even a mailing address. You're made welcome to his studio, where his cartoon-style paintings are done in bright tropical pastels. 'I hope the worms eat my bones here,' he says of the country he loves.

Flanders' canvases and his paintings on driftwood boards sell for US$30 to US$600 on commission. He can paint from photos. You can write to him c/o Tarpum Bay, Eleuthera, The Bahamas.

Places to Stay

Ingraham's Beach Inn (☎ 242-334-4285/4066, fax 242-334-2257), is a modern beachfront property with eight air-con rooms and four apartments, the latter with kitchens. A game room has a pool table and exercise equipment. Room rates are US$70 in summer, US$86 in winter. Apartments cost US$110 summer, US$145 winter.

Hilton's Haven (☎ 242-334-4231, fax 242-331-4020; in the US 800-688-4752, hilhaven@batelnet.bs), in town, has 10 no-frills rooms with private bathrooms. Downstairs rooms have air-con; upstairs rooms have ceiling fans. The owner, Mary Hilton, is a delight. The restaurant serves native fare. Year-round rates are US$55/60 single/double, plus US$10 for an extra person. Apartments cost US$75. The postal address is PO Box N-4616, Tarpum Bay, Eleuthera, The Bahamas.

Cartwright's Ocean View Cottages (☎ 242-334-4215, cartwright@hotmail.com) has four simple units on the oceanfront.

Club Venta Eleuthera (☎ 242-334-4054, 800-457-8167, fax 242-334-4057), on Winding Bay, is an all-inclusive, self-contained village run by Italians and for Italians (it is not talked of highly by locals because of its aloof, elitist ways), who make up most of the clientele and arrive via direct charter flights from Milan to Rock Sound Airport. It has 144 tastefully decorated, air-con rooms with TVs and verandas, plus a full range of facilities, including tennis, swimming pool, and watersports. Per person rates range from US$170 single, US$115 double occupancy in summer to US$215/165 in winter.

Places to Eat
Shine's Famous Seafood is a tiny bayside gem with whitewashed walls and sky-blue shutters, a stone floor, and heaps of time-worn charm. Try the tuna salad and scrambled egg and johnnycake breakfast. Marsha, the robust chef, cooks up seafood and grits. It also serves sandwiches and conch- and fish-burgers for US$3.

The menu at *Hilton's Haven* features continental and full breakfasts and native dinners, plus pork chops and roast beef, and homemade cake and pie.

Entertainment
To hang out with the locals, head to the *Gallery Sports Bar*, on Queen's Hwy on the south side of town.

ROCK SOUND
This small, charming village lies on Rock Sound, a deep U-shaped bay, where early townsfolk set out on their prime occupation – wrecking. Hence the settlement's early name, Wreck Sound. There are several historic buildings of note, plus the Ocean Hole (see below) and, on the bay shore south of town, the **Blow Hole,** which erupts like a geyser during strong swells.

Rock Sound famously comes alive each summer during the All-Eleuthera Regatta (see below), one of The Bahamas' liveliest let-your-hair-down affairs, and the setting for all-out dinghy races. There are few beaches hereabouts.

Information
Scotiabank has a branch on Queen's Hwy, open 9 am to 3 pm Monday to Thursday and 9 am to 5 pm Friday.

The medical clinic (☎ 242-334-2226) has a nurse and doctor; it's open 9 am to 1 pm weekdays.

You can have clothes washed at CC's Laundromat (☎ 242-334-2236).

For the police, call ☎ 242-334-2244.

Ocean Hole
This crater-like curiosity, along Fish Rd on the south edge of town, is a landlocked, 100-yard-wide, tidal blue hole populated by salt-water fish that move to and fro through subterranean sea tunnels. Take some bread to attract the fish, or descend the steps and hop in for a cool swim.

Be sure to lock your car, as I've heard reports that some of the local kids have taken to stealing.

Special Events
Each July or August, islanders flock to Rock Sound for the All-Eleuthera Regatta, a three-day festive occasion highlighted by regatta sailing. It also features live entertainment and family fun.

Another three-day event – the North Eleuthera Regatta – is held in October. This is one of the granddaddies of Bahamian sailing events and *the* highlight of the Eleutheran year, when islanders with their locally built sloops descend for three days of racing. Ashore the action is just as lively, with native songs and bands whipping up a storm, while Bahamian lovelies strip down to bathing suits for beauty contests. Special air and boat charters depart from Nassau. Contact the Ministry of Youth and Culture (☎ 242-322-3140) for more information.

Junkanoo traditionally begins at 5 am on Boxing Day (December 26), when groups from the various settlements come together at Rock Sound.

Places to Stay & Eat
The only place to stay is *Sammy's Place* (☎ 242-334-2121), the most popular restaurant in town. It has four air-con rooms with

ELEUTHERA

satellite TV for US$60, plus two two-bedroom cottages with kitchenettes for US$80. Owner Kathleen Cummer serves up everything from conch fritters and burgers to cheese omelets and grouper creole for US$2 to US$11.

Take your pick among several down-home eateries serving native fare. Try the *Palm Garden Restaurant & Bar* or *Down Home Pizza*, and *The Haven Bakery* (☎ 242-334-2155), which doubles as a pastry shop; it's open 8 am to 6 pm Monday to Friday and 8 am to 7 pm Saturday.

The Marketplace Supermarket is north of town near the Shell gas station.

Shopping
Several gift stores line Queen's Hwy, including Almond Tree Arts & Crafts, Goombay Gifts, and Arlicia's Souvenirs.

Getting There & Around
Rock Sound Airport is 3 miles north of town. A taxi from the airport to Rock Sound settlement costs US$10.

For international flights, see the Getting There & Away chapter. Bahamasair has daily flights from Nassau (US$60 each way).

The *Bahamas Daybreak III* mail boat calls here once a week from Nassau, leaving at 5 pm Monday (five hours, US$30 one-way). The boat also calls at Davis Harbour. Call ☎ 242-393-1064 or ☎ 242-335-1163 to inquire about or confirm schedules.

Dingle Motor Service (☎ 242-334-2031) rents cars.

COTTON BAY
This mile-long bay, off a spur of Queen's Hwy 6 miles south of Rock Sound, is favored by wealthy expats who own fancy villas above the shore. The homes are part of the Cotton Bay Club. Once beloved by hobnobbing socialites, the club has had a troubled history and closed in 1995. Talk of resurrecting the property has thus far come to naught.

The 18-hole Cotton Bay Golf Club (☎ 242-334-6156, 800-334-3523), designed by Robert Trent Jones, Jr, was operating at press time, albeit with reduced facilities. It

boasts 129 bunkers. Vital statistics: 72-par, 7000 yards. Green fees are US$70 (US$50 for nine holes). Caddies cost US$20 plus tips. You can rent clubs for US$15 per bag.

COTTON BAY TO CAPE ELEUTHERA
South of Cotton Bay, the island flares out in a lopsided, inverted 'T.' At Wemyss Bight (pronounced 'WIMS-es'), a nondescript settlement 2½ miles southwest of Cotton Bay, Queen's Hwy splits. One branch leads north 10 miles to Cape Elethera via Davis Harbour and the settlement of Deep Creek; the shore is lined by mangrove swamps.

Cape Eleuthera is a good spot to dive for conch.

Places to Stay & Eat
The *Cape Eleuthera Marina* (☎ 242-334-6327, fax 242-334-6326) planned on building apartments to be ready by 2002.

You'll find grub at *D&N Pizza*, at Davis Harbour; or, in Deep Creek, at *Sharil's Inn*, which serves native dishes such as peas 'n' rice and cracked conch.

Getting There & Away
When open, Cape Eleuthera Marina (see above) has slips, fuel, water, and electricity, as does the Hobo Yacht Club (☎ 242-334-6101) at Davis Harbour Marina, which has showers, laundry, and a bar and lounge.

The mail boat *Bahamas Daybreak III* calls at Davis Harbour Marina weekly from Nassau, also stopping at Rock Sound; see the Rock Sound section earlier in this chapter for details.

ELEUTHERA POINT
South of Wemyss Bight, the paved road runs to the funky settlements of Millars and Bannerman, forlornly set amid scrub and mangroves.

Beyond Bannerman, the vastly deteriorated road loops back to Millars. Midway, a challenging dirt track (for 4WD only) leads south to exquisite **Lighthouse Bay**, at Eleuthera Point. Offshore reefs and two small islands immediately south of the point are good for snorkeling and scuba diving. During tide changes, currents can be strong, so be careful.

At the east end of the bay, a short trail leads up to the **East Point Lighthouse**, atop the dramatic headland of Eleuthera Point, the southernmost point of Eleuthera. The lighthouse is now derelict, courtesy of Hurricane Floyd.

On the windward side of Eleuthera Point, a stunner of a beach runs north, unbroken, for 6 miles (it also can be reached by side roads from Queen's Hwy). *It doesn't get any more beautiful than this!*

Exumas

• pop 3700

This trail of stepping-stone isles is strewn along the eastern edge of the Great Bahama Bank. The Exuma Cays – a necklace of 365 cays – begins 40 miles southeast of Nassau and continues in that direction for more than 100 miles, ending at the distant pendants of Great Exuma and Little Exuma, the two largest islands.

Most of the cays are small uninhabited slips of land. Many are microcays, no bigger than helicopter pads, poking out of the ocean. Some are low and barren. Others, like Highborne Cay, are rolling and smothered with dense pine forest and thatch palms and scrub. All are unified by glittering beaches and snug harbors – a boater's dream! Many are inhabited by iguanas, with several subspecies unique to their particular isles. A section of the cays is protected as the Exuma Cays Land & Sea Park.

Great Exuma, which is 40 miles long, and Little Exuma are the two main islands in the chain. George Town, on Great Exuma, is the administrative center and the only town of significance. Other settlements are few and far between and primitive, albeit picturesque. Another necklace of off-the-beaten-track isles, the Ragged Island Range, runs south of Little Exuma toward Cuba. This chain includes the Jumento Cays and Ragged Island.

During the 17th century, many residents of New Providence settled Great Exuma to escape ruthless buccaneers. They lived as wreckers and salt rakers. By the 18th century the island's salt pans were figuratively producing gold dust. Following the American Revolution, Loyalists under Lord Denys Rolle arrived with 140 slaves aboard a ship named the *Peace & Plenty*. Rolle was granted 7000 acres on which he planted cotton. His plantations blossomed until the chenille bug arrived, destroying the cotton crop. The salt industry also evaporated, done in by more profitable operations on neighboring islands. In 1834, the year of emancipation, most whites uprooted and left. The newly freed slaves, who were in revolt from 1828 to 1834, stayed and took over Rolle's land.

It was common back then for slaves to adopt the name of their master. Today every second person is a Rolle (locals, however, have a good grip on who their blood relatives are). And since the 1890s every Rolle has been permitted to build and farm on common land. Rolleville and Rolle Town, the two most important historic settlements on Great Exuma, are worth perusal. And forts and ruined plantations lie scattered like pirate treasure, though now reclaimed by bush.

Highlights

- Exuma Cays Land & Sea Park, great for kayaking, sunning, and snorkeling
- Family Island Regatta, the time to let your hair down with the locals
- Stocking Island, a day-tripper's paradise
- Thunderball Grotto, a premier dive and snorkel spot, where James Bond swam
- Eddy's Edgewater Club, a great place for dinner and dancing to rake 'n' scrape music

EXUMAS

Most locals still earn a living from farming and fishing. Sponging, once an important source of income, seems to be enjoying a bit of a revival.

Many Exumas residents are born to take to the sea in their shallow-draft sloops. Regattas are definitely the high points on the social calendar. The tradition began more than 40 years ago when Bahamian sailors gathered to race in every conceivable craft, all built at home. Hundreds of islanders still make the annual pilgrimage to George Town's Elizabeth Harbour for the Family Island Regatta (see the boxed text, 'Family Island Regatta,' later in this chapter). The dinghies are shipped from other islands aboard mail boats.

Regattas have helped to revive the spirit of the local population as well as its interest in traditional boatbuilding. Most of the action revolves around the capital city of George Town, a yachter's haven and one of The Bahamas' leading hubs for chartering boats for island-hopping. Jackie Onassis was a regular visitor and the New England yachting crowd still has a penchant for the Exumas.

The millennium has brought a spate of dramatic development to Great Exuma in the form of five deluxe resort estates, including three with championship golf courses and one with a casino...all under construction at press time.

The Exumas are as good as anywhere in The Bahamas for diving and snorkeling. There are dozens of superb reef sites and wrecks. Dolphins, hammerhead and nurse sharks, and the occasional whale cruise the deep waters. See the 'Dive & Snorkel Sites' boxed text later in this chapter for details on the Exumas' underwater world.

The vast flats west and south of the Exumas are bonefish habitat supreme, and you will find good fishing lodges and operators in both George Town and Rolle Town. The Exumas Guides Association (☎ 242-336-2222) can provide recommendations for private guides.

Kayaking is also superb in the Exumas. In particular, see the Exuma Cays Land & Sea Park section of this chapter, and turn to

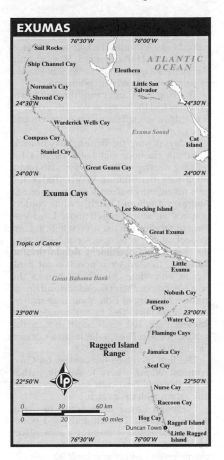

Kayaking in the Outdoor Activities chapter for details on operators offering package trips through the cays.

Great Exuma

GEORGE TOWN
• pop 1000

The main settlement on Great Exuma stands on the west shore of Elizabeth Harbour, a 15-mile-long protected sound sheltered from the Atlantic by Stocking Island, a tantalizing sliver of land lined by fine beaches almost its entire length. George Town is really a village, with one street that encircles a body of water named Lake Victoria. The lake is connected to Elizabeth Harbour by a 50-yard-long channel. It's a quaint, hilly settlement shaded by palms and draped with poinciana.

The Tropic of Cancer runs through town. You may feel the bump as you drive over it. If not, drive around the one-way system and try again!

In days of yore the British Navy utilized Elizabeth Harbour and Lake Victoria for refitting warships. The US Navy also had a small base here during WWII. Today the only noteworthy buildings are the serene **St Andrew's Anglican Church**, a white confection in stone atop the bluff above Lake Victoria (it's well worth the stroll uphill, at least to peek at the gravestones out back), and the waterside **Government Administration Building**, fronted by a neoclassical pink facade with white columns (it houses the post office, police station, customs and immigration, Ministry of Education, magistrates' court, and jail). The rather nondescript **Regatta Park**, 100 yards south, boasts the weather-beaten *Patsy*, a diminutive wooden dinghy that first raced in 1953.

The hub of village life centers on Government Wharf, where townsfolk gather when the mail boat calls and when fisherfolk return with their catch.

Flamingo Bay, 2 miles south of town, boasts a beautiful beach and good bonefishing and is the setting for a new resort development that will add an 18-hole championship golf course by 2002.

Information

Ona Bullard runs the Bahamas Tourist Office (☎ 242-336-2430, fax 242-336-2431), opposite St Andrew's Anglican Church; it's open 9 am to 5:30 pm Monday to Friday.

Scotiabank (☎ 242-336-2651) has a branch in the town center; it's open 9:30 am to 3 pm Monday to Thursday and 9:30 am to 5 pm Friday.

The post office is in the Government Administration Building. You can send packages via UPS at Wally's Photographic Studio (☎ 242-336-2148), opposite Regatta Park; it's

open 8:30 am to 5:30 pm weekdays and 10 am to 3 pm Saturday. The BaTelCo office (☎ 242-336-2011) is at the south end of town. Exuma Markets (☎ 242-336-2033, fax 242-336-2645) has a fax and phone message service. You can have mail delivered here.

Above Scotiabank, HL Young (☎ 242-336-2703) is a full-service travel agent open 9 am to 5 pm weekdays.

A tiny library, opposite the straw market, is open 10 am to noon weekdays May to December. From December to May, it's open 10 am to noon Monday to Saturday.

You can have clothes laundered or dry-cleaned at Exuma Cleaners (☎ 242-336-2038), just off the main street near Exuma Markets. There's also a laundromat at Exuma Docking Services & Marina.

The George Town clinic (☎ 242-336-2088) has three nurses and a resident doctor and dentist. The private Island Med Medical Clinic (☎ 242-336-2220) is 2 miles north of town.

The police station (☎ 919, 242-336-2666) is in the government building.

Diving & Snorkeling

The following companies offer dive trips, including PADI certification:

ExumaSCUBA Adventures, Club Peace & Plenty
☎ 242-336-2893, 800-223-6961
Web site www.exumascuba.com

Exuma Fantasea ☎/fax 242-336-3483

Exuma Dive Centre ☎ 242-336-2390, 800-874-7213, fax 242-336-2391

Exuma Fantasea specializes in blue-hole dives and has a full-service dive shop. You even can join Ed Haxby, a noted marine biologist, in an ecodive and in specialty courses focusing on marine ecology.

The *Nekton Pilot*, a state-of-the-art, twin-hulled, dedicated dive vessel operated by Nekton Diving Cruises (in the US ☎ 954-463-9324, 800-899-6753, fax 954-463-8938, nekton1@aol.com) is based here in winter. The company offers weeklong trips departing Saturday.

The three dive companies above all offer snorkeling excursions and rent snorkel

GREAT & LITTLE EXUMA

PLACES TO STAY
1 Fisherman's Inn
3 Emerald Bay Resort; Four
  Seasons Resort Great
  Exuma; Emerald Bay
  Golf Course & Marina
4 The Palms at Three Sisters
8 Island Club
9 Juliana Apartments
10 Tradewinds Apartments
12 Mt Pleasant Suites
13 Palm Bay Beach Club &
  Spa
14 Coconut Cove Hotel;
  Coconut Cove Restaurant
15 Peace & Plenty Beach Inn
16 Higgin's Landing
17 Latitude Exuma Resort &
  Rolle Yacht Club
19 February Point Resort;
  Bistro & Bar
22 Master Harbour Villas

23 Peace & Plenty Bonefish
  Lodge
26 La Shanté Beach Club

PLACES TO EAT
2 Kermit's Hilltop Tavern
7 Iva Bowe's Central
  Highway Inn
21 Cheater's Restaurant & Bar

OTHER
5 Kermit's Airport Lounge
6 Gas Station
11 Island Med Medical Clinic
18 Flamingo Bay Golf Course
  (proposed)
20 Crab Cay Blue Hole
24 'Shark Lady' Museum
25 St Christopher's
  Anglican Church
27 Doric Pillar

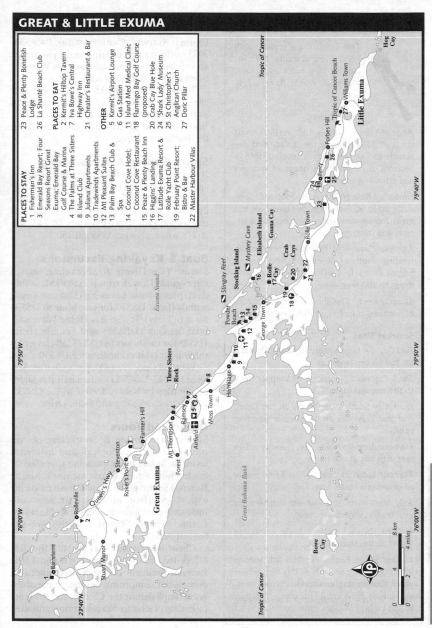

Dive & Snorkel Sites

The Exumas are replete with good dive and snorkel sites, including blue holes and caves, many of which have safety lines.

Dive Sites

Angelfish Blue Hole – This vertical shaft starts at 30 feet below the surface and descends to 90 feet before leveling into a network of caves. It has heaps of sponges and schooling angelfish.

Crab Cay Blue Hole – A 40-foot-wide crevasse up to 90 feet deep, this blue hole has great archways inhabited by lobsters, snappers, and stingrays.

Mystery Cave – At this vast complex extending south of Stocking Island, access begins at 15 feet below the surface and drops to 100 feet.

Stingray Reef – This shallow reef has hordes of snapper, angelfish, grunts, and stingrays.

Snorkel Sites

Bird Cay – A large variety of small fish jostle for turf on this small cay.

Duck Cay North – Schools of snapper flock to this unusual formation.

Duck Cay South – Life teems on this tiered reef that looks like an underwater wedding cake.

Harbour Buoy Portside – This is a very active reef with lots of marine life.

Harbour Buoy Starboard – You'll find plenty of large brain corals here.

Jolly Hall – This is a favored hatchery for grunts and yellowtail snapper.

Liz Lee Shoals – Lots of brain corals are found on this shallow reef.

Loaded Barrel Reef – Plentiful fish species inhabit the wide seabeds of this reef, where you'll also see staghorn coral.

Three Sisters – These three shallow reefs are flooded with schooling fish.

gear, as does Cooper's Charter Services (☎ 242-336-2711), for US$20. Starfish: The Exuma Activity Center (☎/fax 242-336-3033) offers snorkel trips and gear rental and specializes in eco-tourism. Its Web site is www.kayakbahamas.com.

The Crab Cay Blue Hole is conveniently close to George Town, so you might give it a shot if you're up for an adventurous dive. Blue holes are described in the Facts about the Bahamas chapter.

Sport Fishing & Bonefishing

Rolle's Charters (☎ 242-358-0023) offers sport-fishing charters. Cooper's Charter Services (☎ 242-336-2711) will take you deep-sea fishing for US$400/600 half/full day, as will Fish Rowe Charters (☎ 242-345-0074), which charges US$550/750.

Boat & Kayaking Excursions

Starfish (see Diving & Snorkeling, above) offers guided kayak trips (US$45/75 half/full-day), plus a basic kayaking class and kayak rentals (from US$10 for one hour to US$30 for a full day). It also has Hobie Wave sailboat lessons (US$30) and rentals (from US$35 for two hours to US$75 full-day), plus three-hour boat excursions for US$30.

Wendall Cooper of Cooper's Charter Services (☎ 242-336-2711) offers half-day sightseeing trips by boat to Crab Cay for US$35, as well as snorkeling and fishing trips.

Organized Tours

Starfish (see Diving & Snorkeling, above) offers cultural, ecological, and historical tours, including bush medicine tours led by guide Philip Smith, whose mentor is Marlie Kemp, a septuagenarian and bush medicine expert. Starfish also can arrange all-inclusive packages at Peace & Plenty or Latitude Exuma Resort. Visit the Web site for full details.

Christine's Island Tours (☎ 242-358-4016) offers two tours to Barreterre and Little Exuma, focusing on bush medicine; one departs in the morning, another in the afternoon. Trips depart the Club Peace & Plenty (see the Places to Stay section) and cost US$15.

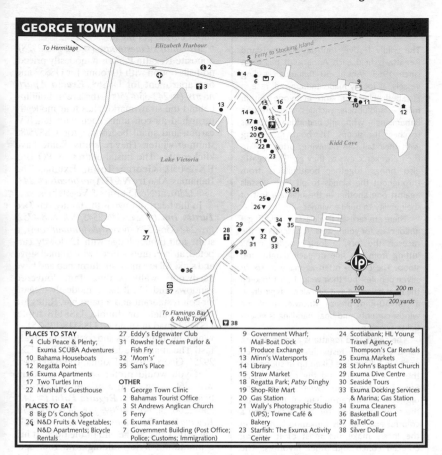

GEORGE TOWN

PLACES TO STAY
4   Club Peace & Plenty;
    Exuma SCUBA Adventures
10 Bahama Houseboats
12 Regatta Point
16 Exuma Apartments
17 Two Turtles Inn
22 Marshall's Guesthouse

PLACES TO EAT
8   Big D's Conch Spot
26 N&D Fruits & Vegetables;
    N&D Apartments; Bicycle
    Rentals

27 Eddy's Edgewater Club
31 Rowshe Ice Cream Parlor &
    Fish Fry
32 'Mom's'
35 Sam's Place

OTHER
1   George Town Clinic
2   Bahamas Tourist Office
3   St Andrews Anglican Church
5   Ferry
6   Exuma Fantasea
7   Government Building (Post Office;
    Police; Customs; Immigration)

9   Government Wharf;
    Mail-Boat Dock
11 Produce Exchange
13 Minn's Watersports
14 Library
15 Straw Market
18 Regatta Park; *Patsy Dinghy*
19 Shop-Rite Mart
20 Gas Station
21 Wally's Photographic Studio
    (UPS); Towne Café &
    Bakery
23 Starfish: The Exuma Activity
    Center

24 Scotiabank; HL Young
    Travel Agency;
    Thompson's Car Rentals
25 Exuma Markets
28 St John's Baptist Church
29 Exuma Dive Centre
30 Seaside Tours
33 Exuma Docking Services
    & Marina; Gas Station
34 Exuma Cleaners
36 Basketball Court
37 BaTelCo
38 Silver Dollar

Seaside Tours (☎ 242-336-2091, fax 242-336-2092) also has guided tours daily, south and north of George Town. It offers a visit to Crab Cay, plus snorkeling and fishing trips. Its postal address is PO Box EX-29034, George Town, Exuma, The Bahamas.

Special Events

The last week of April, visiting yachts congregate for the annual Family Island Regatta in Elizabeth Harbour. The premier regatta in the Bahamian islands, it's a general excuse for the hoi polloi to hobnob with the social elite, downing copious amounts of rum and beer and cheering on the sailboats whizzing along in the harbor. For information, contact either the Bahamas Tourist Office (BTO; ☎ 242-336-2430, fax 242-336-2431), Kermit Rolle (☎ 242-345-6032), or Marilyn Dames (☎ 242-336-2176).

The Annual Bahamas Bonefish Bonanza, one of The Bahamas' prime fishing tournies, is held in George Town in October.

Another great time to visit is Christmas, when Junkanoo traditionally starts at 3 am on December 26 (Boxing Day). The colorful and noisy festival builds beneath the stars as

EXUMAS

Family Island Regatta

The wildly festive, four-day Family Island Regatta is held each April, as it has been since 1953. About 50 Bahamian sailing vessels, all locally made and crewed, race in Elizabeth Harbour, and everyone within miles – landlubbers, yachties, and far-flung Bahamians – who isn't bedridden descends to cheer the sloops. The boats race along with their tall sails billowing, often spilling their drunken crews as they go. The regatta also brings together boatbuilders from throughout the islands to pit their vessels against one another in the ultimate test of their ability to build a winner.

There are races in five classes, including a junior class for youngsters. A hallmark of the races is the 'pry,' a long wooden plank jutting from the side of each dinghy and sloop. The crew – often as many as six or seven people – put their weight on it to keep the boat balanced as it zips along, typically in a stiff 30-knot breeze. Knowledge of the winds, currents, and boat-handling is essential to winning.

The celebrated regatta is also an excuse for a bash! The festivities are massaged until the full week is taken up in support of the Kalik brewery and the rum industry. Sound systems are tweaked until the reggae and African-Bahamian riffs create their own ripples on the bay, assisted by a colorful and raucous Junkanoo band. And the locals make the most of it, selling cracked conch and other favorites. The party gets in the groove the week before the regatta, when liquor companies sponsor related events and parties.

islanders take to the streets for an outpouring of joy and bonhomie.

Places to Stay

For visits during the Family Island Regatta, reserve well in advance: Chances for last-minute accommodations are nil.

The tourist office (see the Information section) provides a list of individuals with guesthouses and rental villas starting at about US$40 per night.

Marshall's Guesthouse (☎ 242-336-2328), opposite Regatta Park, is a modestly priced, no-frills option with 10 rooms for US$52 and one apartment for US$68. *Exuma Apartments* (☎ 242-336-2506), the green building behind the straw market, has four modestly furnished air-con units, each with fan, TV, carpet, and small bedrooms, for US$75/80 summer/winter. They're stuffy. Some have kitchenettes. The postal address is PO Box EX-29050, George Town, Exuma, The Bahamas. Also try *N&D Apartments* (☎ 242-336-2236), at N&D Fruits & Vegetables.

In the heart of town is the family-run *Two Turtles Inn* (☎ 242-336-2545, 800-688-4752, fax 242-336-2528, twoturtl@hotmail.com), a stone and timber lodge with 12 dowdy, carpeted, air-con units – three with a small stove and sink. All are modestly furnished and have hardwood walls, ceiling fan, louvered windows, and TV. It has a modestly elegant air-con restaurant and a patio bar. Rates are US$106 single or double, US$118 triple, US$128 quad in summer; US$118/135/151 in winter, including taxes and continental breakfast. The mailing address is PO Box EX-29251, George Town, Exuma, The Bahamas.

If you would prefer self-catering units with 360° views and a private pocket-size beach, I recommend *Regatta Point* (☎ 242-336-2206, 800-688-0309, fax 242-336-2046, RegattaPoint@BahamasVG.com), overlooking Kidd Cove at the end of the dock. It has a plantation-style building with four spacious waterfront units, each with high ceiling, ceiling fans, kitchen, and patio. Breezes ease through jalousied windows. There are also two exquisite apartments, one with wooden floors and pinewood paneling, plus lofty ceilings and mosquito netting over the master bed. There's no TV here but you'll find a book exchange, free bicycles, boat rentals, Sunfish, and fishing charters. Summer room rates range from US$114 to US$132 for one-bedroom apartments to US$172 for two-bedroom apartments (four people). Winter rates are US$148 to US$164, and US$210, respectively. The postal address is PO Box EX-29006, George Town, Exuma, The Bahamas.

Club Peace & Plenty (☎ *242-336-2551, fax 242-336-2093, pandp@peaceandplenty.com; in the US* ☎ *800-525-2210), at the harbor's edge, has 35 modern, boxy, air-con rooms facing either a small oval-shaped pool or Stocking Island. Each has a small TV and balcony. The property was in need of refurbishment at last visit; the bar, formerly decorated with nautical miscellany, was closed for remodeling. If offers sailboats, scuba diving, snorkeling, and fishing by arrangement. Poolside rooms cost US$115 single or double, US$145 triple, and US$175 quad in low season, US$150/185/220 in the winter. Waterfront and garden suite rooms cost US$104 single or double and US$128 triple in the summer and US$128/152 in the winter. They also have more expensive bay-view rooms. A MAP plan (breakfast and dinner) costs US$36 per day. Children under six are not allowed in winter. The postal address is PO Box EX-29055, George Town, Exuma, The Bahamas.

Fancy a home on the water? *Bahama Houseboats* (☎ *242-336-BOAT, fax 242-336-2629, info@bahamaboats.com)* offers 35- and 42-foot boats with double beds, bathrooms with showers and flushing toilets, and dining area, plus air-con, fridge, microwave, toaster, coffee-machine, and barbecue. The boats sleep six people. Each has a 100hp motor plus a 'runaround' (small Zodiak with outboard motor). Weekly rates are US$1500/1950 35/42-foot in summer; US$1850/2100 winter. Its mailing address is PO Box EX-29031, George Town, Exuma, The Bahamas.

Places to Eat
Club Peace & Plenty is open for breakfast, lunch, and dinner. Its dinner menu includes blackened mahi-mahi and baked chicken; entrees range from US$17 to US$28.

The *Two Turtles Inn* air-con restaurant is open daily for lunch, and for dinner from 6 to 9 pm. It also hosts a barbecue on the patio on Tuesday and Friday evenings.

The nonsmoking *Towne Café & Bakery* (☎ *242-336-2194)*, behind Wally's Photographic Studio, is the place for breakfast: you can opt for a delicious fresh-baked muffin and fresh-squeezed OJ or sample a Bahamian breakfast: boil' fish with onions and hot peppers or chicken souse with grits or mildly spiced johnny cake.

Sam's Place (☎ *242-336-2579)*, with a breezy upstairs deck at the Exuma dock, serves cracked conch, grouper fingers, and blackened dolphin (the fish, not Flipper). It serves breakfasts for US$7 and sandwiches and salads at lunch for US$5.

Gladstone Davis will crack and deftly cut out fresh conch before your eyes. He runs *Big D's Conch Spot* on the mail-boat dock; ceviche or 'conch salad' costs US$3.

My favorite spot is *Eddy's Edgewater Club* (☎ *242-336-2050)*, on the south side of Lake Victoria. It's run by one of the Family Islands' best young chefs, Kevin Brown, who serves splendid Bahamian fare, notably turtle steak but also broiled grouper, steamed chicken, sauteed liver and onions, and a worthy pea soup with dumplings. The restaurant is hidden away at the back behind the bar. Most dishes cost less than US$10. Native breakfasts cost US$5 and lunch specials cost US$8.

Pining for a hotdog? *Jean's Dog House* serves hotdogs from a converted school bus that usually parks outside the government building around midday.

Rowshe Ice Cream Parlor & Fish Fry is on the main street opposite Exuma Dive Centre. It has a fish fry at 9 pm every Friday and Saturday.

In the mornings, 'Mom' sells fresh-baked breads and confections from her van parked outside Exuma Docking Service.

You can buy groceries and household goods at *Exuma Markets*, and fresh produce at *N&D Fruits & Vegetables* and at the *produce exchange* on the mail-boat dock.

Entertainment
The famous English-pub–style bar at *Club Peace & Plenty*, once *the* place to be, was closed and under renovation at last visit. There's usually some action to be found at its poolside bar and at the patio bar of the *Two Turtles Inn*. Both come alive during Family Island Regatta.

EXUMAS

Otherwise, **Eddy's Edgewater Club** is the best bet, especially on Saturday when a rake 'n' scrape band pulls 'em in and everyone works up a sweat on the dance floor. It sometimes has live music on Monday, too. The bar is open nightly.

The **Silver Dollar** (☎ 242-336-2615) bar has dancing every Wednesday evening.

Shopping

First stop is the straw market, where women gather beneath the cool dappled shade of a large fig tree.

The boutique across from Club Peace & Plenty sells resortwear and Androsia batik clothing. A similar array of clothing can be had next door at the Sandpiper, which also sells jewelry, fine art, quality locally made souvenirs, and books. Similarly, Art & Nature has batik fabrics, native hardwoods, and embroidered T-shirts; it's in front of the Two Turtles Inn.

Rod and Mary Page (☎ 242-336-2706) keep an early 19th-century craft alive; they make intricate shell mosaics and 'sailor's valentines,' wooden boxes affixed with shells bearing personalized messages of love.

Getting There & Away

Air The airport is at Moss Town, 6 miles north of George Town. There's a snack bar at the airport, plus Kermit's Harbour Lounge across the road. Taxis meet all flights.

No US carriers flew direct to George Town at press time, although this will undoubtedly change with the opening of the new resorts.

Bahamasair (in Moss Town ☎ 242-345-0035) flies between Nassau and George Town twice daily (US$60 one-way). Lynx Airlines (☎ 242-345-0108) serves Exuma from other Bahamian islands.

Private pilots must clear customs and immigration (☎ 242-345-0073) at the airport.

Boat The *Grand Master* mail boat departs Nassau for George Town at 2 pm Tuesday (12 hours, US$35 one-way).

George Town is the official port of entry to the Exumas. You'll need to call ahead to arrange clearance with customs (☎ 242-345-0071) and immigration (☎ 242-345-2569).

Exuma Docking Services & Marina (☎ 242-336-2578, fax 242-336-2023) has 50 slips with water, electricity, and gas, plus laundromat and store; it charges US60¢ per foot. Exuma Fantasea's marina (☎/fax 242-336-3483) also has slips and facilities, including a marine railway for hauling.

Getting Around

Bus Norman Forbes (☎ 242-336-2857) runs a minibus from George Town to Moss Town and beyond at 8:15 am and 2:30 pm. The fare to Barreterre is US$20. Ona Bullard at the Bahamas Tourist Office can provide information on other possibilities.

Car, Moped & Scooter Thompson's Car Rentals (☎ 242-336-2442, fax 242-336-2445), above Scotiabank, rents cars for US$15 per hour, US$50 for four hours, and US$70 daily. It also has minivans. It's open 9 am to 5 pm Monday to Saturday.

Sam Gray's Exuma Transport (☎ 242-336-2101) has cars at a similar rate. You can rent scooters from Exuma Dive Centre (☎ 242-336-2390) for US$35/240 daily/weekly.

Taxi Several folks run taxis. Try Louise's Taxi 10 (☎ 242-336-2220), Leslie Dames Taxi Service (☎ 242-357-0015), or Luther Rolle Taxi Service (☎ 242-345-5003).

Bicycle Starfish: The Exuma Activity Center (☎ 242-336-3033) rents 21-speed mountain bikes for US$10 for one-hour, US$15 half-day, US$25 full day, including helmet. N&D Fruits & Vegetables (☎ 242-336-2236) also rents bikes.

Boat Exuma Fantasea (☎/fax 242-336-3483) rents Boston Whalers for US$75 to US$105 daily, US$375 to US$525 weekly. If all you want to do is beach-hop to Stocking Island, then Exuma Dive Centre (☎ 242-336-2390, fax 242-336-2391) will rent you a 17-foot Polar with Bimini top for US$75/375 daily/weekly, plus security deposit; its postal address is PO Box EX-29261, George Town, Exuma, The Bahamas.

STOCKING ISLAND & ROLLE CAY

Stocking is a 600-acre, pencil-thin island paralleling Great Exuma about a mile offshore. It's rimmed by talcum-fine beaches and makes a fabulous day trip from George Town.

Many expats have homes on the island, which is owned by John H Perry, a publisher and communications entrepreneur dedicated to the environment.

There are no roads on the island and access is by boat. The main hub is a beach club, run by Club Peace & Plenty, which offers sailing and snorkeling. The club also hosts Out Island Snorkeling Adventures (see the Outdoor Activities chapter). The best snorkel spots are at the cuts between Stocking Island and Elizabeth Island and between Elizabeth Island and Guana Cay.

Rolle Cay is a smidgin-size isle midway between George Town and Stocking Island, and is the center of a deluxe resort development facing onto a white-sand beach.

Mystery Cave

This 400-foot-deep blue hole on the Atlantic side is said to be one of only two living intertidal stromatolite reefs in the world (the other is near Perth, Australia). Stromatolite? Yes, a growing reef of layered limestone – a living fossil – dating back 3½ million years.

Exuma Fantasea (☎/fax 242-336-3483) runs dive trips to the reef from George Town.

Places to Stay & Eat

Higgins' Landing (☎ 242-336-2460, fax 242-357-0008, stockisl@aol.com) is an upscale, environmentally friendly guesthouse with four rooms. It has five handsomely appointed cottages full of antiques, each with a wide balcony and fantastic views. Rates are US$225/175 single/double per person, including breakfast and dinner, transfers, and water sports. There's a beach bar and restaurant; a single-sitting dinner is offered at 6:30 pm Tuesday to Sunday for US$45, including free shuttle from George Town. Reservations must be made by noon. The transfers are provided from the Exuma Fan-

tasea dock in George Town. The postal address is PO Box EX-29146, George Town, Exuma, The Bahamas.

Latitude Exuma Resort & Rolle Yacht Club (☎ 242-357-0340; in the US ☎ 910-256-0610, fax 910-256-0589) is a cottage resort hotel slated to open in 2001 on Rolle Cay, with 16 one-bedroom and 18 two- and three-bedroom cottages in an eco-sensitive, rustic, out-island design and done up in Caribbean pastels. Elevated off the ground, the clapboard cottages catch the breezes. Each has cathedral ceiling, oversize windows, ceiling fans, overstuffed sofas, chaise lounges, and decks or patios with rockers, and exquisite touches such as bathrobes, quality fabrics, and mosquito netting over the beds. Some have intimate loft bedrooms. Activities are provided by Starfish in George Town. Its mailing address is PO Box EX-1349, George Town, Exuma, The Bahamas.

The *Chat & Chill Beach Club* (☎ 242-358-5010) serves sandwiches, picnic items, and drinks.

Getting There & Away

A ferry runs twice daily to the beach club from Club Peace & Plenty in George Town, departing at 10 am and 1 pm and returning at 12:45 and 3:45 pm (US$8 roundtrip; free for the hotel's guests). If you're north of George Town, a separate ferry departs the Peace & Plenty Beach Inn at 10 am and 12:30 pm, returning at 1 and 4 pm.

BOWE CAY

This 220-acre 'Gilligan's Island,' about 10 miles east of Great Exuma, was struck a mighty blow by Hurricane Floyd, which trashed the camp where formerly you could discover the Robinson Crusoe within you, just you and the sun-baked iguanas.

The cay, which is 5 miles around, has a lagoon ringed by mangroves and trails that lead over the blackened coral. Alas, you can no longer rent the lone cabaña…it ain't there no more!

NORTH OF GEORGE TOWN

Queen's Hwy runs north of George Town through a string of small settlements (see

EXUMAS

the Great & Little Exuma map at the beginning of this chapter) with prim little homes painted in Caribbean pastels and shaded by palms. Most are associated with plantation estates that now lie in ruins.

About a mile offshore from the town of Mt Thompson is the Three Sisters Rock, a trio of craggy boulders rising from the sea. They're supposedly named for three sisters who each drowned herself here for the shame of bearing a child out of wedlock (the story is apocryphal: The *majority* of children are born so in The Bahamas).

Beautiful beaches line the shore, including Emerald Bay, the site of major resort development between Farmer's Hill and Steventon, about 15 miles north of George Town. The 450-acre luxury community will feature villas, townhouses, hotels, a marina, and Greg Norman–designed golf course. A similar, albeit smaller project – the Island Club, about 7 miles north of George Town – will add a Tom Weiskopf–designed course.

Information

There's a BaTelCo station beside the road in Farmer's Hill. Coastline Laundromat is beside the road in Roker's Point. The private Island Med Medical Clinic (☎ 242-336-2220) is two miles north of George Town. There's also a medical clinic (☎ 242-358-0053) in Steventon. In an emergency call ☎ 919. The Rolleville police station can be reached at ☎ 242-345-6066.

Kermit Rolle (☎ 242-345-6038) can guide you on a lore-filled tour of the island. Try him at Kermit's Hilltop Tavern (see Places to Eat, below) or Kermit's Airport Lounge (☎ 242-345-0002).

Rolleville

This historic settlement, 28 miles north of George Town, sits atop a hill at the northern end of Great Exuma. It's a poor village with many meager shacks and former slave homes, most in tumbledown condition, but it's brightened in late spring and early summer by flame-of-the-forest trees. The hamlet is the site of the Rolleville Regatta, held the first Monday in August. Several locals still make boats.

Barreterre

About 2 miles south of Rolleville, a pot-holed side road off the Queen's Hwy leads west to Stuart Manor then north to the twin Barreterre Cays. The road ends at Barreterre, a sleepy, nondescript hamlet that stirs only with the monthly arrival of the mail boat. A few locals still make sailboats. Ask Hughrie Lloyd (☎ 242-355-5015) to show you his regatta-winning dinghies. Everyone seems to be called McKenzie, after a plantation owner.

Keep your ears attuned for the voice of Sonny Lloyd, a blind square-box player and bass singer with a laugh like Ray Charles'. He sings gospel, accompanied by his sister-in-law Evalena, who, says author-photographer Harvey Lloyd, sings the melody in 'a sweet high soprano voice – her face lit up like sunshine on the mountain top, her eyes looking straight in the face of God.'

You can rent a 17-foot Boston Whaler from Reverend AA McKenzie (☎ 242-345-7003). Hedley Smith (☎ 242-345-2326), in Stuart Manor, advertises scuba and deep-sea fishing trips.

Places to Stay

The *Peace & Plenty Beach Inn* (☎ 242-336-2250, 800-525-2210, fax 242-336-2253, pandp@peaceandplenty.com), a sibling to the Club Peace & Plenty, is 1½ miles north of George Town in a suburban section named Jolly Hall. It has 16 deluxe, air-con, waterfront rooms, each exotically done up with Italian tile floors and wicker furniture and boasting a private balcony. There's a small pool, plus a two-story restaurant and lobby. Water sports include scuba diving, snorkeling, and Sunfish sailing. A bar hangs over the water. The restaurant is open 7:30 am to 9:30 pm and has Bahamian and continental dishes with a French twist. Summer rates range from US$135 single or double for a sea-view room to US$145 deluxe or efficiency. Winter rates are US$155/180. Packages are also offered. A shuttle bus operates to George Town. The beach here isn't the best, due to sea grasses.

The *Coconut Cove Hotel* (☎ 242-336-2659, fax 242-336-2658), next door, is a more romantic nook amid a garden with a pond full of reef fish. The mahogany structure has sliding glass doors opening to Elizabeth Harbour. The 11 tastefully decorated air-con rooms each have a ceiling fan, fresh flowers, mosquito nets suspended above the bed, a small TV, minibar, and thoughtful extras such as his-and-hers bathrobes. The 'Paradise Suite' has a king-size bed, marble bathtub, and a hot tub on its own private deck. Rates range from US$90/100 single/double to US$110/130 in summer; US$120/140 to US$145/165 in winter. The Paradise Suite costs US$180/200 in summer, US$230/250 in winter. Add US$30 for a third person and US$38 for a MAP plan. It has bonefishing and dive packages. Barman 'Fuzzy' Beneby can mix more than 300 cocktails. An elegant dining room overlooks the pool and the ocean. The restaurant, with options for indoor or alfresco dining, offers white-glove service. It specializes in Italian cuisine and nouvelle Bahamian dishes such as crab fritters, chicken breast with green pepper sauce, and Bahamian lobster tail, followed by crème brulée or banana flambé. The menu varies daily and can be prepared to order. Breakfasts average US$6; dinner entrées are US$15 to US$30. Free shuttles are offered. The postal address is PO Box EX-29299, George Town, Exuma, The Bahamas.

Palm Bay Beach Club & Spa (☎/fax 242-336-2997, 888-396-0606) was under construction in 2000, immediately north of Coconut Cove Hotel.

Mt Pleasant Suites (☎ 242-336-2960, fax 242-336-2964) is a small hotel with modern, modestly furnished, air-con suite units with satellite TV and kitchen. Single rooms cost US$75/90 summer/winter; doubles cost US$85/105. Its address is PO Box EX-29019, George Town, Exuma, The Bahamas.

About a half mile northwest is *Tradewinds Apartments (☎ 242-336-2697)*, with 16 fully furnished, air-con apartments with TV. Nearby, *Juliana Apartments (☎ 242-336-2114)* has self-catering units for daily, weekly, and monthly rental.

The motel-style *Palms at Three Sisters (☎ 242-358-4040, 800-688-4752, fax 242-358-4043)* looks over a deserted, palm-lined beach in Mt Thompson. It has 12 large, air-con beachfront rooms and two cottages, all modestly albeit nicely furnished, with patios or balconies and satellite TV. Facilities include a weather-worn tennis court, indoor bar, and ocean-view restaurant. Summer rates are US$75 single or double, US$95 triple for a beachfront room, US$100 single or double for a cottage. Winter rates are US$105/125/125, respectively. The mailing address is PO Box EX-29215, George Town, Exuma, The Bahamas.

Ground was broken in 2000 on the *Island Club (in the US ☎ 800-772-7995, fax 305-392-3971)*, a 274-acre golf resort and luxury vacation community about 7 miles north of George Town, near Moss Town. It will feature privately owned villas for vacation rentals, a fishing lodge, full-service marina, health and fitness center, swimming pool, shopping village, and 18-hole golf course with separate practice range and putting greens.

Likewise, the 235-room *Four Seasons Resort Great Exuma (☎ 800-332-3442)* is slated to open in late 2001 at Emerald Bay, as a highlight of a 470-acre development – *Emerald Bay Resort (☎ 800-947-9410)* – centered on a second championship golf course. The resort complex will also feature vacation townhouse rentals and beachfront villas, all in plantation-style architecture, plus gourmet restaurants, a health and fitness club, and a full-service marina. Its mailing address is PO Box EX-29005, George Town, Great Exuma, The Bahamas.

The *Fisherman's Inn (☎ 242-355-5017)*, on the waterfront to the left as you enter Barreterre, has two simple rooms with ceiling fans and bathroom for about US$50. The inn has a seafood restaurant and bar; dinner reservations are recommended.

Places to Eat

The hotels all have recommended restaurants or casual lounges.

A no-frills eatery popular with locals is *Iva Bowe's Central Highway Inn (☎ 242-345-7014)*, about 9 miles north of George Town near Ramsey. Iva is acclaimed for her

EXUMAS

conch dishes. She also serves tasty shrimp and a crawfish salad with peas 'n' rice.

In Roker's Point you can enjoy a meal at the *Rhodriquez Neighbourhood Club & Restaurant*.

Kermit's Hilltop Tavern (☎ 242-345-6006) serves steamed conch, curried mutton, and pan-fried grouper with fresh vegetables. Reservations are required for dinner. A seat at one of the rooftop tables with a marvelous view makes it well worth the drive. The tavern has open-air dancing and live music on weekends.

You can buy goods at *McKenzie's* grocery store in Barreterre.

Getting There & Around

Norman Forbes (☎ 242-336-2484/2444) operates a minibus westbound to Mt Thompson (US$5 one-way). Call Mr Forbes or the tourist board for the latest schedules.

The *Etienne & Cephas* mail boat calls at Barreterre weekly from Nassau; see the Staniel Cay section, later in this chapter, for details.

Smitty's Taxi (☎ 242-358-4045) is in Farmer's Hill. There's a gas station opposite Iva Bowe's near Ramsey.

Kermit Rolle (☎ 242-345-6038) of Rolleville offers taxi tours. Check with the tourism office in George Town for private minibus service.

SOUTH OF GEORGE TOWN

Running south of George Town, Queen's Hwy does not pass as many brand-new or up-and-coming resort developments, but it will take you past some great views and lead to one of the Exumas' great bonefishing lodges.

Rolle Town
• pop 300

This small settlement sits magnificently atop a hill with a stunning view over the coastal plains where villagers grow crops of onions, mangoes, and bananas. Vast turquoise bone-flats extend beyond. Many of the sun-bleached pastel buildings and clapboard shacks, some of which are in shambles, date back over a century. Goats graze between the homes.

You can follow a wooden path to three 18th-century tombstones, one of which is shaped like a double bed with headboard and footboard. Here, according to the marble plaque dating to 1792, the 26-year-old wife of an overseer, Captain Alexander McKay, slumbers with her infant child.

Bonefishing

The Peace & Plenty Bonefish Lodge (see below) is one of the best fishing lodges in The Bahamas. It charges US$290 per day with boat, guide, and tackle for two. The hotel has an intensive seven-day 'bonefish school' package each April and November, with 16 hours of instruction over four days. It's billed as 'the ultimate fly fishing school challenge.' The Peace & Plenty Boutique sells fishing gear.

Places to Stay & Eat

In Rolle Town, a chap called Charlie (☎ 242-345-5042) rents a fully furnished *two-bedroom home* with lounge and dining room. The bedroom has satellite TV and air-con; US$100/500 daily/weekly double (US$20 each extra person). It comes with a Boston Whaler for an additional US$50 daily.

You also can rent air-con cottages at *Master Harbour Villas* (☎ 242-345-5076, fax 242-345-5140), about 2 miles north of Rolle Town, for US$150 (one-bedroom) and US$200 (two-bedroom).

A few miles south of George Town, *February Point Resort* (☎ 242-336-2661, fax 242-336-2660, february@grouper.batelnet.bs), a dramatic remake of the former Flamingo Bay Hotel & Villas, sits on a peninsula jutting into Flamingo Bay. It features new two- and three-bedroom villas in Bahamian colonial style, some under construction at press time. The main building has a graciously appointed lounge with New Mexico–style throw rugs, deep-cushion sofas, and Spanish-style antique glass cabinets. The terrace lounge has lofty views over the bay. Facilities will eventually include a freshwater pool, marina, private yacht club, tennis court, basketball court, a golf course, and a cruiser for island-hopping. Rates for rooms in the main house are US$110; the suite costs US$155. Two-bedroom villas cost US$250 (summer) to US$355 (peak season); three-bedroom units cost US$295 to US$415. The mailing address is PO Box EX-29090, George Town, Exuma, The Bahamas.

The *Bistro & Bar* (☎ *242-336-2400*), at February Point, serves native seafood, plus international cuisine, and is open 11 am to 11 pm. It provides a free shuttle to and from George Town.

Serious anglers should head to *Peace & Plenty Bonefish Lodge* (☎ *242-345-5555, fax 242-345-5556, pandp@peaceandplenty.com*), about 3 miles south of Rolle Town. The stone and timber lodge overlooks landscaped grounds and a stone sun deck. A handsome lounge-cum-bar sports a video library, a pool- and card-room, plus a restaurant and pro shop. Upstairs, a second restaurant and lounge with a satellite TV and fax is reserved for fisherfolk. The eight nicely appointed air-con rooms have two queen-size beds and balconies with views over the flats. Three-night all-inclusive packages cost US$1624 single (one person per room and boat) and US$914 per person double. A similar weeklong package costs US$4176/2326. One-night all-inclusive rates are US$200 single or double. The restaurant is not open for lunch (box lunches are provided). The lodge is closed August and September. Its mailing address is PO Box EX-29100, George Town, Exuma, The Bahamas.

The *Traveller's Rest Restaurant & Bar*, on Queen's Hwy as you enter Rolle Town, has a pool table, satellite TV, and music and dancing.

Cheater's Restaurant & Bar (☎ *242-336-2535*), 1 mile south of February Point, serves Bahamian dishes and is popular with locals. It opens at 6:30 am for breakfast of stewed fish, sheeps' tongue souse, etc.

Little Exuma

Little Exuma is separated from the more developed Great Exuma by a 200-yard bight; the two are linked by a 564-foot-long bridge. The subtropical climate will entice you to relax on the white-sand beaches and linger in the perfectly clear water.

FERRY

This small hillside settlement lies immediately across the bridge from Great Exuma.

A highlight is **St Christopher's Anglican Church**, a whitewashed chapel festooned with a bougainvillea bower. Supposedly it's the smallest church in The Bahamas.

'Shark Lady' Museum

The hamlet is most famous for 'Tara,' the home-boutique-museum of Gloria Patience (☎ 242-345-5055), alias 'The Shark Lady of the Exumas,' a sun-baked old dame whose home abounds with her collectibles and other artistic creations, such as jewelry made from sharks' teeth and spines. For seven years, she captained a yacht with an all-female topless crew! Amazingly, too, this youthful septuagenarian used to snare sharks from her Boston Whaler using a 10-inch hook on a 150-foot hand line! The jaws she sold to tourists; the carcasses she conjured into fertilizer.

Her simple clapboard house is fronted by a garden full of bougainvillea. It's roadside, 400 yards south of the bridge and just before the settlement of Ferry.

FERRY TO WILLIAMS TOWN

Forbes Hill, 12 miles southeast of George Town, has a 100-yard-wide scimitar of pure white sand and turquoise shallows cusped by tiny headlands. *Idyllic!* Two miles south of Forbes Hill a side road leads east to **Tropic of Cancer Beach**, another true stunner that runs south, unblemished, for several miles.

The southernmost settlement is **Williams Town** (pop 300), populated predominantly by Kelsalls, descended from or named for the foremost Loyalist family that founded the settlement. The Kelsalls established a cotton plantation and sold salt drawn from nearby salt ponds. The brush-entangled ruins of the plantation home – **Hermitage Estate** – still stand amid pinkish brine ponds.

You can watch locals dressing their fresh catch of fish and conch at the rickety wharf

EXUMAS

EXUMA CAYS

Sail Rocks

Tarpum Bay

Rock Sound

Ship Channel Cay

Allan's Cays

Highborne Cay
1

Eleuthera

Norman's Cay
2

Little San Salvador

Wax Cay Cut

Shroud Cay

Exuma Cays Land & Sea Park

Hawksbill Cay

Cistern Cay

Warderick Wells Cay
3

Hall's Pond Cay

Conch Cut

Fowl Cay

Compass Cay

Sampson Cay
4

Staniel Cay   5 *see inset map*

Black Point

Great Guana Cay

PLACES TO STAY
4 Sampson Cay Club & Marina
5 Farmer's Cay Yacht Club & Marina
8 Staniel Cay Yacht Club & Resort
12 Happy People Marina; Royal Entertainer's Restaurant

PLACES TO EAT
7 Club Thunderball
15 Isles General Store

OTHER
1 Highborne Cay Marina
2 DC-3 Plane Wreck
3 Ranger Station/Park Headquarters
6 Caribbean Marine Research Centre
9 St Luke's Clinic
10 BaTelCo
11 Post Office
13 Library
14 Church

Little Farmer's Cay
5
Big Farmer's Cay

Lee Stocking Island
6

Great Exuma

Majors Spot

0   250   500 m
0   250   500 yards

7

Thunderball Grotto

Great Bahama Bank

Staniel Cay

8

9
10
11
Airstrip

12   13
14   15

Bowe Cay

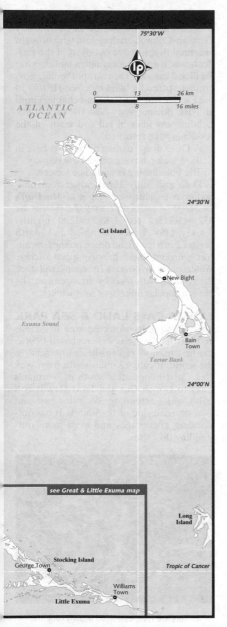

behind and just south of St Mary Magdalene's Church. North of town, on the bluff to the side of the road, you'll pass a tall **Doric pillar** transporting you (metaphorically) to ancient Greece. This column and a rusty cannon stand high above the rocky shore. The hulk of a ship lies dramatically on a white-sand beach fronting the village, within calling distance of the column meant to guide mariners.

Places to Stay & Eat
La Shanté Beach Club (☎ 242-345-4136, fax 242-345-4134), at Forbes Hill, has three modestly furnished air-con rooms with kitchenette and separate dining room, and each has a satellite TV. It's no-frills, but what an enviable and lonesome position, right on the scimitar beach. Rates are US$85/92 summer/winter. It serves sandwiches, burgers, and Bahamian dishes. Breakfast (about US$5) and dinner are provided for guests on request. A seafood platter costs US$25, a T-bone steak costs US$14. There's a free shuttle to George Town. The postal address is PO Box EX-29082, George Town, Exuma, The Bahamas.

Doris Rahming ('Mom') runs *Mom's Bakery* in Williams Town. She bakes tempting rum cake, banana bread, coconut tarts, and bread. Here, too, is *Nelson's Point* (☎ 242-345-4043) restaurant and lounge. *Bullard's Supplies* sells groceries.

Exuma Cays

The cays begin at the barren Sail Rocks, 40 miles southeast of New Providence. Though they may seem alike, each has its own quirky character. Many are privately owned.

These waters are acclaimed as the 'finest cruising grounds in the Western Hemisphere.' *The Exuma Guide: A Cruising Guide to the Exuma Cays* by Stephen Pavlidis is a must-read for sailors.

SHIP CHANNEL CAY & ALLAN'S CAYS
Long, narrow Ship Channel Cay is the northernmost cay after Sail Rocks. Allan's

Cays, immediately south, comprise about a dozen cays popular with boaters and fisherfolk; one of the prettiest is Leaf Cay, with a splendid beach. An endemic subspecies of iguana, the yellowish 'Bahamian dragon,' lives here. Boaters must keep dogs on board (dogs don't realize that iguanas are a protected species!).

Getting There & Away
Powerboat Adventures (☎ 242-327-5385, fax 242-328-7029, info@powerboatadventures .com) offers a thrilling powerboat adventure from Nassau at 9 am daily; it costs US$159/99 adults/children. Hang on to your toupee as you zip along first to Allan's Cays for snorkeling. Then it's on to Ship Channel Cay for a nature hike and barbecue lunch on the beach. The postal address is PO Box CB-13315, Nassau, The Bahamas.

Yachters will find an exceptionally good anchorage at Leaf Cay.

HIGHBORNE CAY
This private cay, 2 miles south of Leaf Cay, is favored by yachters, who are permitted ashore. A pathway leads from the marina to a small provisions store and pay phone where weathered sailors lounge around swapping shaggy-dog stories while basking in the chairs set outside. You can climb the hill topped by waving palm trees for a view of the most beautiful beach you have ever seen.

Highborne Plantations (☎/fax 242-355-1003) has four oceanside cottages for rent from US$200 for up to six people. Only yachters and people staying in the cottages are allowed access to the cay. Its mailing address is PO Box SS-6342, Nassau, New Providence, The Bahamas.

The Highborne Cay Marina, which has a *grocery store*, caters to yachts up to 130 feet. Contact Peter and Alison Albury (☎ 242-355-1008, fax 242-355-1003, VHF channel 16), PO Box N-6342, Nassau, New Providence, The Bahamas.

NORMAN'S CAY
One look at the stunning beaches and you'll understand why 4-mile-long Norman's Cay was once an idyllic hideaway for the winter-

ing wealthy. In the 1970s most of the island was purchased by Carlos Lehder, a key German-Colombian drug lord who brought in armed thugs, drove out most of the residents, and turned the cay into a landing strip for illegal cargoes. The corrupt Pindling government turned a blind eye (see History in the Facts about The Bahamas chapter) until an NBC documentary blew the lid in 1983. Lehder now idles in jail and many of the residents have returned.

A DC-3 drug-running plane rusts here in shallow water, having missed the runway.

The bonefishing is said to be superb.

Dale and Sally Harshbarger rent one-bedroom beachfront cottages at *MacDuff's* (☎ 242-357-8846; in the US ☎ 937-845-0498, fax 937-845-7351) for US$200/1200 nightly/weekly; US$25 each per third and fourth person. Each has island decor, ceiling fans, aircon bedroom, and a fully equipped kitchen. Water sports are offered. The couple will stock the cottages with food by arrangement. The bar is a popular lunch spot for yachters.

EXUMA CAYS LAND & SEA PARK
This 175-sq-mile protected area of islands and surrounding seas was created in 1958 as the first marine 'replenishment nursery' in the world. It runs 22 miles south from Wax Cay Cut (immediately south of Norman's Cay) to Conch Cut and Fowl Cay. It is 8 miles wide, extending 3½ miles east and west on each side of the islands. It has outstanding anchorages and even more outstanding dive sites.

Hutias are rare, cat-sized brown rodents.

All commercial fishing and collecting is banned. (No marine or plant life, whether dead or alive, may be taken, including shells.) The waters teem with marine life, and snorkeling (with an average depth of about 10 feet) doesn't get any better than this – there are miles of sun-dappled coral reefs where groupers and turtles huddle. The waters lap against beaches as private as your innermost thoughts. On land, you may spot the Bahamian mockingbird, Bahamian banana quit, or the rare red-legged thrush. Seabirds abound, including terns, waders, and the elegant, long-tailed tropicbird, which nests in high bluffs. Land animals include curly-tailed lizards, blue-tailed lizards, plump iguanas and, on several isles, hutias so endangered that messing with them is good for a hefty fine and up to six months in the pokey.

Uninhabited Hawksbill Cay, ringed by stunning beaches, has marked nature trails that lead to the ruins of an old Loyalist plantation. Little Hawksbill's Cay is a major nesting site for ospreys. Hall's Pond Cay has a recyclable library (take a book, leave a book) at the abandoned Exuma Cays Club. Warderick Wells Cay, which has 4 miles of nature trails, is said to be haunted by the tormented spirits from a slave ship. Shroud Cay has 'Driftwood Village,' an ever-expanding piece of flotsam folk art. And the Rocky Dundas, two rocks in Conch Cut, have a cave full of stalactites and stalagmites.

The ranger station on the northwest side of Warderick Wells Cay is open 9 am to noon and 1 to 5 pm Monday to Saturday and 9 am to 1 pm Sunday. Trail maps are available and there's a library. The Bahamas National Trust has posted information leaflets on several cays.

Park access is free.

Kayaking

This is an excellent area for sea kayaking. Imagine paddling through the crystal-clear waters by day and camping under the stars by night – heavenly. Bring aquasocks and snorkel fins for exploring the sea outside of your kayak.

Turn to the Outdoor Activities chapter for kayaking outfitters that offer complete-package, guided trips.

Places to Stay

You can rent a deluxe *house and two cottages* sleeping up to 10 people on Cistern Cay. The place comes with a gourmet chef, all meals, and as much booze as you can down, plus water sports, a fishing guide, and other extras. Call ☎ 242-326-7875 for information.

Getting There & Away

Several cays have airstrips, many of which are private.

The best access to the park is from Staniel Cay, where you might be able to hitch a ride with the park warden on his daily patrol. He monitors VHF channel 16 from his headquarters at the Warderick Wells Cay anchorage.

Out Island Voyages (☎ 242-394-0951, 800-241-4591, fax 242-394-0948, balymena@ bahamas.net.bs), on Paradise Island, offers four- and seven-day 'Exuma Exploration' cruises aboard its 124-foot luxury yacht, the sleek *Ballymena*, beginning at about US$1125 for a three-day cruise. It also offers day trips from Paradise Island to the Exuma Cays for snorkeling and hiking, including gourmet meals.

Island World Adventures (☎ 242-394-8960, fax 242-363-1657, cruise@bahamas.net .bs) offers daylong excursions from Paradise Island to Saddleback Cay on the 45-foot, high-powered speedboat *EcoTime*. Trips also stop at Leaf Cay. Its postal address is PO Box N-7366, Paradise Island, The Bahamas.

Boaters must anchor at Hog Cay at the south end of Warderick Wells Cay. Moorings cost from US$15 daily, depending on your vessel's length. Call 'Exuma Park' on VHF 16 at least 24 hours in advance to check availability.

COMPASS & SAMPSON CAYS

These popular yachter's havens, south of the Exuma Land & Sea Park, each boast a small harbor with a beach, beach-lined coves, and trails.

The Lodge is a three-bedroom house at Compass Cay Marina (*☎/fax 242-355-2064, compasscay@aol.com*). There's a deck and a complete kitchen. It rents for US$1650 weekly for two people, including use of a boat; US$100 per extra person. You also can rent a 'Treehouse apartment' with wrap-around porch. The marina has 13 slips and charges US$1 per foot daily. Potluck suppers and beach parties are hosted.

Sampson Cay Club & Marina (*☎ 242-355-2034, VHF channel 16*) was closed for renovation and planned to reopen in 2001. It will offer beachside cottages and at least one two-bedroom villa as well as marina services and water sports.

STANIEL CAY
• pop 80

This mite of a cay is the main settlement in the Exuma Cays and the main base for visiting the Exuma Cays Land & Sea Park. The small village has a post office, church, library (in a 1776 building), and grocery stores. There are peaceful beaches and bonefishing is said to be tops.

There's a BaTelCo station and a few phonecard booths, plus St Luke's Clinic (*☎ 242-355-2010*) staffed by a nurse.

The time to visit is during the New Year's Day Regatta, when locally built dinghies compete for prizes (contact Kenneth Rolle, *☎ 242-355-2008*). There's also the Annual Staniel Cay Bonefish Tournament in August (call Tony Gray, *☎ 242-355-2018*).

Thunderball Grotto

A highlight of any visit to Staniel Cay is a snorkel or dive trip into this grotto, just northwest of the cay. The exquisite cavern, which is lit by shafts of light pouring in from holes in the ceiling, is named for the James Bond movie *Thunderball*, scenes from which were filmed here. So, too, were scenes from *Splash* and another 007 movie, *Never Say Never Again*. A panoply of colorful fish crowds the crystalline waters. The current is very strong – inexperienced swimmers beware!

Places to Stay

The cay's two waterfront hotels play to the boating crowd. *Happy People Marina* (*☎ 242-355-2008*) has eight air-con rooms with ceiling fans and a decor of rainbow pastels. Upstairs rooms boast marvelous views and have private bathrooms; those downstairs share bathrooms. Rooms cost US$75 to US$90. A two-bedroom efficiency costs US$200.

The *Staniel Cay Yacht Club & Resort* (*☎ 242-355-2024, fax 242-355-2044, info@ stanielcay.com; in the US ☎ 954-467-8920, fax 954-522-3248*) has an exceptional oceanfront setting. There are four cozy air-con, waterfront, two-person cottages plus two four-person cottages. All have refrigerators and coffeepots. The resort offers free use of Boston Whalers, plus Sunfish sailboats and scuba gear rentals. Rates are US$95/200 for small/large cottages in summer; US$125/235 in winter. Weekly rates are US$625/1250 and US$800/1400, respectively.

You can rent a two-bedroom cottage for US$1200 weekly (Saturday to Saturday), including use of a Boston Whaler. Contact ☎/fax 242-355-2052; in the US ☎/fax 603-868-2663.

Places to Eat

Singer Jimmy Buffett drops in on occasion to play Happy People's *Royal Entertainer's Restaurant*, where locals hang out. It's open for breakfast and lunch by request; reservations are needed for dinner. Theazel Rolle, the cook, conjures up cracked conch, lobster, pork chops, and other native fare. For lunch, try Theazel's 'Theazelburger.' The place has a pool table and music.

The restaurant at the *Staniel Cay Yacht Club* serves three meals daily; it's closed Sunday except for dinner for cottage guests. Reservations are required for yachters. You can order a boxed lunch for excursions. It, too, has a pool table.

Club Thunderball, at the north end of the cay, sits atop the bluff overlooking the Thunderball Grotto and is open for lunch and dinner (closed Monday). It serves native fare and has beach barbecues on Friday night (by reservation), plus occasional pig roasts, and a Super Bowl party in January. The club also features a pool table, satellite TV, and dancing on weekends.

Several stores sell groceries. You can buy fresh-baked bread at Berkie Rolle's *Isles General Store*. Other local women sell bread. To cool off, head to *Frosty's Ice Cream* on the waterfront.

Getting There & Away

Professional Flight Transport (☎ 954-938-9508, fax 954-938-9509) charges US$320 per person roundtrip for charters from Fort Lauderdale to Staniel Cay.

Charter flights from George Town cost about US$360 roundtrip for up to five people; flights from Nassau cost US$500. The Getting Around chapter lists many small plane charter companies. You can charter a plane on Staniel Cay from Solomon Robinson (☎ 242-355-2012) or John Chamberlain (☎ 242-355-2043).

The *Ettienne & Cephas* mail boat sails here from Nassau at 2 pm Tuesday (21 hours, US$30 one-way), also stopping at Black Point, Little Farmer's Cay, Barreterre, and Ragged Island.

Staniel Cay Yacht Club and Happy People Marina have slips, water, electricity, and fuel (see Places to Stay, above).

GREAT GUANA & LITTLE FARMER'S CAYS

The largest of the Exuma Cays, 12-mile-long Great Guana Cay also has the cays' largest settlement – **Black Point** (pop 300) – where the main attraction is **Willie Rolle's Sculpture Garden**. Many women still weave plaited straw. There is a deep cave worth exploring (Martin Rolle acts as a guide).

Facilities include an airstrip, post office, BaTelCo station, and clinic (☎ 242-355-0007). Clayton Rolle (☎ 242-355-3301) will take you bonefishing. An Emancipation Day Regatta is held here each 'August Monday.'

Little Farmer's Cay, a stone's throw off the southwest tip of Great Guana, hosts the Annual Farmer's Cay Five F's Festival each first weekend of February (call ☎ 242-324-2093) and the Full Moon Beer Festival – *oooww-uuwww!?* – in July. It also has a post office, BaTelCo station, and clinic (☎ 242-355-4015). Cely Smith (☎ 242-345-2341) will take you fishing.

Places to Stay & Eat

At Black Point, *De Shamons* (☎ 242-355-3009) has three rooms over its restaurant for US$80. The restaurant specializes in freshly caught fish.

Scorpio's Cottages (☎ 242-355-3003) has five gaily painted air-con cottages for US$75; you can dine across the road at the *Scorpio Inn*, where local residents gather to play pool and dominoes and to dance.

The *Farmer's Cay Yacht Club & Marina* (☎ 242-355-4017), on Little Farmer's Cay, has three rooms for US$80, and a restaurant and bar (reservations needed for dinner). A new 16-room hotel and marina was in the works. The *Ocean Cabin Restaurant* (☎/fax 242-355-4006, oceancbn@batelnet.bs), in the hamlet up the hill, offers two cottages for US$100, serves native fare, and bakes bread to order. It has pre-dinner crab races on Wednesday and chicken races on Saturday.

On Great Guana Cay, *Lorraine's Café* (☎ 242-355-2201) is recommended for inexpensive native fare and fresh-baked bread and cookies. Call the day before to order breakfast.

Adderley's Friendly Store sells groceries.

Getting There & Away

The *Ettienne & Cephas* mail boat sails to Black Point and Little Farmer's Cay from

Nassau weekly; see the Staniel Cay section for details.

Allan Rolle (☎ 242-355-4003) and Cecil Smith (☎ 242-355-4003) run folks to Barraterre on Great Exuma.

LEE STOCKING ISLAND

About 5 miles north of Great Exuma, Lee Stocking has an airstrip and the **Caribbean Marine Research Centre** (CMRC). This 100-acre scientific research facility (☎ 242-345-6039; in the US ☎ 561-471-7552) is funded by grants from the US National Oceanic & Atmospheric Administration. Its mission is to study underwater ecosystems and broaden understanding to ensure the vitality of the reefs and aquatic life. Visitors are welcome; short tours are given.

Ragged Island Range

This remote range of tiny islands forms a mini-archipelago poking up along the southeastern edge of the Great Bahama Bank. The crescent of a dozen or so isles

and a score of smaller cays begins with the Jumento Cays, about 25 miles south of Little Exuma, and arcs west and south for about 100 miles, ending with Ragged Island, the largest of the half-moon chain.

During the 19th century its flats were utilized for salt-crystal farming. Today they are virtually uninhabited.

Most of the cays here are windswept and barren, increasingly so to the south. The birdlife is varied and prolific. And the cruising is spectacular, though few boaters make it this far. A lighthouse still stands on Flamingo Cay.

The largest and southernmost island, Ragged Island (pop 89) has the only settlement of any consequence, **Duncan Town**. It's a bit of a flyblown place, and most of the houses are abandoned and boarded up. Most folks who remain eke out a living from fishing.

Duncan Town has a 3000-foot paved airstrip. There is no scheduled air service, and the only visitors are the few sailors who call in, often bound for a circuit of Cuba.

The *Ettienne & Cephas* mail boat calls here weekly from Nassau; see the Staniel Cay section for information.

Cat Island

• pop 1800

This little-visited island, south of Eleuthera and 130 miles southeast of Nassau, is one of the most interesting islands in The Bahamas, a true gem for people hoping to discover traditional African-Bahamian culture.

The island is shaped like a long, slender boot, with New Bight, the capital, as the boot's buckle. Cat averages 1 to 4 miles wide before broadening along its 12-mile-wide sole.

How the island got its name is a source of controversy (it was officially known as San Salvador until 1926, when that name was transferred to Watling Island, today's San Salvador). Locals always have called their home 'Cat Island,' for Arthur Catt, a notorious pirate who supposedly had his base here. Local historian Eric Moncur says it was named by the English for the cats that the Spanish introduced to the island.

A single, well-paved road – Queen's Hwy – runs down the west shore, lined by plantation ruins and ramshackle settlements where goats wander amid fallen stone walls. So provincial is the island that many of its inhabitants have never ventured to either its north or south end.

Dirt tracks lead from Queen's Hwy to the Atlantic shore (called the 'north' shore by locals), boasting miles-long pinkish beaches. The scenery here is often dramatic, with cliffs that plunge to the breakers. The south offers tranquil sugar-white beaches. The west shore is memorable for bonefish swarming the creeks opening to Exuma Sound. Cat Island is also blessed with rolling hills, crowned by Mt Alvernia (206 feet), topped by a hermitage looking like it was dropped in from King Arthur's Cornwall.

The island is swampy in places, and elsewhere is densely forested with mangrove, scrub, and broadleaf woodland boasting mahogany and cascadilla, a heavily scented tree whose bark is shipped to Italy to be used in wine and perfume manufacture. Many caves, blue holes, and freshwater lakes dot the island, which is known for a species of freshwater turtle. The creatures – called 'Peter' by locals – are endangered but still are taken as a local delicacy or for domestic garden pools. Good places to see them are the shallow freshwater ponds between Tea Bay and Knowles. Small, non-poisonous snakes abound. You're sure to see giant land crabs with pincers the size of plumber's grips; at night, you might see flickering lights amid the undergrowth, those of locals hunting crabs for tomorrow's supper. And Cat Island is famed for ubiquitous monarch moths, dark brown and as large as small bats. Locals call them 'money

Highlights

- Father Jerome's quaint Tolkeinesque hermitage atop Mt Alvernia, the highest peak in The Bahamas

- Fernandez Bay, with a divine beach, great snorkeling, and a splendid resort

- Island culture that still revolves around African ritual magic, bush medicine, straw-plaiting, and slash-and-burn agriculture

- The Cat Island Regatta, a time for sailboat races and rum-induced fun in the sun

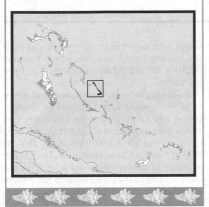

CAT ISLAND

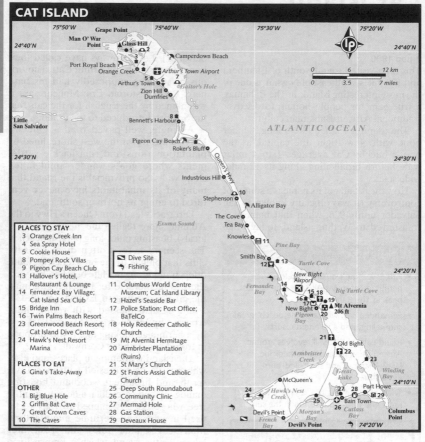

PLACES TO STAY
3   Orange Creek Inn
4   Sea Spray Hotel
5   Cookie House
8   Pompey Rock Villas
9   Pigeon Cay Beach Club
13 Hallover's Hotel,
      Restaurant & Lounge
14 Fernandez Bay Village;
      Cat Island Sea Club
15 Bridge Inn
16 Twin Palms Beach Resort
23 Greenwood Beach Resort;
      Cat Island Dive Centre
24 Hawk's Nest Resort
      Marina

PLACES TO EAT
6   Gina's Take-Away

OTHER
1   Big Blue Hole
2   Griffin Bat Cave
7   Great Crown Caves
10 The Caves

11 Columbus World Centre
      Museum; Cat Island Library
12 Hazel's Seaside Bar
17 Police Station; Post Office;
      BaTelCo
18 Holy Redeemer Catholic
      Church
19 Mt Alvernia Hermitage
20 Armbrister Plantation
      (Ruins)
21 St Mary's Church
22 St Francis Assisi Catholic
      Church
25 Deep South Roundabout
26 Community Clinic
27 Mermaid Hole
28 Gas Station
29 Deveaux House

⌐ Dive Site
↰ Fishing

bats' in the belief that if one lands on you, you'll come into some dough.

The islanders' simple limestone homes are old and foursquare, with steep shingled roofs. Many are dilapidated and seemingly ready to tumble in the next heavy wind. (Many did so when Hurricane Floyd struck in September 1999, ruining the water table when storm water surged inland. Floyd also tore off the roofs of two medical centers and swept away three miles of coastal road that remained passable but unrepaired at press time.) Other homes are gaily painted in faded pastels. Many homes retain tradi-

tional African ovens in their yards, still used for baking bread and teacakes. Another oddity is the old public outhouses built over the shore.

Following the American Revolution, many Loyalists brought their slaves and established cotton and cattle estates. In its heyday Cat Island had more than 40 plantations. There were several slave revolts, notably that of 1831 at Golden Grove plantation. In 1834 the abolition of slavery rang a death knell for the estates. Most of the estate-owners left; others stayed and loaned their names to new emancipation settlements.

Pineapple and sisal farming evolved in the mid-19th century. The island was second only to Eleuthera for pineapples (in 1801, 84 million pineapples were shipped). The ports were full of ships bound for Europe and North America, and the population reached 5000. A railway was even built in the 1880s to transport the produce to port (most of the rails were torn up during WWII).

Materially, since emancipation things haven't changed much for a large percentage of the population, which depends on the slight income derived from selling tomatoes, onions, and succulent pineapples at the produce market, and on small stipends from the National Insurance Board. Small-scale farming is still more important than fishing. Locals plant in potholes in the limestone base, where nutritious soils gather, aided by guano (bat excrement) gathered from caves for fertilizer. Unemployment is rife and many folks pass their day lying in shady doorways, counting the hours. The islanders are proud and at peace in their poverty.

Cat Islanders are anchored by tradition and have not yet been exposed to swarms of tourists or to TV. Straw-work is still a strong custom; you're sure to pass islanders sitting on the side of the road with bales of silvertip palm, casually waiting for a ride. Bush medicine and obeah – the practice of African-based witchcraft – also are stronger here than anywhere else in The Bahamas. Some of the islanders are said to be skilled witches who always are happy to prescribe a homemade cure from Cat Island's own larder. You won't see dolls pricked by pins, however. Obeah uses bottles as its chief prop. Those trees with bottles dangling from them are not bearing strange tropical fruit – the bottles are spells to protect against thieves. So don't go picking fruit! Also stay clear of graveyards, which are littered with bottles meant to indulge the spirits of the dead, who like a tipple and otherwise would come bothering the living for rum. Many houses, especially those north of New Bight, are topped by spindles (like lightning rods) meant to ward off evil spirits. (See the Boxed text 'Obeah' later in this chapter.)

Cat Island boasts more than 12 miles of wall diving along its south coast as well as exceptional dive sites on all quarters. Most sites are virtually unexplored. The island also has excellent hiking along old logging and plantation trails. The Fernandez Bay Village resort (see the New Bight section later in this chapter) can provide maps and a guide, if needed.

Experienced anglers proclaim the fishing off Cat Island to be as good as anywhere in The Bahamas, especially for white marlin and wahoo. Yet sport fishing has hardly been developed. The main grounds are the waters along the island's 'sole', off Devil's Point and east to Columbus Point. Here currents create rip tides that trap schools of baitfish. The edge of Tartar Bank, to the southwest, is a hotspot for wahoo and yellowfin tuna.

South Cat Island

NEW BIGHT

Three-quarters of the way down Cat Island, New Bight is the usual gateway for travelers. It sprawls along several miles of the Queen's Hwy.

New Bight originated as a free-slave settlement named Freetown. Its original inhabitants had been aboard British slave ships from Africa when the abolition of the trade was announced. They were put ashore on Cat Island. Much of the land hereabouts has belonged to the Armbrister family since 1780. In the 1950s Frances Armbrister and her son, Tony, returned to the ancestral property and built a serene retreat from stone recycled from the plantation. Today their home, Fernandez Bay Village, is a hotel and the acknowledged center of affairs.

There are several beautiful casuarina-lined beaches, including Fernandez Bay.

New Bight extends 4 miles north to the tiny settlement of Smith Bay, where there's a hut made entirely of conch shells just north of town, and a bat cave amid the bush behind Hazel's Seaside Bar. A goat track leads east from Smith Bay to Pine Bay, a good surfing beach.

Obeah

Obeah is the practice of interacting with the spirit world. Its equivalents are Haitian Voodoo and Cuban Santería, although it differs from both. Obeah is part folklore, part superstition, and part magic ritual, and it is deeply imbedded in the national psyche.

Obeah (the word is Ashanti, from West Africa) was once prevalent throughout the English-speaking Caribbean islands, and the 'obeah man' inspired respect and fear among fellow villagers. He was hired to work magic, much as a modern doctor (or lawyer!) is sought out today. Obeah was prohibited and severely suppressed by colonial authorities.

Father Jerome, Cat Island's saintly hero (see the boxed text on him earlier in this chapter), fought a constant battle to eradicate obeah. Once, for example, upon hearing that a woman lay dying because she had eaten vegetables from a garden into which an enemy had tossed a cursed rotten banana, Jerome came down from his monastery and ate a sample of every vegetable growing there. Then, to the gasps of the crowd, he ate the rotten banana, too!

The practice of obeah has diminished somewhat, and few Bahamians speak openly of it. But obeah still coexists alongside Christianity. There are no formal gatherings or group worship, and the practice has no formal priests. On Cat Island in particular, Bahamians (regardless of their Christian faith) still consult practitioners. Some practitioners operate as 'balmists,' using magic for medicinal purposes, to enact revenge, to influence impending court cases, or to ensure a successful romance on behalf of a supplicant. Firm believers sometimes heal, fall sick, or even die due to their faith in the power of obeah.

'Fixing' is the deploying of a spell to protect property; it also means casting a spell or preventing a casting on or by other people. Fixers advertise in the yellow pages under the heading 'Spiritual Healers' or 'Psychic Readers.' Many fixers ascribe their powers to God and place their 'fix' through directions derived from the Bible. For example, an alcoholic can be cured by giving a fixer money; the fixer then reads psalms, places the money in the Bible between the pages of the psalms, and shuts the Bible, thus taking away the spirit of drunkenness.

On Cat Island the center of obeah is The Bight; Mrs Armbrister – 'Missus A' – at Fernandez Bay Village delights in telling tales of the island's witchcraft. On New Providence it's the working-class area of Fox Hill, once home to Zaccharias Adderley, 'king' of obeah in Nassau.

Obeah is still legally banned, mostly due to pressure from the Baptist church. In recent years obeah has been given a new lease on life by a flood of Haitian immigrants.

Those with an adventurous spirit can hike east to Turtle Cove, a splendid cove on the Atlantic shore where marine turtles graze in the shallow waters. It's a harpy to get there along a tenuous dirt road.

Information

There are no banks on Cat Island. The post office and BaTelCo (☎ 242-342-3060) are in the government administrative complex on Queen's Hwy. The island's main medical clinic (☎ 242-342-3026) is in Smith Bay. The police station (☎ 242-354-5039) is also in the government administrative complex.

Holy Redeemer Catholic Church

The main attraction in town gleams white beside the main road and looks like it belongs on Mediterranean shores. The church was built by Father Jerome, who also blessed Cat Island with its most famous landmark, the Mt Alvernia Hermitage.

Mt Alvernia Hermitage

Scrub-covered Como Hill, formally called Mt Alvernia, the name bestowed by Father Jerome on this incomparably peaceful spot, rises immediately southeast of New Bight. Here the hermit built himself a simple blanched-stone structure in exquisite medieval style. It is reached by a rock staircase hewn into the side of the hill. Not forgetting his purpose, Father Jerome added simple stone stations of the cross that you pass as you climb. From the top, you can marvel at the spiritually reviving 360° view. Try to make it at sunrise or sunset.

The hermitage, which has a bell tower with a pointed fool's-cap roof, looks like something Merlin might have conjured up in the days of King Arthur. You can enter the small chapel, tiny cloister, and a guest cell the size of a large kennel. The only furniture is a writing desk, a stool, and a single cot for guests (Jerome slept on a straw mat on the cloister floor), perfectly befitting its ascetic function. The brass sundial in the grounds to the rear still gleams and hummingbirds flit about amid the engulfing foliage.

The rough track to the hermitage begins immediately south of the government administrative complex on Queen's Hwy, north of the ruins of the old **Armbrister Plantation**. You also can take a parallel track, 50 yards south, that squeezes through the plantation estate house's archway. (Also see 'Father Jerome' later in this chapter.)

Activities

There are several superb dive and snorkel sites locally. Dry Head, in shallow water close to shore, has prolific marine life.

Fernandez Bay Village has snorkel gear, free for guests' use. Guided snorkeling trips cost US$25. It also rents canoes.

Favored bonefishing spots include the flats of Joe's Sound Creek, a 20-minute boat ride south of Fernandez Bay, and Pigeon Creek, a 20-minute ride to the north. Captain Mark Kaeslar charges US$175/240 half/full day for bonefishing. Sport fishing costs US$250/350. You can ask for him in Fernandez Bay Village.

Fernandez Bay Village offers guided trips to the bat caves and blue holes.

Special Events

The biggest happening of the year is the Cat Island Regatta on Emancipation Day (the first Monday in August), when scores of Cat Islanders return from afar, and the population quadruples. The highlight of this homecoming is the sailboat races. There are domino tournies, fashion shows, and sometimes a beauty contest, and plenty of deafening music while rake 'n' scrape bands scratch out narcotic tunes.

In 1999, the four-day Annual Rake 'n' Scrape Music Festival was initiated, held each June and bringing together many of the islands' best traditional musicians. It is organized by Pamela Poitier, daughter of homegrown hero, Sydney Poitier. For information call the George Town, Exumas, BTO office (☎ 242-336-2430) or the Bahamas Out Islands Promotion Board (in the US ☎ 305-931-6612, 800-688-4752, fax 305-931-6867, info@bahama-out-islands.com).

Places to Stay

Hallover's Hotel, Restaurant & Lounge (☎ 242-342-2028), about 2 miles north of New Bight Airport, has three modern rooms and a suite, plus a restaurant and bar.

The Russells run the simple, motel-style *Bridge Inn* (☎ 242-342-3013, fax 242-342-3041; in the US ☎ 800-688-4752), 200 yards from the western shore, from which it is separated by a mangrove estuary. It has four single rooms, four double rooms, and four triple rooms. All are handsomely and modestly furnished, with air-con, bare native-stone walls and lofty wooden ceilings. Each has a private bathroom, porch, TV, potted plants, and ceiling fan. There's a swimming pool, hot tub, and an airy restaurant and bar that doubles as a nightclub. Rooms cost US$100/110 single/double, including airport transfers.

Nearby, on the shore, is the *Twin Palms Beach Resort* (☎ 242-342-3108, fax 242-342-3108), with four units, each with two bedrooms, tile floors, and full kitchen for US$200/night.

Worth a trip in its own right is *Fernandez Bay Village* (☎ 242-342-3043, fax 242-342-3051, catisland@fernandezbayvillage.com; in North America ☎ 954-474-4821, 800-940-1905, fax 954-474-4864), on a scimitar of sand just north of New Bight Airport (around one arm of the bay lies an even more private beach, Skinny Dip; two knotty islets rise off-shore – perfect for snorkeling over the reefs). Tony and Pam Armbrister pamper you as if you were family down for the week, helping garner a loyal repeat clientele. Hurricane Floyd blasted the property. A fabulous remake has enhanced it with terra-cotta tile floors and tasteful contemporary decor. The six one-bedroom cottages and six two-bedroom villas with fully equipped kitchens are of simple stone and timber, with plate-glass doors opening onto patios, and open-air 'garden baths' surrounded by stone walls so you can shower or linger on the pot while ad-miring the stars. Some rooms have four-poster beds. None have air-con, but you don't need it, as ceiling fans and cross-ventilation do the job. Guests and hosts mingle together at the thatched bar and in the cozy lounge-cum-library and breeze-swept dining room overlooking the beach.

It offers free use of sailboats and canoes, plus diving and snorkeling; bicy-cles can be rented for US$7 daily. Rates are US$160 to US$170 single or double in summer and US$180 to US$190 in winter for cottages, and US$235 to US$250 in summer and US$270 to US$285 in winter for villas, including two meals daily, plus 15% service charge. The hotel offers air charters. The local mailing address is New Bight, Cat Island, Bahamas; in North America write 1507 S University Dr, suite A, Plantation, FL 33324, USA. The Web site is www.fernandezbayvillage.com.

Places to Eat

The restaurant at the *Bridge Inn* specializes in island-style seafood and Yankee fare such as burgers for US$5 and chicken and fries. It serves breakfast, lunch, and dinner, and has a Friday-night fish fry for US$8.

The *Blue Bird Restaurant & Bar* (☎ 242-342-3095), on Queen's Hwy near the gov-ernment complex, serves local fare, with entrees from US$7.

Fernandez Bay Village (☎ 242-342-3043) has a nightly torch-lit buffet dinner served in the handsome stone-and-timber main house. Dinner, for US$32, is by reservation. It's open 8 am to 9:30 pm.

You can buy groceries and other supplies at *New Bight Food Store* (☎ 242-342-3011) or several other convenience stores. *McKin-ney's Bakery* has fresh bread daily.

Entertainment

The *Blue Bird Restaurant & Bar* (☎ 242-342-3095) is a good place to play pool with locals and catch up on 'sip-sip,' or gossip. So, too, are the *First & Last Chance Bar*, nearby on Queen's Hwy, known for its lively games of dominoes, and *Hazel's Seaside Bar*, hosted by octogenarian Hazel Brown, in Smith Bay.

The modern *Hallover's Hotel, Restau-rant & Lounge* has a pleasant bar with TV and pool table. The *Bridge Inn* has dancing on Saturday night, plus a pool table and a jukebox with an A-list of favorite tunes, from Nat King Cole and the Isley Brothers to Conway Twitty and Kenny Rogers; some nights, a local rake 'n' scrape band some-times plays.

Fernandez Bay Village sometimes hosts music, poetry, and storytelling.

Shopping

Iva Thompson makes baskets and mats at her small store next to the First & Last Chance Bar.

If island holidaying puts you in a roman-tic mood, check out Gina's array of Victo-ria's Secret lingerie at her store opposite the Bridge Inn.

Getting There & Away

Air New Bight Airport is 2 miles north of town.

Air Sunshine (in New Bight ☎ 242-342-3117) flies from Fort Lauderdale for about US$235/350 one-way/roundtrip, for up to six people.

Cat Island Air (in New Bight ☎ 242-342-3318) offers direct prop-jet flights between Fort Lauderdale and New Bight three times weekly (US$350 roundtrip).

Bahamasair (in New Bight ☎ 242-342-2017) flies Monday and Friday from Nassau (US$60 one-way). Don't try to call before the day of your flight, as the office is staffed only on flight days.

Sandpiper Air (☎ 242-377-5751) and Lynx Air (☎ 242-345-0108) offer charters to Cat Island; the latter links New Bight with George Town, Exuma.

New Bight is the only port of entry for private pilots. The customs and immigration office (☎ 242-342-2106) is here; private pilots can clear customs here before flying on to Arthur's Town Airport or the Hawk's Nest Airstrip.

Boat The *North Cat Island Special* mail boat departs Nassau at 1 pm Wednesday for New Bight, Bennett's Harbour, and Arthur's Town (14 hours, US$40 one-way). The *Sea Hauler* leaves Nassau at 3 pm Tuesday (17 hours, US$40 one-way), also calling at Old Bight and Smith Bay. This converted tug has 10 bunks in a small cabin that resembles a sauna (I'm speaking *heat*, not pinewood decor).

There are no marina facilities. Most yachties anchor in Fernandez Bay.

Getting Around

There's no bus or taxi service from the airport. Your hotel will arrange a free airport pickup with advance notice.

Jason Russell, owner of the New Bight Shell station, rents cars for US$85 (plus gas at US$3 per gallon) for 24 hours, though rates are negotiable. You're asked to sign accepting responsibility for *all* damage that may be done to the car. His hours are 7:30 am to 6:30 pm Monday to Saturday.

Fernandez Bay Village rents small boats for US$25 per hour; larger boats with captain cost US$50 per hour.

OLD BIGHT

This slightly down-at-the-heels settlement, beginning 4 miles south of New Bight, is also called 'The Village.' It straggles along the road for several miles. Plantation ruins lie to its east, shaded by trees festooned with Spanish moss.

St Francis Assisi Catholic Church, a mossy stone legacy of Father Jerome, sits atop a little ridge beside the road. It has a Gothic facade topped by a cross and an engraving of St Francis with a flock of birds. Its interior

has frescoes and sculptures. Mrs Burrows, across the road, has the key.

Worth a visit, too, is **St Mary's Church**, fronted by an African flame tree. The church is claimed to be the only monument to emancipation in The Bahamas. It was a gift of the family of Blaney Balfour, the British governor who read the emancipation proclamation.

A track that begins at the rear of the Old Bight primary school leads you along the edge of **Great Lake**. If you keep on along the northeast shore (avoiding side paths), you'll reach an old stone wall that descends into the lake. By following the wall uphill, you'll ascend **Mt View** (150 feet), topped by the ruins of an old home. Continue east along a dirt path (which crosses a semipaved road) to reach the sea. Refreshments can be had at the Greenwood Beach Resort, 2 miles south along the sandy shore. The hike is about 5 miles one way.

Check out *Beaches Delight Restaurant & Bar*, on the beach; it's accessed by a dirt road opposite the school on Queen's Hwy.

Armbrister Creek

This creek-laced mangrove estuary, near Old Bight, is fabulous for exploring by canoe. It leads inland to a crystal clear lake called 'Boiling Hole' that bubbles and churns under certain tide conditions, fueling local fears that it is haunted by a monster. Baby sharks and rays can be seen cruising the sandy bottom. Birdlife also abounds.

You can rent canoes at Fernandez Bay Village (see Places to Stay in the New Bight section) for exploring the mangroves. They're free to its guests. A guided canoe trip from Fernandez Bay costs US$25.

Getting There & Away

The *Sea Hauler* mail boat sails here from Nassau once a week. See Getting There & Away in the New Bight section earlier in this chapter for details.

BAIN TOWN

About 13 miles south of New Bight on the Queen's Hwy, you emerge by the south shore at a traffic circle, the Deep South

Father Jerome

John Hawes – hermit and humanitarian – was born in England in 1876 to an upper-middle-class family. He practiced as a visionary, prize-winning architect before entering theological college in 1901, preparing to becoming an Anglican minister.

Once ordained, he vowed to emulate the life of St Francis of Assisi and lived briefly as a tramp. In 1908 he came to The Bahamas and traveled around the islands rebuilding churches destroyed by a hurricane, utilizing thick stone and Roman arches. Hawes offended local sensibilities, however, while preaching on Harbour Island. He asked the congregation why the whites were sitting at the front and the blacks at the back, when all men are created equal. 'The congregation nearly fainted with shock and I was rushed out of the church as quickly as possible,' Hawes recorded.

Between bouts of preaching, the eccentric Englishman did duty as a mule-driver in Canada, a fox-terrier breeder, a cow-puncher, and a sailor. In 1911 he converted to Catholicism and studied in Rome for the priesthood before moving to Australia to serve as a gold-rush bush priest. He stayed there for 24 years and built a renowned reputation until suffering a heart attack.

In 1939 Hawes returned to The Bahamas, washing ashore on Cat Island to live as a hermit. The following year, he began work on his hermitage atop Como Hill, which he renamed Mt Alvernia after the site in Tuscany where St Francis received the wounds of the cross. Meanwhile, like a good hermit, he lived in a cave amid snakes, tarantulas, and crabs, and took unto himself the name Father Jerome.

On weekdays Jerome meditated alone (he also read newspapers, painted, drew cartoons, and wrote essays with a George Bernard Shaw flavor); on weekends he worked in the village. He built four churches on Cat Island, as well as a medical clinic, convent, monastery, technical school, and other projects throughout The Bahamas, all featuring his trademark medievalist architectural motif. His buildings were made of rock quarried on-site, with nothing that could rot or rust away.

Undoubtedly, locals considered him a saintly figure. He strolled around barefoot and lavished charity on the islanders, many of whom climbed the steps to his monastery to ask for money (during this period most Cat Islanders were incredibly poor, described by Father Jerome as 'in a state verging on destitution'). None were denied, and at other times, such as during drought, the charity flowed uphill. Jerome became the conscience of the island, acting as a salve to settle disputes. Locals of all denominations attended his sermons, although apparently he converted only five people to Catholicism, as the locals resisted his strictures against 'extracurricular sex.'

He died in 1956 and was buried, per his request, barefoot and without a casket in the cave that had once been his home.

Roundabout, ringed by 570 rosy conch shells. Bain Town, 2 miles east of Deep South Roundabout, lies along the shore south of the main road. The town has a community medical clinic (☎ 242-342-5057). There's a gas station east of town halfway to Port Howe.

Bain Town has several sites of interest, including **St John the Baptist Catholic Church**, another inspired Father Jerome creation. At the turnoff for town is House Rebecca, built of local limestone and conch shells; owners Mr and Mrs Bain (☎ 242-342-5012) may invite you in to peek at the sitting room ceiling, made of 966 shells.

Lotto-Man Hole

This cave is hidden behind St John the Baptist Catholic Church. It got its name, apparently, after an Indian sailor was marooned here and chose the cave as his home. If you intend to explore beyond the entrance, take a guide.

Mermaid Hole

Many locals firmly believe that this 20-meter-wide blue hole is inhabited by a mermaid. The lake is 10 feet deep, but four holes in its bed lead down into vast underwater chambers and passageways. Your guide may tell you to be quiet as you approach through the brush, as he will want to get a glimpse of the mermaid; she is sure to flee at the sound of humans.

Places to Stay & Eat
Mr and Mrs Bain (☎ 242-342-5012) occasionally welcome guests to *House Rebecca*.

PORT HOWE AREA
A hamlet 5 miles east of Deep South Roundabout, Port Howe is the most historically important area on Cat Island. Historians believe that Columba, the first Spanish settlement in the New World, was established here in 1495 as a terminus for Lucayan Indians shipped as slaves to Hispaniola. A huge tract that spread from today's Port Howe to Old Bight was cleared for cattle ranches. Columba was later abandoned.

Around 1670 a small group of English settlers arrived from Bermuda and established themselves here, earning a living as wreckers. Then, in 1783, 60 English Loyalists arrived from Florida. Their leader, Lt John Wilson, laid out a town named Carlyle. Several important plantations evolved nearby. The harbor later became known as Port Howe, named for Admiral James Howe, a British naval commander during the American Revolution.

The ruins of several fortresses still stand, much overgrown in the years since they were erected to protect against pirates. Take time to browse the old overgrown cemetery on the west side of town.

There's a gas station west of Port Howe, where you can rent a car at Gilbert Car Rental (☎ 242-342-3011).

Deveaux House
This mansion looms foursquare – albeit in advanced dereliction – over the settlement. The two-story edifice was the center of a once-thriving 1000-acre cotton plantation owned by Colonel Andrew Deveaux, the American Loyalist who was granted land here as a reward for saving Nassau from

Spanish occupation in 1783 (see History in the Facts about The Bahamas chapter). Note the old slave quarters just alongside.

Columbus Point
The southeasternmost point of Cat Island, Columbus Point lies 2 miles southeast of Port Howe at the south end of Churney Bay. Cat Islanders cling to the belief – effectively debunked by recent evidence – that Columbus anchored here on October 12, 1492.

The shoreline has old coral heads embedded with brain coral. There's a cave said to be worth exploring (it was once inhabited by Lucayan Indians, who left artifacts for posterity) and a tidal geyser in Churney Bay.

There's no road access. You can hike from Port Howe along a dirt track (you may be able to make it at least part of the way in a 4WD vehicle) that leads east via

the ruins of another old Loyalist settlement, Bailey Town. Here, follow the track that begins to the right of the House of Zion Church (keep right at the Y-fork, and after 2 miles, follow the old plantation farm walls to Churney Bay). You also can continue on the main (but potholed) road via Baily Town to Winding Bay and then walk south to Columbus Point.

Activities

The diving off the south shore is superb along a 12-mile front. The wall begins at 50 feet and drops to 6000 feet, and there are caves and coral canyons to explore. Cat Island's prime dive site is **Tartar Bank**. A 5-mile boat ride southwest of Port Howe, it's a columnlike plateau covered by coral, sponges, and sea fans. The plateau slopes to a drop-off beginning at 80 feet. Winding Bay offers fabulous gorgonians and black coral.

The Cat Island Dive Centre, at Greenwood Beach Resort (see below), is the island's most complete full-service dive shop. It offers tank fills and maintains two boats in Port Howe. Dives cost US$40/65 one/two-tank; an open-water certificate costs US$370. It offers PADI certification and resort courses and has day and night dives. Snorkeling costs US$20, including equipment.

There's good bonefishing in the bay off Port Howe. Charles Zonicle (☎ 242-342-5005) offers fishing from Port Howe. The

Greenwood Beach Resort charges US$140 to US$200 for bonefishing; sport fishing aboard a 25-foot Bimini top boat costs US$460.

Places to Stay

The lonesome *Greenwood Beach Resort & Dive Centre* (☎/fax 242-342-3053; in the USA ☎ 877-228-7475, gbr@grouper.batelnet .bs), 5 miles north of Port Howe, is a delightful resort run by a friendly German family. It edges up to an 8-mile-long pink-sand beach running south to Winding Bay. It's favored by divers. The 20 simply furnished and recently refurbished rooms are in whitewashed cottages with pastel trim. They feature king-size beds, small patios, ceiling fans, and spacious bathrooms. Facilities include an exquisitely decorated TV lounge-cum-dining-room and bar, a swimming pool and whirlpool, and a full-service dive shop. Bicycles can be rented. Rates are US$70/90 single/double in summer, US$79/99 in winter, including airport transfers from Arthur's Town or New Bight. The resort also has air charters to New Bight Airport. A 15% service charge is added. A MAP plan (breakfast and dinner) costs US$40. The postal address is Port Howe, Cat Island, The Bahamas. Visit the resort's Web site at www.greenwoodbeachresort.com.

Places to Eat

The *Greenwood Beach Resort* offers European dishes and local fare, plus specialty buffet dinners on the outside terrace or in the modest dining room. Lunch costs US$5 to US$10.

Otherwise, pickings are slim. Try the *Rockum Palace Bar* in Port Howe.

MORGAN'S BAY TO HAWK'S NEST CREEK

A badly potholed road leads west (to the right) from the Deep South Roundabout, heading along the shore of Morgan's Bay to Devil's Point. Five miles southwest of Deep South Roundabout, needle-sharp Devil's Point is the southernmost tip of Cat Island. There's a hard-pressed fishing village – also named Devil's Point – nearby, at the end of the road. The scant remains of an octagonal fortress atop the bluff are now foundations for a navigation light.

Just before Devil's Point, an unmarked side road leads north to **McQueen's**. The lonesome settlement, 4 miles north of Devil's Point, faces Exuma Sound. It was founded in the 18th century by a Scottish Loyalist, Alexander McQueen, and has several paltry yet intriguing old buildings adorned with ornate chimneys.

From McQueen's, a dirt road runs southwest along the shore of Exuma Sound to Hawk's Nest Resort Marina (see Places to Stay & Eat, below), at the toe of the island. Hawk's Nest is a 15-mile drive from Deep South Roundabout.

Activities
The flats and tidal creeks that meander inland for several miles from Hawk's Nest Creek are 'bonefish city!' Other good sites include the bight east of Hawk's Nest and the lagoon at the entrance to Hawk's Nest Creek.

A 26-foot Dusky can be rented from Hawk's Nest Resort Marina (see below) for US$75 hourly or US$350 daily, with captain. At Devil's Point, Nathaniel Gilbert (☎ 242-342-7003) rents a 14-foot Whaler.

The reefs offshore from Hawk's Nest are splendid for diving and snorkeling. And Devil's Point is noteworthy for large formations of elkhorn and staghorn, tube sponges, and brain coral. Snorkeling is said to be especially good in Morgan's Bay. Hawk's Nest Resort Marina offers diving (US$65/75 one/two-tank) and snorkeling.

Places to Stay & Eat
Hawk's Nest Resort Marina (☎ 242-342-7050, 800-688-4752, fax 242-342-7051, info@hawks-nest.com, Unicom VHF 122.8 channel 16), at the western toe of Cat Island, has 10 clean air-con rooms, all ocean-view with a king-size bed or two queen-size beds, plus a ceiling fan and a patio. It also has two-bedroom houses with full kitchen and housekeeping service. There's a bar and restaurant, plus a beach-volleyball court. Fishing, diving, and snorkeling are offered, and bicycles,

mopeds, and golf carts can be rented. Rooms cost US$100/124 single/double, including breakfast and dinner. Houses cost US$275 single or double and US$315 three or four people. A full meal plan costs US$50 daily. Lunches cost US$10 to US$15.

Getting There & Away
Hawk's Nest has a 4600-foot hard-surface airstrip with tie-downs, plus its own plane for charters.

It also has a protected, deep-water, eight-slip marina with full services. It charges US$1 per foot daily.

If you're coming from abroad, you must clear customs and immigration in New Bight (see Getting There & Away in the New Bight section).

North Cat Island

KNOWLES TO INDUSTRIOUS HILL
North of New Bight, Queen's Hwy hugs the west shore. Little boats lie upturned beneath spread-fingered palms, and tumbledown slave-era homes dot the shore.

Knowles, 8 miles north of New Bight, is the first of a half-dozen small settlements. It boasts the tiny **Columbus World Centre Museum**, which tells the history of the island; and the **Cat Island Library & Resource Centre** (☎ 242-342-6031), where locals have use of computers with Internet hook-up.

Mary Saymore (☎ 242-342-6008) rents a one-bedroom cottage, *Old Dad*, in Knowles, at the north end of Smith Bay.

For conch, check out *Bachelor's Restaurant* (☎ 242-342-6014) in Knowles.

Farther north, the scenery is splendid as you pass through **Tea Bay** and **The Cove**. Endemic freshwater turtles inhabit the inland lakes and ponds.

At Stephenson, a dirt road leads east to a splendid beach at **Alligator Bay**, on the Atlantic.

The Caves, a multi-chambered system just south of the settlement of Industrious Hill and 12 miles north of New Bight, have traditionally been used as a hurricane shelter. They're framed by dramatic fig trees beside the road. Goats prefer the shady entrance and will flee into the dark recesses at your approach. At least one person has disappeared while exploring. You'll need a guide (ask around locally) and a strong flashlight.

ROKER'S BLUFF

This small settlement (also called 'Zanicle,' or The Bluff), 20 miles north of New Bight, was one of the largest settlements in the mid-19th century. It was founded by Scottish settlers, and many of the locals still have Scottish surnames: McKenzie, McDonald, Hepburn.

A dirt road leads northwest 1 mile to beautiful **Pigeon Cay Beach**.

Places to Stay & Eat

The relaxing, American-run *Pigeon Cay Beach Club* (☎ 242-354-5084, pigeoncay@ aol.com), between Roker's Bluff and Bennett's Harbour, straddles a bluff overlooking an exquisite beach. It has seven airy one- to three-bedroom cottages – some octagonal – atop a raised limestone patio with shade umbrellas. Each cross-ventilated unit is distinct, but all have terra-cotta tile and hardwood floors, beam ceilings, ceiling fans, and endearing decor, including twee bathrooms with Mexican ceramic sinks and tiles. Two units are studios; three are one-bedroom units with kitchenettes; two are two-bedroom units with full kitchens. There's a thatched beach bar with grill, and local women will cook meals on request. You can rent boats for fishing, snorkeling, and kayaking; there's a three-hole chipping course; and bikes are available, as is a canoe on Alligator Creek…good for bonefishing. Rates range from US$125 to US$320.

For native fare, locals recommend *Triple X Bar & Restaurant*, just south of Roker's Bluff, and *Tito's Seafood*, about 1 mile north of Pigeon Cay Beach Club.

The *Island Shopping Centre*, about 1 mile south of Pigeon Cay Beach Club, sells groceries and produce.

BENNETT'S HARBOUR

North of Roker's Bluff, the highway climbs Thurston Hill, on whose north slope the settlement of Bennett's Harbour sprawls beneath blazing-bright flame trees that flow down to a picturesque harborfront. The sheltered cove was once favored by pirates waiting to pounce on passing treasure-laden ships. The settlement was founded in the 1830s for slaves freed from captured slavetraders, and it later became a port for the salt trade (you still can see the old salt ponds in the lake to the east).

Little San Salvador, a small, uninhabited island 15 miles west of Bennett's Harbour, has a lagoon good for bonefishing, and there are virtually tame iguanas and plenty of seabirds.

Places to Stay & Eat

At Bennett's Harbour, *Pompey Rock Villas* (☎ 242-354-5222) was under construction at press time. It will have six 12-sided units overlooking the shore, plus a restaurant and a marina.

Cat Island Cottages (in the US ☎ 813-915-1045, fax 813-289-014, BahamasDoc@ aol.com) comprises a one-bedroom cottage, a two-bedroom cottage with wood-burning fireplace (both from US$800 weekly), and a two- and a four-bedroom home (from US$900 and US$1800, respectively). Each is built of coral limestone and has ceiling fans, portable fans, TV/VCR, and CD sound system. A van can be rented and boats are available. Each additional person costs US$100. Nearby, Ginny and Richie Henn (in the US ☎ 516-785-7326, fax 516-221-4695, bahamacat@aol.com) rent a beautiful two-bedroom stone house beside the secluded beach. Each bedroom has king-size beds. There's a TV/VCR with movie library, a patio with barbecue, plus a motorized inflatable raft. It rents for US$900 weekly. A vehicle rents for US$100. The Web site is www .10kvacationrentals.com/catislandcottages/ index.htm.

Peas 'n' rice and conch are served at the *Beverage Restaurant & Disco*, which comes alive on weekends. You can buy foodstuffs at *Len's Grocery*.

Getting There & Away
The *North Cat Island Special* mail boat sails here from Nassau; see Getting There & Away in the New Bight section for details.

Amazing Grace, the supply ship for Windjammer Barefoot Cruises' sailing fleet, calls on Little San Salvador during its island-hopping voyages, offered twice monthly between Grand Bahama and Trinidad. See the Boat section of the Getting There & Away chapter for details and contact information.

DUMFRIES
Named for the hometown of Loyalist settlers who emigrated from Scotland to Virginia to Cat Island, Dumfries lies on the inner shore of a saline lake separated from the sea by the Gossip Bar. A mile-long track that begins just north of the bar leads to **Great Crown Caves**, a vast cave system hidden amid the mangroves. Finding them ain't easy: An old-timer named Ishmael Gaitor will guide you (to find him, try the Turning Point Club).

At Zion Hill, 1 mile north of Dumfries, ruins of a Loyalist mansion can be seen, surrounded by stately silk cotton trees.

You can buy straw hats from Minerva Thompson (☎ 242-354-5077), who makes them.

Gaitor's Hole
This blue hole is reached by a rough mile-long track running east from Dumfries. It is often a deep purple color, due to a dense bacterial population that thrives on a thick hydrogen-sulfide layer.

Ishmael Gaitor loves to regale visitors with the tale – he sounds sincere – of a young island girl who disappeared years ago while visiting the hole to do laundry. Several months later she reappeared…very pregnant! It seems she had encountered a merman (the male equivalent of a mermaid). He had seduced her and she had lived blissfully with her aquatic lover in his home beneath the waters until homesickness drew her away. Her family was less broadminded than she, and her father and brother stormed off to the lake, armed with shotguns. They trapped the distraught merman and shot him

dead. Some weeks later the girl gave birth to a baby merman, with a tail just like a fish's. Mr Gaitor, alas, has no idea what happened to the creature.

Places to Eat
You might catch Mr Gaitor telling his merman stories in the **Turning Point Club**, where a sign advises 'Eat Before Drinking!' Try the mutton souse. Another option is the **Gossip Bar & Restaurant**.

ARTHUR'S TOWN
The island's second-largest settlement, 30 miles north of New Bight, is centered on grassy Symonette Square, lorded over by prim St Andrews Anglican Church, dating from the early 1870s but badly battered by Hurricane Floyd. There are several other historic buildings.

The hamlet's main claim to fame is that it was the boyhood home of Sidney Poitier, the Academy Award–winning actor. You can read about his childhood in his autobiography, *This Life*, but there is no museum and his childhood home is now derelict.

The road to the airport, just north of the hamlet, continues east to Camperdown Beach on the Atlantic shore.

There's a medical clinic (☎ 242-354-4050). For the police, call ☎ 242-354-2046.

Arthur's Town hosts a heritage festival during the first weekend in May.

Places to Stay & Eat
Pat and Dell Rolle rent six basic efficiency units at **Cookie House** (☎ /fax 242-354-2027), 50 yards north of Symonette Square. Each small unit has all-around sliding glass doors, but comes meagerly furnished with sofabed, toilet, and shower in the same room. It's overpriced at US$70 single or double (the seventh day is free).

Nellie Rolle rents three *apartments* (☎ 242-354-2031). Also try **Dean's Inn** (☎ 242-354-2121), with 10 apartments.

Cookie House also sells fresh-baked breads and pineapple and coconut tarts, plus burgers, fish and chips, and other snack lunches costing about US$6, as well as lobster, conch, and grouper dinners for US$15.

Native dishes also are served at *Hard Rock Café*, named for the rocky outcrop on which it rests. *Gina's Take-Away*, a tiny US-style roadside diner near the square, serves hot dogs and burgers.

You can buy groceries and produce from *Jabon Convenience Store* or *Campbell's Big Bull* food store.

Entertainment

The *Boggy Pond Bar* has a pool table, as does *Lover's Boulevard Satellite Lounge*, with TV and disco on weekends.

Getting There & Away

Arthur's Town has a small airport. Bahamas-air (☎ 242-354-2049) flies here from Nassau on Sunday, Tuesday, and Thursday (US$60 each way). Don't try to call before the day of your flight, as the office is staffed only on flight days.

The *North Cat Island Special* mail boat calls from Nassau; see the New Bight section of this chapter for information.

ORANGE CREEK

Near the north end of the island, 3 miles northwest of Arthur's Town, Orange Creek stretches along Queen's Hwy for 2 miles. There's an old and a new section.

Activities

There's good bonefishing in the mouth of Orange Creek, where it spills onto a beach. Farther inland it is scum-covered and smells like something the cat fetched up. Willard and Lincoln Cleare (☎ 242-354-4052) can take you bonefishing.

The turquoise waters offshore are superb for snorkeling, with beautiful fan-coral formations.

From the head of Orange Creek, a trail leads west half a mile to Port Royal Beach. Another leads north past Oyster Lake (good for spotting ducks and cormorants) to Sea Cave and Man O' War Point; take the left-hand trail at the Y-fork just south of the lake. The right-hand trail leads to a beach

(good for snorkeling) east of Man O' War Point.

A third track leads east from the head of Orange Creek to Glass Hill (162 feet), where you'll have beautiful views.

From Queen's Hwy between Sea Spray Hotel and Orange Creek Inn, Dickie's Rd runs east to **Griffin Bat Cave**. Once a home to slaves who built walls and windows into the entrance, the cave is now occupied by leaf-nosed bats. Take a flashlight. The track also leads to a series of blue holes. You can loop north to **Big Blue Hole** and Glass Hill or continue east to the Atlantic shore and then head south 2 miles to Camperdown Beach.

Willard Cleare (see above) acts as a guide.

Places to Stay & Eat

The *Sea Spray Hotel* (☎ *242-354-4116, fax 242-354-4161*) was devastated by Hurricane Floyd in 1999, which destroyed 13 of the 15 rooms. The property was open and rebuilding at press time; the remaining rooms and one suite each have air-con, cable TV, fans, and sliding glass doors opening onto a waterfront patio inset with a tiny man-made beach with hammock. There's an elegant restaurant and bar. Rooms cost US$65 single or double; a small suite costs US$75. The hotel accepts Visa but not MasterCard.

The modern *Orange Creek Inn* (☎ *242-354-4110*) sits above the creek and has 16 spacious, well-lit but modestly furnished efficiency rooms with ceiling fans and kitchenettes; some have air-con. There's a TV lounge and a laundry, plus a grocery store, but no restaurant or bar. Rooms cost US$65, or US$75 with air-con.

Getting Around

The Sea Spray Hotel rents cars for US$65 and bicycles for US$7 per day. The Orange Creek Inn also rents cars. There's a gas station in town.

Lincoln Cleare (☎ 242-354-4052) will take you sightseeing.

San Salvador, Rum Cay & Conception Island

Tiny San Salvador, 200 miles southeast of Nassau, is the nation's outermost island. The name, meaning 'holy savior,' was bestowed by Christopher Columbus on the first land he sighted in 1492. The island had been known as Guanahaní to the Lucayan Indians. There is little evidence to support the persistent claim that the explorer landed here, but the belief has become so entrenched that it's accepted as religiously as was the belief Columbus set out to disprove: that the earth was flat. The island was named Watling Island until 1926, when the name was changed to honor the Columbus claim.

Recent discoveries of Spanish artifacts are said to support the landfall claim. It was nonetheless effectively debunked by a study published in *National Geographic* in 1986 that convincingly concluded that Columbus first landed at Samana Cay, 65 miles to the southeast. (However, in 1989 English around-the-world yachtsman Robin Knox-Johnson retraced Columbus' route using 15th-century instruments and ended up at…San Salvador!)

San Salvadoreans are partisan on the issue and couldn't give a damn for the Samana Cay theory. See further details of the controversy in the 'First Landfall' boxed text in the Facts about the Bahamas chapter.

Rum Cay, a small isle with beautiful beaches, lies 25 miles to San Salvador's southwest. Uninhabited Conception Island is a protected park northwest of Rum Cay.

Highlights

- Gazing over the panoramic view from Dixon Lighthouse
- Diving The Wall…or casting a line for prize-size wahoo at The Hump
- Skinny-dipping at Snow Bay
- Letting it rip at the Friday night 'rip' at the Harlem Square Club

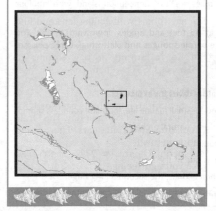

San Salvador

- **pop 1200**

In the 17th century a British pirate, George Watling, claimed the island for himself and loaned his name to it. In the 18th and 19th centuries Watling Island's history was similar to that of neighboring islands. A fistful of settlers established ill-fated cotton plantations (one of the slave-owners, Henry Storr, was himself black) that faded into obscurity. The remote island wallowed in neglected torpor until the 1930s, when Nassau entrepreneur Sir Harry Oakes built a short-lived hotel. In WWII the hotel was leased to the Royal Navy as a submarine reconnaissance base (it was later turned into a teacher training facility; Club Med Columbus Isle now occupies the site). Later the US government set up a missile-tracking station, which was disbanded in the mid-1970s and turned into a biological research station.

The island economy limped along until 1975, when a retired treasure salvager, Bill McGehee, discovered the most beautiful drop-offs he'd seen in his 20 years of Caribbean diving. He began a dive operation. In addition to superb wall diving there are about a dozen shipwrecks, including the *Frascate*, less than a mile off Riding Rock Point. The canyons and reefs to the southwest are especially awesome. For details on the area's best diving and snorkeling, see the 'Dive & Snorkel Sites' boxed text.

In 1992 Club Med opened its exclusive resort, which has finally put 'San Sal,' as the island is known, on the map.

San Sal is the tip of a mountain peak that rises 13,000 feet from the ocean floor. Small – 12 miles long by 6 miles wide – and undistinguished, it is nonetheless ringed by

superb reefs. Its 41-mile circumference also is ringed by 30 miles of beaches. Inland it's waterlogged, with acres of mangroves and briny lakes. The two major settlements are Cockburn Town and United Estates. Queen's Hwy girds the island. It's a 90-minute drive, or a four- or five-hour bicycle ride. In recent decades part of the population has drifted to Nassau, and settlements along the windward shore have been abandoned. The island was whammied by Hurricane Floyd in September 1999.

San Sal offers excellent bird watching. Ospreys (locally called 'chicken hawks') are everywhere. The cays off the north shore are

Dive & Snorkel Sites

Dive Sites

San Sal is one of the best wall-dive destinations in the world. There are more than 40 dive sites within 30 minutes of shore, and more near Rum Cay and Conception Island. The island's waters are known for visibility to 200 feet; on special days it can exceed a miraculous 250 feet! There are more than 20 miles of vertical walls, which begin as little as 40 feet below the surface.

The best sites include the following:

Basket Case – This site is named for the massive basket sponges along a vertical wall beginning at about 30 feet. There's also a deep grotto.

Frascate – This 261-foot-long ship (which sank in 1902) lies just 20 feet down. It's great for novice divers, and there's superb visibility.

Rum Cay Wall – The wall drops from 40 feet to eternity. Nearby are the partial remains of the HMS *Conqueror*, a 19th-century British steam-powered battleship.

Southampton Reef – This massive reef begins 9 miles north of Conception Island, with fabulous elkhorn and staghorn corals.

Telephone Pole – This party-line dive begins at 45 feet and angles downward at 45°. You emerge at 100 feet on a wall crowded with large purple sponges and plate coral. Large pelagics abound.

Snorkel Sites

Flower Gardens – These scattered coral heads feature caves for exploring.

The Hump – This formation is a vast undersea condo for small marine life, including countless shrimp.

Natural Bridges – This unusual reef formation features natural arches.

The Rookery – Queen and king helmet conch abound.

Sandy Point – This site, south of Cockburn Town, is one of the best.

Split Reef – Two reefs in one: The first has huge brain corals, the second a long ridge.

Staghorn Reef – You'll find star and staghorn corals aplenty, as well as heaps of other marine life.

SAN SALVADOR, RUM CAY & CONCEPTION ISLAND

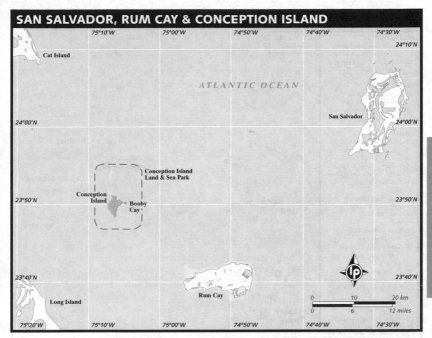

favored as nest sites by boobies and other seabirds. And egrets and herons pick in the brine pools. Flamingos were relocated from Great Inagua to San Sal in 1992, when the **Brice Memorial Flamingo Park** was created in an effort to reintroduce the national bird to the island. Alas, the birds were later removed.

Besides diving and birding, there's not much to do.

A warning: Beaches are infested with no-see-'ums, the sand flies so tiny that you never see them. Take Avon Skin So Soft. And be careful if you explore amid the brush. There are quicksands! Poisonwood and manchineel – poisonous to the touch – are ubiquitous.

COCKBURN TOWN
• pop 300

San Sal's major settlement and administrative center, midway down the west coast, is named for Sir Francis Cockburn, governor of the Bahamas from 1837 to 1844. Cockburn (pronounced 'Coburn') Town is a motley affair comprising two parallel roads (1st Ave and 2nd Ave) criss-crossed by five narrow lanes. Tumbledown stone cottages and clapboard shacks in faded pastels mingle with new, often stylish houses squatting in unkempt yards picked at by goats and cockerels.

A 12-foot plastic iguana guards the entrance to town where locals gather under the 'Lazy Tree,' a gnarled almond tree whose shade is preferred for loafing.

Information
The Bank of The Bahamas (☎ 242-331-2237) is open 9 am to 3 pm on Friday.

There's a BaTelCo office (☎ 242-331-2571) and a post office (☎ 242-331-2232) in town. The new, well-equipped medical clinic (☎ 242-331-2105), on the north side of the airport, is open 9 am to 5:30 pm weekdays. You can get prescriptions filled and buy

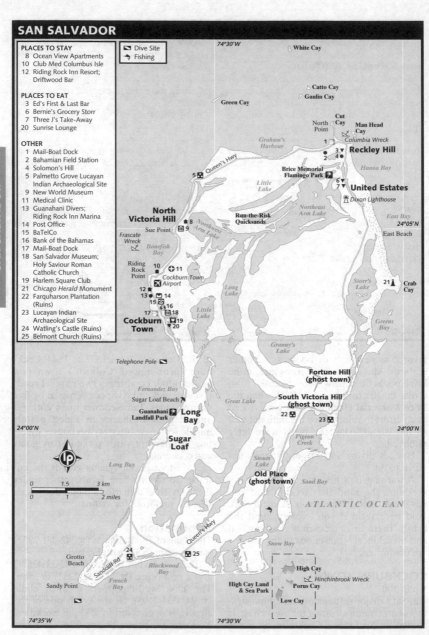

SAN SALVADOR

PLACES TO STAY
8 Ocean View Apartments
10 Club Med Columbus Isle
12 Riding Rock Inn Resort;
    Driftwood Bar

PLACES TO EAT
3 Ed's First & Last Bar
6 Bernie's Grocery Storr
7 Three J's Take-Away
20 Sunrise Lounge

OTHER
1 Mail-Boat Dock
2 Bahamian Field Station
4 Solomon's Hill
5 Palmetto Grove Lucayan
   Indian Archaeological Site
9 New World Museum
11 Medical Clinic
13 Guanahani Divers;
    Riding Rock Inn Marina
14 Post Office
15 BaTelCo
16 Bank of the Bahamas
17 Mail-Boat Dock
18 San Salvador Museum;
    Holy Saviour Roman
    Catholic Church
19 Harlem Square Club
21 *Chicago Herald* Monument
22 Farquharson Plantation
    (Ruins)
23 Lucayan Indian
    Archaeological Site
24 Watling's Castle (Ruins)
25 Belmont Church (Ruins)

Dive Site
Fishing

74°30'W
White Cay
Catto Cay
Gaulin Cay
Green Cay
Cut Cay
Man Head Cay
North Point
Columbia Wreck
Graham's Harbour
1
3
4
2
Reckley Hill
Hanna Bay
Brice Memorial
Flamingo Park
Little Lake
6
7
United Estates
Dixon Lighthouse
5 Queen's Hwy
Run-the-Risk
Quicksands
Northeast
Arm Lake
East Bay
24°05'N
East Beach
North Victoria Hill
8
Sue Point
9
Frascate Wreck
Bonefish Bay
Riding Rock Point
10
11
Cockburn Town
Airport
12
13 14
15 16
17 18
19
20
Cockburn Town
Little Lake
Long Lake
Starr's Lake
21 Crab Cay
Greens Bay
Granny's Lake
Fortune Hill (ghost town)
Telephone Pole
Fernandez Bay
Sugar Loaf Beach
Long Bay
Great Lake
South Victoria Hill (ghost town)
22
23
24°00'N
24°00'N
Guanahani Landfall Park
Sugar Loaf
Pigeon Creek
Stouts Lake
Old Place (ghost town)
Sand Bay
ATLANTIC OCEAN
Long Bay
0   1.5   3 km
0   1   2 miles
Grotto Beach
24 25
Sandcliff Rd
Snow Bay
Blackwood Bay
High Cay
Hinchinbrook Wreck
Porus Cay
Sandy Point
French Bay
High Cay Land & Sea Park
Low Cay
74°35'W
74°30'W

over-the-counter drugs at J's Discount Drugs (☎ 242-331-2570).

To reach the police, call ☎ 242-331-2010.

San Salvador Museum
This small museum is housed in the old jail, in the two-story pink-and-bottle-green building near the north entrance to town. One room displays Lucayan Indian remains, dug up locally. The second room is dedicated to Columbus' conquest of the New World. Note the ceramic mural on the outside wall, bearing a childlike depiction of Columbus paddling ashore.

The doors are usually locked; to visit, ask at the BaTelCo office 50 yards north or call Clifford 'Snake Eyes' Fernandez (☎ 242-331-2676).

Holy Saviour
Roman Catholic Church
This pretty pink structure, behind the museum, was established by the Catholic Archdiocese of Nassau in 1992. It looks much older and fits right in with the museum.

Diving & Snorkeling
Guanahani Divers (☎ 242-331-2631, 800-272-1492), at the Riding Rock Inn Resort, has complete scuba facilities, including the Underwater Photo Center, offering camera and video rentals and daily E-6 processing. A one-day underwater photo course costs US$99. It uses custom boats with walk-through transoms and dive platforms. Dives cost US$40/60 one/two-tank. A night dive is US$45. A beginner's resort course costs US$105; certification costs US$400. It rents scuba gear. You can have your dives filmed and prepared with music on VHF tape.

Guanahani Divers also offers snorkel trips for US$20, rents snorkel gear for US$10/50 daily/weekly, and participates in Jean-Michel Cousteau's Out Island Snorkeling Adventures (see the Outdoor Activities chapter for details).

Club Med Columbus Isle (see Places to Stay, below) has a full-service dive center offering equipment rental, three 45-foot dive catamarans, and an on-site recompression chamber. Certification costs US$275. Several past guests have complained about its dive programs, however, in *The Travelin' Diver's Chapbook* (see the Operators section under Diving in the Outdoor Activities chapter). Common gripes are the excess of divers (dozens at a time) and supercilious staff.

Bottom Time Adventures (in the US ☎ 800-234-8464, fax 954-920-5578, info@bottomtimeadventures.com) offers occasional scuba diving trips from George Town, Exuma (US$1395). Its Web site is www.bottomtimeadventures.com.

Sport Fishing
In winter, flying fish gather over a group of underwater pinnacles named The Hump, north of San Sal, drawing yellowfin tuna as well as wahoo, which feed on the tuna. At times the waters boil as tunas crash the flying fish, driving them to the surface where frigate birds scoop them up in flight and boobies and terns wheel thickly over the water. Then the wahoo come in for lunch. (In 1996 three world records for wahoo were set here.) September through April is the prime wahoo season. In summer blue-marlin fishing is excellent.

You can rent a 30-foot boat and guide from Guanahani Divers at the Riding Rock Inn Resort (see above) for US$300/500 half/full day, including tackle. A 42-foot sport-fishing boat costs US$100 extra.

Club Med has half-day deep-sea fishing excursions for US$95 per person.

Organized Tours
Club Med Columbus Isle offers half-day island excursions for US$25, 'Sunset Cruises' for US$25, and full-day flight excursions to Nassau for US$300.

The Riding Rock Inn Resort (see Places to Stay, below) offers an island excursion, as well as an excursion to the Exumas (US$150 per person, with a minimum of four people). You also can arrange excursions to Low Cay, where you'll see iguanas, and High Cay, where you'll be chased by playful ospreys.

Places to Stay

The **Riding Rock Inn Resort** (☎ 242-331-2631, fax 242-331-2020, info@ridingrock.com; in the US ☎ 305-931-1555, 800-272-1492, fax 305-931-3005) is southwest of the airport. It's popular with divers. It has 42 nicely furnished air-con rooms, all with cool tile floors, cable TV, couch, and small private patio. Eighteen rooms are classified as 'deluxe' and have a refrigerator and phone. Year-round rates are US$114 single or double for a standard room and US$141 for a deluxe room. Triple rooms cost US$129/156 standard/deluxe. There are also five handsome stone cottages with a phone and efficiency kitchen, plus a restaurant, bar, swimming pool, and tennis court. The resort has dive packages. A nice beach lies a stone's throw away. The postal address is c/o Out Island Service Co, 19495 Biscayne Blvd, suite 809, Aventura, FL 33180, USA.

Club Med Columbus Isle (☎ 242-331-2000, fax 242-331-2222; in North America ☎ 800-453-2582, fax 602-443-2086), 200 yards west of the airport, is one of the French hotel chain's flagship properties, spanning 80 half-wild acres along 3 miles of shoreline. Scuba Diving magazine has rated it the 'Best Dive Resort in the World.' The low-slung resort, painted in bright Caribbean pastels, boasts exotic antique art valued at more than US$2½ million: carved Nepalese doorways, Pakistani urns covered with a rich-colored patina, Indonesian temple gods, Brazilian headdresses, Turkish rugs, and African statues and masks. The resort is centered on a vast sun deck and pool. It has 286 spacious rooms in two-story beachfront units, all with custom-fashioned furniture, TV, phone, refrigerator, and safe; some have ocean views from gingerbread-trimmed private balconies. There are three gourmet restaurants, 12 tennis courts, a fitness center, water sports, and recreational activities including lively nocturnal entertainment led by the party-hearty 'GOs' (quasi–camp-counselors for adults). Nightly rates for standard rooms begin at US$162/174 summer/winter, per person. A seven-night package begins at US$1134/1218.

Ocean-view rooms cost more. Children under 12 are not permitted.

Places to Eat

In town the clean and tidy **Three Ships** (☎ 242-331-2787) serves boil' fish and grits for breakfast on request, plus burgers, turtle soup, and native dinner specials from US$8; dinner reservations are required; it's closed Sunday. **The Sunrise Lounge**, on Queen's Hwy south of town, also serves native dishes, as does **Harlem Square Club** (☎ 242-331-2777), which has Friday night buffets.

The **Riding Rock Inn** restaurant serves set meals. Breakfast costs US$11; lunch is US$14; dinner, including wine, is US$27. A 15% service charge is added. Two entree options are offered. The moderate-quality fare is filling. Get there by 8 pm or you may be out of luck. Pizzas are served on Wednesday and Saturday nights until midnight.

Club Med charges nonguests US$45 for an evening pass, including a splendid buffet dinner, entertainment, and access to its nightclub. A bargain!

You can buy groceries at **Jake Jones Food Store**, next to the Sunrise Lounge.

Entertainment

The atmospheric **Driftwood Bar**, at the Riding Rock Inn Resort, is adorned with driftwood carved with names and salacious comments. Popcorn is served. There's a TV. It hosts a party on Wednesday and Friday nights, when it can get lively and noisy.

On Friday night, a bash called 'The Rip' is hosted at the **Harlem Square Club**, a lively place with live music and revelry. There's dancing, too, on Saturday, and you can join the locals for a fast-paced game of dominoes and pool. An alternative is the nearby **Ocean View Club** (☎ 242-331-2676).

Chris McLaughlin, director of the Underwater Photo Center at Guanahani Divers, offers free weekly **slide shows**.

Shopping

Gwen, the 'Straw Lady,' sells shell crafts and plaited straw-work under the Lazy Tree. Iris

Fernandez also sells straw goods, at her San Salvador Gift Shop.

Getting There & Away

Air The airport is 1 mile north of Cockburn Town.

Bahamasair (in Nassau ☎ 242-377-5505, fax 242-377-7409) flies daily from Nassau (US$74 one-way). You can buy tickets or make changes with the Bahamasair agent, in the basement of the Riding Rock Inn Resort.

Club Med operates charter flights from Miami on Friday, Saturday, and Sunday, and from New York on Saturday; fares vary according to season, but are included in the accommodations packages.

Riding Rock Inn Resort also offers private charters from Fort Lauderdale on Saturday (US$165 one-way, US$300 roundtrip). Divers on prepaid diving packages are permitted 70lb of luggage; everyone else gets 44lb.

Boat The mail boat *Lady Frances* sails here from Nassau at 6 pm Tuesday (US$40 one-way). It also calls at United Estates and Rum Cay.

Riding Rock Inn Marina is a 10-slip, full-service facility. Dockage costs US90¢ per foot daily and US$4.80 weekly. Water and electricity each begin at US$10 per day, depending on the size of the vessel.

Getting Around

You can rent cars for US$85 per day at the airport or Riding Rock Inn Resort. K's Scooters (☎ 242-331-2125), at the airport, rents scooters for US$50. Riding Rock Inn Resort rents bicycles for US$6.50/10 half/full day.

NORTHWEST COAST

North of the airport, Queen's Hwy skirts the scrub-lined shore. Bonefish Bay has a fabulous beach that Club Med likes to claim as its own; you can gain access from Sue Point, 3 miles north of Cockburn Town, at the north end of the bay near the settlement of North Victoria Hill. The hamlet has the tiny New World Museum, displaying Lucayan Indian artifacts unearthed at the Palmetto Grove archeological site north of town. You'll need to find the curator, Mervin Benson (☎ 242-331-2126), to be let in. Admission costs US$1.

See if you can hire a local guide and boat to take you bird watching on the lakes.

North of North Victoria Hill, the road swings around the north shore along sand-rimmed Graham's Harbour. The harbor is calm and good for swimming. A Columbus Day Homecoming is traditionally held here on the beach on Discovery Day (October 12). The island bursts into life with music, feasting, dinghy ('smack boat') races, and fun games.

The annual Columbus Bay Regatta is held at Graham's Harbour. The wreck of the *Columbia*, which ran aground in 1980, is just off North Point.

Bahamian Field Station

This research station (☎ 242-331-2520, fax 242-331-2524), at the east end of Graham's Harbour, welcomes visitors. The station, a branch of the New York state college system, is officially known as the Center for the Study of Archaeology, Biology, Geology & Marine Sciences. It primarily hosts scientific conferences and field courses for student groups. Scientists also run a coral-reef monitoring project. Its own two-week course in tropical marine biology, cosponsored by Oklahoma State University, is offered each June and is open to students worldwide. The station also hosts an annual symposium on the natural history of The Bahamas. You can write the station c/o Twin Air, 1100 Lee Wagener Blvd, suite 113, Fort Lauderdale, FL 33315, USA.

Elderhostel (in the US ☎ 617-426-7788, 800-426-8056), 75 Federal St, Boston, MA 02110-1941, has 12-day springtime study trips of the 'Cultural and Physical Geography of San Salvador' for folks over 60 (US$1308 including airfare from Fort Lauderdale). For more details visit the Web site at www.elderhostel.org.

Earthwatch (in the US ☎ 978-461-0081, 800-776-0188, fax 978-461-2332, email: info@earthwatch.org), 3 Clock Tower Place, suite

100, Box 75, Maynard, MA 01754, a non-profit organization, houses volunteers at the Bahamian Field Station in its programs to preserve San Sal's reef. It needs volunteer divers. You'll snorkel four or five hours daily and make observations about coral health. It has three trips annually (from US$1495). The Web site is www.earthwatch.org.

Places to Stay & Eat
You can rent the **Blue House** (☎ /fax 242-331-2306, sansal.house@wanadoo.fr), a three-bedroom home on a rocky perch about a mile north of Club Med. It has an exquisitely decorated lounge with cathedral ceiling, a vast porch, and a 19-foot fishing boat (Floyd, the skipper, can take you fishing or lobstering). It rents for US$190/1170 daily/weekly in summer, US$210/1300 in winter. Two two-bedroom apartments are also available for US$100/640 summer, US$110/700 winter.

Cliff Fernandez (☎ 242-331-2676) rents three modern air-con cottages – **Ocean View Apartments** – in North Victoria Hill.

Club Arawak, next to the New World Museum, has basic native fare and does double duty as the local nightspot.

NORTHEAST COAST
The east shore is lined with lonesome beaches, including 5-mile-long East Beach, with its pinkish sands, and Snow Bay, at the far south, where you can be alone with the gentle lapping of the waves and the cry of sea birds. The road, however, runs inland from the shore for most of the way, passing a series of briny lakes smelling like backed-up toilets.

United Estates (locally called 'U-E'), the main settlement in the area, is 8 miles' drive northeast of Cockburn Town. It's a motley affair strung out for a mile along Queen's Hwy and hemmed in between a limestone ridge and a brine pool that doubles as a resting place for dozens of rusting car hulks. Note the blue house called **Solomon's Hill,** decorated with dozens of plastic buoys. It's very picturesque, especially at Christmas when the owner, Solomon Jones, adorns his home with lights.

Dixon Lighthouse
U-E is pinned by this magnificent lighthouse, nestled atop Dixon Hill (it's a stiff five-minute climb up a potholed road from Queen's Hwy). The gleaming-white structure rises 67 feet from its hilltop base, 163 feet above sea level. It was raised in 1856 and still flashes its beam twice every 25 seconds, fired by a superbly maintained Hood pelcum vapor burner, reflected and magnified to 400,000 candlepower by a huge Fresnel (or bull's-eye) lens. A poster dating from 1921 shows its workings.

The lighthouse is tended by Joyce Hanna, a delightful lady with pigtails who lives in the handsome cottage beneath the light. She is responsible for ensuring that the clocklike rotating mechanism that turns the light is wound by hand every 90 minutes throughout the night. You can climb the 80 steps to admire the internal workings and step out onto the balcony for a panoramic bird's-eye view of the entire island. It's open 9 am to noon and 2 to 5 pm daily.

The Bahamas' Port Dept plans to replace the historic light with an automated light. You can help preserve the magnificent structure by contacting (and sending donations to) the Bahamas Lighthouse Preservation Society; call David Gale (☎ 242-366-0282) for details.

Chicago Herald Monument
This weather-worn monument stands at the south end of East Bay, 1 mile from Queen's Hwy and about 3 miles southeast of U-E. The crude stone marker, topped by a marble globe, sits on a slender isthmus named **Crab Cay**. A plaque reads: 'On this spot Christopher Columbus first set foot upon the soil of the New World. Erected by the *Chicago Herald*, June 1891.' There is no evidence whatsoever to support the lofty claim…and, in any event, the offshore reefs make this an unlikely spot for anyone to come ashore. A dirt track leads to East Bay from the highway; you can slog south along the beach until you find the monument.

Places to Eat
The only two eateries in the area are **Three J's Take-Away** and **Ed's First & Last Bar,**

both funky clapboard shacks, the first in U-E and the second in Reckley Hill. Both serve native dishes such as cracked conch and peas 'n' rice, but neither is guaranteed to be open.

You can buy food at *Bernie's Grocery Storr* in U-E.

Getting There & Away
The *Lady Frances* mail boat calls at United Estates weekly from Nassau. See the Cockburn Town section earlier in this chapter for details.

SOUTHEAST COAST
In the 1800s, this quarter of the island was the center of cotton and citrus plantations. Several small yet once-thriving settlements have been abandoned in recent decades. Only their ghostly old stone houses remain, slowly turning to dust behind fieldstone boundary walls. It's a desolate stretch. The most notable site is the ruins of **Farquharson Plantation**, established in the 1820s by Charles Farquharson, a justice of the peace who recorded plantation life in his journals.

The road dips and rises inland, paralleling **Pigeon Creek**, an 8-mile-long ecological treasure (baby sharks, for example, swim here) that opens to the ocean at **Snow Bay**, to the southeast. The creek is good for bonefishing. There's an important but unmarked Lucayan Indian archaeological site along the shore at the north end of Pigeon Creek.

Breathtakingly beautiful Snow Bay has a snow-white beach and sheltered turquoise waters good for skinny-dipping. A dirt track leads to Snow Bay from Queen's Hwy at Blackwood Bay. The ruins of the Belmont Church are near the turnoff.

High Cay Land & Sea Park, offshore to the southeast, protects High Cay, Porus Cay, and Low Cay, important nesting sites for ospreys, boobies, and other seabirds. Endangered iguanas cling to Low Cay. The reef-girt cays, half a mile southeast of Snow Bay, have claimed several ships, notably the *Hinchinbrook*, which went down in 1913 and is today favored by scuba divers.

Endangered iguanas live on Low Cay.

SOUTHWEST COAST
South of Cockburn Town, Fernandez Bay and Long Bay – boasting beautiful Sugar Loaf Beach – sweep south to Sandy Point, the hilly, pendulous southwest tip of the island, reached off Queen's Hwy by Sandcliff Rd. The peninsula's leeward shore is fringed by beautiful Grotto Beach. Several foreigners have built homes along the breezy coast. The residential community is known as Columbus Estates. There are several caves.

Watling's Castle
Columbus Estates occupies the site of a plantation said to have been established by George Watling but actually founded by a Loyalist settler, Cade Matthews, who named it for the pirate. It remained operational until 1925. The ruins sit atop a hill with goods views of the sea. There's not much to see, just a lookout tower, ruined slave quarters, and other crumbling structures entwined with shrubbery. Long pants are a good idea to guard against thorny scrub.

Guanahani Landfall Park
Years ago some supposedly knowledgeable folks stuck a pin in a map to determine the *exact* spot of Columbus' first landfall in the

'new' world and – *hey, presto!* – here you are at Long Bay, 2 miles south of Cockburn Town. The historic event is commemorated by four uninspired monuments beside the shore. The oldest, a swirly plinth, was created in 1968 and also marks the Olympic Games in Mexico. The chunk of metal on top is a bowl that held the Olympic flame on its journey from Greece to Mexico City.

Alongside it is a simple, 10-foot-tall cement cross, dedicated on Christmas Day, 1956. The government of Spain dedicated its own monument to the visit of three Columbus caravel replicas on February 10, 1992. The cement block, with a ceramic plaque, is backed by an ugly metal sculpture.

Lastly, there's a small chunk of concrete inset with a bronze plaque, dedicated in October 1991 when a replica of the *Santa María*, built by the Nao Santa María Foundation of Japan, made landfall here on its journey from Barcelona to Kobe. (An identical edifice – the Tappan Monument –

was erected in 1951 half a mile farther north.)

A ceremony is held each Discovery Day, when the Olympic flame is rekindled.

Places to Eat

There's a **grocery store** and the **Stansheka Bar** on Queen's Hwy in Sugar Loaf, half a mile south of Guanahani Landfall Park.

Rum Cay

- **pop 60**

This small island – incorrectly claimed by locals to be Santa María de la Concepción, Columbus' name for his second landfall – is 20 miles southwest of San Salvador but shares the same administration. Ten miles long and 5 miles wide, Rum Cay is entirely off the tourist beat. The coasts are lined by stunning beaches and the entire isle wears a necklace of coral. There's a wreck, the HMS

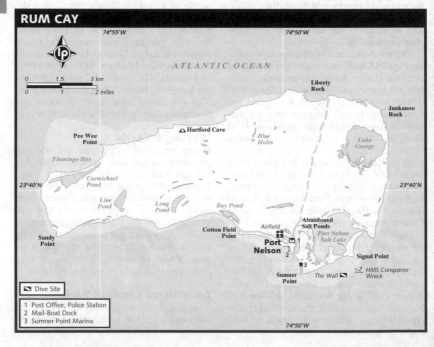

RUM CAY

ATLANTIC OCEAN

0   1.5   3 km
0   1   2 miles

74°55'W   74°50'W

Liberty
Rock

Junkanoo
Rock

Pee Wee
Point

⌂ Hartford Cave

*Blue
Holes*

*Lake
George*

Flamingo Bay

Carmichael
Pond

23°40'N

Line
Pond

Long
Pond

Bay Pond

Abandoned
Salt Ponds

23°40'N

Sandy
Point

Cotton Field
Point

Airfield

**Port
Nelson**

⌂1

2

*Port Nelson
Salt Lake*

Signal Point

⌂3

Sumner
Point

The Wall ⬍

⬍ HMS Conqueror
Wreck

74°50'W

⬍ Dive Site

1 Post Office; Police Station
2 Mail-Boat Dock
3 Sumner Point Marina

Conqueror, a 101-gun British man o' war that sank in 1861 in 30 feet of water off Signal Point.

The only settlement is **Port Nelson**, just west of Sumner Point on the south coast. It is backed by disused salt ponds that provided salt bound for the fishing fleets of Nova Scotia in the 19th century. Hurricanes in 1908 and 1926 destroyed the ponds and killed the industry; afterward many residents drifted away. Hurricane Lily in 1999 did further damage.

The rest of the isle is a virtual wilderness of rolling hills browsed by feral cattle and donkeys.

There's a post office and police station in Port Nelson.

Places to Stay & Eat

Sumner Point Marina (☎ *242-331-2923, fax 242-331-2824*) has a one-bedroom air-con studio and a two-bedroom cottage, plus a fine restaurant beloved of sailors for its 'New World Caribbean' cuisine; call ahead on VHF 16 for dinner.

Constable Ted Bain (☎ 242-331-2818) and Hermie, the local midwife, rent rooms at **Ocean View Restaurant**, which is recommended for basic native fare. Call ahead on VHF 16 for dinner reservations.

The **Rum Cay Club** remained closed at press time.

Two Sisters Take-A-Way sells fresh bread, conch, grouper, and chicken.

Getting There & Away

There's a private airstrip in Port Nelson. There are no scheduled flights.

The *Lady Frances* mail boat calls weekly from Nassau. See the Cockburn Town section earlier in this chapter for details.

The Sumner Point Marina has 18 slips and full services. It charges US95¢ per foot daily.

Conception Island

This uninhabited, reef-rimmed speck on the map, 15 miles northeast of Long Island and 25 miles southeast of Cat Island, is protected as the Conception Island Land & Sea Park under the jurisdiction of the Bahamas National Trust.

The isle – a mere 3 miles by 2 miles – is an important nesting site for endangered green turtles as well as migratory seabirds, particularly boobies, which give their name to Booby Cay, east of the island.

A briny creek dominates the interior and opens to the sea. It's a haven for divers and yachters.

Amazing Grace, the supply ship for Windjammer Barefoot Cruises' sailing fleet, calls on Conception during its island-hopping voyages, offered twice monthly between Grand Bahama and Trinidad. See the Getting There & Away chapter for details.

CONCEPTION ISLAND

Long Island

• pop 3200

Long Island, 28 miles south of Cat Island, is relatively undeveloped, yet it's one of the prettiest Family Islands. The drive along its main road, the Queen's Hwy, offers stupendous sights, from deep caves and a fishing village where you still can see wooden sailing dinghies being made by hand, to plantation ruins and beautiful churches – the divinely inspired handiwork of Father Jerome (see the boxed text, 'Father Jerome,' in the Cat Island chapter). The island is 60 miles from north to south and less than 2 miles wide. (When you're given directions by locals, remember

Highlights

- Cape Santa Maria's beach, blindingly white with bathtub-warm shallows extending forever
- Shark Reef, where you can watch sharks feast in front of your eyes
- Long Island Regatta, *the* time to party-hearty with locals
- Lochabar Beach Lodge, an unpretentious, cozy, down-home inn...and what a setting!
- Hamilton's Cave, boasting stalactites, stalagmites, and leaf-nosed fruit bats

that they say 'up south' and 'down north,' the opposite of what you might expect.)

Scenic side roads lead to magnificent bays, blue holes, and miles and miles of beach. In places along the windward, or eastern, shore, Atlantic rollers crash against dramatic cliffs (other beaches are protected by offshore reefs). Cape Santa Maria, to the north, has especially superb beaches and reefs. The west coast consists of a string of shallow bays. In late spring hundreds of thousands of yellow butterflies appear, dancing merrily along in streams like ribbons.

The island has Lucayan Indian caves to explore (they called their island 'Yuma'). The caves have yielded *duhos* (wooden seats) that archaeologists believe suggest chieftainship and ceremony, and *zemi* figurines bearing religious connotations. To the south, the island – Columbus' 'Fernandina' – ends at Cape Verde, where Columbus supposedly anchored on October 24, 1492.

The island's inhabitants are scattered among about 35 settlements. A large percentage are whites or 'brights' (people of mixed black and white ancestry), including many descendants of the 18th-century Loyalists. The colonists established a plantation system that was as viable as any in the archipelago. Uniquely, sheep-rearing remained profitable well into this century, and a few sheep remain. Farming, too, endures today in large groves of bananas and rows of corn (especially around Deadman's Cay), in stock-rearing, and in cultivation of vegetables and pineapples in limestone potholes.

Long Island is acclaimed as a diving paradise, most famously for its wall dives and the fast-paced action of Shark Reef (see the 'Dive & Snorkel Sites' boxed text later in this chapter). The island also has hot fishing year-round. Seasonal highs include March to May for rainbow runners, March to June for dolphin (dorado), April and May for yellowfin tuna, July to December for blackfin tuna, and September to November for wahoo.

Bottom fish are abundant year-round. And bonefishing is splendid; you can even cast while wading in 1 foot of water near the beaches.

North Long Island

STELLA MARIS AREA

Most visitors fly to Stella Maris. This settlement, near the north end of the island, is an upscale residential community that stretches for about a mile along the coast amid palms and scrub. An irregular warren of narrow lanes has been lain out for future homes. Dominating the scene is the Stella Maris Resort, atop a bluff that descends to a rocky shoreline with beach-lined coves. The beach is not protected by reefs and the waters sometimes can be turbulent, producing a severe undertow.

The best beaches are the four Love Beaches, at the end of a dirt road that runs a mile northeast from Ocean View Dr, the shoreline road. Construction of a new residential resort was slated to begin here in 2001.

For bonefishing enthusiasts, there's excellent sport in the shallow bay on the leeward shore off Adderley Point, where the remains of Adderley Plantation are smothered in vegetation, as are the graves in the slaves' cemetery.

Stella Maris is served commercially by the settlement of **Burnt Ground** (a mile north along the main highway) and its smaller twin community, **Glinton**, immediately north. The two hamlets are speckled with brine pools littered with town refuse. The road continues 3 miles to **Seymours** – a hilltop settlement – then winds downhill and ends at the shores of **Columbus Harbour**, a shallow bay lined by mangroves. You can cross the narrow tidal creek on a footbridge to reach **Newton Cay**, a small island with a beach on the Atlantic shore. There are caves around the headland to the north.

Information

There's a Scotiabank (☎ 242-338-2057) in Stella Maris at the airport; it's open 9:30 am to 1 pm Monday through Thursday, and 9 am to 5 pm Friday. The post office (☎ 242-338-2010) is at Stella Maris Airport, as is the police station (☎ 242-338-2222).

The Speed Queen Laundromat (☎ 242-338-2016), opposite Stella Maris marina, is open 8:30 am to 6:30 pm Thursday, 8:30 am to 5:30 pm Friday, and 8:30 am to 2:30 pm Sunday.

Columbus Memorial

This remote, 15-foot-tall stone obelisk is surrounded by thick stands of thatch palm and sea grape at the northern tip of Long Island. It bears a plaque dedicated to 'the peaceful aboriginal people of Long Island and to the arrival of Christopher Columbus.' It is topped by a rusty globe skewered by a cross. The vistas out to sea are sublime, as are the views over a beautiful, jade-colored, sand-rimmed bay. Snorkeling is good around the headlands and you can body-float with the tide.

The rocky path that leads 1 mile to the monument is signed at Seymours. *Beware the steep cliffs!*

Galliot Cay

This pencil-thin 3-mile-long peninsula is connected to Long Island by a narrow isthmus with mangrove creeks. The isthmus' west shore is lined along its entire length with a gorgeous white-sand beach shelving into turquoise shallows. Snorkeling is especially good at the reef gardens at the southern end, and at the northern ends close by the Cape Santa Maria Beach Resort. The Stella Maris Resort (see the Places to Stay section, later in this chapter) has shade umbrellas midway down the bay. It offers free shuttles each morning for its guests. Access is via a dirt road (signed) from Seymours.

Diving & Snorkeling

Stella Maris Resort (see Places to Stay, below) is a dedicated dive resort that charges US$75 for a day's diving, including two or three dives; a PADI certification course costs US$405. It also offers free snorkeling. Cape Santa Maria Beach Resort (see Places to Stay, below) also offers diving

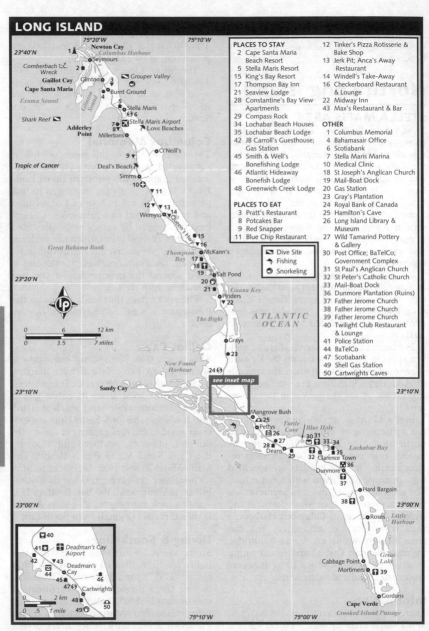

LONG ISLAND

PLACES TO STAY
2 Cape Santa Maria Beach Resort
5 Stella Maris Resort
15 King's Bay Resort
17 Thompson Bay Inn
21 Seaview Lodge
28 Constantine's Bay View Apartments
29 Compass Rock
34 Lochabar Beach Houses
35 Lochabar Beach Lodge
42 JB Carroll's Guesthouse; Gas Station
45 Smith & Well's Bonefishing Lodge
46 Atlantic Hideaway Bonefish Lodge
48 Greenwich Creek Lodge

PLACES TO EAT
3 Pratt's Restaurant
8 Potcakes Bar
9 Red Snapper
11 Blue Chip Restaurant
12 Tinker's Pizza Rotisserie & Bake Shop
13 Jerk Pit; Anca's Away Restaurant
14 Windell's Take-Away
16 Checkerboard Restaurant & Lounge
22 Midway Inn
43 Max's Restaurant & Bar

OTHER
1 Columbus Memorial
4 Bahamasair Office
6 Scotiabank
7 Stella Maris Marina
10 Medical Clinic
18 St Joseph's Anglican Church
19 Mail-Boat Dock
20 Gas Station
23 Gray's Plantation
24 Royal Bank of Canada
25 Hamilton's Cave
26 Long Island Library & Museum
27 Wild Tamarind Pottery & Gallery
30 Post Office; BaTelCo; Government Complex
31 St Paul's Anglican Church
32 St Peter's Catholic Church
33 Mail-Boat Dock
36 Dunmore Plantation (Ruins)
37 Father Jerome Church
38 Father Jerome Church
39 Father Jerome Church
40 Twilight Club Restaurant & Lounge
41 Police Station
44 BaTelCo
47 Scotiabank
49 Shell Gas Station
50 Cartwrights Caves

◹ Dive Site
↯ Fishing
↯ Snorkeling

(US$45/75 one/two-tank dive) and snorkeling (US$10 per hour), and rents scuba and snorkeling equipment. Both resorts participate in Jean-Michel Cousteau's Out Island Snorkeling Adventures (see details in the Outdoor Activities chapter).

Want to be with sharks in a feeding frenzy? Stella Maris Resort offers its famous dive at Shark Reef weekly. Caribbean reef sharks gather and begin circling the dive vessel even before it has moored. (Nurse sharks and hammerheads sometimes visit, too.) Divers go down together – quickly! – accompanied by a divemaster. The sharks swim around and between the divers, expectantly anticipating the moment, five minutes later, when a lead-weighted bucket of chum (fish remains) is thrown in. The frenzy is over almost before the bucket hits the bottom, 30 feet down. *Awesome!* Nondivers can watch events from above through a glass-bottomed boat.

See the 'Dive & Snorkel Sites' boxed text for some of Long Island's other underwater highlights.

Bonefishing & Sport Fishing

Guided bonefishing is offered by Bonafide Bonefishing, at the Stella Maris Resort, for US$275 full-day for two people; check out its Web site at www.bonefishinglongisland.com. Alternately, contact 'Docky' Smith (☎ 242-338-2018, docky@bonefishinglongisland.com), one of the best local guides, in Burnt Ground. Reef fishing costs US$350 full-day; deep-sea fishing costs from US$650. Cape Santa Maria Beach Resort charges US$200/250 half/full-day for bonefishing, US$450/600 for reef fishing, and US$550/800 for deep-sea fishing, for up to 6 people.

Other Activities

Stella Maris Resort offers water-skiing for US$40, and free sailing using Sunfish. It also rents boats for overnight excursions from US$350 for a 27-footer to US$1110 for a 65-foot cruiser capable of sleeping 20 people.

Cape Santa Maria Beach Resort offers boogie boards (US$2 hourly), bicycles (US$2.50 hourly), kayaks (US$5 hourly),

---

Dive & Snorkel Sites

Dive Sites

Most visitors to Long Island come for the acclaimed diving, based at Stella Maris. Prime sites include the following:

Cape Santa Maria Ship's Graveyard – Two wrecks, a small pleasure cruiser and the 103-foot *Comberbach*, lie 100 feet down.

Conception Island Wall – The wall begins just off a leeside beach at 45 feet and plunges down, down, down.

Grouper Valley – Every November thousands of groupers gather in this valley, which also draws other pelagic species.

Grouper Village – Don't arrive without food: The half-dozen or so resident groupers expect to be fed. 'Brutus,' a mammoth jewfish, also lives here.

Ocean Blue Hole – This cavern is a dramatic, ever-widening funnel.

Shark Reef – Sharks habitually come here to be fed.

Snorkel Sites

Coral Gardens – Hawksbill turtles favor these awesome caves, overhangs, and valleys.

Eagle Ray Reef – Yes, rays frequent this beautiful coral formation guarded by a friendly grouper.

Flamingo Tongue Reef – Countless species of corals and fish are on show.

Newton Cay – Scores of coral heads are found on this reef.

Poseidon Point – This is one of very few places to watch large tarpon amid the reefs.

Rainbow Reef – This reef is famous for elkhorn corals and sponges.

Rock Pools – Crabs inhabit these tidal pools and swim-in coral formations.

Turtle Cove – It's named for the turtle grass, not the animals. Still, there's lots of splendid shells.

Watermelon Beach – Plenty of colorful parrotfish and damsels are amid acres of staghorn coral.

LONG ISLAND

windsurfers (US$7 hourly), and Hobie Wave catamarans (US$15 first hour; US$10 hourly thereafter). Cape Santa Maria Beach Resort offers a nature cruise and snorkeling trip (US$60). It also offers a guided nature cruise and snorkeling trip (US$60).

Special Events
The Model Boat Fest takes place at Bridge Beach, near Seymours, each August. For information, call Alvin Smith (☎ 242-338-5273).

Places to Stay
The German-owned *Stella Maris Resort* (☎ *242-338-2050, fax 242-338-2052, smrc@ stellamarisresort.com; in the US* ☎ *954-359-8236, 800-426-0466, fax 954-359-8238)* enjoys a breezy perch atop the ridge and stunning views over the Atlantic. The handsome stone and timber lodge has a fine dining room and large bar-lounge. There are 30 pink-and-white rooms and apartments on the ridge and two dozen one- to four-bedroom cottage-villas with kitchens scattered in a half-mile arc on the coral shore. Rooms have ceiling fans, tile floors, rattan furniture, and glass sliding doors that open to patios or verandas. Some villas have their own pools. Accommodation units were urgently in need of renovation at last visit; a piecemeal renovation was underway. Room rates are US$100/120 single/double in summer, US$115/145 winter. Cottage-villas range from US$120/140 summer, US$135/165 for a one-bedroom unit to US$495 summer, US$555 winter for a four-bedroom unit. Rates include water sports and bicycle use. The resort features tennis courts, a freshwater pool, and an uninspired sun deck and saltwater pool by the beach. Its mailing address is PO Box LI-30105, Stella Maris, Long Island, The Bahamas. The Web site is www.stellamarisresort.com.

The best resort on the island – and one of the most appealing in The Bahamas – is the plantation-style *Cape Santa Maria Beach Resort* (☎ *242-338-5273, fax 242-338-6013, obmg@pinc.com; in North America* ☎ *250-598-3366, 800-663-7090, fax 250-598-1361)*, enjoying a sublime setting at the north end of Galliot Cay. The resort's 20 deluxe air-con cottages, in 10 units, are widely spaced amid lawns a stone's throw from the stunning beach. Each has beautiful tile floors, rattan furniture, ceiling fans, wooden ceilings, bright tropical prints, and simply yet colorfully tiled bathrooms. All rooms open to screened porches facing the beach. Wooden walkways lead to an airy and handsome two-tier restaurant and bar in gingerbread plantation style and offering vast views. Fun amenities include catamarans, sailboats, sailboards, volleyball, diving, and snorkeling. Fishing can be arranged. Rates are US$195/295 one/two-bedroom cottages June to mid-November, US$245/370 mid-November through May. A meal plan costs US$75/40 adult/child. All-inclusive packages are also offered. The resort has its own private airstrip and charters. Full details can be found on the Web site at www.capesantamaria.com.

Places to Eat
Nonguests can dine at *Stella Maris Resort*, which serves buffet breakfasts (US$12) and continental-inspired cuisine catering to its mostly European clientele. Dinners cost US$31; US$21 for entree only.

To dine with locals, try *Pratt's Restaurant* (☎ *242-338-7022)* in Burnt Ground; it serves Bahamian seafood and native dishes. Alternately, try *Potcakes Bar* (☎ *242-338-2018)* next to the Stella Maris Marina. It has an upscale restaurant, and a bar by night.

There's an *ice cream parlor* at the north end of Glinton.

You can stock up your kitchen at the *Stella Maris General Store*; at *Adderley Supply* or the *Burnt Ground Convenience Store*, in Burnt Ground; *Rose Haven & Meat Market* (☎ *242-338-5017)* in Glinton; or *Long Island Meat & Fish* (☎ *242-338-2016)* in Culmers, south of Stella Maris.

Entertainment
Stella Maris Resort has a handsome bar where local residents gather. It has a shuffleboard and billiards. The resort hosts a Saturday night dance with live music, plus uses a cave as a nightclub on Monday night,

with a barbecue and dancing to a rake 'n' scrape band.

There are a few funky satellite lounges in Burnt Ground and in Glinton, good for supping with locals. Check out the *Playboy Club* and *Sabrina's Bar*.

Shopping

Stella Maris has a well-stocked boutique. You can purchase handmade straw-work at Bert's Dry Goods in Burnt Ground and Adderley Straw Work in Glinton.

Getting There & Away

Air Stella Maris Airport serves northern Long Island. For customs and immigration, call ☎ 242-338-2012. Island Express (in the US ☎ 954-359-0380) flies daily from Fort Lauderdale.

Bahamasair (☎/fax 242-338-2015) flies daily from Nassau (US$64 each way). Cat Island Air (☎ 242-377-3318) flies from Nassau Wednesday and Friday (US$60 one-way).

Stella Maris Resort offers private charters for hotel guests (US$90 one-way with hotel booking). If you are holding a Bahamasair ticket, you can use it to fly on the charter.

Boat The mail boat *Sherice M* calls at Seymours weekly from Nassau, also stopping at Salt Pond and Deadman's Cay (see the Salt Pond section for details).

The Stella Maris Marina is an official port of entry and has slips for boats up to 70 feet; it charges US75¢ per foot.

Getting Around

Bus Matthias Pratt (☎ 242-338-7051/7022) operates a minibus charter service. He charges about US$150 for a ride for four people from Stella Maris to Clarence Town, in the southern part of the island.

Car & Scooter Stella Maris Resort rents cars for US$75 a day plus mileage (US35¢ a mile), which can add up to well over US$100 as Queen's Hwy runs 60 miles north to south. Joe Williams (☎ 242-338-5002), in Glinton, charges US$65 daily, including unlimited mileage, and will deliver to Cape Santa Maria Beach Resort.

Stella Maris Resort rents scooters for US$30/46 half/full-day. Inell Ditez, in Burnt Ground, rents scooters for US$40 daily.

Burnt Ground has a tiny gas station.

Taxi All flights are met by taxis. A taxi to the Stella Maris Resort costs US$4 per person. A taxi to Cape Santa Maria Beach Resort costs about US$15 for two. Matthias Pratt (☎ 242-338-7051/7022) charges about US$25 to drive four people from Stella Maris to the memorial.

Jerry and Jennifer Knowles (☎ 242-336-2106) will act as guides.

STELLA MARIS TO SALT POND

Queen's Hwy runs south from Stella Maris along the leeward shore. The beach about 2 miles south of Stella Maris is backed by a 200-year-old cemetery where members of the Knowles family slumber beneath blankets of pine needles. The cemetery is opposite Knowles Straw Works, just north of Millertons, where you can buy handbags and straw-work from the Handicraft Manufacturing Outlet, which also makes Christmas gifts.

Another mile brings you to 2-mile-long Deal's Beach, where the Stella Maris Resort has a picnic cabaña and open grill, plus sailboats for hotel guests (free transfers are offered twice daily from the hotel). The snorkeling, over a sea-fan garden, is splendid. You can follow a road east from here to O'Neill's, a tiny hamlet with two beaches that also offer good snorkeling.

Simms, a quaint seaside hamlet about 10 miles south of Stella Maris, is lent charm by its old cottages behind stone walls, dating back to the plantation era. It is dominated by well-kept **St Peter's Anglican Church**. The most endearing structure is a prim little **post office** and, nudging up behind it, an equally diminutive **jail** still bearing the sign 'HER MAJESTY'S PRISON.'

There's a medical clinic at the south end of Simms.

South of Simms, the road moves inland until it touches the shore again at Thompson Bay, about 5 miles farther south. The bay is scenic, but far more spectacular is the one at McKann's, about half a mile east; turn east at the sign for King's Bay Resort. Here a 200-yard-wide crescent beach is enclosed by low headlands, with a reef about 100 yards offshore. The tall dunes are backed by sea grape and palm and lagoons good for birding.

Captain Bowe at Thompson Bay Inn rents cars for US$65 daily (US$70/75 large sedan/minivan). He'll also take you bonefishing and on guided cave tours.

Places to Stay & Eat

The grandly named *King's Bay Resort* (☎ *242-338-8945, fax 242-338-8012*) enjoys a fabulous and breezy location atop the dunes on the Atlantic shore north of McKann's. There are eight meagerly furnished rooms; each costs about US$60. It has a large restaurant and bar serving three meals daily (Bahamian fare; typically US$5 to US$10), with a concrete patio overlooking the beach. The place is a bit rundown and gets little business…but what a setting for a reclusive no-frills escape! Free airport transfers and a free island tour are offered. A renovation was planned.

Just south of McKann's, the roadside *Thompson Bay Inn* (☎ *242-337-1264*) is favored by locals. It has eight basic rooms with no furnishings except a double bed and dressing table, with two shared bathrooms down the hall. Rates are US$50/60 single/double (US$5 more for air-con) in summer, US$55/65 in winter. The hotel offers a fish-fry on Wednesday. It has a dark bar and restaurant, plus a large dance hall with a Ladies' Night on Thursday, happy hour at 7 pm on Saturday, and dancing on weekends. You also can 'enjoy a rollicking game of pool.' Its postal address is PO Box LI-30133, Thompson Bay, Long Island, The Bahamas.

The *Red Snapper* serves native dishes at Deal's Beach.

Just past Simms, you can grab a bite to eat and drink at the *Blue Chip*, the local hangout of choice that specializes in seafood platters. *Tinker's Pizza Rotisserie & Bake Shop* (☎ *242-338-8170*), about 4 miles south of Simms, will deliver.

For spicy chicken, try the open-air *Jerk Pit*, 2 miles farther south. The air-con *Anca's Away Restaurant* (☎ *242-338-8593*), next door, serves steaks and seafood.

If hunger gets the better of you, check out either the very casual *Windell's Take-Away* or the local's hangout, the *Checkerboard Restaurant & Lounge*, near McKann's.

You can get jerk chicken south of Simms.

SALT POND

Twenty miles south of Stella Maris, Salt Pond is the main commercial node of the island, despite its diminutive size. A small lobster fleet is based here and a mail boat calls in weekly. There's a fish-processing plant, a major supply store (Harding's), and a gas station…about the only place on the island that's open on Sunday.

Just north of Salt Pond is **St Joseph's Anglican Church**, enjoying a sublime setting on a ridge above the beach and boneflats. Break out your camera!

Immediately north of Harding's, a road leads east to the Atlantic shore. It turns to sand after half a mile, but follow this through the thatch palm and sea grape and it suddenly will deposit you atop a headland with blush-pink beaches and craggy, untouched shoreline spreading as far as the eye can see. Tall dunes back the shore. You can hike trails that lead south for several miles.

At Pinders, about 2 miles south of Salt Pond, another road (this one in terrible condition) leads to **Guana Key**, a beautiful, well-protected, shallow bay; Guana Key Island is a short swim offshore. In good weather you can snorkel over the wreck of an old freighter in 15 feet of water.

The *Sherice M* mail boat sails from Nassau to Salt Pond at 1 pm Tuesday (17 hours, US$45 one-way), also stopping at Seymours and Deadman's Cay.

Special Events

The highlight of the island's annual calendar is the Long Island Regatta, held at Salt Pond in mid-May. Sloops from throughout the islands compete during the festive four-day event. You can hop aboard the spectator boat for a close-up view of the action. For information, call Raphael Cartwright (☎ 242-337-0223), Larry Cartwright (☎ 242-337-2761), or Margo Harding (☎ 242-338-0333).

Places to Stay & Eat

The *Seaview Lodge (☎ 242-337-0000)* is a modern guesthouse with four efficiency apartments facing The Bight. It was due to open in late 2000.

The *Midway Inn*, 3 miles south of Salt Pond at Pinders, has a fish-fry on Friday.

South Long Island

DEADMAN'S CAY AREA
• pop 1000

Deadman's Cay, 35 miles south of Stella Maris, is Long Island's main settlement and the site of its second airport. It stretches along Queen's Hwy for several miles. To the north is the subdivision of Lower Deadman's Cay. The locals in this middle-class haven like to top their garden walls with cement griffins, lions, and swans.

Information

There's a Royal Bank of Canada (☎ 242-337-1044) in Lower Deadman's Cay; it's open 9 am to 1 pm Monday to Thursday and

9 am to 5 pm Friday. The Scotiabank branch in Deadman's Cay has similar hours.

There's a BaTelCo office (☎ 242-337-1337) in Deadman's Cay. You can whiten your undies at Cartwright's Laundromat (☎ 242-337-0315). There's a clinic (☎ 242-337-1222) at the south end of Deadman's Cay. The police can be reached at ☎ 242-337-0999.

Wild Tamarind Pottery & Gallery

This pottery studio just south of Pettys is a *must see*. It displays the work of Denis Knight, a septuagenarian who came to The Bahamas from England in the 1960s and became head of the art department at the College of The Bahamas before retiring here. He conjures up exquisite ceramic miniatures of Bahamian cottages and outhouses (US$50 to US$120), as well as mugs, bowls, and vases fired in a propane kiln (or occasionally in an old wood-fired kiln). You also can buy painted sea-urchin shells, Junkanoo figurines, birdhouses shaped like bees' nests, *duhos* (replicas of concave Indian stools and corn-grinding tables), and tiny chickcharnies (US$7), the legendary mischief-makers of Andros. His works are sold only on-site. Denis also is known throughout The Bahamas for his ceramic murals, which adorn several public buildings.

Denis' wife, Marina Darville, loves to show her marvelous collections of shells and old bottles. Marina was born on Long Island to a family that has lived here for 300 years.

The couple host local children for summer camps at their exquisite home, with inspirational views and a setting described as a 'sanctuary of plum, gumelemi, and wild tamarind.'

You'll see the sign for their place by Queen's Hwy south of town; it's 400 yards up a rocky dirt road.

Turtle Cove

This 2-mile-wide bay near Deans, about 4 miles north of Clarence Town, is the future site of a hotel, golf course, and marina. It boasts a fabulous beach and turquoise shallows. Its real treasure, however, lies to the southeast beyond a headland, where the

world's deepest blue hole (660 feet) leads to the world's eighth-largest underwater cavern. The setting is exquisite, surrounded on three sides by cliffs with a ledge favored by locals – filthy litterers! – for shady snoozing and barbecues. The neck of the aquamarine hole opens to a beautiful cove rimmed by gorgeous white sands. *Magnificent!* Bring a picnic.

The turnoff from Queen's Hwy is marked. Turtle Cove also can be reached by a shoreline trail from Mangrove Bush, north of Pettys.

Other Things to See

History buffs might enjoy the overgrown ruins of **Grays Plantation**, 2 miles north of Lower Deadman's near Grays.

Lower Deadman's Cay is dominated by **St Athanatius Church**, which dates from 1929.

Cartwrights Caves, near the settlement of Cartwrights, immediately south of Deadman's Cay, were once used by Lucayan Indians. Harmless bats now live in the 150-foot-long caves. They're on private property, half a mile east of the main road. You'll see

the sign. **Hamilton's Cave**, at the hamlet of Pettys, 4 miles southeast of Deadman's Cay, is 1500 feet long…one of the largest caves in The Bahamas. It, too, contains bats, stalactites, stalagmites, and a stone walkway with salt water on one side and fresh water on the other. Leonard Cartwright (☎ 242-337-0235, VHF 16 'Cave Man') offers guided tours of the caves for US$5.

Reached from Queen's Hwy by a side road beginning at the Hillside Tavern, 1 mile south of Cartwrights, the fishing hamlet of **Mangrove Bush** is a center for traditional boatbuilding. Today the

wooden vessels are built exclusively for racing regattas.

The **Long Island Library & Museum**, in Pettys, has a collection of photographs and artifacts (glass bottles and the like) that chronicle the island's history and culture.

Bonefishing

The sound west of Deadman's Cay is superb for bonefishing. The Greenwich Creek Lodge (see below) charges US$250/600/800 per day for bone/reef/deep-sea fishing.

Places to Stay

The modest two-story *JB Carroll's Guesthouse* (☎ 242-337-1048), next to JB Carroll's gas station, has six rooms for rent; two have a kitchen.

The *Greenwich Creek Lodge* (☎ 242-337-6278, fax 242-337-6282, info@greenwichcreek .com) is a dedicated bonefishing lodge overlooking The Bight at Cartwrights. This handsome, twin-structure complex is built in Caribbean style with broad shaded verandas. It has 12 air-con rooms with ceiling fans, tile floors, mahogany antique reproductions or more modern rattan furniture, and step-up bathrooms with modern amenities. Four rooms each have a king-size bed. Facilities include a modest restaurant and a swimming pool. Meals for nonguests are by prior request (four-person minimum). Rates are US$140/190 'superior'/'deluxe' in summer, US$175/225 in winter. A MAP plan costs US$50/25 adults/children. Special fishing packages are offered. Its mailing address is PO Box CT-3035, Clarence Town, Long Island, The Bahamas. The lodge's Web address is www .greenwichcreek.com.

Alternately, try the *Smith & Wells Bonefishing Lodge* (☎ 242-337-1056), 1 mile north. It was not open for inspection when I visited.

Don't be misled by the name of the *Atlantic Hideaway Bonefish Lodge* (☎ 242-337-1050), on the Atlantic shore due east of Deadman's Cay. This uninspired option has four modest air-con rooms for about US$65, and offers a ho-hum restaurant and bar popular with locals for its video machines and pool table. The breeze-swept location above the rocky shore, however, is marvelous. If you book in here, expect to be by your lonesome.

For a nondescript but adequate option try the recently built **Keva's Villa Apartments & Rooms** (☎ 242-337-1054) in Lower Deadman's Cay. It has six air-con units. Likewise, **Glen's Inn** has eight similar units; it's next to the Smith & Wells Bonefishing Lodge. And **Constantine's Bay View Apartments** (☎ 242-337-0644), at Deans, has 15 units. All charge about US$65.

Places to Eat
Tinker's Pizza Rotisserie has a small, colorful outlet 200 yards south of St Athanatius Church in Lower Deadman's Cay.

For native dishes, try the clean, modern, air-con **Dew Drop Inn Restaurant & Bar** (☎ 242-337-0044) at the north end of Deadman's Cay; or **Max's Restaurant & Bar** (☎ 242-337-0056) for conch.

You can buy groceries at the **J&M Food Store** (☎ 242-337-1446), 400 yards north of BaTelCo. On Sunday when the entire island closes shop, you can buy basic foodstuffs at the Shell gas station south of Cartwright.

In Mangrove Bush, the air-con **Hillside Tavern** (☎ 242-337-1628) is the local place to be. It's full of trophies won in local sailing regattas. At Deans, **Coco's Restaurant & Lounge** is the nicest place for miles; it serves native dishes.

Entertainment
Check out **Moonglow Bar** or the **Twilight Club Restaurant & Lounge** (☎ 242-337-1076) in Lower Deadman's Cay. The **Hillside Tavern** has music and dancing.

Getting There & Around
The airport is between Lower Deadman's and Deadman's Cay, 1 mile east of the Queen's Hwy. It has a snack bar.

Bahamasair (☎ 242-337-0877) flies between Nassau and Deadman's daily (US$68 each way).

The *Sherice M* mail boat sails from Nassau to Deadman's Cay each Tuesday (see the Salt Pond section for details).

Gladstone Taylor (☎ 242-337-1055) rents cars at the airport. Or try Ophelia's Rent-a-Car (☎ 242-337-1042). There's a Shell gas station near Cartwrights.

CLARENCE TOWN AREA
The peaceful harbor settlement of Clarence Town, Long Island's administrative headquarters, has a stupendous setting on a hillside that falls gently to the harbor, where jade-colored flats deepen to Atlantic blues.

Information
The post office and BaTelCo are in the government complex (☎ 242-337-3030) on the north side of Clarence Town, as is the police station (☎ 242-338-3919). The clinic (☎ 242-337-3333), by the dock, is open 9 am to 3:30 pm Monday to Friday.

Things to See
Two twin-spired mission-style churches rise above the town. **St Paul's Anglican Church**, on a hill north of town, is accented with red trim and is pretty enough, but it's outshined by its Catholic counterpart – **St Peter's Catholic Church** – on a hill south of town. Ironically, both were designed by Father Jerome, the enigmatic architect-hermit-cleric of Cat Island. The first was designed prior to, and the second after, his conversion to Catholicism. Father Jerome conjured up a visionary confection in stone with sparkling St Peter's, white with blue trim, reminiscent of Greek buildings. You can climb the ladders within one of its two medievalist spires for a marvelous bird's-eye view over Clarence Town. Portly folks should forgo the climb; you could get stuck! The church, beside Queen's Hwy, is open all hours.

Immediately east of town is **Lochabar Bay**, a stunning half-mile-wide, flask-shaped cove that funnels east to a vast blue hole. It is rimmed by a splendid and lonesome white-sand beach, surrounded on three sides by dense thickets of thatch palm and scrub. Coral reefs lie just offshore, with staghorn at 30 feet.

Places to Stay & Eat
Compass Rock (☎ 242-337-1094), 1 mile north of Clarence Town, offers 8 modest

LONG ISLAND

efficiency rooms on Lowes Beach. It's a magnificent albeit lonesome setting with spectacular ocean vistas of the craggy shore with tidepools and jade colored flats and fine sand.

The all-timber *Lochabar Beach Lodge* (☎ *242-327-8323, 337-3123, fax 242-327-2567, lochabar@hotmail.com*), PO Box 30330, Clarence Town, Long Island, a wonderfully lonesome cottage-inn nestling up to Lochabar Bay, is one of the sweetest finds in the Family Islands. This small, utterly charming guesthouse offers two air-con studio apartments and a one-bedroom full apartment; the studios sleep up to four and the apartment sleeps five. All are spacious and exquisitely decorated, with homemade furniture, sponge-painted wooden walls, tile floors, ceiling fans, fully stocked kitchen or kitchenette, and wide French doors that open to a patio facing the bay. Studios cost US$115 single or double, plus US$20 for each extra person; US$150 apartment; US$750/1000 weekly, plus US$75 per extra person. *Highly recommended!*

You can rent two- and three-bedroom units – *Lochabar Beach Houses* (☎ */fax 242-337-0331*) – on the shore 1 mile south of town.

The best place to eat is the *Harbour Restaurant, Bar & Satellite Lounge* (☎ *242-337-3247*), a clean, modern eatery down by Clarence Town harbor. For a more down-to-earth offering, try *Skieta's OK Bar*, where locals hang out under a shady palapa.

You can stock up at *Harbour Grocery* (☎ *242-337-3934*).

Getting There & Around

The *Abilin* mail boat sails from Nassau to Clarence Town at noon on Tuesday (17 hours, US$45 one-way), also stopping at Great Inagua.

A 15-slip marina, under completion at press time, will make Clarence Town an official port of entry. Contact the Flying Fish Marina (☎ 242-337-3430, fax 242-337-3429, flyingfishmarina@batelnet.bs) for a progress report. It has a provisions store, laundry, bathrooms and showers, plus accommodations for sailors.

Red Major (☎ 242-337-3004) rents cars, as does Millander's Auto (☎ 242-337-3227). Seaside Scooter Rentals (☎ 242-337-3458) rents scooters at the marina in Clarence Town; ask for Jouiette or Vincent.

DUNMORE TO CAPE VERDE

The southern quarter of Long Island is scenically uninspired, although the 15-mile route leads past three exquisite **Father Jerome churches,** whitewashed and painted in trademark blue, in Dunmore, Hard Bargain, and Mortimers.

It also passes overgrown **plantation ruins,** such as Dunmore, named for a former governor of The Bahamas who had an estate producing sisal, cotton, and pineapples. You can follow a dirt track half a mile to the ruined hilltop mansion; look for the gates beside the road just north of the church at Dunmore, about 3 miles southeast of Clarence Town.

Great salt ponds (accessible by side roads) lie hidden from view between the road and west shore. The Diamond Crystal Salt Co produced salt and shrimp here until the 1970s. A Taiwanese company reportedly plans to resurrect shrimping.

Another side road leads to **Roses**, a quaint hilltop village that overlooks Little Harbour.

Income levels decrease progressively to the south, with modern bungalows giving way to mostly clapboard homes and tumbledown emancipation-era houses. The road ends at Gordons, a small, down-at-the-heels hamlet.

From Gordons, you can hike a mile to Cape Verde, which is the island's southernmost point.

Crooked Island District

Crooked Island, Acklins Island, Long Cay, and outlying Samana and Plana Cays make up the Crooked Island District. The three main islands form a rough triangle enclosing the shallow Bight of Acklins – superb for tarpon and bonefish – to the north, east, and west, respectively. By all accounts, Columbus sailed down the leeward side of the islands in 1492, passing through the Crooked Island Passage, which later became a major route for Spanish treasure fleets. Columbus referred to the islands as the 'Fragrant Isles,' perhaps because of the aromatic scent of the cascarilla tree's bark (also called 'Eleuthera bark').

Highlights

- Taking a trip to Bird Rock Lighthouse and the Bat Caves
- Shelling at Shell Beach and skinny-dipping at Bathing Beach
- Dining with locals at Ms Gibson's Lunch Room when the mail boat is in
- Diving the Million Dollar Mistake – maybe you'll rustle up some unclaimed money
- Bonefishing in the Bight of Acklins. It doesn't get better than this!

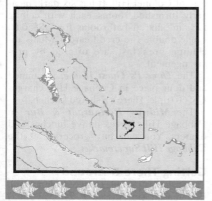

In the late 18th century the islands, like their northern neighbors, were settled by Loyalists from North America who attempted to develop a cotton industry. About 50 plantations were founded. By the 1830s depleted soils, weevils, and emancipation of the slave-labor workforce doomed the plantations forever. The white landowners left. The black laborers remained and turned to subsistence fishing and farming. Their descendants still fish, tend the land, and draw an income from stripping cascarilla bark and selling it to the manufacturers of Campari liquor (it is also used in medicines). Says one islander: 'Around 'ere everyone get up early to figure out a way to get by. You got to be creative, mon, to make a living 'ere.'

These southerly islands are relatively backward. Electricity still hasn't reached many areas, and tourism is almost nonexistent. But other adventurers come calling: Cubans and Haitians make the desperate run for a new life, and, not infrequently, drug-runners rush in aboard small planes to offload bales of cocaine that some locals – despite their God-fearing ways – will disperse to Nassau and abroad. Many locals who, for example, won't eat figs because Jesus cursed the fig tree are up to their necks in trafficking because Jesus never spoke out against drugs.

The islanders' idiosyncrasies are related in *Out Island Doctor*, the autobiography of Evans Cottman, a Yankee teacher who came under the Crooked and Acklins spell in the 1940s and settled here, where he was adopted as a doctor. Many of today's adult islanders were youngsters back then and scamper about in various chapters. Locals will tell you that the doctor stretched the truth: ''im spice it up so it sell well…'e put a lot of tricks in that book.'

A 50-mile barrier reef rings the entire island chain, offering drop-offs beginning at about 50 feet and plunging to 3600 feet in the Crooked Island Passage. I recommend bringing your own dive equipment.

In summer the mosquitoes are ferocious. Bring repellent.

Crooked Island

• pop 436

Crooked Island, about 250 miles southeast of Nassau, is the main island although only a few hundred souls inhabit its 92 sq miles. They're concentrated in Landrail Point and Colonel Hill, the motley capital.

Locals on several other islands claim brazenly that Columbus landed on their pieces of turf. But Crooked Island, which recent evidence suggests was the explorer's second New World landfall (he named it Santa María de la Concepción after the Virgin Mary), modestly makes no claims. There are no plaques.

The island's irregular shoreline is indented with deep inlets and sounds and lined by beautiful beaches. The main road runs along the north shore. Inland, briny lagoons and swamps cover much of the island. The rest is scrub and dense pockets of woodland. Bird watchers are in for a treat! Herons, ospreys, egrets, mockingbirds, finches, wild canaries, hummingbirds, and flamingos abound. And lepidopterists can spot approximately 28 endemic subspecies of butterflies. Spring is a good time to visit.

About 60% of the islanders are Seventh-Day Adventists (the rest are Baptists and Presbyterians)…and a devout lot they are, too! From Friday sundown to Saturday sundown, the island comes to a virtual halt.

COLONEL HILL AREA

The only major settlement flanks a hill midway along the north coast. The scrub-covered plain below slopes down to a beach-rimmed bay. The village comprises a few dozen ramshackle clapboard huts, emancipation-era houses, and pastel-painted modern concrete homes. The only building of note is **St John's Baptist Church**, atop the hill.

The road leads northwest 1½ miles to the twin settlements of Cabbage Hill and Church Grove and, 2 miles farther, to Cripple Hill. The only buildings of interest in these villages are lime-green **All Saints Church**, surrounded by *Spathodea* (flame-of-the-forest) in Cabbage Hill, and the small **Baptist church**, fronted by a tiny bell tower, in Cripple Hill.

From All Saints Church, a hilly dirt road leads southwest to a small ferry dock – Church Grove Landing – jutting into Turtle Sound, good for bonefishing.

Information

There are no banks in the Crooked Island District. The post office, beside the police station (☎ 242-344-2599) in the administration building in Colonel Hill, may provide basic banking transactions. The BaTelCo office (☎ 242-344-2590) is in Church Grove.

The medical clinic is in Landrail Point (see the Landrail Point Area section later in this chapter), but there's a nurse in Colonel Hill in the pink building opposite the school, at the base of the village.

The island is policed by a 'great whale of a man' named Constable Elijah; he can be reached at the commissioner's office (☎ 242-344-2197).

Places to Stay & Eat

Hardy budget travelers might check out the Reverend Ezekiel Thompson's spartan *Crooked Island Beach Inn* (☎ 242-344-2321), fronting a tiny beach half a mile east of Colonel Hill. It has six dark, meagerly furnished rooms, each with ceiling fan and shared bathrooms for US$50/60 single/double (no credit cards). Meals, including breakfast, are offered by prearrangement.

The *Three Ps Guest House*, a cramped and dour place in Cabbage Hill, charges US$60 triple. There's a shared kitchen.

The *Midway Restaurant & Bar*, in Cabbage Hill, serves native lunches and dinners. You can buy groceries at the *Cabbage Hill Supermarket*.

Getting There & Around

The airfield is 1½ miles east of Colonel Hill. Bahamasair (in Nassau ☎ 242-377-5505)

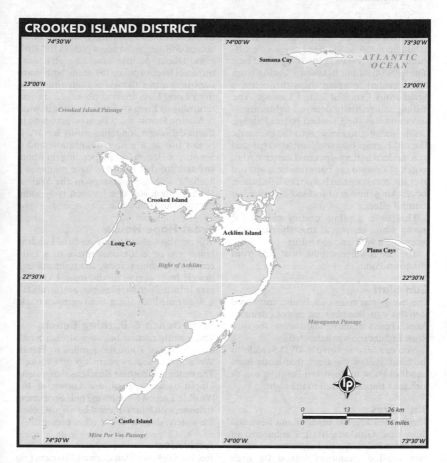

CROOKED ISLAND DISTRICT

flies between Nassau and Colonel Hill twice weekly (US$86 one-way), also stopping at Acklins Island. Charter airlines also fly to Colonel Hill; see the Turks and Caicos introductory chapter for some suggestions.

A small passenger ferry runs between Church Grove Landing and Albert Town (Long Cay) on Wednesday and Saturday.

You can negotiate a car rental with locals, any of whom also will run you about for a small fee. The Reverend Ezekiel Thompson (see Places to Stay & Eat, above) rents cars for US$60 to US$80 per day, plus deposit. There are no taxis.

LANDRAIL POINT AREA
• pop 50

This hamlet, 9 miles northwest of Colonel Hill, has a teeny harbor where the mail boat calls, announcing its arrival with two blasts of the horn.

A sandy 4WD track leads north 1½ miles to Pittstown Point, the northwestern tip of the island. Most local sites of interest are here.

There's a medical clinic in Landrail Point. The local phone booth is at Ms Gibson's Lunch Room (☎ 242-344-2676). She'll time your call on a stopwatch!

Bird Rock Lighthouse

Crooked's most impressive site is a small, coral-encrusted, sand-edged cay a mile offshore from Pittstown Point. It is pinned by a stately 115-foot-tall lighthouse dating from 1876, erected to guide ships through the treacherous Crooked Island Passage. The rusting and partially decayed lighthouse – also known as the Crooked Island Passage Light – today struggles against the elements. The old Fresnel lens was long ago replaced by a modern battery-operated lantern. Alas, scores of disused car batteries lie scattered over the coral cay and inside the lighthouse, too, leaking their acid to God knows what harmful effect.

The cay is a prime nesting colony for snowy white terns and tropicbirds, which caterwaul a welcome to visitors.

The cay is a five-minute boat ride from Pittstown Point.

Gun Bluff

The overgrown ruins of a British fort stand atop this shoreline bluff just east of Pittstown Point. There's a quarry where stone for Bird Rock Lighthouse was extracted.

You can hike or drive a 4WD vehicle to the bluff. Follow the track that leads from Landrail Point to Pittstown Point; at the Y-fork take the sandy trail to the right.

Bat Caves

These caves are 100 yards inland from the shore near Gordon's Bluff, 2 miles east of Pittstown Point. A small entrance opens to vast vaulted chambers linked by high tunnels. They're easily explored and the walking is level. Some of the walls are festooned with mosses, and there are stalactites in the depths. Land crabs find the cool retreats accommodating and bats squint down from their rooftop perches. Take mosquito repellent; clouds of ravenous insects lick their proboscises at your approach, especially after heavy rains.

Brine Pool

This amoeba-shaped lagoon, stretching from Landrail Point north to Pittstown Point, is separated from the sea by a narrow tombolo (sandspit beach), along whose shore several expats have built modest homes. Stilt-legged waders pick in the shallows. Ducks paddle atop the glistening surface. Ospreys police the scene with sharp eyes. In summer flamingos sometimes flock from Long Cay, arriving about sunset and returning to Long Cay shortly after dawn.

Marine Farms, a salt farm on an island in the midst of the pond, has a long history. It began life as a cotton plantation and a Spanish or British fort (depending on whom you talk to) that is said to have managed a firefight with US warships in the War of 1812. Cannon still can be seen lying amid the ruins and salt pans.

Great Hope House

This mansion, about a mile south of Landrail Point, was once the centerpiece of a 19th-century plantation. Today the ruins are embraced by towering jumby trees, blooming sage brushes, periwinkle vines, and scrub. It's a 30-minute hike along an overgrown track.

Shell Beach & Bathing Beach

These aptly named beauties stretch south from Landrail Point for 7 miles to **French Wells** at the southwestern tip of Crooked. The waters off Bathing Beach, as shallow and limpid as a spa pool, are known as the 'World's Largest Swimming Pool.' Snorkeling is divine, with fabulous coral heads just below the water. Alas, sharks are often present.

Activities

Robbie Gibson's Thunderbird Charters (c/o the marina ☎ 242-344-2676; c/o Robbie's wife at the BaTelCo office ☎ 242-344-2590) offers fishing for US$300/500 half/full-day for up to six people. Elton 'Bonefish Shakey' McKinney also guides for US$175/325 half/full-day.

Robbie offers scuba diving for US$35 per dive and rents scuba gear (mask and snorkel, US$5; flippers, US$5; regulator, US$10).

Places to Stay

Daisy Scavella's *Scavella Bonefish Lodge* (☎ 242-344-2598; in the US c/o Buccaneer Travel ☎ 307-674-9442, fax 307-674-6051,

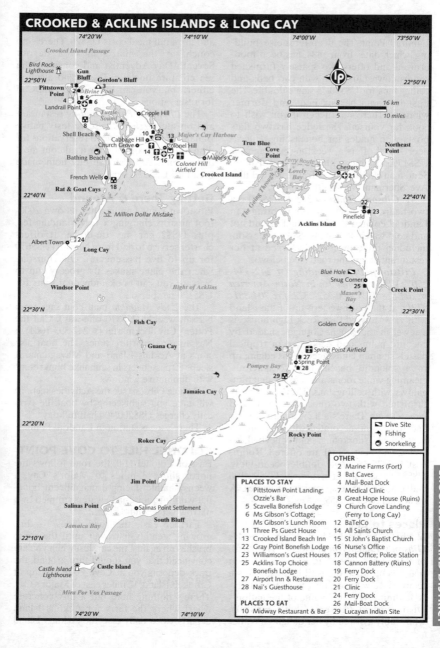

CROOKED & ACKLINS ISLANDS & LONG CAY

Crooked Island Passage

Bird Rock Lighthouse

Gun Bluff

Gordon's Bluff

Pittstown Point

Brine Pool

Landrail Point

Turtle Sound

Cripple Hill

Shell Beach

Cabbage Hill

Church Grove

Major's Cay Harbour

True Blue Cove Point

Northeast Point

Colonel Hill

Major's Cay

Ferry Route

Chesters

Bathing Beach

Colonel Hill Airfield

Crooked Island

Lovely Bay

French Wells

Rat & Goat Cays

Million Dollar Mistake

Ferry Route

The Going Through

Acklins Island

Pinefield

Albert Town

Long Cay

Windsor Point

Bight of Acklins

Blue Hole

Snug Corner

Creek Point

Mason's Bay

Fish Cay

Golden Grove

Guana Cay

Spring Point Airfield

Pompey Bay

Spring Point

Jamaica Cay

Roker Cay

Rocky Point

Jim Point

Salinas Point

Salinas Point Settlement

South Bluff

Jamaica Bay

Castle Island Lighthouse

Castle Island

Mira Por Vos Passage

0   8   16 km
0   5   10 miles

Legend:
- Dive Site
- Fishing
- Snorkeling

OTHER
2 Marine Farms (Fort)
3 Bat Caves
4 Mail-Boat Dock
7 Medical Clinic
8 Great Hope House (Ruins)
9 Church Grove Landing (Ferry to Long Cay)
12 BaTelCo
14 All Saints Church
15 St John's Baptist Church
16 Nurse's Office
17 Post Office; Police Station
18 Cannon Battery (Ruins)
19 Ferry Dock
20 Ferry Dock
21 Clinic
24 Ferry Dock
26 Mail-Boat Dock
29 Lucayan Indian Site

PLACES TO STAY
1 Pittstown Point Landing; Ozzie's Bar
5 Scavella Bonefish Lodge
6 Ms Gibson's Cottage; Ms Gibson's Lunch Room
11 Three Ps Guest House
13 Crooked Island Beach Inn
22 Gray Point Bonefish Lodge
23 Williamson's Guest Houses
25 Acklins Top Choice Bonefish Lodge
27 Airport Inn & Restaurant
28 Nai's Guesthouse

PLACES TO EAT
10 Midway Restaurant & Bar

david@buccaneertravel.com) is a simple yet endearing guesthouse facing the harbor in Landrail Point. The deep-turquoise building, which dates from 1884, has been modernized and offers two sparsely furnished rooms downstairs, each with two beds and ceiling fans, for US$50/75 single/double. The upstairs room has six beds and dormer windows. There's a kitchen if you wish to cook for yourself. The lodge has two flats boats with guides for bonefishing. Buccaneer Travel offers a weeklong package for US$1795 double, with meals and fishing. Send mail c/o Buccaneer Travel, 406 Schiller Ave, Sheridan, WY 82801, USA.

Ms Gibson's House (☎ 242-344-2676) is a two-bedroom, one-bathroom cottage in Landrail Point, with wood paneling and hot and cold water. It costs US$80 per person, including three meals daily served at her restaurant across the road (see below).

Pittstown Point Landing (☎ 242-344-2507, VHF channel 16; in North America ☎ 704-878-8724, 800-752-2322, fax 704-881-0771), at the northwestern tip of the island with views toward Bird Rock Lighthouse, is a jewel in the rough. Cottages shaded by coconut palms and decorated in tropical pastels sit amid landscaped lawns edging up to a splendid beach. The 12 spacious, gleaming-white rooms are in four squat bungalows with ceiling fans. They're sparsely furnished with two queen-size beds and large closets. There's a handsome little bar and restaurant, decorated with fishermen's nets. Diving, snorkeling, sand volleyball, bicycles, and boat rental are offered. Rooms cost US$75/85 single/double ocean-view, US$85/95 oceanfront in summer; US$90/100 and US$105/115, respectively, in winter. A meal plan costs US$55.

Places to Eat

Much of the local chit-chat occurs at *Ms Gibson's Lunch Room* (☎ 242-344-2676), or 'Mama's Kitchen,' an island institution that fills up when the mail boat calls. It's a teeny place with one long table for family-style dining. It's run by one of the nation's Distinguished Citizens (that's official), who – ably assisted by her daughter Wilhe-

mena – serves fried fish, lobster, peas 'n' rice, and johnny cake. Dishes cost US$10 and up; a full meal costs US$20. There's no conch, as the matriarch is a devout Seventh-Day Adventist and considers the sea creature unclean. There's no alcohol, either…but you can bring your own. Call for reservations.

The *Pittstown Point Landing* restaurant and on-site *Ozzie's Bar* serve tasty native Bahamian fare. You'll need reservations for dinner. Locals come by for a takeout meal or to drink. You also can buy homemade bread for US$3.50 per loaf.

Getting There & Around

Pittstown Point Landing has its own 2000-foot airstrip, charging a US$5 landing fee, plus US$2 per day tie-down. It offers charter service to and from Nassau (US$670 for up to five passengers). On Thursday when the plane makes its grocery run to Nassau, you can book individual seats for US$120 per person.

The *Lady Mathilda* mail boat sails from Nassau weekly (US$70 one-way). Call the Potter's Cay dockmaster (☎ 242-393-1064) in Nassau for departure times. The boat also stops at Acklins Island and Mayaguana. It sleeps 50 passengers in saunalike bunkrooms with diminutive windows.

Robbie Gibson (see the Activities section) will take you sightseeing by boat; he typically charges US$200/400 half/full-day.

There's a gas station in Landrail Point.

COLONEL HILL TO COVE POINT

East of Colonel Hill, the road follows the north shore 3 miles to **Major's Cay**, a weensy hamlet facing a magnificent bone-flat with turquoise-jade waters rimmed by a narrow yet splendid beach.

Farther east, the road fades to dirt, growing steadily narrower until the scrub brushes up against the car. Just when you are convinced that you should turn around, the track deposits you at **Cove Point**, the tip of Crooked Island, 12 miles east of Major's Cay. There's nothing here but a tiny concrete wharf where the ferry for Acklins Island departs twice daily (see the Acklins Island section later in this chapter for details), as well as a two-seat outhouse.

There are no services east of Colonel Hill.

Long Cay

• pop 30

This small island hangs like a wattle below Crooked Island, from which it is separated by a mile-wide channel. Columbus, it seems, landed here on October 19, 1492. The explorer named the island Isabela after the Spanish queen.

The island was later known as Fortune Island (it still is shown on charts as such, though few Bahamians know it by that name) and once boasted thriving sponging and salt industries. In the 19th century Long Cay also was used as the central Royal Mail station for mail traveling between England and the Caribbean.

Flamingos wade in the bight on the south side of the island. In summer they migrate – often daily – between Long Cay and Crooked Island. And an endemic subspecies of iguana inhabits two tiny cays – Fish Cay and Guana Cay – that lie 7 and 10 miles southeast of Long Cay.

In the 19th century **Albert Town** (also called 'Windsor'), the island's only settlement, was the main base in the archipelago for transatlantic mail and freight ships hiring and dropping off stevedores, or 'coast crew.' The port town was lively with bars and, presumably, illicit brothels. In the 20th century the town's population fell from 3000 to just 30 people. Wild goats have taken over the intriguing ruins, though the largest Anglican church south of Nassau still stands.

Albert Town still has a clinic and post office, although they may be closed by the time you visit. Stephen Rose has a small grocery and acts as a bonefishing guide.

Million Dollar Mistake

This famous plane wreck lies in 12 feet of water about 50 yards offshore. The plane was on a drug run when it crashed at sea. Locals found a suitcase containing about US$1,000,000. It was handed to an official from Nassau who, it seems, pocketed the money and went on to live the life of Riley.

Places to Stay & Eat

Steven Rolles has a basic **guesthouse**. And Ruth May will prepare food with advance notice. In this town of only 30 souls, you'll be able to find her.

Getting There & Away

Crooked Island's Robbie Gibson (c/o the marina ☎ 242-344-2676; c/o his wife at the BaTelCo office 242-344-2590) will take you to Long Cay by boat from Landrail Point (30 minutes, about US$100). He also includes Long Cay on a full-day sightseeing trip.

Acklins Island

• pop 430

Decidedly undeveloped and offbeat Acklins is separated from Crooked Island by a shallow passage called 'The Going Through.' The 45-mile-long island tapers southwest. It is low and sandy, except to the north and along the east coast, which are hilly and rugged areas. Reefs lie offshore to the east and there are fabulous and lonesome beaches along the shore. To the west, the bight extends for miles; bonefish gather in vast schools near shore, and catching 'em is a no-brainer. Flamingos also inhabit the briny flats.

Many of the locals still rely on fishing and beating bark for Campari. Public electricity arrived in 1998 (although plenty of homes still use a small generator). And most people still use public wells for their water source; to bathe, most locals dip water from barrels.

The main settlement is Spring Point, midway down the west coast. A rugged dirt road leads north to the smaller settlements of Snug Corner, 12 miles from Spring Point, and Chesters, at the northern tip of Acklins. The road runs nearly 20 miles south from Spring Point to Roker Cay.

A partially excavated **Lucayan Indian site** along the shore of Pompey Bay, immediately south of Spring Point, may have been the largest Lucayan settlement in The Bahamas. The only other site of interest is the remote

Castle Island Lighthouse, erected in 1867 at the southern tip of the island.

The annual Acklins Homecoming & Regatta is held during the first weekend in August.

Information

The police station (☎ 242-344-3666) is at Spring Point. There are clinics in Mason's Bay (☎ 242-344-3169) and Spring Point (call BaTelCo at ☎ 242-344-3550), plus a nurse in Mason's Bay. The Spring Point BaTelCo office also can be reached at ☎ 242-344-3536.

Fishing

The bonefishing is as good as it gets, as the Bight of Acklins has more than 1000 sq miles of knee-deep water. Most hotels can arrange fishing trips.

Fishing International (in the US ☎ 707-542-4242, fax 707-526-3474, fishint@ fishinginternational.com), PO Box 2132, Santa Rosa, CA 95405, USA, offers week-long fishing packages (US$1095 to US$2095 per person double occupancy; US$1400 to US$3366 single occupancy).

Places to Stay & Eat

Gray Point Bonefish Lodge (in the US ☎ 800-993-5287) in Pinefield, has new rooms. Here, too, the Williamson family rents two *guesthouses* (☎ 242-344-3210).

Acklins Top Choice Bonefish Lodge (☎ 242-344-3628; in the US ☎ 810-415-9750, fax 810-415-8577, bn1fsh2@aol.com), is at Mason's Bay, 10 miles north of the airport. It has eight air-con rooms for about US$50 nightly. One-week packages cost US$1950 all-inclusive (excluding airfare). The lodge's Web site is www.fishinginternational.com.

Locals gather at Curtis Hanna's *Airport Inn & Restaurant* (☎ 242-344-2590), in Spring Point, with two rooms with ceiling fans and shared bathroom for about US$50. Native dishes cost about US$6. Nearby, in the same price range, *Nai's Guesthouse* (☎ 242-344-3089) has four rooms and offers meals by appointment. Its restaurant has a bar with pool table and TV, plus music.

If you're catering for yourself, *McKinney's Grocery & Meats (☎ 242-344-3614)*, in Spring Point, can supply.

Getting There & Around

The airfield is immediately northeast of Spring Point. Bahamasair (in Nassau ☎ 242-377-5505) flies from Nassau via Crooked Island twice weekly. Alternately, a private charter plane should cost about US$900 for a five-seater plane (US$1500 for a nine-seater); turn to the Getting Around chapter for a list of small plane charter companies.

The government runs a passenger ferry from Cove Point (Crooked Island) to Lovely Bay, 3 miles west of Chesters, at 8 am and 4 pm daily except Sunday, returning at 8:30 am and 4:30 pm. It costs US$5.

The *Lady Mathilda* mail boat calls at Spring Point weekly from Nassau (see the Landrail Point Area section earlier in this chapter for details).

Leonard Cooper (☎ 242-344-3614) acts as a local guide and may rent out his car. Ethelyn Bain (☎ 242-344-3628), at Acklins Top Choice Bonefish Lodge, also has a car for rent.

Samana Cay

This uninhabited cay, 25 miles north of Acklins Island, still fits Columbus' description of the island that welcomed the explorer to the New World in 1492: 'quite large...flat...green...[with] many waters and white cliffs facing south.' The island's claim to first landfall has been hotly disputed for two centuries, but in 1986 a National Geographic Society field study concluded that Samana should indeed have that honor. If the claim is true, the *Niña*, *Pinta*, and *Santa María* anchored on Samana's southwest side, at a spot where the reef opens. Columbus explored inside the reef in a rowboat and recorded the features of the island that he named San Salvador.

Archaeological digs led by the National Geographic Society have unearthed at least 10 Lucayan sites (along with a Spanish earthenware vessel) and an ancient causeway of conch shells.

Crooked and Acklins Islanders visit seasonally to crab by torchlight and to collect conch meat and cascarilla bark. Otherwise no one has claimed the isle or settled it in the more than 500 years since Columbus landed.

Plana Cays

This string of small cays, beginning 15 miles east of Acklins Island, is a protected reserve for endangered great iguanas and the endangered hutia, The Bahamas' only endemic mammal. (The Facts about The Bahamas chapter has more on these animals.) An estimated 5000 hutias survive here in splendid isolation. No dogs are allowed ashore.

Amazing Grace, the supply ship for Windjammer Barefoot Cruises' sailing fleet, calls on Plana Cays during its twice-monthly island-hopping voyages between Grand Bahama and Trinidad. American Canadian Caribbean Line's cruise ships also stop here during their island-hopping trips. See the Getting There & Away chapter for details.

Inaguas & Mayaguana

Great Inagua, suspended just above Cuba and Haiti, 325 miles from Nassau and virtually off the tourist map, is the southernmost Bahamian island and a tremendous offbeat escape. Little Inagua is a diminutive isle to its northeast. Mayaguana, the easternmost and one of the most lonesome of all Bahamian islands, is 50 miles east of Acklins Island and 50 miles northwest of Providenciales (Turks and Caicos).

Great & Little Inagua

Great Inagua, 35 miles east to west and 20 miles north to south at its widest, is a parched limestone platform that narrows to the northeast. Uninhabited Little Inagua lies to the northeast.

Great Inagua's interior is covered in brush and cactus, with vast acres of exceedingly briny lakes. Though the trade winds blow here strongly and consistently, the island is scorchingly hot. About half of the island lies within Inagua National Park, protecting the hemisphere's largest flock of West Indian flamingos. The eastern two-thirds of the island are inaccessible except by arduous trek. There is only one settlement: Matthew Town, once a major seaport and trading center, which retains much of its rugged charm.

The human population is outnumbered five to one by wild horses and burros. By day they stay in the brush, wandering into the open at night to evade the mosquitoes (in years when the mosquito plague is particularly bad, the burros escape it by wading up to their necks in the ocean). The burros are said to be descended from wild asses sent here laden with gold by Henri Christopher, the Haitian revolutionary, when France attempted to retake that island in 1802. Locals say the treasure is still buried here. In truth the burros were simply imported as beasts of burden.

Great Inagua's human settlement was financed and supported by salt. 'Crystal farming' was initiated in the late 18th century and the island became a major salt exporter. For the tale of salt and Great Inagua, read *Great Inagua* by Margery O Erickson (Capriole Press, New York). Great Inagua also became a pony-breeding center. During the early 20th century, merchant vessels called in at Matthew Town to pick up crews, draining the population during a time when salt production was in decline.

In 1935 three Yankee brothers – the Ericksons – revived salt processing and began its mechanization. The industry was boosted during WWII by attempts to extract magnesium (a highly flammable metal) from brine. In 1954 the Ericksons' West Indian Chemical

Highlights

- Taking a fascinating tour of Morton Salt Works
- Counting flamingos in Inagua National Park
- Volunteering at the marine turtle research station at Union Creek Reserve
- Bunking at Camp Arthur Vernay in the midst of Inagua National Park

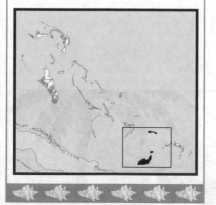

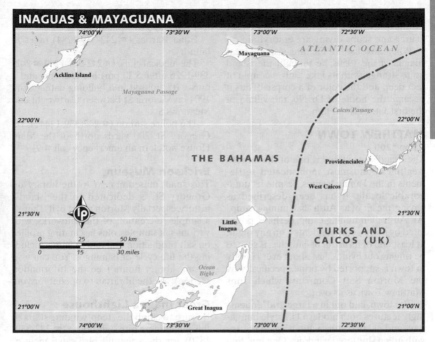

INAGUAS & MAYAGUANA

Company was bought by the Morton Salt Company, which still pretty much runs the island. Today Morton produces about 1 million tons of salt a year locally. Most is bulk-shipped for the industrial and chemical markets, for highway de-icing, and for northern European fisheries. The vast mountains of salt change hue throughout the day, turning pastel-pink and even purple at dawn and dusk. It makes you pine for a glass of water! Great Inagua, however, has no potable water supply; water currently is shipped in aboard Morton's M/S *Cecile Erickson* salt freighter and distributed by truck.

Lying only 50 miles north of Cuba and Haiti (Great Inagua is closer to both countries than to its nearest Bahamian neighbor), the island sometimes sees refugees washing ashore. Great Inagua's southernmost position also makes it a prime piece of real estate for drug-runners heading in from Colombia and other drug-producing nations. So many islanders profited from the drug trade in the 1980s that when a policeman became overzealous, locals burned down the police station and took him hostage. A riot squad was flown in. Things are calmer now that the US Coast Guard has a facility here.

So why the heck visit? First, how about 50,000 West Indian, or roseate, flamingos? (The locals say 'fillymingos.') In season – November through June – the birds can be seen in great flocks in Inagua National Park, strutting around like prima donnas, dabbling their toes in the water, wheeling in to land, or, most magnificently, taking off en masse in a pink blizzard. The birds mate in December and January and nest February to April. They migrate annually to Cuba. There are other rare birds, too, including the reddish egret, to entice even the most jaded bird watcher.

Hawksbill turtles come ashore to nest. Freshwater turtles inhabit ponds. There are plenty of wild boar, which the locals like to hunt (foreign visitors are barred from hunting). And the saltworks make an interesting study. There are few beaches. Sport fishing and scuba diving are embryonic.

When novelist Ian Fleming visited Great Inagua in the 1950s, he thought the island quite strange, with its lake 'only a couple of feet deep and the color of a corpse.' Thus it became the home of Dr No, the villain of the first James Bond film.

MATTHEW TOWN
• pop 1200

The island's only town is one of the largest, wealthiest, and most sophisticated settlements in the Family Islands, despite its unfavorable locale. It has been described as having 'the air of an Australian mining camp.' An Australian mining camp, perhaps, populated by more godly residents – on any night, at least one of its fistful of churches is sure to be ringing out hymns. Just about every family in town is supported by brine, specifically by the Morton Salt Company, which runs Matthew Town as its own.

The town, laid out in a large grid, endearingly features both modern US-style bungalows and old two-story whitewashed houses with green shuttered windows. One building stands out: the gleaming-white, two-story colonial structure on Gregory St (the main street), topped by a clock tower and housing the island commissioner's office. There's a small beach to the south, with shade trees and picnic benches.

Information

There's no tourist office. A local named David Hanna sells videos of Great Inagua.

The Bank of the Bahamas (☎ 242-339-1264) is one block north of the Main House hotel on Gregory St; it's open 9:30 am to 2 pm weekdays except Wednesday.

The post office (☎ 242-339-1248) is on the ground floor of the commissioner's office. Public telephone booths are scattered around town. The BaTelCo office (☎ 242-339-1000, fax 242-339-1323) is a half-mile north of the town's center; it's open 9 am to 5:30 pm weekdays.

The Erickson Public Library (☎ 242-339-1863), on Gregory St, is modestly stocked.

It's open 10 am to 1 pm weekdays and 9 am to 1 pm and 3 to 7 pm Saturday.

Edna Barbes (☎ 242-339-1284) takes in laundry.

The medical clinic (☎ 242-339-1249, ☎ 242-339-1226 after 5:30 pm) has a doctor and a nurse. It's housed in a building dating from 1904 on Victoria St between Cartwright and Meadows Sts.

The police station (☎ 242-339-1444) is on Gregory St, 200 yards north of the Main House hotel. In an emergency call ☎ 919.

Erickson Museum

This small museum, next to the library on Gregory St, is dedicated to the island's history, especially Morton's part in it. There's a simple re-creation of the saltworks, with various salt samples, plus fascinating profiles on salt production and native fauna, including the life cycle of flamingos. You can visit during library hours (see the Information section); ask the librarian to open it for you.

Great Inagua Lighthouse

Be sure to climb the steep, winding stairs of this gleaming-white lighthouse (☎ 242-339-1370) for the splendid bird's-eye view of the island from the observation platform at the top. The tower, a mile south of central Matthew Town, occupies the southernmost point in The Bahamas. It's one of three ancient lighthouses in the country that feature a rotating mechanism, similar to a grandfather clock, that must be wound by hand every 90 minutes throughout the night. Its beautiful Fresnel (or bull's-eye) lens focuses and magnifies light from a kerosene vapor lantern; its light is visible from up to 20 miles offshore. It's splendidly preserved by the keeper, who lives in one of two sextagonal buildings at the base.

On an especially fine day, Cuba can be seen temptingly on the horizon, 50 miles to the south.

Below the lighthouse, note the cut in the shore where a noisy generator turns an Archimedes screw that 'pumps' seawater into a channel to be conveyed to the Morton salt pans. Pelicans may be seen scooping fish from the channel, which is often chock-full

GREAT & LITTLE INAGUA

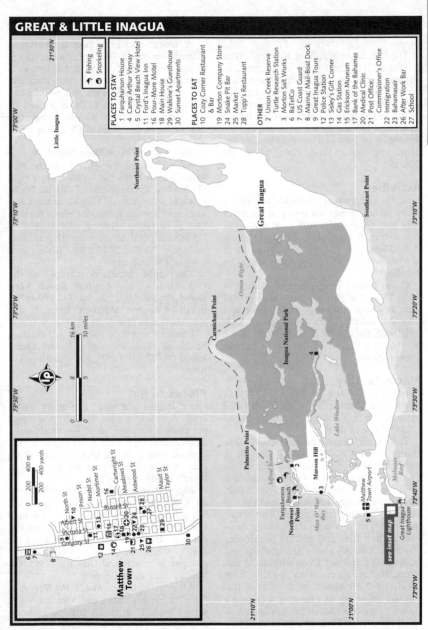

Fishing

Snorkeling

PLACES TO STAY
1 Farquharson House
4 Camp Arthur Vernay
5 Crystal Beach View Hotel
11 Ford's Inagua Inn
16 Pour-More Motel
18 Main House
29 Walkine's Guesthouse
30 Sunset Apartments

PLACES TO EAT
10 Cozy Corner Restaurant & Bar
19 Morton Company Store
24 Snake Pit Bar
25 Market
28 Topp's Restaurant

OTHER
2 Union Creek Reserve
   Turtle Research Station
3 Morton Salt Works
6 BaTelCo
7 US Coast Guard
8 Marina; Mail-Boat Dock
9 Great Inagua Tours
12 Police Station
13 Sisley's Gift Corner
14 Gas Station
15 Erickson Museum
17 Bank of the Bahamas
20 Medical Clinic
21 Post Office;
   Commissioner's Office
22 Immigration
23 Bahamasair
26 After Work Bar
27 School

Little Inagua

Northeast Point

Great Inagua

Southeast Point

Ocean Bight

Carmichael Point

Inagua National Park

Lake Windsor

Palmetto Point

Alfred Sound

Farquharson Beach
Northwest Point

Man O' War Bay

Maroon Hill

Molasses Reef

Matthew Town Airport

Great Inagua Lighthouse

see inset map

16 km
10 miles

Matthew Town

400 m
400 yards

North St
Prison St
Nesbit St
Mortimer St
Cartwright St
Meadows St
Astwood St
Russell St
Albert St
Victoria St
Gregory St
Maud St
Taylor St

of shad, barracuda, and other species. Locals gather in the early evening to catch their supper.

The lighthouse is fighting for its life. The Bahamas' Port Dept plans to automate it, but the Bahamas Lighthouse Preservation Society hopes to sway the government to save this maritime landmark and elevate it to the same status accorded other historic structures. Donations are welcome. For information on how you can help to save the lighthouse, contact David Gale (☎ 242-366-0282).

Activities

Isaac Cartwright rents boats. He also offers scuba diving (bring your own gear) and will take you bonefishing. Any local can point you to him. A good place for snorkeling is Alfred Sound, at the end of the road north of town, where bonefishing also is said to be excellent.

Great Inagua Tours offers snorkeling at Alfred Sound as part of a three-hour guided tour. It also can arrange bonefishing and deep-sea fishing. Larry Ingraham (☎ 242-339-1862), the quality control inspector for Morton, runs most of the Great Inagua Tours outings.

Places to Stay

Ford's Inagua Inn (☎ 242-339-1277), at Prison and Victoria Sts, is the most basic option, with four meager rooms for about US$45 single or double.

The endearing and well-maintained *Main House* (☎ 242-339-1267), on Gregory St in the heart of town, is run by Morton Salt Company. There are six rooms (including a triple) in the old two-story clapboard home. Most have private bathrooms and central air-con fed by the noisy power plant across the road. The two downstairs rooms have only ceiling fans and private bathrooms down the hall. All rooms are spacious and adequately furnished, albeit with dated furniture. Bathrooms are clean and large with plenty of fluffy towels and – taking Bahamian religiosity to extremes – Gideon's Bibles in the loos! Meals are not served. A small room costs US$55 single or double; a

large room is US$70 single, double, or triple. No credit cards are accepted.

A more modern option is *Walkine's Guesthouse* (☎ 242-339-1612), on Gregory St at the corner of Maud St. It has five well-maintained rooms, all with crisp, attractive decor, pin-neat bathrooms, and modern furniture, including TVs. Light is limited by small windows. Rooms with two single/two double beds cost US$55/65; credit cards aren't accepted.

The modern *Pour-More Motel* (☎ 242-339-1361), on Kortwright St (as the sign says – the street is actually called Cartwright St), has five air-con rooms, all with tile floors, private bathroom, and TV plus modern furnishings. There's a restaurant, plus a bar with two pool tables. Rooms cost US$65 to US$85, depending on size. The mailing address is PO Box 27, Matthew Town, Great Inagua, The Bahamas.

The only beachside hotel is the Colombian-owned *Crystal Beach View Hotel* (☎ 242-339-1550, fax 242-339-1670), north of central Matthew Town. It was closed at press time.

Ezzard Cartwright also has self-catering beachside efficiencies called *Sunset Apartments* (☎ 242-339-1362), in the south end of town.

Places to Eat

Great Inagua is a bit of a culinary wasteland. Most fare is fried. Health food hasn't yet made it here, and since few locals make an income from the sea, don't expect a wide seafood menu. Vegetables are rare. Even peas 'n' rice is hard to come by. At least there's no shortage of salt.

Topp's Restaurant (☎ 242-339-1465/1293), on Astwood St between Albert and Russell Sts, is run by a happy-go-lucky fella named Cleveland Palacious. For breakfast, you can get pig's-feet souse or eggs and toast for US$5; for lunch or dinner, try okra soup and grouper or conch and fries for US$5. On Sunday it serves dinner only.

Alternately, try the *Snake Pit Bar*, alias 'The Pit,' at Meadows and Victoria Sts. It serves basic fare: conch fritters, grouper, and hamburgers, all with fries, for US$5.

Similarly, there's **Cozy Corner Restaurant & Bar** (☎ 242-339-1440), on North St, which opens at 10 am.

The **Morton Company Store**, on Gregory St, is well stocked. A **market** is held intermittently by the beach.

Entertainment

The place to hang is the **Snake Pit Bar**, where the music is loud, the satellite TV is always on, and a pool table keeps locals amused. It hops on weekends. **Topp's** is a less moody place with a jukebox and dartboard as well as satellite TV.

Alternatives include the **After Work Bar**, down by the shore on Gregory St near the foot of Astwood St. It has a pool table.

Shopping

You'll find a small array of local crafts at Sisley's Gift Corner at the corner of Victoria and Mortimer Sts, and at BBB's Souvenirs on Nesbit St, one block inland from Gregory St.

Getting There & Away

The airport is 2 miles north of town. It has a telephone but no other facilities.

Bahamasair has service between Nassau and Matthew Town three times weekly (US$120 one-way). The local office (☎ 242-339-1415) is on Gregory St at the foot of Astwood St.

Private pilots clear immigration (☎ 242-339-1602) at the airport.

The *Abilin* mail boat sails here from Nassau at noon Tuesday (17 hours, US$45 one-way), stopping first at Clarence Town (Long Island).

Matthew Town Harbour (☎ 242-339-1427) has slips for US$8 daily plus fuel, and services. You'll need to clear immigration; there's an office (☎ 242-339-1271) next to the commissioner's office on Gregory St.

Getting Around

There's no bus service. Rocklyn 'Rockie' Barbes (☎ 242-339-1284) acts as an unofficial taxi driver in his beat-up old Yankee car that he drives at about 15mph.

You can rent single-gear bicycles for US$10 daily from Bertram Ingraham at Ingraham's Variety Store (☎ 242-339-1232) on Kortwright St.

NORTH OF MATTHEW TOWN

The road turns to dirt 2 miles north of Matthew Town. About 2 miles farther on, you pass between vast briny flats, the southernmost of the Morton Salt Works' mirrorlike salt pans, contained by dikes that connect them to equally briny natural lakes. Farther north, the dirt road passes sporadic beaches, the ruins of an old sisal plantation, and an abandoned Loyalist settlement.

About 4 miles north of Morton Salt Works, the road ends at Farquharson Beach, lining Albert Sound, a protected bay and a prime snorkeling and bonefishing spot where the abandoned US Aerostat station is located. Breakers crash over the coral reef about a mile from shore. A turnoff here leads east – inland – to the Union Creek Reserve (see the reserve's section later in this chapter).

Morton Salt Works

This facility is the second-largest solar saline plant in North America. It comprises 34,000 acres of reservoirs and salt pans surrounding a cleaning, storage, and bulk-freight loading facility.

Seawater drains into canals that feed the lagoons (the canals teem with barracuda, lobster, and bonefish), which spread inland for miles, separated by low dikes that channel brine between the vast flats. As water circulates, algae (fostered by flamingo droppings) grow and darken the water, hastening evaporation by absorbing more sunlight. Meanwhile tiny brine shrimp feed on the algae, filtering and cleaning the water. More impurities are removed via controlled movement of water, which is eventually channeled into 60 huge rectangular pans. There the supersaturated brine is evaporated to a specific gravity at which sodium chloride precipitates out. The water is pumped back into the sea, leaving a vast carpet of snow-white salt crystals – called 'salina,' or solar salt – about 6 inches deep. The whole process takes about seven months.

Each pan is 'harvested' once a year between March and June, and its salt is transported and washed. The soggy crystals then are stacked into huge mountains to dry in the sun before being loaded by conveyor belt into bulk-freighters tied up at the nearby wharf. Each pile of salt contains crystals of a specific size and shape; the different grades of salt are each intended for a different purpose.

The Morton Salt Company doesn't offer a formal tour, but any of the senior executives will be happy to show you around. Contact Carl Farquharson, the company president, or the general manager at ☎ 242-339-1847.

Places to Stay

Larry Ingraham (☎ 242-339-1204/1862) rents the four-bedroom *Farquharson House* at Farquharson Beach – a splendidly lonesome setting if you want a self-catering option.

INAGUA NATIONAL PARK

This 287-sq-mile national park protects the world's largest breeding colony of West Indian (or roseate) flamingos. It owes its existence to Robert Porter Allen, research director of the National Audubon Society, who arrived on Great Inagua in 1952 and dedicated his life to saving what might have been the last breeding colony of endan-

Some pink pals

gered roseate flamingos (see Ecology & Environment in the Facts about The Bahamas chapter). The park was created in 1963 and is administered by the Bahamas National Trust. Most of the vegetation is thorny, drought-resistant scrub. Bonsai forest also graces much of the interior. However, the brine concentration can overcome even the hardiest plants, and there are vast acres of deceased, leafless trees amid circular pools, looking like the Somme after an infernal bombardment.

The super-salty soup teems with brine shrimp and larval brine flies, foods favored by flamingos and a parade of other waders. Dominating the park is Lake Windsor, a precious mirror reflecting the antics of roseate spoonbills, endemic reddish pink egrets, avocets, cormorants, tricolored Louisiana herons, and about 50,000 flamingos strutting around in hot pink.

The roseate flamingo is restricted to Great Inagua, the Turks and Caicos, Bonaire, portions of the Yucatán Peninsula, and Cuba. The gangly birds visit Lake Windsor each spring.

Flamingos have started to repopulate neighboring islands…a sure sign of success. The birds have been hunted ruthlessly for meat and milliners' stores during the past 200 years. Locals still have a taste for flamingo steak (the flesh is said to taste like partridge) and occasionally shoot the birds for meat, despite a US$1000 fine and a penalty of three months' imprisonment. Hogs are the birds' other main enemies.

Sometimes you can see flamingos in the brine pools on the edge of the Morton Salt Works, outside the park boundary. But the large flocks are within the park, far from traffic and other disturbances. The best times to visit are early morning and late evening.

There are also burrowing owls, Bahamian pintails, endemic Bahamian woodstar hummingbirds, brown pelicans, stripe-headed tanagers, American kestrels, and endangered Bahama parrots.

Each spring a bird count is undertaken. You're welcome to volunteer. Contact Henry Nixon, the warden (☎ 242-339-

1616, fax 242-339-1850, VHF channel 16) for information.

Places to Stay

There's a bunkhouse at *Camp Arthur Vernay* on Long Cay in Lake Windsor – a beautiful, silent place in the midst of a foreboding landscape. The rather dour bunkhouse (called Basil's Bunkhouse) sleeps nine people in a dormer room and has two shared showers with cold and lukewarm water. There's an outdoor kitchen with wood-fired stove. Sheets and mattresses are provided. It costs US$25 per person. Arrangements must be made through the warden, Henry Nixon (☎ 242-339-1616, fax 242-339-1850, VHF channel 16), who may or may not overnight with you. You should take your own food, but Nixon will cook for you on request; be prepared to tip extra.

Getting There & Away

The park entrance, 20 miles from central Matthew Town, is reached via a dirt road that passes the southernmost of Morton's salt ponds and Maroon Hill (see below). The park gate is kept locked. You must be accompanied by Henry Nixon, the park warden, who charges US$50 for up to four people (US$10 each extra person) for a tour that includes the saltworks. Otherwise you can accompany Nixon on his rounds of the park 'for a donation.' See the previous section for contact information.

AROUND INAGUA NATIONAL PARK
Maroon Hill

This linear, cactus-covered limestone ridge stretches east to west at the south end of the Morton salt pans. Its ecosystem is different from that of the surrounding flats. There's a cave full of bats at its westernmost end beside the road. The hill is a good vantage point for spying the location of flamingos, which usually can be seen in the brine ponds immediately to the west.

Union Creek Reserve

This separately administered area lies at Inagua National Park's northwest corner and encompasses 7 sq miles of tidal creeks and beach where sea turtles – notably green turtles – feed and come ashore to nest. The sanctuary is the only natural feeding ground in the Caribbean region and mid-Americas where sea turtles are not hunted or exploited in any way.

Important research is undertaken at the **Archie Carr Research Center**. Donations and volunteers are needed. If you're interested, contact the Caribbean Conservation Corporation (☎ 352-373-6441, 800-678-7853, ccc@cccturtle.org), 4424 NW 13th St, suite A1, Gainesville, FL 32609, USA. The Web site is www.cccturtle.org.

Union Creek Reserve is accessed by a dirt road that leads 2 miles east from Albert Sound.

LITTLE INAGUA

This 30-sq-mile island, 5 miles northeast of Great Inagua, is uninhabited, despite its relatively rich soils, which support a dense stand of plump Cuban royal palm, the only such stand in The Bahamas. It, too, harbors a large population of wild burros and goats, as well as prolific birdlife. Marine turtles also nest here.

Amazing Grace, the supply ship for Windjammer Barefoot Cruises' sailing fleet, calls at Little Inagua during its island-hopping voyages, offered twice monthly between Grand Bahama and Trinidad. See the Getting There & Away chapter for details.

Mayaguana

• pop 308

Visiting Mayaguana, 65 miles north of Great Inagua, is about as offbeat an adventure as you can find in The Bahamas. Occasionally the island is favored by budget travelers, mostly European backpackers.

The remote, bow-tie-shaped island is 25 miles east to west and 6 miles at its widest, in the west. To the east, the deep Caicos (or Windward) Passage separates Mayaguana from the Turks and Caicos. The ties between the two are strong, and

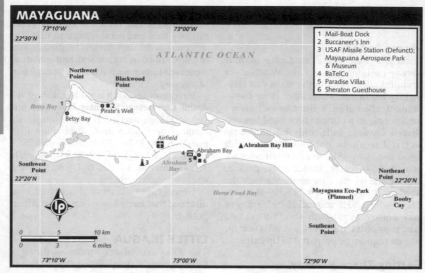

MAYAGUANA

ATLANTIC OCEAN

Northwest Point
Blackwood Point
Betsy Bay
Pirate's Well
Betsy Bay
Airfield
Abraham Bay
Abraham Bay Hill
Southwest Point
Abraham Bay
Northeast Point
Horse Pond Bay
Mayaguana Eco-Park (Planned)
Booby Cay
Southeast Point

1 Mail-Boat Dock
2 Buccaneer's Inn
3 USAF Missile Station (Defunct);
   Mayaguana Aerospace Park
   & Museum
4 BaTelCo
5 Paradise Villas
6 Sheraton Guesthouse

0   5   10 km
0   3   6 miles

many Turks and Caicos islanders settled on Mayaguana in the mid- and late 19th century.

The US Air Force (USAF) had a missile-tracking station – now defunct – here during NASA's Apollo and Mercury programs (apparently it was initiated during the Cuban Missile Crisis). Since it closed, many islanders have drifted away. The Bahamian government is planning a 25,000-acre eco-tourism project (see the Mayaguana Eco-Park section, below) that, when completed, may boost Mayaguana's fortunes.

Abraham Bay, on the south coast, is the largest of three small settlements on the island. Islanders have erected the motley Mayaguana Aerospace Park & Museum around NASA's theodolite pedestal, which once helped keep US astronauts on track.

Roads lead to the other settlements: Pirate's Well, 10 miles northwest, and Betsy Bay, 12 miles northwest.

BaTelCo has an office here in Abraham Bay (☎ 242-339-3203). Everyone else communicates by radio on VHF channel 16. Electricity and full telephone service arrived here only in 1997.

Mayaguana Eco-Park

Still in the planning stages, this vast park, at the pristine east end of the island, will have a botanical garden, an experimental farm, nature trails for hikers and cyclists, and sea kayaks for canoeing through the mangrove creeks. There are beaches, rocky shores, and reefs good for snorkeling, plus **Booby Cay**, an important nesting site for seabirds, offshore.

It will be several years before the planned tourist facilities are in place.

Places to Stay & Eat

Paradise Villas, in the heart of Abraham Bay, offers 20 simple rooms surrounding a small swimming pool, plus a restaurant and bar with pool table and TV. The hostess, Emmeline, cooks hearty native meals. Rooms cost US$85 including breakfast. Nearby, Doris and Cap Brown run the *Sheraton Guest House*, with two rooms for US$85, plus a restaurant. Both can be reached through BaTelCo (☎ 242-339-3203).

The funky *Mayaguana Inn Guest House* has five basic rooms of cement and wood for about US$40.

The beachside ***Buccaneers' Inn*** (☎ 242-339-3605), at Pirate's Well, offers 16 simple rooms for US$75. It has a restaurant and bar.

If cooking for yourself, ***Brook's***, ***Brown's***, and ***Farrington's*** are all tiny groceries open daily.

Getting There & Away
The airfield is 2 miles west of Abraham Bay.

Bahamasair (☎ 242-377-5505) flies from Nassau to Mayaguana three times weekly via Great Inagua.

The mail boat *Lady Mathilda* sails from Nassau weekly, calling at Betsy Bay after stopping at Crooked and Acklins Islands (US$70 one-way). For departure times, call the dockmaster's office (☎ 242-393-1064) on Potter's Cay in Nassau. Note that the mail boat now docks at Betsy because of navigational problems in Abraham Bay.

'Papa' Charlie and Bosie Brooks both offer on-demand water-taxi service; you can ask about it when you stop by their little grocery stores.

Turks and Caicos

Though constitutionally separate from The Bahamas, the Turks and Caicos are geographically part of the Bahama Banks. This oddity is a British crown colony with its own government, yet the US dollar is the coin of the realm. The islands have their own identity, different from that of The Bahamas.

The chain consists of eight islands and 41 small cays, of which only nine are inhabited. Though it's just a 75-minute flight from Miami (closer than Puerto Rico or the US Virgin Islands), this obscure outpost has begun to appear on tourist maps only in the past few years. The Turks and Caicos are like a hidden pearl, and an offbeat one at that. For many years the islands' tourist slogan was, 'Where on earth are the Turks and Caicos?'

Still, things are moving and on my last visit I sensed that the Turks and Caicos was about to swim into tourism's main current. Hotels sprinkled throughout the islands add up to about 2500 hotel rooms, but the Turks and Caicos Islands Tourist Board would like to double that number.

Ashore, they are not the prettiest of the region's islands, being rocky, semi-barren, and covered with cacti and thorny acacia trees. But there *are* notes of astounding beauty, such as Chalk Sound (Providenciales). The islands are also a bird watcher's and whale watcher's paradise. There are 200 miles of powdered-sugar beaches. (It's still an item of local lore – endorsed by Turks and Caicos tourism officials – that in 1962 John Glenn sighted the beaches from space and maneuvered his Mercury capsule to splash down in paradise.) The beaches shelve gently into emerald-green, sand-bottomed shallows that grade into Prussian blues where the ocean floor falls off into the depths. The waters offer fishing to rival The Bahamas. Wahoo, dolphin fish, sailfish, and kingfish are among the many game species that cruise the troughs within a half-mile of shore. The bonefishing is both superb and untapped. And a 230-mile-long coral reef with plummeting walls explains

why the Turks and Caicos is listed as one of the world's top 10 dive sites. If you're not an investment banker, reinsurance executive, or drug smuggler, chances are you've come here to dive the wall.

'Development' has come late to the islands. In Cockburn Town (Grand Turk), the funky capital, as late as 1965 the telephone operator was the jailer…and the telephone exchange was a hand-cranked phone in a wooden shack! But now, even karaoke has arrived. But no major cruise ship has yet called. And though resort development is proceeding apace on Providenciales (locally known as 'Provo'), where condos on Grace Bay now sell for US$1 million and up, the other islands retain a sleepy, bucolic mood. You don't come to the Turks and Caicos to live it up – you come for beautiful beaches, good fishing, and the down-to-earth charm of the place.

Facts about the Turks and Caicos

HISTORY

The early history of the Turks and Caicos parallels that of The Bahamas. Recent discoveries of Indian artifacts on Grand Turk have shown that the islands evolved much the same indigenous culture as did their northern neighbors. A ball court similar to those of the far more advanced Maya culture in Central America has been found on Middle Caicos.

Locals even claim that the islands were Christopher Columbus' first landfall in 1492. Some argue for Grand Turk, where a monument attempts to cast the claim in stone. Experts, however, have debunked the theory (see the Facts about The Bahamas chapter for more on Columbus' first landfall).

Colonial Era

The island group was a pawn in the power struggles between the French, Spaniards,

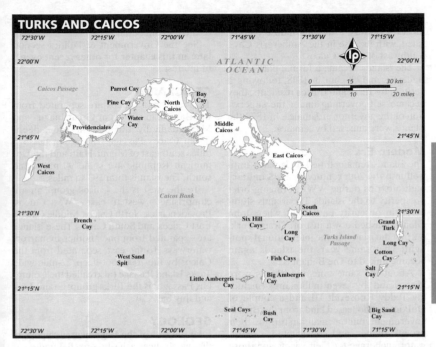

TURKS AND CAICOS

ATLANTIC OCEAN

Caicos Passage

Parrot Cay
Pine Cay
Water Cay
North Caicos
Bay Cay
Providenciales
Middle Caicos
West Caicos
East Caicos
Caicos Bank
South Caicos
French Cay
Six Hill Cays
Long Cay
Grand Turk
Long Cay
Turks Island Passage
West Sand Spit
Fish Cays
Cotton Cay
Salt Cay
Little Ambergris Cay
Big Ambergris Cay
Seal Cays
Bush Cay
Big Sand Cay

and British. For several centuries, ownership bounced like a ping-pong ball, landing finally with Great Britain. But lying to windward of the main sailing routes, possessing no gold or decent anchorages, and lacking sufficient rain for growing sugar, the islands were viewed as unimportant specks. They remained virtually uninhabited until 1678, when a group of Bermudians settled and began to extract salt and timber. Salt traders cleared the land and created the *salinas* (salt-drying pans) that still exist on several islands. Most of the salt went aboard swift sloops to supply the codfishing industries of New England and Canada's Maritime Provinces.

In 1710 the Spaniards captured the islands, then sailed away. The Bermudians returned and prospered. Like their northerly neighbors, the islands became a base for notorious pirates, who were not averse to sacking the wealthy salt merchants' homes. Some people claim that piracy accounts for

the islands' name: 'Turks' for the name of a group of Mediterranean pirates and 'Caicos' for the name of the boats. ('Baloney!' say others: 'Turks' refers to the species of native cactus whose scarlet blossom resembles a Turkish fez; 'cayos' is for the Spanish word for 'tiny isles.')

The pirates' depredations invoked a French attack in 1753, and France claimed the islands. Though repelled the following year by a British warship from the Carolinas, the French briefly occupied Grand Turk again in 1778 and 1783.

Following the American Revolution, the Bermudians were joined by a wave of colonial Loyalists. They brought their slaves, established cotton plantations throughout the islands, and built the King's Rd, which ran across North Caicos to the end of East Caicos. But the plantation era was short-lived. By 1820 the cotton crop had failed. The majority of planters moved on. Many left their slaves behind, and eventually they, too, became salt rakers. About the middle of the 19th century, a whaling industry flourished, with its base in the Ambergris Cays, southwest of South Caicos.

The islands became a formal part of the Bahamas in 1799, but in 1848, following a petition by Turks and Caicos residents, they became self-governing under the supervision of the governor of Jamaica. In 1872 the islands were annexed by Jamaica.

Modern Era

The islands remained tied to Jamaica until well into the 20th century. The US military built airstrips during WWII, bringing brief prosperity to the islands. The islands slumbered in obscurity until 1962, when John Glenn splashed down just off Grand Turk, putting the islands in the international spotlight. That same year, the islands again became linked to The Bahamas.

About the same time, the islands were 'discovered' by seven millionaires (including Teddy Roosevelt III and a couple of DuPonts), who leased land from the British government, built a small airstrip for their private planes, and constructed a deepwater anchorage for their yachts and those of friends escaping the rigors of East Coast winters. When those friends arrived in larger numbers than their hosts could accommodate, the intimate Third Turtle Inn was built to relieve the pressure. By the 1970s Provo was the near-private domain of a group of wealthy escape artists from longjohn climates.

In 1973 the Turks and Caicos became a separate crown colony of Great Britain. Meanwhile, Count Ferdinand Czernin, son of the last prime minister of the Austro-Hungarian Empire, ferreted out a tiny dot on the map – Pine Cay, northeast of Provo – on which he planned a Walden Pond–like resort. After his death, it became the exclusive Meridian Club, a prize-winning resort still frequented by the sophisticated elite.

In 1984 Club Med opened its doors on Provo, and the Turks and Caicos started to boom. In the blink of an eye, the islands, which had had no electricity, acquired satellite TV. Today bulldozers and half-poured foundations line the roads of Provo, center of the tourism boom.

See the Government & Politics section later in this chapter for other recent events of interest.

GEOGRAPHY

The Turks and Caicos are separated from the Bahamian islands of Great Inagua and Mayaguana by the 30-mile-wide, deep-ocean Caicos Passage. The group lies 575 miles southeast of Miami. Haiti and the Dominican Republic are some 90 miles due south. The islands total 193 sq miles.

To the west is the Caicos group, an arc comprising – west to east – West Caicos, Providenciales, North Caicos, Middle Caicos, East Caicos, and South Caicos. These islands are separated from one another by narrow waterways. To the east, separated from the Caicos by the 7000-foot-deep, 22-mile-wide Turks Island Passage (also called the Columbus Passage) is the Turks group: Grand Turk and tiny Salt Cay.

GEOLOGY

Like the rest of the Bahamian archipelago, the two groups each sit atop a flat underwater mountain surrounded by its own barrier reef. Separating the islands are shallow, sand-covered banks that cover an area 10 times larger than the islands' land area. As in The Bahamas, there are sinkholes, notably Ocean Hole, a 1200-foot-wide, 200-foot-deep blue hole off the south shore of Middle Caicos.

See the Geology section in the Facts about The Bahamas chapter for details on geological formations in the region.

CLIMATE

The Turks and Caicos' climate is similar to that of the southern Bahamas, though slightly warmer and drier. Temperatures average 77° in winter and rise to an average of 90° in summer. The hottest months are August to November, when trade winds can die and temperatures can soar to 100° or more. Average humidity is 35% (significantly less than most Bahamian islands). Average annual rainfall is 21 inches (less in

Quiet moment at Arthur's Beach on Eleuthera

Little Exuma gospel singers

Secluded beach on Twin Cay in the Exumas

Conch salad

The Queen Conch

Juicy limes and hot peppers

Lunch! Catch of the day

Conch salad fixin's

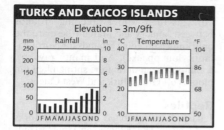

TURKS AND CAICOS ISLANDS

Elevation – 3m/9ft

the Turks group and slightly more in North, Middle, and East Caicos). Most falls in summer.

Official announcements of hurricanes are broadcast on Turks and Caicos Radio (on Grand Turk 94.9 FM; on Provo 105.9 FM). Hurricane-shelter locations are listed on page 28 of the telephone directory. There is a Hurricane Command Centre (☎ 649-946-1425) on Grand Turk and another on Provo, at the Myrtle Rigby Health Complex. (For more on hurricanes, turn to Climate in the Facts about The Bahamas chapter, as well as the boxed text 'Big Blows.')

ECOLOGY & ENVIRONMENT

The Turks and Caicos (whose official slogan is 'Beautiful by Nature') bear similarities to the southernmost Bahamian islands, in particular Great Inagua and Crooked and Acklins Islands. They are predominantly semi-arid, notably Salt Cay and much of South Caicos and Grand Turk, which were denuded of vegetation to dissuade rainfall during the heyday of the salt industry. The larger, middle islands of North, Middle, and East Caicos are more lush.

Much of the islands, notably the southern halves of North, Middle, and East Caicos, is composed of creeks, sand flats, lagoons, and marshy wetlands. Most of the sandy beaches – some of the finest on the planet – are on the north and west shores, facing the open ocean.

More than 30 protected areas have been set aside to conserve delicate ecosystems and wildlife habitat (see the National Parks section later in this chapter). Spearfishing, diving for lobster and conch, and Jet Skiing are outlawed within the preserves.

FLORA

The vegetation is tenacious and well adapted to drought. Cacti thrive. Native vegetation varies from island to island according to variations in rainfall; North Caicos is the lushest island. Salt Cay and West Caicos are virtual deserts.

Typical species include the sweet acacia, prickly pear, doughboy cactus, and cinicord, with its fuzzy, lollipop-like yellow flowers. Unique to the islands is the Turk's head cactus, which you'll see on the national flag. It's easily recognizable: a short, stubby cactus topped by a red flower shaped like a fez. Aloe and sisal are also common.

You'll recognize wild cotton plants by the lint given off in spring, and the gumbo limbo tree by its coppery bark. Buttonwood, candlewood, and aptly named poisonwood are abundant. Dwarf silver palm is common along the shore. Wild mahogany, bay cedar, and lignum vitae can still be found. The

Turk's head cactus

TURKS AND CAICOS

coconut palm is not native; it was only recently introduced by resort developers.

There are many flowering trees and bushes, including the false frangipani and the bonsai-like red mangrove, whose white and yellow blossoms emit a deep fragrance in summer. Wild orchids bloom in winter. The bougainvillea, the magnificent royal poinciana, and casuarina are among the more common exotic species introduced to the islands, as is the Geiger tree, with its bright orange blossoms, and the golden shower tree, a native of India named for its cascade of brilliant yellow blossoms in late spring.

Other trees bear fruits, such as the pigeon plum (good for making jams), passion flower, canip (known in the Florida Keys as 'Spanish lime'), and wild dilly, whose gummy fruit is favored by iguanas (humans prefer its domesticated cousin, which produces chicle, once the main ingredient in chewing gum).

Seagrasses and seaweeds flourish in the vast banks south of the Caicos islands. The dense meadows extend for miles. The most common species is turtle grass, so-called because it is a favorite food of green turtles. The grassy ocean meadows support huge populations of mollusks, sea urchins, sea cucumbers, and other animals, notably conch, a favorite food of stingrays, octopi, and loggerhead turtles.

FAUNA

There are almost as many donkeys, wild horses, and cattle as humans, though they stay in the wilds. Their forebears once carried 25lb burlap bags of salt from the ponds to the warehouses and docks. Having earned their rest, they were set free.

Marine Life

A flourishing population of bottle-nosed dolphins lives in these waters. The islands' unofficial and much-cherished mascot is JoJo, a 7-foot male bottle-nosed dolphin, who has been playing with tourists off Provo's Grace Bay Beach and Pine Cay since leaving his pod in 1983.

As many as 7000 North Atlantic humpback whales use the Turks Island Passage and the Mouchoir Banks, south of Grand Turk, as their winter breeding grounds between January and March (these are the only known breeding grounds for North Atlantic humpbacks). And manta rays are commonly seen during the spring plankton blooms off Grand Turk and West Caicos.

Reptiles

Iguanas once inhabited much of the Turks and Caicos. The colonies on larger islands were wiped out by development, which destroyed their natural habitats, and by newly introduced predators – domestic cats and dogs. Today they're endangered.

The Turks and Caicos National Trust (see the National Parks section later in this chapter) has a 'Little Water Cay Initiative' to raise US$50,000 annually for preservation of the rock iguana (Cyclura carnata), the endangered endemic species found only on Little Water Cay, northeast of Provo. The 1500 or so iguanas have become a major

---

JoJo, the Friendly 'Flipper'

For more than a decade, a 7-foot bottle-nosed male dolphin called JoJo has cruised the waters off Provo and North Caicos. When he first appeared, he was shy and he limited his human contact to following or playing in the bow waves of boats. He soon turned gregarious and has become an active participant whenever people are in the water. In 1995 JoJo crossed the Turks Island Passage and appeared off Grand Turk, where he spent a month.

JoJo is now so popular that he has been named a national treasure by the Ministry of Natural Resources. JoJo even has his own warden, who studies his behavior and looks out for him as part of the JoJo Dolphins Project (☎/fax 649-941-5617), PO Box 153, Providenciales, Turks and Caicos, BWI. Web site: www.jojo.tc

It is important to remember that JoJo is wild and therefore unpredictable. See the cautions in the Outdoor Activities chapter.

tourist lure for the 150-acre cay, part of Princess Alexandra National Park, which also comprises Mangrove Cay and Donna Cay. Fort George Cay (between Provo and North Caicos) and the Ambergris Cays (south of South Caicos) also are protected iguana reserves.

A rare endemic snake species, the Turks Island boa *(Epicrates chrysogaster)* inhabits Big Ambergris Cay.

The waters are favored by four species of turtle. Hawksbills are an endangered species, although locally they are a dime a dozen and nest on many of the cays; alas, the Turks and Caicos do *not* recognize the hawksbill's endangered status. Green turtles visit the inshore waters and tidal creeks of North and Middle Caicos to graze on seagrass beds. Loggerheads are also common, and even leatherbacks are occasionally seen.

Birds
The vast wetlands in the southern portions of the Caicos islands are ideal feeding grounds for shorebirds and waders, and the numerous uninhabited cays throughout the chain make perfect nesting sites for seabirds. More than 175 species have been sighted, of which 78 are migratory land birds. Ospreys are numerous and easily spotted, as are sparrow hawks and barn owls. Flamingos – once numerous throughout the chain – are now limited to West, North, and South Caicos, where you may also see Cuban herons.

Frigate birds are more commonly seen here than in The Bahamas. The most important nesting site is Vine Point (Middle Caicos), but they also nest on Penniston Cay (near Grand Turk) and other islands. Pelicans are ubiquitous, more so than in The Bahamas. Many cays are important nesting sites for sooty and roseate terns, Audubon's shearwaters, and brown noddy terns.

Insects
These islands are home to two endemic lepidoptera: the Erebus and Oleander moths. The former is a dark chocolate giant that hangs out around frangipani trees and which can reach a wingspan of up to 11 inches; the latter is fond of poisonous oleander bushes (to which they have developed an antidote) and resembles a giant, bright orange wasp.

NATIONAL PARKS
Native flora and fauna are protected within 33 areas set aside as national parks, nature reserves, sanctuaries, and sites of historical interest under the aegis of Turks & Caicos Islands National Parks, which administers 23 national parks and nature reserves. The Dept of Environment & Coastal Resources (dccr@tciway.tc) has jurisdiction. It has offices on Grand Turk (☎ 649-946-2855, fax 649-946-1895), Providenciales (☎ 649-946-4017, fax 649-941-3063), and South Caicos (☎/fax 649-946-3306).

The Turks and Caicos National Trust (TCNT, ☎ 649-941-4258, fax 649-941-5710, tc.nattrust@tciway.tc), PO Box 540, Providenciales, is a non-governmental organization dedicated to the preservation of the cultural, natural, and historical heritage of the islands.

The Trust has established three underwater snorkeling trails: two off Provo and another off Grand Turk. It has initiated countrywide studies of bird populations, and in 1999 gained international funding to manage the Ramsar wetlands in North, Middle, and East Caicos.

Parks and reserves include the following (west to east):

West Caicos
West Caicos Marine National Park – Superb diving amid the coral reefs
Lake Catherine Nature Reserve – Protects breeding grounds of flamingos, osprey, and waterbirds

Providenciales
Northwest Point Marine National Park – Majestic stands of elkhorn coral and superb wall diving; inland saline ponds attract roseate spoonbills and other waterfowl
Chalk Sound National Park – A cay-studded lagoon of stunning turquoise
Princess Alexandra National Park – Protects the shore and offshore environment along Grace Bay and the cays northeast of Provo

North, Middle & East Caicos
Ramsar Site – Protects a vast expanse of marsh

and intertidal wetlands, a breeding site and nursery for waterfowl, lobster, conch, and fish; the Middle Caicos Reserve & Trail System is part of this park

North Caicos

Three Mary Cays National Park – Another important seabird nesting site

East Bay Islands National Park – Protects numerous small cays off North Caicos, favored sites for seabirds

Middle Caicos

Conch Bar Caves National Park – An extensive cave system, some with lagoons and most with colonies of bats and Indian petroglyphs

Middle Caicos Reserve & Trail System – Pristine beaches, freshwater lakes, and pine forests are accessed by 10 miles of trails inside the Ramsar Site

Vine Point & Ocean Hole Nature Reserve – Protects vast intertidal swamplands along the south shore, a frigate-bird breeding colony, and a huge blue hole

South Caicos

Admiral Cockburn Land & Sea Park – Protects the scrub-covered shore and offshore coral reefs of western South Caicos

Belle Sound & Admiral Cockburn Cays Nature Reserve – Encompasses the mangroves and bonefish flats west of South Caicos

Grand Turk

Columbus Landfall National Park – Protects the western shore and coral reefs off Cockburn Town, which some argue was the site of Columbus' first landing in the New World; the ocean deep begins within 400 yards of shore

South Creek National Park – Protects mangroves and wetlands along the island's south shore, home to migrating shorebirds and waders

Grand Turk Cays Land & Sea Park – Comprises a series of tiny cays – Gibb's, Penniston, Long, and Martin Alonza Pinzon – off the southeast shore, important nesting sites for seabirds, with abundant iguanas and Turk's head cactus

GOVERNMENT & POLITICS

The Turks and Caicos Islands (TCI) are a British crown colony, a dependency of the UK. The existing constitution dates from 1988. A governor from the UK is appointed as the Queen's representative, with responsibility for internal security, external affairs, and certain judicial matters. The governor also presides over the Executive Council of Ministers.

Local self-government is administered by the 13-member Legislative Council, an elected body headed by the chief minister (appointed by the governor) and empowered to enact local statutes and run the show on a daily basis, with a good deal of power to determine the islands' future. The last general election was on March 4, 1999. The legal system is based upon English common law, supplemented by UK statutes designed to apply to the islands, and local ordinances of the Legislative Council that are approved by the UK government. The judicial system is administered by a resident magistrate and a resident judge.

Relations between the islanders and the governor have been strained for some years. Governor Martin Bourke was appointed in 1993 with a US$35 million budget to combat corruption. In January 1996 Bourke suggested that government and police corruption had turned the islands into a haven for drug trafficking. When his comments appeared in the *Offshore Finance Annual*, opponents accused him of harming investment. Growing opposition threatened to spill over into civil unrest. In April 1996 the British government sent the warship HMS *Brave* to cruise the coast, and a squad of specially trained policemen arrived. In the end the much-ballyhooed popular uprising turned out to be just another lazy day in the sun.

The Turks and Caicos Crest

In 1860 artists were asked to submit a design for the territory's colonial crest. The selected design showed a schooner in the background and two men in the foreground, raking heaps of salt – a typical island scene of the 19th century. Unfortunately, the London flagmaker assumed that the salt heaps were igloos and added entrances to the white mounds!

In 1967 the flag was changed to include a new crest, depicting the country's indigenous spiny lobster, the queen conch, and the Turk's head cactus.

The issue created a resurgence in calls for independence, but so far these have been just agitated conversation over rum cocktails.

In October 1996 Bourke was recalled to England after his stormy term. He was replaced by John Kelly. A Jamaican national, Kipling Douglas, was appointed chief justice. At press time the chief minister was Derek Taylor, appointed on January 31,1995.

The government offices are in Cockburn Town, the capital, on Grand Turk.

ECONOMY

Historically the Turks and Caicos relied upon salt export and, to a lesser degree, upon whatever booty came their way from pirates. Salt remained the backbone of the British crown colony until the 1950s, when the industry collapsed.

Today the finance, tourism, and fishing industries generate most private-sector income. The Turks and Caicos are a tax-free offshore finance center, offering services such as company formation, offshore insurance, banking, trusts, and limited partnerships. Still, the industry is a mere minnow compared to that of The Bahamas, and you will no doubt be astonished to discover that Grand Turk, the much-hyped financial center, is just a dusty backwater in the sun.

The Turks and Caicos are experiencing a tourism boom: up from 87,794 visitors in 1996 to 110,855 in 1998, the last year for which such data was available. The government has grand plans for tourism, including a much-touted cruise-ship terminal on East Caicos, to be linked to Provo by a major causeway.

Still, income from tourism and offshore investment is not yet sufficient for the islands to survive without British aid. Practically all consumer goods and foodstuffs are imported. Agriculture is limited to small family gardens and teeny farms. The islands' most important exports are conch and lobster (about 750,000lb annually). Commemorative coins and souvenir-issue stamps bring in considerable revenue. And illegal drug trafficking, a major problem, is also a source of significant revenue for many islanders, whose per capita GDP in 1999 was estimated at US$7900.

POPULATION & PEOPLE

The population totals a mere 17,502 (July 2000 estimate). The growth rate is 3.65% per annum. Turks and Caicos islanders (called 'TIs' or 'Belongers,' or 'black Turkish people' in self-deprecating jest) are descended from the early Bermudian settlers, Loyalist settlers, slave settlers, and salt rakers.

Many whites are 'retirement-aged swashbucklers and goldbugs' and shady expat characters who, if you ask their profession, will tell you, 'Uh, I have some – er – investments.' Many expats, particularly Brits, are employed in the hospitality and finance industries.

More recently, hundreds of Haitians have fled their impoverished island and landed in the Turks and Caicos seeking opportunity: some come here having been told – I jest not – that a land bridge links Provo to Miami, and that they can catch a bus to the USA!

ARTS

Though slow to develop, the arts scene in the Turks and Caicos has begun to blossom. Traditional music, folklore, and sisal weaving evolved during colonial days and have been maintained to this day.

The local art scene is dominated by the Haitian community. However, now other artists are also well represented. Much of the work is inspired by the islands' scenery and marine life, with vibrant colors redolent of the Caribbean. The Bamboo Gallery, in Provo, promotes the work of local artists, including Dwight Outten, from Middle Caicos, whom some people consider the leading artist in the islands. Another family member, Phillip Outten, a Rastafarian, produces naive acrylic works (some in gay primary colors, others more somber) inspired, he says, by his meditations and 'concept of daily reality.'

The North Caicos Art Society in Whitby (North Caicos) sponsors local art, emphasizing silkscreen painting. Perhaps the leading artist in this genre is Anna Bourne, one of many expat artists, who lives on Provo and paints on silk with French dyes.

SOCIETY & CONDUCT

Turks and Caicos islanders are gracious, warm-spirited, friendly, and entrepreneurial. Occasionally you meet some taciturn, even cantankerous, figures.

The islanders are as devoutly religious as their northern neighbors. This doesn't stop some from philandering or having a tipple, for example, on Sunday, when the pubs (strictly speaking) aren't serving: 'We might be drinking, but we are conscious of our religion.'

Also see Society & Conduct in the Facts for the Visitor chapter in the Bahamas section.

LANGUAGE

The official language is English. The local islanders' distinct dialect bears much resemblance to the Bahamian dialect. The Haitians speak their own French-based creole patois.

Facts for the Visitor

See The Bahamas' Facts for the Visitor chapter for tips on planning your trip, such as when to go and what to bring.

THE BEST

Salt Cay This tiny cay, the southernmost major isle, retains an otherworldly charm loaned by the architectural remains of the salt industry and historic Balfour Town. Two splendid guesthouses and a deluxe resort add to the appeal. And there's whale watching in winter.

Cockburn Town (Grand Turk) The colony's capital is a charming enclave of old Bermudian architecture, including old inns. Wild burros and horses roam the sand-blown streets. The beaches are nice. And there's great sport fishing and windsurfing. But it ain't for everyone. You'll either love it or hate it (see The Worst, below).

Whale Watching Humpback whales mate and give birth in the warm waters north and east of Salt Cay...close enough for you to swim out from the scintillating beaches to be in their midst. *Wow!*

Swimming with JoJo The islands' resident mascot is sure to put a smile on your face if he shows up unannounced while you're snorkeling off Provo.

Diving the Wall What a rush to don scuba gear and drop down the sheer-faced walls – festooned with gorgonians and other corals – of the submarine plateaus upon which the islands sit.

Chalk Sound (Provo) It's hard to believe the beauty of this narrow, 3-mile-long inlet, whose waters are colored an impossibly uniform turquoise and studded with a zillion mushroomlike islets.

Grace Bay Who couldn't love Provo's miles-long stretch of white sand? It's one of the world's most spectacular beaches.

Flamingo Pond This brine lake, the highlight of North Caicos, is named for the flock of flamingos that are resident year-round.

Cuba Excursions For a description, see the '¡Cuba Sí!' boxed text in the New Providence chapter.

THE WORST

Grand Turk Despite my comments above, there's a second side to Grand Turk. Some of the locals are sullen, the sights can be seen in a day, and it gets infernally hot and barren in summer. You can almost read the thought, 'Oh, my God...what have I gotten myself into?' on the faces of expats who believed the glossy brochures and have just arrived for a two-year posting.

SUGGESTED ITINERARIES

The overwhelming majority of visitors restrict their stay to Provo and, to a lesser degree, Grand Turk. A few offbeat travelers make it to the more remote cays. If you really want to experience the heart and soul of the islands, take time to explore South Caicos or Salt Cay.

Here's a recommended offbeat approach to taking in the best of the islands, assuming a 10-day itinerary. Any combination will do.

Day One Arrive on Provo. Sunbathe, drink cocktails, make love.

Day Two Hire a 4WD jeep. Explore the island, visiting the Caicos Conch Farm, Chalk Sound, and Northwest Point Marine National Park. Take snorkel gear and a picnic lunch to be enjoyed at the Tiki Huts.

Day Three Enjoy water sports at Grace Bay. This afternoon, perhaps you'll play a round of golf or go horseback riding. Or you can sunbathe, drink cocktails, and make love.

Day Four Take a flight excursion to North and Middle Caicos (be sure to visit the flamingos) or a dive excursion to West Caicos.

Day Five Fly to South Caicos for bonefishing at Belle Sound or diving the wall.

Day Six Fly to Grand Turk. Explore Cockburn Town. Hire a boat for sport fishing, or dive the wall.

Day Seven Charter a boat for an excursion to Salt Cay for a prearranged lunch at Mount Pleasant Guest House. Take a tour by golf cart or dive the wall. If you're visiting in winter, go whale watching or even *swimming* with whales.

Day Eight Sunbathe, drink cocktails, make love.

Day Nine Treat yourself to a one-day excursion to Cuba!

Day Ten Home, sweet home!

TOURIST OFFICES

The Turks and Caicos Islands Tourist Board has its headquarters (☎ 649-946-2321, 800-241-0824, fax 649-946-2733, tci.tourism@tciway.tc) on Front St in Cockburn Town, Grand Turk; its mailing address is PO Box 128, Cockburn Town, Grand Turk, Turks and Caicos, BWI. The board is under the jurisdiction of the Ministry of Tourism (☎ 649-946-2801, fax 649-946-1120).

The board also has two information bureaus on Provo: at Providenciales Airport (☎ 649-941-5496) and at Turtle Cove Marina Plaza (☎ 649-946-4970, fax 649-941-5494).

The board maintains offices abroad at the following locales:

UK

Turks and Caicos Information Office, c/o MKI, Mitre House, 66 Abbey Rd, Enfield, Middx EN1 2RQ (☎ 020-8350-1017, fax 020-8350-1011, tricia@ttg.co.uk)

USA

Turks and Caicos Islands Tourist Board, 11645 Biscayne Blvd, suite 302, Miami, FL 33181 (☎ 800-241-0824)

VISAS & DOCUMENTS

US citizens need proof of citizenship (a valid passport, voter's registration card, or birth certificate) and photo identification to enter the Turks and Caicos. Everyone else, including UK citizens, needs a valid passport. No visas are required for citizens of the US, Canada, UK and Commonwealth countries, Ireland, and most Western European countries. Citizens of most other countries require visas, which can be obtained from British embassies, High Commissions, or consulates abroad (see below).

For information on work, residence, or stays longer than three months, contact the Turks and Caicos Immigration Dept (☎ 649-946-2929, fax 649-946-2924), South Base, Grand Turk, Turks and Caicos, BWI.

Proof of onward transportation is required upon entry.

To rent a car, citizens of the US, Canada, and the UK and Commonwealth countries are required to have a valid driver's license for stays of up to three months. Everyone else requires an International Driving License (see the Facts for the Visitor chapter in the Bahamas section for information on how to obtain one). You must get this permit *before* you arrive in the Turks and Caicos.

EMBASSIES & CONSULATES

Turks and Caicos Representation Abroad

As a British crown colony, the Turks and Caicos are represented through British embassies and consulates abroad. For a complete listing, the Web site www.embassyworld.com/embassy/uk1.htm is usually up-to-date.

In the USA, contact the British Embassy (☎ 202-588-6500, fax 202-588-7870), 3100 Massachusetts Ave NW, Washington, DC 20008-3600, or the Consular Section (☎ 202-588-7800, fax 202-797-2929), Observatory Circle, Washington, DC 20008-3600.

There are also British Consulate-Generals in many US cities, including Atlanta, Boston, Chicago, Houston, Los Angeles, Miami, New York, and San Francisco.

In Canada, contact the British High Commission (☎ 613-237-1530, fax 613-237-7980), 80 Elgin St, Ottawa K1P 5K7, ON. The Web site is www.britain-in-canada.org/.

In Canada, you can also contact the following consulates:

Montreal

British Consulate-General (☎ 514-866-5863, fax 514-866-0202, bcgmtl@videotron.ca), 1000 De La Gauchetiere St W, suite 4200, Montreal, Quebec H3B 4W5

Toronto
British High Commission (☎ 613-237 2008, fax 613-237 6537, passportenquiries@ottawa.mail. fco.gov.uk), 80 Elgin St, Ottawa, Ontario K1P 5K7

Vancouver
(☎ 604-683-4421, fax 604-681-0693, british_consulate@ telus.net), 1111 Melville St, suite 800, Vancouver, BC

Embassies & Consulates in the Turks and Caicos

There are no foreign embassies or consulates in the Turks and Caicos.

The US Embassy & Consulate (☎ 242-322-1181/2/3, fax 242-328-7838), on Queen St in Nassau in The Bahamas, also serves the Turks and Caicos.

CUSTOMS

Visitors may each bring in duty free one carton of cigarettes or 50 cigars, one bottle of liquor or wine, and 50 grams of perfume. The importation of all firearms is forbidden, except upon written authorization from the Commissioner of Police. Spear guns, drugs, and pornography are also illegal.

For further information, contact Turks and Caicos Customs (☎ 649-946-2993).

MONEY

The Turks and Caicos are unique: a British-dependent territory with the US dollar as its official currency. The treasury also issues a Turks and Caicos crown and quarter. There are no currency restrictions on the amount of money that visitors can bring in.

The country is pricey. Credit cards are readily accepted on Provo and Grand Turk, as are traveler's checks. Elsewhere you may need to operate on a cash-only basis.

Foreign currency can be changed at local banks, which can also issue credit-card advances. Barclays Bank has branches in Provo, Grand Turk, and South Caicos. Scotiabank has branches in Provo and Grand Turk.

There are no direct taxes on either income or capital for individuals or companies. Indirect taxation is limited to telephone charges (10%), customs duties (33%), car (US$10) and scooter rental (US$5), plus the

9% hotel tax and a 1% surcharge to fund the new National Parks Service, and US$15 air departure tax.

POST & COMMUNICATIONS
Sending & Receiving Mail

The post office headquarters (☎ 649-946-1334) is on Grand Turk. There's at least one post office on each island. Most are open 8 am to 12:30 pm and 2 to 4:30 pm Monday to Thursday and 8 am to 12:30 pm Friday. All the caveats mentioned regarding sending and receiving mail in The Bahamas apply here as well (see the Facts for the Visitor chapter in the Bahamas section).

DHL Worldwide Express (☎ 649-946-4352) has an office in Butterfield Square, Provo; Federal Express (in Provo ☎ 649-946-4682; in Grand Turk ☎ 649-946-2542) is also represented.

Telephone & Fax

Cable & Wireless operates a digital network using state-of-the-art equipment. Its offices are on Grand Turk and Provo. Direct dial is standard.

Public phone booths are located throughout the islands. Many booths require phonecards, issued in denominations of US$5, US$10, and US$20 (plus 10% government tax).

You can also bill calls to your American Express, Discover, Visa, or MasterCard by dialing ☎ 111 on any touchtone phone and giving the operator your card details (there's a three-minute minimum).

Calls to the US and Caribbean cost US$2.50 per minute; to the UK and Canada, US$3.30; to The Bahamas, US$1.95; to Europe, US$4; and to the rest of the world, US$5. Rates drop on weekdays between 7 pm and 6 am, and all day on weekends.

When calling from abroad, dial the country code (☎ 649), then ☎ 94, and then the five-digit local number. When dialing within the Turks and Caicos, dial the seven-digit local number only.

For the local operator, call ☎ 110; for the international operator, call ☎ 115.

Cellular Phones You can rent a cellular phone at Cable & Wireless offices for US$10 a day. There's no long-distance charge if you bring your own phone card. National calls cost US$1 per minute. Calls to the US and Caribbean cost US$2.15 to US$2.95 per minute; to Canada and the UK, US$2.45 to US$3.70; and to Western Europe, US$2.70 to US$4.50.

Fax Most major hotels have a fax machine. Faxes can also be sent via Cable & Wireless offices, as can telexes. Telexes are billed at the same rate as telephone calls. Telegrams cost US55¢ a word. A 10% government tax is charged.

BOOKS
The *Turks and Caicos Pocket Guide*, edited by Julia Blake (Domy Graphix, Providenciales), is a handy compendium-style guide to the islands. It is not a sightseeing guide.

Diving and Snorkeling Guide to the Turks and Caicos Islands by Susanne Cummings and Stuart Cummings (Lonely Planet's Pisces Books) includes detailed, illustrated descriptions of 30 dive sites, with ratings.

The Turks and Caicos Islands – Beautiful by Nature by Julia Davies and Phil Davies is a beautiful coffee-table book. And *Turks Islands Landfall* by HE Sadler is an illustrated, large-format text regaling the history of the Turks and Caicos.

Water and Light by Stephen Harrigan is a splendid memoir by a Texan who 'followed his bliss' and spent several months diving off Grand Turk. A reader recommends Amelia Smithers' *The Turks and Caicos Islands: Land of Discovery*.

Doing Business in the Turks and Caicos Islands is a 32-page booklet published by Times Publications, PO Box 234, Providenciales, Turks and Caicos, BWI. The company also publishes *Turks and Caicos Islands Real Estate Guide*. Each costs US$6, including shipping.

Several stores and hotel shops stock books. The largest selection is at Unicorn Bookstore in the Market Place on Provo (see the Caicos Islands chapter).

NEWSPAPERS & MAGAZINES
There are two newspapers: the biweekly *Free Press* (☎ 649-941-5615, frepress@tciway.tc)

and the weekly *Turks and Caicos News*. *Times of the Islands* (timespub@tciway.tc) is a slick, full-color, quarterly magazine serving both the tourist and the investor. Subscriptions cost US$28, plus US$4 for orders *outside* the USA; write PO Box 234, Providenciales, Turks and Caicos, BWI.

Provo and Grand Turk are each served by a free monthly visitors' guide: *Where, When, How: Turks & Caicos Islands* (☎ 649-946-4815) and a new competitor, *Turks & Caicos: The Magazine* (☎ 649-946-1994).

RADIO & TV
The official government radio station is Radio Turks and Caicos (106 FM) on Grand Turk. There are several private stations. For contemporary light rock, try 92.5 FM. You'll find country and western on 90.5 FM, easy listening on 89.3 FM, and classical music on 89.9 FM. WPRT at 88.7 FM is a religious and public announcement channel, as is WIV at 96.7 FM.

Multichannel satellite television is received from the US and Canada. The islands have one private television station.

INTERNET RESOURCES
The CIA's Factbook provides specifics on the islands at the following Web site: www.odci.gov/cia/publications/factbook/geos/tk.html.

Web Directories & Tourist Information
The following Web sites offer detailed information that will help you plan your trip to the islands:

North Caicos www.northcaicos.tc
Provo.net www.provo.net
TCISearch www.tcisearch.com
TCI Online http://milk.tciway.tc/
Turks and Caicos Islands Getaways www.tcimall.tc
The Turks and Caicos Hotel Association www.tcimall.tc/tcresorts.
Turks and Caicos Islands Tourist Board www.turksandcaicostourism.com

TIME
Turks and Caicos are on Eastern Standard Time (EST), five hours behind Greenwich Mean Time (GMT).

ELECTRICITY

The Turks and Caicos use 110 volts, 60 cycles, suitable to all US appliances.

HEALTH

There are no endemic tropical diseases in the Turks and Caicos. No vaccinations are required. See the Facts for the Visitor chapter in the Bahamas section for general travel-health advice.

The only full-service public hospital is Grand Turk Hospital (☎ 649-946-2233), which has an emergency room but is dour. It is considered a last resort by locals, who advise using the private medical centers on Provo: the Associated Medical Practices clinic (☎ 649-946-4242) on Leeward Hwy and the New Era Medical Centre in Blue Hills. For an emergency in Grand Turk call (☎ 649-946-2333).

There are also government clinics on each of the islands:

Grand Turk	☎ 649-946-2328
Middle Caicos	☎ 649-946-6145
North Caicos	☎ 649-946-7194
Provo	☎ 649-941-3000
South Caicos	☎ 649-946-3216

A government doctor pays a weekly visit to Salt Cay.

In medical emergencies beyond the capacity of the local hospital, patients are flown by air-ambulance to full-service hospitals in Nassau or Miami.

The Associated Medical Practices clinic on Provo has a recompression chamber.

EMERGENCIES

For the police, fire, or ambulance, call ☎ 911 or ☎ 999.

Other important numbers include the following:

Island	Police	Fire
Grand Turk	☎ 649-946-2499	☎ 649-946-2233
Middle Caicos	☎ 649-946-6111	
North Caicos	☎ 649-946-7116	
Provo	☎ 649-946-4259	☎ 649-946-4444
Salt Cay	☎ 649-946-6929	
South Caicos	☎ 649-946-3299	

DANGERS & ANNOYANCES

Crime is rare and muggings virtually unknown. The odd incident of drunkenness is about as bad as things get. Nonetheless, be cautious of petty theft.

The most sinister – dare I say asinine – threat may be the donkeys. Occasionally an unruly villain such as Buster, a frisky black jackass on Grand Turk, will think it quite fun to strike terror into unsuspecting pedestrians and cyclists.

BUSINESS HOURS & PUBLIC HOLIDAYS

Government offices are generally open 8 am to 12:30 pm and 2 to 4 pm Monday to Friday. Private offices and businesses are usually open 8:30 am to 5 pm. Banks are open 8:30 am to 2:30 pm Monday to Thursday and 8:30 am to 12:30 pm and 2:30 to 4:30 pm Friday.

Holidays that fall on Saturday or Sunday are usually observed on the following Monday.

New Year's Day January 1

Commonwealth Day March 13

Good Friday Friday before Easter

Easter Monday Monday after Easter

National Heroes' Day May 29

Her Majesty The Queen's Official Birthday June 14 (or nearest weekday)

Emancipation Day August 1

National Youth Day September 26

Columbus Day October 13

International Human Rights Day October 24

Christmas Day December 25

Boxing Day December 26

There are also numerous local special events; see the island chapters for details.

ACCOMMODATIONS

Lodgings in the Turks and Caicos, as in The Bahamas, range from quaint inns to fancy resorts. The variety is greatest in Provo, where you can choose among modern 'boutique' hotels, intimate guesthouses, condominiums, and Club Med and other all-inclusive resorts.

Rates range from about US$60 to more than US$400 nightly. A 9% hotel-room tax plus 1% surcharge apply. Most hotels impose their own surcharge (usually about 20%) during the Christmas season. Many hotels also add a 10% to 20% service charge, also assessed on anything charged to your room.

The Turks and Caicos Hotel Association has a Web site at www.tcimall.tc/tcresorts.

Also see Accommodations in the Facts for the Visitor chapter in the Bahamas section; most of those comments apply in the Turks and Caicos as well.

The following agencies arrange villa rentals:

Elliot Holdings
 ☎ 649-946-5355, fax 649-946-5176, Elliot@Provo.net

Prestigious Properties
 ☎ 649-946-4379, fax 649-946-4703, Sales@PrestigiousProperties.com

Market Place Villas
 ☎ 649-946-4919, fax 649-941-5880

Turks & Caicos Real Estate
 ☎ 649-946-4474, fax 649-946-4128, Sales@TCRealty.com

FOOD

Local fare is unnoteworthy. As in The Bahamas, conch, lobster, soft-shell crab, and fresh fish (often blackened with Cajun seasoning) are the island favorites, along with spicy Jamaican jerk chicken and fresh fruits, such as sapodillas and sugar apples.

See Food in the Facts for the Visitor chapter in the Bahamas section for more details on local cuisine.

ENTERTAINMENT

Night life is relatively subdued, except in Provo where a large number of lively bars and other options cater to the tourist trade. Several bars – especially in Grand Turk – are filled with chummy English expats and their colorful 'mates.' On Provo bars range from quiet cocktail lounges to Texas–style sports bars with live bands. All the islands have funky bars where bands play traditional rake 'n'

scrape music and the locals (mostly men) engage in dominoes or watch TV.

The only cinema complex is on Provo, although South Caicos has a small cinema on Stubbs Rd. Several resort hotels on Provo feature dance clubs. Live bands also do the hotel rounds.

There's a casino on Provo.

SHOPPING

The handcrafted plait-and-sew style of straw weaving survives. Handmade rag rugs and baskets are a great buy. The art scene is lively on Provo; you can pick up some splendid Haitian art. And you can stock up on Cuban cigars (but see the warning for US citizens concerning the purchase of Cuban cigars in the Shopping section of the Facts for the Visitor chapter in the Bahamas section).

Getting There & Away

AIR
Scheduled Service

There are international airports to Grand Turk and Provo, and most international flights arrive at Provo. Other islands have local airstrips.

A departure tax of US$15 is payable on all international flights. No tax is levied on children under 12.

American Airlines (☎ 649-946-4948; in the US ☎ 800-433-7300) flies two daily 90-minute non-stops from Miami from about US$185 roundtrip in low season. American has an office in Butterfield Square.

Delta Air Lines flies daily, nonstop from Atlanta (high-season fares were about US$760).

InterIsland Airways (☎ 649-946-5481) has service between Fort Lauderdale and Provo; you can also make connections through Nassau and Freeport, The Bahamas. And Lynx Air International (in the US ☎ 954-772-9808, 888-596-9247, info@lynxair.com) flies to Grand Turk from Fort Lauderdale.

Air Canada (☎ 800-776-3000) serves Provo from Toronto.

Bahamasair (in the US ☎ 800-222-4262, fax 305-937-6461) serves Provo from Nassau.

Turks and Caicos Airways (☎ 649-946-4255) flies to Provo from Miami and Nassau.

Charters

Sandals' Beaches Turks and Caicos resort offers charter flights to Provo from numerous North American cities (see the Provo chapter for details).

Canada 3000 (☎ 416-674-2661) offers charters from Canada. From Europe, you'll need to fly to Miami or New York and connect to flights to the Turks and Caicos.

Private Plane

If you're piloting a private plane, you can buy aerial charts in the Turks and Caicos at the Unicorn Bookstore on Provo. See the Books section of the Facts for the Visitor chapter in the Bahamas section for recommended flight guides.

SEA
Cruise Ship

The major cruise lines bypass the Turks and Caicos, although this may change – the government has been talking of building a cruise-ship terminal on East Caicos.

At press time, two cruise companies offered regular cruises to the islands: American Canadian Caribbean Line and Windjammer Barefoot Cruises. See the Getting There & Away chapter in the Bahamas section for details.

Private Yacht

Yachters are welcome and served by marinas. Yachters are permitted seven days in the islands, after which they can obtain a cruising permit good for three months.

Many of the approaches and landfalls lie within protected areas where anchoring is strictly controlled (moorings within such areas are for dive boats only, although visiting yachts can moor while diving). No firearms may be brought into the Turks and Caicos (you must surrender them for the duration of your stay). And no conch or lobster may be taken. The latest regulations can be obtained from the Dept of Environment & Coastal Resources (☎ 649-946-2855/2970/4017). See the island chapters for details on marinas.

An excellent guide to sailing the Turks and Caicos is the *Yachtsman's Guide to The Bahamas and Turks and Caicos* edited by Meredith Helleberg Fields (Tropic Isle Publishers). See the Books section of the Facts for the Visitor chapter in the Bahamas section for details and ordering information.

Tides swirl across the shallow sea bottom and around the sandbanks, making the shallows treacherous for boaters. Nautical charts are sold in the Turks and Caicos at the Unicorn Bookstore on Provo. You should obtain US Defense Mapping Agency charts 25720, 26260/1/2, and 26268, or British Admiralty charts 409, 1266, and 1441. You can order them from Bluewater Books & Charts (☎ 954-763-6533, 800-942-2583), 1481 SE 17th St, Fort Lauderdale, FL 33316, USA. The Web site is www.bluewaterweb.com.

Boaters should use VHF channel 16 (and VHF 09 or 13 as a last resort) for communications.

ORGANIZED TOURS

A few companies offer air-hotel packages to the Turks and Caicos. Check with the companies listed under Organized Tours in the Getting There & Away or Outdoor Activities chapters in the Bahamas section.

Scuba operators also offer packages from North America. Otherwise organized tours to the islands are rare.

From the Turks and Caicos, daylong excursions to Cuba and the Dominican Republic are offered by travel agencies; see the island chapters for details.

Getting Around

AIR

All the islands except West and East Caicos are served by air from Grand Turk and Provo. Most flights island-hop; planes land merely to drop off and pick up passengers, and they're usually back in the air before you can blink. Flights are often fully booked, and you may be placed on a waiting list.

Three local companies fly between the islands on a quasi-scheduled basis. The largest and most professional operator is

Sky King (☎ 649-941-5464), with about 10 flights daily between Provo and Grand Turk.

Turks and Caicos Airways (☎ 649-946-4255) offers regular scheduled interisland service between all the inhabited islands, as does InterIsland Airways (☎ 649-941-5481).

The smaller cays can be accessed only by charter plane. Fares are usually based on five passengers. The three airlines listed above offer charter flights between all islands and nearby destinations, as does Provo Air Charter (☎ 649-941-0685) on Provo.

BUS

Public bus service is limited to a single line in Provo. There are no buses on the other islands.

CAR & MOTORCYCLE

Driving is on the *left*. Speed limits in the Turks and Caicos are 20mph in settlements and 40mph on main highways.

Because local transportation is limited, renting a car or motorcycle makes sense on Provo if you plan to explore the island. Otherwise, stick to taxis (expensive) or bicycles for 'scooting' around locally. See the island chapters for details.

A government tax of US$10 is levied on car rentals (US$5 on scooter rentals). Mandatory insurance costs US$14.

BICYCLE

As in The Bahamas, bicycles can be rented at many hotels and concessions, but they're unwieldy beach cruisers. They're fine for tootling around but not for serious touring.

TAXI

Taxis are available on all the inhabited islands. Most are minivans. They're a good bet for touring; most taxi drivers double as guides. Be sure to negotiate an agreeable price before setting out. Fares are usually quoted according to the number of passengers; each additional passenger reduces the per-capita fare.

ORGANIZED TOURS

Sky King and Turks and Caicos Airways (see the Air section) offer island-hopping excursions.

See island sections for more details. For special-interest and outdoor activities, see the Outdoor Activities chapter.

Caicos Islands

The Caicos chain is an arc comprising, west to east, the islands of West Caicos, Providenciales (the main tourist gateway and hot spot), North Caicos, Middle Caicos, East Caicos, and South Caicos, as well as numerous small isles and cays.

Providenciales

- **pop 8000**

As recently as 1964, the island of Providenciales (colloquially called 'Provo') did not have a single wheeled vehicle. In 1990 the 230-room Turquoise Reef Resort & Casino

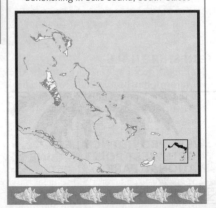

Highlights

- Parasailing over Grace Bay
- Diving The Wall at West Caicos or South Caicos
- Exploring Northwest Point Marine National Park, Chalk Sound National Park, and the beach at Malcolm Roads. Bring your camera!
- Swimming with stingrays at French Cay
- Hiking and bird watching on Middle Caicos and North Caicos
- Bonefishing in Belle Sound, South Caicos

(now the Allegro Resort & Casino) opened on Grace Bay, giving the island its first large hotel and casino. Provo is now the most developed island, boasting an 18-hole golf course, many resort hotels, and burgeoning residential development.

The island is shaped like a wedge, narrowing to the northeast. The north shore is a gentle, concave curve lined with beaches. The south shore is indented by sounds and lakes.

The main town, sprawling, soulless namesake Providenciales, sits in the middle of the island. It's a modern town with a haphazard layout. There are pockets of makeshift shacks – the homes of Haitians – interspersed among more upscale homes. Turtle Cove, about a mile northeast of downtown, is a node for tourist services and has Provo's premier marina.

The resort scene grips the north shore along 5-mile-long Grace Bay, with its blindingly white sand and unbelievably turquoise waters. The bay begins east of Turtle Cove and is lined with an unbroken, snow-white beach backed by well-spaced hotels. Smith's Reef lies offshore, providing good snorkeling. Grace Bay curves toward the northeastern tip of the island, ending at Leeward Marina. Secluded Leeward Beach is good for beachcombing. East of Provo, the entire north shore and offshore waters are protected within Princess Alexandra National Park.

Along the south shore, Juba Point Salina, a large lake surrounded by mangrove flats, spreads inland of the coast. East of the lake, the Long Bay Hills, an upcoming residential area, rises over the shore. Long Bay Beach, 3 miles long, is accessible by trails from Long Bay Beach Dr.

Away from the beaches, Provo's charm lies in its rugged hills and ridges, carpeted with prickly pear cacti and scrub unfolding down to the sea. The western half of Provo is mostly barren wilderness, dramatic and well worth exploring, with two national parks.

Provo is surrounded by uninhabited cays that you can easily reach by chartered boat or excursion. Miles and miles of coral reefs are temptingly close to shore.

ORIENTATION
The main highway, Leeward Hwy, runs east from downtown along the island's spine, ending near Bird Rock. A coastal highway, Grace Bay Rd, parallels Grace Bay.

A separate coast road runs northwest from downtown to Blue Hills and Wheeland settlements, beyond which it continues as a dirt track to Northwest Point. A fourth road runs south from downtown to Sapodilla Bay.

INFORMATION
Tourist Offices
The tourist office (☎ 649-946-4970) is at Turtle Cove Marina Plaza; it's open 9 am to 5 pm weekdays (see the Turtle Cove to Grace Bay map). There's also a tourist information booth in the arrivals hall at Provo's airport.

Money
Barclays Bank (☎ 649-946-4245) is in Butterfield Square, the main downtown plaza, on Leeward Hwy. Scotiabank (☎ 649-946-4750), also in Butterfield Square, has a 24-hour ATM. You can receive money by wire transfer through Western Union (☎ 649-941-3702) in the Town Centre Mall on Leeward Hwy, or in Ports of Call (see the Turtle Cove to Grace Bay map).

Post & Communications
The post office (☎ 649-946-4676) is next to the police station on Old Airport Rd; it's open 8 am to noon and 2 to 4 pm Monday to Thursday and 8 am to 12:30 pm and 2 to 5:30 pm Friday. Federal Express (☎ 649-946-4682) is in the Center Complex on Leeward Hwy. DHL Worldwide Express (☎ 649-946-4352) has an office in Butterfield Square.

There are public phone booths at several roadside locations. Dial ☎ 111 to place credit-card calls. A telephone exchange is on Leeward Hwy near Turtle Cove (see the Turtle Cove to Grace Bay map).

Travel Agencies
Try Provo Travel (☎ 649-946-4035) in Central Square Plaza on Leeward Hwy. There are several other agencies downtown.

Bookstores
The Unicorn Bookstore (☎ 649-941-5458), at the Market Place on Leeward Hwy, has a large selection of books, newspapers, and magazines. Most resort boutiques also sell a small supply of books and magazines.

Laundry
Try Pioneer Cleaners (☎ 649-946-4388) in Butterfield Square.

Medical Services
The Associated Medical Practices clinic (☎ 649-946-4242), on Leeward Hwy, has several private doctors. The clinic has a recompression chamber.

The government-run Myrtle Rigby Health Clinic (☎ 649-941-3000, VHF channel 82) is downtown on Leeward Hwy.

The Provo Discount Pharmacy (☎ 649-946-4844), in Central Square Plaza on Leeward Hwy, is open 8 am to 10 pm daily.

Colette Pepperell offers treatments, massage, and aerobics classes at Spa Tropique (☎ 649-941-5720, fax 649-946-4632, spa@provo.net), in three locations. Mobile service is available.

Emergency
Dial ☎ 911 for emergencies, ☎ 649-946-4259 for the police, and ☎ 649-946-4444 for the fire department.

CHESHIRE HALL
Pickings for sightseers are rather slim downtown, but history buffs might check out the ruins of this 1790s plantation house, constructed by British Loyalists. It's on Leeward Hwy.

WEST PROVIDENCIALES & NORTHWEST POINT MARINE NATIONAL PARK
A rugged dirt road (for 4WD vehicles only) leads from the settlement of Wheeland, northwest of downtown, to **Malcolm Roads**,

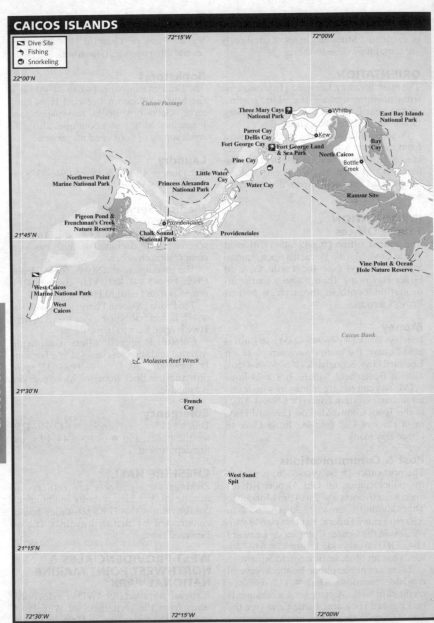

CAICOS ISLANDS

- ⬚ Dive Site
- ⚓ Fishing
- ◉ Snorkeling

72°15'W

72°00W

22°00'N

Caicos Passage

Three Mary Cays 🏯
National Park

Whitby

East Bay Islands
National Park

Parrot Cay
Dellis Cay
Fort George Cay

Kew

Pine Cay

Fort George Land
& Sea Park

North Caicos

Bay
Cay

Bottle
Creek

Little Water
Cay

Northwest Point
Marine National Park

Princess Alexandra
National Park

Water Cay

Pigeon Pond &
Frenchman's Creek
Nature Reserve

Ramsar Site

21°45'N

Providenciales

Chalk Sound
National Park

Providenciales

Vine Point & Ocean
Hole Nature Reserve

West Caicos
Marine National Park

West
Caicos

Caicos Bank

⚓ *Molasses Reef Wreck*

21°30'N

French
Cay

West Sand
Spit

21°15'N

CAICOS ISLANDS

72°30'W

72°15'W

72°00'W

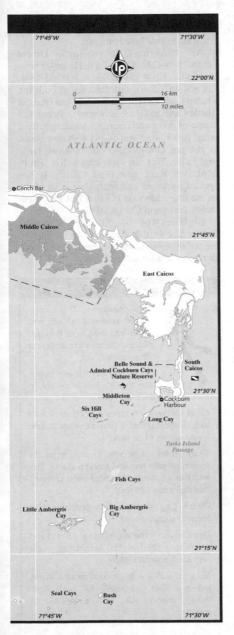

a superb 2-mile-long beach good for snorkeling and popular with locals on weekends. Following this arduous, windy, hilly, rocky track, you're soon amid cacti, with views over the inland saline lakes.

The **Tiki Huts**, at the south end of the beach, is a tumbledown Polynesian village sitting over a coral shore. It was erected by a French TV company that used it for an adventure game show until a contestant was killed while diving for conch. There are no facilities.

Another dirt road leads from Crystal Bay Resorts, northwest of Wheeland, to **Northwest Point**. From here you can walk east to a lighthouse. It's a desperate drive, with deep sand and potholes, and you shouldn't attempt it unless you have a large 4WD. Many people who attempt the track in small jeeps get stuck!

Protecting reefs off Provo's west shore, Northwest Point Marine National Park also encompasses several saline lakes that attract breeding and migrant waterfowl. The largest is **Pigeon Pond**, inland. This part of the park is the Pigeon Pond & Frenchman's Creek Nature Reserve. Other ponds – notably Northwest Point Pond and Frenchman's Creek – encompass tidal flats and mangrove swamps along the west coast, attracting fish and fowl in large numbers. You'll have to hike to get there.

There are no facilities.

CHALK SOUND NATIONAL PARK
The waters of this 3-mile-long bay, 2 miles southwest of downtown, define 'turquoise.' The color is uniform: a vast, unrippled, electric-blue carpet eerily and magnificently studded with countless tiny islets, like mushrooms. Incredible!

A slender peninsula separates the sound from the sea. The peninsula is scalloped with beach-lined bays, notably **Sapodilla Bay**. A horribly potholed road runs along the peninsula, which is lined with vacation homes.

ROCK CARVINGS
At the far eastern end of the Sapodilla Bay peninsula, a rocky hilltop boasts carvings on slabs of rock, like the Ten Commandments.

In fact they date back only to 1844. The slabs are intricately carved with Roman lettering that records the names of sailors apparently shipwrecked here and the dates of their sojourns. The carvings are reached via a rocky trail that begins 200 yards east of the Mariner Hotel; it leads uphill 200 yards to the summit, which offers wonderful views over the island and Chalk Sound.

CAICOS CONCH FARM & INLAND SEA CENTRE

This smelly place (☎ 649-946-5643/5330, fax 649-946-5849), near the northeastern tip of Provo, claims to be 'the world's only conch farm.' It strives to protect the Caribbean queen conch *(Strombus gigas)* from extinction and also raises the mollusks commercially for export and local use. The farm was the brainchild of Chuck Hesse, an environmentalist who after years of research can now produce a consumable mollusk in 28 months, from egg to adult conch. Chuck reckons he has two million conchs in the ponds and another million offshore in 80 acres of 'pasture' fenced to keep predators at bay. (He further reckons that in the wild only one in 500,000 conch eggs matures to adulthood, due to predation; at the farm more than 80% of larvae survive.) Annual production is more than 750,000 conchs a year, with 10,000 harvested weekly.

The farm briefly closed due to financial problems, but had reopened at press time.

You can learn how conchs are grown from eggs to adults on a tour. You'll see the hatchery and metamorphosis facility, onshore nursery ponds, 'sub-sea maturation pasture,' and conch-processing facility. The facility is rather boring unless you have a guide to bring it to life. Call ahead. It's open 9 am to 4 pm daily; the tour costs US$6 (children US$3). The mailing address is PO Box 286, Providenciales, Turks and Caicos, BWI.

DIVING & SNORKELING

See the 'Dive & Snorkel Sites' boxed text for highlights of Provo's underwater world. All the dive operators offer a range of dive options, from introductory 'resort courses' to PADI certification (US$350 to US$395). Most offer free hotel pick-up.

Art Pickering's Provo Turtle Divers (☎ 649-946-4232, ProvoTurtleDivers@Provo.net; in the US ☎ 954-467-3460, 800-833-1341, fax 954-467-7544), with facilities at both the Ocean Club and the Turtle Cove Inn (see the Turtle Cove to Grace Bay map), offers a full range of dives and courses, including nitrox, using two 30-foot and one 41-foot dive boats. It charges US$45/75/70 one-tank/two-tank/night dive. You can even take a dive trip to Molasses Reef and West Caicos. It has special packages and rents dive equipment; its mailing address is PO Box 219, Providenciales, Turks and Caicos, BWI.

Big Blue (☎ 649-946-5034, bigblue@tciway.tc), at Leeward Marina on the far eastern side of the island, offers nitrox dives plus underwater scooter safaris.

PROVIDENCIALES

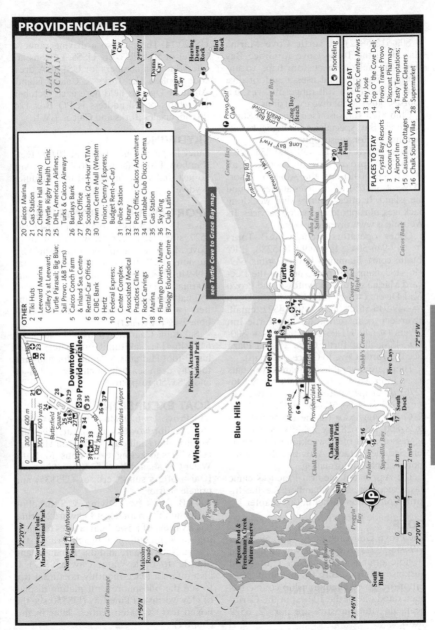

OTHER
2 Tiki Huts
4 Leeward Marina
(Gilley's at Leeward;
Turtle Parasail; Big Blue;
Sail Provo; J&B Tours)
5 Caicos Conch Farm
& Inland Sea Centre
6 Rental-Car Offices
8 CIBC Bank
9 Hertz
10 Federal Express;
Center Complex
12 Associated Medical
Practices Clinic
17 Rock Carvings
18 Marina
19 Flamingo Divers; Marine
Biology Education Centre

20 Caicos Marina
21 Gas Station
22 Cheshire Hall (Ruins)
23 Myrtle Rigby Health Clinic
25 DHL; American Airlines;
Turks & Caicos Airways
26 Barclays Bank
27 Post Office
29 Scotiabank (24-Hour ATM)
30 Town Centre Mall (Western
Union; Denny's Express;
Budget Rent-a-Car)
31 Police Station
32 Library
33 Post Office; Caicos Adventures
34 Turntable Club Disco; Cinema
35 Gas Station
36 Sky King
37 Club Latino

PLACES TO STAY
1 Crystal Bay Resorts
3 Coconut Grove
7 Airport Inn
15 Casuarina Cottages
16 Chalk Sound Villas

PLACES TO EAT
11 Go Fish; Centre Mews
13 Hey José
14 Top O' the Cove Deli;
Provo Travel; Provo
Discount Pharmacy
24 Tasty Temptations;
Pioneer Cleaners
28 Supermarket

Downtown Providenciales

CAICOS ISLANDS

Caicos Adventures (☎ 649-941-3346, email: divucrzy@caribsurf.com; in the US ☎ 800-513-5822), at Turtle Cove Marina Plaza (see the Turtle Cove to Grace Bay map), specializes in custom trips to uncharted dive sites and uses a 36-foot dive boat. It also has a full range of dives and courses, plus special dive excursions.

Club Med Turkoise (see Places to Stay), on Grace Bay, specializes in diving, but its facilities are for guests only.

Dive Provo (in the US 800-234-7768, diving@diveprovo.com), at Ports of Call (☎ 649-946-5040) and the Allegro Resort (☎ 649-946-5029), offers dives at sites around the island. It offers courses and weeklong packages, plus photo and video services. Its Web site is www.diveprovo.com.

Other operators include J&B Tours (☎ 649-946-5047, fax 649-946-5288, jill@jbtours.com), Flamingo Divers (☎/fax 649-946-4193, flamingo@provo.net), in the Leeward Marina south of downtown, and Provo Wall Divers (☎ 649-941-5441), Silver Deep (☎ 649-946-5612, fax 649-946-4527, email: silverdeep_dean@tciway.tc), and Turtle Inn Divers (☎ 649-941-0643; in the US ☎ 800-359-3483), all at Turtle Cove Marina Plaza (see the Turtle Cove to Grace Bay map).

There are several live-aboard dive boats based in Provo. *Sea Dancer* (☎/fax 649-946-5276, divetrip@bitstream.net; in the US ☎ 612-953-4124, fax 612-431-5023) and *Turks & Caicos Aggressor* (in the US ☎ 504-385-2628, 800-348-2628, fax 504-384-0817, info@aggressor.com) offer weeklong dive charters. See the Outdoor Activities chapter for more complete information.

The Associated Medical Practices clinic has a recompression chamber; see the Information section earlier in this chapter.

GOLF

The Provo Golf Club (☎ 649-946-5991, fax 649-946-5992, provgolf@tciway.com) is an 18-hole course across from Club Med Turkoise on Grace Bay. The beautiful, Karl Litton–designed championship course has been rated one of the 10 best in the Caribbean. Its vital statistics are par 72, 6529 yards.

The course charges US$120/70 for 18/nine holes. Club rental and cart rental each cost US$20/14. There's also a driving range; a bucket of 50 balls costs US$5. Lessons are offered to nonmembers for US$40. A dress code applies. The Turks & Caicos Islands Amateur Open is held here each October. The club's postal address is PO Box 124, Providenciales, Turks and Caicos, BWI.

SKYDIVING

Fancy leaping from a plane at 10,000 feet? Rainbow Flyers (☎ 649-946-4201) let you do just that while harnessed to a qualified skydiver.

SPORT FISHING & BONEFISHING

Silver Deep (☎ 649-946-5612, fax 649-946-4527, silverdeep_dean@tciway.tc), at Turtle Cove Marina Plaza, specializes in fishing excursions. J&B Tours (☎ 649-946-5047, fax 649-946-5288, jill@jbtours.com), at Leeward Marina, has bonefishing excursions (US$240/450 half/full-day), as does Bonefish Unlimited (☎ 649-946-4874, fax 649-946-4960, bonefish@provo.net).

Sakitumi Charters (☎ 649-946-4065, fax 649-946-4141, sakitumi@provo.net) offers his 43-foot Hatteras, *Sakitumi*, for half- and full-day deep-sea fishing charters (US$400 and US$750, respectively).

BOAT EXCURSIONS

Sail Provo (☎ 649-946-4783, fax 649-946-5527, sailprovo@tciway.tc), at Leeward Marina, offers half-day (US$45) and full-day (US$79) snorkeling excursions to Little Water Cay aboard 36- to 52-foot catamarans. It also offers sunset cruises (US$35) and private charters.

J&B Tours (see Diving & Snorkeling earlier in this chapter), at Leeward Marina, has a variety of powerboat cruises to outlying cays, including a beach cruise, the 'Provo Native Tour,' and the 'Iguana Island Shuttle' to Little Water Cay (US$27). It also offers a twice-monthly nocturnal trip to see the phosphorescent mating display of glowworms off Pine Cay (US$50; see the boxed text 'X-Rated Antics,' later in this chapter).

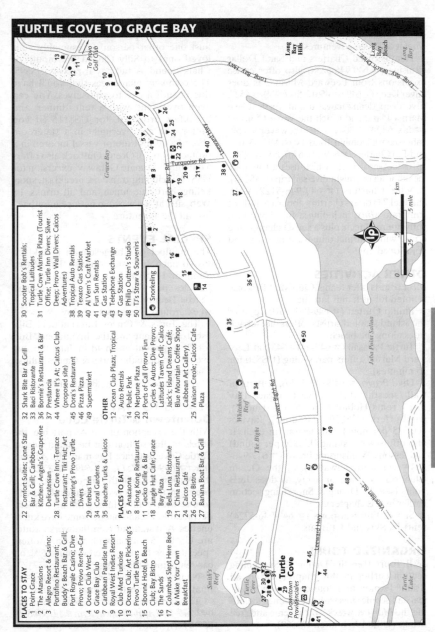

TURTLE COVE TO GRACE BAY

CAICOS ISLANDS

PLACES TO STAY
1 Point Grace
2 The Mansions
3 Allegro Resort & Casino;
   Portofino Restaurant;
   Buddy's Beach Bar & Grill;
   Port Royale Casino; Dive
   Provo; Provo Rent-a-Car
4 Ocean Club West
6 Grace Bay Club
7 Caribbean Paradise Inn
9 Royal West Indies Resort
10 Club Med Turkoise
15 Ocean Club; Art Pickering's
   Provo Turtle Divers
15 Sibonné Hotel & Beach
   Club; Bay Bistro
16 The Sands
17 Columbus Slept Here Bed
   & Make Your Own
   Breakfast

22 Comfort Suites; Lone Star
   Bar & Grill; Caribbean
   Kitchen; Angela's Grapevine
   Delicatessan
28 Turtle Cove Inn; Terrace
   Restaurant; Tiki Hut; Art
   Pickering's Provo Turtle
   Divers
29 Erebus Inn
34 Coral Gardens
35 Beaches Turks & Caicos

PLACES TO EAT
5 Anacaona
8 Hong Kong Restaurant
11 Gecko Grille & Bar
18 Jungle Hut Cafe; Grace
   Bay Plaza
19 Bella Luna Ristorante
21 China Restaurant
24 Caicos Café
26 Coco Bistro
27 Banana Boat Bar & Grill

32 Shark Bite Bar & Grill
33 Baci Ristorante
36 Bonnie's Restaurant & Bar
37 Prestancia
44 Where It's At; Catcus Club
   (proposed site)
45 Dora's Restaurant
46 Pizza Pizza
49 Supermarket

OTHER
12 Ocean Club Plaza; Tropical
   Auto Rentals
14 Public Park
20 Neptune Plaza
23 Ports of Call (Provo Fun
   Cycles & Autos; Dive Provo;
   Latitudes Tavern Grill; Calico
   Jack's; Island Dreams Shop;
   Blue Mountain Coffee Shop;
   Caibbean Art Gallery)
25 Maison Creole; Caicos Cafe
   Plaza

30 Scooter Bob's Rentals;
   Tropical Latitudes
31 Turtle Cove Marina Plaza (Tourist
   Office; Turtle Inn Divers; Silver
   Deep; Provo Wall Divers; Caicos
   Adventures)
38 Tropical Auto Rentals
39 Texaco Gas Station
40 Al Vern's Craft Market
41 Fun Sun Rentals
42 Gas Station
43 Telephone Exchange
47 Gas Station
48 Phillip Outten's Studio
50 TJ's Straw & Souvenirs

 Snorkeling

Big Blue (☎ 649-946-5034, bigblue@ tciway.tc), also at Leeward Marina, offers what it calls 'eco-adventures.'

Hammerhead Charters and Sand Dollar Cruising (☎ 649-946-5238) also offer cruise excursions from Leeward Marina, as does Silver Deep (☎ 649-946-5612, fax 649-946-4527, silverdeep_dean@tciway.tc), at Turtle Cove Marina Plaza; and Catch the Wave Charters (☎/fax 649-941-3047, catchthewaveprovo@ yahoo.com); Dolphin Tours (☎ 649-946-5102); and Tao Charters (☎ 649-231-6767, fax 649-941-5510, tao@provo.net), which uses a trimaran, including an overnight dive-sail trip (US$235).

Minx Charters (☎ 649-946-5122, VHF channel 74) offers charters aboard a 41-foot trimaran, *Minx*, including a full-day cruise with catered lunch, plus a sunset champagne cruise with gourmet dinner for just you and your loved one!

OTHER ACTIVITIES

Most resorts offer tennis. Club Med Turkoise is noted for its tennis facilities.

Phillip Outten (☎ 649-941-3610), one of the island's noted artists, offers horseback rides along the beach.

Turtle Parasail (☎ 649-941-0643), at Leeward Marina, offers parasailing (US$50 for 15 minutes).

Dive Provo (☎ 649-946-5040), at Ports of Call (see the Turtle Cove to Grace Bay map), rents Hobi-cats (US$20 first hour), windsurfers (US$20 first hour), kayaks (US$15 per hour), plus lessons in each. It also offers water-skiing (US$20 per round) and lessons. Windsurfing Provo (☎ 649-946-5649, windpro@tciway.tc), at the Ocean Club, offers a similar array, as does J&B Tours (see the Diving & Snorkeling section earlier in this chapter).

Sun & Fun Seasports (☎ 649-946-5724) rents Jet Skis and Jet Boats.

ORGANIZED TOURS

J&B Tours (see the Diving & Snorkeling section earlier in this chapter) offers an 'Island Exploration' tour combining historical and scenic sites with snorkeling (including the *Marifax* wreck), plus picnic and free drinks (US$119; children US$69).

Ocean Outback (☎ 649-941-5810, oceanoutback@provo.net) will take you and 'just one other person' (presumably your loved one) to Silly Cay, at the mouth of Chalk Sound. A full-day trip costs US$95. The company guarantees that you'll have this beautiful cay to yourselves. You can even overnight, with a tent, dinner, and breakfast provided, for US$115 (if you prefer, you can overnight in a stateroom aboard a 70-foot motor vessel moored in a protected cove). Ocean Outback also offers a daylong 'Ultimate Getaway' excursion for US$79, including transfers, breakfast, snorkeling, barbecue lunch, and all drinks. Its Web site at www.provo.net/oceanoutback lists all the adventures.

SPECIAL EVENTS

The archipelago's biggest bash is held on Provo each July and August. The Provo Summer Festival features regattas, float parades, partying, and a 'Miss Turks and Caicos Beauty Pageant,' all spread over a week around Emancipation Day.

The Turks & Caicos International Billfish Tournament and the Invitational Billfish Tournament are held in July; the two events comprise the Turks & Caicos Billfish Challenge.

A Culture Night is held in mid-May.

PLACES TO STAY
Downtown & Turtle Cove

With the exception of the Airport Inn, the hotels in this section can be found on the Turtle Cove to Grace Bay map. The *Airport Inn* (☎ 649-941-3514, fax 649-941-3281), in the Airport Plaza at the airport, is perfect if you're in transit between islands. It has 19 rooms with ceiling fans, calming modern decor, cable TV, and phone; some have kitchenettes. A restaurant is in the works. Rates are US$65/75 without/with air-con. It offers special rates for airline crew, plus 15% off car-rental rates for guests.

Nearby, the *Travellers Rest Inn* was in final stages of construction at press time.

The *Turtle Cove Inn* (☎ 649-946-4203, fax 649-946-4141, tcinn@tciway.tc; in the US ☎ 800-887-0477), near the Turtle Cove Marina, is an

CAICOS ISLANDS

intimate property centered on an amoeba-shaped pool and stone-paved sundeck surrounded by lush tropical gardens. It bills itself as a dive and tennis center and has its own dock. There are 30 air-con rooms, all with tile floor, patio, a lively tropical motif, cable TV, phone, and ceiling fan. Bathrooms were refurbished in 1999. Rates (summer/winter) are US$98/118 poolside, US$120/145 waterfront, and US$150/185 suite. A nine-night minimum stay is required at Christmas, when prices rise 20%. There are two restaurants – the Tiki Hut is a lively little spot – a dive shop, and scooter rentals on-site. The postal address is PO Box 131, Providenciales, Turks and Caicos, BWI.

For the best views, check into *Erebus Inn* (☎ 649-946-4240, fax 649-946-4704, erebus@ tciway.tc; in the US ☎ 800-323-5655), amid landscaped grounds on the hill overlooking Turtle Cove. It has 21 spacious air-con rooms with a tropical motif, tile floors, cable TV, rattan furniture, ceiling fans, and a choice of king-size bed or two doubles. Sliding glass doors open to patios with fine views along the coast. Better yet are the four handsome chalets and the two-bedroom villa perched on the hillside. They have marvelous ambience, with large French doors opening to wooden decks. Facilities include a panoramic restaurant and sun deck, two pools, clay tennis courts, miniature golf, and a shuttle service by boat to the nearby beach. Rates are US$100/140 poolside, US$125/170 ocean-view, US$150/ 190 ocean-view cottage low/high-season. The mailing address is PO Box 238, Providenciales, Turks and Caicos, BWI.

The Turtle Cove marina office (☎ 649-946-4106, fax 649-941-3440) rents efficiency units.

Grace Bay & East Providenciales

Alas, Louise Fletcher, the owner of the delightful *Columbus Slept Here Bed & Make Your Own Breakfast* (☎/fax 649-946-5878, louisa@tciway.tc) guesthouse planned to pack up her bags in late 2000, driven out by 'overdevelopment.'

The *Caribbean Paradise Inn* (☎ 649-946-5020, toll free 877-946-5020, fax 649-946-5022, fax 419-821-8175, inn@paradise.tc) is a

twee, family-oriented place run by a charming German couple. At its heart is a small, attractive pool surrounded by bougainvillea. There's a bar in a canopied patio where buffet breakfasts are served (no lunch or dinner, though occasional barbecues are offered). Rooms have rattan furnishings, terra-cotta tile floors, king-size beds, and heaps of light pouring in through French windows opening onto wide balconies. It's 300 yards from the beach. Rates are US$119 to US$135 in summer, US$135 to US$149 in winter; suites cost US$199 and US$238, respectively.

Sibonné Hotel & Beach Club (☎ 649-946-5547, 800-528-1905, fax 649-946-5770, info@Sibonne.com) is a small, informal, recently renovated inn with 26 luxury air-con rooms set around a flower garden. Each has an iron-framed bed, telephone, cable TV, and ceiling fan. Bathrooms are small. Junior suites, upstairs, have vaulted ceilings. The hotel has a dive center offering certification courses. There's a freshwater pool, plus a restaurant and bar overlooking the beach. Standard rooms cost US$110/160 single/ double in summer; junior suites cost US$170/185 in winter. One-bedroom condos cost US$210/260 in winter and US$295 in peak season. Dive and golf packages are offered. The postal address is PO Box 144, Providenciales, Turks and Caicos, BWI.

An exquisite option – and a bargain! – is *Coral Gardens* (☎ 649-941-3713, fax 649-941-5171, coralgardn@tciway.tc), at Whitehouse, offering huge, well-lit two-bedroom suites with king-size beds and wrap-around plate-glass windows opening to verandas over a twin-pool complex. Room rates range from US$135 for a junior bedroom to US$670 for a two-bedroom suite, depending on season. The Coyaba restaurant is here. The Whitehouse Reef – perfect for snorkeling – is directly offshore.

Comfort Suites (☎ 649-946-8888, fax 649-946-5444, comfort@tciway.tc; in the US ☎ 888-678-3483), inland of the beach, has 100 air-con junior suites set around a lush courtyard with small swimming pool. All rooms have king-size or two double beds, plus sofabed, refrigerator, coffeemaker, cable TV, in-room safe, and ceiling fans. Some have balconies. Seasonal rates range from US$140 to US$235, depending on season.

Club Med Turkoise (☎ *649-946-5500, 800-258-2633, fax 649-946-5497*) is spread over 70 acres toward the eastern end of Grace Bay. It's built around an open-air bar, theater, casino and nightclub, and an asymmetrical pool with volleyball and water polo. It's more downscale than many other Club Meds, but it's still adults-only. Facilities include tennis courts, a dive center, and an 'Intensive Circus Workshop.' Specialty weeks are offered, such as a Pro-Beach Volleyball week in January. The recently renovated 298 air-con double rooms are in two-story beachfront units; some have king-size beds. Per-person nightly rates begin at US$145/179 summer/winter. Weeklong packages begin at US$1015/1253. Single supplements (for a private room) cost 20% to 100% extra. Special package rates are offered, including airfare from various US gateways. The Web site is www.clubmed.com.

The ***Ocean Club*** (☎ *649-946-5880, fax 649-946-5845, oceanclb@tciway.tc; in the US* ☎ *800-457-8787*) is a deluxe all-suite oceanfront resort at the east end of Grace Bay centered on two freeform pools set in beautifully manicured grounds. It has a range of 83 suites, from studio suites (from US$180/225 summer/winter) to three-bedroom deluxe suites for up to six people (from US$550/835). All have a telephone, cable TV, en-suite kitchen, and washer and dryer. Children under 12 stay free with parents. Seniors over 55 get a 10% discount in low season. Low season discounts on interisland flights and local businesses are offered. There are shaded hammocks slung between the palms, a swim-up bar, fitness room, night-lit tennis court, and a dive operation. The mailing address is PO Box 240, Providenciales, Turks and Caicos, BWI.

Ocean Club West is an extension a mile down the beach from its sister property, with 90 suites from studios to three-bedroom units. Rates began at US$180 for studios.

The Sands (☎ *649-946-5199, 877-777-2637, fax 649-946-5198, vacations@thesandsresort.com*) is a gracious three-story,

neo-Georgian property in elegantly landscaped grounds with 69 one-, two-, and three-bedroom luxury suites. Facilities include tennis, a cabaña-style restaurant, water sports, and beachside pool, plus use of bicycles. Rates range from US$195 for a studio to US$785 for a three-bedroom oceanfront suite. Its mailing address is PO Box 681, Providenciales, Turks and Caicos, BWI.

The recently remodeled ***Allegro Resort & Casino*** (☎ *649-946-5555, 800-858-2258, fax 649-946-5522*) operates as an all-inclusive. It has 191 air-con rooms centered on a huge sun deck and massive pool with two Jacuzzis. Each has a tropical motif, contemporary rattan furniture, terra-cotta tile floors, fans, oversize bathrooms, and patios or balconies with ocean views. It attracts a mixed clientele of oldsters and young couples as well as families, catered to with the 'Kids on Vacation Club' and supervised babysitting. There's tennis, volleyball, and water sports, plus nightly entertainment. Garden-view rooms cost US$254/400 to US$287/468 single/double and ocean-view rooms cost US$267/454 to US$300/494, depending on season. The local postal address is Grace Bay Rd, PO Box 205, Providenciales, Turks and Caicos, BWI; in the USA, c/o Icon Hotel Marketing, 9200 S Dadeland Blvd, suite 518, Miami, FL 33156.

The Mansions (☎ *649-946-5863, fax 649-946-5862, themansions@tciway.tc*) is a private condominium complex; some owners rent their units. A seven-day minimum stay is required, and children under 12 are not accepted. Weekly rates per night range from US$650 to US$850, based on season.

Beaches Turks & Caicos is part of the Sandals chain, which has been voted 'Top Caribbean Hotel Group' *every* year in the World Travel Awards. To contact Sandals, call the following numbers:

Turks and Caicos ☎ 649-946-8000, fax 649-946-8001

Canada ☎ 416-223-0028, 800-545-8283, fax 416-223-3306

UK ☎ 020-7581-9895, fax 020-7823-8758

USA ☎ 305-284-1300, 800-726-3257, fax 305-667-8996

The 45-acre resort – which caters primarily to families – has 466 large, elegantly furnished, air-con, ocean-view rooms in seven categories, including two standards of suites. Some have king-size beds; all have private verandas, cable TV, clock radio, and telephone. There are also 36 one- and two-bedroom villas with kitchens. A US$100 million extension in the style of Versailles, named the French Village, opened in spring 2000 around a lush formal garden with fountains centered on a 4000-sq-foot gradual-entry swimming pool surrounded by neoclassical columns. It has six restaurants, numerous bars and lounges, water sports, recreational activities, plus a top-rated spa. Kids are catered to with Pirates Island, a $4 million kiddy's complex set around a mock galleon, with a kid's pool, restaurant, disco, movie theater, Sega center, and more. A casino was planned. Per person all-inclusive room rates range from US$315 to US$380 low season, US$340 to US$395 high season. Suites range from US$400 to US$595, and US$425 to US$610. Most people book three- to seven-night packages. Beaches accepts singles, couples, and families with children. Sandals' guarantees you a free vacation if a hurricane strikes. It offers charter flights; see the Getting There & Away section for details. The postal address is Light Bight Rd, Providenciales, Turks and Caicos, BWI.

A more luxurious offering, and one popular with the international A-list, is **Point Grace** (☎ 649-946-5096, 888-682-3705, fax 649-946-5097, pointgrace@tciway.tc). Opened in March 2000, this luxury boutique hotel offers 30 oceanfront suites and breathtaking penthouses, plus three cottages – each with three one-bedroom suites – tucked in a courtyard sanctum centered on a handsome pool. Suites feature full kitchens, washers and dryers, handmade Indonesian teak furniture, 37-inch TV, DVD/CD player with surround-sound, king-size four-poster beds, Indonesian fabrics and embossed Italian linens, and expansive becolumned balconies. Cottages have bathtubs and separate walk-in showers. One of the penthouses has a rooftop solarium with private Jacuzzi; the other has its own massage room and a baby grand piano. Point Grace has underground parking with elevator access to rooms. Espressos and cappuccinos are served, as are complimentary wines and hors d'oeuvres in the evening. Sorbets are served on the beach, where the umbrellas are Indonesian silks! A gourmet chef prepares meals in your suite on request. A business lounge has laptops with Internet hookup and secretarial service. Rates run from US$345 to US$435 for a one-bedroom cottage suite, to US$2500 to US$3500 for the three-bedroom penthouse, including membership to the golf club. The postal address is PO Box 158, Providenciales, Turks and Caicos, BWI.

Equally divine is the **Grace Bay Club** (☎ 649-946-5757, 800-946-5757, fax 649-946-5758), a lush 5-acre world centered on an Andalusian-style mansion and a plaza with fountain, waterfall, and real frogs. The entire complex – brimful of tasteful artwork and antiques – is like stepping inside the Louvre or British Museum. The 21 suites are done up in cool igloo-white, with exquisite furnishings and artwork, monogrammed bathrobes, fine toiletries, and cable TV/VCR. Facilities include a clover-shaped swimming pool, Jacuzzi, two tennis courts, water sports (including Sunfish and Hobie Cats), and the intimate, candlelit Anacaona Restaurant. Service is impeccable. There are eight types of rooms, from junior suites (US$385 to US$595, depending on season) to a two-bedroom penthouse (US$925 to US$1395). The postal address is PO Box 128, Providenciales, Turks and Caicos, BWI.

Point Grace also rents two top-end villas – **Sunset Villa** and **Sunnyside Villa** – with their own pools, security, and refined luxe. They rent from US$7500 and US$10,500, respectively, weekly.

There's no shortage of private cottages for rent. See the Accommodations section in the Turks & Caicos introduction chapter for information on agencies that arrange villa rentals.

The **Royal West Indies Resort** was under construction at press time.

West Providenciales

An upscale condominium resort complex – *Crystal Bay Resorts* (☎ 649-941-5555, fax 649-946-4825, crystalm@tciway.tc) – sits on 98 acres near the far northwestern end of the island. It offers 160 privately owned deluxe units, most available for rent. These include junior suites and one-, two-, and three-bedroom apartments along the shore amid the low scrub. The resort has two freshwater pools, a Jacuzzi, and a restaurant and bar. Rates range from US$220 to US$280 for one-bedroom, to US$395 to US$520 for a three-bedroom. Its postal address is PO Box 101, Providenciales, Turks and Caicos, BWI, and its Web site address is www.crystalbay.tc.

Several dozen villas are available for rent along Chalk Sound and the Sapodilla peninsula. A good source of information is *Where, When, How: Turks & Caicos Islands*, which has a Web site: www.WhereWhenHow.com. Also visit the following Web sites: www.provo.net/Listings/Lodging and www.tcimall.tc/villas.

PLACES TO EAT
Downtown & Turtle Cove

Unless noted otherwise, these places to eat are on the Turtle Cove to Grace Bay map. A good place for breakfast is the congenial *Tiki Hut* (☎ 649-941-5341) cabaña bar and grill at the Turtle Cove Inn. It has a wide menu, from Belgian waffles to 'El Tiki Burritos,' burgers and salads, plus pastas and pizzas for dinner (US$5 to US$15). The inn's *Terrace Restaurant* specializes in creative conch dishes and other seafood; it's closed Sunday.

The atmospheric and gaily painted *Banana Boat Bar & Grill* (☎ 649-941-5706), near Turtle Cove Marina Plaza, specializes in seafood and steaks. It also has burgers for US$6. It has an oyster bar, plus a happy hour 4 to 7 pm. Tuesday night is seafood night.

Where It's At Restaurant (☎ 649-941-3673), downtown near Butterfield Square, is a quaint Haitian-run restaurant popular with locals. It serves barbecue, seafood, and chicken from US$9, plus Jamaican patties, fish and chips, and sandwiches, for US$2 to US$8. It planned to move to a site opposite Dora's (see below).

You can even find Mexican food, plus sandwiches, pizzas, and treats such as curry lime chicken breast (US$13) at *Hey José* (☎ 649-946-4812) in Central Square Plaza on Leeward Hwy downtown near Provo Travel; it's run by Californians. Meals cost US$6 to US$18.

Baci Ristorante (☎ 649-941-3044), at Turtle Cove, is upscale with terra-cotta tile floors and wrought iron furnishings, plus a bougainvillea-shaded patio. It serves Italian fare and seafood such as mahi mahi provençale (US$15 to US$24). It's open Tuesday to Friday, and on weekends for dinner only. *Shark Bite Bar & Grill* (☎ 649-941-5090), next door, is a waterfront bar serving burgers and the like.

The restaurant at the *Erebus Inn* offers a view over Turtle Cove and specializes in Asian-Caribbean cuisine, such as sesame seared tuna with wok-fried veggies, baby bok choy, and coconut wasabi with mashed potato (US$26). Brunch costs US$9.

Downtown, *Fast Eddie's* (☎ 649-941-3176), on Airport Rd, serves island dishes, as does unpretentious *Dora's Restaurant* (☎ 649-946-4558) on Leeward Hwy near Turtle Cove; the ambience is somewhat forlorn until the evening crowd arrives. Dora's has a seafood buffet Monday to Thursday for US$24, including taxi transfers (minimum four people).

Also on the Leeward Hwy downtown, try *Go Fish* (☎ 649-941-4646), at Centre Mews, for fish specials to eat in or to go. It also has herb roast chicken.

For snacks, try *Top O' the Cove Deli* (☎ 649-946-4694), on Leeward Hwy. If you have a pizza craving, try *Pizza Pizza* (☎ 649-941-3577), to the east in Provo Plaza on Leeward Hwy.

Tasty Temptations (☎ 649-946-4049), in Butterfield Square downtown, serves coffee, cappuccinos, and pastries, plus sandwiches and cold cuts for lunch.

You can stock up on groceries and produce at *Island Pride Supermarket* (☎ 649-941-3329) in Town Centre Mall.

Grace Bay & East Providenciales

At the far eastern end of town, *Gilley's at Leeward* (☎ 649-946-5094) has a waterfront setting but uninspired decor. It serves breakfast and lunch (mostly salads and sandwiches) for about US$5. Budget US$20 for a seafood dinner.

Jungle Hut Café, in Grace Bay Plaza, offers such dishes as grilled chicken with roasted red pepper sauce, grilled shark, and ribeye, plus ice cream with Baileys. Entrees range from US$10 to US$20.

The lively, German-run *Calico Jack's* (☎ 649-946-5120), upstairs in Ports of Call, offers dishes from gazpacho (US$4.50) and Caesar salad (US$6.75) to fresh seafood, pizzas, and a veggie rasta burger (US$6.75). On Wednesday night fish and chips are served English-style in newspaper for US$9. It's open 6 am to midnight daily (Wednesday to Saturday only in summer).

The *Latitudes Tavern Grill* (☎ 649-946-5832), also at Ports of Call, is a sports bar with three large-screen TVs. It serves Tex-Mex food and has special theme nights. Monday and Thursday are all-you-can-eat 'Fajita Rita' nights, and a prime rib special is offered on Friday.

Bonnie's Restaurant & Bar (☎ 649-946-4660) is a good option for seafood, jerked chicken, and curry goat.

Provo has its share of fine dining, as at the *Caicos Café* (☎ 649-946-5278), opposite the entrance to the Grace Bay Club. This French-run charmer has tremendous ambience, assisted by lively artwork, tasteful music, and the hip clientele. You dine on a deck shaded by a dazzling, flamboyant tree. It serves entrees from steak au poivre to seafood, averaging US$20. *Do* try the profiteroles. The lunch menu features lobster-salad sandwiches, grilled fish, and hamburgers. Budget about US$10 for lunch.

Nearby, *Coco Bistro* (☎ 649-946-5369) is an exquisite villa with tropical motif, terracotta tile floors, and abundant art, options for breeze-swept indoor dining or alfresco dining on a palm-shaded patio, plus creative dishes such as mussels in curry (US$9), lamb tajine (US$20), and hurricane ginger shrimp (US$22).

Likewise, sophisticates might head to *Gecko Grille & Bar* (☎ 649-946-5885) in the Ocean Club Plaza. It's renowned for such

dishes as Chilean salmon, 'Voodoo Jalapeño Shooters,' and grouper macadamia with pureed avocado and pineapple-tomato salsa. Entrees begin at US$15. Soups, salads, and appetizers average US$7. You can choose air-con indoor dining in upscale, contemporary surrounds or romantic alfresco dining in a courtyard. It's open 6 to 9:30 pm nightly except Wednesday. In summer it's open Wednesday to Sunday *only*.

For Italian, head to the *Portofino Restaurant* at the Allegro Resort; entrees cost about US$20. It has nightly specials, including pizzas on Monday. The elegantly casual *Bella Luna Ristorante* (☎ 649-946-5214), a futuristic building on Grace Bay Rd with massive plate-glass windows all around, offers dishes such as clams sauteed with mushrooms in garlic with olive oil. Entrees average US$15.

Mediterranean cuisine has also found its way to the islands at *Prestancia* (☎ 649-941-4417) on Leeward Hwy. You can dine in the lounge or on the terrace overlooking Grace Bay. Ottoman delights include kebabs, pita bread, and pizza. Reservations are recommended.

The most stylish – and most expensive – place to eat in town is the ultra-elegant *Anacaona* (☎ 649-946-5050) by the Grace Bay Club. It serves nouvelle cuisine with a Caribbean flair. It's very romantic…but I've heard conflicting reviews, from 'sublime' to 'poor.'

Coyaba, at the Coral Gardens Hotel, offers elegant dining under a canopy, highlighted by such dishes as Atlantic salmon wrapped in filo stuffed with goat cheese, anise, lobster mushroom, saffron, and vanilla (US$26).

China Restaurant (☎ 649-946-5377), on Turquoise Rd, serves Szechwan cuisine amid suitable decor. The house specialty is pork in hot sauce. The simple, unpretentious *Hong Kong Restaurant*, on Grace Bay Rd, is also good, with more than 100 dishes on its menu.

The *Pasta House Restaurant* aims 'to provide good, healthy meals at family-affordable prices.' Go on Monday or Thursday nights, when it offers all-you-can-eat.

The **Fairways Bar & Grill**, at the Provo Golf Club, is a popular brunch spot on weekends.

For coffees, try **Island Dreams Café**, which serves ice cream, cappuccinos, and espressos; and **Blue Mountain Coffee Shop**; both are in Ports of Call. **Angela's Grapevine Delicatessen**, also in Ports of Call, sells pastries, meats, cheeses, etc, as well as cappuccinos and dinners-to-go.

ENTERTAINMENT
Dance Clubs & Casinos

Most of the upscale resorts in Grace Bay have dance clubs, including **Beaches** and **Allegro Resort**. **Club Med Turkoise** permits outside visitors with a pass for US$25, including US$20 worth of bar tokens. It gives you full access to the dance club, bars, and nightly show.

You can gamble at the **Port Royale Casino** (☎ 649-946-5508) at Allegro Resort. It has roulette, blackjack, Caribbean stud poker, and slot machines. Drinks are free. It's open 6pm to 2am. A casino was to be added at Beaches.

Pubs & Bars

At the Sands Resort, **Hemingways on the Beach** has live music on Tuesday and Thursday evenings. The **Banana Boat Bar & Grill** also has live music on Tuesday (see Places to Eat, above). On a more upscale note, the **Anacaona** also has live music on Saturday.

At Turtle Cove, the **Shark Bite Bar & Grill** has live entertainment most nights; it's **the** in spot on Saturday night, which is Ladies Night, when gals get in free. The **Jungle Hut Café** also has Ladies Night on Thursday and Saturday until 9 pm. **Hey José** has Ladies Night on Tuesday, with drinks for half price.

At Ports of Call, the unpretentious and distinctly Texan **Latitudes Tavern Grill** is the number-one sports bar, with three games at once on the three satellite TVs, and funk and disco on Friday night. Happy hour is 5 to 6:30 pm Monday to Friday. **Calico Jack's** is also a happening spot on Friday night, with live calypso, reggae, and soca.

For local color, head to **Turntable Club Disco** on Airport Rd downtown. It has a dartboard, pool table, and one-armed bandits (slot machines). The disco on Thursday night is popular with Haitians and can sometimes get rowdy. Bingo is offered at 8 pm Saturday and on Sunday afternoon. It was planning to move to a site on Leeward Hwy opposite Dora's Restaurant, and will be renamed the oddly spelled **Catcus Club**.

Also downtown, the **Club Latino** is a down-to-earth dance club with video slots and go-go dancers on weekends.

North of town, in the Blue Hills neighborhood, there are several spots filled with locals, including **Three Queen's**, where you can catch a game of dominoes. Nearby, the **Pub on the Bay** is another popular jive spot. And **Dolphin's Sports Bar & Grill**, in Blue Hills' Neptune Plaza, is a simple satellite lounge popular with locals.

SHOPPING

A large selection of beachy items, casual clothing, and batiks is offered at Tattooed Parrot (☎ 649-946-5829), Marilyn's Crafts, and the Night & Day Boutique, all in the Ports of Call complex (see the Turtle Cove to Grace Bay map).

The Caribbean Art Gallery, also in Ports of Call, sells mostly Haitian art, including painted wooden animals. Check out Maison Creole, near the Caicos Café, boasting fabulous contemporary art, model ships, and an eclectic miscellany of decorative pieces. It's open 10 am to 5 pm Tuesday to Saturday and 7 to 9 pm Thursday to Saturday.

Tropical Latitudes (☎ 649-946-4311), at Turtle Cove Marina Plaza, is an Aladdin's Cave selling hammocks, reconditioned antique furniture, exquisite pottery, etc (see the Turtle Cove to Grace Bay map).

If you're driving along Leeward Hwy, look for the sign saying 'Local Artist's Studio' opposite the Shell gas station. The sign points the way to the studio of Phillip Outten, a Rastafarian whom some people consider the leading artist in the Turks and Caicos. Take the first right onto Venetian Rd (see the Turtle Cove to

Grace Bay map); his home – gaily painted in Rasta colors – is the first house on the right. (See the Turks and Caicos introductory chapter for more information on Outten.)

You can buy Cuban cigars and expensive jewelry at Koko Tok, next to Maison Creole in Grace Bay. The best places for duty-free jewelry are The Goldsmith's in Central Square Plaza on Leeward Hwy and the jewelry store in the Allegro Resort & Casino.

To support the local economy, pop into Nell's Gift Shop (☎ 649-941-3228), Al Vern's Craft Market, or TJ's Straw & Souvenirs, all on Leeward Hwy.

GETTING THERE & AWAY
Air
The recently expanded Providenciales Airport is 1 mile west of town on Airport Rd. There's a tourist information desk by baggage claim, and car rental offices beyond customs. See the Getting There & Away section of the Turks and Caicos introductory chapter for airline phone numbers.

American Airlines (☎ 649-946-4948; in the US ☎ 800-433-7300) flies two daily nonstops from Miami from about US$185 roundtrip in low season. American has an office in Butterfield Square. Turks & Caicos Airways (☎ 649-946-2455 at the airport) has daily service from Miami.

InterIsland Airways (☎ 649-941-5481) flies from Fort Lauderdale; you can also make connections through Nassau and Freeport, The Bahamas.

Sandals' Beaches Turks & Caicos offers nonstop weekend charter flights from Atlanta, Boston, Chicago, New York's JFK, Newark, and Philadelphia. Fares include complimentary champagne.

Bahamasair flies from Nassau three days a week (US$120 one-way, US$220 roundtrip). Turks & Caicos Airways (☎ 649-946-4255) also operates between Provo and Nassau. It also flies between Provo and the Dominican Republic, Haiti, Jamaica, and Puerto Rico. Sky King offers charters to Cuba, Haiti, and the Dominican Republic. It has an office (☎ 649-941-5464) downtown.

Boat
Windjammer Barefoot Cruises' *Amazing Grace* calls in Provo twice monthly during 13-day cruises between Grand Bahama and Trinidad (see the Getting There & Away chapter in the Bahamas section for more details).

Turtle Cove Marina (☎ 649-941-3781, fax 649-941-5782, TCMarina@provo.net) has 65 deep-water slips plus full services; it charges US90¢ per foot daily. Leeward Marina (☎ 649-946-5000, marina@tciway.tc), at the eastern end of the island, has limited services and dockside berths only (US50¢ per foot); it was planning a major expansion. There's also the South Side Basin Marina (☎ 649-946-4200) and the Caicos Marina (☎ 649-946-5416/5600, fax 649-946-5390).

GETTING AROUND
To/From the Airport
There are no buses from the airport. A taxi to Grace Bay costs US$10 to US$15 one-way for two people; each extra person costs US$5.

Beaches Turks & Caicos and the Ocean Club have their own minibus transfers.

Bus
A public minibus runs along Leeward Hwy; it also runs southwest as far as South Dock and Sapodilla Bay. The fare is US$2.

Car, Motorcycle & Scooter
Mandatory insurance costs US$14. Most rental companies offer free drop-off and pick-up.

Hertz (☎ 649-941-3910; in the US ☎ 800-654-3131), Avis (☎ 649-946-4882, avis@provo.net; in the US ☎ 800-831-2847), Budget (☎ 649-946-4079; in the US ☎ 800-527-0770), and Provo Rent-a-Car (☎ 649-946-4404, fax 649-946-4993, rentacar@provo.net) are at the airport. Hertz also has an outlet at Southern Shores Centre, and Budget has an outlet at Town Centre Mall, both on Leeward Hwy. Provo Rent-a-Car also has an office at the Allegro Resort.

Tropical Auto Rentals (☎ 649-946-5300, fax 649-946-5456) charges US$49 to US$80 for six types of vehicles, including minivans.

It has an office in the Ocean Club Plaza on Grace Bay and another at Tropicana Plaza on Leeward Hwy at Turquoise Rd; they're open 8 am to 5 pm daily. Turks & Caicos National Car Rental (☎ 649-941-3514, fax 649-941-3281), at Airport Plaza, charges US$37 to US$64. Island Rent-a-Car (☎ 649-946-4475) also has an office at the airport.

You'll want a 4WD vehicle if you're planning on traveling to Malcolm Roads. Driving on the beaches is prohibited; if you get stuck, you'll be charged US$500 for recovery! Suzuki Jeep Rental (☎ 649-946-4158), on Leeward Hwy, rents jeeps from US$52/312 daily/weekly. Rent a Buggy (☎ 649-946-4158) charges similar rates.; it also has Mustang convertibles for US$65/390.

Provo Fun Cycles & Autos (☎ 649-946-5868), at Ports of Call, rents Honda scooters for US$29/39 single/double seat. It also has 250cc enduro motorcycles, plus jeeps for US$69.

Scooter Bob's (☎ 649-946-4684, scooter@provo.net), in Turtle Cove Marina Plaza, rents Yamaha scooters for US$35, plus Jeeps for US$55. It also has an office at Grace Bay Plaza (☎ 649-946-5684).

Taxi
There are several taxi companies. Most use minivans. Allow plenty of time, as they often take ages to arrive. You can call VHF channel 06 for the dispatcher or contact companies at the numbers below.

Island's Choice Taxi	☎ 649-941-0409
Nell's Taxi Service	☎ 649-941-3228
Paradise Taxi	☎ 649-941-3555
Provo Taxi & Bus Group	☎ 649-946-5481

Bicycle
Provo Fun Cycles & Autos and Scooter Bob's (see Car, Motorcycle & Scooter, above) rent mountain bikes for US$15 and US$12.50 daily, respectively. Tropical Auto Rentals has bikes for US$3.50/12 hourly/daily.

Boat
Boat trips can be arranged from any of the marinas (see Getting There & Away,

earlier in this section), or through Catch the Wave Charters (☎ 649-941-3047, catchthewaveprovo@yahoo.com) and Sail Provo (see the Boat Excursions section, earlier in this chapter).

You can charter *Beluga*, a 37-foot catamaran (call Tim Ainley at ☎/fax 649-946-4396).

West Caicos

This small island, 6 miles southwest of Provo, is renowned for its diving. The 10-mile-long, 2-mile-wide, virtually uninhabited isle is fringed by the **Molasses Reef**, which harbors the remains of the oldest known shipwreck in the Western Hemisphere, dating from 1513. The reefs off the west shore are protected within **West Caicos Marine National Park**.

Other prime dive sites include Elephant Ear Canyon, named for the biggest sponges found in the Turks and Caicos, at 95 feet. One 10-foot-wide monster masks a cave. There's also the Magic Mushroom: A sand chute leads to a precipice where sponges and black coral anchor the coral buttresses. Lobsters pack the cracks.

Inland, **Lake Catherine** is a nature reserve that attracts flamingos, ospreys, ducks, and waders.

There's no scheduled transport to West Caicos. To get there, you'll need to hire a boat or take a scuba diving excursion. See the other sections of this chapter for options.

French Cay

This tiny cay, about 15 miles due south of Provo, is an uninhabited wildlife sanctuary protecting over 2000 nesting and migrating species of birds, including frigate birds and ospreys. Stingrays gather to give birth, and nurse sharks are drawn in summer. Supposedly it is an old French pirate lair.

Caicos Adventures has a full-day snorkel trip to French Cay, as does J&B Tours. See the Provo section for more information. Trips include swimming and snorkeling with the friendly sharks in summer, and with stingrays year-round. Both companies charge US$109.

Cays East of Providenciales

LITTLE WATER CAY

Northeast of Provo and separated from it by the 400-yard-wide Leeward Going Through channel, Little Water Cay is a nature reserve within Princess Alexandra National Park and is the home of about 2000 endangered rock iguanas. It's a popular destination for day-trippers. (See the Providenciales map.)

Visitors can bathe, snorkel, line-fish, or walk the nature trails, which have board-walks and interpretive signs. The 170-yard-long **North Shore Trail** leads from the beach to a shallow mangrove estuary where you can learn about this vital ecosystem. A lookout deck offers views over a pond and large osprey nest. Iguanas frequently forage along the 225-yard-long **South Shore Trail**, which passes through a lush coastal coppice and also has a lookout deck.

It's illegal and harmful to feed the 2000 or so endangered rock iguanas, though so many people do it that they'll come waddling down to the boat to greet you. *Don't feed or touch the iguanas!* And stay to the trails to avoid trampling the iguanas' burrows and the ecologically sensitive plants.

Mangrove Cay was joined to Little Water Cay before a hurricane in 1960 gouged out the channel that now separates the two. The cay (also known as Big Water Cay) boasts an unbroken span of sand where the 1987 *Sports Illustrated* swimsuit edition was shot.

Visitors on private boats are not charged; people arriving by commercial boat pay a US$3 fee. See the Boat Excursions section in the Providenciales section for details on tours to Little Water.

PINE CAY

Two miles northeast of Provo, Pine Cay is an 800-acre private cay that welcomes visitors by prior arrangement. It has a small cadre of seasonal residents that includes Bill Cosby, Denzel Washington, and Jimmy Buffett, who has a passion for bonefishing here.

The cay was the site of the first tourist development in the islands – the snooty Meridian Club – planned in the 1950s by Count Ferdinand Czernin but not brought to fruition until the '70s by his widow, Helen Czernin, and the Polish-born architect George Nipanich (both of whom still live on the island). Today there's a second hotel and about 30 affiliated houses, but no cars, roads, TVs, or telephones (there *is* a fax, however). So far out is the cay that it doesn't take note of daylight saving time, thereby constituting its own little time zone.

About two-thirds of the island, which is named for the native Cuban pine that thrives at the edge of the freshwater ponds,

---

X-Rated Antics

No, I'm not talking sex on the beach. I'm referring to glowworm sex, which takes place in the channel between Pine Cay and Fort George Cay near the Aquarium snorkel spot.

Here millions of the teeny glowworm (*Odontosyllis enopla*) copulate by the clock, 55 minutes after sundown, five days after each month's full moon. Lesser displays are seen on the fourth and sixth nights. Voyeurs may journey by boat to witness the fabulous 15-minute-long performance. First the females, then the males, light up in an outburst of phosphorescent fireworks as the males chase the glowing white egg sacs enclosed within the hindquarters of the females. Talk about a sexual flush! Alas, the males' brief but ecstatic neon-green display is their last gasp: The females devour the males after mating.

is set aside as a nature preserve, accessed by 9 miles of nature trails. There are semi-tame iguanas and 120 species of birds, including white-tailed tropic birds.

A fabulous beach runs almost the full length of the west shore. At its northern end, Sand Dollar Point, you can wade out 400 yards in knee-deep water, searching for the eponymous shells. A 70-foot wreck lies partially submerged a stone's throw from shore, with cannon on the seabed. And snorkeling is superb at the Aquarium, a cove on the east shore of Pine Cay, with two coral arms embracing a sandy floor covered with anemones pulsing like little translucent green hearts.

Pine Cay has a packed-sand airstrip.

Places to Stay

The *ultra*-exclusive **Meridian Club** *(in the US ☎ 203-602-0300, 800-331-9154, fax 203-602-2265, rmiresorts@juno.com)*, which has acquired a cult status among the super-rich, is both barefoot casual – even the manager hangs out in rumpled shorts – and pricey, appealing to travelers with a taste for luxurious and unpretentious isolation. There are 13 one-bedroom cabañas tucked amid the dunes, each with lounge and screened porch fronting the beach. Rooms are grandly austere, with neither telephones nor TVs. For total seclusion, you can opt for the one-room Sand Dollar Cottage nestled under casuarinas on the beach. There's also a pool and tennis court. Rates are US$525 to US$750 double, depending on season. Single occupancy costs US$90 less, as does the Sand Dollar Cottage. Rates include transfers for certain flights, plus use of sailboats, sailboards, and bicycles, and boating excursions on the spiffy launch, with crew decked out in yachting whites. Special package rates are offered. No credit cards or kids under 12. Write the club c/o RMI Marketing, 456 Glenbrook Rd, Stamford, CT 06906, USA.

FORT GEORGE CAY

This tiny cay, a stone's throw north of Pine Cay, is a national historic site, with the remains of an 18th-century British fort built to protect the Caicos islands from attack. Divers and snorkelers can inspect barnacle-encrusted cannon lying on the bottom of the ocean. The site is protected within **Fort George Land & Sea National Park**.

DELLIS CAY

Next north in the necklace, Dellis is one of the best isles for shelling, thanks to a combination of tide patterns and current. *No shells may be taken away!* Leave them for others to admire.

PARROT CAY

This private cay, just west of North Caicos, is said to have been the lair of the pirate Calico Jack in the 1720s. The only guarded treasure today is a deluxe resort once owned by a Kuwaiti shah…and the scintillating 3-mile-long beach, glinting like dusted diamonds. Bring bug spray.

The boat leaves from Leeward Marina on Provo. To arrange a ride, you call ahead to Parrot Cay club. It's by demand.

Places to Stay

Opened to fanfare in 1998, *Parrot Cay (☎ 649-946-7788, 800-628-8929, fax 649-946-7789, mneutelings@parrot-cay.com)* is favored by the chicest of chic, such as Donatella Versace. The 56 air-con rooms and six villas (two with private swimming pools) are done up in blazing whites, furnished with an Indonesian motif, sisal rugs, and four-poster beds enveloped in romantic linens. Each has a CD/radio, ceiling fan, direct dial telephone, hairdryer, in-room safe, minibar, modem hookup, and separate bath and shower. You can cool off in the infinity pool and relax in the super-luxe Asian spa. The staff provides exemplary service, though the Asian-influenced food served in the overly air-con dining room is overly expensive and, by some claims, ho-hum. Standard rooms cost from US$360 to US$530 for garden-view, US$1900 to US$2900 for suites, and US$2300 to US$3100 for a three-bedroom villa. Rates include breakfast and dinner. It's closed in September.

Dixon Lighthouse, San Salvador

Typical Bahamian sloop

Cape Santa Maria Beach Resort, Long Island

Abandoned home

Columbus Plaza, Cockburn Town

Old salt warehouse in Provo

Main drag, downtown Cockburn Town, Grand Turk

CHRISTOPHER P BAKER

CHRISTOPHER P BAKER

CHRISTOPHER P BAKER

CHRISTOPHER P BAKER

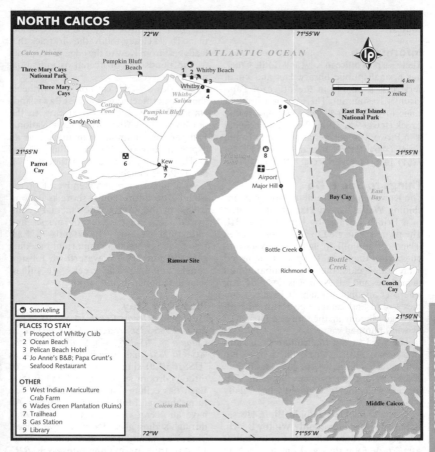

NORTH CAICOS

PLACES TO STAY
1 Prospect of Whitby Club
2 Ocean Beach
3 Pelican Beach Hotel
4 Jo Anne's B&B; Papa Grunt's
   Seafood Restaurant

OTHER
5 West Indian Mariculture
   Crab Farm
6 Wades Green Plantation (Ruins)
7 Trailhead
8 Gas Station
9 Library

North Caicos

• pop 1375

Little-visited North Caicos appeals to eco-tourists. It gets more rainfall than other islands and hence has lusher vegetation. It has traditionally been the bread basket of the island chain and in the last century was the seat of government for these islands, while Bellfield Landing was the principal port for loading Sea Island cotton. Farms evolved in colonial times and sloops were built to transport the crops to the other islands. Mangoes, oranges, and other fruits and vegetables still thrive beside sea grapes and sugar apples.

There are four tiny settlements, notably Kew, near the island's center, and Bottle Creek, on a breezy coastal bluff 2 miles south of the airport.

The island is becoming popular with expats who have settled here in recent years. There's a sense of development in the air.

North Caicos hosts the Festarama Festival each July. This annual regatta includes beach parties and the Miss Festarama Beauty Pageant. In October, the North Caicos Extravaganza features a

Junkanoo and Miss Extravaganza beauty contest.

Information

There's a post office in Kew, and Bottle Creek has a small public library. Fax and email service is available in the office of Papa Grunt's Restaurant. There's a government clinic in Kew (☎ 649-946-7397) and Bottle Creek (☎ 649-946-7194). The nearest hospital is in Provo. The police stations are in Bottle Creek (☎ 649-946-7116) and Kew (☎ 649-946-7261). In an emergency dial ☎ 999 or ☎ 911.

Things to See & Do

The Kew area has several historic ruins, including **Wades Green Plantation**, granted to a British Loyalist by King George III. The owners struggled to grow sisal and Sea Island cotton until drought, hurricanes, and bugs drove them out. The plantation lasted a mere 25 years; the owners abandoned their slaves and left. Nearby is **Cosmic Farm**, where a Canadian nicknamed 'Farmer John' raises okra and cantaloupe fertilized with seaweed raked from the shore and irrigated by wind-pumped water.

The **West Indian Mariculture Crab Farm** (☎ 649-946-7213), on the northeast shore, is a commercial venture where you can observe crabs in various stages of development. Visitors are welcome. It supposedly has a daily boat tour.

Beaches include Pumpkin Bluff, Horsestable, and most importantly, Whitby Beach. On any one, yours will be the only Robinson Crusoe footprints, and I guarantee you will find pluperfect shells. Pumpkin Bluff Beach is especially beautiful and the snorkeling is good, with a foundered cargo ship adding to the allure.

Cottage Pond, a 150-foot-deep blue hole on the northwest coast, attracts waterfowl such as West Indian whistling ducks, grebes, and waders. Bellfield Landing Pond, Pumpkin Bluff Pond, and Dick Hill Creek also attract flamingos, as does a large brine lake, **Flamingo Pond**, which floods the center of the island. Here the gangly birds strut around in hot pink. You can see them from a distance: Three cabañas have been erected

on the main road, and they offer views over the pond, 400 yards away. You'll need binoculars. To get closer, follow the dirt track that leads east from Kew to the edge of the pond.

The ponds are protected as individual nature reserves.

A series of small cays off the northeast shore are protected within **East Bay Islands National Park**, and a trio of cays to the northwest form **Three Mary Cays National Park**, another flamingo sanctuary and an osprey nesting site. The snorkeling is good at Three Mary Cays and farther west at Sandy Point Beach.

Vast bonefish flats extend east of the island. The entire south shore is encompassed by the **Ramsar Site** sanctuary, comprised of a vast series of marsh and inter-tidal wetlands. It extends to East Caicos and protects an important breeding site and nursery for waterfowl, lobster, conch, and fish. The creeks are full of schooling bonefish and tarpon.

Places to Stay

The homey **Ocean Beach** (☎ 649-946-7113, fax 649-946-7386, reservations@tciway.tc; in Canada ☎ 905-336-2876, 800-710-5204, fax 905-336-9851) has 10 units featuring rooms (US$105/120 single/double) and two- or three-bedroom suites (from US$130/150). Each has ceiling fans, rattan and bamboo furnishings, and fully equipped kitchen. All have an ocean view and a patio accessed through sliding glass doors. It's overpriced. There's a restaurant and bar. Children under 12 stay free. Its mailing address is RR3 Campbellville, Ontario, LOP 1BO, Canada.

Nearby is the **Pelican Beach Hotel** (☎ 649-946-7112, fax 649-946-7139, email: reservations@tciway.tc), with 12 spacious, modestly furnished oceanfront rooms and two suites with wood-paneled walls, tile floors, and patios with lounge chairs. The bathrooms are small but enhanced by hand-painted motifs. There are no telephones or TVs. Breakfasts and sandwich lunches are provided, and native meals are prepared on request. It has a nice bar. It's a good escape for nongregarious types. Rates range from US$100 to US$150 double.

Jo Anne's Bed & Breakfast (☎ 649-946-7184, fax 649-946-7301, joannesbnb@tciway.tc) is a modest affair run by Jo Anne Selver, a Peace Corps volunteer from Michigan who chose to stay. Two rooms – one without windows – share an outside bathroom and cost US$70. She also has six rooms fashioned of bare cement block and meagerly furnished with handmade plywood furniture, though there are some romantic touches; they cost US$90. Two 'suites' with ocean views, fridge, and king-size or double beds cost US$105. She also has a two-bedroom 'villa' for US$200, including housekeeping service, and a two-bedroom apartment with kitchen for US$120/600 daily/weekly. The beach is a 15-minute walk away. Jo Anne also offers a courtesy van service and runs a small gift shop at Prospect of Whitby Club (see below). She does *not* take walk-ins: You'll need to make reservations with a 50% deposit.

The *Ocean Beach Hotel Condos* (☎ 649-946-7113), at Whitby, is a 10-unit complex with single rooms and two- and three-bedroom suites, modestly furnished with rattan, and all with kitchens and ocean views. There's a dining room. Rooms cost US$105/120 single/double; two-room suites cost US$130/150; three-bedroom suites cost US$215 single or double.

The nicest place is the *Prospect of Whitby Club* (☎ 649-946-7119, fax 649-946-7114, prospwhit@tciway.tc; in Italy ☎ 02-66982006 in Milan, 06-4814041 in Rome, info@clubvacanze.it), run by Club Vacanze and serving a predominantly Italian clientele. The 23 spacious, air-con rooms and four suites are set amid parched lawns, thatch palms, and casuarinas. Each has terra-cotta tile floors, wicker furniture, two double beds, minifridge, and telephone. A TV lounge has live music some nights. There's a sun deck and pool, plus archery, scuba diving, and sea kayaks. Rates are US$340 to US$390 double, all-inclusive.

A newcomer is *Bottle Creek Lodge* (☎ 649-946-7080, bottlecrkldg@tciway.tc), a small, modern-style ecolodge perched on a ridge on the northeastern side of Flamingo Pond. It's simple and airy, and features

modest furnishings. All rooms face the sea and prevailing tradewinds. It has Hobi-cats, kayaks, and bicycles free of charge. Rates, including full breakfast, are US$100/140 low/high season for a room; US$125/175 for a cabin.

Datai Villa (☎ 649-946-7248, dataivilla@aol.com) on Whitby Beach has two separate units with fine furnishings, and a garden courtyard between. The lounge has a TV/VCR. It rents for US$1300 (two people) to US$1600 (six people) in summer.

Seabreeze Villa (☎/fax 649-946-7308, info@seabreezevilla.tc) fronts Whitby Beach and has two bedrooms, each with king beds. The lounge has a TV/VCR. It rents for US$150/1050 nightly/weekly.

See the Accommodations section in the Turks & Caicos introduction chapter for information on agencies that arrange villa rentals.

Places to Eat
Jo Anne Selver offers salads, sandwiches, burgers, and seafood at her no-frills *Papa Grunt's Seafood Restaurant*; open 7 am to 7 pm daily. Dinners are by reservation. The fare ranges from pizza (US$3 per slice) to lobster (US$24).

For steamed conch and native fare, try the *Super D Cafe* (☎ 649-946-7528) at the airport. Better yet, head to *The Shoal*, a funky bar in Kew, with green turtles swimming along the walls.

The restaurants in both the *Pelican Beach Hotel* and the *Ocean Beach* serve lunch and dinner by reservation only. *Prospect of Whitby Club* serves quality meals catering to Italian tastes; expect to pay US$30 or so for dinner.

You can buy produce and groceries at *KH's Food Store* in Whitby and at *Al's Grocery* in Bottle Creek. Or head out to Bellfield Landing Rd to buy organically grown fruit and veggies at *Cosmic Farm*.

Getting There & Away
North Caicos' airport is just north of Major Hill.

Global (☎ 649-946-7093, fax 649-946-7290, global@tciway.tc) and InterIsland

Airways each have daily flights from Provo to North Caicos (US$30 one-way). Turks & Caicos Airways also flies to North Caicos on Monday, Wednesday, and Friday.

A Lauda Air charter flight flies weekly from Milan to the Provo Airport for guests at the Prospect of Whitby Club.

Getting Around
A taxi from the airport to Whitby costs US$10 one-way. Mac of M&M Tours (☎ 649-946-7338) offers island tours for US$25 per hour. You won't need more than three hours to see the entire island.

You can rent beach-cruiser bicycles at the Prospect of Whitby Club and Whitby Plaza for a steep US$18 a day! No hourly rentals.

Middle Caicos

• pop 300

The largest of the Caicos islands (48 sq miles) is also one of the least developed, although it seems to have been heavily populated in ancient times by Lucayan Indians. There are at least 38 pre-Columbian Lucayan sites on the island, many of which have been excavated by archaeologists.

The fishermen and farmers in the tiny hamlets of Conch Bar, Bambarra, and Lorimers give visitors a warm welcome. Bambarra is named for people from the

Green sea turtle

Bombarras tribe of the Niger River, who were shipwrecked here in 1842 when a slavetrader, the *Gambier*, ran aground.

The island hosts the Middle Caicos Expo each August.

Turks & Caicos Airways operates two flights daily between Provo and Middle Caicos (US$38 each way). Also see the Organized Tours section, below.

Things to See
The southern half of the island is composed of vast inter-tidal swamplands. Offshore, **Vine Point & Ocean Hole Nature Reserve** protects a frigate-bird breeding colony, plus a 210-foot-deep, 400-yard-wide marine blue hole favored as a hangout by turtles and sharks.

Middle Caicos Reserve & Trail System The island boasts miles of beaches, large freshwater lakes, and lavish pine forests accessed by 10 miles of trails along the north coast, created in conjunction with the Turks & Caicos National Trust as part of the Ramsar Site. One trail leads from Mudjen Harbour Beach to join the historic **Crossing Over Trail** that leads from Middle to North Caicos. En route, it passes the ruins of several Loyalist cotton plantations, as well as brine pools favored by cranes and flamingos. Signs at regular intervals point out highlights of the trek.

The north coast is dramatically scenic, with long sandy beaches and scalloped bays held in the cusps of rugged limestone cliffs. Mudjen Harbour Beach features a huge amphitheater carved from the raw limestone bluffs. Here the long unfurling of turquoise waves is broken by tiny **Dragon Cay**, connected to the shore by a sand spit and surrounded by placid sea pools.

Plans call for the trail to be extended eastward along almost the entire north coast.

Conch Bar Caves National Park This park protects 15 miles of underground caverns. Some have lagoons and stalactites and stalagmites. Most have colonies of bats. They were used as sacred sanctuaries by the Lucayan Indians, who left petro-

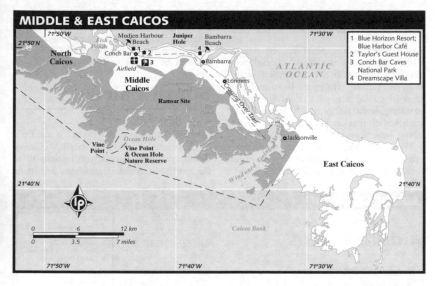

MIDDLE & EAST CAICOS

1 Blue Horizon Resort;
Blue Harbour Café
2 Taylor's Guest House
3 Conch Bar Caves
National Park
4 Dreamscape Villa

glyphs on the walls. The most notable Lucayan site is the **Armstrong Pond Village Historical Site**.

Organized Tours

J&B Tours (☎ 649-946-5047, fax 649-946-5288, jill@jbtours.com) in Provo offers daylong excursions that include Conch Bar Caves (US$135), as do Silver Deep (☎ 649-946-5612, fax 649-946-4527) and Majestic Tours (☎ 649-946-4999, fax 649-946-4040).

Cardinal Arthur (☎ 649-946-6107), at Conch Bar, offers guided tours, as well as bonefishing, reef fishing, snorkeling, and bird watching.

Places to Stay & Eat

Taylor's Guest House (☎ 649-946-6118; in the US ☎ 305-667-0966), in Conch Bar about 300 yards from the beach, has four basic rooms for US$50. Only one room has its own bathroom; the others share. It has a small restaurant. Likewise, *Arthur's Guest House (☎ /fax 649-946-6122)* has two simple rooms with ceiling fans and TVs for US$55 to US$65. Mrs Arthur will cook for an extra fee.

Blue Horizon Resort (☎ 649-946-6141, fax 649-946-6139, bhresort@tciway.tc) is a residential and vacation community in Mudjen Harbour, overlooking Dragon Cay. It includes studio-type rental cottages with screened porches and full modern kitchens. Rates are US$150 to US$225 per night or US$1000 to US$1500 weekly. Its *Blue Harbour Café* offers lunch and dinner by reservation only.

Seascape Villa (no phone) is a three-bedroom, air-con home with cathedral ceiling, pastel rattan furniture, and ceiling fans. One bedroom is a quaint wooden loft. There's a TV/VCR and tape library. It rents for US$1195/1395 per week summer/winter. The Web site is www.caicosvilla.com.

Dreamscape Villa (in the US ☎/fax 802-295-2652, mmilne2652@aol.com) is a three-bedroom option at Bambarra that rents for US$1400/1500 per week summer/winter for up to four people (US$150/175 each additional person). The mailing address is 185 Highland Ave, White River Junction, VT 05001, USA.

See the Accommodations section in the Turks & Caicos introduction chapter for information on rental agencies that arrange accommodations in all types of villas, cottages, and houses.

CAICOS ISLANDS

East Caicos

East Caicos is the least-visited island. You'll often hear it called 'uninhabited,' although there's an impoverished settlement of Haitians. It's home to small herds of wild cattle and flocks of flamingos flaunting their neon-pink liveries. There are miles of beaches perfect for the adventurous beachcomber.

The island could soon boom, thanks to a proposal to build a cruise-ship terminal here. The proposed US$450 million project includes plans for a bridge link with South Caicos, part of a future pan-Caicos highway with bridges linking the entire Caicos chain.

There is no air service; East Caicos can be reached only by boat.

South Caicos

• **pop 1600**

South Caicos, 22 miles west of Grand Turk, is the easternmost and smallest Caicos island. It's ladle-shaped, with its 'handle' to the northeast. First impressions are of an

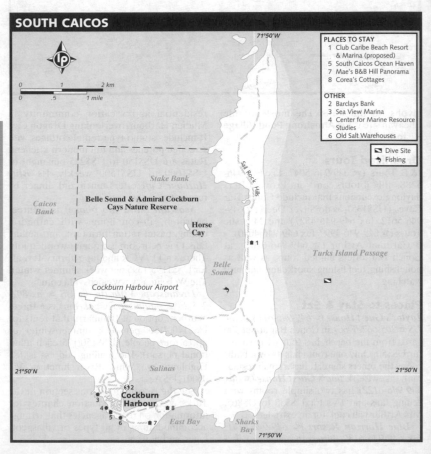

SOUTH CAICOS

0   1   2 km
0   .5   1 mile

71°50'W

PLACES TO STAY
1 Club Caribe Beach Resort
  & Marina (proposed)
5 South Caicos Ocean Haven
7 Mae's B&B Hill Panorama
8 Corea's Cottages

OTHER
2 Barclays Bank
3 Sea View Marina
4 Center for Marine Resource
  Studies
6 Old Salt Warehouses

⬛ Dive Site
↱ Fishing

Stake Bank

Caicos
Bank

Salt Rock Hills

Belle Sound & Admiral Cockburn
Cays Nature Reserve

Horse
Cay

Turks Island Passage

Belle
Sound

Cockburn Harbour Airport

21°50'N   21°50'N

Salinas

2 Cockburn
Harbour
3
4
5   6   8   7   East Bay

Sharks
Bay

71°50'W

CAICOS ISLANDS

arid wasteland and forlorn, sand-blasted streets roamed by wild horses and donkeys. But read on.

The big attraction is diving: A reef and wall run the length of the east coast. **Cockburn Harbour**, the only settlement, is also a perfect spot to launch across the 40-mile-wide Caicos Bank in search of bonefish. Flamingos inhabit the vast salinas (salt ponds) on the northeast edge of Cockburn Harbour; the birds – about 70 total – are resident year-round. And the Annual Commonwealth Regatta is held on South Caicos each May.

South Caicos was historically the most productive isle during the 19th-century heyday of salt raking. The population now lives exclusively off conch and lobster fishing, but the lobstering industry is in crisis. It is highly competitive and the last few seasons have not been good. Locals have even begun using bleaches to drive scarce lobster out of their hiding places, destroying both the coral reefs and the lobster stock. Many islanders have drifted to Provo in the past decade.

South Caicos may soon be put on the map by a massive 1000-room resort development, High Point, atop the Sail Rock Hills, though the project was stalled at last visit.

Cockburn Harbour itself is a rough-edged place with a somewhat sullen population and a rakishly appealing down-in-the-dumps shantytown feel. Corrugated-tin-and-driftwood shacks are interspersed amid modern bungalows and handsome, albeit weathered, colonial-era wooden structures left from the salt-trade days.

Drug traffic is a problem (signs posted in town remind locals that trade or possession of drugs is good for 14 years in the pokey). In the 1980s the trade was fostered by the annual Plane Exchange, when aircraft came in from South and North America, ostensibly for an aircraft swap-meet...a customs nightmare! The pilots gathered at the former Admiral Arms Hotel (now the Center for Marine Resource Studies), where aircraft serial numbers are etched on the roof beams.

The South Caicos Regatta is held annually the last weekend in May.

Information
Barclays Bank has a branch in town, open 9 am to 1 pm on Thursday. For the police, call ☎ 649-946-3299.

Youland Mills (☎ 649-946-3369), the District Commissioner, can provide information.

Center for Marine Resource Studies
This research center, in the center of Cockburn Harbour, undertakes ecological studies with the aim of helping Turks and Caicos islanders to develop sustainable fishing practices. It is run by the School for Field Studies (☎ 649-946-3246, info@fieldstudies.org; in the US ☎ 978-927-7777, 800-989-4418, fax 978-927-5127), 16 Broadway, Beverly, MA 01915-4499, USA, a nonprofit organization that gives young students practical education in environmental studies. Visitors are welcome, as are donations.

Month- and semester-long courses are offered. For more information, visit the school's Web site at www.fieldstudies.org.

Town Landmarks
Most historic buildings are at the southeast end of town, centered on the old **Wesleyan church** with its tall spire. By its lonesome atop Tucker's Hill at the south end of town is the **old commissioner's house**, now Mae's Bed & Breakfast Hill Panorama (see Places to Stay, below).

Belle Sound & Admiral Cockburn Cays Nature Preserve
Much of the island is within this park, north and west of Cockburn Harbour. It encompasses the **Sail Rock Hills**, a ridge extending along the panhandle and rising to 178 feet. The hills offer spectacular views east over the Turks Island Passage and west over **Belle Sound**, a vast turquoise bay opening to the flats of the Caicos Bank. The reserve extends west for several miles to protect the mangroves and bonefish flats, and extends windward to protect the offshore coral reefs.

Activities
South Caicos is known for its wall diving, plus you're sure to see plenty of pelagics,

CAICOS ISLANDS

including eagle rays, Atlantic rays, blacktip sharks, and – the highlight – humpback whales in January and February.

South Caicos Ocean Haven (see Places to Stay, below) is a full-service dedicated dive resort offering advanced diving, with three dives daily. It does *not* offer resort or certification courses.

Octogenarian Julius 'Goo the Guide' Jennings (☎ 649-946-3444) will take you fishing on Belle Sound.

Organized Tours
J&B Tours (☎ 649-946-5047, fax 649-946-5288, jill@jbtours.com) in Provo offers a full-day powerboat excursion from Provo, including diving for conch and lobster in season and a visit to a frigate-bird colony (US$168).

Places to Stay
A basic option is *Corea's Cottages*, east of town. It offers simple bunk-type beds for about US$50 nightly.

Mae's Bed & Breakfast Hill Panorama (☎ 649-946-3207), in the old commissioner's house atop Tucker's Hill, is an offbeat gem. The place is run by a delightful old dear named Mae, who has a renewable lease on the government-owned property that she shares with her numerous dogs and cats. The place is thoroughly charming, with a parlor and music room and three clean, well-lit bedrooms (two with shared bathroom) offering views over town. They're simply furnished, with romantic lace bedspreads and pillowcases, and cost US$70 each, including breakfast. Mae makes lunch and dinner on request and will even give up her splendid large bedroom. The breezy patios in front and back are perfect for savoring sunrise and sunset.

South Caicos Ocean Haven (☎ 649-946-3444, fax 649-946-3466, divesouth@tciway.tc; in Canada ☎/fax 905-898-0982), a dedicated dive resort that's also perfect for nondivers, sits over the ocean at the edge of town. It has 22 modestly furnished air-con rooms, each with cable TV, refrigerators, ceiling fan, couch, and small bathroom. Rates are US$100/175 town-view/ocean-view, including meals. There are two large elevated sun decks and a pool. Bicycles and kayaks are available. It also has two octagonal two-story 'villas,' each with four units, about a mile north on a lonesome beach. They have fans but no air-con or kitchens. Its mailing address is 350 Davis Dr, Unit 6, Newmarket, ON L3Y 2N6, Canada.

Places to Eat
South Caicos Ocean Haven (*see above*) serves set meals; they're tasty and filling. Reservations are required for nonguests. The basic *Eastern Inn Restaurant* (☎ 649-946-3301) serves seafood and chicken.

Other good spots to eat with locals include *Muriel's Restaurant* (☎ 649-946-3535), on Graham St; and *Dora's Restaurant* (☎ 649-946-3247) at the airport. Dora's serves a great lobster sandwich.

Entertainment
The tiny *Trench Town Club*, 100 yards from South Caicos Ocean Haven, has a pool table and music (usually cranked to full bore). There's a *cinema* on Stubbs Rd.

Getting There & Around
The airport is about a mile north of town. See the Getting There & Away section of the Turks and Caicos introductory chapter for flights from the US.

Sky King flies thrice daily between Provo and South Caicos (US$50 one-way), with onward service to Grand Turk (US$30 oneway), and vice versa. Turks & Caicos Airways also has daily flights from Provo and Grand Turk (US$50 one-way, US$90 roundtrip).

InterIsland Airways flies between South Caicos and all the other inhabited islands.

Sea View Marina (☎ 649-946-3219), in Cockburn Harbour, has a fuel dock, water, and the Sea View grocery.

There are usually no taxis at the airport; you'll have to call for one on arrival.

Turks Islands

The Turks group comprises Grand Turk and its smaller southern neighbor, Salt Cay, in addition to several tiny cays. The islands lie east of the Caicos, separated from them by the 22-mile-wide Turks Island Passage.

Grand Turk

Grand Turk – a charming, off-beat gem with a rare sense of innocence – is a brush-covered, bean-shaped dot of an island, just 6½ miles long and 1½ miles across at its widest. Cockburn Town, the main settlement, has been the administrative and political capital of the archipelago for more than 400 years. Today it also claims to be the business and financial center (banks are

Highlights

- Hanging out in funky Cockburn Town, sandblown and strewn with weathered colonial edifices
- Diving The Wall!
- Picturesque, sun-baked Salt Cay, a fascinating day trip
- Swimming with humpback whales in the bay on the north side of Salt Cay

registered here, but don't have a physical presence), yet it remains as sleepy as a capital can be. Semi-wild horses, cattle, and donkeys roam the streets. You'll either love it or hate it, think it desolate and suffocating or calming and quaint.

The island's middle is dominated by several *salinas*, or salt ponds, from which a peculiar odor sometimes arises. Salt – 'white gold' – was the island's most important export until the industry collapsed in 1962. Pocketed limestone cliffs rise along the north and east shores. There are nice beaches along all shores; inland, caves once used by Lucayans await your discovery. A series of tiny isles – Gibb's, Penniston, Long, and Martin Alonza Pinzon Cays – begins about 1 mile off the southeast shore, forming Grand Turk Cays Land & Sea Park.

A few hundred yards off Grand Turk's leeward shore, the ocean abruptly changes hue, the luminous turquoise close to shore shading to an abyssal shade of Prussian blue where the shallow seabed opens into a chasm more than 8000 feet deep. There's excellent diving and fishing. Tuna, wahoo, and dolphin fishing are all fabulous, and bonefish can be caught off Long Cay and in North Creek, which also offers great windsurfing.

COCKBURN TOWN
- **pop 3500**

Cockburn Town belies all notions of a nation's 'capital.' Everything happens on the two main streets, lined with old street lamps and colonial buildings, some of them salt warehouses built of limestone. Others are fine wooden structures, usually painted white, with steep roofs, shuttered windows, and shaded doorways. These were erected by the wealthy Bermudian expatriates who once dominated the salt trade. Many of the houses are hemmed in by stone walls to keep out wild cattle and donkeys.

Sand smothers the streets, blowing into yards and gathering against walls. Shanties,

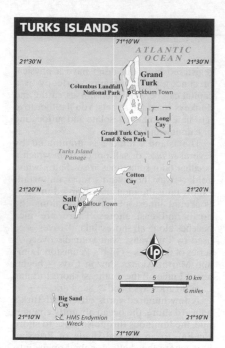

TURKS ISLANDS

71°10'W

ATLANTIC OCEAN

21°30'N   21°30'N

Grand Turk

Columbus Landfall
National Park   Cockburn Town

Long
Cay

Grand Turk Cays
Land & Sea Park

*Turks Island
Passage*

Cotton
Cay

21°20'N   21°20'N

**Salt
Cay**   Balfour Town

0   5   10 km
0   3   6 miles

**Big Sand
Cay**

21°10'N   HMS Endymion
Wreck   21°10'N

71°10'W

huts fashioned of cardboard, bits of wood, and tin, have been erected on spare plots in the heart of the dusty downtown.

Immediately inland, a latticework of old salt ponds runs the length of downtown. Pillory Beach runs along the Cockburn Town shorefront, pierced by salt piers that point toward the reef a quarter-mile from shore. Most people live in more modern homes in the eastern 'suburbs,' where the land rises to Colonel Murray's Hill.

The town attracts some colorful characters, including one man of importance who everyone agrees ran two hotels into the ground and turned another into a bordello before disappearing, they say, with a suitcase full of taxpayers' cash.

Cockburn Town is still as death on Sunday.

Orientation

The heart of town is sandwiched between the ocean and the salt pond named Red

Salina. Front St runs along the waterfront. Front St narrows and becomes Duke St three blocks south of the government plaza. Pond St runs parallel 50 yards to the east, along Red Salina. Osborne Rd, Mission Folly, and Moxie Folly run east from Pond St over Red Salina to the residential area known as Back Salina.

To the north Pond St divides: Hospital St runs north to the hospital and Lighthouse Rd runs northeast to the lighthouse at Northeast Point. It divides to the south, too: One road follows the waterfront to Governor's Beach and the dock; the other – Airport Rd – runs southeast to the airport.

Information

The Turks & Caicos Islands Tourist Board (☎ 649-946-2321, fax 649-946-2733) is on Front St at Market St; its mailing address is PO Box 128, Cockburn Town, Grand Turk, Turks and Caicos, BWI.

T&C Travel (☎ 649-946-2592), on Pond St, provides full travel services.

Scotiabank (☎ 649-946-2507), on Front St at Osborne Rd, is open 8:30 am to 2:30 pm Monday to Thursday and 8:30 am to 4:30 pm Friday. There's a Barclays Bank (☎ 649-946-2831) a few blocks south, with an ATM where you can get cash advances on Visa, MasterCard, and cash cards.

The post office (☎ 649-946-1334) is on Front St next to Barclays Bank in the plaza. Federal Express (☎ 649-946-2542) has an office in Harbour House. The Cable & Wireless telephone office (☎ 119, fax 649-946-2209) on Front St is open 8:30 am to 4 pm Monday to Thursday and 8:30 am to 3 pm Friday. It offers Internet access.

The Victoria Public Library is on Front St; it's open 8 am to 5 pm Monday to Thursday, 8 am to 4 pm Friday, and 9 am to 1 pm Saturday. It has recent international newspapers and magazines.

Locals say the small Grand Turk Hospital (☎ 649-946-2333), a mile north of town, is best avoided. It has an emergency room. There's also a clinic (☎ 649-946-2328).

For the police, call ☎ 911 (emergency) or ☎ 649-946-2299. There are two stations, one on Hospital Rd on the north side of town

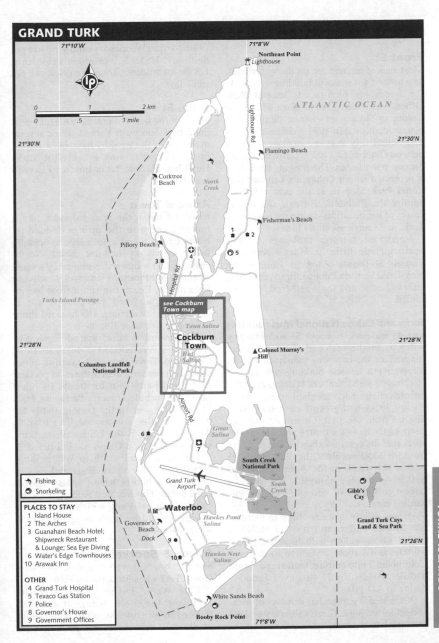

GRAND TURK

71°10'W · 71°8'W

Northeast Point
Lighthouse

ATLANTIC OCEAN

0 · 1 · 2 km
0 · .5 · 1 mile

21°30'N · 21°30'N

Lighthouse Rd

Flamingo Beach

North Creek

Corktree Beach

Fisherman's Beach

1 · 2

Pillory Beach · 4

5

3

Hospital Rd

Turks Island Passage

see Cockburn Town map

Town Salina

Cockburn Town

21°28'N · 21°28'N

Red Salina

▲ Colonel Murray's Hill

Columbus Landfall National Park

Airport Rd

Great Salina

6

7

South Creek National Park

South Creek

Gibb's Cay

↰ Fishing
○ Snorkeling

Grand Turk Airport

Waterloo

8 · *Hawkes Pond Salina*

Governor's Beach

Dock

9 ●

10 ■

Hawkes Nest Salina

Grand Turk Cays Land & Sea Park

21°26'N

PLACES TO STAY
1 Island House
2 The Arches
3 Guanahani Beach Hotel;
 Shipwreck Restaurant
 & Lounge; Sea Eye Diving
6 Water's Edge Townhouses
10 Arawak Inn

OTHER
4 Grand Turk Hospital
5 Texaco Gas Station
7 Police
8 Governor's House
9 Government Offices

● White Sands Beach

Booby Rock Point
71°8'W

TURKS ISLANDS

and one on Airport Rd near Great Salina. For the fire department, call ☎ 649-946-2233.

Front St

Most sites of interest are on the waterfront. The historic government buildings – notably the handsome blue-faced **General Post Office** – surround a small plaza where the Columbus Monument – a small plinth with a plaque, dedicated in 1990 – claims cheekily and definitively that the explorer landed here on October 12, 1492. Nearby, four large cannon point to sea. The fringing coral reef is protected within **Columbus Landfall National Park**. Stop in at the post office to admire the Philatelic Bureau, displaying scores of the beautiful stamps for which the Turks and Caicos are justly famous.

Important historic buildings farther north include little St Mary's Anglican Church, St Thomas Anglican Church, the pink-faced Victoria Public Library, the Oddfellows Lodge, and the weathered Masonic Lodge.

Turks and Caicos National Museum This superb museum, at Front St and Murphy Alley, is in the restored Guinep House (named for the imposing guinep tree in its forecourt), a historic building constructed of salvaged ship's timbers. It displays eclectic miscellany such as shell tools, beads, stamps, locks, and greenstone celts (tools) dug up from the past. Other sections are devoted to the salt industry and life on the coral reef. Its central exhibit is the remains from the Molasses Reef, the oldest authenticated shipwreck in the Americas, whose hull is on display alongside the world's largest collection of wrought-iron breech-loading cannon.

A new gallery upstairs offers an incredible, lifelike underwater display in 3D; a natural history gallery with displays on local wildlife; and a room dedicated to the pre-Columbian Taino culture, featuring a Taino paddle – one of only two ever found – dating to AD 1100.

An adjacent garden has displays of local and imported flora. There's a library and research lab to the rear.

The museum (☎ 649-946-2160, museum@ tciway.tc) is open 9 am to 4 pm weekdays (9 am to 6 pm Wednesday) and 9 am to 1 pm Saturday; US$5/2 nonresidents/residents; US50¢ for students. Tours are given at 2 pm weekdays.

Duke St

South of the heart of downtown, Duke St is lined by stone walls behind which several mansions of the wealthy have been turned into rakish little inns, notably the Turks Head Inn and Salt Raker Inn (see Places to Stay, later).

Around Town

North of town, the island divides like a tuning fork, with the prongs divided by North Creek, a 2-mile-long lagoon opening to the sea via a pencil-thin mouth. Northeast Point, to windward, is pinned by a small cast-iron **lighthouse**. Flamingo Beach and Fisherman's Beach run south from Northeast Point; seaweed and choppy waters detract from swimming. The leeward shore is lined by Corktree Beach.

The government dock and administrative complex at **Waterloo**, 1½ miles south of Cockburn Town, boasts beautiful, pine-shaded Governor's Beach, the most popular picnic and party spot for locals. Its other highlights include Governor's House, built in 1815, the year of the famous battle for which the village is named. The island's dock is here, as is the US missile-tracking station where John Glenn was debriefed.

Dirt roads lead south to White Sands Beach (good for snorkeling) and east to three prime **bird-watching spots**: Hawkes Pond Salina, Hawkes Nest Salina, and South Creek National Park, which protects the mangroves and wetlands along the island's southeast shore.

Diving & Snorkeling

See the boxed text for a description of Grand Turk's best underwater spots.

Blue Water Divers (☎/fax 649-946-1226, mrolling@tciway.tc), at the Salt Raker Inn on Duke St, offers a full range of dives. It has weeklong packages for

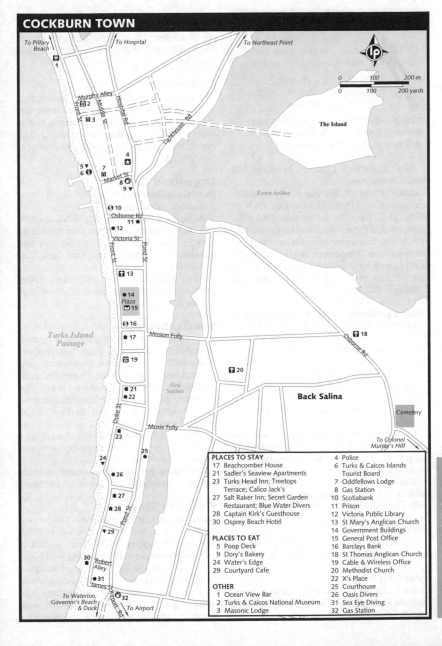

COCKBURN TOWN

To Pillory Beach
To Hospital
To Northeast Point

The Island

Town Salina

Turks Island Passage

Osborne Rd

Mission Folly

Back Salina

Red Salina

Cemetery

To Colonel Murray's Hill

Moxie Folly

To Waterloo, Governor's Beach & Dock
To Airport

PLACES TO STAY
17 Beachcomber House
21 Sadler's Seaview Apartments
23 Turks Head Inn; Treetops
   Terrace; Calico Jack's
27 Salt Raker Inn; Secret Garden
   Restaurant; Blue Water Divers
28 Captain Kirk's Guesthouse
30 Osprey Beach Hotel

PLACES TO EAT
5 Poop Deck
9 Dory's Bakery
24 Water's Edge
29 Courtyard Cafe

OTHER
1 Ocean View Bar
2 Turks & Caicos National Museum
3 Masonic Lodge

4 Police
6 Turks & Caicos Islands
   Tourist Board
7 Oddfellows Lodge
8 Gas Station
10 Scotiabank
11 Prison
12 Victoria Public Library
13 St Mary's Anglican Church
14 Government Buildings
15 General Post Office
16 Barclays Bank
18 St Thomas Anglican Church
19 Cable & Wireless Office
20 Methodist Church
22 X's Place
25 Courthouse
26 Oasis Divers
31 Sea Eye Diving
32 Gas Station

TURKS ISLANDS

Dive Sites

Black Forest – Five types of black coral cling to an undercut festooned with sponges.

McDonald's – Everything from groupers to angelfish hang out near this coral arch.

Tunnels – Sand chutes slope down to the entrance of twin tunnels that drop to 100 feet and emerge in a sponge theme park.

US$650, including 12 dives. It offers full PADI instruction.

Oasis Divers (☎ 649-946-1128, oasisdiv@ tciway.tc; in the US ☎ 770-645-8163, 800-892-3995, fax 770-640-7461), also on Duke St, specializes in three- to seven-day dive packages. It also has mid-winter whale trips. (See the boxed text 'Humpback Whales' for some details on these leviathans' migration to Salt Cay.) Prices start at US$295. Its mailing address is PO Box 137, Grand Turk, Turks and Caicos, BWI.

Sea Eye Diving (☎/fax 649-946-1407, ci@ tciway.tc; in the US ☎ 305-670-6149, 800-725-2822), at the Guanahani Beach Hotel at Pillory Beach and in town at the south end of Duke St, offers a full range of dives (prices start at US$35 for a one-tank dive) and courses. It has a full-service photo center with rental gear. Snorkel trips to Gibb's Cay cost US$35. The postal address is PO Box 67, Grand Turk, Turks and Caicos, BWI.

The hearsay during my last visit was that Blue Water and Sea Eye 'have antiquated equipment and that Oasis does not have the greatest reputation for following all rules and regulations.' On the other hand, Oasis was rated the 'Top Dive Operator in the World' with the 'Top Staff' in the 2000 Readers' Choice Award in *Rodale's Scuba Diving* magazine.

If you're into snorkeling, bring a mask, fins, and snorkel. Rentals are scarce.

Sport Fishing

You can charter a boat for fishing from Dutchie's (☎ 649-946-2244), on Airport Rd, for US$250 to US$350 daily.

The annual Grand Turk Game Fishing Tournament is held at the end of July or in early August. The annual Turks & Caicos International Billfish Tournament is held each July.

Golfing

The new governor, John Kelly, has conjured a nine-hole, par-three golf course from the grounds of the governor's residence in Waterloo. Green fees for visitors are US$25. For information call ☎ 649-946-2308, fax 649-946 2903.

Organized Tours

Provo Air Charter (☎ 649-941-0685) offers 35-minute aerial safaris.

Majestic Tours (☎ 649-946-4999, fax 649-946-4040) offers a daylong excursion to Grand Turk from Provo (US$149) and another to Grand Turk and Salt Cay (US$209).

See the '¡Cuba Sí!' boxed text in the New Providence chapter for information on trips to Cuba.

Special Events

The island hosts a Spring Garden Festival each April. In June, a two-day 'Summerjam' features live bands, beauty contests, and general festivities; and the Queen's Official Birthday Celebration features the police marching band playing with jingoistic fervor.

Traditional music highlights the Rake 'n' Scrape Festival in July.

There's a Cactus Fest in August, plus a weeklong carnival with reggae music and general festivities.

The lights go on in mid-December at the annual Christmas Tree Lighting Ceremony.

Places to Stay

Downtown Cockburn Town The folks at *Solomon Porches B&B* (☎ 649-946-2094) rent one room for US$50/70 single/double.

Sadler's Seaview Apartments (☎ 649-946-2569), on Duke St, has three one- and two-bedroom bungalow units, each with kitchen, living room, cable TV, ceiling fans, and outdoor patio, for US$50 to US$85. Housekeeping service is provided and there's a laundry. Write c/o Marjorie Sadler, PO Box 31, Grand Turk, Turks and Caicos, BWI.

The *Beachcomber House* (☎ 649-946-2470), also called 'The Gordons,' rents a spacious oceanfront suite for US$60/80 single/double, including a splendid breakfast. Its mailing address is PO Box 110, Grand Turk, Turks and Caicos, BWI.

The *Turks Head Inn* (☎ 649-946-2466, fax 649-946-1716, turkshead@tciway.tc), an 1869 charmer on Duke St, offers eight spacious rooms with lofty ceilings and creaky wooden floors. It has recently been renovated in tropical pastels and the rooms now boast antique reproduction furniture, throw rugs, satellite TVs, phones, and minibars. Three rooms on the ground floor have their own garden; upstairs rooms have balconies. Rates are US$65/80 single/double. The postal address is PO Box 58, Grand Turk, Turks and Caicos, BWI.

Captain Kirk's Guesthouse (☎ 649-946-2227, cellular ☎ 649-941-0376, tciyama@ticway.com.tc), on Duke St, has rooms in an idyllic old wooden home with polished wood floors. It has three rooms and two apartments sleeping up to four people each. It boasts romantic Caribbean pastels and tasteful decor combined with screened, louvered windows, throw rugs, ceiling fans, and air-con. The apartments are lined with pine; one has an exquisite, cross-ventilated attic bedroom with dormer windows. No children under 12 are allowed. Rooms, which share a simple bathroom, cost US$70/80 single/double; apartments cost US$1300 to US$1500 weekly.

The *Salt Raker Inn* (☎ 649-946-2260, fax 649-946-2432, sraker@tciway.tc), on Duke St, is a 150-year-old Bermudian shipwright's home turned into an intimate, oceanfront inn. Modern conveniences meld with Caribbean charm. It offers three suites plus 10 air-con rooms, all individually decorated. Four face the ocean and have telephone and cable TV; six face a tropical garden. All have ceiling fans, refrigerators, and verandas. Upstairs suites have an ocean-view balcony with hammocks. The Secret Garden Restaurant is set in a quaint patio. Rates are US$80/90 low/high-season garden-view; US$90/120 for sea-view; US$105/150 for the suites. Its mailing address is PO Box 1, Grand Turk, Turks and Caicos, BWI.

The *Osprey Beach Hotel* (☎ 649-946-2260, fax 649-946-2817, info@ospreybeachhotel.com), on Duke St, has 16 no-frills rooms in oceanfront units, each with carpeted floor, wooden ceiling, rattan furniture, ceiling fan, quirky plumbing, and glass sliding doors opening to a patio or balcony facing the beach. Some have a tiny kitchenette. A renovation was needed at last visit. Rooms begin at US$95 single/double low-season, US$150 high-season. The mailing address is PO Box 42, Grand Turk, Turks and Caicos, BWI.

Around Cockburn Town The uninspired *Guanahani Beach Hotel* (☎ 649-946-2440, fax 649-946-2817), at the north end of Front St, has 16 spacious air-con rooms, each with two double beds, telephone and cable TV, ceiling fans, and ocean-view balcony. The Sea Eye dive center is here, and there's a small pool, sun deck, and beach bar. Kayaks are available. It was in need of refurbishment at last visit. Rates are US$75/90 single/double mid-April to mid-December and US$110/125 the rest of the year. Special three- to seven-night dive packages are offered.

The family-run *Island House* (☎ 649-946-1519, fax 649-946-2646, ishouse@tciway.tc) is a Mediterranean-style, whitewashed villa-hotel wrapping around an effusive garden on the ridge 800 yards northeast of town. It has eight spacious, contemporary air-con suites with wooden floors, homey decor, full kitchens, cable TV, and balconies with hammocks. There's a swimming pool in a garden that sweeps down to North Creek. Room rates include use of bicycles or a golf cart. Island House has no restaurant. Boats and windsurfers were to be added. Studios range from US$105 to US$125; one-bedroom suites range from US$125 to US$150. Its mailing address is PO Box 36, Grand Turk, Turks and Caicos, BWI.

Nearby, *The Arches* (☎ /fax 649-946-2941, archesgrandturk@tciway.tc) enjoys a breeze-swept ridgetop setting with views over the Atlantic. Rooms have air-con bedrooms,

TURKS ISLANDS

cable TV, and kitchenettes. The modern, three-story structure has 24 units that rent for US$150/225 summer/winter for two people. Weekly rates are available, as are bicycles.

The modern *Arawak Inn* (☎ *649-946-2277, fax 649-946-2279, arawakinn@tciway.tc*), by its lonesome 2 miles south of town, has 15 self-catering air-con suites. Each has a kitchen and sofa bed and can sleep up to four people. There's a freshwater pool and beach bar-cum-restaurant. Horseback riding is offered. The inn has a daily shuttle service to town. Weeklong per-person package rates cost US$825/580 single/double. Dive packages are available. The postal address is PO Box 140, Grand Turk, Turks and Caicos, BWI.

Water's Edge Townhouses (☎ *649-946-2055, fax 649-946-2911*), a half-mile south of town, is a self-catering option. It comprises three two-bedroom units with dining room and full kitchen. Each costs US$2500 weekly for up to four people.

The erstwhile Coral Reef Hotel & Beach Club, on Flamingo Beach 2 miles northeast of Cockburn Town, still stands but was closed at press time after briefly serving as a bordello.

Places to Eat

For conch and native fare, try *Regal Beagle* (☎ *649-946-2274*), on Hospital Rd. The *Poop Deck*, on Front St near Market St, is said to have the best fried chicken in the islands.

The *Water's Edge* (☎ *649-946-1680*), on Duke St, is an atmospheric restaurant and bar with a wooden deck overhanging the beach. It's a good place for buffalo wings, nachos, and conch salad, starting at US$5, and entrees such as curried conch, surf 'n' turf for US$29, and a superb snapper with garlic butter sauce for US$18. Try the key lime pie or carrot cake for US$4. It also has pizzas from US$7, a 'brown bag special' lunch, and nightly specials: all-you-can-eat pasta (Monday), Tex-Mex (Tuesday), pizza (Wednesday), and a fish fry (Thursday).

The *Courtyard Café*, near the Osprey Beach Hotel, serves snacks such as tuna sandwiches outside in a bougainvillea-shaded patio. Waffles, cinnamon rolls, and bagels and cream cheese are breakfast staples.

At the Turks Head Inn, you can opt for the breezy outdoor *Treetops Terrace* or *Calico Jack's* on the patio beside the English pub, with its brass plaques, sea charts, and china. It serves island and continental cuisine, including fish and chips (US$8), chicken curry (US$10), spiced lamb (US$10), and tuna and crab salad. The menu also has creative dishes such as smoked chicken and mango served with a raspberry coulis (US$6.50), and crispy duck on bubble and squeak with spinach and caramelized onions in a rich wine sauce (US$18). It offers a Sunday brunch.

The Salt Raker Inn's *Secret Garden Restaurant* has entrees such as blackened grouper for US$18 and curry chicken for US$16, plus splendid desserts such as cherry pie and ice cream (US$5). An English breakfast costs US$9.

You can buy freshly baked items at *Dory's Bakery* on Pond St next to the gas station. For groceries, head to *Sarah's*, off Moxey Rd.

Entertainment

Nookie Hill (named for the highest point of the island or for the activity?) has a disco with ultra-violet lights from 10 pm to 5 am on Friday and 9 pm to midnight on Saturday (entrance costs US$5). The booming beat of hip-hop will guide you.

Mitch Rollings plays guitar at the *Salt Raker Inn*. The *Turks Head Inn* also has live music. The 'boys' club,' a clique of prominent males that many consider a kind of informal government, meets every Friday night on the patio to debate the week's events and plot the island's future. All comers are welcome to join the games of intellect.

A more earthy place to drink with locals is the *Poop Deck* on Front St, or the waterfront *Ocean View Bar*, at the north end of town, which has slot machines.

Shopping

X's Place (☎ 649-946-1299), on Duke St, is a trove of Haitian art, antiques, handdrawn antique maps, and carved items. X is Xavier Tonneau, an extroverted Frenchman. There's a store selling fine batiks, T-shirts, and resortwear at Sea Eye Diving at the south end of Duke St.

A-1 Business, on Front St, sells cameras, but they're *not* duty-free.

Getting There & Away
Air Grand Turk Airport is 1 mile south of Cockburn Town. See the Getting There & Away section of the Turks and Caicos introductory chapter for flights from the US. If you're traveling to Grand Turk from elsewhere abroad, you'll need to transfer in Provo.

Sky King (in Provo ☎ 649-941-5464) flies between Provo and Grand Turk nine times daily (US$65 one-way, US$120 roundtrip), and between South Caicos and Grand Turk three times daily (US$30 one-way, US$50 roundtrip). InterIsland Airways (☎ 649-946-1667) and Turks & Caicos Airways (☎ 649-946-2709) also fly several times daily from Provo and South Caicos.

Boat Windjammer Barefoot Cruises' *Amazing Grace* includes Grand Turk on its cruises. See the Getting There & Away chapter in the Bahamas section for details.

Flamingo Cove Marina (☎/fax 649-946-2227) has a couple of berths.

Getting Around
To/From the Airport A taxi usually meets incoming flights. If not, you can call for one from the airport (see the Taxi section, below). A taxi to or from downtown costs US$4 one-way. There are no buses.

Car & Scooter You're hardly likely to need a car, but you *can* hire one from Mitchell's Car Rental (☎ 649-946-1879) or Dutchie's Car Rental (☎ 649-946-2244, fax 649-946-2799), near the airport on Airport Rd. If you do drive, pay attention to the one-way system.

Island Fun Cycles (☎ 649-946-1680), near Water's Edge restaurant on Duke St, rents scooters for US$25 (single) and US$40 (double) per day.

Taxi Several locals operate taxis. Try Mrs K (☎ 649-946-2239). If you hire a taxi for an island tour, be sure to negotiate the fare beforehand.

Bicycle You can rent a bicycle at Sea Eye Diving on Duke St for US$5 half-day, US$10 full-day. Island Fun Cycles (see Car & Scooter, above) has bicycles for the same price.

GRAND TURK CAYS LAND & SEA PARK
Gibb's, Penniston, Long, and Martin Alonza Pinzon Cays make up this small park southeast of Grand Turk. It protects important nesting sites for seabirds. There are also large numbers of Turk's head cacti. Penniston is an important nesting site for frigate birds, and boobies and noddy and sooty terns abound on Gibb's. The terns come to Gibb's each May and June to breed (the females lay a single egg in a thick carpet of cactus spines). Human visitation is discouraged during these months. Long Cay is a separate sanctuary with a population of iguanas.

There's no scheduled transport. You'll need to rent a boat and guide in Cockburn Town.

Dive and tour operators in Provo and Grand Turk offer trips; refer to the relevant sections, below.

Salt Cay

• pop 125

Sun-drenched Salt Cay, 8 miles southwest of Grand Turk, is shaped like a triangle. It's a mere speck of land but it's steeped in character and to my mind is the most interesting Turks and Caicos island. The modern history of the archipelago began here in the 17th century, when Bermudian salt traders settled and a salt industry emerged. They constructed ponds linked to the sea by canals and sluice gates and built windmills to control water flow. Salt Cay once was the world's largest producer of salt – in the industry's heyday, over 100 vessels a year departed the isle for the US, bulging with 'white gold.'

The island provides a picturesque vision of 19th-century life. It could be a living museum of industrial archeology, with its decrepit windmills, salt sheds, and salinas, now smelly and scummed with wind-whipped froth. And the beaches and swimming are superb. It has been proposed that Salt Cay be made a UNESCO World Heritage Site.

The main settlement, historic **Balfour Town**, boasts old two-story homes with wide verandas and jalousied windows, like buildings from a Tennessee Williams play. Many

have been bought of late by expats, who are gradually bringing them back to life with fresh coats of paint.

Donkeys and wild cattle far outnumber human inhabitants, as do iguanas, including 'Iggy,' a semi-tame giant who resides at the north end of the island.

Big Sand Cay, 8 miles south of Salt Cay (see the Turks Islands map), once was a habitat for now-endangered West Indian monk seals and manatees. Both have long since disappeared here, due to hunting and habitat destruction. The cay is also a haven for diminishing numbers of green and hawks-

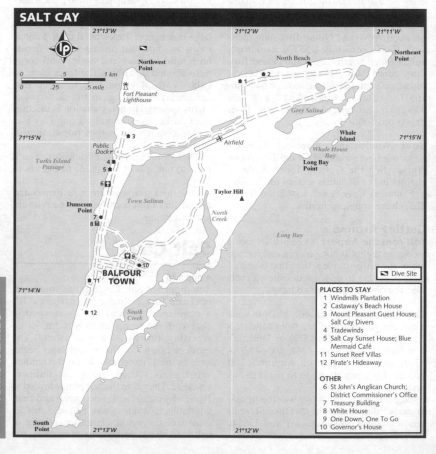

SALT CAY

PLACES TO STAY
1 Windmills Plantation
2 Castaway's Beach House
3 Mount Pleasant Guest House;
   Salt Cay Divers
4 Tradewinds
5 Salt Cay Sunset House; Blue
   Mermaid Café
11 Sunset Reef Villas
12 Pirate's Hideaway

OTHER
6 St John's Anglican Church;
   District Commissioner's Office
7 Treasury Building
8 White House
9 One Down, One To Go
10 Governor's House

Map labels: Northwest Point, North Beach, Northeast Point, Fort Pleasant Lighthouse, Grey Salina, Whale Island, Public Dock, Airfield, Whale House Bay, Turks Island Passage, Long Bay Point, Taylor Hill, Dunscom Point, Town Salinas, North Creek, Long Bay, BALFOUR TOWN, South Creek, South Point, Dive Site

bill turtles, which come ashore to lay their eggs in the sand.

Salt Cay has a post office (☎ 649-946-6985), open Monday through Thursday 8 am to 12:30 pm and 2 to 4 pm, Friday from 8 am to 3:30 pm. There's a small clinic (☎ 649-946-6970) with two nurses; a doctor visits once every two weeks. You can reach the police at ☎ 649-946-6929.

The Fun in the Sun Festival is held on Salt Cay each June.

Things to See

The most noteworthy attraction is the splendidly preserved **White House** in north Balfour Town, a salt merchant's stately manor with a stepped (Bermudian) stone roof and chimney. It is still owned by the Harriott family, who built the house in 1835 from stone brought here as ballast. Next door is the old wooden **Treasury Building**, where salt workers once collected their pay. Nearby are **St John's Anglican Church** and the **District Commissioner's Office**, housing the old jail.

Rusting 18th-century cannons sit atop **Fort Pleasant**, in ruins, about 400 yards north of Mt Pleasant Guest House.

Activities

In the Salt Cay area, choice dive sites include Wanda Lust, known for its plankton-rich waters that attract whales and eagle rays; Kelly's Folly, a rolling coral garden with hawksbill turtles, morays, and parrotfish; and HMS *Endymion*, a never-salvaged, 18th-century British warship bristling with cannon and massive anchors in a

Humpback Whales

Salt Cay is perhaps the best spot in the Caribbean region to see humpback whales during the winter months. Scores of leviathans arrive to breed in the warm waters of the Silver and Mouchoir Banks, east and south of Salt Cay. They gather each January, February, and March to mate and give birth in these waters, so close to shore that you can literally swim out to touch them!

Whaling was an important industry on the cay in the late 19th century, when whales were dragged ashore and butchered at Whale House Bay.

corals, and Point Pleasant, a shallow cove crowded with coral heads topped with elkhorn.

Salt Cay Divers (☎ 649-946-6906, email: scdivers@caribsurf.com), at the Mount Pleasant Guest House (see Places to Stay, below), uses two boats, including a 38-foot WWII-era landing craft. The company has package deals.

The *Turks & Caicos Aggressor* (see Live-Aboard Dive Boats in the Outdoor Activities chapter) offers swim-with-the-whale dives January through March.

Bottom Time Adventures (☎ 800-234-8464, fax 954-920-5578, info@bottomtimeadventures .com) offers weeklong swim-with-the-whales trips. You'll live aboard the luxurious 90-foot catamaran *Bottom Time II*. Its mailing

coral canyon just 25 feet down. The sea mound here has swim-throughs. The wreck is south of Big Sand Cay (see the Turks Islands map). There's also the Northwest Wall, plunging from 50 feet to 120 feet and covered with

address is PO Box 11919, Fort Lauderdale, FL 33339-1919, USA. In 2001, the trips with the whales will be offered from February to April in the Silver Banks.

Oasis Divers (see Diving in the Cockburn Town section earlier in this chapter) offers whale-watching trips from Grand Turk.

Mount Pleasant also offers bicycling, horseback riding (free for guests, US$20 half-day for others), plus shelling and snorkeling trips.

Places to Stay

The timber-beamed ***Mount Pleasant Guest House*** (*☎/fax 649-946-6927, mtpleasantinfo@ yahoo.com*) is an unpretentious gem north of Balfour Town run by Tim Dunn, descendant of the original Harriott family, the main landowners in the 1800s. His home-turned-hostelry dates back to 1830, when it was a salt merchant's house. The seven air-con rooms all have wooden floors, lively tropical pastel decor, and heaps of charm. A nearby cottage holds four more rooms. Hammocks are slung between shade trees. Rates are US$65/85 single/double for upstairs; US$105 for a larger room downstairs. A weekly dive package costs US$895. Bicycles are provided for guests.

The ***Salt Cay Sunset House*** (*☎ /fax 649-946-6942, seaone@tciway.tc*), a colonial structure north of Balfour Town on the west shore, has three rooms for US$73/95 single/double. This lovingly restored historic home has a wrap-around veranda and patio dining area. Each lofty-ceilinged bedroom boasts a sofa bed in addition to one or two double beds. Breezes and ceiling fans keep things cool. The vast living room has cable TV and VCR, plus period furnishings.

Pirate's Hideaway (*☎ 649-946-6909, pirates@tciway.tc; in the US ☎ 800-289-5056*), run by Candy, an amiable and forthright Englishwoman, is a Hansel-and-Gretel–style B&B abounding with stained glass, Haitian artwork, and murals on a pirate theme. There are two units – one up, one down – boasting dark hardwood floors, nautical-themed bathrooms (including shell-lined tubs), and lively tropical decor. Rooms cost US$85/120 single/double. You can opt for the three-bedroom *Blackbeard's Quarters*, a self-contained unit with throw rugs and exquisite Italian fabrics, a child's room with bunks, and four-poster beds with orthopedic

mattresses. It rents for US$85 per room, or US$200 nightly for up to six people. Candy prepares gourmet cuisine. You won't want to leave!

The ***Castaway's Beach House*** (*☎ 649-946-6921, fax 649-946-6922; in the US ☎ 315-536-7061*), on the north shore, rents six one-bedroom self-catering apartments for US$110 to US$150. It doesn't have a restaurant. It's open mid-November to mid-April.

The self-contained ***Sunset Reef Villas*** (*☎ 649-946-6901, sunsetreef@aol.com; in the US ☎ 410-889-3662, 888-889-3662*) overlooks the beach in Balfour Town. This modern home features air-con, water purifier, cable TV and VCR, CD and stereo, and washer and dryer, plus a full kitchen and outdoor grill on a deck with hammocks. It has a one-bedroom apartment sleeping four people (US$900 to US$1100) and a two-bedroom unit for six (US$1000 to US$1200). The owners, when not in residence, rent the cottage for US$150/1000 nightly/weekly double in peak season. Rates include a bicycle; you can rent a golf cart for US$40 daily. The US mailing address is 45 Holmehurst Ave, Baltimore, MD 21211.

Tradewinds (*cellular ☎ 649-941-0071*) has five modern, self-contained air-con apartment units with kitchenettes, rattan furniture, fans, tile floors, and a shared screened veranda. For information, contact Debbie at Salt Cay Divers (*☎ 649-946-6906, scdivers@ caribsurf.com*).

The ***Windmills Plantation*** (*☎ 649-946-6962, 800-822-7715, fax 649-946-6930*) is a small deluxe resort in a stunning beachside location about a mile and a half northeast of Balfour Town. It boasts a delightfully bizarre West Indian motif and a palette of Caribbean pastels (it was recently the locale of a Victoria's Secret fashion shoot). It has eight romantically appointed suites with terra-cotta floors, handcarved four-poster beds (king-size), old lanterns, and private outdoor patio with shower and Jacuzzi. Columned walkways, lined by alcoves with hammocks, radiate out from the Romanesque pool. It has its own restaurant and bar, and diving and water sports are offered. Daily rates range from US$625 to US$995 double. It's open mid-October to May only.

Places to Eat

The choice option is *Mount Pleasant Guest House*, serving native seafood and other gourmet fare. Try the superb carrot cake and ice cream…or homemade sherry trifle.

Similarly super fare can be had at *Pirate's Hideaway*, where lobster doubloons and recherché seafood are served on an exquisite patio lit by flaming torches at night. Here, too, you can sup grog at the *Smuggler's Tavern*.

The *Blue Mermaid Café* at Sunset House also offers an exciting menu, with whopping breakfasts and such dinner treats as Cajun pork chops and stuffed sweet peppers (US$12).

The owners of the *Windmills Plantation* pride themselves on their Caribbean cuisine.

For local color, head to *Leggetts' Brown House (☎ 649-946-6936)* in town.

Entertainment

Locals gather to play dominoes at the *One Down, One to Go* bar. It has a pool table.

The bars at the *Mount Pleasant Guest House* and *Pirate's Hideaway* offer more sophistication.

Getting There & Away

The airfield is northeast of Balfour Town.

InterIsland Airways (in Grand Turk ☎ 649-946-1667), Sky King (in Provo ☎ 649-941-5464), and Turks & Caicos Airways (in Grand Turk ☎ 649-946-2709) have flights from Provo (US$70 one-way, US$130 round-trip). InterIsland Airways and Turks & Caicos Airways also fly from Grand Turk (US$25 one-way). A private charter plane from Grand Turk will cost about US$75; check out the Getting Around chapter for charter options.

The trip to the cay is much more fun by boat. A government ferry runs from the South Dock on Grand Turk four days a week (US$8 roundtrip). It's a 45-minute journey. Call the harbormaster in Grand Turk (☎ 649-946-2325) for information.

Getting Around

One of the island's only two taxis will inevitably show up after the driver sees the plane land at the Salt Cay Airfield.

Acknowledgments

THANKS

Many thanks to the travelers who used the last edition and wrote to us with helpful hints, useful advice and interesting anecdotes:

Anthony Allan, Timothy E Armesy, Mr J P Barett, Linda Billings, Suisie Brocks, Glenn Havelock, Mike Hibbert, Tammy Kraeger, Renee & Mike Kramer, Carolyn McGowan, Miss S McInnes, Chris Mirakian, Loekie Schonthaler, Barbara Stickler, Todd Varble

LONELY PLANET

You already know that Lonely Planet produces more than this one guidebook, but you might not be aware of the other products we have on this region. Here is a selection of titles which you may want to check out as well:

Diving & Snorkeling Bahamas
ISBN 1 86450 181 2
US$16.99 • UK£10.99

Florida
ISBN 0 86442 745 X
US$19.95 • UK£13.99

Cuba
ISBN 0 864442 750 6
US$19.99 • UK£11.99

Jamaica
ISBN 0 86442 780 8
US$17.95 • UK£11.99

Puerto Rico
ISBN 0 86442 552 X
US$15.95 • UK£9.99

Dominican Republic & Haiti
ISBN 0 86442 647 X
US$15.95 • UK£10.99

Available wherever books are sold.

Index

Bold indicates maps.

Bold indicates maps.

Bold indicates maps.

Boxed Text

MAP LEGEND

ROUTES

City   Regional

................Freeway
................Toll Freeway
................Primary Road
................Secondary Road
................Tertiary Road
................Dirt Road

................Pedestrian Mall
................Steps
................Tunnel
................Trail
................Walking Tour
................Path

TRANSPORTATION

................Train
................Metro

................Bus Route
................Ferry; Water Taxi

HYDROGRAPHY

................River; Creek
................Canal
................Reef
................Water

................Spring; Rapids
................Waterfalls
................Dry Lake
................Salt Lake

BOUNDARIES

................International
................State

................County
................Disputed

AREAS

................Beach
................Building
................Campus

................Cemetery
................Forest
................Garden; Zoo

................Golf Course
................Park
................Plaza

................Reservation
................Sports Field
................Swamp; Mangrove

POPULATION SYMBOLS

○ **NATIONAL CAPITAL** ...National Capital
◉ **State Capital** ....State Capital

● **Large City** ....Large City
● **Medium City** ....Medium City

● Small City ....Small City
● Town; Village ....Town; Village

MAP SYMBOLS

■ ....Place to Stay
▼ ....Place to Eat
● ....Point of Interest

................Airfield
................Airplane Wreck
................Airport
................Archeological Site; Ruin
................Bank
................Baseball Diamond
................Battlefield
................Bike Trail
................Bus Station; Terminal
................Cable Car; Chairlift
................Campground
................Canoeing; Kayaking
................Castle
................Cathedral
................Cave

................Church
................Cinema
................Dive Site
................Embassy; Consulate
................Fishing
................Footbridge
................Fountain
................Gas Station
................Hospital
................Information
................Internet Café
................Lighthouse
................Lookout
................Monument
................Mountain

................Museum
................Observatory
................Park
................Parking Area
................Pass
................Picnic Area
................Police Station
................Pool
................Post Office
................Pub; Bar
................RV Park
................Shelter
................Shipwreck
................Shopping Mall
................Skiing - Cross Country

................Skiing - Downhill
................Snorkeling
................Stately Home
................Surfing
................Synagogue
................Taxi
................Telephone
................Theater
................Toilet - Public
................Tomb
................Trailhead
................Tram Stop
................Transportation
................Volcano
................Winery

Note: not all symbols displayed above appear in this book

LONELY PLANET OFFICES

Australia
Locked Bag 1, Footscray, Victoria 3011
☎ 03 8379 8000 fax 03 8379 8111
email talk2us@lonelyplanet.com.au

USA
150 Linden Street, Oakland, California 94607
☎ 510 893 8555, TOLL FREE 800 275 8555
fax 510 893 8572
email info@lonelyplanet.com

UK
10a Spring Place, London NW5 3BH
☎ 020 7428 4800 fax 020 7428 4828
email go@lonelyplanet.co.uk

France
1 rue du Dahomey, 75011 Paris
☎ 01 55 25 33 00 fax 01 55 25 33 01
email bip@lonelyplanet.fr
www.lonelyplanet.fr

World Wide Web: www.lonelyplanet.com *or* AOL keyword: lp
Lonely Planet Images: lpi@lonelyplanet.com.au